Norma Alarcón

Forced by Circumstance

Chicana Feminist Essays
(1981-2024)

Edited by
Norma E. Cantú
Marisa Belausteguigoitia
Dionne Espinoza

Copyright © 2025 Norma Alarcón

All rights reserved. This book, or parts thereof, must not be reproduced in any form or by any means, electronic or mechanical, including photocopying and recording, or by an information storage and retrieval system, without written permission from the publisher.

Aunt Lute Books, P.O. Box 410687, San Francisco, CA 94141
www.auntlute.com

Cover design: Sarah Lopez
Text design: Sarah Lopez
Cover Art: Liliana Wilson, "Migrante en la cuerda" © 2025
Editorial: Shay Brawn and Emma Rosenbaum
Production Team: María Mínguez Arias, Isis Asare, Golda Sargento, Elizabeth Martínez

The production of this book was made possible by support from California Arts Council, the Council on Literary Magazines and Publishers, the Poetry Foundation, the San Francisco Arts Commission, Sara and Two C-Dogs Foundation, and the Zellerbach Foundation.

English translations of "Chicana Literature: A Sexual and Racial Challenge from the Proletariat to the Patriarchy," "On Feminine Culture according to Rosario Castellanos," and "Nymphomania: The Discourse of Difference" published here with permission from Universidad Nacional Autónoma de México (UNAM)/Centro de Investigaciones y Estudios de Género (CIEG) © 2023.

Print ISBN: 978-1-951874-10-0
eBook ISBN: 978-1-939904-46-1

Library of Congress Cataloging-in-Publication Data
Names: Alarcón, Norma author | Cantú, Norma E., 1947- editor | Belausteguigoitia, Marisa editor | Espinoza, Dionne editor
Title: Forced by circumstance : Chicana feminist essays (1981-2024) / Norma Alarcón ; edited by Norma E. Cantú, Marisa Belausteguigoitia, Dionne Espinoza.
Description: San Francisco, CA : Aunt Lute Books, 2025. | Includes bibliographical references. | Summary: "Forced by Circumstance gathers foundational essays by, and interviews with, Norma Alarcón, noted scholar of Chicana/o, Latina/o, and Feminist Studies. The volume includes essays written/published between 1981 and 2024 and include both literary criticism and broader cultural analysis"— Provided by publisher.
Identifiers: LCCN 2025032250 (print) | LCCN 2025032251 (ebook) | ISBN 9781951874100 trade paperback | ISBN 9781939904461 ebook
Subjects: LCSH: American literature—Mexican American authors—History and criticism | American literature—Women authors—History and criticism | Mexican American women in literature | Mexican Americans in literature | Feminism in literature | Mexican American women—Intellectual life |
LCGFT: Literary criticism | Essays
Classification: LCC PS153.M4 A434 2025 (print) | LCC PS153.M4 (ebook)
LC record available at https://lccn.loc.gov/2025032250
LC ebook record available at https://lccn.loc.gov/2025032251
10 9 8 7 6 5 4 3 2 1

ACKNOWLEDGMENTS

WE ACKNOWLEDGE SUPPORT OF individuals and institutions who have contributed in various ways along the way.

BIG THANKS TO THE Humanities Research Institute, UC Irvine for the sponsorship of the Minority Discourse Seminars, and UC Berkeley for the opportunity to be a participant in Advanced Critical Thinking and Intellectual Praxis that were offered during my tenure there. I want to also thank ChaeRan Freeze, Chair of Women's, Gender and Sexuality Studies at Brandeis University, for her support and hospitality. Also, Paola Bacchetta, Women's, Gender and Sexuality Studies, UC Berkeley, for her unwavering support of my work and myself throughout the years. A great shout of gratitude to Yolanda Venegas, a stalwart supporter and worker for Third Woman Press (TWP) for the long haul, as well as the many undergraduate and graduate students who helped to keep TWP going. A debt of gratitude to Norma E. Cantú for her invitation to teach at the University of Texas in San Antonio. Most of all I want to acknowledge the great Trifecta—Norma E. Cantú, Marisa Belausteguigoitia, and Dionne Espinoza—that enabled the production of this book. A big shout of gratitude for longtime support of my work to Angela O'Byrne and Marc Neikurg. Also, last but never least, my son and kindred spirit, Joseph McKesson, whose support has been invaluable.

Norma Alarcón

AT TRINITY UNIVERSITY, I acknowledge our work-study students, Kim Granados, Natasha Nahu, and Kathryn McKinney my administrative assistants, Lupita Domníguez and especially Corrine Castillo; Coates Library humanities librarian, Lacey Brooks-Canales. Thank you also to the amazing editorial staff at Aunt Lute Books, especially Shay Brawn. Years ago, at the University of Texas at San Antonio, Christina Gutiérrez helped track down and gather the essays dispersed in various publications. I want to thank my fellow "triangle" members—Marisa and Dionne—for their patience and diligence. Also, gracias to my tocaya, for a sustained friendship of over 40 years and for trusting me to amadrinar this amazing collection. To my family, especially Elvia and Elsa, for their support and understanding.

Norma E. Cantú

WE ACKNOWLEDGE AND ARE grateful to the Universidad Nacional Autónoma de México/Centro de Investigaciones y Estudios de Género (CIEG) for their support and for providing translation from Spanish to English of the following: "The Discourse of Difference" translated by Ariadna Molinari Tato; "On Feminine Culture" translated by Mónica Mansour; and "Chicana Literature" translated by Ariadna Molinari Tato and Alí Siles. We also acknowledge the work of Paulina Barrios, Modesta García Roa, and Alejandra Tapia, as well as others on the staff at CIEG. Marisa gives a special thanks to Jasbir Puar for being an enthusiastic part of the origins of this project.

Marisa Belaustiguigoitia

I WOULD LIKE TO thank Norma Alarcón, Norma Cantú, and the Chicana feminist activists, educators, and critical theorists who have given me a body of work and tools to visibilize Chicana lives and herstories.

Dionne Espinoza

To all of my students who enjoyed the critical challenge and in turn challenged me.

Norma Alarcón

→ TABLE OF CONTENTS ←

Foreword: "Traversing Bordered Lands"—*Norma E. Cantú* — xiii
Preface: "Forced by Circumstance"—*Norma Alarcón* — xix
Introduction: "Making Chicana Critical Theory from Scratch: Norma Alarcón's
    Malintzin Praxis and Feminist Studies"—*Dionne Espinoza* — xxv

PART I ⁂ HAY QUE INVENTARNOS

Chicana's Feminist Literature: A Re-Vision through Malintzin or, Malintzin,
    Putting Flesh Back on the Object — 5
"What Kind of Lover Have You Made Me, Mother?": Towards a Theory of
    Chicana Feminism and Cultural Identity through Poetry — 15
Making *Familia* from Scratch: Split Subjectivities in the Work of Helena
    María Viramontes and Cherríe Moraga — 39
The Sardonic Powers of the Erotic in the Work of Ana Castillo — 55
Traddutora, Traditora: A Paradigmatic Figure of Chicana Feminism — 71
Chicana Literature: A Sexual and Racial Challenge from the Proletariat to the Patriarchy — 101
Chicana Feminism: In the Tracks of "The" Native Woman — 111
On Feminine Culture According to Rosario Castellanos — 123

PART II ⁂ THEORETICAL SUBJECTS

The Theoretical Subject(s) of *This Bridge Called My Back* and Anglo-American Feminism — 153
Nymphomania: The Discourse of Difference — 169
Cognitive Desires: An Allegory of/for Chicana Critics — 179
Tropology of Hunger: The Miseducation of Richard Rodríguez — 197
Anzaldúa's *Frontera:* Inscribing Gynetics — 213
Conjugating Subjects in the Age of Multiculturalism — 231
Anzaldúan Textualities: A Hermeneutic of the Self and the Coyolxauqui Imperative — 257

PART III ⁂ IMBRICATIONS/CONJUGATIONS/MEDIATIONS

...But You Don't Look Mexican — 283
Imbrications — 295
Anzaldúa's Insurrection of Subjugated Knowledges: An Interview with Norma Alarcón — 305
Nepantla—Productions of Pathologies and Healing: Under Construction — 337
Conjugations: The Insurrection of Subjugated Knowledges and Exclusionary Practices — 357

Epilogue: Critical Thinking as a Pedagogical Movida: Double-Binds, Accents,
    and Contradictions for Student Speaking-Subjects"—*Marisa Belausteguigoitia* — 377

Foreword

TRAVERSING BORDERED LANDS

Norma E. Cantú

SOMETIME IN THE MID-1980S I drove up from my hometown of Laredo, Texas, to a literary event in San Antonio hosted by Sandra Cisneros, who had moved to San Antonio to be the Literary Coordinator at the Guadalupe Cultural Arts Center (GCAC). San Antonio's flourishing art scene with a concomitant literary renaissance inspired and prodded us creatives to gather at various venues, but the Guadalupe was at the center of such activity. Cisneros's friend, Norma Alarcón, was visiting. Perhaps it was at an early small press book festival that Cisneros had founded or a conference at the GCAC, I cannot recall. While I am certain that I saw and heard writers and critics, and I am certain I heard readings, I don't recall any one particular reading. But I do remember meeting Alarcón, my tocaya. I remember a bunch of us at a picnic table outdoors swatting at Texas-size mosquitoes at the Brooklyn Bar off the busy south Alamo Street. Artist Terry Ybañez was there as were a number of regulars who hung out at the GCAC. Alarcón, cigarette in hand, talked about Chicago and Indiana, and Spain where her son, Joe, an opera singer, was either about to go to or was already. I had just come back from a Fulbright studying fiestas in Spain, so we talked and talked. And we laughed. Yes. We laughed. I loved her wry wit and sarcasm. We talked about mutual friends, including Ana Castillo, whom I had just met in Spain. I knew about Third Woman Press and her work to publish Chicana and other "third women" writers. That fateful meeting cemented our now decades-long friendship.

A short time later, I visited Cherríe Moraga and Ana Castillo in Oakland while out there to attend a meeting of Amnesty International. I was eager to see other Chicanas in the Bay Area, including Alarcón and Lucha Corpi, who were all living in close proximity—by California standards—that is within a 5-10 minute drive of each other. During her post-doc at UC Berkeley, Alarcón lived in what seemed to me, coming from Texas, an ideal community of incredible women, a haven for political and intellectual work. Already she was positioning herself as a leading literary critic; she subsequently accepted a tenure track assistant professor position at Berkeley. I marveled at how a fronteriza raised in the

Midwest was now at UC Berkeley. In my mind, her traversing the many borders offered a model. The other Chicanas I had met while I was in graduate school in Nebraska rarely left the Midwest; similarly, the Tejanas rarely left Texas. Her publishing of cutting-edge Chicana feminist texts through Third Woman Press and her participation in conference presentations that never failed to wow those in attendance brought me closer to her. For several years, we met at various conferences—Modern Language Association, American Studies Association, National Association for Chicana and Chicano Studies, and Mujeres Activas en Letras y Cambio Social—where we discussed ideas, books, people, and of course, politics. And we laughed! Boy did we laugh! We laughed at the absurd antics of politicians and at the foibles and idiosyncrasies of our academic colleagues. We laughed at ourselves, we laughed at puns and jokes, and we laughed at life.

My admiration grew as she published essay after essay, as she opened the path for many of us with bold feminist analyses that elevated the discourse and highlighted Chicana authors and poets. Her work published in journals and as book chapters was not easy to find in those days before the internet, and I am sure I missed quite a few. As I read the essays for this book, I reminisced. I was struck by how pathbreaking they were back then and how timely they still are today.

Forced by Circumstance gathers Alarcón's feminist essays published over a span of more than forty years and seeks to bring these foundational essays of literary and cultural criticism to a new generation of readers. By making Alarcon's work available in one volume, our intent was to highlight the work of one of the most important critics of our time and to make the essays available in one tome for scholars and students. Readers new to her work as well as those of us already familiar with it will find the book to be a treasure trove of insights and analysis of our literary and cultural production, all through a feminist lens. But Alarcón's feminist tools go far beyond the usual ones of second wave feminism as she engages and deploys brilliant analysis. Sometimes she turns to the usual suspects—European thinkers and scholars like Kristeva or Lacan. Invariably, she turns her well-trained literary critical eye to the work of Chicanas. While she may harken back to Eurocentric theories, she does so sieved through her own lens, a Third World Women's perspective.

In Alarcón's work we find a fiercely political and insightful analysis of texts and of the often conflicted and contradictory realities of the Chicane and Latine populations in general, and of the academic in particular. Like a sonar reading below the waters, Alarcon's analysis goes beneath the obvious to offer views that elucidate and uncover the feminist project of Chicanas in the late 20th and early 21st centuries.

Within the Chicane literary panorama, critics and thinkers often remain unrecognized despite the fact that it is their work that shines a light on the highly significant work of the writers. It is the thinkers whose critical analysis and vision illuminate the key factors and insights that bring us a sense of context and texture, to borrow from folkloristics, to the literary enterprise. This long-overdue volume presenting decades of Norma Alarcón's work gathers essays that have withstood the test of time and still have something to teach us.

Reading Alarcon's early work on Rosario Castellanos we sense the fierce feminist approach that develops and matures in later work. In the canonical articles that are often referenced, she has given us a language and an approach that continues to situate our literature as central to the study of American literature in general and women's studies and Chicane studies, specifically. In her humor and wit, we find the core of her brilliant thinking. The work on Castellanos is from her graduate school days, but Alarcón reads Castellanos with a feminist acuity that offers us paths to recover Castellanos as an integral voice for Chicana feminist thought.

When Alarcón was living in San Antonio, after her retirement from UC Berkeley, she taught graduate seminars in the English Department at the University of Texas at San Antonio; her students from Berkeley and from UTSA are now forging their own paths in academia. Her influence as a professor in and out of the classroom, goes way back to her teaching in Indiana as a graduate student and at UC Berkeley. Students drawn to her brilliant lectures and engaging classroom discussions invariably came back for more. Through mentorship and support of students, she has created a cadre of professors who are now contributing to the literary scholarly narrative in Chicane, Latine, and Women's Studies.

Reading her work thirty or forty years later, I am surprised, and yet not, at how relevant and spot on her observations remain in our contemporary world with the current political climate and the dearth of thinkers delving deeply into our literary production. When we contemplate the systemic attacks on faculty of color in academic settings, the dismissal and erasure of our work, we relish the voice of a critic and truthsayer who will elucidate and deconstruct the underpinnings that sustain and maintain the stranglehold on our work. When Critical Race Theory is attacked, it is the work of Alarcón that comes to mind. We may not have been using the terminology that has found its way into the common discourse, but the concepts of intersectionality and of settler colonialism exist in the essays published before Kimberlé Crenshaw gave it a name.

I recall a late-night conversation with Alarcón several decades ago. I was still teaching in Laredo at what is now Texas A&M International University and she was at Berkeley. Her student evaluations had come in and the students were complaining that she was too theoretical. I laughed because my students were similarly challenging my pedagogy with comments such as "she expects us to read too much" or "I had never heard of the names Prof. Cantú mentioned in her lectures." I remember saying to her, "Well, if you can't be theoretical at Berkeley, then where?" Of course, many of her students not just relished her theoretical interventions but ran with them and went ahead and wrote dissertations and books that built on her work.

As we have grown older, we have sustained our friendship and our discussions, most recently via zoom. When I retired from UTSA and relocated to Kansas City to start a Latinx Studies program at the University of Missouri, Kansas City, I felt I was abandoning her; Sandra Cisneros had also left San Antonio and moved to San Miguel de Allende. Although she had family in San Antonio, I still felt we were as close or perhaps even closer. Working on *Forced by Circumstance* has brought us together in a different way as the "triangle" as Marisa began calling our trio of coeditors evolved with Alarcón at the center.

What happens next? Presumably our work will be done as the book is published but in reality, our work continues as we spread the word. As we continue doing what Anzaldúa urged us to do, work that matters. Indeed, Alarcon's work mattered and it matters still as we confront the realities of our time. Many of the elders have passed on; we have become the elders, those of us in our 70s and 80s. It is up to the younger generations to go forth and keep fighting to right the injustice of our world armed with Alarcón's keen insights. As is her wont, she will continue to think, and to think deeply, about who we are and what we have become in this neoliberal capitalist purgatory that the post-pandemic world has created. The bizarre and illogical rise of the right-wing ideologies threaten our world as we know it. Yet, I remain optimistic. We have been here before. It is not new. Nor will it be resolved as expeditiously as we hope, for it is a system rife with technologies of destruction and of discrimination against brown and black bodies that surface time and again and dismantle the landmark advances of the 20th century: a woman's right to an abortion, every citizen's right to vote, etc. Flawed as it may be, the system serves a purpose and while the ideal is a totally egalitarian, non-sexist, non-discriminatory world, the reality is far different. Perhaps the only way to make it right, is to do away with it all, and start from scratch, and given the climate change crises, we may be headed that way.

Where do we go from here? Forward! There is no option. Time will tell if our work survives, if la lucha que aún sigue will yield the results we dreamed of back then. I have an image in my mind of Alarcón walking alongside several of us on the Women's Day March in San Antonio wearing a straw hat under the scorching sun. As we arrive at Milam Plaza, a historic space where gatherings have taken place for well over a hundred years, the speeches begin. We listen. Seems we've heard it all before. The heat becomes intolerable—Alarcón never did well in the heat of South Texas. We are in solidarity. We are tired, hungry. We listen, clap with others as speakers go up and offer hope, challenges. Finally, she turns to me and suggests we leave and go eat. And that's what we do. As we leave, I think of the many other women who have marched, who have been en la lucha here and elsewhere. I feel a kinship with them and with the women who have marched with us, and with my tocaya. We are part of a long line of dreamers, of activists.

She may not remember, but she has been there for me when I've encountered my own self-doubts. Her reading *Canícula* and her praise for one of my poems inspired me to keep writing. My intellectual sister brings all of herself, difficult and obstinate as she can be, yet always honest, sin pelos en la lengua. Once her razor sharp tongue—or pen—is engaged, she will zero in and cut to the chase. Her acumen precise and lucid shows us how to read our work but also through her thinking demonstrates an engaged and active mind and spirit that is ever pointing us forward as she continues doing "work that matters."

I invite you to read this book and build upon the ideas Alarcón presents in the essays, apply the approaches and theoretical framings she provides to create your own reading strategies, your own apparatus for feminist analysis.

¡Adelante, tocaya!

Preface

FORCED BY CIRCUMSTANCE[1]

For Sor Juana Inés de la Cruz

NORMA ALARCÓN

to be a woman, I've had to live far from your scent
far from your calloused lips

and smoke-stained hands
The day I left

I heard the miscrack of a wishbone
I longed to pull your flesh off every rib putting off a kill I felt fated
to fulfill

I held back   I held back
gestures   glances   even sounds
I've had to let you go to evoke my name
though your face follows me
reminding me of the unsaid

Enveloped by the silence of a mushroom cloud
I left with cardboard boxes arm in arm and
Joined the endless lines of hapless immigrants
Who gather up their threadbare breath and walk

I've walked everywhere
I've walked everywhere you've walked
Following your tracks on pressed down dirt
I've lived inside your every move
Your every thought

---

1. This poem was first published as "Forced by Circumstance," in "Chicanas and Chicanos en Diálogo," *Quarry West*, no. 26 (1989): 20. Subsequently, it was published in *Telling to Live: Latina Feminist Testimonios*, ed. Latina Feminist Group (Durham, NC: Duke University Press, 2001), 289-90.

Forced by circumstance to be a woman
I've lived far from your scent
Though your face follows me
Reminding me of the unsaid

THE POEM IS DEDICATED to Sor Juana Inés de la Cruz. Literary cognoscenti can hear traces, not only of Sor Juana but also of more contemporary thinkers and writers, like Virginia Woolf, Simone de Beauvoir. Rosario Castellanos, and Audre Lorde. In the long run, since adolescence, I have acquired many library shelves of mentors like them, as I sought my place in letters broadly speaking and more specifically in feminist letters. I had to look to books for entertainment, for sociality, and most importantly for "answers." Books were my soulmates/friends/advocates, and adversaries.

Once a colleague posed to me the question "Don't you have a thought of your own?" I was stunned at the time, sometime at the end of the 1990s. I wondered, does she think that there is an originality of thought when we build on the "head and shoulders" of others? In point of fact in the 1970s I wrote an essay for myself, now somewhere in a box, called "without a word to my name." Well, if I was meditating on that line of thought, why would I not, in the 90s, not be conscious of the fact that I may not have a thought of my own beyond the assemblage of helpful thinkers? One may have an "issue" of one's own, and it may well be the issue that determines the thinking with the help of others who have worked with the "issue." After thousands of years of archives, can one individual have a thought that is all her own, especially in the midst of a hegemonic phallic patriarchy? It is the challenge to and the fugue from those patriarchal structures that can produce the thought of one's own as one faces the issues that beleaguer our ability to even speak, let alone write and think.

So, what is a word or a thought of one's own, what can it be, with so much verbal rubbish continuing to bury the so-called "feminine condition," when, indeed, it may well be a condition conditioned in those branded as a woman from birth, and constructed in accordance with her reproductive organs? These mentors, as well as many others I cite in the work that follows, constructed "thoughts of their own" by challenging the misogynistic heteropatriarchal regime that continues to brand and plague women. I was not alone. Mistakenly, I think, my colleague believed that *she* could have a thought of her own, all of her own.

It is hard to have a thought of one's own when one does not have a word, not even a family name, of one's own, and no matrilineality to carry the name. Yet I don't think that our historical moment is calling for matrilineality. However, we do recall the conquest, domination, and vanishment that fell upon women after the patrilineal takeover thousands of years ago.

We have been heirs to preconceived notions of what a "woman" is supposed to be. Those notions have been challenged for thousands of years; however, it is recent developments like the pursuit of the vote, equity, and full citizenship in democratic societies and its achievement in 1920 that have enabled women to acquire full citizenship rights in pursuit of freedom, self-determination, and, in 1973, possession of our own bodies by controlling socio-biological reproduction at our discretion (a civil right until the Supreme Court took it away in 2022, with the Dobbs decision). The misogynistic heteropatriarchy has defined itself against the backdrop of the control of women's reproductive and sexual capacities and the curtailment of our freedom for centuries. In effect, these men, who appear to be a minority, want their "sovereignty" over women back. Their effort has relied on preconceived and extensive definitions of womanhood and/or femininity which have been challenged by a multitude of women across centuries. The misogynistic-patriarchal definitions encompass all areas of a woman's life: physical appearance, dress, behavior, linguistic practices, parameters of movement, education, work, childbearing, domestic responsibilities, and care. Failing to comply brings on shaming, guilting, and punishing. Brothers have not shared in domestic responsibilities of work and care, nor have they been subjected to this level of bodily control; in fact, many are asked to play vigilante with female siblings. In brief, her life has been defined by her family, secular and religious institutions, and the State. This is still true in many countries, though the imprisoning walls are cracking for some; however, some men and women in the United States are on a Christian crusade to repress the civil rights of women that includes LGBTQ+ people and racism. That is, the white supremacist Christian heteropatriarchy wants to have control over all forms, representations, and expressions of sexuality believing that there are only two forms, representations, and expressions of sexuality. The patriarch is in charge of the determination of sexual expression. He is in charge of that determination as the bible dictates, that is HIS interpretation of the bible which is veiled by scientific claims that may be the battle cry of our times! One mistakenly thinks that ALL women would want to challenge the horrors of misogynistic patriarchies, but as exemplified by U.S. women, some want to submit and even call themselves "Moms for Liberty,"² a right-wing group promoting book bans, guns, and no-choice prenatal clinics. I think of these women as phallic mothers, like my own mother. The phallic mother makes her daughter submit to a misogynistic heteropatriarchal agenda, which in the Anglo-European ethnic U.S. ultimately relies on the King James Bible for its interpretations of sexuality itself. In part, these paragraphs count as some of the "unsaid" alluded to in the poem. It takes a while to learn the grammars, logic, and rhetoric one needs to challenge the patriarchy and its phallic mothers, the handmaidens. Some of those analytic tools are buried in the dustbins of history, other chunks have to be unscrambled, and other slices have to be tossed. The "feminine mystique" Betty Friedan alluded to is now being justified under religious fundamentalist tortured thought. In other words, timelines have to be redrawn, epistemologies revised, and ontologies rewritten.³ That is, in fact, part of what my work entails.

I knew in the 1970s that I did not have a word of my own. I did not even have my own last name. I had, though, achieved Virginia Woolf's ambition to "have a room of one's own."⁴ This was due to the fact that my parents did not think I should sleep in the same room as my brothers! I may have gotten privacy, but I also got a prison of my own! Had I been born in the urbanite 1960s, I would probably have become a runaway adolescent, but I was born in the 1940s which imprisoned me in traditions that my Mexican family cherished for women. Most children are helpless in light of parent and church indoctrinations until they begin to question the restrictions foisted upon them. I had to leave home to eventually get the education I wanted. It is in universities that I learned that I may not have a single word of my own. That the misogynistic heteropatriarchy had sewed up the rhetorical and genealogical legacy. However, the 1970s made it clear to me that education, the library, and the archives had treasures to learn from. There had to be as Rosario Castellanos said, "otro modo de ser humana y libre," that is, another way of being human and free.⁵

Feminism is the pursuit of women's rights and equality in the family, society, politics, and the economy. In the United States, the hegemonic standard bearers

---

2. Moms for Liberty is an extremist right-wing group in the U.S. It has recently emerged to play "phallic mothers" for women who would rather have an abortion. They offer shaming and guilt-tripping as care along with prayers to sweeten the visit to their own right-wing clinics. No medical care is available as in Planned Parenthood. Note how they abuse terms like "liberty." It is neither liberty nor freedom not to have choices.

3. Betty Freidan, *The Feminine Mystique* (New York: WW Norton & Company, Inc., 2001).

4. Virginia Woolf, *A Room of One's Own* (London: Hogarth Press, 1935).

5. Rosario Castellanos, *Poesía no eres tú* (México: Fondo de Cultura Económica, 1972), 295-297.

of power have been white Christian males. Apparently, these men and some of their handmaidens, especially if they are members of the Republican party, have decided that it is their mission to restore the misogynistic heteropatriarchy, to normalize it again 100 years since women got the vote, and 50 years since acquiring the right to have rights, and even as women are still fighting to get equality along with minorities of color. However, there's nothing normal about it from a feminist point of view. Letting "you go to evoke my name," the poem above says. That is, I do want a thought of my own, but I cannot have it without letting you go. Yours may be the loudest voice in the room, but it does not necessarily make sense. Some have remarked on the "poverty of language," such as the citation from Sor Juana. What one has to say or write or think does not fit into the words available. Sor Juana did not have the language at hand with which to express the devastation she underwent when the CHURCH rejected her and deprived her of the tools of her labors. Imagine a sculptor, an architect, a fisherwoman without the tools for the job. One has to take apart the Master's and Mistress's House. One has to rebuild and we have to do it over and over again as Gloria Anzaldúa tells us in the call for the Coyolxauhqui Imperative.[6] One can use some of his "bricks" and make others in our kilns, reducing the poverty of language as we go. The poverty of language presents itself as a fact when we attempt to express our confoundedness with the language available. If nothing more for starters we have to unscramble the rhetoric that traps and imprisons us.

---

6. Gloria Anzaldúa, "Let Us Be the Healing of the Wound: The Coyolxauhqui Imperative—la sombra y el sueño," in *One Wound for Another: Una herida por otra. Testimonios de Latin@s in the U.S. through Cyberspace* (11 de septiembre de 2001-11 de marzo de 2002), ed. Claire Joysmith and Clara Lomas (México City: UNAM – CISAN / Colorado College/Whittier, 2005).

BIBLIOGRAPHY

Alarcón, Norma. "Forced by Circumstance." In "Chicanas and Chicanos en Diálogo." *Quarry West* no. 26 (1989).

Alarcón, Norma. "Forced by Circumstance" In *Telling to Live: Latina Feminist Testimonios.* 289-90. Edited by the Latina Feminist Group. Durham, NC: Duke University Press, 2001.

Anzaldúa, Gloria. *Borderlands/La Frontera: The New Mestiza.* San Francisco: Spinsters/Aunt Lute, 1987.

Anzaldúa, Gloria. "Let Us Be the Healing of the Wound: The Coyolxauhqui Imperative—la sombra y el sueño." In *One Wound for Another: Una herida por otra. Testimonios de Latin@s in the U.S. through Cyberspace (11 de septiembre de 2001-11 de marzo de 2002)*, edited by Claire Joysmith and Clara Lomas. México City: UNAM – CISAN / Colorado College/Whittier, 2005.

Castellanos, Rosario. *El Eterno Femenino.* México, DF: Fondo de Cultura Económica, 1975.

Freidan, Betty. *The Feminine Mystique.* New York: WW Norton & Company, Inc., 2001.

Woolf, Virginia. *A Room of One's Own.* London: Hogarth Press, 1935.

Introduction

MAKING CHICANA CRITICAL THEORY FROM SCRATCH

NORMA ALARCÓN'S MALINTZIN PRAXIS AND FEMINIST STUDIES

Dionne Espinoza

IN THE LATE 1980S, I had the opportunity to witness Norma Alarcón presenting a talk on Chicana literature that exists in my historical consciousness as a fierce representation of Chicana power in the academy and as a catalyzing moment in my own coming to voice as a Chicana academic. To a first-generation Chicana college student who was beginning to understand our marginalization in the academy, Alarcón appeared as a towering figure with an awesome presence, a Chicana intellectual in the space of the Human/ities. Her talk discussed Malintzin Tenepal, the indigenous woman translator for Cortés who is viewed as a traitor within Chicano and Mexicano culture and society.[1] Reflecting upon this event now, I see how Alarcón's presence in a predominantly White academic institution invoked a multilayered sense of historical or *her*storical déjà vu as she spoke eloquently in "their/our" language and engaged in the acts of translation required of women of color within the spaces of the U.S. academy. As Alarcón herself has written, to be a Chicana critical theorist in academic space is to navigate a speaking space from within and against "the crossfire of multiple patriarchies."[2] She had entered the academy at a time when there was little representation of Chicanas in the disciplines (including Chicano Studies) nor were there frameworks and theories that could effectively and accurately diagnose the dimensions of Chicana subordination given the colonialities that continue to foster the persistent silencing and erasure of Chicana and women of color voices and experiences.[3]

---

1. Alarcón may have been presenting an excerpt from an earlier version of what she soon published as "Traddutora, Traditora: A Paradigmatic Figure of Chicana Feminism," *Cultural Studies* 13, (1989): 57-87. Malintzin Tenepal was an Aztec woman who was sold to the Maya by her mother. She was among the group of Indigenous women slaves who were given to Cortés and the Spanish men who accompanied him.

2. Norma Alarcón, "Conjugations: The Insurrection of Subjugated Knowledge and Exclusionary Practices," *Chicana/Latina Studies* 13, no. 2 (2014): 223.

3. While this layered understanding of the meanings of Alarcón's presence in the academy did not fully register for me at the time, thanks to the invitation to write this introduction to her feminist essays and the experience of my own academic travels/travails over the years, I can appreciate even more the challenges Alarcón faced as a first-generation Chicana feminist academic, critic, and theorist.

Alarcón enacted her own critical agency and academic survivability through a Malintzin praxis. Malintzin praxis invokes the indigenous woman as a Chicana feminist who deploys multiple languages to fight for her survival within White supremacist settler colonial capitalist hetero-patriarchy, Chicano/Mexicano nationalist patriarchy and in, Alarcon's case, the academy. Alarcón's work centers Chicanas as resistant subjects who push against the ongoing mechanisms, rooted in history, that subordinate Chicanas and women of color.[4] Working within the given terms, but also challenging them, Alarcón's Malintzin praxis could be described as *bricolage* with a Chicana twist.[5] As a Chicana *bricoleur*, Alarcón employed her voice often in dialogue and tension with a variety of contemporary critical languages and vocabularies. She set about translating and pressing multiple languages of dominant critical theories (written in English, Spanish, and French) into the project of creating Chicana feminist critical theory. In this way, Alarcón subverted the theories by appropriating them in order to analyze Chicana and women of color queer and feminist writing.

Through these acts of translation and interpretation Alarcón advanced and ensured Chicana and women of color visibility in critical conversations about race/ethnicity, class, gender, and sexuality as these conversations deepened after the civil rights movements and feminist movements of the sixties and seventies. Alarcón's interpretive praxis produced new vocabularies of experience that advanced conversations about Chicana and women of color subjectivities and agency. As I worked on this introduction, it became clear to me that the challenge of Alarcón's Malintzin praxis have yet to be fully fleshed out and processed. This may not be surprising given that Alarcón's essays and theoretical work have often been deemed opaque and in need of translation, almost in-credible. How audacious for a Chicana to take up the tools of dominant

---

4. Alarcón discusses how Chicana writers have "helped to lay bare Malintzin's double etymology..." in "Traddutora, Traditora," 83.

5. *Bricolage* is a term drawn from the structuralist theory of Claude Lévi-Strauss and popularized by theorist Jacques Derrida. It was a widely discussed concept in the late eighties through the nineties in poststructuralist critical theory. I use it here to describe the process of taking from a variety of existing terms and languages to create a new novel analysis. See Jacques Derrida, "Structure, Sign, and Play in the Discourse of the Human Sciences," in *Modern Criticism and Theory: A Reader*, ed. David Lodge (Longman, 1988), 114-115.

theories, re-appropriate them, critique them, and move beyond them to create new vocabularies and interpretations![6]

Beginning and ending with Malintzin, a colonized, indigenous woman with compromised agency, whom Alarcón has called "a paradigmatic figure of Chicana feminism," this essay surveys Alarcón's canonical essays in Chicana feminist studies following a logic that is roughly chronological and thematic. My hope is that this expository and exegetical introduction will re-activate an engagement with the implications of Alarcón's Malintzin praxis for Chicana feminist studies. Even as Chicana feminist studies has shifted to engage with other figures to explore healing and decolonization such as Coyolxauhqui, Chicana feminist writing about Malintzin has empowered us to speak to/of the contradictions, paradoxes, and "double-binds" (following Alarcón) that face Chicana critics, their intellectual labor, and their institutional pedagogies. Placing Alarcón's canonical essays in the political, literary, theoretical, and institutional contexts in which she claimed her critical agency as she was "making Chicana feminist theory from scratch," we can understand her drive to visibilize Chicana/women of color experiences at the intersection of race/ethnicity, class, gender, and sexuality. Finally, it is crucial to declare that while this introduction, and this volume of her essays, centers Alarcón as an individual scholar-activist, her work cannot be understood outside of her embeddedness within Chicana/Latina and women of color collectives and scholar-activist networks that she participated in and that she contributed to as a scholar, a poet, and founder of Third Woman Press, all of which are crucial to any genealogy of Chicana/Latina and women of color critical thought and literature in the academy from the eighties to the present.

TRANSLATING EXPERIENCE: FOUNDATIONS OF MALINTZIN PRAXIS IN THE CHICANA LITERARY BOOM AND THE WOMEN OF COLOR EIGHTIES

> In my own work, I'm interested in translating our experience, however painful. My essay in *This Bridge Called My Back* (1983), which was later translated

---

6. I would also like to note the significance of tone in Alarcón's essays. She writes in a philosophical mode with rage as an undercurrent that some readers can grasp (as it resonates with our own). She commented openly that she was driven by rage in a panel at the sesquiannual *El Mundo Zurdo* Conference. The El Mundo Zurdo conferences celebrate the influences and theories of Gloria Anzaldúa. See Norma Alarcón, Marisa Belausteguigoitia, and Romana Radlwimmer. "Nepantla–Production of Pathologies and Healing: Under Construction," in *El Mundo Zurdo 6. Selected works from the 2016 meeting of the Society for the study of Gloria Anzaldúa*, ed. Sara A. Ramírez, Larissa M. Mercado-López, and Sonia Saldívar-Hull (San Francisco: Aunt Lute Books, 2018), 86-87.

under the title *Esta Puente, mi espalda* (1988) was kind of a breakthrough in this sense. Because I was claiming my own voice at the same time that I was recuperating a female historical space, and establishing a discursive formation within which to ground that tradition.[7]

WHILE THE EIGHTIES HAVE been characterized (rightly so) as an era of conservativism, antifeminism, and "backlash" within feminist political history, that narrative often overlooks the resistance project of women of color feminism that began to flourish at the beginning of the decade. The publication of *This Bridge Called My Back: Writings by Radical Women of Color* in 1981, co-edited by Chicana lesbian writers Cherríe Moraga and Gloria Anzaldúa, an anthology of voices including Chicana, African America, Asian American, and Native American women authors, reframed the period between the so-called "second wave" and "third wave" of the long feminist movement as a "bridging" period during which women writers of color raised their voices against racism and sexism in social movements and in US society. At the same time, the *U.S. News & World Report* in 1978 declared the eighties would be the "Decade of the Hispanic" adding to the overlapping and multiple currents that swirled around the emergence of a Chicana feminist literary movement.[8] The combination of the societal declaration of the "Decade of the Hispanic" and the publication of *This Bridge Called My Back* visibilized the Chicana/Latina literary boom and the women of color feminist movement in the eighties and beyond.

This is the context for Alarcón's reflections on her "breakthrough" as a Chicana critic in the late seventies to early eighties when she inaugurated her work of "claiming," "recuperating," and "establishing" a Chicana feminist praxis. She was working on her dissertation and teaching during the late seventies and early eighties when she connected with Chicana/Latina writers in the Midwest, including Ana Castillo, Sandra Cisneros, and Luz María Umpierre, among

---

7. Alarcón quoted in Angie Chabram-Dernersesian, "Chicano Critical Discourse: An Emerging Cultural Practice," *Aztlán: A Journal of Chicano Studies* 18, no.2 (1989): 53. In the extended quote, Alarcón speaks about why she chose to create Third Woman Press. It's also important to note that *This Bridge Called My Back: Writings by Radical Women of Color,* ed. Cherríe Moraga and Gloria Anzaldúa, is listed here as published in 1983, but it was first published in 1981 by Persephone Press. The second edition was published by Kitchen Table: Women of Color Press in 1983 after they reclaimed the book from Persephone. For more on the story of the publication of *Bridge* see Kayann Short, "Coming to the Table: The Differential Politics of *This Bridge Called My Back*," *Genders* no. 19 (June 30, 1994): 3. Alarcón also referenced Cherríe Moraga and Ana Castillo *eds., Esta Puente, Mi Espalda: Voces de Mujeres Tercermundistas en Los Estados Unidos,* trans. Ana Castillo and Norma Alarcón (San Francisco: ism Press, 1988).

8. Frank Del Olmo, "Commentary: Latino 'Decade' Moves into 90s," *Los Angeles Times*, December 14, 1989. https://www.latimes.com/archives/la-xpm-1989-12-14-ti-1-story.html accessed April 12, 2024.

many others. These circles of Latinas and women of color feminists were doing insurgent critical and cultural work in the region. The lack of Latina writing outlets publishing Latina work inspired her to found Third Woman Press in 1979.[9] In 1981, Third Woman Press produced the first issue of *Third Woman* journal featuring Latina writers in the Midwest. In her introduction to this inaugural issue Alarcón declared "Hay Que Inventarnos/We Must Invent Ourselves" citing Mexican poet Rosario Castellanos. That same year, Alarcón's first major work of Chicana feminist literary theory appeared in *This Bridge Called My Back: Writing by Radical Women of Color* entitled, "Chicana's Feminist Literature: A Re-Vision through Malintzin/or Malintzin: Putting Flesh Back on the Object."[10]

"Chicana's Feminist Literature" laid out several themes that would recur in Alarcón's Chicana feminist critical canon, starting with a robust critique of patriarchy. As a work of literary criticism, "Chicana's Feminist Literature" frankly confronted the master narrative of Malintzin as the "bad woman" that had pervaded the Chicano movement's masculinist constructions of womanhood. She argued that Chicana poetry countered the movement's masculinist narrative with responses, re-visions, and objections to its misogynistic implications. Unsurprisingly "Chicana's Feminist Literature" ruffled feathers. Alarcón testified that an early employer had described the essay as too "shrill" and "'too' militant."[11] As Alarcón noted, these terms translated to "feminist." Accusations of "shrill" and "militant" tones and rhetoric were often attributed to feminist literary criticism circulating in an academy that had only begun to reckon with women's or feminist literature.

Feminist philosophers and literary critics of the time readily confronted the "myth of woman," the "enigmatic feminine," and the "eternal feminine" as patriarchal constructs. A central point of reference for feminist critiques was French philosopher Simone de Beauvoir's *The Second Sex,* in which she denounced the construction of woman as the fixed "other" to the neutral, universal man. Alarcón's attendance at *The Second Sex —Thirty Years Later: A Commemorative Conference on Feminist Theory* in 1979 as a graduate student underscored this

---

9. Third Woman Press paralleled the founding of other independent feminist publication outlets in late second wave feminism to counter the exclusion and erasure of women writers' literature in dominant publishing houses.

10. Norma Alarcón, "Chicana's Feminist Literature: A Re-vision through Malintzin/or Malintzin: Putting Flesh Back to the Object" in *This Bridge Called My Back: Writings by Radical Women of Color*, ed. Cherríe Moraga and Gloria Anzaldúa (Persephone Press, 1981), 182-190.

11. Alarcón, "Conjugations: The Insurrection of Subjugated Knowledges and Exclusionary Practices," 210.

influence.¹² Although Beauvoir appeared often in Alarcón's Chicana feminist literary criticism, her more direct companion muse at the time was Mexican feminist writer Rosario Castellanos, a contemporary of Beauvoir, whose poetry, novel, and essay writing deconstructed the "eternal feminine" in the search for a subjectivity for women outside of patriarchal discourses.¹³ Similar to the "myth of woman" that patriarchy upholds, Alarcón named the "male myth of Malintzin" as a Mexican and Chicano patriarchal project that subordinated Chicanas.¹⁴

A short and powerful essay with many layers and theoretical depth, characteristics that are easily applied to all of Alarcón's canonical essays, "Chicana's Feminist Literature" debuted a Chicana feminist literary critic whose primary objective was to restore the value of indigenous women's lives and to reclaim agency. She refused to apply the pejorative "Malinche" to the indigenous woman in the title of her landmark essay and insisted on calling Malintzin by her name, a practice followed by several Chicana writers of the seventies. She candidly declared that "Her historicity, her experience, her true flesh and blood were discarded" in dominant "master" narratives that maintained a construction of Malintzin as a sexualized figure of betrayal in a narrative intended to regulate Chicana sexuality and agency.¹⁵ For Alarcón, "putting flesh back on the object" involved thinking through the complexities of history, experience, and the body to reclaim Malintzin's agency and that of all indigenous women and Chicanas, as "descendants" of Malintzin. This is where Alarcón issued her central challenge to the limitations of dominant critical theories for interpreting Chicana

---

12. This was the conference at which Audre Lorde called out White feminists for tokenization in a talk that served as the basis for her classic essay "The Master's Tools Will Never Dismantle the Master's House," which appeared in *This Bridge Called My Back: Writing by Radical Women of Color*, 98-101. In the conference program, Alarcón is listed as a panelist at a workshop entitled "Contemplative Women, the Cloister in Creativity" with Electa Arenal and Susan Potters. See the *Second Sex Thirty Years Later Program* posted on Michelle Moravec, "Unghosting Apparitional (Lesbian) History, Erasures of Black Lesbian Feminism," scalar.usc.edu/works/unghosting-apparitional-lesbians/it-began-with-audre-lorde-1?origin=note, retrieved March 24, 2025.

13. Alarcón wrote her dissertation on Rosario Castellanos and published her dissertation as a book entitled *Ninfomanía: El discurso feminista en la obra poética de Rosario Castellanos* (Madrid: Editorial Pliegos, 1992). Castellanos's book, *El Eterno Femenino*, published posthumously, was one of Alarcón's inspirations for the journal *Third Woman*. See Rosario Castellanos *El Eterno Femenino* (México, Fondo de Cultura Económica, 1975). She cited Castellanos' concept of "Self-Invention," as the "third way" in "Hay Que Inventarnos/We Must Invent Ourselves," *Third Woman: of Latinas in the Midwest* 1, no. 1, (1981): 1. This introduction is discussed in Catherine S. Ramírez, "Alternative Cartographies: *Third Woman* and the Respatialization of the Borderlands, 1981-1986," *Midwestern Miscellany XXX* (Fall 2002): 50-51. See also Sara A. Ramírez and Norma E. Cantú, "Publishing Work that Matters: Third Woman Press and Its Impact on Chicana and Latina Publishing," *Diálogo*, 20, no. 2 (Fall 2017): 77-85.

14. Alarcón, "Chicana's Feminist Literature," 183.

15. Alarcón, "Chicana's Feminist Literature," 182.

experience and agency: These theories adopted humanism and its accompanying model of the subject and consciousness without regard for (or perhaps because of) humanism's colonialist, racist, and patriarchal assumptions. Against a "male ideologized humanism devoid of female consciousness" that erased Chicanas by reading their agency through the lens of European men, Alarcón argued for locating resistance, critical knowledge, and agency in a "female consciousness" that allowed for "envisioning how as women we would like to exist in the material world."[16] For Alarcón, this project could lead Chicanas toward the possibility of "repossessing ourselves" from the narratives that subordinated us so that we could move toward liberation.[17]

Further uplifting Chicana literature as a vehicle for "female consciousness" and deploying her Malintzin praxis as a critic "translating experience," Alarcón's early literary criticism unpacked the teachings about feminism and gender socialization communicated in Chicana poetry that surged in Latine and feminist presses of the time such as Third Woman. Her essay "What Kind of Lover Have You Made Me Mother? Towards a Theory of Chicanas' Feminism and Cultural Identity Through Poetry," cited a veritable roll call of Chicana poets, including Evangelina Vigil, Lorna Dee Cervantes, Carmen Tafolla, Barbara Brinson-Pineda, Cherríe Moraga, Gloria Anzaldúa, Rina Rocha, Margarita López Flores, Olivia Castellano, Alma Villanueva, and Tey Diana Rebolledo. In alignment with Audre Lorde's "Poetry is not a Luxury," Alarcón emphasized that the Chicana poets whose work she interpreted were working class, bicultural, and bilingual women.[18] Analyzing and interpreting the work of these poets, she asserted the role of the Chicana feminist literary critic as a partner in theorizing from, and supporting the visibility of, Chicana writers. To this end, she explored how their work conveyed a Chicana feminism rooted in a woman of Mexican descent's working-class experience of living "on the cutting edge of two languages both of which threaten to silence her with their apparent unbridgeable discourses."[19] She argued that as Chicana poets reflected on the women in their lives ("mothers

---

16. Alarcón, "Chicana's Feminist Literature," 188-189. Alarcón quoted Adrienne Rich, lesbian feminist poet and theorist, who commented on tokenism under patriarchy. Adrienne Rich's ideas were influential among feminists at the time including several writers in *This Bridge Called My Back*.

17. Alarcón, "Chicana's Feminist Literature," 188.

18. Audre Lorde, "Poetry Is Not a Luxury," in *Sister/Outsider: Essays & Speeches* (The Crossing Press, 1984), 36-39.

19. Alarcón, "What Kind of Lover Have You Made Me, Mother: Toward a Theory of Chicanas' Feminism and Cultural Identity Through Poetry," in *Women of Color: Perspectives on Feminism and Identity*, ed. Audrey Thomas McCluskey (Women's Studies Program, Indiana University, 1985), 105.

and female friends"), they charted the internalized patriarchal gender scripts that were passed down generationally by mothers and grandmothers who struggled to identify paths of agency for themselves.[20] It is up to the daughters to understand these fraught struggles and to take a different path, however difficult that may be. By focusing on the lineages of Chicana patriarchal socialization, Alarcón wrote, these poets complicated the idea of feminism as defined primarily in opposition to men.

The essay "What Kind of Lover Have You Made Me Mother?" also introduced Alarcón's first elaboration of a Kafka parable as an analytic to conceptualize the forces pushing against Chicanas in their search for agency, self-determination, and liberation. Her adaptation of the parable for Chicanas—for which she stated, "(I took the liberty of changing all the he's to she's and it's)"—described a Chicana protagonist caught between two antagonistic forces, the past pushing toward the future and the future pushing toward the past.[21] In this version of Alarcón's telling, the past and the present represented two cultural forces, México and the U.S. "Anglo American world," respectively.[22] The goal of the protagonist caught between these forces was to somehow become the umpire who could determine the outcome of the epic battle, perhaps going beyond or outside of history. But for Alarcón history has always been part of the big picture: She did not imagine the Chicana outside of history as a form of liberation. Instead, according to Alarcón, Chicana poets and writers rehearsed the umpire role in their work as they documented the struggle and imagined liberation could be possible.[23]

In addition to Kafka, Alarcón utilized French feminist theory to interpret Chicana texts, specifically the work of philosophers Julia Kristeva and Luce Irigaray. French feminist theory traveled in the mid-eighties as part of the

---

20. Alarcón, "What Kind of Lover Have You Made Me, Mother: Toward a Theory of Chicanas' Feminism and Cultural Identity Through Poetry," 105.

21. Alarcón describes the parable in "What Kind of Lover Have You Made Me, Mother?" 86-87. Alarcón cited Hannah Arendt's version of the parable in *Between Past and Future: Eight Exercises in Political Thought* (London: Penguin Books, 1978), 7. Alarcón framed the Chicana writer as a possible umpire in "What Kind of Lover Have You Made Me Mother," 87 and 105.

22. Alarcón, "What Kind of Lover Have You Made Me, Mother?" 87.

23. Alarcón, "What Kind of Lover Have You Made Me, Mother?" 88.

continental theory boom in the U.S. academy.²⁴ Alarcón deployed Kristeva's concepts of the "sociosymbolic contract," "crisis of meaning," and "speaking subject" to describe the embattled agency of Chicanas in her essay "Making *Familia* from Scratch: Split Subjectivities in the Work of Helena María Viramontes and Cherríe Moraga." Extending the conversation she began in "What Kind of Lover Have You Made Me, Mother?" Alarcón argued that patriarchy, the gender binary, and heterosexuality conspired to ensure that the female body would be "pressed" into the appropriate gender as a "woman."²⁵ The "sociosymbolic contract" dictated an expression of gender and sexuality that left Chicanas very little space to "invent themselves." Alarcón argued that the characters in Moraga's "Giving Up the Ghost" bristled against this gendering process in a society ruled by a gender binary that "allows only one or the other" (man or woman), hinting at the possibility of refusal: "The speaking subject today has to position herself at the margins of the 'symbolic contract' and refuse to accept definitions of 'woman' and 'man' in order to transform the contract."²⁶ As Alarcón traced the mechanisms of gendering, she included queer gender identity and sexuality, placing queer Chicanas within Chicana feminist literary theory and criticism, although she did not delve into transgender identity except in the epigraph of the essay.²⁷

Alarcón's investment in theorizing refusal and resistance as well as her understanding of ideology and socialization as forms of entrapment from which Chicanas must be liberated appeared further in "The Sardonic Powers of the Erotic in the Work of Ana Castillo." She decoded Castillo's commentary

---

24. Kristeva and Irigaray engaged poststructuralist theorists of language and psychoanalysis as figures of the *écriture féminine* movement. See Luce Irigaray, *This Sex Which is Not One*, trans. Catherine Porter (Cornell University Press, 1985) and *The Julia Kristeva Reader*, ed. Toril Moi (Columbia University Press, 1986). Alarcón is not the only Chicana who drew on French Feminist theories. Historian Emma Pérez also cited and engaged with this work, especially in her influential essay, "Sexuality and Discourse: Notes from a Chicana Survivor," in *Chicana Lesbians: The Girls Our Mothers Warned Us About*, ed. Carla Trujillo (Third Woman Press, 1991), 159-184.

25. Alarcón, "Making *Familia* from Scratch: Split Subjectivities in the Work of Helena María Viramontes and Cherríe Moraga," in *Chicana Creativity and Criticism: Charting New Frontiers in American Literature*, ed. María Herrera-Sobek and Helena María Viramontes (Houston: Arte Público Press, 1988), 147-159. This essay implicitly dialogues with the work of philosopher Judith Butler, whose essays grappling with French feminist theories had been circulating prior to her book *Gender Trouble* (New York: Routledge, 1990).

26. Alarcón, "Making *Familia* from Scratch," 157.

27. The epigraph to the essay raises the question of gender identity. See Alarcón, "Making *Familia* from Scratch," 147-148. New work on transgender Chicanx experience can be found in Francisco J. Galarte's *Brown Transfigurations: Rethinking Race, Gender, and Sexuality in Chicanx/Latinx Studies* (Austin: University of Texas Press, 2021).

on "sexual/erotic oppression" upheld by an idealized heterosexual romantic narrative that led to disillusionment and cynicism.[28] Invoking Kristeva once again, Alarcón specified the "traditional heterosexual speaking subject" (who articulated potential bisexual leanings) as the protagonist "trapped in a variety of ideological nexuses that she, and we, need to question and disrupt."[29] Alarcón again raised the question of how to narrate and interpret our life experiences outside of *a priori* cultural images that stifled sexual liberation. Ultimately, the protagonist in Castillo's novel *The Mixquiahuala Letters* "inhabits a shooting gallery in which she must wear many a mask to survive and to understand where she has been."[30] For Alarcón, refusal and resistance require the mask or, in reality, many masks as a method for dodging the oppressive narratives.

The appearance of the Kafka parable or French feminists in Alarcón's literary critical readings of Chicana literature indexed Alarcón's intellectual trajectory as consonant with the "heyday" of contemporary theory and receptivity to European critical theories by Chicana/o literary critics. In "Chicano Critical Discourse: An Emerging Critical Practice" Chicana/Riqueña literary critic Angie Chabram-Dernersesian documented and interviewed Chicana/o literary critics, primarily men, who dominated the field of Chicano literary criticism. Alarcón was one of the few women among the slew of male critics Chabram-Dernersesian interviewed for her account of the field. She singled out Alarcón for noteworthy recognition: "Norma Alarcón's work forms part of an unprecedented and culturally significant Chicana critical enterprise which rivals cultural nationalism as a motivating social and political force in Chicano letters."[31] By this time Alarcón had moved to California for a position as a Chancellor's Postdoctoral Fellow at UC Berkeley and had been subsequently hired as a tenure-track faculty member in the Chicano Studies program within the Department of Ethnic Studies. Receptivity to Alarcón's critical project was evident in its circulation in a variety of literary anthologies and journals in Women's Studies, Chicana Studies, and Latina/o Studies. Alarcón's Chicana *bricolage* and construction of novel critical frameworks to theorize Chicana experiences helped to amplify the Chicana/Latina literary boom considerably.

---

28. Norma Alarcón, "The Sardonic Powers of the Erotic," in *Chicana Critical Issues,* ed. Norma Alarcón, Rafaela Castro, Emma Pérez, Beatriz Pesquera, Adaljiza Sosa Riddell, and Pat Zavella. Series in *Chicana/Latina Studies,* Mujeres Activas en Letras y Cambio Social (Berkeley: Third Woman Press, 1993), 5-19.

29. Alarcón, "Sardonic Powers of the Erotic," 5.

30. Alarcón, "Sardonic Powers of the Erotic," 18.

31. Angie Chambram-Dernesesian, "Chicano Critical Discourse: An Emerging Cultural Practice," 53.

As the eighties closed, Alarcón circled back to Malintzin in "Traduttora, Traditora: A Paradigmatic Figure of Chicana Feminism," a capstone essay that revisited many of the same questions raised in "Chicana's Feminist Literature" more extensively but expanded the scope of the analysis considerably. Published in the popular academic journal *Cultural Critique*, "Traduttora, Traditora" offered a sweeping cultural and transnational literary analysis of depth and breadth that explored the politics of modern interpretations of the meanings and applications of Malintzin's story and experience, from the historic reality to the various imaginings, mythifications, and re-imaginings across three groups of writers (Mexican men, Chicano men, and Chicanas). She declared that in contrast to the Virgen de Guadalupe, who was valued within patriarchy, "Malintzin stands in the periphery of the new patriarchal order and its sociosymbolic contract" a position from which she undermined and disturbed that patriarchal order.[32] Alarcón asserted that Chicana writing about Malintzin engaged in the literary, intellectual and feminist labor of calling her forth from the colonial and postcolonial condition of marginalization in which she, an indigenous enslaved woman, had been defamed as a bad mother and a traitor. With Chicana poets to hand, Alarcón saw the possibility of Malintzin's redemption: "Because Malintzin's sociosymbolic existence has affected the actual experience of so many Mexicanas and Chicanas it became necessary for 'her daughters' to revise her scanty biography."[33] Implicating Marxist theories of appropriation associated with capitalist acts of claiming ownership (and surfacing another theoretical influence in Alarcón's critical toolkit), Alarcón applauded Chicana poets' "reappropriation" of Malintzin from the problematic appropriations by mostly male writers. By claiming Malintzin as "one's own," Chicana writers change Chicano/Mexicano traditions and constructs of gender "from within culture."[34] Such an approach could enable Chicanas to "repossess ourselves" as Alarcón had called for in "Chicana's Feminist Literature."

As she concluded "Traddutora, Traditora," Alarcón sounded a hopeful note about the state of the field of Chicana feminist studies at the end of the decade. She observed, "since Chicanas have begun the appropriation of history, sexuality, and language for themselves, they find themselves situated at the cultural edge of a new historical moment involving a radical though fragile change in

---

32. Alarcón, "Traddutora, Traditora," 59.
33. Alarcón, "Traddutora, Traditora," 83.
34. Alarcón, "Traddutora, Traditora," 71.

consciousness."[35] At this juncture in her career, Alarcón modeled the *chingona* scholar-activist navigating the individualized demands of the academy while consistently and insistently collaborating with Chicanas/Latinas and women of color writers and scholars to produce new works that developed the field. Within ten years, she had not only published significant articles contributing to Chicana literary theory and criticism, she had completed a co-translation (with Ana Castillo) of *This Bridge Called My Back* as *Esta Puente, Mi Espalda: Voces de Mujeres Tercermundistas en los Estados Unidos*. Third Woman Press was also poised to publish a series of field-defining and now canonical texts. There would be many reasons to celebrate this Chicana feminist leap forward (and her role as a crucial instigator of that leap). She also observed a shift that had taken place in Chicana feminist studies: "Much of the Chicana feminist work of the seventies, like Anglo-American feminist work, was launched around the assumption of a unified subject organized oppositionally to men from a perspective of gender differences"; however, she wrote, Chicana feminism in the eighties recognized "differential experiences that cannot be contained under the sign of a universal woman or women."[36] It was time for the Chicana critic as the "figure in the periphery" to vindicate Malintzin not only by becoming "speaking subjects" in literary work but also by "repossessing ourselves" from feminist and other theories that erased Chicana's "differential experiences" and political agency. She called for nothing less than the liberation of Chicana theories.

Making Sense of It All: Chicana/Women of Color Consciousness, Subjectivity, and Political Agency in the Era of Identity Politics

> Thus, current political practices in the United States make it almost impossible to go beyond an oppositional theory of the subject, which is the prevailing feminist strategy and that of others; however, it is not the theory that will help us grasp the subjectivity of women of color.
>
> —Alarcón, "The Theoretical Subject(s) of *This Bridge Called My Back* and Anglo-American Feminism."[37]

---

35. Alarcón, "Traddutora, Traditora," 83.
36. Alarcón, "Traddutora, Traditora," 86-87.
37. Norma Alarcón, "The Theoretical Subject(s) of *This Bridge Called My Back* and Anglo-American Feminism," in *Making Face, Making Soul/ Haciendo Caras: Creative and Critical Perspectives by Feminists of Color*, ed. Gloria Anzaldúa (San Francisco: Aunt Lute Books, 1990), 366. *Making Face, Making Soul* is an interdisciplinary volume of poetry, political essay, short story, literary analysis, and critical theory.

AS THE NINETIES LAUNCHED, Alarcón more directly engaged questions of subjectivity, consciousness, experience, and agency that had surfaced in cultural studies, social movement studies, and social theory by calling attention to the misrepresentation of Chicana and women of color experiences in existing theories and debates in the academy. Two of her characteristically short, dense, and richly layered essays published in 1990 "The Theoretical Subject(s) of *This Bridge Called My Back* and Anglo-American Feminism" and "Chicana Feminism: In the Tracks of 'the' Native Woman" challenged dominant theories and sketched out alternative theories of Chicana/women of color subjectivity, consciousness, experience, and political agency under oppression. "Theoretical Subject(s)" was first published in Gloria Anzaldúa's anthology *Making Face, Making Soul: Haciendo Caras: Creative and Critical Essays by Women of Color* and "Chicana Feminism: In the Tracks of 'the' Native Woman," appeared in a special issue of the journal *Cultural Studies* dedicated to "Chicana/a Cultural Representations: Reframing Alternative Critical Discourses." Alarcón's theorizing about experience, identity, and agency was always grounded in acknowledging the historical, cultural, sociopolitical and material dimensions of Chicana and women of color lives. In other words, from "Chicana's Feminist Literature" to her later essays, Alarcón maintained her commitment to "putting the flesh back on the object," contrary to claims that she had uncritically embraced postmodernism's removal of any and all grounding for identity (which would certainly be a damaging prospect for Chicanas and women of color).[38] In fact, both "Theoretical Subject(s)" and "Chicana Feminism" cited *This Bridge Called My Back* and the lived experiences recounted within its pages as a generative text that set the terms for evaluating existing feminist theories vis-á-vis their relevance for women of color. *This Bridge Called My Back* overtly guided her theory-building project as rooted in "the 'flesh and blood' experiences of women of color."[39]

"The Theoretical Subject(s) of *This Bridge Called My Back* and Anglo-American Feminism" continued Alarcón's dialogue with theories of experience, consciousness, and knowledge but now shifted from her earlier criticism of universalist humanism to White feminist theories of the "subject" and their implications for women of color.[40] Answering her own insistence, stated at the end of "Traddutora, Traditora," upon theories that ethically represent

---

38. Paula M.L. Moya, "Chicana Feminism and Postmodernist Theory," *Signs* 26, no. 2 (Winter 2001): 441-483.
39. Norma Alarcón, "Chicana Feminism: In the Tracks of 'the' Native Woman," *Cultural Studies* 4. No. 3 (October 1990), 254.
40. Alarcón, "The Theoretical Subject(s) of *This Bridge Called My Back* and Anglo-American Feminism," 356.

"differential experiences," such as those communicated by women of color in *This Bridge Called My Back*, Alarcón confronted Anglo-American standpoint epistemology as inadequate for understanding women of color. Anglo-American standpoint theory claimed to represent "women's experience" and knowledge, but its assumptions excluded women of color or "subsumed" them into its theory. Alarcón observed, "Anglo-American feminist theory assumes a speaking subject who is an autonomous, self-conscious individual woman," that is, a subject modeled on privileged White man who had access to self-determination and full sociopolitical agency within the U.S. ideology of liberal individualism.[41] Additionally, Anglo-American feminist standpoint epistemology assumed gender as the primary oppression of women and therefore a rallying point or a "common denominator" for feminist politics that "set aside" other oppressions and inequalities such as those of race and class.[42]

In place of this version of standpoint epistemology and its assumptions about agency and consciousness, Alarcón called for "alternative theories of consciousness" based on women of color lives.[43] In what is an overlooked contribution to intersectionality studies that complemented Kimberlé Crenshaw's groundbreaking concepts of legal, structural, political, and representational intersectionality based on race and gender, Alarcón grappled with the *experiential* and *agential* dimensions and dilemmas of intersectional consciousness.[44] She sketched out parameters of an alternative theory drawing from the writings of the women of color activists in *This Bridge Called My Back*. She started with the premise that "[c]onsciousness as a site of multiple voicings is the theoretical subject par excellence of *Bridge*."[45] Building on her idea of "multiple voicings" she argued

---

41. Alarcón, "The Theoretical Subject(s) of *This Bridge Called My Back* and Anglo-American Feminism," 363.

42. Alarcón, "The Theoretical Subject(s) of This Bridge Called My Back and Anglo-American Feminism," 357-359.

43. Alarcón, "The Theoretical Subject(s) of *This Bridge Called My Back* and Anglo-American Feminism," 364.

44. On intersectionality studies see Sumi Cho, Kimberlé Williams Crenshaw, and Leslie McCall, "Toward a Field of Intersectionality Studies: Theory, Applications, and Praxis," *Signs* 38, no 4 (Summer 2013): 785-810. Black feminist and critical race theorist Kimberlé Crenshaw's coining of the term "intersectionality" was rooted in her brilliant critiques of the single axis logic of antidiscrimination doctrine and legal outcomes for Black women. She elaborated on the heuristic and problematic of the single axis in "Demarginalizing the Intersection of Race and Sex: A Black Feminist Critique of Antidiscrimination Doctrine, Feminist Theory, and Antiracist Politics," *University of Chicago Legal Forum* 1, Article 8 (1989): 139-167. Black feminist political scientist Ange-Marie Hancock writes about "intersectionality like" ideas in her intellectual history of intersectionality but does not include Alarcón. However, she does cite Anna Nieto-Gómez and Cherríe Moraga in her pre-history of intersectionality alongside Black women intellectuals and activists. See *Intersectionality: An Intellectual History* (Oxford University Press, 2016).

45. Alarcón, "The Theoretical Subject(s) of *This Bridge Called My Back* and Anglo-American Feminism," 365.

that the multiple systems women of color have to confront challenge their process of claiming consciousness, knowledge, and agency. Because women of color consciousness was situated in relation to multiple "thematic threads" of race, ethnicity, gender, and sexuality, "making sense" of experience involved grabbing hold of these "discourses that traverse consciousness" to claim their agency within and in relation to these "thematic threads" and "discourses."[46] When she described the multiple-voiced subjectivity coming from a woman of color who has to manage "competing notions for one's allegiance or self-identification," we can understand why Alarcón theorizes the agential work of managing the "thematic threads" as a weaving project.[47] Such a project is challenging for any individual oppressed person which explains why collective activist praxis (as reflected by the writers of *This Bridge Called My Back*) would be crucial. The women of color in *This Bridge Called My Back* grabbed hold of the "thematic threads" of race, ethnicity, class, gender, and sexuality, naming them and their positionalities as they wrote about their life experiences in a collective project.

Alarcón's "Theoretical Subject(s)" appeared as women of color scholars began to describe alternative epistemologies beyond the limitations of Anglo-American standpoint theory. Patricia Hill Collins published *Black Feminist Thought* in which she proposed a Black feminist epistemology. In the later nineties, Dolores Delgado Bernal outlined a Chicana feminist epistemology as a guiding principle for conducting research. Black and Chicana feminist epistemologies would be compatible with Alarcón's assertion of an ethical imperative for feminist theories that accounted for Black, Chicana, Asian American, and Native American experiences and consciousness.[48] Hill Collins and Delgado Bernal's work validated research conducted by, for, about, and *with* women of color, that is, research that started from the lives of Black women and Chicanas. At the same time, Alarcón

---

46. Alarcón, "The Theoretical Subject(s) of *This Bridge Called My Back* and Anglo-American Feminism," 366. Anzaldúa's description of the "[juncture] where the mestiza stands is where phenomena tend to collide" is from *Borderlands/La Frontera: The New Mestiza* (Aunt Lute Books, 1987), 79. See Alarcón, 369, n. 57. This description also resonates deeply with Crenshaw's imagery of the intersection, another example of parallel theorizing and one in which different forms of imaging give rise to the richness of intersectionality theories that bear deeper consideration.

47. Alarcón, "The Theoretical Subject(s) of *This Bridge Called My Back* and Anglo-American Feminism," 365. Alarcón's "weave" here is reminiscent of Chela Sandoval's notion of the differential consciousness that shifts strategies of resistance. See Sandoval, "US Third World Feminism: The Theory and Method of Oppositional Consciousness in the Postmodern World," *Genders* 10 (Spring 1991): 1-24.

48. See Patricia Hill Collins, *Black Feminist Thought: Knowledge, Consciousness and the Politics of Empowerment* (Routledge, 1990) and Dolores Delgado Bernal, "Using a Chicana Feminist Epistemology in Educational Research," *Harvard Educational Review* 68, no. 4, (December 1998): 555-582.

concluded "Theoretical Subject(s)" with a reminder that claiming agency may be a privilege of academics, writers, and activists. For this reason, women of color scholars, critics, activists, and researchers are compelled to uplift the knowledges and experiences of women of color who did not have access to the academy by drawing on or developing theories and frameworks, such as those proposed by Alarcón, Hill Collins and Delgado Bernal, that made their lives visible.

Published in the same year as "Theoretical Subject(s)," "Chicana Feminism: In the Tracks of 'the' Native Woman," described as a "position paper" by Alarcón, pivoted to focus on the meanings and mobilizations of the term "Chicana" in Chicana Studies. Moving beyond her earlier work in which she described Chicana writers as generally working class and bicultural Mexican American women she now defined Chicana as "the name of resistance that enables cultural and political points of departure and thinking through the multiple migrations and dislocations of women of 'Mexican' descent."[49] "The" native woman in this essay called back to Malintzin Tenepal but also referenced Indigenous women, past and present, whose lives and stories have been (and continued to be) erased and submerged through colonialisms and patriarchies. Underneath the many layers of shifting cultural, national, and political projects on race, a Chicana was more than a woman of "Mexican descent": "She is the descendant of native women who are continuously transformed into mestizas, Mexicans, emigrés to Anglo-America, 'Chicanas,' Latinas, Hispanics —there are as many names as there are namers."[50] Because there are so many names, it would be a challenge to mobilize a unified consciousness among Chicanas, according to Alarcón. Moreover, these names have historically occluded the native woman. Therefore, a complex Chicana identity politics required "The strategic invocation and recodification" (and reclamation, I would add) of the native woman (i.e., the hand outstretched in "Traddutora, Traditora") as the basis for Chicana identities.[51]

The core of Alarcón's "position paper" on Chicana identity politics was the assertion that "Chicana" constellated layered, multiple, and diverse histories of racialized (and gendered) bodies across two countries and two colonialisms that could not easily be categorized or contained. First, she recounted the Spanish colonialist project that attempted to identify and control racial mixture through diverse and extensive classifications (*las castas*). Then, she described how the

---

49. Alarcón, "Chicana Feminism: In the Tracks of 'the' Native Woman," 250. In "What Kind of Lover Have You Made Me, Mother?" Alarcón had referenced the earlier definition of Chicana, 105 and see 106, n. 1.
50. Alarcón, "Chicana Feminism: In the Tracks of 'the' Native Woman," 253.
51. Alarcón, "Chicana Feminism: In the Tracks of 'the' Native Woman," 252.

Mexican project of *mestizaje* ideologically homogenized racial constructions in a version of the melting pot thereby erasing African and Indigenous descendancy. Finally, in a U.S. context where *mestiza* signals non-white, the homogeneity of *mestizaje* takes on a different tone and meaning. Ultimately, Alarcón maintained, all of these dynamics of racialization, a dizzying narrative of multiplicities and historical disjunctures, informed Chicana identities. For this reason, there could be no ahistorical or universal Chicana because Chicana indexed multiple "embodied histories," which is why she declared that the *mestiza* concept, despite attempts by the Mexican nation-state to mobilize it for a homogenizing project, was "always already bursting its boundaries."[52]

In addition to redefining "Chicana," Alarcón proposed an interdisciplinary Chicana feminist scholar-activist agenda to document and to interpret Chicana social, cultural, and political agency. A critical point in Alarcón's social and political theory was the importance of relationality, which meant considering Chicanas in relation to other groups including "all men and some Anglo-European women."[53] (Her insistence on relationality here and in "Theoretical Subject(s)" named a hallmark of intersectional analysis that required attention to the dynamics of differential positioning in society based on race, ethnicity, class, gender, nation, and sexuality.[54]) As sites for interpreting and documenting Chicana agency and subjectivity, Alarcón pointed to literature, social science studies, and autobiography, or all of these at once. In this way, through research and activism driven by a commitment to "read" Chicana individual and collective political agency (The "We's" and "I's" she refers to), Chicana feminist studies could empower Chicanas and her *hermanas*. In the decades since Alarcón published this essay, Chicana and Latina scholars, educators, and critics have elaborated and adopted methods of auto-ethnography, *testimonio*, and *autohistoria teoría* in ethnic and gender studies.

It is important to underscore here that in both "Chicana Feminism: In the Tracks of 'the' Native Woman" and "The Theoretical Subject(s) of *This Bridge Called My Back* and Anglo-American Feminism" Alarcón maintained a wariness about any assumptions of homogeneity of knowledge or experience among groups of women—including women of color—such as those implied by references

---

52. Alarcón, "Chicana Feminism: In the Tracks of 'the' Native Woman," 250.
53. Alarcón, "Chicana Feminism: In the Tracks of 'the' Native Woman," 254.
54. In "Theoretical Subject(s)" she stated that there was a need for "a reconfiguration of the subject of feminist theory, and her relational position to a multiplicity of others, not just white men," 359.

to a "unified subjectivity" or "shared consciousness."[55] In "Chicana Feminism" she defined "Chicana" as a collectivity and solidarity across borders rather than an identity based on sameness of experience. Acknowledging the need for collective action while simultaneously recognizing that difference could function to "destabilize group or collective identities" she argued for a more productive approach to organizing through "provisional solidarities" or coalitions, such as those named by the concept of "women of color."[56] "Provisional solidarities" would be distinguished from literary theorist Gayatri Spivak's "strategic essentialism" that circulated in the nineties at the height of contentious debates in identity politics.[57] Where "strategic essentialism" suggested a temporary capitulation to an idea of inherent characteristics of a particular identity for the sake of unity, "provisional solidarities" would be formed with difference as a given and would welcome the idea of "diverse, multiply-constructed subjects and historical conjunctures."[58]

Alarcón's two essays published at the dawn of the nineties emphasized her insistence upon themes of intersectionality, relationality, and solidarity against reductive, simplistic, and essentialist identity politics. Going beyond "oppositional" positions, Alarcón not only criticized the limitations of existing theories, whether universalist humanist (as in "Chicana's Feminist Literature") or Anglo-American feminist, she also created new critical vocabularies and analytics for interpreting Chicana and women of color feminisms, theories, and social movements such as relationality, "flesh and blood experiences," "consciousness as a weave," and "thematic threads." In short, these two essays offered a way to "make sense of it all" so that Chicanas and women of color, or any feminist of color scholars writing about Chicanas and women of color, could "grasp" Chicana and women of color lives. By doing so, Alarcón expanded the genealogies of intersectionality in feminist political theory and forged a Chicana feminist critical theory praxis "of her own."

---

55. See Alarcón "Theoretical Subject(s), 64, and Alarcón, "Chicana Feminism," 252.
56. Alarcón, "Chicana Feminism," 252.
57. Spivak's first use of the term "strategic essentialism" appeared in an interview she conducted with Australian scholar Elisabeth Grosz in 1984. It was reprinted in Gayatri Chakravorty Spivak, *The Post-Colonial Critic, Interviews, Strategies, Dialogues*, ed. Sarah Harasym (New York: Routledge, 1990), 11-12.
58. Alarcón, "Chicana Feminism," 252.

Resisting Subjects: Identity-in-Difference vs. Multiculturalism

> The very emergences of syncretic new subjects, recodified on their own terms and rehistoricized anew are dismissed without taking up the task of piercing beneath, uncovering the structure, relations and possibilities that present themselves as the conditions of the possibility of the [new subject's] appearing as it does. The maneuver to avoid the probing is done through a reobjectification of the "new subject," a reification or a denial of the historical meaning posited by the differential signifier. As a result the difference is not fully engaged as a resistance to the monologizing demands of the West.
>
> —Alarcón, "Conjugating Subjects in the Age of Multiculturalism." [59]

WITHIN A FEW YEARS of proposing new languages and paradigms for interpreting Chicana and women of color experiences, Alarcón ventured into the culture wars around multiculturalism that raged in the late eighties to nineties. At the national level, multiculturalism was largely seen as a liberal ideology meant to acknowledge cultural pluralism and difference within the nation-state. These debates over multiculturalism had been sparked within higher education when the "great books debate" at Stanford University questioned the centering of (White) Western men and Western civilization in the curriculum by calling for a curriculum that was more inclusive of "women, minorities, and class."[60] To conservatives, multiculturalism threatened the status quo of White supremacy and patriarchy in academic institutions where the canons of disciplines such as history and literature had not changed after the Ethnic Studies and Gender Studies revolution of the sixties and seventies. As a result, multiculturalism and the accompanying demands to revise the curriculum became the target of conservative wrath as reflected in books such as Allan Bloom's *The Closing of the American Mind* and Dinesh D'Souza's *Illiberal Education* that asserted the superiority of Western civilization over the voices of non-Western peoples

---

59. Norma Alarcón, "Conjugating Subjects in the Age of Multiculturalism," in *Mapping Multiculturalism*, ed. Avery F. Gordon and Christopher Newfield (Minneapolis: University of Minnesota Press, 1996), 132-133. This essay is an extended version of Norma Alarcón, "Conjugating Subjects: The Heteroglossia of Essence and Resistance," in *An Other Tongue: Nation and Ethnicity in the Linguistic Borderlands*, ed. Alfred Arteaga (Durham, NC: Duke University Press), 125-138.

60. Barbara Vobejda, "The Great Books Debate: Colleges and Universities Ask What Does It Mean to be an Educated Person," *Washington Post*, August 7, 1988. The debate included disciplines such as anthropology. Anthropologist Renato Rosaldo offered his analysis of culture in *Culture and Truth: The Remaking of Social Analysis* (Beacon Press, 1999). At UC Berkeley, the movement to diversify the curriculum congealed into an American Cultures requirement rather than an Ethnic Studies requirement.

and literatures.[61] In California, Stanford University and UC Berkeley were two major sites of this activism. However, while multiculturalism initially rendered an insurgent challenge to the overwhelming dominance of White and Western voices in the curriculum, it was quickly co-opted in the liberal academy as an apolitical pluralism.

In "Conjugating Subjects in the Age of Multiculturalism," Alarcón approached these debates from the perspective of difference. She argued that, while postwar shifts in the racial and gender landscape required new ways of thinking about difference, for the most part progressive or "liberal" cultural critics and social theorists persisted in applying outdated paradigms, political philosophies, and theories to understand the resistance signified by difference. These recycled paradigms shut down (whether intentionally or not) the implications of this historical shift and the meanings of difference for societal reimagining. Additionally, the concept of identity politics and criticism of essentialism dominated contentious academic debates around difference. Alarcón cited examples of European and White American social philosophers and political theorists who, in their wish to avoid the appearance of essentializing difference, instead offered what she called, "recodified appropriations" that undermined the critical edge of the languages of race and gender put forward by critics of color. For example, French philosopher Jean-Luc Nancy universalized the difference implied by *mestizaje* ("We are all part of *mestizaje*" or "We are all *mestizas*") while Jean-Paul Sartre proposed that *negritude*, referencing the difference of Blackness, be understood as a variation of class. Alternatively, Anglo-American feminist Diana Fuss promised to address "the problem of essentialist identity politics" in her book *Essentially Speaking*. Nonetheless, Alarcón argued, Fuss reinscribed the "autonomous, self-determining, liberal bourgeois subject" rather than come to terms with the fractured or multiple subject. As with the Anglo-American feminist standpoint theory Alarcón earlier evaluated, Fuss put aside the question of differences between or among women.[62] In Alarcón's estimation, each of these examples failed to grasp the concepts of race and resistance articulated by people of color, much less consider the intersectionality experiences of women of color..[63]

---

61. Allan Bloom, *The Closing of the American Mind: How Higher Education Has Failed Democracy and Impoverished the Souls of Today's Students* (New York: Simon & Schuster, 1987) and Dinesh D'Souza, *Illiberal Education: The Politics of Race and Sex on Campus* (New York: Free Press, 1991).
62. Alarcón, "Conjugating Subjects in the Age of Multiculturalism," 134.
63. Alarcón, "Conjugating Subjects in the Age of Multiculturalism," 133.

Returning to her central preoccupation with the lack of theories that accurately interpreted the "flesh and blood experiences of women of color," Alarcón countered the "charge of essentialism" weaponized against women of color such as essayist Gloria Anzaldúa by suggesting a phenomenology of women of color experience, difference, and resistance. For Alarcón, a woman of color phenomenology of experience, difference, and resistance would be shaped by history, race, class, gender, sexuality, ethnicity, and nation while also pushing against these determinations toward a future that would validate difference outside of the pre-existing, outdated narratives and beyond the "charge of essentialism." The central figure of this phenomenology would be the "subject-in-process" who navigated "signifying practices and structural experiences imbricated in the historical and imaginary shifting national borders of México and the United States for Chicanas, for example."[64] The complexities of this phenomenology required the concepts of identity-in-difference (which she cited from Lorde rather than Hegel) and the "cultural politics of difference" (citing Cornel West) as more accurate descriptions of the social landscape postwar rather than multiculturalism. To think through her proposed woman of color phenomenology, Alarcón introduced the concept of conjugating, a participle whose etymology means "a joining together" that also refers to the process of changing person and verb tense. In a discussion of Jacques Derrida's *différance,* she argues that two approaches or interpretations of difference can be understood as both "simultaneous *and* irreconcilable" thereby creating a space for the meanings of difference.[65] While the actual participle "conjugating" only appears twice in the essay, the concept provided a crucial clue to Alarcón's phenomenology of women of color agency by shifting the focus not only to the politics of interpretation but also to the multiple forces acting upon subjects who could only maneuver from within these forces (like the woman in the Kafka parable).[66]

While it is not easy to piece together Alarcón's theory of resistance, an alternative theory was required due to the complicity of multiculturalism with the nation-state and liberalism. In the second part of "Conjugating Subjects in the Age of Multiculturalism" Alarcón rendered a harsh and lucid critique of the partnership between liberalism and multiculturalism: "The term 'multiculturalism'

---

64. Alarcón, "Conjugating Subjects in the Age of Multiculturalism," 137.
65. Alarcón, "Conjugating Subjects in the Age of Multiculturalism," 134.
66. "Conjugating" appears twice in the essay, in the title and then in the context of her critique of anti-essentialists who show their "own resistance to conjugating both interpretations of interpretation and its significance for the present," 134.

appears to be a quick metaphoric fix signaling inclusion that both comprehends the commodifications of difference and refuses to hear the implications for the production of knowledge and the material grounds that give rise to revised social and political histories as well as the 'cultural politics of difference.'"[67] Nonetheless, despite her misgivings about political, social, and cultural theorists who misidentify difference, Alarcón entertained the "politics of recognition" coined by philosopher Charles Taylor and taken up in *Multiculturalism and the Politics of Recognition*.[68] In *Multiculturalism and the Politics of Recognition*, a group of political theorists and philosophers registered their understandings of multiculturalism and difference. Alarcón perceived that Taylor moved closer to understanding the "cultural politics of difference" only to be overtaken by Habermas's construction of equality within the terms of liberal individualism and legal procedures. Since the already existing frame of liberal individualism is more readily embraced, the result is that those operating from these assumptions would consistently reduce difference to the terms of the liberal nation-state.[69]

In addition to registering her objections to multiculturalism as the preferred ideology of difference within the terms of liberalism, Alarcón addressed yet another dimension of the culture wars debate when she explored how a "minority" subject might suppress their difference to fit within or to fortify the dominant narratives of the nation-state. In "Tropology of Hunger: The 'Miseducation' of Richard Rodríguez," published in David Palumbo-Liu's anthology, *The Ethnic Canon*, Alarcón scrutinized *Hunger of Memory: The Education of Richard Rodríguez*, an autobiography published in 1981 that gained some traction in the eighties as a representation of an "ethnic" voice. *Hunger of Memory* narrates an individual Mexican-American man's path of assimilation through higher education and his argument that his ethnicity was irrelevant—as long as he disavowed it. The autobiography was widely viewed as a response to the programs established after the civil rights and social movements of the sixties and seventies such as Affirmative Action and bilingual education that acknowledged difference and inequality. In her reading, Alarcón traced Rodríguez's affirmation of the dominant, bourgeois, liberal political subject and the accompanying presumption of juridical equality that depended on perceiving his difference as a private matter. In fact, he attempted to represent ethnicity as a matter of aesthetics,

---

67. Alarcón, "Conjugating Subjects in the Age of Multiculturalism," 139.
68. Taylor, Charles et al., *Multiculturalism: Examining the Politics of Recognition*," ed. by Amy Gutmann (Princeton: Princeton University Press, 1994).
69. Alarcón, "Conjugating Subjects in the Age of Multiculturalism," 145-146.

but belied his own sense that difference goes deeper than that. Indeed, the real issue is racialization: "the hidden episteme in Rodríguez's pastoral is the rage at our embodied history, for while his wit may pass muster, his face does not."[70] Finally, he distanced himself from *los pobres*, the (im)migrant "others" to the nation-state, in a subtext that perhaps inadvertently implicated anti-immigrant rhetorics in the U.S.[71]

Alarcón's "reading" of Rodríguez offered a rejoinder to the neoconservatives of color, primarily Black, South Asian, and Latinx, who offered their narratives as examples to demonstrate that meritocracy, bootstrap analogies, and assimilation allowed for the assimilation of "ethnics" especially during a time of increased legislative warfare waged on immigrants and on affirmative action.[72] Both of these essays cited the social justice issues at stake in debates about racial and ethnic (and to some extent, gender) difference. Alarcón's frame of reference included court cases, ballot measures, and propositions that legislated ongoing inequality in California from the late seventies to the mid-nineties: the "not guilty" verdict in the trial of the policeman who brutally beat Rodney King, Proposition 187 that was backed by the anti-immigrant "Save Our State" movement (and was later deemed unconstitutional), Proposition 227 "the Civil Rights Initiative" that overturned Affirmation Action in California, and an earlier case, Bakke vs. the UC Regents, in which a White man claimed that he was denied admission to UC Davis medical school due to the existence of racial quotas. Within a national frame, she cited the *Hernández v. Texas* decision that recognized Mexicans as a group that could experience discrimination. Alarcón's reference to these court cases and legislative actions nodded to LatCrit, the Latine based formation of Critical Race Theory, a school of legal thought that emerged in the late eighties to examine juridical and legislative processes as they impact Latine people.

In sum, Alarcón responded to the misidentifications of difference by even well-meaning scholars who engaged in "reification," "denial," and "prohibition," by re-asserting the importance of building a theory from the experiences of people of color rather than re-apply outworn paradigms and frameworks that proved to domesticate or deny cultural resistance. Additionally, "Conjugating

---

70. Norma Alarcón, "Tropology of Hunger: The 'Miseducation' of Richard Rodríguez" in *The Ethnic Canon: Histories, Institutions, and Interventions*, ed. David Palumbo-Liu (Minneapolis: University of Minnesota Press, 1995), 150.

71. Alarcón, "Tropology of Hunger," 144.

72. See, for example, Shelby Steele, *The Content of Our Character: A New Vision of Race in America* (New York: St. Martin's Press, 1990) and Linda Chávez, *Out of the Barrio: Toward A New Politics of Hispanic Assimilation* (New York: Basic Books, 1992).

Subjects" and "Tropology of Hunger" pointed to the limits and problems of multiculturalism in a context in which the project of interpreting resistant subjects and acknowledging difference within the nation-state had been pushed aside. Ultimately none of the critics she contended with had accurately applied the interpretive labor needed to make difference visible on its own terms. It was up to the Chicana and woman of color critic to do this work. That meant that the Chicana critic doing the labor had to be visible and therein lay the dilemma.

Repossessing Ourselves: Chicana Intellectual Labor and Interpretive Agency

> To pursue the nexus or the intersectionality of the multiple discourse structures that surround the Chicana critic is in a sense to come to terms with the modes through which her disappearance is constantly promoted through the speech of others no matter how unintentional and against which she struggles through counter —and disidentificatory discourses.
>
> —"Cognitive Desires: An Allegory of/for Chicana Critics"[73]

As Alarcón had predicted, the nineties was a watershed decade for the production of Chicana feminist theory. It would not be an exaggeration to suggest that Third Woman Press pushed forward the "cultural edge" with anthologies and special journal issues that compiled dense and rich analysis, creative writing, and cultural theory by, for, and about Chicanas and Latinas including *The Sexuality of Latinas* (1989), *Chicana Lesbians: The Girls Our Mothers Warned Us About* (1991), *Chicana Critical Issues* (1992), *Chicana (W)rites on Word and Film* (1995), and *Living Chicana Theory* (1997).[74] A number of essays in these anthologies had been previously published, but here they were compiled intentionally as a Chicana body of thought. Placed firmly within the frame of the "Third Wave" of feminism and pushing the wave further (although without acknowledgement in

---

73. Norma Alarcón, "Cognitive Desires: An Allegory of/for Chicana Critics," in *Chicana (W)rites On Word and Film*, ed. María Herrera-Sobek and Helena María Viramontes (Berkeley: Third Woman Press, 1995), 187.

74. *The Sexuality of Latinas* was a themed issue of the journal *Third Woman IV* (Berkeley: Third Woman Press, 1989); Carla Trujillo, ed. *Chicana Lesbians: The Girls Our Mothers Warned Us About* (Berkeley: Third Woman Press, 1991); Norma Alarcón et al. eds. *Chicana Critical Issues*. Series in Chicana/Latina Studies, Mujeres Activas en Letras y Cambio Social. (Berkeley: Third Woman Press, 1993); María Herrera-Sobek, and Helena María Viramontes, eds. *Chicana (W)Rites: On Word and Film* (Third Woman Press, 1995); and Carla Trujillo, ed. *Living Chicana Theory* (Third Woman Press, 1997).

the mainstream), these works announced a renaissance of Chicana knowledge, expression, and celebration.

In spite of the proliferation of Chicana scholarship that could ground our existence in the academy, Alarcón found herself contending with the devaluation of her intellectual labor. As she theorized the challenges of grasping agency and the meanings of experience for Chicanas and women of color, she was to a large degree describing —through her readings of Chicana literary texts —her own experiences as a Chicana academic and critic within the academy. In a masterful analysis of the forces that conspired to hold a Chicana intellectual in her place, Alarcón's "Cognitive Desires: An Allegory of/for Chicana Critics" mapped out the difficulties not only of speaking but also of being heard as a Chicana intellectual in the academy. In "Cognitive Desires," she testified to the exasperating and exhausting institutional and interpretive gatekeeping that disappeared the Chicana intellectual, her texts, and her labor, exposing the hidden mechanisms of exclusion experienced by women of color in the academy.

The "cognitive desire" of the Chicana critic in this essay is for "interpretive agency"—that is, the ability to tell her own story, to have her difference recognized, and to analyze her texts with her own critical apparatus.[75] This critical agency continued to be suppressed by iinstitutional sites of academic knowledge production such as conferences, disciplinary boundaries and, especially Euro-American interpretive frameworks that misread or domesticated texts and critics of color. Alarcón charged the academy with wielding a heavy hand to control Chicana critical voicings: "It is often the institutionalized prerogative of both the Angloamerican and the European to decide where we belong, which may foreclose almost all possibilities for self-propelled inquiry on the part of Chicanas."[76] To add to the disenfranchisement of the Chicana critic, Alarcón writes—in her matter of fact tone that barely hides rage and disappointment— both established disciplines such as Spanish and English as well as the newer insurgent fields of Ethnic and Gender Studies required Chicana critical work to follow preconceived terms of engagement.[77] Additionally, Alarcón pointed out that nation-states (U.S. and México) and their political economies of race, class, and gender contributed to Chicana disappearance in transnational spaces. This brief sketch of her argument only scratches the surface of the profound

---

75. Alarcón, "Cognitive Desires," 193.
76. Alarcón, "Cognitive Desires," 193.
77. Alarcón, "Cognitive Desires," 193-194.

achievement of this essay, a *tour de force* that, more than twenty-five years later, may still ring painfully true for many Chicana scholars.

"Cognitive Desires" introduced yet another iteration of "Chicana," a category and identity that became successively more layered and nuanced in Alarcón's work over time. Alarcón consistently referenced the Chicano movement and the Chicana feminist organizing that emerged within and from the movement as the framing historical context for the production of Chicana feminist discourse.[78] Where "Chicana Feminism: In the Tracks of 'the' Native Woman" had added more layers to the term Chicana, "Cognitive Desires" deepened her framework of Chicana resistance through the concept of memory:

> In my view, then, the academic allegory of/for Chicana critics refers to that woman of Mexican descent who claims the name Chicana, lives in the United States, may even be a descendant of native or long-time residents, and most importantly, *refuses to forget* that she is also the descendant of peoples, some of whose names have disappeared, who have been engaged in continuous conflict with state and institutional powers that wish to *repress the memory* of the unsavory consequences of conquest, colonization, dislocation, discrimination, and their historical transformations.[79] (emphasis mine)

Memory and refusal are two less obvious elements of Alarcón's conceptualization of Chicana critical history and praxis. The Chicana critic's memory, embedded within her critical praxis, functioned as a site of resistance to the erasure of history.

"Cognitive Desires" maintained Alarcón's argument for a provisional practice of Chicana identity politics as she had previously outlined in "In the Tracks of 'the' Native Woman." In other words, these identities, with all the layers, histories, and intersectionalities mobilized "through the term Chicana" were not homogenous, rather they were "differentially theorized experiences," a force of resistance articulated through the "speaking subjects-in-process."[80] In a dense paragraph that reiterates the phenomenology of Chicana resistance she put forward in "Conjugating Subjects in the Age of Multiculturalism," Alarcón positioned the Chicana critic and writer as a "subject-in-process" whose written

---

78. For an overview of the emergence of Chicana feminism in the movement, see Alma M. García, "The Development of Chicana Feminist Discourse, 1970-1980," *Gender and Society* 3, no. 2. (1989): 217-238.

79. Alarcón, "Cognitive Desires," 185.

80. Alarcón, "Cognitive Desires," 198-200. These two pages are crucial to an understanding of Alarcón's theory of Chicana resistance.

interventions could effect change on multiple registers of praxis that she had referred to previously (and reiterated here) as reconfiguration, transculturation, and transcodification.[81] In this way, Alarcón tracked Chicana methods of resistance as wide-ranging and multiple. She also acknowledged, drawing on references to Marxist concepts of use and exchange value, that this "speaking subject-in-process" grappled with dynamics of textual commodification, (de)valuation of her intellectual labor, and discourses of authenticity.

In this context, and in dialogue with "Cognitive Desires" Alarcón turned to Gloria Anzaldúa's pathbreaking work, *Borderlands/La Frontera: The New Mestiza* as proffering an antidote to disappearance and a new theoretical vision for Chicana critical theory. Alarcón began "Anzaldúa's *Frontera*: Inscribing Gynetics" by noting that the ways that the theory project—whether from the dominant Anglo-American side or the minoritized ethnonationalist side— excluded women of color or used them to "rematerialize their discourse."[82] Instead, Alarcón proposed that Chicana literary texts, and specifically, Gloria Anzaldúa's *Borderlands/La Frontera,* reflected a project of Chicana self-inscription that went beyond literary criticism to engage with historical, material, phenomenological, and juridical forces. Taking Anzaldúa's *Borderlands/La Frontera: The new mestiza* as a generative text for Chicana critical theory raised the question: Was Anzaldúa the "umpire" in the Kafka parable? Or was Anzaldúa the "she" in the parable, fighting the past and the future in the present? She would, indeed be both ("the stand-in"). Through her stunning interpretation of *Borderlands*, Alarcón showcased a methodology to identify the many "thematic threads"—representing the discourses, structures, and narratives—embedded in Anzaldúa's text and their relation and response to multiple forces. These embedded narratives (woven?), Alarcón asserted, were "inscribing gynetics," by recovering the feminine through mestiza consciousness. Alarcón deftly sketched out how Anzaldua's work pushed against Western and colonialist narratives and, driven by queer epistemologies, narrated a path to self-recovery (repossessing ourselves?) that might now be understood as a form of decolonization.[83]

As Alarcón crafted her interpretation of *Borderlands*, the concepts of the weave, cognitive (dis)locations, the speaking subject, counterdiscourse, disidentification, and the polyvalent guided the way. She specified finer points

---

81. Alarcón, "Cognitive Desires," 199.

82. Norma Alarcón, "Anzaldúa's *Frontera:* Inscribing Gynetics," in *Displacement, Diaspora, and Geographies of Identity,* ed. Smadar Lavie and Ted Swedenburg (Durham, NC: Duke University Press, 1996), 41-42.

83. Alarcón, "Anzaldúa's Frontera," 49-52.

of resistance when she chose disidentification more definitively over counter identification: "The desire is not so much a counterdiscourse as that for a disidentificatory one that swerves away and begins the laborious construction of a new lexicon and grammars."[84] Disidentification moved her critical praxis away from battling the dominant primarily on their terms to centering—as she did in her earliest critical essay—the Chicana critical text as a text of theory. In "The Theoretical Subject(s) of *This Bridge Called My Back* and Anglo-American Feminism," she had already tracked disidentification as the method of resistance: "It is a process of *disidentification* with prevalent formulations of the most forcefully theoretical subject of feminism."[85] Alarcón also re-introduced a new key word in her interpretive tool kit. She applied polyvalent to name the multiple feminine manifestations of goddesses that constellated into *mestiza* and *Indígena* subjectivity. In science, valence relates to the combining capacity of atoms. Polyvalent suggested the combinations of meanings, discourses, and the creation of new connections. As applied in "Anzaldúa's *Frontera*," the polyvalent brought into view the many histories and "many names" of the Chicana subject as well as how she was racialized, ethnicized, gendered, and classed.[86] In short, Alarcón's interpretation of *Borderlands/La Frontera* demonstrated how to conduct a decolonial as opposed to a multicultural reading of a Chicana text—an act of critical and scholarly repossession of the text and its meanings.

As a coda to this discussion and honoring that Alarcón at times slightly revised and republished several of her essays, a later version of "Anzaldúa's *Frontera*" (the version included in this book) incorporated a familiar note of self-reflection from Alarcón when she reminded us of the many women of color who might not have ready access to critical and interpretive agency. According to Alarcón, the charge of the Chicana critic was to represent and to surface women of color resistance. At the end of this later version of "Anzaldúa's *Frontera*," she declared:

> The contemporaneous question, then, is how this [Anzaldúa's critical theory] can continue to be rewritten in multiple ways from a new ethical and political position, and what might it imply for the feminine

---

84. Alarcón, "Anzaldúa's Frontera," 53.
85. Alarcón, "Theoretical Subject(s)," 366. Alarcón draws on Michel Pêcheux's *Language, Semantics, and Ideology* (New York, St. Martin's Press, 1982) for this formulation. As part of his genealogy of disidentification, Latinx Queer Theorist and Performance Studies scholar José Esteban Muñoz refers to Alarcón's work in *Disidentifications: Queers of Color and the Performance of Politics* (Minneapolis: University of Minnesota Press, 1999), 22.
86. In "Anzaldua's *Frontera*," the terms polyvalent or polyvocal appear on 355, 359, 360, 365.

in our historical context, especially for women of Mexican descent and for others for whom work means migration to the electronic, high-tech assembly work on both sides of the U.S.-Mexican border.[87]

Alarcón returned our attention to the women of color who did not have access to their agency, often women workers.[88] Certainly, another context for Alarcón's work in the mid-nineties was the reports of violence against maquiladora workers on the US-Mexican border, or what we now call femicides, that called attention to the lives of Mexicana workers.[89] Alarcón's question was part of what she would call a "mandate" for the knowledges of women workers and women of color to be surfaced and visibilized as political agency. She acknowledged that despite the oppressive structures, discourses, symbolics, and histories that can shut her down, the Chicana critic in the academy had access to privileges that many women workers did not have.

LIBERATING CHICANA CRITICS AND OUR THEORIES: TOWARD SELF DECOLONIZATION

> One thing is still certain: we queer and feminist women of color are wedged in or caught in the crossfire of multiple patriarchies inside and outside of the university. [...] I believe that we continue to be part of the insurrection of subjugated knowledges and that our mere existence is transgressive.
>
> —From "Conjugations: The Insurrection of Subjugated Knowledges and Exclusionary Practices"[90]

THE POLITICAL CONTEXT OF events of the late nineties and into the new millennium impacted Alarcón's personal/political, institutional, and scholarly life. In California, ballot measures targeting immigrants in the early to mid-nineties and the overturning of Affirmative Action after the passage of Proposition 209 in 1996 led to student discussions with faculty in Ethnic Studies about the impact of these

---

87. See *Chicana Feminisms: A Critical Reader*, ed. Gabriela F. Arredondo, Aída Hurtado, Norma Klahn, Olga Nájera-Ramírez, and Patricia Zavella (Durham, NC: Duke University Press, 2003), 367. In "Chicana Feminism: In the Tracks of 'the' Native Woman" she lays out the scholar activist project as empowering "actual subaltern native women in the US/México dyad," 254.

88. See also "Chicana Feminism," 248-256.

89. See *Terrorizing Women: Feminicide in the Americas*," ed. by Rosa Linda Fregoso and Cynthia Bejarano (Durham, NC: Duke University Press, 2010) and *Making a Killing: Femicide, Free Trade, and La Frontera*, ed. Alicia Gaspar de Alba and Georgina Guzmán (Austin: University of Texas Press, 2010).

90. Alarcón, "Conjugations," 223.

legislative actions and how they could undermine Ethnic Studies.⁹¹ Along with these events and actions by students, the UC Berkeley administration threatened budget cuts to Ethnic Studies that precipitated intense student activism and a hunger strike in April-May 1999. Students demanded more faculty and more funding for the programs in Ethnic Studies. Alarcón was among those faculty who expressed solidarity with the students' efforts, a fact that would not be forgotten by the administration.⁹² Maintaining her focus on advocacy for the voices of feminist and queer women of color, Alarcón continued to lead Third Woman Press and to participate in Latina and women of color writing and scholarship collectives. These projects demonstrated her unrelenting commitment as a scholar, activist, and publisher even as she experienced turmoil in her institutional life (as well as her personal life) that culminated in her departure from the academy as an Emeritus Professor in 2004.

Against this fraught backdrop, Alarcón never stopped collaborating with feminists of color and Chicana/Latina feminists to create spaces in the academy and to activate conversations among Latinas and women of color within a global/transnational context.⁹³ The Telling to Live Collective convened a series of cross-national dialogues among Latinas in the academy in the mid-nineties, after which, through dialogue and consensus, participants agreed to share their testimonies in the book *Telling to Live: Latina Feminist Testimonios*.⁹⁴ Alarcón contributed her previously published poem "Forced by Circumstance" (the title of this collection and reprinted in the preface) to that effort. When "transnationalism" emerged as a new analytic of feminist thought in the nineties, Alarcón ensured Chicanas and Latinas were part of this conversation when she co-edited *Between Woman and Nation: Nationalisms, Transnational Feminisms, and the*

---

91. For the background to the various factors that led to the student hunger strike, see Jennie M. Luna, "1999 twLF at UC Berkeley: An Intergenerational Struggle for Ethnic Studies. *Ethnic Studies Review* 42. no. 2 (2019): 83–98.

92. See Luna, "1999 twLF at UC Berkeley"; Ellie Hernández, "Norma Alarcón," in *The Oxford Encyclopedia of Latinos and Latinas in the United States*, ed. Suzanne Oboler and Deena J. González (Oxford: Oxford University Press, 2005) 52-53; Jared Sexton and Frank B. Wilderson III, "The twLF Hunger Strike: A Critical View—On Tactics and a Broader Mission," in *Against the Current: A Socialist Journal* 83 (November-December 1999). https://againstthecurrent.org/atc083/p1733/.

93. Collaborating to facilitate new voices and scholarship was central to the mission of Third Woman Press. In 1994, Alarcón and Asian American feminist literary scholar Elaine Kim co-edited a collection of essays on Theresa Hak Kyung Cha's *Dictée* (Berkeley: Third Woman Press, 1994). The collection showcased literary criticism by established and emerging Asian American scholars.

94. "Introduction, Papelitos Guardados: Theorizing Latinidades through Testimonio," in *Telling to Live: Latina Feminist Testimonios*, Latina Feminist Group (Durham, NC, Duke University Press, 2001), 6-21.

State. Five essays by Chicana/Latina scholars were included in this collection, among them a republication of Alarcón's "In the Tracks of 'the' Native Woman."[95]

Alongside these collaborative and collective projects that elevated Chicana/Latina narratives and scholarship, Third Woman Press published a new edition of *This Bridge Called My Back*. To celebrate this third edition, a conference entitled *Practicing Transgression: Radical Women of Color for the 21st Century* was organized at UC Berkeley, featuring keynote speakers such as Angela Davis and the original editors Gloria Anzaldúa and Cherríe Moraga.[96] The conference took place in February 2002, early in the Bush "W" presidency that was an outcome of a deeply contested election and amidst a resurgence of zealous patriotism and Christian fundamentalism that followed the September 11 terrorist attack. As described by the organizers, the conference meditated on the relevance of *This Bridge Called My Back* twenty years later through panel discussions of healing, decolonial praxis, globalization, and state terror. Panel themes and plenaries proclaimed a revival of the radical politics and perspectives of *This Bridge Called My Back* for a new era by addressing topics that had not been present in the first or second editions of *This Bridge Called My Back*.

However, behind the scenes of these projects in the late nineties to early aughts, Alarcón had been struggling with institutional micro-macro aggressions as the "only out feminist Chicana" faculty member at UC Berkeley.[97] Her powerful *testimonio*/memoir essay "Conjugations: The Insurrection of Subjugated Knowledges and Exclusionary Practices" takes us to the Chicana critic twenty years after "Cognitive Desires: An Allegory of/for Chicana Critics" to reckon with the reality of her conditions of existence and struggle for space, voice, and validation in the academic industrial complex. While "Cognitive Desires" offered a thinly veiled analysis of the Chicana critic's experience, "Conjugations" more directly addressed concrete practices of exclusion, including misreadings of her work and tone, lesbian baiting/homophobia, race and gender microaggressions,

---

95. Caren Kaplan, Norma Alarcón, and Minoo Moallem, eds., *Between Woman and Nation: Nationalisms, Transnational Feminisms and the State*, (Durham, NC: Duke University Press, 1999). The five essays by Chicanas were Laura Elisa Pérez, "*El desorden*, Nationalism and Chicana/o Aesthetics," 19-46; Norma Alarcón, "Chicana Feminism: In the Tracks of 'The' Native Woman," 63-71; Rosa Linda Fregoso, "Re-Imagining Chicana Urban Identities in the Public Sphere, *Cool Chuca Style*," 72-91; Emma Pérez, "Feminism-in-Nationalism: The Gendered Subaltern at the Yucatán Feminist Congresses of 1916," 219-239; and Angie Chabram-Dernersesian, "'Chicana! Rican? No, Chicana Riqueña!' Refashioning the Transnational Connection," 264-295.

96. See Martha Arevalo Duffield and Karina Lissette Cespedes, "Practicing Transgression: Radical Women of Color for the 21st Century," *Meridians: feminism, race, transnationalism* 3, no. 1 (2002): 125-132.

97. Alarcón, "Conjugations," 217.

and dismissal of her intellectual labor by colleagues. "Conjugations" also commented on the institutional limitations of ethnic and women's/gender studies. While these fields were conceived as critical sites for empowering "subjugated knowledges," they existed under the constraints of an increasingly corporate and neoliberal university. In this context, no department was a home for Alarcón, a self-described "idealist Chicana feminist."[98] Seeking different home bases, she held appointments in Ethnic Studies, Chicano Studies, Women's and Gender Studies (including a stint as department chair), and Spanish. Essentially, she was living in a *nepantla* of the institution's making.

To manage the constant microaggressions in her daily work life as well as the macroaggressions of the institution, Alarcón admitted to taking anti-depressants that numbed her out so that these harms would have less effect on her mind, body, and spirit. When she decided to stop taking anti-depressants, she lifted the lid to a barely suppressed anger. In the face of the evaluation process for faculty, the historical barrage of racism and sexism, and rejection from Ethnic Studies/Chicano Studies when she sought to revert back to holding a single appointment, the culmination of years of constant micro/macro aggressions led her finally to walk off the job in a lone strike, a refusal of a phenomenal proportion when it comes to the academy and its norms and a powerful statement of valuing oneself and one's labor. Alarcón ends "Conjugations" by stating that she had "no regrets," but the reality of her shocking actions, breakdown, and the aftermath of forced retirement, remind us of the toll of daily life in a hostile environment for Chicanas and women of color, a story that is not new in the herstory of Chicana feminist thought.

Alarcón's self-disclosures, available in an "Institutional Violence"-themed issue of the *Chicana/Latina Studies* journal, courageously broke silences around Chicana experiences in the academy and launched an era of healing for Alarcón. It therefore made sense that one of Alarcón's next publications after almost ten years of healing and relative silence—during which she was teaching in San Antonio while managing various health concerns—was "Anzaldúan Textualities: A Hermeneutic of the Self and the Coyolxauhqui Imperative," a lucid exegesis of Gloria Anzaldúa's epistemological project. I would venture to say that Alarcón's own "Coatlicue state" and its aftermath solidified her perspective on Anzaldúa as a theorist of decolonial thought, or what Alarcón more specifically defined as self-decolonization. Anzaldúa's system of thought, worked through in her

---

98. Alarcón, "Conjugations," 202.

writings from "La Prieta" through *Borderlands/La Frontera* and subsequent essays, exemplified "alternative theories of consciousness" and epistemology that Alarcón had been seeking. For Alarcón, Anzaldúa's work was a "theory of our own" and a "visionary political philosophy drawn from praxis and theory of praxis."[99]

In "Anzaldúan Textualities" Alarcón teased out the elements of Anzaldúa's episteme from their individual/personal aspects to the political project of the spiritual activists or *nepantleras*. She saw Anzaldúa's proposal for new tribalism as a primer for *nepantleras* to collectively go up against larger structures such as imperialism. Alarcón unpacked the implications of the Shadow Beast as a theory of oppression/oppressiveness both within the self and within larger political structures that could contribute to discourses of restorative justice. Among the conclusions Alarcón drew from this work was that decolonization was not completed in one act, but required a constant, repetitive praxis of self-decolonization since, in the world we live in, we are constantly bombarded by colonial structures and ideologies.

"Anzaldúan Textualities" was a full circle moment that harkened back to her earlier work as a literary critic but now positioned as an interpreter of Chicana political philosophy invested in restorative and healing justice and self-decolonization. Features of this essay distinguish it markedly in language from others by Alarcón. For example, Alarcón engaged here less with European thinkers, with the exceptions of brief references to Simone de Beauvoir or Sigmund Freud, both of whom represented traditions of feminist and psychological thought that Anzaldúa's theories superseded. She embraced Anzaldúa's "concept-metaphors" to theorize the praxis of consciousness under colonization, that is, she allowed Anzaldúa to "speak" for herself through the concepts of *el cenote, nepantla, la naguala,* the Shadow, Coatlicue, Coyoalxauqui, *conocimiento,* and *arrebatamiento*. Anzaldúa as "speaking subject" created a Chicana hermeneutics that could lead toward self-decolonization with Alarcón as the collaborating interpreter and, yes, translator, of Anzaldúa's texts. In effect Alarcón found a path for Chicanas to "repossess ourselves" through the strategies she earlier referred to as "biographical" and "self mythologizing" to what we now call *autohistoria teoría,* automythography, and *testimonio*. Through Anzaldúa, Alarcón found a healing

---

99. Norma Alarcón, "Anzaldúan Textualities: A Hermeneutic of the Self and the Coyolxauhqui Imperative," in *El Mundo Zurdo 3: Selected works from the 2012 Meeting of the Society for the Study of Gloria Anzaldúa,* ed. Larissa M. Mercado-López, Sonia Saldívar-Hull, and Antonia Castañeda (San Francisco: Aunt Lute Books, 2013), 195.

space both in Anzaldúa's work and in the community that came together around the continued exploration of Anzaldúa's theories and philosophies of praxis.[100]

As she endured the micro and macroaggressions of the academy, Alarcón always reached back to *Bridge*, women of color feminism, and to Chicana feminist literature as the pillars of her scholarship and teaching. In "Conjugations" she writes "In a sense, the classroom was the only space of self-expression for me where my own voice could be mediated by and through the discussion of texts by queer and feminist women of color."[101] Throughout her career in the academy, Alarcón never backed down on asserting Chicana and women of color feminist and queer perspectives and experiences as the basis for critical theories that countered dominant paradigms of experience, agency and knowledge. Her ideas about resistance and agency have inspired new generations of feminist and queer scholars of color. Her essays continue to be taught in Chicana Studies and in feminist theory courses. She has received several awards that testify to her influence and legacy including the Tortuga Award from Mujeres Activas en Letras y Cambio Social (2005). She was recognized as a National Association for Chicana and Chicano Studies (NACCS) Scholar (2011), the highest honor for a scholar in the field.

Toward the end of "Conjugations," Alarcón wrote "If in ES and Chicano Studies I seemed to be performing a latter-day Malinche, among many a white progressive I had become a tokenized part of their dog and pony shows."[102] The only way Alarcón could escape the institutional *nepantla* was to leave the academy. Was she pushed out or did she walk out? This is the forever paradox of Chicana feminist resistance when our choices are reduced and the "death of [our] spirit" is at stake.[103] Chicanas who become speaking subjects—writers,

---

100. Norma Alarcón, Marisa Belausteguigoitia, and Romana Radlwimmer, "Nepantla–Productions of Pathologies and Healing: Under Construction," in *El Mundo Zurdo* 6. Selected works from the 2016 meeting of the Society for the study of Gloria Anzaldúa, ed. Sara A. Ramírez, Larissa M. Mercado-López, and Sonia Saldívar-Hull (San Francisco: Aunt Lute Books, 2018), 73-88. explores pedagogy, rage, and healing. The panel transcription offers a glimpse of the kind of space that exists at the Mundo Zurdo Conferences hosted by the Society for the Study of Gloría Anzaldúa. Marisa Belausteguigoitia with Alarcón and Romana Radlwimmer created an inspiring dialogue touching on critiques of academia and patriarchy, "cognitive desire," and the productive potential of embracing pathologies. Alarcón states, "One of my methodological problems has been anger and rage" (86) and that she seeks "to conjugate pleasure, anger, and power, inside and outside the classroom" (86-87).

101. Alarcón, "Conjugations," 209.

102. Alarcón, "Conjugations," 221.

103. Alarcón writes "In my view, the death of my spirit was at stake" when she chose to detox from the numbing effects of the anti-depressants. See "Conjugations," 219.

academics, activists—are working against repressive/oppressive mechanisms and forces of subordination. Publications such as *Presumed Incompetent: The Intersections of Race and Class for Women in Academia, Telling to Live: Latina Feminist Testimonios*, and a slew of essays by Chicana scholars on the challenges of the academic industrial complex communicate the ongoing struggle for women of color in the US academy.[104] Perhaps it is this challenge and experience that led Alarcón to further update her description of Chicana as "A self-decolonized critical political subject who is simultaneously aware of being both inside modernity and postmodernity as well as a subject-in-excess to both."[105] Chicana feminist scholars continue to navigate, weave, and live in *nepantla* because there is no other way to exist as Chicana intellectuals and feminists in the given configuration of the academy, even today. Alarcón's Malintzin praxis empowered her to "make Chicana feminist theory from scratch" constructing a legacy of critical and theoretical praxis that charted a path toward our future. We cannot allow ourselves to be pushed back.

---

104. Gabriella Gutiérrez y Muhs, Yolanda Flores Niemann, Carmen G. González, and Angela P. Harris, *Presumed Incompetent: The Intersections of Race and Class for Women in Academia*, (Denver: University Press of Colorado, 2012).

105. Norma Alarcón, "…But You Don't Look Mexican," in *Cien años de lealtad: en honor a Luis Leal/One Hundred Years of Loyalty: In Honor of Luis Leal*, ed. Luis Leal, Sara Poot Herrera, Francisco Lomelí, María Herrera-Sobek (University of California, Santa Barbara, Universidad Nacional Autónoma de México, Instituto Tecnológico y de Estudios Superiores de Monterrey, Universidad del Claustro de Sor Juana, 2007), 269.

BIBLIOGRAPHY

Alarcón, Norma. "Anzaldúan Textualities: A Hermeneutic of the Self and the Coyolxauhqui Imperative." In *El Mundo Zurdo 3: Selected works from the 2012 Meeting of the Society for the Study of Gloria Anzaldúa*, edited by Larissa M. Mercado-López, Sonia Saldívar-Hull, and Antonia Castañeda, 189-208. San Francisco: Aunt Lute Books, 2013.

Alarcón, Norma. "Anzaldúa's *Frontera:* Inscribing Gynetics." In *Displacement, Diaspora, and Geographies of Identity,* edited by Smadar Lavie and Ted Swedenburg, 41-53. Durham, NC: Duke University Press, 1996.

Alarcón, Norma. "…But You Don't Look Mexican." In *Cien años de lealtad: en honor a Luis Leal/One Hundred Years of Loyalty: In Honor of Luis Leal*, edited by Luis Leal, Sara Poot Herrera, Francisco Lomelí, and María Herrera-Sobek, 269. University of California, Santa Barbara, Universidad Nacional Autónoma de México, Instituto Tecnológico y de Estudios Superiores de Monterrey, Universidad del Claustro de Sor Juana, 2007.

Alarcón, Norma. "Chicana Feminism: In the Tracks of 'the' Native Woman." *Cultural Studies* 4. no. 3 (October 1990), 248-256.

Alarcón, Norma. "Chicana's Feminist Literature: A Re-vision through Malintzin/ or Malintzin: Putting Flesh Back to the Object." In *This Bridge Called My Back. Writings by Radical Women of Color*, edited by Cherríe Moraga and Gloria Anzaldúa, 182-190. Persephone Press, 1981.

Alarcón, Norma. "Cognitive Desires: An Allegory of/for Chicana Critics," in *Chicana (W)rites On Word and Film*, edited by María Herrera-Sobek and Helena María Viramontes, 185-200. Berkeley: Third Woman Press, 1995.

Alarcón, Norma. "Conjugating Subjects in the Age of Multiculturalism." In *Mapping Multiculturalism*, edited by Avery F. Gordon and Christopher Newfield, 127-148. Minneapolis: University of Minnesota Press, 1996.

Alarcón, Norma. "Conjugating Subjects: The Heteroglossia of Essence and Resistance," in *An Other Tongue: Nation and Ethnicity in the Linguistic Borderlands*, edited by Alfred Arteaga, 125-138. Durham, NC: Duke University Press, 1994.

Alarcón, Norma. "Conjugations: The Insurrection of Subjugated Knowledges and Exclusionary Practices." *Chicana/Latina Studies* 13, no. 2 (2014): 202-224.

Alarcón, Norma. "Hay Que Inventarnos/We Must Invent Ourselves." *Third Woman: of Latinas in the Midwest* 1, no. 1, (1981): 1.

Alarcón, Norma. "Making *Familia* from Scratch: Split Subjectivities in the Work of Helena María Viramontes and Cherríe Moraga." In *Chicana Creativity and Criticism: Charting New Frontiers in American Literature*, edited by María Herrera-Sobek and Helena María Viramontes, 147-159. Houston: Arte Público Press, 1988.

Alarcón, Norma. *Ninfomanía: El discurso feminista en la obra poética de Rosario Castellanos*. Madrid: Editorial Pliegos, 1992.Alarcón, Norma. "The Sardonic Powers of the Erotic in the Work of Ana Castillo." In *Chicana Critical Issues*, edited by Norma Alarcón, Rafaela Castro, Deena González, Margarita Melville, Emma Pérez, Tey Diana Rebolledo, Christine Sierra, and Adaljiza Sosa Riddell. Series in *Chicana/Latina Studies,* Mujeres Activas en Letras y Cambio Social, 5-19. Berkeley: Third Woman Press, 1993.

Alarcón, Norma, ed. *The Sexuality of Latinas Third Woman IV*. Berkeley: Third Woman Press, 1989.

Alarcón, Norma. "The Theoretical Subject(s) of *This Bridge Called My Back* and Anglo-American Feminism," in *Making Face, Making Soul/Haciendo Caras: Creative and Critical Perspectives by Feminists of Color*, edited by Gloria Anzaldúa, 356-369. San Francisco: Aunt Lute Books, 1990.

Alarcón, Norma. "Traddutora, Traditora: A Paradigmatic Figure of Chicana Feminism." *Cultural Studies* 13, (1989): 57-87.

Alarcón, Norma. "Tropology of Hunger: The 'Miseducation' of Richard Rodríguez." In *The Ethnic Canon: Histories, Institutions, and Interventions*, edited by David Palumbo-Liu, 140-153. Minneapolis: University of Minnesota Press, 1995.

Alarcón, Norma. "What Kind of Lover Have You Made Me, Mother: Toward a Theory of Chicanas' Feminism and Cultural Identity Through Poetry." In *Women of Color: Perspectives on Feminism and Identity*, edited by Audrey Thomas McCluskey, 85-110. Women's Studies Program, Indiana University, 1985.

Alarcón, Norma, Marisa Belausteguigoitia, and Romana Radlwimmer. "Nepantla–Productions of Pathologies and Healing: Under Construction." In *El Mundo Zurdo 6. Selected works from the 2016 meeting of the Society for the study of Gloria Anzaldúa*, edited by Sara A. Ramírez, Larissa M. Mercado-López, and Sonia Saldívar-Hull, 73-88. San Francisco: Aunt Lute Books, 2018.

Alarcón, Norma, Rafaela Castro, Emma Perez, Beatriz Pesquera, Ada Sosa Riddell, and Pat Zavella, editors. *Chicana Critical Issues.* Series in *Chicana/Latina Studies,* Mujeres Activas en Letras y Cambio Social. Berkeley: Third Woman Press, 1993.

Anzaldúa, Gloria. *Borderlands/La Frontera: The New Mestiza*. San Francisco: Aunt Lute Books, 1987.

Arendt, Hannah. *Between Past and Future: Eight Exercises in Political Thought*. London: Penguin Books, 1978.

Arredondo, Gabriela F., Aída Hurtado, Norma Klahn, Olga Nájera-Ramírez, and Patricia Zavella, eds. *Chicana Feminisms: A Critical Reader*. Durham, NC: Duke University Press, 2003.

Bernal, Dolores Delgado. "Using a Chicana Feminist Epistemology in Educational Research." *Harvard Educational Review* 68, no. 4 (December 1998): 555-583.

Bloom, Allan. *The Closing of the American Mind: How Higher Education Has Failed Democracy and Impoverished the Souls of Today's Students*. New York: Simon & Schuster, 1987.

Butler, Judith. *Gender Trouble*. New York: Routledge, 1990.

Castellanos, Rosario. *El Eterno Femenino*. México: Fondo de Cultura Económica, 1975.

Chabram-Dernersesian, Angie. "'Chicana! Rican? No, Chicana Riqueña!' Refashioning the Transnational Connection." *In Between Woman and Nation: Nationalisms, Transnational Feminisms and the State*. 264-295. Edited by Caren Kaplan, Norma Alarcón, and Minoo Moallem (Durham, NC: Duke University Press, 1999).

Chabram-Dernersesian, Angie. Chicano Critical Discourse: An Emerging Cultural Practice." *Aztlán: A Journal of Chicano Studies* 18, no. 2 (1987): 45-90.

Chávez, Linda. *Out of the Barrio: Toward A New Politics of Hispanic Assimilation*. New York: Basic Books, 1992.

Cho, Sumi, Kimberlé Williams Crenshaw, and Leslie McCall. "Toward a Field of Intersectionality Studies: Theory, Applications, and Praxis." *Signs* 38, no. 4 (Summer 2013): 785-810.

Collins, Patricia Hill. *Black Feminist Thought: Knowledge, Consciousness and the Politics of Empowerment*. London: Routledge, 1990.

Crenshaw, Kimberlé. "Demarginalizing the Intersection of Race and Sex: A Black Feminist Critique of Antidiscrimination Doctrine, Feminist Theory, and Antiracist Politics." *University of Chicago Legal Forum* 1, Article 8 (1989): 139-167.

Del Olmo, Frank. "Commentary: Latino 'Decade' Moves into 90s." *Los Angeles Times*, December 14, 1989.

Derrida, Jacques. "Structure, Sign, and Play in the Discourse of the Human Sciences." In *Modern Criticism and Theory: A Reader*, edited by David Lodge. Longman, 1988.

D'Souza, Dinesh. *Illiberal Education: The Politics of Race and Sex on Campus*. New York: Free Press, 1991.

Duffield, Martha Arevalo and Karina Lissette Cespedes. "Practicing Transgression: Radical Women of Color for the 21st Century." *Meridians: feminism, race, transnationalism* 3, no. 1 (2002): 125-132.

Fregoso, Rosa Linda. "Re-Imagining Chicana Urban Identities in the Public Sphere, Cool Chuca Style." *In Between Woman and Nation: Other: Nationalisms, Transnational Feminisms, and the State*. Edited by Caren Kaplan, Norma Alarcón, and Minoo Moallem. 72-91. Durham, NC: Duke University Press, 1999.

Fregoso, Rosa Linda and Cynthia Bejarano, editors. *Terrorizing Women: Feminicide in the Americas*. Durham, NC: Duke University Press, 2010.

Galarte, Francisco J. *Brown Transfigurations: Rethinking Race, Gender, and Sexuality in Chicanx/Latinx Studies*. Austin: University of Texas Press, 2021.

García, Alma M. "The Development of Chicana Feminist Discourse, 1970-1980." *Gender and Society* 3, no. 2 (1989): 217-238.

Gaspar de Alba, Alicia and Georgina Guzmán, eds. *Making a Killing: Femicide, Free Trade, and La Frontera*. Austin: University of Texas Press, 2010.

Gutiérrez y Muhs, Gabriella, Yolanda Flores Niemann, Carmen G. González, and Angela P. Harris, editors. *Presumed Incompetent: The Intersections of Race and Class for Women in Academia.* Denver: University Press of Colorado, 2012.

Hancock, Ange-Marie. *Intersectionality: An Intellectual History.* Oxford University Press, 2016.

Hernández, Ellie. "Norma Alarcón." In *The Oxford Encyclopedia of Latinos and Latinas in the United States,* edited by Suzanne Oboler and Deena J. González, 52-53. Oxford: Oxford University Press, 2005.

Herrera-Sobek, María and Helena María Viramontes, eds. *Chicana (W)Rites: On Word and Film.* Berkeley: Third Woman Press, 1995.

Irigaray, Luce. *This Sex Which is Not One.* Translated by Catherine Porter. Ithaca: Cornell University Press, 1985.

Kaplan, Caren, Norma Alarcón, and Minoo Moallem, eds. *Between Woman and Nation: Nationalisms, Transnational Feminisms and the State.* Durham, NC: Duke University Press, 1999.

Kim, Elaine H., Hyun Yi Kang, Lisa Lowe, and Shelley Sunn Wong. *Writing Self, Writing Nation: A Collection of Essays on Dictée by Theresa Hak Kyung Cha.* Edited by Norma Alarcón. Berkeley: Third Woman Press 1994.

Kristeva, Julia. *The Julia Kristeva Reader.* Edited by Toril Moi. New York: Columbia University Press, 1986.

Latina Feminist Group. "Introduction, Papelitos Guardados: Theorizing Latinidades through Testimonio." In *Telling to Live: Latina Feminist Testimonios,* 1-24. Durham, NC, Duke University Press, 2001.

Lorde, Audre. "The Master's Tools Will Never Dismantle the Master's House." In *This Bridge Called My Back. Writings by Radical Women of Color,* edited by Cherríe Moraga and Gloria Anzaldúa, 98-101. Watertown, MA: Persephone Press, 1981.

Lorde, Audre. ""Poetry is Not a Luxury." In *Sister/Outsider: Essays & Speeches,* 36-39. Berkeley: The Crossing Press, 1984.

Luna, Jennie M. "1999 twLF at UC Berkeley: An Intergenerational Struggle for Ethnic Studies." *Ethnic Studies Review* 42, no. 2 (2019): 83-98.

Moraga, Cherríe, and Ana Castillo, eds. *Esta Puente, Mi Espalda: Voces de Mujeres Tercermundistas en Los Estados Unidos.* Translated by Ana Castillo and Norma Alarcón. San Francisco: ism Press, 1988.

Moraga, Cherríe, and Gloria Anzaldúa, eds. *This Bridge Called My Back. Writings by Radical Women of Color.* Watertown, MA: Persephone Press, 1981.

Moya, Paula M.L. "Chicana Feminism and Postmodernist Theory." *Signs* 26, no. 2 (Winter 2001): 441-483.

Muñoz, José Esteban. *Disidentifications: Queers of Color and the Performance of Politics.* Minneapolis: University of Minnesota Press, 1999.

Pêcheux, Michel. *Language, Semantics, and Ideology*. New York: St. Martin's Press, 1982.

Pérez, Emma. "Feminism-in-Nationalism: The Gendered Subtaltern at the Yucatán Feminist Congresses of 1916," *In Between Woman and Nation: Nationalisms, Transnational Feminisms and the State*, edited by Caren Kaplan, Norma Alarcón, and Minoo Moallem, 219-239. Durham, NC: Duke University Presss, 1999.

Pérez, Emma. "Sexuality and Discourse: Notes from a Chicana Survivor." In *Chicana Lesbians: The Girls Our Mothers Warned Us About*, edited by Carla Trujillo, 159-184. Third Woman Press, 1991.

Pérez, Laura Elisa. "*El desorden*, Nationalism and Chicana/o Aesthetics." *In Between Woman and Nation: Nationalisms, Transnational Feminisms and the State*, edited by Caren Kaplan, Norma Alarcón, and Minoo Moallem, 219-239. Durham, NC: Duke University Presss, 1999.

Ramírez, Catherine S. "Alternative Cartographies: *Third Woman* and the Respatialization of the Borderlands, 1981-1986." *Midwestern Miscellany* 30, no. 2004 (Fall 2002): 47-62.

Ramírez, Sara A., and Norma E. Cantú, "Publishing Work that Matters: Third Woman Press and Its Impact on Chicana and Latina Publishing." *Diálogo* 20, no. 2 (Fall 2017): 77-85.

Rosaldo, Renato. *Culture and Truth: The Remaking of Social Analysis*. Beacon Press, 1999.

Sandoval, Chela. "US Third World Feminism: The Theory and Method of Oppositional Consciousness in the Postmodern World." *Genders* 10 (Spring 1991): 1-24.

Sexton, Jared, and Frank B. Wilderson III, "The twLF Hunger Strike: A Critical View—On Tactics and a Broader Mission," *Against the Current: A Socialist Journal* 83 (November-December 1999).

Short, Kayann. "Coming to the Table: The Differential Politics of *This Bridge Called My Back*." *Genders* no. 19 (June 30, 1994): 3.

Spivak, Gayatri Chakravorty. *The Post-Colonial Critic, Interviews, Strategies, Dialogues*. Edited by Sarah Harasym. New York: Routledge, 1990.

Steele, Shelby. *The Content of Our Character: A New Vision of Race in America*. New York: St. Martin's Press, 1990.

Taylor, Charles, Kwame Anthony Appiah, Jürgen Habermas, Steven C. Rockefeller, Michael Walzer, and Susan Wolf. *Multiculturalism: Examining the Politics of Recognition*. Edited by Amy Gutman. Princeton: Princeton University Press, 1994.

The Second Sex Thirty Years Later Program. Posted on Michelle Moravec, "Unghosting Apparitional (Lesbian) History, Erasures of Black Lesbian Feminism." scalar.usc.edu/works/unghosting-apparitional-lesbians/it-began-with-audre-lorde-1?origin=note, retrieved March 24, 2025.

Trujillo, Carla, ed. *Chicana Lesbians: The Girls Our Mothers Warned Us About*. Berkeley: Third Woman Press, 1991.

Trujillo, Carla, ed. *Living Chicana Theory*. Berkeley: Third Woman Press, 1997.

Vobejda, Barbara. "The Great Books Debate: Colleges and Universities Ask What Does It Mean to be an Educated Person." *Washington Post*, August 7, 1988.

PART I

HAY QUE INVENTARNOS

CHICANA'S FEMINIST LITERATURE

A RE-VISION THROUGH MALINTZIN/OR MALINTZIN: PUTTING FLESH BACK ON THE OBJECT[1]

→ ←

MALINTZIN (OR LA MALINCHE) was an Aztec noble woman who was presented to Cortés upon landing in Veracruz in 1519. She subsequently served Cortés as lover, translator and tactical advisor. She is a controversial figure in the Conquest of México. Her name is often called forth to reenact, symbolically, the Conquest or any conquest. Part of this drama, analogically so, is now being played out also in Aztlán.

Malintzin's history, her legend and subsequent mythic dimensions as evil goddess and creator of a new race—the mestizo race, embroils her in a family quarrel, where many male members often prefer to see her as the mother-whore, bearer of illegitimate children, responsible for the foreign Spanish invasion; and where female members attempt to restore balance in ways that are sometimes painfully ambivalent, and at other times attempt to topple the traditional patriarchal mythology through revision and re-vision.

This essay will explore the traditional image of Malintzin in Chicano culture and will provide examples of the ways contemporary Chicana feminist writers have reacted to and used this image in their work.

In our patriarchal mythological pantheon, there exists even now a woman who was once real. Her historicity, her experience, her true flesh and blood were discarded. A Kantian, dualistic male consciousness stole her and placed her on the throne of evil, like Dante's upside down frozen Judas, doomed to moan and bemoan. The woman is interchangeably called by three names: Malintzin, Malinche, Marina. Malintzin's excruciating life in bondage was of no account, and continues to be of no account. Her almost half century of mythic existence, until recent times mostly in the oral traditions, had turned her into a handy

---

1. *Editors' Note:* This essay was first published in *This Bridge Called My Back: Writings by Radical Women of Color*, ed. Cherríe Moraga and Gloria Anzaldúa (Watertown, MA: Persephone Press, 1981), 182-190. It was republished in all subsequent editions of *This Bridge Called My Back: Writings by Radical Women of Color*. Most recently it was published in *This Bridge Called My Back, Fortieth Anniversary Edition: Writings by Radical Women of Color* (Albany, NY: SUNY University Press, 2022), 181-189.

reference point not only for controlling, interpreting or visualizing women, but also to wage a domestic battle of stifling proportions.[2]

Unlike Eve whose primeval reality is not historically documentable and who supposedly existed in some past edenic time, Malintzin's betrayal of our supposed pre-Columbian paradise is recent and hence almost palpable. This almost-within-reach past heightens romantic nostalgia and as a consequence hatred for Malintzin and women becomes as vitriolic as the American Puritans' loathing of witches-women.

The focus of the betrayal is not a lofty challenge to a "god" who subsequently unleashed evil upon the world as punishment. Disobedience to a "god" might place the discussion at times on an ideal plane and relieve tension momentarily as one switches from an intense dialogue about one's body to a "rarefied" field at least in terms of the vocabulary used. However, the male myth of Malintzin is made to see betrayal first of all in her very sexuality, which makes it nearly impossible at any given moment to go beyond the vagina as the supreme site of evil until proven innocent by way of virginity or virtue, the most pawnable commodities around.[3]

Because the myth of Malintzin pervades not only male thought but ours too as it seeps into our own consciousness in the cradle through their eyes as well as our mothers', who are entrusted with the transmission of culture, we may come to believe that indeed our very sexuality condemns us to enslavement. An enslavement which is subsequently manifested in self-hatred. All we see is

---

2. Insofar as feminine symbolic figures are concerned, much of the Mexican/Chicano oral tradition as well as the intellectual are dominated by La Malinche/Llorona and the Virgin of Guadalupe. The former is a subversive feminine symbol which often is identified with La Llorona, the latter a feminine symbol of transcendence and salvation. The Mexican/Chicano cultural tradition has tended to polarize the lives of women through these national (and nationalistic) symbols thereby exercising almost sole authority over the control, interpretation and visualization of women. Although the material on both figures is vast, the following serve as guides to past and present visions and elucidations: Eric R. Wolf, "The Virgin of Guadalupe: A Mexican National Symbol," *The Journal of American Folklore* 71, no. 279 (1958): 34–39. Américo Paredes, "Mexican Legendary and the Rise of the Mestizo: A Survey," in *American Folk Legend*, ed. Wayland D. Hand (Berkeley: University of California Press, 1971): 97-107; Richard M. Dorson, "Forward," in *Folktales of Mexico*, ed. Américo Paredes (Chicago: University of Chicago Press, 1970), xvi-xxxvii; and Octavio Paz, "The Sons of la Malinche," in *The Labyrinth of Solitude*, trans. Lysander Kemp (New York: Grove Press, 1961): 65-88. Paz takes the traditional male perspective of woman as enigma and mystery and then proceeds to disclose the culture's (men's) mentality *vis-à-vis* these figures. Women in their assigned roles as transmitters of the culture have often adhered to these views; however, they have not created them.

3. Bertrand Russell, *Marriage and Morals* (New York: Liveright Publishing Corporation, 1929) affirms that the conception of female virtues has been built up in order to make the patriarchal family as we have known it possible.

hatred of women. We must hate her too since love seems only possible through extreme virtue whose definition is at best slippery.

The poet Alma Villanueva must have realized, understood the insidiousness of the hate syndrome. Her whole book *Bloodroots* is a song to the rejection of self-loathing. The poem "I sing to myself" states:

> I could weep and rage
> against the man who never
> stroked my fine child hair
> who never felt the pride of
> my femininity...[4]

It is not just the father that is a source of pain; a mother figure appears also. The mother is impotent to help the daughter. All of her energies seem directed, spent in her desire and need for man, a factor that repulses and attracts the daughter. Love for mother is an ambivalence rooted in the daughter's sense of abandonment by her mother and her apparently enormous and irrational need:

> Never finding a breast to rest
> and warm myself.[5]

As the daughter proceeds to repeat her mother's experience, she ironically discovers and affirms a "mounting self/love" as a combative force against the repetition of the mother's abnegation, and irrational need of and dependency on men. Self-love as a tool of survival, however leads the male lover to reject her. Her conclusion leaves no doubt as to what woman may be forced to do:

> l/woman give birth:
> and this time to
> myself[6]

The sexual abuse experienced leaves the daughter no choice but to be her own mother, to provide her own supportive, nurturing base for physical and psychic survival. To escape the cycle of loathing and self-loathing. Villanueva's woman has no alternative, even though she would have wanted more options, but to first love the self and then proceed to regenerate and nurture it by becoming her own mother. She is forced to transform the self into both mother and daughter

---

4. Alma Villanueva, "I sing to myself," in *Third Chicano Literary Prize: Irvine 1976-1977* (Irvine: Dept. of Spanish and Portuguese, University of California, Irvine, 1977), 99-101.

5. Villanueva, "I sing to myself," 100.

6. Villanueva, "I sing to myself," 101.

and rejects the male flesh which at this point in time "is putrid and bitter." He must be transfigured.

The end effect could be seen as narcissistic, a perennial accusation directed at woman's literature. Yet, if it be narcissistic, never has a motive force for it been revealed so tellingly and clearly, never have the possible roots been exposed so well: starvation for self-reflection in the other: man or woman.

The male myth of Malintzin, in its ambivalent distaste and fear of the so-called "enigmatic feminine," echoes in this poem as it does in many Mexican/Chicanas poems, even when her name is not mentioned. The pervasiveness of the myth is unfathomable, often permeating and suffusing our very being without conscious awareness.

The myth contains the following sexual possibilities: woman is sexually passive, and hence at all times open to potential use by men whether it be seduction or rape. The possible use is double-edged: That is, the use of her as pawn may be intracultural—"amongst us guys"—or intercultural, which means if we are not using her then "they" must be using her. Since woman seen as highly pawnable, nothing she does is perceived as a choice. Because Malintzin aided Cortés in the Conquest of the New World, she is seen as concretizing woman's sexual weakness and interchangeability, always open to sexual exploitation. Indeed, as long as we continue to be seen in that way we are earmarked to be abusable matter, not just by men of another culture, but all cultures including the one that breeds us.

Lorna Dee Cervantes addresses herself to the latter point in her poem "Baby you cramp my style." In the poem Malintzin is mentioned by her other name: Malinche. The poet is asked to bestow her sexual favors; the lover's tone implies that her body/self is as available as the mythic Malinche is thought to be by male consciousness:

> You cramp my style, baby
> when you roll on top of me
> shouting, "Viva La Raza"
> at the top of your prick.
>
> . . .
>
> Come on Malinche
> Gimme some more![7]

---

7. *El Fuego de Aztlán*, no. 4 (1977): 39.

He cramps her style; she refuses sexual exploitation for herself and her daughters yet to come, in a way Malintzin could not do because of the constraints of the slave society into which she was born.

The Mexican poet Rosario Castellanos reminds us in "Malinche"[8] that Malintzin was sold into slavery by complicitous parents to enhance her brother's inheritance. The mother eager to please her new husband agrees to sell her daughter, and therefore enchains her destiny. Castellanos speculates, in the poem, that this is the result of the mother's own self-loathing. A mother who cannot bear to see herself reflected in her daughter's mirror/sexuality, prefers to shatter the image/mirror, negate the daughter and thereby perpetuate rejection and negation.

Bernal Diaz del Castillo, a brilliant chronicler of the Conquest with a great eye for detail, reveals to us that when Malintzin re-encounters her mother and brother years later and during the very process of the Conquest, she is merely polite. It seems that Malintzin, instead of offering them protection within the folds of the victorious, leaves them to their own devices for survival in an embattled country. In a way she condemns them to servitude just as she had been condemned. Why is there no forgiveness? Within what context can we analyze Malintzin's behavior at this point? We have a reversal, the daughter negates the mother.

Within the complex mother-daughter relationship, the mother keeps bearing quite a bit of the responsibility for the daughter's emotional starvation, abandonment or enslavement and yet paradoxically both are subordinate and subjected to a male culture and tradition. Perhaps our sexual identification with our mothers leads us to expect greater understanding from her as well as psychic/sexual protection. Villanueva tells us it is a false expectation—mothers are powerless, looking to satisfy their own hunger through men, which is agonizing for the daughter: "her pain haunted me for years."[9]

Simone Weil suggests that the conscious slave is much superior, and I would add that a woman who is conscious of being perceived as pawn is much superior. I doubt that the historical Malintzin was a truly conscious slave. In her ambiance slavery was a cultural norm, it was not unusual for men or women to be royalty one day and slave, vanquished or sacrificial victim the next. It was a norm within which she had to seek accommodation. It is also quite possible that

---

8. Rosario Castellanos, *Poesía no eres tú* (México: Fondo de Cultura Económica, 1972), 295-297.
9. Villanueva, "I sing to myself," 99.

what is seen as Malintzin's allegiance to Cortés—hence purposeful betrayal of "her people"—may be explained by Weil's perception of the slave-master relationship. She says, "... the thought of being in absolute subjection as somebody's plaything is a thought no human being can sustain: so if a man [I add woman] is left with no means at all of escaping constraint he [she] has no alternative except to persuade himself [herself] that he [she] is doing voluntarily the very things he [she] is forced to do; in other words, he [she] substitutes *devotion* for *obedience*... devotion of this kind rests upon self-deception, because the reasons for it will not bear inspection."[10]

In our religiously permeated and oriented indo-hispanic minds, it is often the case that devotion is equated with obedience and vice versa, particularly for women and children, so that disobedience is seen as a lack of devout allegiance, and not necessarily as a radical questioning of our forms of life. This factor makes it almost impossible to sense a shift from obedience to devotion; they have been one and the same for hundreds of years. As such, we are a greater unconscious prey to subjugation which we then proceed to call devotion/love. To be obedient/devoted is proof of love, especially for women and children.

Consciously and unconsciously the Mexican/Chicano patriarchal perspective assigns the role of servitude to woman particularly as heterosexual relationships are conceived today and in the past. In an "Open Letter to Carolina ... or Relations between Men and Women" the Chicano poet Abelardo Delgado testifies as follows: "Octavio Paz in *El Laberinto de la Soledad*[11] has much to say as to how we as Chicanos see our women ... For now let it suffice to say that as far as our wives and mothers we make saints of them but remain always in search of a lover with macho characteristics *(sic)*." Obviously when the wife or would-be-wife, the mother or would-be-mother questions out loud and in print the complex "servitude/devotion/love," she will be quickly seen as false to her "obligation" and duty, hence a traitor. Delgado also points to the creation of a different category of women—macho-lover—who will provide comforts beyond those that fall within the purview of wives and mothers. What is a macho/lover kind of woman?

Delgado goes on to tell Carolina that "All it takes is a simple refusal on the part of women to be abused by us men." However, he cautions about the manner in which it is done, "You must show them all that your mind is on par

---

10. Simone Weil, *First and Last Notebooks*, trans. Richard Rees (London: Oxford University Press, 1970), 41.
11. See note 2 for my commentary on this text.

or above theirs. You must be careful that you do this with some grace, dignity and humility... Men might accept your challenges a few times and let it go but if our ego happens to be wounded, then watch out, Carolina, because what follows is a cold rejection and a new assigned role as a feme-macho."[12] (Will this new role of a "feme-macho" then provide the macho/lovers that are sought above and beyond the wife and mother?)

It seems that what is wanted here is for all women to be a kind of Sor Juana,[13] which leaves out the majority of us who are not fortunate enough to be a woman of genius. But because we know Sor Juana's dreadful fate as a result of her intellectual endeavors, we also know that genius is hardly enough. Even genius needs a political base, a constituency. Since many Mexican/Chicana poets' challenges are straightforward, not humble, I shudder to think at our marginalization; how are we being shunned?

When our subjection is manifested through devotion we are saints and escape direct insult. When we are disobedient, hence undevout, we are equated with Malintzin; that is, the *myth* of male consciousness, not the *historical* figure in all her dimensions doomed to live in chains (regardless of which patriarchy might have seemed the best option for survival).

Carmen Tafolla's poem "La Malinche"[14] makes it quite clear that Malintzin as woman is dispossessed of herself by every male ideology with which she was connected. Tafolla would simply like to see Malintzin recognized as a visionary and founder of a people. Yet as I have noted, the realities that this figure encompasses are much too complex to simply replace them with the notion of a matriarch. However, each implicit or explicit poem on Malintzin emphasizes the pervasive preoccupation and influence of the myth and women's need to demythify.

The mythic aspects of disavowal, and the historical ambiance of Malintzin merge in Chicana's literature to bring out the following sexual political themes: 1) to choose among extant patriarchies is not a choice at all; 2) woman's abandonment and orphanhood and psychic/emotional starvation occur even in the midst of tangible family; 3) woman is a slave, emotionally as well as economically;

---

12. Abelardo Delgado, *Revista Chicano–Riqueña* 6, no. 2 (1978): 35, 38.

13. Sor Juana Inés de la Cruz is a famous poet-nun of the Mexican Colonial Period. A highly creative and intellectual woman, she was forced by the church to abandon her writing after penning a treatise that challenged a prelate's notions on the nature of Love and Christ.

14. Carmen Tafolla, "La Malinche," in *Canto al Pueblo: An Anthology of Experiences*, ed. Leonardo Carrillo (San Antonio: Penca Books, 1978), 38-39.

4) women are seen not just by one patriarchy but by all as rapeable and sexually exploitable; 5) blind devotion is not a feasible human choice (this is further clarified by the telling absence of poems by women to the Virgin of Guadalupe, while poems by men to her are plentiful); 6) when there is love/devotion it is at best deeply ambivalent as exemplified by Rina Rocha in "To the penetrator:"

> I hate the love
> I feel for you.[15]

Feminist women agree with Hegel, despite his relentless use of man as universal, that the subject depends on external reality. If she is to be fully at home this external reality must reflect back to her what she actually is or would want to be. When we don't participate in creating our own defined identity and reality as women, when the material and spiritual realities do not reflect us as contributors to the shaping of the world, we may feel as in Judy Lucero's poem "I speak in an illusion:"

> I speak but only in an illusion
> For I see and I don't
>
> It's me and It's not
> I hear and I don't
>
> These illusions belong to me
> I stole them from another
>
> Care to spend a day in my House of Death?
> Look at my garden . . . are U amazed?
> No trees, no flowers, no grass . . . no gardens . . .
> I love and I don't
> I hate and I don't
> I sing and I don't
> I live and I don't
>
> For I'm in a room of clouded smoke
> and a perfumed odor
>
> Nowhere can I go and break these bonds
> Which have me in an illusion
>
> But the bonds are real.[16]

---

15. Rina Rocha, "To the Perpetrator," *Revista Chicano-Requeña* 3, no. 2 (1975): 5.
16. Judy Lucero, "I speak in an illusion," *De Colores* 1, no. 1 (Winter 1973): 52.

Feminism is a way of saying that nothing in patriarchy truly reflects women unless we accept distortions—mythic and historical. However, as Chicanas embrace feminism they are charged with betrayal *a la* Malinche. Often great pains are taken to explain that our feminism assumes a humanistic nuance. The charge remains as a clear image imprinted on Chicanas (and I believe most Third World women, in this country or outside of it) by men. It continues to urge us to make quantum leaps towards a male ideologized humanism devoid of female consciousness. The lure of an ideal humanism is seductive, especially for spiritual women such as we have often been brought up to be; but without female consciousness and envisioning how as women we would like to exist in the material world, to leap into humanism without repossessing ourselves may be exchanging one male ideology for another.

As women we are and continue to be tokens everywhere at the present moment. Everywhere in a Third World context, women invited to partake in the feast of modeling humanism can be counted among the few, and those few may be enjoying what Adrienne Rich calls "a false power which masculine society offers to a few women who 'think like men' on condition that they use it to maintain things as they are. This is the meaning of female tokenism: that power withheld from the vast majority of women is offered to the few."[17]

Even as we concern ourselves with Third World women's economic exploitation, we have to concern ourselves with psychosexual exploitation and pawnability at the hands of one's brother, father, employer, master, political systems and sometimes, sadly so, powerless mothers. As world politics continues the histrionics of dominance and control attempting to figure out just who indeed will be the better macho in the world map, macho politics' last priority is the quality of our lives as women or the lives of our children.

---

17. Adrienne Rich, "On Privilege, Power and Tokenism," *MS.* 8 (September 1979): 42-44 43.

BIBLIOGRAPHY

Castellanos, Rosario. *Poesía no eres tú*. México: Fondo de Cultura Económica, 1972.

Cervantes, Lorna Dee. "Baby you cramp my style." In *El Fuego de Aztlán*, 1 no. 4 (1977): 39.

Delgado, Abelardo. "Open Letter to Carolina... or Relations between Men and Women." *Revista Chicano-Riqueña* 6, no. 2 (1978).

Dorson, Richard M. "Foreword" to *Folktales of Mexico*. Edited by Américo Paredes, Chicago: University of Chicago Press, 1970.

Lucero, Judy. "I speak in an illusion." *De Colores* I, no. 1 (1973): 52.

Paz, Octavio. "The Sons of la Malinche." In *The Labyrinth of Solitude*. Translated by Lysander Kemp. New York: Grove Press, 1961.

Paredes, Américo. "Mexican Legendary and the Rise of the Mestizo: A Survey." In *American Folk Legend*. Edited by Wayland D. Hand. Berkeley: University of California Press, 1971.

Rich, Adrienne. "On Privilege, Power and Tokenism." *MS.* 8 (September 1979): 42-44.

Rocha, Rina. "To the Penetrator." *Revista Chicano-Riqueña* 3, no. 2 (Spring 1975): 5.

Russell, Bertrand. *Marriage and Morals*. New York: Liveright Publishing Corporation, 1929.

Tafolla, Carmen. "La Malinche." In *Canto al Pueblo: An Anthology of Experiences*. Edited by Leonardo Carrillo, 38-39. San Antonio: Penca Books, 1978.

Villanueva, Alma. "I sing to myself." In *Third Chicano Literary Prize: Irvine 1976-1977*. 99-101. Irvine: Department of Spanish and Portuguese, University of California, 1977.

Weil, Simone. *First and Last Notebooks,*. Translated by Richard Rees. London: Oxford University Press, 1970.

Wolf, Eric R. "The Virgin of Guadalupe: A Mexican National Symbol." *The Journal of American Folklore* 71, no. 279 (1958): 34–39.

"WHAT KIND OF LOVER HAVE YOU MADE ME, MOTHER?"

TOWARDS A THEORY OF CHICANAS' FEMINISM AND CULTURAL IDENTITY THROUGH POETRY[1]

→ ←

TO DATE, POETRY HAS been the single most important genre employed by Chicanas in order to grasp and give shape to their experience and desire.[2] With few exceptions, most of the poets writing today were born between 1945 and 1955. Most of them, then, acquired a consciousness of being women of Mexican descent during that tumultuous decade, 1965-1975. This period gave rise to questions of Chicano economic and sociopolitical disenfranchisement, as well as of cultural identity. Moreover, the Chicano Movement was male-dominated so that many of the questions framed did not include women's concerns as women. Either her reality was taken for granted or interpreted from a masculine point of view. Sensing that nationalistic politics could well leave her without voice, the Chicana quickly took pen to paper and dashed off poetry and essays of protest that questioned men's narrow interpretation of culture and most particularly of her. (This was compounded by the fact that Anglo-American literature had also stereotyped her.)

---

1. *Editors' Note:* This essay was first published *in Women of Color Perspectives on Feminism and Identity*, ed. Audrey T. McCluskey (Bloomington: University of Indiana Press, Occasional Papers Series 1, 1985), 85–110.

2. The first part of the title is taken from Cherríe Moraga's poem "La Dulce Culpa," in *Loving in the War Years: Lo que nunca pasó por sus labios* (Boston: South End Press, 1983), 14-15.

The term *Chicana* is used to refer to women of Mexican descent whose lives are inextricably linked to an Anglo-American context. Also, the reader may want to consult the following essays for additional perspectives on the poetry of Chicanas: Elizabeth Ordoñez, "Sexual Politics and the Theme of Sexuality in Chicana Poetry," in *Women in Hispanic Literature: Icons and Fallen Idols,* ed. Beth Miller (Berkeley: University of California Press, 1983), 316-339; Miriam Bornstein, "La poeta chicana: vision panorámica," *La Palabra* 2, no. 2 (1980): 43-66; Eliana Rivero, "Escritura Chicana: la mujer," *La Palabra* 2, no. 2(1980): 2-9; Tey Diana Rebolledo, "Soothing Restless Serpents: The Dreaded Creation and Other Inspirations in Chicana Poetry," *Third Woman* 2, no.1 (1984): 83-102; Tey Diana Rebolledo, "Abuelitas: Mythology and Integration in Chicana Literature," in *Woman of her Word: Hispanic Women Write,* special issue of *Revista Chicano-Riqueña* 11, nos, 3-4 (1983): 148-158; Marta Sánchez, "Gender and Ethnicity in Contemporary Chicana Poetry," *Critical Perspectives* 2, no.1 (1984): 10-19.

Poetry, and secondarily the essay, continues to be the most powerful mode of communication for her concerns, her self-discovery, and her self-definition.[3] Ultimately, we are speaking about the birth of a written record of women who could not easily lay claim to a past literature of their own. Previous writings by women who may be claimed as Chicanas by literary historians have, unfortunately, been of little or no account, to the contemporary group I speak of.[4] Their work has not been accessible to them. Though we may find some similar concerns between past writers and present writers, it may only serve to prove Tillie Olsen's observation that without access to the written record of the past, women are doomed to repeatedly go over the same ground instead of forging ahead with additional explorations.[5] In any case, there are two major differences between past writers that may be claimed as Chicanas and the contemporary writer. The former were middle-class Spanish-speaking and Spanish-writing women closely adhering to Mexican rooted literary canons and discourse. The current writer by dint of historical circumstance often writes in English, and traces her economic background to the working class. Most of them are the first in their family—for as long as they can remember—to have had some access to institutions of higher education.[6]

The poet more than any other kind of writer is free to explore her sense of self, her situation, and her conditions of being. The Chicana poet is no exception, though she often does so in relation to a very complex ambience. And, when these writers are viewed as a group that shares a past and is engaged in a struggle to stake out a future, the limitations of personal experience, perspective, and vision may be surmounted to discover a multifaceted existential mosaic. A study of these poets with an eye to some salient and repeated concerns may help us in assessing how Chicanas are inventing a literature, a feminism, and a cultural identity of their own.

---

3. It is important to note that poetry has served as a strong vehicle of communication among women everywhere in the U.S. regardless of ethnicity. See Jan Clausen, *A Movement of Poets: Thoughts on Poetry and Feminism* (Brooklyn: Long Haul Press, 1982).

4. On the reclamation of past writers—male and female—see Juan Rodríguez, "Notes on the Evolution of Chicano Prose Fiction," *Modern Chicano Writers*, ed. Joseph Sommers and Tomas Ybarra-Frausto (Englewood Cliffs, NJ: Prentice-Hall, 1979), 67-73.

5. This theme is repeatedly taken up in Adrienne Rich, *Silences* (New York: Delta Press, 1979).

6. The reader may want to consult the sociohistorical overview given in Alfredo Mirande and Evangelina Enriquez, *La Chicana* (Chicago: University of Chicago Press, 1979). The book is problematic most particularly in the idealization of the maternal figures and its prescriptive point of view.

In general, the modes of poetic expression as well as language choices are as varied as each poet's concrete situation. The modes range from the most prosaic of utterances composed on the run, to those that pay close attention to rhythms, images, and structure. Languages used may comprise a mixture of Spanish and English, or adherence to one or the other. To construct her personal aesthetic each poet has drawn upon the information and canons available to her—oral traditions, speech patterns common to her social milieu, Latin-American or Anglo-American written models, etc. What most concerns me presently is not so much to dictate an aesthetic nor even to thoroughly describe Chicanas' current aesthetics, as to assess the subjects that give configuration to the urgent desire to conserve and reconstruct strengthening elements from the ruins of a fragmented past, as well as the desire to redirect and transform her future. Paradoxically, her desire unfolds towards the past and the future, but often these forces converge upon her and clash with her and each other in a fashion similar to that depicted in Kafka's parable, (I take the liberty of changing all the *he's* to *she* or *it*):

> She has two antagonists: The first presses her from behind, from the origin. The second blocks the road ahead. She gives battle to both. To be sure the first supports her in her fight with the second, for it wants to push her forward, and in the same way the second supports her in her fight with the first, since it drives her back. But it is only theoretically so. For it is not only the two antagonists who are there, but she herself as well, and who really knows her intentions? Her dream, though, is that some time in an unguarded moment—and this would require a night darker than any night has ever been yet—she will jump out of the fighting line and be promoted, on account of her experience in fighting, to the position of umpire over her antagonists in their fight with each other.[7]

The allegorical nature of Kafka's parable obviously lends itself to multiple interpretations depending on the situation of the reader, and how she reads herself into the parable. I would, however, like to suggest some names for the conflictive forces that conspire to make her capitulate and remain silent, and against which she has to struggle in order to say anything at all. Given Chicanas' life experience in an Anglo-American context, México itself represents

---

7. Cited in Hannah Arendt, *Between Past and Future: Eight Exercises in Political Thought* (London: Penguin Books, 1978), 7.

the past, the origin, while the future lies in a nebulous Anglo-American world full of obstacles to her self-determination, and definition. Given her sexual self-awareness, an unquestioned Mexican, and Chicano male culture represent a past that may lock her into some crippling traditional stereotypes, while the future has been represented within an Anglo-American feminist promise. It is a promise and a dream derived from what to a Chicana is an alien culture and rhetoric riddled with barriers to her attempt to articulate her sense of herself.[8] Language comes into play as well. Spanish, when lost, occupies a past reality which nonetheless is constantly real through older family members, and of course México's nearness. English appears as a tempting future, and is usually represented as opening the doors to the future. But does it open the doors to poetry? Cherríe Moraga, for example, notes "I have been translating my experience out of fear of an aloneness too great to bear. I have learned analysis as a mode to communicate what I feel the experience itself already speaks for."[9] Caught within these lines of fire, some Chicana poet-protagonists have chosen writing as a medium to facilitate the leap into the role of umpire. Through the poem she can reflect upon some of the forces that threaten to eradicate her, and those that are strengthening in considering the tension-ridden battlefield. How does she imagine and name some of these forces, what are her intentions, and does the poem truly promote her "to the role of umpire?"

The potential effects of these murky forces that push and pull, and may entrap Kafka's poet-protagonist, are aptly captured by the title of Evangelina Vigil's first chapbook, *Nade y Nade*.[10] (Though the title is in Spanish, the poems are largely in English. A few employ a mixture of both.) The immediate impact of the title is enigmatic. It takes the reader or utterer of the title a moment to orient herself with respect to it. Quickly uttered in Spanish, it could lead one to confuse it with "nada y nada." (Nothing and nothing.) Upon reflection, however, several significations begin to suggest themselves. "Nade" as a command form of the verb to swim; or "nade" as the first or third person singular of the present subjunctive. The possible significations thus range from an order to "swim and swim," to "I swim and swim," and "she swims and swims." If the command condemns the person to constant motion, it is at least clear. The subjunctive

---

8. This point of view is articulated in many of the essays compiled in Cherríe Moraga and Gloria Anzaldúa, eds., *This Bridge Called my Back: Writings by Radical Women of Color* 2nd ed. (New York: Kitchen Table Press, 1983).

9. Cherríe Moraga, *Loving in the War Years: Lo que nunca pasó por sus labios* (Boston: South End Press, 1981), vi.

10. Evangelina Vigil, *Nade y Nade* (San Antonio: M & A Editions, 1978).

form is problematic. The subjunctive phrase impels us to imagine a closure by referring to some principal event to which it is related. One of the essences of a subjunctive form is relation, denoted or implied, to some other event, which in this instance is potentially in the past, the present, or the future. The attempt to complete the relation between the swimmer's constant motion and the events to which it may be subordinated is precisely the theme of the chapbook. Vigil trusts that writing will take her out of the line of fire, or as it were will keep her from drowning due to exhaustion. *Nade y Nade,* a collection of telegraphic meditations, succeeds in clarifying for Vigil the strategies for her quest: recollection, and attention to the present. Her subsequent book *Thirty an' Seen a Lot* makes a full use of those strategies.[11] Here Vigil puts into effect her intention to transform actuality into something illuminating, new and valuable by portraying all of those people who have surrounded her all of her life, past and present. Vigil's former confusion, and paradoxically so, suspension begin to evaporate,

An analogous aquatic image of constant wandering is evoked by Lorna Dee Cervantes in "Refugee Ship":

> I feel I am a captive
> aboard the refugee ship.
> The ship that will never dock.[12]

Though she is not doing the swimming, she is imprisoned by a vehicle in perpetual motion. In order to put a stop to her exile, she would have to jump ship, swim to shore, and build the dock herself. The docks she builds will correspond to the poems written. That indeed no one else can build the dock is confirmed when she asserts that she trusts "only what I have built/with my own hands."[13] The notion of making things for one's self, and creating a literature of one's own is an ongoing concern. In "Declaration in a Day of Little Inspiration," a poem that Cervantes did not include in *Emplumada,* the restless movement shifts from aquatic wanderings to "street pounding." The quest is for "ripe literature." It is, however, fruitless since nothing she sees "will own up." All objects are locked into their solitude and maintain a frustrating silence. What she seeks in the poem itself is the unfolding of the other. To make the other speak, give up its secrets, and thus find the relation between self and other, ship and dock.

---

11. See Julian Olivares, "Seeing and Becoming: Evangelina Vigil, in *Thirty an' Seen a lot,*" *The Chicano Struggle: Analyses of Past and Present Efforts,* ed. John A. García et al. (Binghamton, NY: Bilingual Press, 1984), 152-765.

12. Lorna Dee Cervantes, *Emplumada* (Pittsburgh: University of Pittsburgh Press, 1981), 41.

13. Cervantes, *Emplumada,* 14.

Perhaps she did not include it in *Emplumada* because it is not "ripe literature" It is, as Vigil's *Nade y Nade, a* recognition of the difficulties in making the other unfold, instead of staying "shut like a wet piece of paper." Cervantes' keenest insight in this poem is that if the poem does not yield the relation between self and other, the self may be reduced to writing the same poem of rage, and frustration at the imponderable "Who am I?" As she says "Flushing this anger is easy." The difficulty lies in deciphering the others, to which any amplification of the self is subordinate.[14]

If Cervantes would want the others to unfold through her invented lyric voice, there are poets like Carmen Tafolla who record the actual speech of the other. She does so by imitating the oral Spanish speech patterns of people in the Mexican barrio in "Los Corts."[15] Unfortunately for the listener or reader who is not bilingual *and* bicultural, this wonderful portrayal is not accessible. But inaccessibility cuts both ways, which means that there are areas of experience lost to the speakers in the poems as well. Thus, it is that the bilingual/bicultural poet posits herself as a bridge between two worlds that could theoretically remain silent and closed to each other. The poet wants to eliminate the isolation between these two worlds. Yet, this is an arduous task because these areas of experience are not exclusively outside the poet's self but may refractorily coexist within her, violently splitting the core of her being:

> and I am
> back,
> a stranger,
> english/spanish making knots of
> my tongue.[16]
>
> or:
> I'm orphaned from my Spanish name[17]
> They give me a name that
> fights me.[18]

The "knots" and the orphanhood from a "name that fights" thrust the poet into a linguistic line of fire that pushes into the past armed with words that do not

---

14. Lorna Dee Cervantes, "Declaration on a Day of Little Inspiration," *Mango*, no.1 (Fall 1976): 4.
15. Carmen Tafolla, *Curandera* (San Antonio: M&A Editions, 1983), 19-23.
16. Alma Villanueva, *Blood Root* (Austin: Place of Herons Press, 1977), 67.
17. Cervantes, *Emplumada*, 41.
18. Cervantes, *Emplumada*, 44

belong to it and vice versa. Hence, for example, Moraga's fear that she may "Speak in a language that maybe no 'readership' can follow."[19] The consensus among some of these writers is that they have emerged from a long line of illiterates. The introduction to *Cuentos: Stories by Latinas*, for example, states that the writers presented in the collection are largely "first generation writers. This means that your mother couldn't have written this story—or even helped you write it."[20] Indeed, the mother portrayed by Tafolla in "Los Corts" is doomed to the oral repetition of her life. If she stops uttering it out loud to herself and others, her life will elude her. In a sense Tafolla recorded it for her so that she can rest assured of her life's permanency as she lived it, but that mother could not have helped Tafolla write it. From this perspective the poet's own past is concretely linked to the biological mothers. As a pivotal sexual person, symbol, and image in the poet's experience, the mother is simultaneously within the poet and without, is herself and is not herself, is part of a cherished and a rejected past. She stands as a Spanish-speaking Janus-like illumination facing the past, and the future through her daughter who is largely an English-writing poet. Thus, at the subjective level the poet's core is split (or ambivalent) precisely at the point where she glimpses her own mother. Perhaps for the writer, sexual and cultural disjunctions between herself and her mother take place at the linguistic level. The daughter learns to reconsider the mother through a dissimilar discourse, that in the end make them unintelligible to each other. The unintelligibility is exacerbated when one considers the cultural assumptions in which each discourse is drenched. This, I think, leads to Moraga's earlier cited observation as well. The mother may reject the daughter's hard-won insights on the grounds that they were acquired through another discourse's vision. Simultaneously, the daughter may discover that the world created by English style discourse also finds her alien. At this juncture, I believe, there occurs a terror of total disjunction between daughter and mother beginning with the language each speaks. However tumultuous and troubled, the writer desires relationship and communication with the mother for she is at the source of her sexual continuity, and experience. The Chicana poet wants to capture the mother's reality, either by recording what she says or has said, or by interpreting her as best she can through her own voice; a voice that demands that she invent a discourse which furthermore will invent them both.

---

19. Moraga, *Loving in the War Years*, vi.
20. Alma Gómez, Cherríe Moraga, Mariana Romo-Carmona with Myrtha Chabrán, "By Word of Mouth," in *Cuentos: Stories by Latinas*, ed. Alma Gómez, Cherríe Moraga, and Mariana Romo-Carmona (New York: Kitchen Table Press, 1983), ix.

The excruciating torture involved in such an act is captured by Cherríe Moraga in "It's the poverty:"

> I *lack imagination* you say
>
> *No.* I lack language.
>
> The language to clarify
> my resistance to the literate.
> Words are a war to me.
> They threaten my family.
> To gain the words to describe the loss,
> I risk losing everything.
> I may create a monster
> the word's length and body
> swelling up colorful and thrilling
> looming over my *mother*, characterized.
> Her voice in the distance
> *unintelligible illiterate.*
> These are the monster's words.[21]

Anglo-American style literacy with a discourse in place to assess its male or female realities, disjunctions, and continuities may lead to the loss of the mother, and the erasure of a part of the poet's self. Moraga fears that this literacy will make of her a monster that her mother (by extension her culture) will not recognize at all, nor will she. She will be totally disconnected from that being that willed her a sexual and cultural identity that at the moment appears elusive. The disjunction through the agency of language will make her unintelligible to herself inside herself. Yet, if she accepted the whole of her mother's world held in place by a discourse to which the poet has a reduced access, and that further locks her into questionable, even crippling ways of being, she would end up silent, most particularly because she has no control of literacy in her mother's language. Words, in either language, threaten to make a monster of her, as they sever continuity with her mother and parts of herself. The daughter may become alien: to herself at the bifurcating root of the languages that have shaped her experiences, and her desires. Thus, words proceeding from two very distinct discourses, labelled illiterate (oral Spanish) and literate (written English), become a "war to me." At this point the poet, who deals in words as vehicles

---

21. Moraga, *Loving in the War Years*, 62-63.

of expression, is forced to forge ahead with the creation of a discourse that may make it appear even to herself that she is "speaking in tongues," as Gloria Anzaldúa puts it.[22] But, as Anzaldúa goes on to say, for the writer the fear of the unintelligibility of her own words must be transcended and "hope we don't have to repeat the performance."[23] She must clear the ground for the creation of herself and her discourse because "We are not reconciled to the oppressors who whet their howl in our grief. We are not reconciled."[24]

Resistance to oppressors is in effect resistance to the future as it is represented by them. Thus, the future drives her back into herself, the source of her own invention. For many Chicana poets, that self-invention begins with the family—biological, historical, and symbolic. In the family complex, a review of the literature reveals that for her the female members, friends and lovers are of crucial importance. Although the grandmother is important as Diana Tey Rebolledo has noted,[25] the mother figure looms just as large. Moreover, the mother is central to the daughter-poet in a very immediate way. Due to the intimate relations between mother and daughter, their relationship is as fraught with strife as that with lovers, male or female, though the dynamics are quite different in each instance.

The strategies to capture the mother-daughter relationship from the writer's perspective are multiple. First, as I have noted, is the attempt to portray her actual voice, as in Tafolla's poem. There the mother is a figure that frets over the economic and affective sustenance of her family, regretting her lost youth and beauty as she disintegrates in sweat and tears. Or, the mother is urged to speak, as Marina Rivera writes, reminding her mother of the toil that has been the hallmark of her existence. Most of the mothers, however, will not own up. The task falls upon the daughter to invent and interpret the mother's life, and how it spills onto her own life, hoping to sketch out their faces in the process. Indeed, it becomes a necessity for the daughter-writer:

> Collectively, many of us have looked back to our mothers and grandmothers for artistic force, for affirmation of our cultural selves for reinforcement of our identities as women and as writers. Our stories,

---

22. Moraga and Anzaldúa, *This Bridge Called My Back*, 165.
23. Moraga and Anzaldúa, *This Bridge Called my Back*, 165.
24. Moraga and Anzaldúa, *This Bridge Called my Back*, 165.
25. Rebolledo, "Abuelitas...." See note 2.

poems and essays are frequently peopled by these women in an attempt to understand our connection to history, to our people.[26]

In recreating her mother's image and life, the daughter-writer recovers her in two salient modes. One is symbolic, and often converges with myth. The other is a blend of confession and testimony that dovetails with the historical familial bonds, and the biographical. Carmen Tafolla and Pat Mora, for example, employ symbolic strategies in some of their work.

In "Ancient House" Tafolla journeys into that house, symbol of her cultural and racial line. There she happens across the shrunken, "old and silent" body of the mother "thin as onion skin over bones."[27] The family, and most of all herself, is still possessed by that maternal figure. Though silent, she is not dead. She is all breath and eyes, a living deaf and mute living witness:

> Her eyes search us,
> reach like arms,
> dress themselves
> and crawl out of the mattress.
>
> We do not know what to say
> with our sight,
> And her eyes begin to cover us
> with hand-made healing quilts.
> They stroke us with compassion
> and they grow a shade in power.
> They move and dance
> and as I watch
> I am absorbed.
>
> I lean over the still body, still mattress-bound,
>   and wonder who she is & why I care
>   so much.
>
> In this tall-ceilinged ancient eight-walled house
>   owned by cold drafts and volcanic spaces
>   I breathe in through her onionskin lung
>   and know,

---

26. Barbara Brinson-Pineda, "'Onde Estas Grandma: Chicana Writers and the Rejection of Silence," *Intercambios Femeniles*, no. 2(1984): 1.

27. Tafolla, *Curandera*, 32.

with her eyes too old to need vision to see
that she
is
    me [28]

The voyage into that ancient house brings the quester to an alarming self-identification: a silent figure bound to reproduction and healing. For Tafolla, as for others, the image of the silent primordial mother is also very closely linked to the figure of the *curandera*, the traditional professional healer, and repository of folk wisdom. Both are figures whose nurturing and healing skills and knowledge have saved the family line from extinction. Yet, the disturbing element is that self sacrifice and abnegation for the sake of others' survival does not generate a discourse that the daughter can use for her own transformation, rather than one she may learn to imitate and repeat. That, of course, is the case in most oral and traditional cultures. The fact that knowledge is oral dooms the culture to reproduce it over and over again lest it be forgotten and lost. In the absence of records that may preserve a people's wisdom change is near to impossible.[29] The residue of oral tradition in Chicana culture gives us clues to the entrenched and sometimes damaging conservatism endured, as well as a fatalistic outlook. Yet, this cannot be perceived without the conscious search for these figures. The quest to recover and conserve the past is riddled with contradiction and paradox.

On the symbolic plane Pat Mora introduces us to a rebellious Aztec Princess in a poem of the same name. The mother admonishes the daughter to look for her happiness at home, not beyond: "Here. See here. We buried your umbilical/cord here, in the house, a sign that your girl-child would nest inside."[30] The young daughter, however, digs up the cord, takes it outdoors and whispers, "Breathe." In "Mi Madre" Mora's lyric speaker, a daughter, sings in praise of the desert, which stands for the empowering and nurturing mother. The desert-mother is

---

28. Tafolla, *Curandera*, 33. Also see poem on curandera, 26-27. Other poets deal with the curandera figure as well, and her outline is maternal. In the interfacing areas between mother and daughter the figure of La Malinche is also writ large. Any theory of Chicanas' feminism and cultural identity will have to incorporate this figure also. I skip her at this point because there are some considerations on her already to the exclusion of the mother figure. See my own essay "Chicanas' Feminist Literature: A Revision through Malintzin," in Moraga and Anzaldúa eds., *This Bridge Called my Back*, 2nd ed. (New York: Kitchen Table Press, 1983), 182-190. Also see Moraga, *Loving in the War Years*, 98-117.

29. See Walter Ong, *Interfaces of the Word: Studies in the Evolution of Consciousness and Culture* (Ithaca: Cornell University Press, 1977).

30. Pat Mora, *Chants* (Houston: Arte Público Press, 1984), 28.

envisioned as the all giving to the daughter, exclusively. She feeds, teases, frightens, comforts, heals, caresses, beautifies, teaches, and above all sings, "chants lonely women's songs of femaleness."[31]

In "Maria la O," Barbara Brinson-Pineda's approach to the mother highlights both symbolic and historical elements. The name of the woman connotes everywoman; an everywoman who is linked to the Virgin Mother Mary. Also, we should remember that in México the beggar women in the city streets, often of rural and indigenous background, are called "Las Marias." Brinson-Pineda's Maria, with her roots in the Mexican revolution of 1910, can be viewed as the founding mother of many Chicanas today, who is both enshrined and degraded. In giving a first-person account of Maria's travails, Brinson-Pineda is constructing for herself and us an interpretation of her past. Maria was born into the Mexican servant class. Her own mother willed her the appropriate skills. Maria marries and soon flees México's violent revolution because it is a "lover/of women in black." When her husband falls victim to the war, Maria joins her mother in the United States. Her Mexican-style servitude is exchanged for an Anglo-American one:

> Texas cotton,
> Michigan cherry,
> California grape,
>
> to the city's concrete bed,
> to an open road.[32]

Maria joins the ranks of symbolic and legendary women of the revolution, such as the Adelitas and *guerrilleras* who are camp followers, except that now Maria's camps will be those of the migrant and urban workers in the United States.

For the Chicana writing today the historical Maria would be tantamount to a grandmother figure. As Diana Tey Rebolledo has noted in her essay, "Abuelitas: Mythology and Integration in Chicana Literature," poems about the grandmother abound and are central to today's writer's efforts to decipher a cultural past, and central to perceiving a part of self in a distanced and evaporating past. Grandmothers "form a complex of female figures who are nurturing, comforting, and stable. They are linked symbolically and spatially to the house and home, and are often associated with an idealistic, cultural space.... They provide a link

---

31. Mora, *Chants*, p. 9.

32. Barbara Brinson-Piñeda, "Maria la O," in *The Midwest to the West: An Anthology* (Bloomington: A Chicano Riqueño Studies Publication, 1980), 1-5.

to those cultural values ascribed to family, food, and language."[33] The collective nostalgia for, and configuration of, the grandmother as a solid figure that illuminates the writer's present, and secures the past, in effect is raised to a myth that reflects a kinship with Mora's desert mother and provides a historical and creative continuity for the writer. In the absence of apparent literary foremothers and accessible goddesses who may be imitated and/or revised the Chicana writer forges her own myths from legend and history.

By virtue of age, distance, durability, and ultimately death, the grandmother acquires a privileged status. The poet can make the grandmother a positive heroine, but she cannot completely do so for her mother. The mother is too close and constitutes the recent past and present. In a very direct sense the daughter is in the mother's line of fire. The mother has shaped her experience, and may even appear to block her desire. The irony, of course, is that in life the grandmother may have influenced the mother in similar ways. To the daughter-writer the mother figure may give rise to double-binds, ambivalence and further, she may unwittingly repress her as a writer as well, or condemn her to repetition. As such, poems of a confessional and testimonial nature, working with the explosive raw materials of mother-daughter biography break new ground in the poet's quest for a self-discovering discourse.

Rina Rocha, for example, in "Baby Doll" is amazed to discover her need for her mother's love and approval in spite of the fact that her mother denies her words and her view of the world. Rocha defines the mother as follows:

> Mothers can be
> jealous gods
> Just like
> husbands
> Unforgiving and demanding[34]

It is interesting to note the parallel perceived between mothers and husbands. Both are capable of silencing the daughter-wife. All the don'ts uttered by them can render her "fallen/words and action/into a neat clump," a "Neat and Bitter Clump." Though unaware, husbands and mothers may conspire to embitter and paralyze the young woman. Fathers, too, are accomplices as Margarita López Flores notes in "Margarita: What Accounts for the Name:"

> My father would have wanted me

---

33. Rebolledo, "Abuelitas...," 150-151. See note 2.
34. Rina Rocha, *Eluder* (Chicago: Alexander Books, 1980), 20.

> a flower, sitting perhaps
> on a Mexican playa
>
> ...
>
> My mother dreamed me a mother
> Someone's clear woman of family
> She does not want me
>
> ...
>
> I was to have been
> the prize for waiting
> and they had always waited
> for this, what they thought
> would be so pure
> how wrong they were to think of me
> their unity.³⁵

But an awareness of a complicity that defines a common ground for father and mother is not enough for the daughter. She is also desirous of the mother's recognition of her and her presence in the mother's life as we shall see.

Olivia Castellano views the mother as one who waits for the absent husband-father:

> She spends too many years
> watching for car lights in the dark
> waiting for father to come home³⁶

In this instance, however, the mother's loneliness becomes the daughter's comfort. Mother and daughter become each other's solace. Waiting brings them together so powerfully that the daughter-poet anticipates her own future loneliness when her mother goes:

> When she has gone,
> I too will
> lie alone, scan the edges of evening
> remembering her with every light
> that breaks around a ridge,
> and something like her will
> lie beside me, something powerful

---

35. Margarita López Flores, "Margarita: What Accounts for the Name," *Third Woman* 2, no. 1, (1984): 25.
36. Olivia Castellano, *Blue Mandolin, Yellow Field* (Berkeley: Tonatiuh—Quinto Sol International, 1980), 19.

and learned in the waiting art.[37]

For Castellano a sympathetic mother-daughter relationship forged through lonely waiting may result in creativity, as the mother teaches to see beauty:

> She has an eye for perfect things,
> has the power of seeing through darkness."[38]

Some mothers, however, cannot enable the daughter to see as they become absorbed in a darkness all their own. The daughter's greatest terror is to duplicate the mother's dark suffering. As a result, she is compelled to reject her, hover between repulsion and attraction, or redeem her.

Lorna Dee Cervantes clearly finds many a fault with the mother, and appears to reject her in favor of the grandmother. The mother is viewed as someone who like Margarita's "gave birth/ to a blue doll struck dumb/from the start."[39] Some of the "dumbness" is not solely due to paralyzing traditions, but also to the mother's responsibility in the loss of the Spanish language that now alienates the daughter from her own name: "Mama raised me without language./I'm orphaned from my Spanish name."[40] Consequently, for example, in "Beneath the Shadow of the Freeway," the mother appears to be discarded as a constructive influence or role model for the daughter. In this poem we have a woman family portrayed: grandmother, mother, and daughter. Despite adversities that include poverty and an abusive husband, the grandmother preserves her innocence, creativity, and optimism in the face of the future. The mother, however, torn between the desire to be a princess and the enforced role of Warrior, becomes cynical, and warns the daughter: "You're too soft . . . always were. / You'll get nothing but shit . . . / Baby, don't count on nobody."[41] With regard to the grandmother, the mother says: "It's her own fault, / getting screwed by a man for that long, / Sure as shit wasn't hard."[42] The daughter in turn is as idealistic as the grandmother, and wants to share her faith "in myths and birds." Though the mother's anger and cynicism are destructive in the daughter's view, the mother's words are ultimately blended with the perception of the grandmother. The mother's advice not to "count on nobody," and the grandmother who builds with her own hands

---

37. Castellano, *Blue Mandolin, Yellow Field*, 19.
38. Castellano, *Blue Mandolin, Yellow Field*, 20.
39. Cervantes, *Emplumada*, 55.
40. Cervantes, *Emplumada*, 41.
41. Cervantes, *Emplumada*, 13.
42. Cervantes, *Emplumada*, 12.

become one in the daughter's realization that she can trust only what she has built with her own hands. In this way Cervantes uses these figures to discover her own truths which only she can discover. In "Herself" she notes:

> I picked myself up ignoring
> whoever I was   slowly
> noticing for the first time my body's stench
> I made a list in my head
> of all the names who could help me
> and then   meticulously I scratched
> each one
> > *they won't hear me burning*
> > *inside of myself*[43]

For Cervantes the journey to self-discovery is so mysteriously personal that the figures used in poems are others who in their unfolding, primarily unfold her. Intentionally or not, however, the efforts to make others speak through the writer's poetic intervention makes of literature a self-defining journey for almost all of these writers.

In parallel ways Sandra Cisneros like Cervantes discovers that to duplicate the mother-woman role is to become a silent nobody overcome by regret. In *The House on Mango Street*, a collection of poetic vignettes that elaborate a collage of the urban family and barrio, the mother in "A Smart Cookie" is filled with remorse over what could have been. She says to the daughter: "I could've been somebody, you know?"[44] The some bodies she might have been, perhaps, are the ones that populate her fantasies: opera and ballet heroines, visual artists. The daughter, Esperanza—meaning hope—in another vignette imagines that in order not to reproduce such a blighted life full of sighs she must grow up to be "Beautiful and Cruel." She must be the kind of heroine of the cinema that "drives men crazy" and learns to increase her own power by starting out to be as rude as men: "I am one who leaves the table like a man, without putting back the chair or picking up the plate."[45] The notion that to be important and powerful the daughter may have to imitate some masculine behaviors and cruelties underlies some of Cisneros' poems as well, such as "The So-and-So's." If the daughter-child is led to reject the abnegating mother role, in her adulthood

---

43. Cervantes, *Emplumada*, 9.
44. Sandra Cisneros, *The House on Mango Street* (Houston: Arte Público Press, 1984), 83.
45. Cisneros, *The House on Mango Street*, 82.

male lovers complete the rejection process of the mother. They prefer women who "are well-behaved," a true mother's daughter in order to love and accept her. Thus, the latter-day daughter concludes, "I want to be like you. A Who./ And let them bleed."[46] Ironically, the earlier advice from the mother "Got to take care all your own" is unintentionally in some sense turned against the mother with the help of male lovers.

Alma Villanueva, particularly in *Blood Root*,[47] continually hovers between repulsion and attraction to the mother that in her eyes demands resolution. At the source of the ambivalence is the notion that the mother never desired the daughter as well as men. A factor that is coupled with the pain of abandonment of both mother and daughter by the father-husband:

> her pain haunted me for years,
> the way she looked when she
> talked about him, the
> desire and need that rose to her eyes—
> it repulsed me and attracted me.[48]

Villanueva's need for the mother is so fundamentally strong that not even a grandmother's nurturance can assuage it, nor any man. In *Blood Root* the unfolding of the daughter's life drama in relation to the mother is resolved in two steps. The first takes place in youth:

> I vowed
>   to never
>   grow up
>   to be a woman
> and be helpless
>   like my mother[49]

In childhood, then, she desires to be a boy. As an adult, however, she recognizes the mother's courage "to just keep/ standing/where she was."[50] But, the primal need does not cease, hence her desire to love herself, to seek renewal by giving birth to herself, to self-mother.[51]

---

46. Cisneros, *Woman of Her Word*, 2-21. See note 2.
47. Villanueva, *Blood Root*.
48. Villanueva; *Blood Root*, 20
49. Villanueva, *Blood Root*, 50.
50. Villanueva, *Blood Root*, 50.
51. Villanueva, *Blood Root*, see particularly "I Sing to Myself," 2-21; and "I was a skinny tomboy," 49-51.

Blood Root is truly a joyously conceived poem. Though there are titles that separate one poem from another, the unifying autobiographical voice revolves around the Whitmanesque "I Sing to Myself." Villanueva sings to herself as woman, as such she is moved to overlook the vicissitudes of the biographical mother-daughter relationship in favor of an affirmation of their common bonds as sexual beings. Villanueva's second book *Mother, May I?*[52] again uses biographical materials for a voyage of self-discovery that focuses on grandmother-mother-daughter relations. Recalling her own mother's warnings "men come/and go. your friends/ stay. women/ stay,"[53] Villanueva again wants to emphasize the common grounds that enhance women's creativity and permanence—themselves. Notwithstanding the ambivalence produced by the mother-daughter biographical relation, Villanueva aims to heal the wounds by constantly searching for the elements that may create communication among women. On the positive side, she approaches women and nature with an ecological fervor that is exhilarating. On the negative side, she subsumes male negation of women, male physical abuse, and abandonment of women, and male deadly aggression.[54]

Cherríe Moraga is a poet who wants to redeem the mother from her dark suffering plight. Actually, in *Loving in the War Years: Lo que nunca pasó por sus labios*[55] a collection of poems, stories, journal entries, and essays, Moraga appears to want to help to redeem all of her people. The basic drive behind the book is her "Mexican faith that there is meaning to nuestro sufrimiento en el mundo." And, the fundamental question behind the book is what are we "as a people... doing suffering?"[56] In a hopscotch but definitely challenging way, Moraga tackles issues that may yield answers to her faith and questions. Though not necessarily disparate, these are as far ranging as lesbianism, cultural identity, and Anglo-American imperialism. Yet as she herself testifies the quest for self-discovery may also begin in our most private home—the family. For Moraga the women of the family, however, suffer most. Insofar as the book explores personal relations with others, Moraga's mother is writ large, and is followed by other family members, friends and female lovers.

If, as earlier noted, Cervantes refuses to internalize the mother's bitterness and rage in favor of the grandmother's creativity and faith in life, Moraga fears

---

52. Alma Villanueva, *Mother, May I?* (n.p.: Motheroot Publications, 1978).
53. Villanueva, "Mother, May I?" 38.
54. See Marta Sánchez's article cited in note 2 for a different view of Villanueva's work.
55. Cherríe Moraga, *Loving in the War Years: Lo que nunca pasó por sus labios* (Boston: South End Press, 1981).
56. Moraga, *Loving in the War Years*, ii.

that indeed she has already internalized her mother's rage and disappointments. Moraga, then, seeks to understand the nature of the mother's anger, and how it has been assimilated by her. In "For the Color of my Mother," Moraga, "speaking for her" because she wears "the wide-arched muzzle of brown women," portrays the mother's mouth as "pressed into a seam," until finally it bleeds "into her stomach." Socially enforced silence becomes a cancer to her. In that poem what starts out as a biographical mother-daughter relation is by the end raised to symbol:

> I pass thru their hands
> the head of my mother
> painted in clay colors
>
>   touching each carved feature swollen eyes and mouth
>
> they understand the explosion, the splitting
> open   contained within the fixed expression
> they cradle her silence
>
>   nodding to me[57]

But, the lot of those fettered by muzzles is to explode in inarticulate gestures—snarls, violence, rages—as in "La Dulce Culpa:"

> What kind of lover have you made me, mother
> who took belts to whip this memory from me
>   the memory of your passions
>   dark & starving, spilling
>   out of rooms, driving
>   into my skin, cracking
>   & cussing in Spanish
>   the thick dark sounds
>   hsrd *c's* splitting
>   the air like blows
>
>   *you would get a rise out of me*
>   *you knew it in our blood*
>   *the vision   of my rebellion*[58]

---

57. Moraga, *Loving in the War Years*, 60-61.
58. Moraga, *Loving in the War Years*, 14.

Though the daughter's rebellion is prefigured in the mother's violent rage itself, it still is juxtaposed to the memory of early intimate closeness which the anger threatens to eradicate. To prevent the erasure of that early loving contact "as if you never noticed/when they cut me /out/from you," the daughter promises to fight back:

> Strip the belt from your hands
> and take you
>
> into
>
> my arms.[59]

The mother's irascibility has not solely emanated from enforced silence, but also from the inability of her husband to ever assuage her anger, passion, hunger. In short, this represents the failure to find a common ground. Moraga intuits that these complex factors and relations give rise to the questions, what kind of lover have you made me, mother? Her own sense of herself as a lover is in some way connected to the mother's life and image. The prose piece "The Slow Dance" gives us some clues when the daughter declares "I am my mother's lover."[60] Keeping the original question in mind, the phrase is double-edged for it can just as well suggest I am the lover my mother reproduced, and just as needy as she is. Or, I am the kind of lover my mother would have wanted—strong, satisfying, compelling. In "The Slow Dance," then, she alternates between one pose and the other, but neither gives her access to 'the slow dance' with the woman she desires. It is as if there was too much need displayed on the one hand, and too much strength on the other.

Moraga's insight that mothers are closely linked to how the daughter might enact her role as lover is quite novel and fascinating. Further exploration of the literature from this perspective, for both the heterosexual and lesbian daughter, would yield tensions and themes that are presently veiled from us. Poets already discussed in this essay point to a triangle of experience and desire labelled mother-daughter-lover at each point. We have to date, not only in the literature of Chicanas but others as well, examined lovers and love as if they existed in a vacuum. In considering these poets, it is clear that the intimate relations with mothers and lovers are interconnected in ways that help define the daughter. The dynamics that would come into play depending on the daughter's adult

---

59. Moraga, *Loving in the War Years*, 16.
60. Moraga, *Loving in the War Years*, 32.

sexual preferences may be quite different and need additional exploration even in psychological theory."[61] A review of the poetry of Chicanas also shows that the father figure seems somewhat muted when it does appear. He is someone that the mother plays accomplice to; or that abandoned the mother and daughter; or that the mother is obsessed with. Whatever he may be is for the daughter largely reflected through her mother. I suspect that the most salient reason for the father's shadowy presentation in the women's poetry is the fact that male poets (the sons) have been inventing and interpreting him for themselves in modes parallel to those of the daughters' interpretation of the mother. Consequently, in the sons' poetry, the mother is shadowy and muted. To construct a theoretical dialogue between these two perspectives might lay bare the disjunctions and conjunctions between parental figures as interpreted by daughters and sons.[62]

The daughter-poet's efforts to rescue the mother and other women in her life[63] from the silent abyss enables her not only to rescue herself, but to acquire a richer and more varied voice. The voice becomes more luminous and creative as it strives to avoid the pitfalls of sheer reactive modes towards men. Her poetic 'I' which is viewed as a subordinate and subjective contingency in the realm of temporal events that seem more real, emerges to explore and decipher her relations to those others that shape her existence or conspire to keep her silent. In this quest, the mothers, in more paradoxical and contradictory ways than the grandmothers, are made to speak in order to reveal the "dark sufferings" that have made them prisoners of a deferred or suspended time. Though some poets' efforts at self-definitions have made use of symbolic figures, the preference is for biographical strategies that break new poetic grounds for self-interpretation and invention. The future advantages in this strategy lie in the creation of a feminist mythopoeia that lays down the premises for the pattern of beliefs and relations

---

61. See Nancy Chodorow, *The Reproduction of Mothering: Psychoanalysis and the Sociology of Gender* (Berkeley: University of California Press, 1978), 200. In her consideration of the mother-daughter relationship and the consequent relations of the daughter with others (i.e., fathers), she eschews a consideration of lesbian others on the basis that "most women are heterosexual."

62. The male Chicano poet who also claims working-class roots, posits a voice that emerges from Silence as well. Other minority males claim a similar perspective. For this point of view see Juan Bruce-Novoa, "The Other Voice of Silence: Tino Villanueva," in *Modern Chicano Writers*, eds. Joseph Sommers and Tomas Ybarra-Frausto, 133-140 (Englewood Cliffs, NJ: Prentice-Hall, 1979). His claims and hers raise questions about the notion of silence and poetic voice depending on issues of sex, race and class. Cross-sexual and cross-cultural considerations need further examination.

63. Many of the poets considered in this essay have written poems that focus on their relation and connection to other women, i.e., friends and lovers. It is an interfacing area that further aids in her self-definition, and which requires further exploration.

that will henceforth inform her future cultural identity. That is, she explores her life for the purpose of generating her new mythos. It is one that supplants and revises her past mythos. In doing so, it is crucial to emphasize that she does so as a speaker-member of working-class masses on the cutting edge of two languages both of which threaten to silence her with their apparent unbridgeable discourses. It is at this juncture that the impulse to be promoted to the position of umpire takes place (at least in literature). For as a poet engaged in self-discovery and self-invention, she is in the middle of a tense firing line between two disparate teams whose players are wide-ranging. The Chicanas' feminist discourse and cultural identity through poetry take as a central point of departure the poetic exploration of the self's relation to the muted "dark sufferings" of mothers and female friends while standing on a bridge between two cultures.

BIBLIOGRAPHY

Arendt, Hannah. *Between Past and Future: Eight Exercises in Political Thought*. London: Penguin Books, 1978.

Bornstein, Miriam. "La poeta chicana: vision panorámica." *La Palabra* 2, no. 2, (1980): 43-66.

Brinson-Pineda, Bárbara. "Maria la O." 1-5. In *The Midwest to the West: An Anthology*. Bloomington: A Chicano Riqueño Studies Publication, 1980.

Brinson-Pineda, Bárbara. "'Onde Estas Grandma': Chicana Writers and the Rejection of Silence." *Intercambios Femeniles* 2, 1984.

Castellano, Olivia. *Blue Mandolin, Yellow Field*. Berkeley: Tonatiuh—Quinto Sol International, 1980.

Cervantes, Lorna Dee. *Emplumada*. Pittsburgh: University of Pittsburgh Press, 1981.

Cervantes, Lorna Dee. "Declaration on a Day of Little Inspiration," *Mango* 1, (Fall 1976): 4.

Chodorow, Nancy. *The Reproduction of Mothering: Psychoanalysis and the Sociology of Gender*. Berkeley: University of California Press, 1978.

Cisneros, Sandra. *The House on Mango Street*. Houston: Arte Público Press, 1984.

Clausen, Jan. *A Movement of Poets: Thoughts on Poetry and Feminism*. Brooklyn: Long Haul Press, 1982.

Gómez, Alma, Cherríe Moraga, and Mariana Romo-Carmona, editors. *Cuentos: Stories by Latinas*. New York: Kitchen Table Press, 1983.

López Flores, Margarita. "Margarita: What Accounts for the Name." *Third Woman* 2, no. 1, (1984): 25.

Mirandé, Alfredo and Evangelina Enriquez. *La Chicana*. Chicago: University of Chicago Press, 1979.

Mora, Pat. *Chants*. Houston: Arte Público Press, 1984.

Moraga, Cherríe. *Loving in the War Years: Lo que nunca pasó por sus labios*. Boston: South End Press, 1981.

Moraga, Cherríe, and Gloria Anzaldúa, editors. *This Bridge Called My Back: Writings by Radical Women of Color*. 2nd ed. New York: Kitchen Table Press, 1983.

Olivares, Julian. "Seeing and Becoming: Evangelina Vigil, *Thirty an' Seen a lot*." In *The Chicano Struggle: Analyses of Past and Present Efforts*. Edited by John A. García, Teresa Córdova, Juan Ramon García, National Association for Chicano Studies, 152-65. Binghamton, NY: Bilingual Press, 1984.

Olsen, Tillie. *Silences*. New York: Delta Press, 1979.

Ong, Walter. *Interfaces of the Word: Studies in the Evolution of Consciousness and Culture*. Ithaca: Cornell University Press, 1977.

Ordoñez, Elizabeth. "Sexual Politics and the Theme of Sexuality in Chicana Poetry." 316-339. *Women in Hispanic Literature: Icons and Fallen Idols*. Edited by Beth Miller. Berkeley: University of California Press, 1983.

Rebolledo, Tey Diana. "Abuelitas: Mythology and Integration in Chicana Literature." In *Woman of her Word: Hispanic Women Write*, special issue of *Revista Chicano-Riqueña* 11, no. 3-4, (1983): 148-158.

Rebolledo, Tey Diana. "Soothing Restless Serpents: The Dreaded Creation and Other Inspirations in Chicana Poetry." *Third Woman* 2, no. 1 (1994): 83-102.

Rivero, Eliana. "Escritura Chicana: la mujer," *La Palabra* 2, no. 2, (1980): 2-9.

Rocha, Rina. *Eluder*. Chicago: Alexander Books, 1980.

Rodríguez, Juan. "Notes on the Evolution of Chicano Prose Fiction" In *Modern Chicano Writers*. Edited by Joseph Sommers and Tomas Ybarra-Frausto, 67-73. Englewood Cliffs, NJ: Prentice-Hall, 1979.

Sánchez, Marta. "Gender and Ethnicity in Contemporary Chicana Poetry." *Critical Perspectives* 2, no.1 (1984): 10-19.

Tafolla, Carmen. *Curandera*. San Antonio: M&A Editions, 1983.

Vigil, Evangelina. *Nade y Nade*. San Antonio: M&A Editions, 1978.

Vigil, Evangelina. *Thirty an' Seen a lot*. Houston: Arte Público Press, 1985.

Villanueva, Alma. *Blood Root*. Austin: Place of Herons Press, 1977.

Villanueva, Alma. *Mother, May I?* n.p.: Motheroot Publications, 1978.

MAKING *FAMILIA* FROM SCRATCH

SPLIT SUBJECTIVITIES IN THE WORK OF HELENA MARÍA VIRAMONTES
AND CHERRÍE MORAGA[1]

→ ←

What can be our place in the symbolic contract? If the social contract, far from being that of equal men, is based on an essentially sacrificial relationship of separation and articulation of differences which in this way produces communicable meaning, what is our place in this order of sacrifice and/or of language? No longer wishing to be excluded or no longer content with the function which has always been demanded of us (to maintain, arrange, and perpetuate this sociosymbolic contract as mothers, wives, nurses, doctors, teachers . . .), how can we reveal our place, first as it is bequeathed to us by tradition, and then as we want to transform it?

—Julia Kristeva, "Women's Time"

"I carried out my role as a priest always feeling as though I was a woman," Father Paolo told *La Stampa*. "Now I want to be a woman and still feel like a priest. I was looking for the woman inside myself, but trying not to renounce the priest that I was. Then I realized the rules would not permit this and I had to leave." She now is living in a small northern Italian village working as a babysitter, the newspaper said, and her legal status has been altered from male to female, though her canonical status remains unclear.

—Bruce Buursma, *Des Moines Register*

CHICANA WRITERS ARE INCREASINGLY employing female-speaking subjects who hark back to explore the subjectivity of women. Often in their writings this subjectivity takes as its point of departure "woman's" over-determined signification as future wives/mothers in relation to the "symbolic contract within which

---

[1]. *Editors' Note:* This essay was first published in *The Americas Review* 15, no. 3 (October 1, 1987). Subsequently the essay appeared in *Chicana Creativity and Criticism: Charting New Frontiers in American Literature*, ed. María Herrera-Sobek and Helena María Viramontes (Houston: Arte Público Press, 1988), 147-59, and in *Contemporary American Women Writers: Gender, Class, Ethnicity*, ed. Louise Parkinson Zamora (Routledge: New York, 2017), 87-98. We include the version from *Chicana Creativity and Criticism*, 1988.

women may have a voice on the condition that they speak as mothers."[2] The female-speaking subject that would want to speak from a different position than that of a mother, or a future wife/mother, is thrown into a crisis of meaning that begins with her own gendered personal identity and its relational position with others. Paradoxically, as we shall see, a crisis of meaning can ensue even in the case of a female who may have never aspired to speak from a different position than that of a wife/mother.

First, to start the exploration of the question of "woman," I want to discuss Helena M. Viramontes' story "Growing." What young girl can fight a father (and an assenting mother) when he roars "*TÚ ERES MUJER*"?[3] As Naomi, the protagonist notes, the phrase is uttered as a verdict. It is a judgment meant to ensure the paternal law and view of woman's cultural significance. Within this symbolic structure, Naomi is not supposed to counterspeak her sense of herself as different from what her father says it is. In his view her subjectivity has been decided *a priori* by what is perceived as the body of a woman. The fact that she is compelled to report the phrase in Spanish only points to a particular Chicano/ Mexicano rigidity with respect to the signifying system that holds the dyad woman-man in place, and which provides her father with his authority. By switching codes to "mujer," he knows more precisely what his judgment of Naomi ought to signify. If he said "woman," he would be on precarious ground. He is not quite sure what it may mean in Anglo culture, a culture within which he may well feel that he has no authority. Thus, though we may conjecture that Naomi's family transacts some of its communication in English, Spanish is employed in this sentence to guarantee parental authority. Naomi, on the

---

2. "Symbolic contract" is the term Julia Kristeva sometimes employs to refer to the Patriarchal Law and/ or linguistic domain. In her work the subject, who is almost always male, is conjectured as one who finds "his identity in the symbolic, [and] separates from his fusion with the mother"; in "Revolution in Poetic Language," *The Julia Kristeva Reader*, ed. Toril Moi (New York: Columbia University Press, 1986), 101. In Kristeva's theoretical perspective the Mother is posited, for the male subject, as an almost inarticulable site (i.e. a site of the Freudian/Lacanian unconscious). I do not take up that line of inquiry in this essay because in asking what our place as female subjects may be within the symbolic contract, the Mother is more than a theoretical site. We are asked to fill the site symbolically and socially. In "Women's Time," from which my epigraph is taken (23–4), Kristeva suggests that women speaking subjects may want to adopt an attitude where "the very dichotomy man/woman as an opposition between two rival entities may be understood as belonging to metaphysics" (33). That attitude is the one I have attempted to take vis-à-vis the writers discussed in my essay. See Julia Kristeva, Women's Time," *Signs: Journal of Women in Culture and Society* 7, no.1 (Autumn 1981): 13–35.

The second epigraph was written by Bruce Buursma in the *Chicago Tribune* and subsequently reprinted in the *Des Moines Register*, Sunday, October 17, 1987, n.p.

3. Helena Maria Viramontes, *The Moths and Other Stories* (Houston: Arte Público Press, 1985), 32.

other hand, has learned that "woman" is different from "mujer." As a result, she attempts to assert her difference from what is expected of Mexican/Chicana girls by appealing to the Anglo code. Thus, Naomi notes that for the girls "in the United States" experience is different.[4]

Though Naomi is correct in her perception of the difference in social experience between girls due to the relatively different cultural/racial codes (perhaps class-rooted codes as well), she is also too young to apprehend that in the "symbolic contract" virtually all women will sooner or later reach a limit with regard to the speaking position that they may take up as "woman." How rapidly that limit is reached and how she may speak thereafter will vary in accordance with the specific "semantic charters" that her cultural linguistic ground offers her.[5] Often that limit is set by how her father (and assenting mother) perceive her body which is always that of a "woman" and underpinned by what her father perceives as her sexual/maternal function. As a result, Naomi feels increasingly imprisoned by the concept "mujer," which her father wields as a weapon against her. Yet, she is hard put to fight him because his evidence for her meaning as "woman" is her own changing body, that is, menarche and breasts. In a sense, then, her very physical experience is used to press her to live out concepts such as "woman" and make Naomi become "*the practical realization of the meta-physical ... operating in such a way, moreover, that subjects themselves, being implicated through and through, being produced in it as concepts would lack the means to analyze it. Except in an after-the-fact way whose delays are yet to be fully measured....*"[6] Within such a "semantic charter" Naomi is too young to understand what is happening to her. She views her sexuality as a very confused mass. Though it may take her the rest of her life to apprehend what may have taken place as a result of the verdict "Tú eres mujer," the narrator of Naomi's

---

4. Viramontes, *The Moth and Other Stories*, 31.

5. Pierre Maranda suggests that "semantic charters condition our thoughts and emotions. They are culture specific networks that we internalize as we undergo the process of socialization" (185). Moreover, these charters or signifying systems "have an inertia and a momentum of their own. There are semantic domains whose inertia is high: kinship terminologies, the dogmas of authoritarian churches, the conception of sex roles" (184–5). See Pierre Maranda, "The Dialectic of Metaphor: An Anthropological Essay on Hermeneutics," in *The Reader in the Text: Essays on Audience and Interpretation*, ed. Susan R. Suleiman and Inge Crosman (Princeton: Princeton University Press, 1980), 183–204.

6. Luce Irigaray, *This Sex Which Is Not One*, trans. Cahterine Porter (Ithaca, NY: Cornell University Press, 1985), 189. The ellipsis occurs in the original as if calling for measurement itself which is what our research is about. In the chapter "Women on the Market" (170–91), from which I cite Irigaray, she also argues that this process turns women *qua* woman/mother into commodities so as to sustain economic systems and infrastructures that exploit women. Further citations to this work will be noted in the text.

circumstance is not too young to conclude as follows: "Now that she was older, her obligations became heavier both at home and at school. There were too many expectations... She could no longer be herself and her father no longer trusted her, because she was a woman."[7] All manner of things that she is obliged and expected to do are derived from the "fact" that she is a "woman." Her body is enlisted in a stream of sociosymbolic activities which she also experiences as a splitting her from herself. As Irigaray comments,

> Participation in society requires that [her] body submit itself to a specularization, a speculation, that transforms it into a value-bearing object, a standardized sign, an exchangeable signifier, a "likeness" with reference to an authoritative model. A *commodity*—a *woman*—*is divided into two irreconcilable "bodies"*: her "natural" body and her socially valued, exchangeable body, which is a particular mimetic expression of masculine values.[8]

Within Mexican/Chicano culture the authoritative model, however unconscious, to which fathers (masculine values) have recourse is the Catholic Holy Family and its assumed social authority. Viramontes, the constructor of this narrative world, is quite aware of that since many of her stories allude to religious expectations and dogma. Given that Naomi feels split from herself when she is pressed to become a "woman" for social and symbolic purposes, who is that self? If it could speak what would it say? It is at this point that many a woman of letters of Hispanic origin, in her quest for her subjectivity has turned to mysticism. Santa Teresa is our paradigm in that instance. Others, and here Sor Juana Inés de la Cruz is our paradigm, have opted for the convent (a retreat) so that no one could verify she was a "woman": "Yo no entiendo de esas cosas; / sólo sé que aquí me vine / porque, si es que soy mujer, / ninguno lo verifique."[9] In order to avoid these resolutions which are no solution at all for the contemporary Chicana critic and writer as speaking subjects, I want to pursue an alternate course with reference to two very different female-speaking subjects: Viramontes' own Olga Ruiz in "Snapshots" and Cherríe Moraga's Marisa in *Giving Up the Ghost*. I choose these because, unlike Naomi of "Growing," they speak their subjectivity directly, without the intervention of a narrator who has

---

7. Viramontes, *The Moth and Other Stories*, 38.

8. Irigaray, *The Sex Which Is Not One*, 180.

9. For a discussion of Sor Juana's passage from "woman" to "non-woman," see Octavio Paz, *Sor Juana Inés de la Cruz o Las Trampas de la Fe* (México: Fondo de Cultura Económica, 1982), 291.

greater "knowledge." Moreover, in assessing their crisis of meaning with regard to their own gendered personal identity, they have to look back as older women. Naomi is too young to have much to look back to except those moments of play when she experienced herself as forgetting that she was a "woman," though, as we shall see, that in itself can be significant. Both Marisa, who is in her late 20s, and Olga Ruiz, who is past 50, have had an opportunity that Naomi has yet to go through, that is, the increasing pressure to become that "woman" in the sociosymbolic contract. In looking back (and so many Chicana writers have their speaking subjects look back—Sandra Cisneros in *The House on Mango Street*, Ana Castillo in *The Mixquiahuala Letters* and Denise Chávez in *The Last of the Menu Girls* to name a few), Marisa and Olga Ruiz enact, as Irigaray asserts, an analysis "after-the-fact" of the treacherous route on the way to becoming a "woman" or not becoming a "woman."

Virtually all the readers I have talked with are put off by the story "Snapshots." Since there is nothing wrong with the story *qua* story, I ask why? Neither older women nor young women students like Olga Ruiz. Since Olga is the sole speaking subject in the story, as readers we are called upon to enter her world, and her view of it. Only one reader has admitted to me that she feels like Olga Ruiz and she said it with a sigh. Hardly anyone can, or wants to, recognize their subjectivity in Olga Ruiz. Olga Ruiz holds up a deadly mirror for women. If, as Pierre Maranda states, "the text is the light on my face that enables me to see myself in the one-way mirror that I hold in front of it; the text allows me, Narcissus, to marvel at my mind, to believe in myself and, consequently, to have the impression that I live more competently,"[10] then Olga Ruiz holds up to us the potential psychosis that awaits us if we live a life like hers. As readers we refuse to take up her "I" as our own, to fuse our "I" with hers. Female readers could come away feeling that they live "more competently," but they are not sure. Olga Ruiz may well remind us of our mothers, or we may even recognize ourselves in Olga's own daughter Marge, whose only advice to her mother is to keep busy. Marge has brought Olga enough skeins of wool to stock a retail shelf. Even the daughter, that is, younger readers, are caught speechless as to what they may say to help Olga Ruiz out of her crisis of meaning. In short, Olga Ruiz has lived the life of a "woman." How can we help a woman who according to cultural models has lived her life "correctly" and who is now cynical and embittered?

---

10. Maranda, "The Dialectic of Metaphor: An Anthropological Essay on Hermeneutics," 191.

Olga Ruiz has been *framed* by cultural expectations and is now so removed from her sensibility, her contact with her own body and its reality that she states, "I don't know if I should be hungry or not."[11] Was her grandmother right? Did her grandfather's camera, which split the sexes into men who mill "around him expressing their limited knowledge of the invention,"[12] and women whose pictures are taken, cut her from her soul? Given her desperate situation, Olga Ruiz appeals to folk beliefs in order to give closure to her crisis of meaning as wife/mother. If she can accept that she was "killed" since infancy, then maybe she can stop her obsessive-compulsive desire to find clues for meaning in the family album. Yet she will be left to wonder if her grandmother's antidote worked to save her, "My grandmother was very upset and cut a piece of my hair, probably to save me from a bad omen."[13] The grandmother's effort to counter the camera's evil work may have worked, in which case Olga Ruiz may be forced to conclude that she did not save herself, that she colluded with society and thus is responsible for her situation. Obviously, she stops short of completely blaming herself, and leaves a seed of doubt, a very small one, since not to doubt that indeed that is the meaning could throw her over the edge into total psychosis.

According to her own account, Olga stands on the threshold of psychosis after thirty years of marriage. However, as Olga remembers it, she had an earlier crisis of meaning as a "woman" after the birth of her daughter, Marge. The discomforts of pregnancy send her into her first quest for self-meaning in the family album as if it were a bible: "I began flipping through my family's photo albums ... to pass the time and the pain away."[14] She labels her compulsive behavior an "addiction" to "nostalgia." Giving birth becomes for Olga the first occasion in which she feels split from herself. Julia Kristeva has suggested that for many women,

> Pregnancy seems to be experienced as the radical ordeal of the splitting of the subject: redoubling up of the body, separating and coexistence of the self and of an other, of nature and of consciousness, of physiology and speech. This fundamental challenge to identity is then accompanied by a fantasy of totality—narcissistic completeness—a sort of instituted, socialized, natural psychosis.[15]

---

11. Viramontes, *The Moth and Other Stories*, 94.
12. Viramontes, *The Moth and Other Stories*, 98.
13. Viramontes, *The Moth and Other Stories*, 99.
14. Viramontes, *The Moth and Other Stories*, 94.
15. Kristeva, "Women's Time," 31.

According to sociosymbolic "semantic charters," Olga Ruiz should have found her gendered meaning and should surrender herself to a "narcissistic completeness" in the child, which she subsequently does. However, at that moment Olga found herself divided between the past as the moment of separateness from the child and the future which will demand an uneasy and continued coexistence. Though nothing comes of this critical moment, the sense that she should be separate is signaled by the nostalgic neurosis. By contemplating the family photo album, Olga hopes "some old dream will come into my blank mind."[16] She is depressed "because every detail, as minute as it might seem, made me feel that so much had passed unnoticed."[17] What dream or desire should make itself evident in the photographs? Whatever "had passed unnoticed" is not accompanied by any speech that would help Olga grasp the difference between what she wanted and what she got. Her mind is blank with regard to that self who may have dreamed of another life. She already knows that she has been very capable of devoting herself to the details of homemaking. She is so much the automaton that she cannot stop, though it is no longer necessary that she continue homemaking for others. The only words she can come up with, that can describe what might have been different from the muteness that enveloped her life, are nostalgia, indulgence, anticipation. She cannot come to terms with the separate self that could articulate an alternate past, present or future than what she has had.

Her solution to this particular blankness is brilliant given its truth currency: "Both woman and child are clones: same bathing suit, same pony tails, same ribbons."[18] However, truth does not necessarily grant one a new purchase on life. The snapshot of Olga, Marge and Dave is uncannily like the one of Olga with her parents. In a sense it is like that of the Holy Family triad—father, mother and child—except that the child is a girl, and indeed that is what problematizes the "snapshot." The girl-child does not have a sublime transcendent story. Her story according to that "semantic charter" is to duplicate the wife/maternal tale. How can any meaningful memory stand out in the redoubling of this snapshot? Certainly, Olga could not get close to her passionless mother, just as Marge cannot get close to Olga, nor does she appear to want to. They are as distanced from feeling as they are from their core responsive sensibility/sexuality, not only from men but from each other. Mother and daughter are so much alike one would think they could comfort each other, but they cannot. To do so Olga or

---

16. Viramontes, *The Moth and Other Stories*, 94.
17. Viramontes, *The Moth and Other Stories*, 94.
18. Viramontes, *The Moth and Other Stories*, 97.

Marge would have to take up a different speaking position with respect to each other. Before they can see themselves as more than a relational unit of mother-daughter, Olga or Marge would have to take up a different speaking position in their bodies. This position would entail entering into their emotional lives in ways that would strengthen and renew the bond differently, which may shut men out (temporarily?). (Let us remember that the Holy Family is the family of the son not the daughter.) Thus, to contemporanize the situation Marge would have to be capable of speaking to Olga, who is on the verge of madness, in the words of Luce Irigaray, as follows:

> And here you are, this very evening, facing a mourning with no remembrance. Invested with an emptiness that evokes no memories. That screams at its own rebounding echo. A materiality occupying a void that escapes its grasp. A block sealing the wall of your prison. A buttress to a possible future which, taken away, lets everything crumble indefinitely:
>
> Where are you? Where am I? Where to find the traces of our passage? From the one to the other? From the one into the other?
>
> [. . .]
>
> No one to mark the time of your existence, to evoke in you the rise of a passage out of yourself, to tell you: Come here, stay here. No one to tell you: Don't remain caught up between the mirror and this endless loss of yourself. A self separated from another self. A self missing some other self. Two dead selves distanced from each other, with no ties binding them. The self that you see in the mirror severed from the self that nurtures. And, as I've gone, I've lost the place where proof of your subsistence once appeared to you.[19]

Olga's middle-of-the-night phone call to Marge is her cry to have Marge reunite her with herself, "I don't know if I should be hungry." To start from the beginning as if she were a baby, so they can "make *familia* from scratch." Since Marge may not possess the wherewithal to respond, the call is rendered irrelevant. Before a crisis of meaning can be effected in the relationship between Olga and Marge as mother-daughter-mother, the husbands interfere. It is clearly not in their interest

---

19. Luce Irigaray, "And The One Doesn't Stir Without the Other," trans. Helene Vivienne Wenzel, *Signs: Journal of Women in Culture and Society* 7, no. 1 (Autumn 1981): 64-65.

to have these two women renegotiate the sociosymbolic contract by effecting a different dialogue between themselves. If we go on the report that Olga gives us of Marge, Marge herself cannot even begin to grasp that she, too, is abducted from herself, "Immobilized in the reflection he expects of [her]. Reduced to the face he fashions for [her] in which to look at himself. Traveling at the whim of his dreams and mirages. Trapped in a single function—mothering."[20] In short Marge is already also *framed* in her great grandfather's camera-eye which he passed on to the sons. It will be some years before Marge arrives at the speaking position her mother presently holds, by which time it may be too late. For indeed, grasping one's gendered meaning "after-the-fact" entails the removal of the buttress (that is, Mother) which lets everything crumble indefinitely." In the crumbling may be the speaking position from which to transform the sociosymbolic contract.

In *Giving Up the Ghost*, Cherríe Moraga offers us a heroine who has refused to become a "woman" who has refused to be framed by the camera's eye, "immobilized in the reflection he expects of [her]."[21] On the contrary Marisa desires to take up his "camera's eye," his gaze. In short, Marisa wanted to be a "man" when she was a child. Uncannily, as if the lines of communication between Olga Ruiz and Marisa had been inverted, Marisa implicitly uses the metaphor of the camera except, like a "man", she uses it to frame or trap women. Through Corky, her younger "male" self, Marisa "after-the-fact" reports:

> *when I was a little kid I useta love the movies*
> *every saturday you could find me there*
> *my eyeballs glued to the screen*
> *then during the week my friend Tudy and me*
> *we'd make up our own movies*
> *one of our favorites was this cowboy one*
> *where we'd be out in the desert*
> *'n' we'd capture these chicks 'n' hold 'em up*
> *for ransom we'd string 'em up 'n'*
> *make 'em take their clothes off*
> *jus' pretending a'course but it useta make me feel*
> *real tough*
> *strip we'd say to the wall*
> *all cool-like*

---

20. Luce Irigaray, "And The One Doesn't Stir Without the Other," 66.
21. Cherríe Moraga, *Giving Up the Ghost* (Los Angeles: West End Press, 1986).

[...]

I was a big 'n' tough 'n' a dude[22]

Corky's imaginary play, however, the fact that in her mind she was a "dude," is put into action one day. Corky and her friend Tudy (a boy), strip Chrissy down completely, and Corky reports that *"after that I was like a maniac all summer."*[23] In stripping Chrissy down, Corky looks into the vaginal mirror which makes her a little crazy as she also remembers that "deep down inside / no matter how / I tried to pull the other / off,"[24] she always knew she was a girl. As in Naomi's case, Corky is reminded that she is a girl, and consequently a "woman-to-be" through the body, except that Corky refuses to enter the "semantic charter." We are not sure what will come to Naomi, though she did report that she experienced sexual neutrality during childhood play. There is no neutrality for Corky ever, and even as she puts into play the dyad man-woman, it is in some sense unacceptable. However, she first internalizes the dyad in such a way that, though her body always reminds her that she is a girl/woman, her imaginary desire, the site of her subjectivity, is experienced as that of a "man."

Marisa, the adult Corky, is catapulted into a dance of "symbolic identifications" with the concepts of "man" and "woman" that is always too close for any female's comfort, because they constantly run the risk of being socialized into poses. Because Marisa is a lesbian, one of these is the famous lesbian dyad of the "butch-femme" split. In some sense, Marisa is split asunder between her male-like subjectivity and behavior, and her literal female body. For Marisa neither alternative "butch" (man) nor "femme" (woman) is acceptable. At this point, one can say that Marisa, out of necessity, either conjures Amalia into her life or that Amalia appears out of nowhere to save her. Both Marisa and Amalia speak their subjectivity "after-the-fact" of the relationship and hold a conversation that hardly ever is enacted face-to-face. It is as if Moraga knows that in "real" life these two women may not be able to speak to each other directly in any effective way, thus we must enter their sociosymbolic lives, in a dialogue that is always a near miss. Thus, Moraga effects a process of potential transformations between two women as unlike each other as we could ask for the lesbian with the subjectivity of a "man" and the traditional heterosexual "woman," who also may be our mother.

---

22. Moraga, *Giving Up the Ghost*, 5.
23. Moraga, *Giving Up the Ghost*, 12.
24. Moraga, *Giving Up the Ghost*, 6.

There are ways in which one can see the ghostly face of Olga Ruiz in Amalia, except that given the sexual interchange between Marisa and Amalia, Amalia is less repressed than Olga. Yet Amalia is in some ways a stereotypic heterosexual Mexican "woman." Amalia is framed by the of her male lovers, the ones for whom she wanted to be an object eye of desire. Amalia cannot bring herself to desire Marisa until her ideal male lover dies, and his ghost reenters her body so that she may feel enough a "man" to desire Marisa.[25] In this fashion we are cued from a different angle, that active sexual desire has been marked masculine. By the end of this "after-the-fact" indirect dialogue both Amalia and Marisa have learned as much about themselves as we have about the variety of gendered crises of meaning.

The subjective agency of desire, the ineffable energy that may help us transform our world has heretofore been the province of whoever "man" is. As a lesbian-identified woman, Marisa does not want just a "woman" (a "femme"), that is a muted object of desire, but as she says: "It's not that you don't want a man, / you don't want a man in a man. / You want a man in a woman. / The woman-part goes without saying. / That's what you always learn to want first."[26] The implication that a girl learns to want a woman first through her relationship to her mother, and places the girl-child in competition with the boy-child for the body of the mother is very suggestive. It brings us face to face with the fantastic cultural silence, religious or Freudian, with regard to what the girl's position is in the Holy Family or Oedipal triad. This lays bare the fact that in that sociosymbolic contract a girl-child may not speak except as would-be mother or mother. In taking refuge in a male identity, Corky/Marisa acquire a speech that is at odds with the body, thus in a different way they are forced into two irreconcilable selves. Amalia, however, thinks that Marisa wanted her so that Marisa could feel (be) the woman in her: "Sometimes I think, with me / that she only wanted to feel herself / so much a woman / that she would no longer be hungry for one."[27] If this is so, then Marisa goes to Amalia, the maternal/heterosexual, for the reconciliation with her female body. As bereft daughter, Marisa reverses the "narcissistic completeness" that Kristeva suggests mothers are expected to attain through the child: "But then was the beautiful woman / in the mirror of the water / you or me?"[28] Moraga here suggests the daughter's

---

25. Moraga, *Giving Up the Ghost*, 28.
26. Moraga, *Giving Up the Ghost*, 29.
27. Moraga, *Giving Up the Ghost*, 53.
28. Moraga, *Giving Up the Ghost*, 27.

quest to unite with the mother in ways that only sons get to do within a too rigid patriarchy. It is clear at the end of the dramatic monologues, that Marisa's severed pieces have come together to enable her creativity, "so I cling to her in my heart, / my daydream with pencil in my mouth, when I put my fingers / to my own forgotten places."[29]

In my view, in *Giving Up the Ghost*, Moraga puts into play the concepts "man" and "woman" (and the parodic butch/femme"), with the intuitive knowledge that they operate in our subjectivities, so that it is difficult to analyze them, except in the way she has done. Women speaking with each other in a spiraling way, not quite face-to-face, but with the recollection that at least once they were so close to each other that they could effect a transfusion so as to avoid the extremes that is a muted "woman's" speaking position, and a male-identified subjectivity. It is to Moraga's credit that she puts the dyad man-woman into play in such a way that she brings into view three relational trajectories—the lesbian-butch who is killing herself by the implied rejection of her literal body, the mother-daughter relation where the daughter may be forced to take the son (or father's) position so as to get close to her mother, and the hope that the heterosexual woman will not be put off by the lesbian due to homophobia.

For young Chicana writers (and critics) the crisis of meaning as women has increasingly led to a measuring "after-the-fact" of the speaking subject's meanings. The most exciting explorations are those that "measure" the intricacies of relationship between and among women. Yet if actual social experiences have the potential of effecting a complex and heterogeneous subjectivity, the symbolic contract within which "woman" is the repository of meaning and not the agent, constantly presses her to align herself with the symbolic; in this way she is forced to live the life of a "woman/mother." To refuse to live the life of a "woman," which is both literal (body) and symbolic (iconic/linguistic configurations), throws her into a crisis of meaning. As young Corky makes clear, if you don't want to be a girl, society as well as she then takes it that you want to be a boy. Corky's "error" is that she does not refuse both. How could she? Perhaps, as the older and wiser Marisa suggests, we must make "*familia* from scratch."[30] Marisa, who wanted to save her own mother[31] and later Amalia, by having them remember their own "forgotten places" beyond womanly duty, would, unlike Marge, be

---

29. Moraga, *Giving Up the Ghost*, 58.
30. Moraga, *Giving Up the Ghost*, 58.
31. Moraga, *Giving Up the Ghost*, 14.

capable of saying to Olga Ruiz: "Where are you? Where am I? Where to find the traces of your passage? From the one to the other? From the one into the other?"

In my view, Julia Kristeva goes a long way towards charting a course for the dissident (female) speaking subject. The speaking subject today has to position herself at the margins of the "symbolic contract" and refuse to accept definitions of "woman" and "man" in order to transform the contract. However, as Kristeva's critics have pointed out, a female-speaking subject today has to walk with one foot inside and another outside the interstice that would stake the boundary of what a "woman" may speak. Toril Moi's critique reads as follows: "political reality (the fact that patriarchy defines women and oppresses them accordingly) still makes it necessary to campaign in the name of women, it is important to recognize that in this struggle a woman cannot *be*: she can only exist negatively, as it were, through the refusal of that which is given."[32] Moi adds that as a result Kristeva can state "I therefore understand by 'woman,' that which cannot be represented, that which is not spoken, that which remains outside naming and ideologies."[33] Thus, it is that both Naomi and Marisa leave their futures open-ended, and Naomi in her way too can challenge her father, for to believe that one "is a woman" is as absurd and obscurantist as to believe that one "is a man."[34]

As Chicana writers explore the subjectivity of their speaking subjects, they are bound, as most of us are, to explore sexual identities as they have been bequeathed. However, as I hope I have made clear, each speaking subject takes positions that vary according to her self-conscious grasp of the engendering process, which constantly throws girls/women into a crisis of meaning as women. That self-conscious grasp will be very much dependent on age, cultural ground, and on how she understands herself in relation to others, after the fact. The task before us is to continue to measure the delay and its painful implications.

---

32. Toril Moi, *Sexual/Textual Politics: Feminist Literary Theory*, 2nd edition (New York: Methuen,1986), 10.
33. Moi, *Sexual/Textual Politics*, 163.
34. Moi, *Sexual/Textual Politics*, 163.

BIBLIOGRAPHY

Buursma, Bruce. *Chicago Tribune* and subsequently reprinted in the *Des Moines Register*, Sunday October 17, 1987, n.p.

Cahill, Susan, editor. *Writing Women's Lives: An Anthology of Autobiographical Narratives by Twentieth-Century American Women Writers.* New York: Harper Perennial, 1994.

Evans, Mari, editor. *Black Women Writers (1950–1980).* Garden City, NY: Anchor Press, 1984.

Irigaray, Luce. "And the One Doesn't Stir Without the Other." Translated by Helene Vivienne Wenzel. *Signs: Journal of Women in Culture and Society* 7, no. 1 (Autumn 1981): 64–65.

Irigaray, Luce. *This Sex Which Is Not One.* Translated by Catherine Porter. Ithaca: Cornell University Press, 1985.

Kristeva, Julia. "Revolution in Poetic Language." *The Kristeva Reader.* Edited by Tori Moi. New York: Columbia University Press, 1986.

Kristeva, Julia. "Women's Time." *Signs: Journal of Women in Culture and Society* 7, no. 1 (Autumn 1981): 13-35.

Larson, Sidner. "Native American Aesthetics: An Attitude of Relationship." *MELUS* 17, no. 3, (September 1992): 53-67.

Maranda, Pierre. "The Dialectic of Metaphor: An Anthropological Essay on Hermeneutics." In *The Reader in the Text: Essays on Audience and Interpretation.* Edited by Susan R. Suleiman and Inge Crosman. Princeton: Princeton University Press, 1980. 183-204.

Moi, Toril. *Sexual/Textual Politics: Feminist Literary Theory*, 2nd edition. New York: Methuen, 1986.

Moraga, Cherríe. *Giving Up the Ghost.* Los Angeles: West End Press, 1986.

Morrison, Toni, editor. *Race-ing Justice, En-gendering Power: Essays on Anita Hill, Clarence Thomas, and the Construction of Social Reality.* New York: Pantheon Books, 1992.

Paz, Octavio. *Sor Juana Inés de la Cruz o Las Trampas de la Fé.* México: Fondo de Cultura Económica, 1982.

Pearlman, Mickey, editor. *Listen to Their Voices: Twenty Interviews with Women Who Write.* New York: Norton, 1993.

Perry, Donna, editor. *Backtalk: Women Writers Speak Out.* New Brunswick, NJ: Rutgers University Press, 1993.

Tate, Claudia. *Black Women Writers at Work.* New York: Continuum, 1983 (Harpenden: Oldcastle Books, 1985).

Todd, Janet, editor. *Women Writers Talking.* New York: Holmes and Meier, 1983.

Valdés, María Elena de. "In Search of Identity in Cisneros's *The House on Mango Street.*" *Canadian Review of American Studies* 23, no. 1 (Fall 1992): 55-72.

Viramontes, Helena María. *The Moths and Other Stories.* Houston: Arte Público Press, 1985.

Yalom, Marilyn, editor. *Women Writers of the West Coast: Speaking of Their Lives and Careers.* Santa Barbara, CA: Capra Press, 1983.

THE SARDONIC POWERS OF THE EROTIC
IN THE WORK OF ANA CASTILLO[1]

→ ←

ANA CASTILLO, A NATIVE of Chicago, first made an impact on the Chicano writer's community with the publication of her chapbook, *Otro Canto*.[2] Written mostly in English (as is almost all of Castillo's work), it ensured her reputation as a "social protest" poet at a time when it was difficult to be anything else. As a result, some of the ironic tones already present in the early work have been easily over-looked in favor of the protest message, which in fact is re-doubled by irony. It can be argued that irony is one of Castillo's trademarks. Irony often appears when experience is viewed after-the-fact or in opposition to another's subjectivity. In this essay, I would like to explore the ironically erotic dance that Castillo's speaking subjects often take up with men. Thus, my exploration will follow the trajectory of the traditional heterosexual, female speaking subject in Castillo's published works: *Otro Canto*, *The Invitation*,[3] *Women Are Not Roses*,[4] and *The Mixquiahuala Letters*.[5]

Otro Canto portrayed the burdens of the urban poor through the voice of a young woman who had learned the bitter lessons of disillusionment early in life. Thus, in the poem "1975," we hear a sigh of relief when all of those "proletarian talks"—the nemesis of many a left-wing activist—are finally translated into action. The speaker underscores the repetitiveness of mere talk by starting off every stanza with the line, "talking proletarian talks," which subsequently opens the way for details that give rise to such talk. We are not relieved from this tactical monotony "until one long awaited day—/ we are tired/ of talking."[6] Though in "1975" the speaker is not gender-marked but is revealed as being in a

---

1. *Editors' Note:* This essay was first published in *Breaking Boundaries: Latina Writing and Critical Readings*, ed. Asuncíon Horno-Delgado, Eliana Ortega, Nina M. Scott, and Nancy Saporta Sternbach (Amherst: University of Massachusetts Press, 1989), 94-107. It was subsequently published in *Chicana Critical Issues*, ed. Norma Alarcón (Berkeley: Third Woman Press, 1993)), 5-19. We include the version published in *Chicana Critical Issues*, 1993.
2. Ana Castillo, *Otro Canto* (Chicago: n.p., 1977).
3. Ana Castillo, *The Invitation* (Chicago: n.p., 1979; 2d ed n.m. 1986).
4. Ana Castillo, *Women Are not Roses* (Houston: Arte Público Press, 1984).
5. Ana Castillo, *The Mixquiahuala Letters* (Binghamton, NY: Bilingual Review Press, 1986).
6. Castillo, *Otro Canto*, 49-51.

"we-us" speaking position within a Marxist revolutionary stance, that speaker is transformed into a "we-us" who makes "A Counter-Revolutionary Proposition." In this poem we are called upon to make love and "forget/that Everything matters."[7] Given the litany of the things that matter in the stanza preceding the call, however, the poem urges me to ask if the speaker is wryly alluding to the well-known Anglo counterculture slogan of the sixties: "Make Love, Not War." As the poem notes, what matters to the proletarian (i.e., Marxist) revolutionary speaker is the struggle to overcome class oppression, a struggle that is spoken through a supposedly non-gendered we. However, juxtaposing the poem's title, "A Counter-Revolutionary Proposition," with the implicit allusion to the slogan "Make Love, Not War," may help us to unravel a story with a difference for the underclass female speaker who addresses her partner, "Let's forget . . ."[8]

Notwithstanding the recent involvement of women in revolutionary struggles (i.e., Cuba and Nicaragua), it is still the case that in opposition to the erotic, a revolution or a war is especially marked with a traditional male subjectivity that awaits analysis. In order for a female speaker to recover the full meaningful impact of herself, she still must address how that self figures in the "heterosexual erotic contract," revolutions not excepted. Within this contract, the female body continues to be the site of both reproduction and the erotic; despite class position, a speaker and her gendered social experience are imbricated in that age-old contract. Thus, "A Counter-Revolutionary Proposition" may now be understood as a call to explore the politics of the erotic. Let us actively explore the neo-revolutionary implications of erotic relations that have been constantly displaced, undervalued, and even erased by masculine-marked militancy, or at best rendered passively by the male poet, with the woman as the muse, the wife, the mother.

From this point of view, the poem's title acquires a polyvalence that goes beyond the private, where the erotic has often been held "hostage," and is placed in the political arena. In a sense, then, "Let's 'make love'" is taken from the lips of an Anglo, male, left wing activist by the most unexpected speakers—Ana Castillo's poetic persona. In retrospect, Castillo's early work stands out as one of her first attempts to appropriate the erotic and its significances for the female speaker, with ironic repercussions. Given the assumed class position of the speaker herself, affirming the erotic, as she takes pause from the class struggle, is

---

7. Castillo, *Women Are Not Roses*, 63.
8. Castillo, *Women Are Not Roses*, 63.

tantamount to speaking against herself, or so her "brother/lover" may attest. The implicit suggestion that the erotic and the class struggle may be incompatible in a patriarchal world, when both are made public, places the underclass female in a double-bind, since she may be forced to choose between areas of life that, for her, are intertwined or indivisible. In my view, the speakers in Castillo's work refuse to make such choices. Choosing one or the other splits the subject into the domains that heretofore have been symbolically marked feminine or masculine.

In the seventies, Chicanas and other women of color had a difficult time within their fraternal group when they insisted that feminist politics, with its commitment to the exploration of women's sexuality and gendered identities, also applied to them. The supposed contradictory position of women of color, one that was between a male-identified class liberation struggle and a middle-or upper-class, white, female-identified sexual liberation struggle, forced women of color to walk a tightrope in their quest for an exploration of gender.[9] Thus, a poem such as "A Counter-Revolutionary Proposition" was politically risky, as the speaker addresses another, ostensibly male, and asks that he forget that "Everything matters." Yet, it is only within this apparent self-contradictory situation that such a speaker may be able to claim sexuality for herself and explore the significance of the female body that is always, and already, sexually marked. Such a "proposition" simultaneously opens up a gap between the fact of economic oppression and the desire for erotic pleasure and significance that faces us when we perceive the separation between the first and the second stanzas in the poem.

In *The Invitation*, a chapbook-length collection of erotic poems and vignettes, Castillo's speaker no longer requests that her interlocutor forget that "everything matters" but pursues, instead, a sustained exploration of her erotic, at times bisexual desires.[10] The appropriation of the erotic for the female speaker is again a motivating force. The emphasis, however, is not so much on the speaker's uneasy conjunction with "proletarian politics" as it is with "textual politics." That is, the appropriative process resonates respectively against, and with, two important books of our time: Octavio Paz's *The Labyrinth of Solitude*,

---

9. For testimonials regarding this predicament, one of the most accessible books is *This Bridge Called My Back: Writings by Radical Women of Color*, 2nd. ed., ed. Cherríe Moraga and Gloria Anzaldúa (New York: Kitchen Table Press, 1983). Leftist feminists in Latin America encounter similar predicaments when working in a framework of "grassroots feminism." See Magaly Pineda, "Feminism and Popular Education: A Critical but Necessary Relationship," *Isis International*, no. 6 (1986): 111-113.

10. Ana Castillo, *The Invitation* (n.p., 1979).

and María Teresa Horta, Maria Isabel Barreno, and María Velho da Costa's *The Three Marías: New Portuguese Letters*.[11] Consider, for example, that in the second chapter of this book, Paz affirms women's dormant and submissive sexuality that awaits discovery through male efforts, while "The Three Marías" reject this view throughout their book and protest women's political bondage that, at the core, is based on their sexuality. Notwithstanding the different approaches that each of "The Three Marías" would take to liberate women, there is very little doubt that they agree that male perception of women's sexuality pervades all levels of women's existence.

The erotic thematics of *The Invitation* openly declare the influence of those two books.[12] Castillo's text, when viewed in their light, becomes a purposefully glossed negation of Paz's view and an extension of the author's own erotic vision. It is as if the relative absence of any sociopolitical debate of the Chicana/Mexicana's sexuality had made it imperative that Castillo explore instead her speaker's desire in the light of a textual milieu. Moreover, reading Castillo's work in this fashion enables us to clarify her struggle to place her erotic thematics and voices in the interstice of both her sociopolitical and textual experiences. In other words, if, due to her social position, the underclass female is called upon to address her oppression with a ready-made, class-struggle rhetoric, attempting to address her sexual/erotic oppression forces her to see it in relation to texts. Her own response to those texts enables her to give voice to her experience and make it public. If she does not make an effort to bring out that voice herself, it will remain muted, as she is forced to align herself with the heretofore masculine-marked class voice. Thus, she is reconfirming, from another angle, Gilbert and Gubar's call in *The Madwoman in the Attic* for our critical need to explore "the metaphor of experience" (in "1975" and "A Counter-Revolutionary Proposition") and "the experience of metaphor" (in *The Invitation*).[13] The speaker/writer and the critic must discern, insofar as it is possible, between the metaphors female speakers create to represent our sociopolitical and erotic experience and the metaphors these speakers inherit and that *a priori* inscribe our potential experience. Thus,

---

11. For the purpose of this essay, I have used *The Labyrinth of Solitude*, trans. by Lysander Kemp (New York: Grove Press, 1961); and *The Three Marias: New Portuguese Letters*, trans. by Helen R. Lane (New York: Doubleday, 1975).

12. Castillo, *The Invitation*, iii, 9.

13. Sandra M. Gilbert and Susan Gubar, *The Madwoman in the Attic: The Woman Writer and the Nineteenth-Century Imagination* (New Haven: Yale University Press, 1979), xiii. Sigrid Weigel makes a similar suggestion in her essay "Double Focus: On the History of Women's Writing," in *Feminist Aesthetics*, ed. Gisela Ecker, trans. Harriet Anderson (Boston: Beacon Press, 1986), 59-80.

a writer/speaker can unwittingly live out the experiences that the metaphors call upon her to duplicate (i.e., Paz's description of female sexuality) or she can struggle to lay them bare and thus reinscribe her evolving position (i.e., "The Three Marías" struggle to reinscribe women's sexuality).

Paz's work, as well as "The Three Marías" and *The Invitation* itself, are, in a sense, all glossed over in Castillo's epistolary narrative, *The Mixquiahuala Letters*, which more closely approximates the sociopolitical images of *Otro Canto*. In a sense, *Letters* is more aggressive in its conjugation of "the experience of metaphor" and "the metaphor of experience" as it pertains to the erotic, for it is yet another link in Castillo's exploration of sexuality and its significance for women. If in *Letters*, however, the negation of Paz's view of women's sexuality continued, even as it is ironically reconfirmed by some of the males represented in the text, the work of "The Three Marías" is honored by adapting its epistolary form. However, the letters of "The Three Marias" are also supplemented by Castillo's Anglo-American political and sexual angle of vision. Castillo's sole speaking protagonist—Teresa ("Tere")—takes up the position, initially, of a free agent, while the narrative web of "The Three Marías" starts out by recognizing that women are not free agents in any sense whatsoever. Moreover, as Darlene Sadlier's essay makes clear, "The Three Marías" did not have the political freedom to explore women's sexual oppression or question its nature even textually, let alone in practice.[14] As a result, they were placed on trial for publishing their book. Ironically, the trial itself corroborated their point; women have not been free to express an uncensored subjectivity. Ana Castillo's *Letters* supplements "The Three Marias" insofar as her protagonist projects a subjectivity, free to express and practice her sexuality, but still imprisoned by an intangible heterosexist ideology, a heterosexist ideology for which we may posit Paz's view as the model. Thus, in *Letters* we have a protagonist who, by virtue of North American political practices and feminist influence, had "forgotten" what it is like to live in the world of "The Three Marías" or even in Paz's world. As a result, Tere, the main speaker in *Letters*, undergoes a trial by fire when México's cultural configuration is put into play. She is forced to recall that she is not as free as she thought. Since Teresa is a woman of Mexican descent (a Chicana), she should not have forgotten but, insofar as she wants to be a freer agent, she would want to forget. The complexities of her diverse levels of consciousness

---

14. For an excellent discussion of both the political problems and the narrative modes of this book, see Darlene Sadlier, "Form in Novas Cartas Portuguesas," *Novel* 19, no. 3 (Spring 1986): 246-63.

may be located in the push and pull of divergent political countries, i.e., the United States and México. As Gloria Anzaldúa states in "*La Conciencia de la Mestiza*: Towards a New Consciousness":

> Within us and within *la cultura chicana*, commonly held beliefs of the white culture attack commonly held beliefs of the Mexican culture, and both attack commonly held beliefs of the indigenous culture. . . . In a constant state of mental nepantilism, an Aztec word meaning torn between ways, *la mestiza* is a product of the transfer of the cultural and spiritual values of one group to another. . . . and in a state of perpetual transition, the *mestiza* faces the dilemma of the mixed breed: which collectivity does the daughter of a darkskinned mother listen to?[15]

Indeed, this may explain the rationale behind addressing the letters to Alicia, who was Tere's traveling companion and ought to have known what they experienced. Nevertheless, the technique enables Tere to bring out, through Alicia, the Anglo-American cultural influence that, in any case, does not save either of them in the face of the erotic, as we shall see.

Before further consideration of the *The Mixquiahuala Letters*, however, other important points must be brought up that will clarify its social and literary importance as well as my necessarily complex critical approaches. The critical conjugation of "the metaphor of experience" and "the experience of metaphor" is as complex as its literary elaboration.

Selections from both chapbooks, *Otro Canto* and *The Invitation*, as well as sixteen new poems, have been made available to a wider audience in Castillo's book, *Women are Not Roses*. As happens in "selections" books, the evolution of a writer's work is often cut short in favor of the "best" that a writer has produced, a factor that is the prerogative of editors. As a result, *Women Are Not Roses* does not provide the reader with many clues to the intertextual observations made above. Theorists of the text, of course, have taught us that one does not have recourse to direct intertextual sources for the pursuit of such considerations. However, it is also the case that writers do respond consciously to their textual milieus and effect a revisionary dialogue. As such, it is of paramount political importance to identify the textual milieu of culturally marginalized writers such as Chicanas, as

---

15. Gloria Anzaldúa, "*La Conciencia de la Mestiza*: Towards a New Consciousness," in *Borderlands: La Frontera, The New Mestiza* (San Francisco: Spinsters/Aunt Lute Books, 1987), 77-91.

well as to clarify the appropriate strategies at work in the struggle to construct and reconstruct an identity despite its instability, lest a writer appear to speak in a vacuum. Moreover, writers and critics often rely on a textual milieu and an actual experience, insofar as that milieu assists with the verbal translation of our cultural experience. In this fashion, a variety of discourses can be negated, supplemented, modified, and repeated, though it may not always be possible, or even necessary, to make clear-cut source identifications.[16]

Women Are Not Roses does not provide any clues to Castillo's appropriate strategies and experimentations, though the word "rose" in the title points to, and plays upon, the masculine textual production in which women are represented as flowers/nature. In this book, however, there are at least two poems that resonate intertextuality and intratextuality, and their examination may also help us in the reading of *The Mixquiahuala Letters*.

Both "An Idyll"[17] and "The Antihero"[18] warrant a closer look because they not only evoke the Western romantic tradition that has underpinned women's erotic image within patriarchy but also, in this instance, further the female speaker's appropriation of that tradition to explore her sexuality and revise the image. Moreover, since Tere, the letter-writing protagonist of *Letters*, does not explicitly speak of her erotic illusions and ideals but instead reconstructs, from a ten-year distance, a period of her life that she calls a "cesspool" (Letter #2), a consideration of these two poems may help us come to terms with the nature of her failed erotic quest. Though *Letters* represents sexual encounters with men, Tere often assumes a sarcastic, pragmatic, and even distant tone that contrasts sharply with whatever illusions and ideals may have led her (Letter # 1) and her friend Alicia to actively explore their sexuality. This is an exploration that falls short of erotic bliss, to say the least: hence, the label "cesspool." In a sense, the expectations of heterosexual erotic bliss constitute the partially repressed aspects of *Letters*, which on occasion contains such startling confessions as "i was docile"[19] or "i believed i would be placed in the little house and be cared

---

16. I am specifically referring to the work of Julia Kristeva, *Revolution in Poetic Language*, trans. Margaret Waller, intro. Leon S. Roudiez, (New York: Columbia University Press, 1980), 15; as well as the work of M.M. Bakhtin, *The Dialogic Imagination*, ed. Michael Holquist, trans. Caryl Emerson and Michael Holquist (Austin: University of Texas Press, 1981), 259-422.
17. Castillo, *Women Are Not Roses*, 8-10.
18. Castillo, *Mixquiahuala Letters*, 24.
19. Castillo, *Mixquiahuala*, 113.

for..."²⁰ These occasional confessions are barely audible. They tend to get lost in Tere's latter-day, after-the-fact sardonic anger. As we shall see, she has been framed *a priori* by certain "semantic charters,"²¹ and Castillo mocks her further by framing her with the "reading charts" offered to the reader.

"An Idyll" and "The Antihero" reinscribe two aspects of the erotic/romantic hero—the god-like and the demonic—from the point of view of a female speaker. Their representation, however, is complicated by the different spatio-temporal positions that the speaker takes, consequently putting into question how one translates and interprets (writes/reads) the experience. Since "The Antihero" is a significant inversion of the hero in "An Idyll," the speaker's relational position to each becomes very important, adding another dimension to their inscription. A speaker's position in relation to such monumental and heroic figures cannot be all that simple. The speaker is probing not only a relationship to the symbolic, that is, how the romantic hero has figured in textual tradition, but her social experience as well, that is, how she has lived her sexuality in, and through, such figurations.

In these two poems, the speaker filters her position through an intricate use of the first-("An Idyll") and third-("The Antihero") person pronouns in combination with temporal distance and proximity, respectively. These spatiotemporal, positional techniques are employed in *Letters* as well; though most of the letters are first-person accounts, Letters # 21 and # 32 are examples of speaker shifts. "An Idyll" is a first-person narration of past experience that is represented in fantastic terms, a virtual parody of male literary figurations:

>   now
> i   can   tell
> of being swept b
> y a god a michael
> angelo's david a

---

20. Castillo, *Mixquiahuala*, 118. The use of the small "i" pronoun throughout *Letters* is disturbing but something other than an affectation. Weigel (1986) suggests that to use the "I" in public, women will have to learn to speak "without having first to acknowledge the male definition of their gender role." See note 13.

21. Pierre Maranda, "The Dialectic of Metaphor: An Anthropological Essay on Hermeneutics," in *The Reader in the Text: Essays on Audience and Interpretation*, ed. Susan Rubin Suleiman and Inge Crosman (Princeton: Princeton University Press, 1980), 184-85. Maranda suggests that "Semantic charters condition our thoughts and emotions. They are culture specific networks that we internalize as we undergo the process of socialization." Moreover, these charters of signifying systems "have an inertia and a momentum of their own. There are semantic domains whose inertia is high: kinship terminologies, the dogmas of authoritarian churches, the conception of sex roles."

> man of such phys
> ical   perfection,
> one could not be
> lieve him human.[22]

In this poem, the very columnar shape points to a phallic symmetry that distorts the potential plasticity of language for its own sake. It takes a very well programmed machine to reproduce that form. It is akin to a divine hierarchical account that only "now," by stepping outside of it, can be apprehended. The narrator, who only "now" can represent her enthrallment with the beautiful stony hero, assesses that erotic dance as "truer" because it was satisfying, in some measure. Enthrallment itself may have its own temporary erotic rewards. The romantic interlude—an idyll—as a symbolic fantasy may be spellbinding, but the effort to transform it into a social reality literally enslaves her:

> angelo's   david   a
>   i ate
> with   it slept   wi
> th   made   its   b
> ed   in the   mornin
> g when it disapp
> eared   ...   i waited
> for   its   return—
> each night.[23]

Indeed, like language, she is immobilized and transfixed by "it," a god-like man. "It" has turned her into a robot. The murder of this fantastic being is due to her almost sudden awareness that her union with him, despite its insane and masochistic pleasures, is tantamount to her own self-destructive collusion. In the poem, his murder is anonymous, perhaps collective. As a crowd gathers to demand his expulsion, one of them shoots him when he refuses to leave:

> until one of us c
> ould not stand it
> any longer and
> shot him.[24]

---

22. Castillo, *Mixquiahuala Letters*, 8.
23. Castillo, *Women Are Not Roses*, 9.
24. Castillo, *Women Are Not Roses*, 10.

Now that the fantasy, with its perverse truth, is over, the first-person speaker is free to recall her delusion. Indeed, it is the newer, after-the-fact consciousness that makes it possible to see the enthrallment as a delusion. The one who narrates, however, is distanced from the one who lives the fantasy, that distance itself muting the emotional charge of the actual experience that was once lived as true and is now viewed through the lens of fabulous fiction. It is as if there was something inherently ironic in an experience recollected from the now-distant point of a changed consciousness. This is precisely the ironic tone affected in many of the letters (see, for example, Letter #16 where Tere's attraction to Alvaro is later viewed as a weakness). Tere mocks her initial enthrallment. She "Believed that beneath his rebellion was a sensitive human being with an insight that was unique and profound."[25] Years later, however, either Tere's narrative hindsight or that of an unidentified narrator reports, "This is a woman conditioned to accept a man about whom she has serious doubts . . ."[26]

The ironies of "An Idyll" take a more cruel turn in "The Anti-hero," who exhibits a reckless disregard for his partner's erotic desires: "the antihero/always gets the woman/not in the end/an anticlimax instead."[27] If the heterosexual dance in "An Idyll" is paradoxically viewed as a true fiction by the first person narrator, the lyrical speaker of "The Antihero" views him as purposely playing his partner false. He obfuscates erotic desire by rendering sexual experience anticlimactic, as against pressure and denouement. He manipulates her desire so as "to leave her yearning lest/she discover that is all."[28] She is double-crossed by the anticlimactic ruse into continuing to conflate desire with him. It is clear, as Luce Irigaray comments in another context, that "man's desire and woman's are strangers to each other."[29] If she discovered the infinite power of her own desire, then certainly the cruel dance would undergo transformation or come to a stop. The poem presents the anticlimactic sexual event in the present-tense lyrical mode, through the lens of the third person. The couple is objectified in the present tense to suggest an ongoing, unsatisfactory scenario of desire that brings them together, yet keeps them apart. Thus, contrary to the dictates of the lyric, which calls for a personal account of sensual experience, the poem

---

25. Castillo, *Mixquiahuala Letters*, 48.
26. Castillo, *Mixquiahuala Letters*, 48.
27. Castillo, *Women Are Not Roses*, 24.
28. Castillo, *Women Are Not Roses*, 24.
29. Luce Irigaray, *This Sex Which is Not One*, trans. Catherine Porter with Carolyn Burke (Ithaca, NY: Cornell University Press, 1985), 27.

switches the speaker position to suggest a model of contemporaneous behavior that distorts erotic desire. For Castillo, then, angles of perception, which may be both spatial and/or temporal, are sites for discrete eruptions of meaning that may be subsequently juxtaposed, thus effecting additional meanings. In a sense, the significance of any one thing is highly unstable and much depends on the angle of vision.

Conventionally, the letter form has shared at least two important features with the lyric, notwithstanding the fact that the first is prose and the second is poetry.[30] Both reveal the intimate events in the life of the speaker, combined with the speaker's emotional response to them, thus exploring the personal states of mind at the moment of the event or with respect to it. It should be noted, in passing, that *Letters* is a mixture of poetic and prosaic forms, but the speaker, who may not always be identified with Tere, does not feel bound by conventions. This disruption of conventions signals, in my view, a pursuit of narrative approaches that may be beyond Tere's simple "i." In a sense, she is undergoing an inquisition that makes her both the subject of her narrative and the object of someone else's.

Consider how, in recalling events shared with Alicia, her sole interlocutor, Tere almost consistently shifts to a third-person present narration to explore emotional responses to an event. Letter #21 is an example of such an instance, an account telling of Tere's breakdown as a result of her misalliance with Alexis:

> After a while, she adapts to neglecting herself more than he can. Her nails are bitten to the quick. She forgets to eat or eats when she's not hungry. Her inability to sleep makes her face droop like the jowls of an old hound dog. She is twenty-six-years-old. With nervous gestures, she tears an invisible thread from the edge of her slip. If she doesn't watch out, she will quietly go mad and no one will have noticed."[31]

As in "An Idyll," enthrallment again leads to a slavish madness, but it cannot be stated in the first person. Who narrates? An older Tere, who fears to re-enter that period of insanity with a personal "i"? Also, as in "The Antihero," the speaker shifts to the third-person account, thus creating distance with regard to speaking positions, but not to time. As a narrator of her letters, Tere reveals that

---

30. Ruth Perry discusses at length the enactment of "a self-conscious and self-perpetuating process of emotional self-examination," as well as the history of the epistolary genre, in her book *Women, Letters, and the Novel* (New York: AMS Press, 1980), 117.

31. Castillo, *Mixquiahuala Letters*, 112.

she occasionally shifts personae to "create distance with the use of a personal 'i.'"³² As such, it would appear to be an admission that, emotionally, events have a dangerous, contemporaneous power that must be objectified, displaced to a "she/her." Often, Tere can only re-present what has lost the power to hurt her. Romantic love, however, cannot be spoken of, intimately or directly. As she—or is it she?—coldly says: "Love? In the classic sense, it describes in one syllable all the humiliation that one is born to and pressed upon to surrender to a man."³³ In our time, "the classic sense" of love is the erotically romantic one that has been popularized *ad nauseam* through romance novels or, in the case of México and Latin America, *fotonovelas*—as Tere knows.³⁴ It is a genre that cuts across classes and makes many women, regardless of their economic status, sisters under the skin, daughters of patriarchy. In fact, it is the erotic quest that holds Tere and Alicia's friendship together. The true closeness of the friendship is placed in question when we read Letter #13, in which Tere emphasizes her occasional loathing of Alicia. The wedge between them is Alicia's privilege, color, and worldly-wise airs. Clearly, Tere and Alicia's relationship requires further scrutiny. However, what keeps them together is their shared relationship to the romantic. Letter #40 serves to additionally reiterate the erotic common ground.

In Letter #33, to further explore her relations with Alexis, Tere again shifts speaking positions. On this occasion, she switches to her fantasy of his voice. When Tere encounters Alexis five years after the breakup, she imagines what he should be thinking upon seeing her. This is the end to the affair that pleases her.³⁵ The poem, entitled "Epilogue" and attributed to Alexis, is a tribute to Tere's unequaled charms, a testimonial to his lingering affection for Tere, despite the passage of time and his subsequent involvements with other women: "It was her. /... *She* /was there, in the same room ... "³⁶ Tere is effectively converted into his Muse, the one still capable of stirring him into poetic reverie. Indeed, she reveals that being the object of his desire is something in which she is well trained, so well in fact that she can even write poems about that object, herself, and assume his voice. Even as this version of the end pleases her more than the actual reported sordid end of their affair, Tere's self-conscious posing parodies the experience of the romantic metaphor: *She*, the muse, the love object that truly

---

32. Castillo, *Mixquiahuala Letters*, 64.
33. Castillo, *Mixquiahuala Letters*, 111.
34. Castillo, *Mixquiahuala Letters*, 50.
35. Castillo, *Mixquiahuala Letters*, 114.
36. Castillo, *Mixquiahuala Letters*, 115.

moves him; *He*, the desiring lover/poet. In Tere's relationship with Alexis, the gap between the metaphor of experience, insanity and abandonment, and the experience of metaphor, the enchanting muse, provides us with a variation of the chords struck in "The Antihero" and "An Idyll" (see Letter #28 for Tere's initial response to Alexis). As Janice A. Radway has told us in *Reading the Romance*,[37] romantic/erotic bliss is the salient promise that Western patriarchy holds out to women, a bliss that constantly eludes our hapless heroines. Why? I can only conjecture that, while both Tere and Alicia are quite adept at posing as the object of desire, they find it impossible to carry through the subsequent social actualization of that objectification, primarily because it is not an option at all. It spells the death of their subjectivity. Ironically, that is their near-unconscious discovery. The patriarchal promise of romantic/erotic bliss, re-presented in all manner of popular literature, is an ideological maneuver to kill their subjectivity and any further exploration of their own desire.

The understated, failed quest for romantic/erotic bliss effects a blisteringly sardonic tone in the *Letters*, which are an exercise in hindsight. If, in fact, *Letters* represents the struggle to move beyond the quest, the irony is Tere's inability to succeed. In part, this is due to the fact that both the women and their string of men are still operating under a romantic/erotic heterosexist ideology that is hard to shake, notwithstanding Tere's latter-day awareness that this is so. Consider what she says ten years after the quest for "womanhood": "Destiny is not a metaphysical confrontation with one's self, rather, society has knit its pattern so tight that a confrontation with it is inevitable."[38] The quest for "womanhood" is still socially defined in sexual terms under the popular emblem of the romantic/erotic. Both Tere and Alicia are pressed to fulfill the pattern. In a sense, *Letters* offers us a different version of the so-called "star-crossed" lovers.

Destiny, as such, is a socially enforced misrecognition under the guise of love that places Tere in a double-bind: on the one hand, a desire for her own sexual definition, and on the other, an overly determined script in which she takes part. Tere, in short, is bitter over her unwitting, yet unavoidable, folly. The appropriation of the erotic, as enjoyed and desired in the more symbolic book, *The Invitation*, is betrayed in *Letters*. *Letters* makes evident the possibility that an appropriation of the erotic in a heterosexist society may only end up being revealed as a misappropriation.

---

37. Janice A. Radway, *Reading the Romance: Women, Patriarchy, and Popular Literature* (Chapel Hill: University of North Carolina Press, 1984).

38. Castillo, *Mixquiahuala Letters*, 59.

Castillo's experimentations with shifting pronouns and appropriative techniques for the purpose of exploring the romantic/erotic does not stop with Tere's letters, however. If we return to the "real beginning" of *Letters*, we must note that the first letter is to the reader, penned by Castillo. We are directed to undertake a variety of unconventional readings—"The Conformist," "The Cynic," and "The Quixotic"—each tailored to our reading needs. We are also given the option to read each of the forty letters separately, as if they were short fiction. We are alerted that we are in for a variety of ironic and parodic plays but we are ignorant of what they might be. In short, the book brings into question our own reading practices, for the apparently unconventional suggested readings actually lead to resolutions that are more conventional than the handful of letters attributed to Tere. Insofar as each suggested reading by Castillo presents us with a resolution, we are handed an ideological nexus (i.e., The Conformist-idyllic conjugal life) that forces us to reconstruct the meaning of Tere's letters as always and already leading in that direction.[39] Was that Tere's desired end, or is it The Quixotic, or The Cynic's? If, as readers, we play along with the suggested charts, we are forced to come to terms with the notion that Tere is very much trapped by a variety of ideological nexuses that she, and we, need to question and disrupt.

But it is not only our reading and interpretive practices that are in question; Tere's are, too. She constantly shifts voices in an effort to "read" and interpret her own experiences. Which one of the various selves that she explores is she? Is she the vampish one, the docile one, the clever one, the fearful one, the liberated one, or the oppressed one? Insofar as each is connected with her sexuality, she is all of them, and more. Above all, I think she is betrayed by a cultural fabric that presses its images of her upon her, and her response (as well as Castillo's) is to give them all back to us, albeit sardonically. Tere is no longer a sitting duck, as Paz or even "The Three Marías" would have it, but she still inhabits a shooting gallery in which she must wear many a mask to survive and to understand where she has been.

---

39. Frederic Jameson's commentary on "the kind of reading which attaches itself to finding out how everything turns out in the end" provides a helpful perspective for understanding Castillo's parodic plots. See Frederic Jameson, "The Ideology of the Text," *Salgamundi* 31-32 (Fall 1975/Winter 1976): 225.

BIBLIOGRAPHY

Anzaldúa, Gloria. "*La Conciencia de la Mestiza*: Towards a New Consciousness." In *Borderlands/La Frontera*. 99-120. San Francisco: Spinsters/Aunt Lute, 1987.

Bakhtin, Mikhail M. *The Dialogic Imagination: Four Essays*. Translated and Edited by Michael Holquist and Caryl Emerson. Austin: University of Texas Press, 1981.

Castillo, Ana. *Otró Canto*. Chicago: Alternativa Publications, 1977.

Castillo, Ana. *The Invitation*. n.p., 1979.

Castillo, Ana. *Women Are Not Roses*. Houston: Arte Público Press, 1984.

Castillo, Ana. *The Mixquiahuala Letters*. Binghamton, NY: Bilingual Press/Editorial Bilingüe, 1986.

Gilbert, Sandra and Susan Gubar. T*he Madwoman in the Attic: The Woman Writer and the Nineteenth-Century Literary Imagination*. New Haven: Yale University Press, 1979.

Horta, María Teresa, María Isabel Barreno, and María Velho da Costa. T*he Three Marías: New Portuguese Letters*. New York: Doubleday, 1975.

Irigaray, Luce. *This Sex Which is Not One*. Translated by Catherine Porter and Carolyn Burke. Ithaca: Cornell University Press, 1985.

Jameson, Frederic. "The Ideology of The Text." *Salmagundi*, nos. 31/3 (1975): 204–46.

Kristeva, Julia. *Revolution in Poetic Language*, translated by Margaret Waller. New York: Columbia University Press, 1984.

Kristeva, Julia. D*esire in Language: A Semiotic Approach to Literature and Art*, edited by Leon S. Roudiez, translated by Thomas Gora, Alice A. Jardine, and Leon S. Roudiez. New York: Columbia University Press, 1982.

Maranda, Pierre. "The Dialectic of Metaphor: An Anthropological Essay on Hermeneutics." 183-204. In *The Reader in the Text: Essays on Audience and Interpretation*. Edited by Susan Rubin Suleiman and Inge Crosman. Princeton: Princeton University Press, 1980.

Paz, Octavio. *The Labyrinth of Solitude*. Translated by Lysander Kemp. New York: Grove Press, 1961. [Originally published in 1950 by Cuadernos Americanos, México, and revised and expanded in 1959 for the second edition published by the Fondo de Cultura Económica, México, under the title *El Laberinto de la Soledad*.]

Perry, Ruth. W*omen, Letters, and the Novel*. New York: AMS, 1980.

Weigel, Sigrid. "Double Focus: On the History of Women's Writing." In *Feminist Aesthetics*. Translated by Harriett Anderson and edited by Gisela Eckler, 59-80. Boston: Beacon Press, 1986.

TRADDUTORA, TRADITORA

A PARADIGMATIC FIGURE OF CHICANA FEMINISM[1]

→ ←

> When the Spanish conquistador appears, this woman [a Mayan] is no more than the site where the desires and wills of two men meet. To kill men to rape women: these are at once proof that a man wields power and his reward. The wife chooses (sic) to obey her husband and the rules of her own society, she puts all that remains of her personal will into defending the violence [of her own society] of which she has been the object.... Her husband of whom she is the "internal other"... leaves her no possibility of asserting herself as a free subject.
>
> —Tzvetan Todorov, *The Conquest of America*

IN HIS SPLENDID BOOK *Quetzalcóatl and Guadalupe*, Jacques Lafaye gives a fascinating account of the roles those two divine and mythic figures played in the formation of the Mexican national consciousness.[2] Quetzalcóatl was an Aztec god whose name, so the missionaries argued, was the natives' own name for the true Messiah. Guadalupe, on the other hand, was the emerging Mexican people's native version of the Virgin Mary and, in a sense, substituted for the Aztec goddess Tonantzin. By the time of Mexican independence from Spain in 1821, Guadalupe had emerged triumphant as the national patroness of México, and her banner was often carried into battle. In a well-known article which may have inspired Lafaye, Eric R. Wolf comments that:

---

1. *Editors' Note:* The earliest version of this essay appeared as, "Excerpts from Traddutora, Traditora: A Paradigmatic Figure of Chicano Feminism" in *Changing Our Power: An Introduction to Women's Studies*, ed. Jo Cochran and Donna Hightower-Langston (Dubuque, Iowa: Kendall Hunt, 1988), 195-203. Subsequently it was published in *Cultural Critique* 13 (1989): 57-87; debate feminista 8 (1993): 19-48; *Dangerous Liaisons: Gender, Nation, and Postcolonial Perspectives,* ed. Anne McClintock, Aamir Mufti, Ella Shohat (Minneapolis, MN: University of Minnesota Press: 1997), 278-97; and *Perspectives on Las Américas: A Reader in Culture, History, and Representation*, ed. Matthew C. Gutmann, Felix V. Matos-Rodríquez, Lynn Stephen, and Patricia Zavella (United Kingdom: Wiley, 2003), 31-49. We include the version published in *Cultural Critique*, 1989.

2. Jacques Lafaye, *Quetzalcóatl y Guadalupe: La Formación de la conciencia en* México (1531-1813), trans. Ida Vitale (México City: Fondo de Cultura Económica, 1983).

the Mexican War of Independence marks the final realization of the apocalyptic promise... [T)he promise of life held out by the supernatural mother has become the promise of an independent México, liberated from the irrational authority of the Spanish father-oppressors and restored to the chosen nation whose election had been manifest in the apparition of the Virgin at Tepeyac.... Mother, food, hope, health, life; supernatural salvation from oppression; chosen people and national independence—all find expression in a single symbol.[3]

There is sufficient folklore, as well as documentary evidence of a historical and literary nature, to suggest that the indigenous female slave Malintzin Tenepal was transformed into Guadalupe's monstrous double and that her "banner" also aided and abetted in the nation-making process or, at least, in the creation of nationalistic perspectives. On Independence Day of 1861, for example, Ignacio "El Nigromante" Ramírez, politician and man of letters, reminded the celebrants that Mexicans owed their defeat to Malintzin—Cortés' whore.[4] Moreover, Malintzin may be compared to Eve, especially when she is viewed as the originator of the Mexican people's fall from grace and the procreator of a "fallen" people. Thus, México's own binary pair, Guadalupe and Malintzin, reenact within this dualistic system of thought the biblical stories of our human creation and condition. In effect, as a political compromise between conquerors and conquered, Guadalupe is the neorepresentative of the Virgin Mary and the native goddess Tonantzin, while Malintzin stands in the periphery of the new patriarchal order and its sociosymbolic contract.[5]

---

3. Eric R. Wolf, "The Virgen de Guadalupe: A Mexican National Symbol," *Journal of American Folklore* 71, no. 279 (January-March 1958): 38.

4. Cited in Gustavo A. Rodríguez, *Doña Marina* (México City: Imprenta de la Secretaría de Relaciones Exteriores, 1935), 48.

5. I borrow the notion of "sociosymbolic contract" from Julia Kristeva. She uses the notion in the essay "Women's Time," trans. Alice Jardine and Harry Blake, *Signs* 7, no. 1 (Autumn 1981): 13-35. I take it to mean a kind of contract within which the social life of women (and some men) is expected to conform or live up to a metaphysical (essential) configuration of who we ought to become in the socialization process. These metaphysical configurations are accompanied by culture-specific "semantic charters." Pierre Maranda suggests that "(s)emantic charters condition our thoughts and emotions. They are culture specific networks that we internalize as we undergo the process of socialization." Moreover, these charters or signifying systems " have an inertia and momentum of their own. There are semantic domains whose inertia is high: kinship terminologies, the dogmas of authoritarian churches, the conception of sex roles." See Pierre Maranda, "The Dialectic of Metaphor: An Anthropological Essay on Hermeneutics," in *The Reader in the Text: Essays on Audience and Interpretation*, eds. Susan R. Suleiman and Inge Crosman, 184-85 (Princeton: Princeton University Press, 1980).

Indeed, Malintzin and the "false god" and conqueror Hernan Cortés are the countercouple, "the monstrous doubles," to Lafaye's Quetzalcóatl and Guadalupe. These two monstrous figures become, in the eyes of the later generations of "natives," symbols of unbridled conquering power and treachery, respectively.[6] Malintzin comes to be known as *la lengua*, literally meaning the tongue. *La lengua* was the metaphor used, by Cortés and the chroniclers of the conquest, to refer to Malintzin the translator. However, she not only translated for Cortés and his men, she also bore his children. Thus, a combination of Malintzin-translator and Malintzin-procreator becomes the main feature of her subsequently ascribed treacherous nature.

In the eyes of the conquered (oppressed), anyone who approximates *la lengua* or Cortés (oppressor), in word or deed, is held suspect and liable to become a sacrificial "monstrous double." Those who use the oppressor's language are viewed as outside of the community, thus rationalizing their expulsion, but, paradoxically, they also help to constitute the community. In *Violence and the Sacred*, René Girard has observed that the religious mind "strives to procure, and if need be to invent, a sacrificial victim as similar as possible to its ambiguous vision of the original victim. The model it imitates is not the true double, but a model transfigured by the mechanism of the "monstrous double."[7] If in the beginning Cortés and Malintzin are welcomed as saviors from, and avengers of, Aztec imperialism, soon each is unmasked and "sacrificed," that is, expelled so that the authentic gods may be recovered, awaited, and/or invented. While Quetzalcóatl could continue to be awaited, Guadalupe was envisioned, and her invention was under way as the national Virgin Mother and goddess only twelve years after Cortés' arrival. Guadalupe, as Lafaye himself suggests, is a metaphor that has never wholly taken the place of Tonantzin. As such, Guadalupe is capable of alternately evoking the Catholic and meek Virgin Mother and the prepatriarchal and powerful earth goddess. In any case, within a decade of the invasion, both Cortés and Malintzin begin to accrue their dimensions as

---

6. The "natives" that came to hate Cortés and Malintzin are the mestizos—the mixed blood offspring—since the indigenous people at the time of the conquest often welcomed them as liberators. It is of interest to note that throughout the Mexican colonial period the missionaries staged secular plays for the indigenous population in which Cortés and Malintzin were represented as their liberators. Some parishes, even today, continue to reenact these plays in dispersed communities. I draw the preceding comments from Norma Cantú's work in progress, "Secular and Liturgical Folk Drama," presented at the National Association of Chicano Studies, Los Angeles, March 29-April 1, 1989.

7. René Girard, *Violence and the Sacred*, trans. Patrick Gregory (Baltimore: Johns Hopkins University Press, 1977), 273.

scapegoats who become the receptacle of human rage and passion, of the very real hostilities that "all the members of the community feel for one another."⁸ In the context of a religiously organized society, one can observe in the scapegoating of Cortés and Malintzin "the very real metamorphosis of reciprocal violence into restraining violence through the agency of unanimity."⁹ The unanimity is elicited by the chosen scapegoats, and violence is displaced onto them. That mechanism then structures many cultural values, rituals, customs, and myths. Among people of Mexican descent, from this perspective, anyone who has transgressed the boundaries of perceived group interests and values often has been called a *malinche* or *malinchista*. Thus, the contemporary recuperation and positive redefinitions of her name bespeak an effort to go beyond religiously organized Manichaean thought. There is nothing more fascinating or intriguing, as Lafaye demonstrates, than to trace the transformation of legends into myths that contribute to the formation of national consciousness. However, by only tracing the figures of transcendence—the recovered or displaced victims of the impersonators—we are left without a knowledge of the creation process of the scapegoats—whether it be through folklore, polemics, or literature. An exploration of Cortés' role as monstrous double shall be left for another occasion. It is clear that often his role is that of the conqueror, usurper, foreigner, and/or invader.¹⁰ In the course of almost five centuries Malintzin has alternately retained one of her three names: Malintzin (the name given her by her parents), Marina (the name given her by the Spaniards), or Malinche (the name given her by the natives in the midst of the conquest). The epithet *La Chingada*¹¹ has surfaced most emphatically in our century to refer to her alleged ill-fated experience at the hands of the Spaniards. The epithet also emphasizes the sexual implications of having been conquered—the rape of women and the emasculation of men.

Guadalupe and Malintzin almost always have been viewed as oppositional mediating figures, though the precise moment of inception may well elude us.

---

8. Girard, *Violence and the Sacred*, 99.

9. Girard, *Violence and the Sacred*, 96.

10. Córtes' misfortunes with the Spanish Crown may be linked to the need of the successor colonizers and the colonized to extirpate him from their relations with Spain. Certainly, he has been expelled from public life in México where no monuments or mementos to his role in the conquest may be seen. Ironically, he is very much in everyone's mind.

11. *La Chingada* is used to refer, literally, to a woman who is "fucked" or "fucked over." Thus, Paz and others suggest a metonymic relation to rape. When used in the past participle, passivity on her part is implied. The verb and its derivatives imply violent action, and much depends on context and the speaker's inflection. To refer to a masculine actor, the term *chingón* is used.

Guadalupe has come to symbolize transformative powers and sublime transcendence and is the standard carried into battle in utopically inspired movements. Always viewed by believers as capable of transforming the petitioner's status and promising sublime deliverance, she transports us beyond or before time. On the other hand, Malintzin represents feminine subversion and treacherous victimization of her people because she was a translator in Cortés' army. Guadalupe and Malintzin have become a function of each other. Be that as it may, quite often one or the other figure is recalled as being present at the "origins" of the Mexican community, thereby emphasizing its divine and sacred constitution or, alternately, its damned and secular fall. The religiously rooted community, as Girard notes, "is both attracted and repelled by its own origins. It feels the constant need to re-experience them, albeit in veiled and transfigured form . . . by exercising its memory of the collective expulsion or carefully designated objects."[12] Though Guadalupe is thought to assuage the community's pain due to its fall from grace, Malintzin elicits a fascination entangled with loathing, suspicion, and sorrow. As translator she mediates between antagonistic cultural and historical domains. If we assume that language is always in some sense metaphoric, then, any discourse, oral or written, is liable to be implicated in treachery when perceived to be going beyond repetition of what the community perceives as the "true" and/or "authentic" concept, image, or narrative. The act of translating, which often introduces different concepts and perceptions, displaces and may even do violence to local knowledge through language. In the process, these may be assessed as false or inauthentic.

Traditional nonsecular societies, be they oral or print cultures, tend to be very orthodox and conservative, interpreting the lifeworld in highly Manichaean terms. It is common in largely oral cultures to organize knowledge, values, and beliefs around symbolic icons, figures, or even persons, which is a characteristic of both the Spanish and the natives at the time of the conquest, and one that in surprising numbers continues to our day in Mexican/Chicano culture.[13] In such a binary, Manichaean system of thought, Guadalupe's transcendentalism power, silence, and maternal self-sacrifice are the positive, contrasting attributes to those of a woman who speaks as a sexual being and independently of her maternal role. To speak independently of her maternal role, as Malintzin did, is viewed

---

12. Girard, *Violence and the Sacred*, 99.

13. I draw on the work of Walter J. Ong for parts of this discussion, especially *The Presence of the Word: Some Prolegomena for Cultural and Religious History* (New Haven: Yale University Press, 1967) and *Orality and Literacy: The Technologizing of the Word* (New York: Methuen, 1982).

in such a society as a sign of catastrophe, for if she is allowed to articulate her needs and desires she must do so as a mother on behalf of her children and not of herself. Because Malintzin the translator is perceived as speaking for herself and not the community, however it defines itself, she is a woman who has betrayed her primary cultural function—maternity. The figure of the mother is bound to a double reproduction, *strictu sensu*—that of her people and her culture. In a traditional society organized along metaphysical or cosmological figurations of good and evil, cultural deviation from the norm is not easily tolerated nor valued in the name of inventiveness or "originality." In such a setting, to speak or translate in one's behalf rather than the perceived group interests and values is tantamount to betrayal. Thus, the assumption of an individualized nonmaternal voice, such as that of Chicanas during and after the Chicano movement (1965-75),[14] has been cause to label them *malinches* or *vendidas* (sellouts) by some, consequently prompting Chicanas to vindicate Malinche in a variety of ways, as we shall see. Thus, within a culture such as ours, if one should not want to merely break with it, acquiring a "voice of one's own" requires revision and appropriation of cherished metaphysical beliefs.

The Mexican poet and cultural critic Octavio Paz was one of the first to note, in his book *The Labyrinth of Solitude*,[15] a metonymic link between Malintzin and the epithet *La Chingada*, which is derived from the Hispanicized Nahuaátl verb *chingar*. Today, *La Chingada* is often used as a synonym for Malintzin. Paz himself reiterates the latter in his introduction to Lafaye's book by remarking that "entre la Chingada y Tonantzin/Guadalupe oscila la vida secreta del mestizo" (The secret life of the mestizo oscillates between La Chingada and Tonantzin/Guadalupe).[16]

Although Paz's views are often the contemporary point of departure for current revisions of the legend and myth of Malintzin, there are two previous stages in its almost five-hundred-year trajectory. The first corresponds to the chroniclers and inventors of the legends; the second corresponds to the development of

---

14. These dates are highly arbitrary, especially the closing date. There is consensus among Chicano critics that the production of contemporary Chicano literature began in conjunction with César Chávez's National Farm Workers' Association strike of 1965, noting the fact that Luis Valdez's Teatro Campesino was inaugurated on the picket lines. See Marta E. Sánchez, *Contemporary Chicana Poetry: Critical Approaches to an Emerging Literature* (Berkeley and Los Angeles: University of California Press, 1985), 2-6. For the recuperation of the term *vendida* (sellout), see Cherríe Moraga, "A Long Line of Vendidas," in *Loving in the War Years: Lo que nunca pasó por sus labios* (Boston: South End Press, 1983), 90 – 117.

15. Though the Spanish original was published in 1950, I use the Lysander Kemp translation of Octavio Paz, *The Labyrinth of Solitude: Life and Thought in Mexico* (New York: Grove Press, 1961).

16. Lafaye, *Quetzalcóatl y Guadalupe*, 22.

the traitor myth and scapegoat mechanism which apparently comes to fruition in the nineteenth century during the Mexican independence movement.[17] In this study I would like to focus on the third, modernistic stage which some twentieth-century women and men of letters have felt compelled to initiate in order to revise and vindicate Malintzin.

In writing *The Labyrinth of Solitude* to explicate Mexican people and culture, Octavio Paz was also paying homage to Alfonso Reyes' call to explore and discover our links to the past as put forth in *Visión de Anáhuac (1519)*.[18] In that work Reyes suggested that Doña Marina, as he calls her, was the metaphor par excellence of México and its conquest, oppression, and victimization, all of which are very much a part of Mexican life and "historical emotion."[19] Though Reyes' vision was somewhat muted by the decorous language of the beginning of the century, Paz exploits the modernistic break with the sacred in order to expand and clarify Reyes' Doña Marina by transfiguring her into *La Chingada*. In the now-famous chapter "The Sons of La Malinche," Paz argues, as Reyes did before him, that "our living attitude... is history also"[20] and concludes that La Malinche is the key to our Mexican origins. In his view Malintzin is more properly our historically grounded originator and accounts for our contemporary "living attitude." However, Paz is not interested in history per se but in the affective and imaginary ways in which that history is/has been experienced and the ways in which we have responded to it. Paz explores the connections between Malintzin and *La Chingada*, that is, the sexual victim, the raped mother. He argues that as taboo verb (and noun), *chingar* lacks etymological documentation, yet it is part of contemporary speech. Independent of any historical record, the word's existence and significance seem phantasmagorical, illusory. In Terry Eagleton's terms, then, Paz goes to work on the apparently illusory, "the ordinary ideological experience of men,"[21] and tries to demonstrate its connection to historical events and, by implication, men's attitudes towards the feminine. In doing so,

---

17. These stages have suggested themselves to me in reviewing Rachel Phillips, "Marina/Malinche: Masks and Shadows," in *Women in Hispanic Literature: Icons and Fallen Idols*, 97-114, ed. Beth Miller (Berkeley and Los Angeles: University of California Press, 1983). See also Rodríguez's *Doña Marina* and the work of Norma Cantú, "Secular and Liturgical Folk Drama."

18. Though the work was originally published in 1915, I use Alfonso Reyes, *Visión de Anáhuac (1519)* (México City: El Colegio de México, 1953).

19. Reyes, *Visión de Anáhuac (1519)*, 61-62.

20. Paz, *Labyrinth of Solitude*, 71.

21. Terry Eagleton, *Marxism and Literary Criticism* (Berkeley and Los Angeles: University of California, 1976), 19.

however, he transforms Malintzin into the Mexican people's primeval mother, albeit the raped one. To repudiate her, he argues, is to break with the past, to renounce the "origins." Paz believes that he is struggling against "a will to eradicate all that has gone before."[22] He concludes by saying that Cortés' and Malintzin's permanence in the Mexican's imagination and sensibilities reveals that they are more than historical figures: they are symbols of a secret conflict that we have still not resolved. Through the examination of taboo phrases, Paz makes Malintzin the Muse/Mother, albeit raped and vilified—hence, also *La Chingada*. In calling attention to the fact that Malintzin and Cortés are more than historical figures, Paz in effect is implying that they are part and parcel of Mexican ideology—our living attitude; thus, they have been abducted from their historical moment and are continuing to haunt us through the workings of that ideology. In a sense, by making Malintzin the founding mother of Mexicans, Paz has unwittingly strengthened the ideological ground that was there before him while simultaneously desacralizing our supposed origins by shifting the founding moment from Guadalupe to Malintzin. Paradoxically, Paz has displaced the myth of Guadalupe, not with history, but with a neomyth, a reversal properly secularized yet unaware of its misogynistic residue. Indeed, Paz's implied audience is male, the so-called "illegitimate mestizo," who may well bristle at the thought that he is outside the legitimate patriarchal order, like women! In Paz's figurations illegitimacy predicated the Mexican founding order. It is a countersuggestion to the belief that Guadalupe legitimized the Mexican founding order. The primary strategy in Paz's modern (secular) position is to wrest contemporary consciousness away from religious cosmologies.

Unlike Reyes, Paz mentions that "the Mexican people have not forgiven Malinche for her betrayal."[23] As such, he emphasizes the ambivalent attitude towards the origins despite the need for acceptance and a change of consciousness. Carlos Fuentes, too, pleads for acceptance of the "murky" and knotted beginnings of the Mexican people in *Todos los gatos son pardos*.[24] However, if Paz implicitly acknowledges the asymmetrical relationship between that of slave (Malintzin) and master (Cortés) by saying that our neosymbolic mother was raped, Fuentes privileges Malintzin's attributed desire for vengeance against her people—hence her alliance with Cortés. Subsequently, Fuentes has Malintzin

---

22. Paz, *Labyrinth of Solitude*, 87.
23. Paz, *Labyrinth of Solitude*, 86.
24. Though originally published in 1970, I use Carlos Fuentes' *Todos los gatos son pardos* (México: Siglo XXI, 1984).

reveal herself as a misguided fool, thus becoming the ill-fated Mother-Goddess/ Muse/Whore, a tripartite figure who possesses the gift of speech. The gift, in the end, makes her a traitor. She self-consciously declares herself *la lengua*, "Yo sólo soy la lengua," adding that objects ultimately act out the destiny that the logos proposes.[25] In this instance, Fuentes, along with such contemporaries as Rosario Castellanos, Elena Poniatowska, José Emilio Pacheco, and Octavio Paz, is portraying through Malintzin the belief that literature is the intention, through the power of language, to recover memory by recovering the word and to project a future by possessing the word.[26] The underlying assumption is that history, insofar as it obeys ideological and metaphysical constraints, does not truly recover human events and experience, nor is it capable of projecting change—thus literature is allocated those functions. Simultaneously, however, and perhaps unknowingly, this point of view ironically suggests that literature (language) also narrates ideological positions that construct readers. In suggesting that their literary production is a theory of history, these Mexican writers also appear to suggest that it is capable of effecting historical changes. It is clear that both Paz and Fuentes view themselves as catalysts, as movers and shakers of the "academic" historians of their time and country. From a secular perspective Paz and Fuentes see themselves as more radical and as providing a cultural critique. They explode myths with countermyths, or narrative with counternarrative.[27]

In Fuentes' play, Malintzin is the narrator who is in possession of speech. She is, as a result, given the task of recovering the experience of the conquest by spanning the confrontation between powers—that of Cortés and Moctezuma. Thus, for Fuentes, narration is a feminine art in opposition to the masculine "arts of power," a bridge for disparate power brokers, who thus make use of Malintzin's mediating image. One can observe here a romantic artifice—woman the Mother-Goddess/Muse/Whore who is knowledge itself—if only the male artists can decipher it; in this Fuentes falls in line with many other writers from Goethe to Paz. It is, of course, ironic that the narrative should be viewed even symbolically as a feminine art, or an art embedded in the feminine, since few women have practiced it throughout history. But as the fallen goddess in Fuentes, Malintzin recalls patriarchy's Eve, the first linguistic mediator and the primeval biblical mother and traitor, who, of course, is later replaced by the

---

25. Fuentes, *Todos los gatos son pardos* 64, 99.
26. Fuentes, *Todos los gatos son pardos* 5-6.
27. An interesting study of Paz's and Fuentes' work is presented by Edmond Cros, *Theory and Practice of Sociocriticism*, trans. Jerome Schwartz (Minneapolis: University of Minnesota Press, 1988), 153-89.

Virgin Mary, alias Guadalupe, the "go-between" mediating two cultural spaces that are viewed as antithetical to each other.

To suggest that language itself, as mediator, is our first betrayal, the Mexican novelist and poet José Emilio Pacheco writes a deceptively simple yet significant poem entitled "Traddutore, traditori" ("Translator, Traitor"). In the poem, Pacheco names the three known translators involved during the time of the conquest—Jerónimo Aguilar, Gonzalo Guerrero, and Malintzin. Pacheco claims that we are indebted to this trio for the knot called México ("el enredo llamado México").[28] For Pacheco, what might have been "authentic" to each cultural discourse before the collision has now been transformed by language's creative and transformative powers. The translators, who use language as their mediating agent, have the ability, consciously or unconsciously, to distort or to convert the "original" event, utterance, text, or experience, thus rendering them false, "impure." The Mexican cultural and biological entanglement is due to the metaphoric property of language and the language traders. By translating, by converting, by transforming one thing into another, by interpreting (all meanings suggested by the dictionary), the "original," supposedly clear connection between words and objects, is disrupted and corrupted. The "corruption" that takes place through linguistic mediation may make the speaker a traitor in the view of others-not just simply a traitor, but a traitor to tradition which is represented and expressed in the "original" event, utterance, text, or experience. In Pacheco's poem the treacherous acts are rooted in language as mediator, language as substitution, that is, as metaphor.

It is through metaphor and metonymy that Reyes, Paz, Fuentes, and Pacheco have been working to revise, reinterpret, or reverse Malintzin's significations. In the twentieth century, they are the first appropriators "rescuing" her from "living attitudes." To cast her in the role of scapegoat, monstrous double, and traitor as other men have done is to deny our own monstrous beginnings, that is, the monstrous beginnings of the mestizo (mixed blood) people in the face of an ethic of purity and authenticity as absolute value. By recalling the initial translators and stressing the role of linguistic mediation, Pacheco's revisions are the most novel and diffuse the emphasis on gender and sexuality that the others rely on for their interpretive visions. Paz and Fuentes have patently sexualized Malintzin more than any other writers before them. In so doing they lay claim to a recovery of the (maternal) female body as a secular, sexual, and signifying

---

28. José Emilio Pacheco, *Islas a la deriva* (México: Siglo XXI, 1976), 27-28.

entity. Sometimes, however, their perspective hovers between attraction and repulsion, revealing their attitudes towards the feminine and their "origins." For Fuentes, Malintzin's sexuality is devouring, certainly the monstrous double of Guadalupe, the asexual and virginal feminine.

Chicano writers have been particularly influenced by Paz's and Fuentes' revisions of Malintzin. The overall influence can be traced not only to the fascination that their writings exert but to the fact that their work was included in early texts used for Chicano Studies. Two such texts were *Introduction to Chicano Studies* and *Literatura Chicana: Texto y Contexto*.[29] The Chicanos, like the Mexicans, wanted to recover the origins. However, many Chicanos emphasized the earlier nationalistic interpretations of Malintzin as the traitorous mediator who should be expelled from the community rather than accepted, as Paz and Fuentes had suggested. In their quest for "authenticity" Chicanos often desired the silent mediator—Guadalupe, the unquestioning transmitter of tradition and deliverer from oppression. Thus, it should not have come as a surprise that the banner of Guadalupe was one of those carried by the Chicano farm workers in their strike march of 1965.[30]

In discussing women's role in traditional cultures, anthropologist Sherry Ortner has stated,

> Insofar as woman is universally the primary agent of early socialization and is seen as virtually the embodiment of the functions of the domestic group, she will tend to come under the heavier restrictions

---

29. For example, Octavio Paz's "The Sons of La Malinche" may be found in *Introduction to Chicano Studies: A Reader*, ed. Livie Isauro Durán and H. Russell Bernard (New York: Macmillan, 1973), 17-27, and Carlos Fuentes' "The Legacy of La Malinche," in *Literatura Chicana: Texto y Contexto*, ed. Antonia Castañeda, Tomás Ybarra-Frausto, and Joseph Sommers (New York: Prentice-Hall, 1972), 304-06.

30. For a perspective on men's implicit or explicit use of oppositional female figures whose outlines may be rooted in Guadalupe-Malintzin, see Juan Bruce Novoa, "One More Rosary for Doña Marina," *Confluencia* I, no. 22 (Spring 1986): 73-84. In the eighties some Chicana visual artists began experimenting with the image of Guadalupe. Ester Hernández, for example, depicts the Virgin executing a karate kick. Santa Barraza depicts a newly unearthed Coatlicue (Mesoamerican fertility goddess) pushing Guadalupe upward and overpowering her. The contrastive images tell the story of the difference between them—the one small, the other huge. See reproductions of these works in *Third Woman* 4 (1989): 42, 153, respectively. Yolanda M. López has portrayed "Guadalupe Walking" in high-heel sandals. The reproduction that *Fem* 8, no. 34 (Junio-Julio 1984) carried on its cover provoked a large number of hate mail, accusing the editors of being "Zionists." According to Hernandez's personal communication, the exhibit of her Guadalupe ink drawing caused a minor scandal in a small California town. She had to leave the exhibit to avoid a violent attack. Community leaders had to schedule workshops to discuss the work and the artist's rights. Modern revisions of Guadalupe are fraught with difficulty and may well be the reason why Chicana writers have bypassed her. She still retains a large, devoted following.

and circumscriptions surrounding the unit. Her (culturally defined) intermediate position between nature and culture, here having the significance of her mediation (i.e. performing conversion functions) between nature and culture, would account not only for her lower status but for the greater restrictions placed upon her activities.... [S]ocially engendered conservatism and traditionalism of woman's thinking is another—perhaps the worst, certainly the most insidious—mode of social restriction, and would clearly be related to her traditional function of producing well-socialized members of the group.[31]

The woman who fulfills this expectation is more akin to the feminine figure of transcendence, that is, Guadalupe. In a binary, Manichaean society, which a religious society is almost by definition, the one who does not fulfill this expectation is viewed as subversive or evil and is vilified through epithets the community understands. If one agrees with Adrienne Rich, not to speak of others since Coleridge, that the imagination's power is potentially subversive, then, for many Chicanas, "to be a female human being trying to fulfill traditional female functions in a traditional way [is] in direct conflict"[32] with their creativity and inventiveness, as well as with their desire to transform their cultural roles and redefine themselves in accordance with their experience and vision. If literature's intention is, in some sense, the recovery or projection of human experience, as the Mexican writers discussed also suggest, then linguistic representation of it could well imply a "betrayal" of tradition, of family, of what is ethically viewed as "pure and authentic," since it involves a conversion into interpretive language rather than ritualized repetition. It is not surprising, then, that some of the most talented writers and intellectuals of contemporary Chicana culture should be fascinated with the figure most perceived as the transgressor of a previous culture believed to be "authentic." It is through a revision of tradition that self and culture can be radically reenvisioned and reinvented. Thus, in order to break with tradition, Chicanas, as writers and political activists, simultaneously legitimate their discourse by grounding it in the Mexican/Chicano community and by creating a "speaking subject" in their reappropriation of Malintzin from Mexican writers and Chicano oral tradition—through her they begin a recovery of aspects of their experience as well as of their language. In this way,

---

31. Sherry B. Ortner, "Is Female to Male as Nature is to Culture?" in *Woman, Culture, and Society*, ed. Michelle Zimbalist Rosaldo and Louise Lamphere (Stanford: Stanford University Press, 1974), 85.

32. Adrienne Rich, *On Lies, Secrets and Silence: Selected Prose*, 1966-1978 (New York: Norton, 1979), 43.

the traditional view of femininity invested in Guadalupe is avoided and indirectly denied and reinvested in a less intractable object. Guadalupe's political history represents a community's expectations and utopic desires through divine mediation. Malintzin, however, as a secularly established "speaking subject,"[33] unconstrained by religious beliefs, lends herself more readily to articulation and representation, both as subject and object. In a sense, Malintzin must be led to represent herself, to become the subject of representation, and the closest she can come to this is by sympathizing with latter-day speaking female subjects. Language, as Mikhail Bakhtin has noted,

> becomes "one's own" only when the speaker populates it with her own intention, her own accent, when she appropriates the word, adapting it to her own semantic and expressive intention. Prior to this moment of appropriation, the word does not exist in a neutral and impersonal language (it is not, after all, out of a dictionary that the speaker gets her words!), but rather it exists in other people's mouths, in other people's contexts, serving other people's intentions: it is from there that one must take the word, and make it one's own.... Language is not a neutral medium that passes freely and easily into the private property of the speaker's intentions; it is populated—over populated with the intentions of others. Expropriating, forcing it to submit to one's own intentions and accents, is a difficult and complicated process.[34]

Expropriating Malintzin from the texts of others and filling her with the intentions, significances, and desires of Chicanas has taken years. Mexican men had already effected the operation for their own ends; it was now women's turn. (Though in this essay I only deal with the efforts of Chicanas, some Mexican women writers such as Juana Alegría and Rosario Castellanos have also worked with this figure and have contested male representations.)

One of the first to feel the blow of the masculine denigration of Malintzin was Adelaida R. del Castillo. It was a blow that she apparently felt personally on behalf of all Chicanas, thus provoking her to say that the denigration of Malintzin was

---

33. For the notion of the "speaking subject" I am guided by Julia Kristeva's work, especially "The Ethics of Linguistics," in *Desire in Language: A Semiotic Approach to Literature and Art*, trans. Thomas Gora, Alice Jardine, and Leon S. Roudiez, ed. Leon S. Roudiez (New York: Columbia University Press, 1980), 23 – 25.

34. I have taken the liberty of changing all of the he's in Bakhtin's text to she's. Mikhail M. Bakhtin, *The Dialogic Imagination: Four Essays*, trans. Caryl Emerson and Michael Holquist, ed. Michael Holquist (Austin: University of Texas Press, 1981), 293-94.

tantamount to a defamation of "the character of the Mexicana/Chicana female."[35] For Chicanas, as del Castillo implies, Malintzin was more than a metaphor or foundation/neomyth as Paz would have it; she represented a specific female experience that was being misrepresented and trivialized. By extension, Chicanas/Mexicanas were implicated: del Castillo's attempt to appropriate Malintzin for herself and Chicanas in general involved her in vindication and revision. It is not only Malintzin's appropriation and revision that is at stake, but Chicanas' own cultural self-exploration, self-definition, and self-invention through and beyond the community's sociosymbolic system and contract. The process, however, is complicated by Chicanas' awareness that underlying their words there is also a second (if not secondary) sociosymbolic order—the Anglo-American. She leaves herself open to the accusation of "anglicizing" the community, just as Malinche "hispanicized" it, because her attempts at self-invention are "inappropriate" to her culture and her efforts are viewed as alien to the tradition. In other words, changes wreak havoc with the perceived "authenticity." Each writer, as we shall see, privileges a different aspect of Malintzin's "lives"-that is, the alleged historical experience and/or the inherited imaginary or ideological one.

Adaljiza Sosa Riddell, in "Chicanas in El Movimiento,"[36] an essay written in the heat of the Chicano movement of the early seventies, views Malintzin as a cultural paradigm of the situation of contemporary Chicanas. She thinks that the relationship of Chicanas to Chicanos in the United States has paralleled Malintzin's relationship to the indigenous people in the light of the Spanish conquest. Riddell concludes that Chicanas, like Malintzin before them, have been doubly victimized—by dominant Anglo society and by Mexicano/Chicano communities. In turn, these factors account for some Chicanas' ambiguous and ambivalent position in the face of an unexamined nationalism. Riddell's passionate attempt at revision and appropriation is both a plea for understanding some women's "mediating" position and an apology—-an apologia full of irony, for it is the victim's apologia!

Victimization in the context of colonization and of patriarchal suppression of women is a view shared by Carmen Tafolla in her poem "La Malinche."[37]

---

35. Adelaida R. del Castillo, "Malintzin Tenepal: A Preliminary Look into a New Perspective," in *Essays on La Mujer*, ed. Rosaura Sánchez and Rosa Martinez Cruz (Los Angeles: Chicano Studies Center Publications, University of California, Los Angeles, 1977), 141.

36. Adaljiza Sosa Riddell, "Chicanas and El Movimiento," *Aztlán* 5, nos. 1-2 (1974): 155-65.

37. Carmen Tafolla, "La Malinche," in *Five Poets of Aztlán*, ed. Santiago Daydí-Tolson (Binghamton, N.Y.: Bilingual Press, 1985), 193 – 95.

Tafolla's Malintzin claims that she has been misnamed and misjudged by men who had ulterior motives. In Tafolla's poem Malintzin goes on to assert that she submitted to the Spaniard Cortés because she envisioned a new race; she wanted to be the founder of a people. There are echoes of Paz and Fuentes in Tafolla's view, yet she differs by making Malintzin a woman possessed of clear-sighted intentionality, thus avoiding attributions of vengeance.

As Tafolla transforms Malintzin into the founder of a new race through visionary poetry, Adelaida R. del Castillo effects a similar result through a biography which is reconstructed with the few "facts" left us by the chroniclers. In her essay, del Castillo claims that Malintzin "embodies effective, decisive action.... Her actions syncretized two conflicting worlds causing the emergence of a new one, our own.... [W]oman acts not as a goddess in some mythology"[38] but as a producer of history. She goes on to say that Malintzin should be "perceived as a woman who was able to act beyond her prescribed societal function (i.e., servant and concubine) and perform as one who was willing to make great sacrifices for what she believed to be a philanthropic conviction."[39] Del Castillo wants to avoid the mythmaking trap by evading "poetic language" and by appealing to "historical facts." In a sense, unlike the male Mexican writers reviewed, she privileges history as a more truthful account than literature. (This may spell the difference between del Castillo's Anglo-American education and experience and that of Mexican nationals for whom history often is reconstructed anew with each new regime, thereby encouraging a cynical attitude. Perspectives on the disciplines of history and literature differ according to our location, experience, and education.) However, notwithstanding her famed translating abilities, Malintzin has left us no recorded voice because she was illiterate; that is, she could not leave us a sense of herself and of her experience. Thus our disquisitions truly take place over her corpse and have no clue as to her own words, but instead refer to the words of the chroniclers who themselves were not free of self-interest, motive, and intention. Thus, all interpreters of her figure are prey to subjectivized mythmaking once they begin to attribute motives, qualities, and desires to her regardless of the fact that they have recourse to historical motifs regarding her role, a role seen through the eyes of Cortés, Bernal Díaz del Castillo, Tlaxcaltecas, and many others present at the time. For Adelaida R. del Castillo, then, Malintzin should be viewed as a woman who made a variety

---

38. Del Castillo, "Malintzin Tenepal," 125.
39. Del Castillo, "Malintzin Tenepal," 126.

of *choices* (sic) due to a "philanthropic conviction," that is, her conviction that Cortés was Quetzalcóatl and, subsequently, that Christ was the true Quetzalcóatl, or that the true Quetzalcóatl was Christ—hence Malintzin's role in converting the indigenous population and her "sense of deliverance when she recognized that the Spaniards resembled Quetzalcoatl."[40] In other words, Malintzin initially fell victim to a mistaken identity but subsequently recognized Quetzalcóatl in Christ and displaced her devotion onto Cortés, onto Christ, and, subsequently, onto the child who would represent the new race. I think there is as much a revision of Paz and Fuentes as of history (i.e., the chroniclers) in del Castillo's interpretation, as well as a repudiation of Paz's views of woman's passive sexuality. In short, as del Castillo revises a "mythology" (as she names it in opposition to history) with which she feels implicated, she appears to be reading two texts at once, the purported "original" one (the chroniclers) and the "mythology of the original" (Paz and Fuentes). These texts are separated by almost five centuries; however, del Castillo wants to appropriate Malintzin for herself, as one whose face reflects her vision, Malintzin as agent, choice-maker, and producer of history. Actually, the whole notion of choice, an existentialist notion of twentieth-century Anglo-European philosophy, needs to be problematized in order to understand the constraints under which women of other cultures, times, and places live. In trying to make Malintzin a motivated "producer of history," del Castillo is not so much reconstructing Malintzin's own historical moment as she is using her both to counter contemporary masculine discourse and to project a newer sense of a female self, a speaking subject with a thoroughly modern view of historical consciousness.

    A similar strategy is used by Cordelia Candelaria in the essay "La Malinche, Feminist Prototype."[41] For Candelaria, Malintzin is the feminist prototype because she "defied traditional social expectations of woman's role."[42] Candelaria enumerates a variety of roles that she enacted: "liaison, guide to region, advisor on native customs, and beliefs, and strategist ... [T]he least significant role was that of mistress."[43] Though the roles described by the chroniclers may fit within such a description, the verb "defied" does not. It is difficult to know to what extent it was possible to defy either native or Spanish cultures since both adhered to the trinitarian worldview of Authority, Religion, and Tradition. The defiance

---

40. Del Castillo, "Malintzin Tenepal," 130.
41. Cordelia Candelaria, "La Malinche, Feminist Prototype," *Frontiers* 5, no. 2 (1980): 1-6.
42. Candelaria, "La Malinche, Feminist Prototype," 6.
43. Candelaria, "La Malinche, Feminist Prototype," 3.

Candelaria speaks of is rooted in contemporary existentialist philosophy, which has been as yet an unfinished revolt against the former worldview.[44] In revising the image of Malintzin, Candelaria privileges a self capable of making choices and of intellectual acumen over a self-manifesting sexuality and polyglot, thus avoiding in effect the two most significant charges against her. Since sexuality, especially ascribed to the maternal, and language are such powerful aspects of culture, it is in my opinion inadvisable to avoid them; they must be kept in view by the newer sense of a self who challenges traditions.

It is as a redeeming Mother/Goddess that Sylvia Gonzales awaits Malintzin's return in her poem "Chicana Evolution."[45] In this poem Gonzales views the self as a "Chicana/Daughter of Malinche."[46] Gonzales claims to await Malinche's return so that she may deny her traitorous guilt, cleanse her flesh, and "sacrifice herself" in "redemption of all her forsaken daughters"[47]—the New World's Demeter, perhaps, who shall rescue all Chicana Persephones. Whereas Fuentes will have Malintzin redeem the latterday sons/Quetzalcóatl, Gonzales will have her redeem the daughters. This redemptory return will empower Gonzales' creativity, who admires those women who have stripped themselves of passivity with their "pens."[48] At present, however, she feels overwhelmed by her definitions—"a creation of actions/as well as words."[49] For Gonzales, writing itself is empowering, yet she postpones the daughters' actual enablement, as if the appropriation of language were still to take place. As a result, her revision is gloomy—we still await. Our deliverance is viewed in apocalyptic terms, but Malinche has been substituted for Guadalupe.

The intertextual debate between women and men raises the following question implicitly: does Malintzin belong to the sons or the daughters? Each answers for him- or herself, narrowing the quarrel to a struggle for the possession of the neomaternal figure. Malintzin's procreative role is privileged in one way or another by most of these writers. Who shall speak for her, represent her? Is she now the procreator of the new founding order? Who will define that order?

---

44. The unfinished revolt is discussed by Hannah Arendt, *Between Past and Future: Eight Exercises in Political Thought* (London: Penguin Books, 1978).

45. Sylvia Gonzales, "Chicana Evolution," in *The Third Woman: Minority Women Writers of the United States*, ed. Dexter Fisher (Boston: Houghton Mifflin, 1980), 418-22.

46. Gonzáles, "Chicana Evolution," 420.

47. Gonzales, "Chicana Evolution," 420.

48. Gonzales, "Chicana Evolution," 420.

49. Gonzales, "Chicana Evolution," 419.

In the face of patriarchal tradition, Malintzin as Mother-Goddess/Muse/ Whore is viewed by some as the daughters' own redemptress. In the recently published three-part poem called *La Chingada*, Alma Villanueva envisions Malintzin as the displaced and desecrated prepatriarchal goddess who has returned to redeem and empower her daughters and to transform the sons. Villanueva states in a short preface to the poem: "This poem is a furious response centuries later to masculine culture, that is, a patriarchal destructive power that threatens all existence . . ."; the destructiveness emanates from "a strange, disembodied, masculine God" through whom men first "discredited, the first raped woman, when the feminine was forced to abdicate its sacred power."[50] In the previsionary section, Villanueva suggests that the Mexican/Chicana Malintzin, also known as *La Chingada*, is a recent reenactment and parody of the more ancient routing of the Goddess, one of whose names was Demeter.

Within the poem itself, the goddess Malintzin/Demeter calls upon the sons to transform themselves into "loving men capable of reinventing love." That feat can only be achieved by evoking the "girlchild inside" of them, by healing all the nameless wild animals that they killed and watched die due to some masculine quest or ritual.[51] In Part II, titled "The Dead," in opposition to Part I which was titled "The Living," the Goddess, who is now conflated with La Llorona/Mater Dolorosa,[52] mourns her dead daughter. The daughters were prepared for their defeat through socialization. The malediction "Hijos de La Chingada" is reserved for the sons, who in profound irony have been birthed to kill the mourned daughters. Subsequently, the Goddess calls upon the daughters to give birth to themselves, to renew their being. Both sons and daughters are forbidden to look back to old religious models and are urged to recreate themselves with her help. She is willing to sacrifice herself so that "You are born, at last, unto/ yourself!"[53]

---

50. Alma Villanueva, "La Chingada," in *Five Poets of Aztlán*, ed. Santiago Daydi-Tolson (Binghamton, N.Y.: Bilingual Review Press, 1985), 140.

51. Villanueva, "La Chingada," 153.

52. In "La Llorona, The Third Legend of Greater Mexico: Cultural Symbols, Women, and the Political Unconscious," *Renato Rosaldo Lecture Series Monograph*, no. 2 (1984-85) (Tucson: Mexican American Studies and Research Center, University of Arizona, Spring 1986): 59-93. Jose Limón has argued that La Llorona (The Weeping Woman) would make a more effective feminist cultural symbol for women of Mexican descent. In fact, he argues that Chicanas have failed to recognize her potential feminist political importance. In my view, La Llorona fails to meet some of the modern and secularizing factors that Chicanas have felt they've needed in order to speak for themselves. The so-called second wave of global feminism forces contemporary women to deal with the notion of the self and subjectivity that previous feminisms have often bypassed in favor of women's rights on the basis of being wives and mothers. The current debate on La Malinche goes beyond that.

53. Villanueva, "La Chingada," 163. 53.

In her representation of Malintzin, Villanueva tries to fulfill Adrienne Rich's view of the daughter's desire for a mother "whose love and whose power were so great as to undo rape and bring her back from death."[54]

Villanueva's interpretation of Malintzin draws on elements from Paz who, along with Rich in *Of Woman Born: Motherhood as Experience and Institution*,[55] is one of the epigrammatic voices preceding the poem. She also borrows elements from Fuentes; however, she replaces his view of a vengeful Malintzin with a redeeming one, who will not be still until she is recognized as patriarchy's suppressed woman, the one upon whose body Western civilization has been built—hence, the call for erasing religious models which hold daughters and sons back from newer senses of self. In her feminist revision Villanueva differs from Paz and Fuentes in that she does not "plead" for acceptance of Malintzin as Goddess/Raped Mother. On the contrary, Malintzin speaks on her own behalf and is enraged over her suppression, desecration, and rape, all of which have disenabled the female line. A crime has been committed against the Mother/Goddess, and she demands retribution and justice. Villanueva addresses directly the sexual and linguistic aspects of Malintzin's so-called betrayal, precisely what Candelaria avoids in her representation. In reading Villanueva's poem, one is made aware of the powerful charge effected when the speaking subject appropriates language and expresses her rage at the suppression of maternal self-representation.

Lucha Corpi refers to Malintzin by her Spanish name, Marina. This factor is significant because Corpi inscribes Marina into biblical discourses rather than pre-patriarchal ones. Thus, it follows that she should be called Marina as the Spaniards baptized her. For Corpi, Marina is a parody and reenactment of Eve and Mary, a woman who has sacrificed herself for the latter-day daughter and who, because of her experience, presages a renewing and enabling cycle. In four poems, or one poem consisting of four parts, which are in turn titled "Marina Mother," "Marina Virgin," "The Devil's Daughter," and "She (Distant Marina)," Corpi revises the story of Marina/Malintzin.[56] Marta Sánchez, in *Contemporary Chicana Poetry: A Critical Approach to an Emerging Literature*, views Corpi's cycle of poems accurately, I think, when she observes that "Corpi's cultural paradigm leaves readers no alternative but to accept a passive Marina

---

54. Villanueva, "La Chingada," 142.

55. Adrienne Rich, *Of Woman Born: Motherhood as Experience and Institution* (New York: W.W. Norton, 1976).

56. Lucha Corpi, "Marina Mother," "Marina Virgin," "The Devil's Daughter," and "She (Distant Marina)" in her *Palabras de Mediodía/Noon Words: Poems*, trans. Catherine Rodríguez-Nieto (Berkeley: El Fuego de Aztlán Publications, 1980), 118-25.

who can do nothing about her situation."⁵⁷ "Marina Madre" is perceived as victim of her own feminine condition. That is, insofar as women are women and mothers, they are incommensurably vulnerable. Using images that allude to the Old and New testaments, Corpi imagines a Marina made of the "softest clay" by the Patriarchs ("los viejos"): in biblical inscription and creation as either Eve ("her name written on the patriarchal tree") or as Mary ("the fruit of her womb stolen") and, nearer to us in time, the Marina abandoned and vilified by father, husband, and son. The latter three may be seen as an allusion to the male triad in one God—Father, Son, and Holy Ghost—as the Catholic tradition holds. By planting her soul in the earth, Corpi's latter-day Marina reinscribes herself and awaits her own renewal. The "she" in the fourth poem—She (Distant Marina)"—is that contemporary daughter who is imagined as a "mourning shadow of an ancestral figure" crossing a bridge leading to a new time and space, a reconstructed self. The passive, victimized Marina of the first two poems is left behind. Marta Sánchez has also suggested that the bridge is the boundary crossed "between Mexico and the United States."⁵⁸ Both Corpi's reinscription and Sanchez's interpretation of it continue to emphasize the mediating function assigned to Marina, though from a Chicano point of view in which the Spaniards, harbingers of a different existence, are now replaced by Anglo-Americans. It is important to reiterate the value placed by many Chicanas on a primary identification with the indigenous people or recuperations of that identity and the rejection of a Spanish one, despite the use of the language. However, these rhetorical strategies are now often undertaken to underscore our differences from Anglo-Americans.

For Gonzales, Villanueva, and Corpi, the forced disappearance of the Mother/Goddess leads to the daughter's own abjection. The daughter is doomed to repeat the cycle until the ancient powers of the goddess are restored. Of the three, however, Villanueva is the only one who, in appropriating Malintzin, makes her a speaking subject on her own behalf and on behalf of the daughters in a truly powerful way. Gonzales and Corpi objectify her and leave us with a promise of vindication.

Cherríe Moraga also explores the significations of Malintzin in her recent book *Loving in the War Years: lo que nunca pasó por sus labios*.⁵⁹ Moraga feels, on the one hand, a need to recover the race of the biographical mother so that she

---

57. Sánchez, *Contemporary Chicana Poetry*, 190.
58. Sánchez, *Contemporary Chicana Poetry*, 194.
59. Cherríe Moraga, *Loving in the War Years* (Boston: South End Press, 1983).

may recover her ethnosexual identity and, on the other, a need to appropriate her political and literary voice.[60] Simultaneously, however, a search for the identity of, and relation between, self and mother also requires an exploration of the myth of Malintzin who is our "sexual legacy."[61] That legacy is inscribed in cruel epithets such as *"La Chingada," "La Vendida,"* "Traitor." These epithets are in turn used on women to stigmatize, to limit the quest for autonomy, and to limit "The Chicana imagination ... before it has a chance to consider some of the most difficult questions."[62] Moraga points to the double-bind of the Chicana who defies tradition; she is viewed either as a traitor to her race or a lesbian. As such, not only is the lesbian in the Chicano imagination *una Malinchista*, but vice versa. Feminism, which questions patriarchal tradition by representing women's subjectivity and/or interjecting it into extant discursive modes, thereby revising them, may be equated with *malinchismo* or lesbianism. Even as she recognizes the double-bind, Moraga proceeds to identify herself as a lesbian who, as such, represents the "most visible manifestation of a woman taking control of her own sexual identity and destiny, who severely challenges the anti-feminist Chicano/a."[63] Moraga thinks that if she were not a lesbian she would still be viewed as one by a culture that does not understand the pursuit of a sexual identity beyond heterosexism.[64] In a sense, for Moraga, lesbianism in our culture is the ultimate trope for the pursuit of newer gender identities, for anything that smacks of difference in the face of traditional gender values. Rather than try to revise the myths of Malintzin, Moraga accepts them and labels them male myths whose purpose is to exercise social control over women. To escape the double-bind, Moraga has no choice but to declare that, indeed, she comes "from a long line of vendidas."[65] One could, however, opt for Lorna D. Cervantes' sarcastic view of the usual male perception of Malintzin's figure by stating ambiguously, as does the title of her poem, "Baby, you cramp my style."[66] Baby is, of course, a double

---

60. For a complementary essay on the way Chicana writers have reconstructed the relationship between self and mothers in order to redefine their feminine/feminist identity, see Norma Alarcón, "What Kind of Lover Have You Made Me, Mother?" in *Women of Color: Perspectives on Feminism and Identity*, ed. Audrey T. McCluskey (Bloomington, IN: Women's Studies Monograph Series, no. 1, 1985), 85-110.

61. Moraga, *Loving in the War Years*, 99.

62. Moraga, *Loving in the War Years*, 112.

63. Moraga, *Loving in the War Years*, 113.

64. In charging the Chicano community with heterosexism, Moraga relies on Adrienne Rich's sense of the term in "Compulsory Heterosexuality and Lesbian Existence," in *Women, Sex and Sexuality*, ed. Catharine R. Stimpson and Ethel Spector Person (Chicago and London: University of Chicago Press, 1980), 62 – 91.

65. Moraga, *Loving in the War Years*, 117.

66. Lorna D. Cervantes, "Baby, You Cramp My Style," *El fuego de Aztlán* 1, no. 4 (1977): 39.

allusion—to him who would impose his notions on her and to Malinche, whose historical existence and subsequent interpretations are a burden. Moraga and Cervantes, in a sense, become the heroines of their own individualized vision and revision, for it is through their appropriations that we proceed beyond Malinche. However, have they truly integrated the "treacherous" Malintzin whose ascribed attributes are the source of contention—the speaking subject and procreator? Cervantes' sarcasm is a dismissal of the subject in favor of her own future self-creation. On the other hand, if one follows Moraga's reasoning and takes it one step further, then one would have to say that the ultimate trope for the pursuit of new gender identities is not so much lesbianism as it is the speaking subject who is also a lesbian mother, or perhaps one who articulates and visualizes herself and procreation beyond heterosexism. If newer racial and gendered identities are to be forged, the insight arrived at in writing needs to be communicated to millions of women who still live under such metaphoric controls. How are they to be persuaded to accept these insights if they still exist under the ideology "Guadalupe-Malintzin"?

If for the Mexican male writers, the originating rape is of paramount importance because it places in question their legitimacy as sons, Chicanas—with the exception of Villanueva, who accepts Paz's view—do not even mention rape in connection with Malintzin. Paz, as far as I can discern, was the first writer to advance forcefully the metonymic relations between three terms—Malintzin, La Chingada, and rape. Though pillage and rape are almost by definition factors of conquest and colonization, there is no trace of evidence that Malintzin suffered the violent fate of other indigenous women, strictly speaking—though her disappearance from the record is troublesome and puzzling. One may even argue that she performed as she did to avoid rape and violence upon her body, to "choose" negatively between lesser evils. Clearly, in patriarchal and patrilineal societies—which these were—sons stand to lose a great deal more if they are the illegitimate offspring of rapes. Daughters, like their mothers, would still have to struggle to protect themselves from rapists. "Legitimacy" under these circumstances at best grants a female protection from rape; it does not make a woman her father's heir nor even give her a sure claim to her offspring. For the men, the so-called rape is largely figurative, a sign of their "emasculating" loss; for the women, it is literal. There is irony in Paz's insistence that Malintzin should also serve as the figure for "our" rape since it may well be that she saved herself from such a fate through diligent service. There are no choices for slaves, only options between lesser evils.

Because Malintzin's neosymbolic existence in the masculine imagination has affected the actual experience of so many Mexicanas and Chicanas, it became necessary for "her daughters" to revise her scanty biography. Through revisions, many undertaken in isolation, contemporary Chicana writers have helped to lay bare Malintzin's double etymology which until recently appeared illusory and hallucinative: one privileges the sociosymbolic possibilities for signification, the second, the existential and historical implications. Some of the writers discussed have actually, as speaking subjects, reemphasized the patriarchal view of the maternal/ feminine as mediator, even though they wish to represent her themselves. Others have transformed her into the neomyth of the goddess. Still others have foregrounded qualities such as "choice-maker," "history producer," and "self-aware" speaking subject, all of which are part of modern and contemporary experience and desire. In a sense, they sidestep the image of Malintzin as a raped mother and part of the feminine condition. Except for Villanueva, who follows Paz in this respect, no one has explored the full impact—imaginary or not—that such an image may have for us. It emphasizes that our beginnings, which took place barely half a millennium ago, are drenched in violence, not simply symbolic but historically coinciding with European expansionist adventures. It implies that the object of that violence was/ has been feminine (or feminized) and that it barely begins to be recovered as subject or even object of our history. Since the European expansionists of the time were Christians, it implies that indeed the ancient putative suppression of the goddess was reenacted; the missionaries did not have a problem assimilating Quetzalcóatl into their discourse but suppressed Tonantzin. However, since Chicanas have begun the appropriation of history, sexuality, and language for themselves, they find themselves situated at the cutting edge of a new historical moment involving a radical though fragile change in consciousness. It is an era in which we live in simultaneous time zones from the pre-Colombian to the ultramodern, from the cyclical to the linear. The latter is certainly a theme in the work of Carlos Fuentes, Rosario Castellanos, Octavio Paz, and other contemporary Mexican writers. However, I think that the objectified thematics have now passed onto a more consciously claimed subjectivity in the work of Chicanas such as Gloria Anzaldúa's *Borderlands/La Frontera: The New Mestiza*.[67] Moreover, such subjectivity is capable of shedding light upon Chicanas' present historical situation without necessarily, in this newer key, falling prey to

---

67. Gloria Anzaldúa, *Borderlands/La Frontera: The New Mestiza* (San Francisco: Spinsters/ Aunt Lute, 1987).

a mediating role but, rather, catching stunning insights into our complex culture by taking hold of the variegated imaginative and historical discourses that have informed the constructions of race, gender, and ethnicities in the last five hundred years and that still vibrate in our time. Issues of "class" and "color" (i.e., race and ethnicity) per se have not entered the appropriation because, I think, the historical person and textual figure of Malintzin (indigenous female slave in her own society as well as in the one taking shape under the Spaniards) implicitly subsume those as part of her condition—hence the possibility of her suppression as feminine/maternal speaking subject. It could very well signify that anyone *completely* deprived of voice within the Anglo-European and Spanish imperialist projects has by definition been an impoverished and/or enslaved woman of color. Here, then, is a powerful reason why the notion of the "literature of women of color" in the United States is one of the most novel ideas to have arisen in the Anglo-European imperialist context. Such a notion is yet to be part of Mexican or Latin American criticism; we have yet to see how women there begin to resolve their struggle for self-representation. Mexican writers Elena Poniatowska and Rosario Castellanos have many a heroine who is a woman of color. Consciously or unconsciously they have tried, as upper-class Mexican writers, to understand the complexity of the relationship between a woman of color (or native one) and Anglo-European patriarchal history and thought. It is in the vibrations of that distance between them that the appropriation of the many transformations of a woman of color lies.

In a more recent appropriation of Malintzin, Tzvetan Todorov appears to agree with some of the Chicanas discussed, which is an interesting phenomenon since for each the work of the other was unavailable at the time of writing. The agreement appears coincidental for those of us who have been forced for historical, political, and economic reasons to become perennial migrants in search of "home." For Todorov, Malintzin is the

> first example, and thereby the symbol, of the cross-breeding of cultures; she thereby heralds the modern state of México and beyond that, the present state of us all, since if we are not invariably bilingual, we are inevitably bi- or tri-cultural. La Malinche glorifies mixture to the detriment of purity . . . and the role of the intermediary. She does not simply submit to the other . . . ; she adopts the other's ideology and serves it in order to

understand her own culture better, as is evidenced by the effectiveness of her conduct (even if "understanding" here means "destroying").[68]

The reconstruction of ourselves as women or as exiles from "home" due to subjugations is fraught with paradox, contradiction, and unlikely partners, such as Mexican male writers and Todorov. Though Todorov does not mention the role of gender and sexuality in his interpretation, he also readily finds a point of identification for himself.

As a historical subject, Malintzin remains shrouded in preternatural silence, and as object she continues to be on trial for speaking and bearing the enemy's children and continues to be a constant source of revision and appropriation—indeed, for articulating our modern and postmodern condition. The "discovery" and colonization of what is presently called the Third World could just as well be said to have started when the Spaniards conquered México as at any other moment—and also at a time when a significant portion of Europe was about to inaugurate the modern epoch, that is, the Reformation, Copernicus, Galileo, Cartesian philosophy, etc. Thus, the quarrel over the interpretation of Malintzin serves not only as a heuristic device for the assumption of feminism in a traditionalist and essentialist setting where men refuse to let women speak for themselves, or women feel constrained from speaking, but also as the measurement of discursive maneuvers in the effort to secularize or appropriate thought for oneself. It is noteworthy that these have to be undertaken under the auspices of a woman—the one who did not remain the "internalized other" of the European's other. And what about the women who remain the "internalized others," that is, the ones who submit or are "offerings" to the colonizers? What can we make of such gifts? Do they become like the Mayan woman in the epigram, a woman in the service of violence against herself?

Much of the Chicana feminist work of the seventies, like Anglo-American feminist work, was launched around the assumption of a unified subject organized oppositionally to men from a perspective of gender differences. The assumption that the subject is autonomous, self-determining, and self-defining often has been a critical space shared by many feminists because it opens up vistas of agency for the subject. Often that critical space has generated the notion, especially among Anglo-Americans, that women's oppression can be described universally from the perspective of gender differences, as if boundaries of race, ethnicities, and

---

68. Tzvetan Todorov, *The Conquest of America: The Conquest of the Other*, trans. Richard Howard (New York: Harper and Row, 1985), 101.

class had not existed. The fact that Todorov also shares that critical space makes it possible for him to project onto La Malinche observations similar to those of some Chicanas, ironically even more similar than those of Mexican men. The Mexican men do not forget that she is an Indian and a woman, thus making it possible for them to understand the "betrayal" on the grounds that she would not want to remain "in the service of violence against herself." However, to the extent that we know it, the story of La Malinche demonstrates that crossing ethnic and racial boundaries does not necessarily free her from "violence against herself"; moreover, once her usefulness is over she is silenced and disappears from the record, precisely because she is an Indian and a woman. She crosses over to a site where there is no "legitimated" place for her in the conqueror's new order. Crossings over by "choice" or by force become sporadic individual arrangements that do not necessarily change the status of Indian women or women of color, for example. The realization that the "invitation" to cross over, when it is extended, does not ameliorate the lot of women of color in general has led, in the eighties, to a feminist literature by Chicanas and women of color which demonstrates that, despite some shared critical perspectives, boundaries exist and continue to exist, thus accounting for differential experiences that cannot be contained under the sign of a universal woman or women. Yet for Mexicans, Guadalupe is a symbol that continues to exist for the purpose of "universalizing" and containing women's lives within a discrete cultural banner that may be similar to those of other cultures. On the other hand, the diverse twentieth-century interpretations of La Malinche rupture the stranglehold of religion by introducing the notion of historical, sexual, and linguistic agency, though not necessarily available to La Malinche herself at the beginning of the Mexican colonial period.

Postmodern feminist theories have arisen to supplant gender standpoint epistemology and to diffuse explanatory binarisms. However, the critical question arises: do they free women of color from the "service of violence against themselves," or do they only rationalize it well? For those of us who simultaneously assume a critical position and a kinship with "native women" and women of color, the "philosophical bases of political criticism"[69] and cognitive practices are as important as the deployment of critical theories: do they also function to help to keep women from doing service against themselves—if not, why not?

---

69. The gulf between criticism and politics or criticism and cognitive practices is examined by S. P. Mohanty, "Us and Them: On the Philosophical Bases of Political Criticism," *Yale Journal of Criticism* 2, no. 2 (1989): 1-31; Mary E. Hawkesworth, "Knowers, Knowing, Known: Feminist Theory and Claims of Truth," *Signs* 14, no. 3 (Spring 1989): 533-57; Edward W. Said, *The World, The Text, and the Critic* (Cambridge: Harvard University Press, 1983); and Chandra T. Mohanty, "Under Western Eyes: Feminist Scholarship and Colonial Discourse," *Boundary* 2 12, no. 3, and 13, no. 1 (Spring and Fall 1984): 333-58.

BIBLIOGRAPHY

Alarcón, Norma. "What Kind of Lover Have You Made Me, Mother?" In *Women of Color: Perspectives on Feminism and Identity*, edited by Audrey T. McCluskey, 85-110. Bloomington: Women's Studies Monograph Series, no. 1, 1985.

Anzaldúa, Gloria. *Borderlands/La Frontera: The New Mestiza*. San Francisco: Spinsters/Aunt Lute, 1987.

Arendt, Hannah. *Between Past and Future: Eight Exercises in Political Thought*. London: Penguin Books, 1978.

Bakhtin, Mikhail M. *The Dialogic Imagination: Four Essays*. Translated by Caryl Emerson and Michael Holquist. Edited by Michael Holquist. Austin: University of Texas Press, 1981.

Barraza, Santa. "Coatlicue." *Third Woman* 4 (1989): 42, 153.

Bruce-Novoa, Juan. "One More Rosary for Doña Marina." *Confluencia* 1, no. 22 (1986): 73-84.

Candelaria, Cordelia. "La Malinche, Feminist Prototype." *Frontiers* 5, no. 2 (1980):1-6.

Cantú, Norma. "Secular and Liturgical Folk Drama." Community Empowerment and Chicano Scholarship, National Association of Chicano Studies, March 29-April 1, Los Angeles. Presentation.

Cervantes, Lorna D. "Baby, You Cramp My Style." *El Fuego de Aztlán* 1, no. 4 (1977): 39.

Corpi, Lucha. *Palabras de Mediodía/Noon Words: Poems*. Translated by Catherine Rodríguez-Nieto. Berkeley: El Fuego de Aztlán Publications, 1980.

Cros, Edmund. *Theory and Practice of Sociocriticism*. Translated by Jerome Schwartz. Minneapolis: University of Minnesota Press, 1988.

del Castillo, Adelaida R. "Malintzin Tenepal: A Preliminary Look Into a New Perspective." In *Essays on La Mujer*, edited by Rosaura Sánchez and Rosa Martinez Cruz, 124-149. Los Angeles: Chicano Studies Center Publications, University of California, Los Angeles, 1977.

Eagleton, Terry. *Marxism and Literary Criticism*. Berkeley and Los Angeles: University of California, 1976.

Fuentes, Carlos. *Todos los gatos son pardos*. México: Siglo XXI, 1984. Originally published in 1970.

Fuentes, Carlos. "The Legacy of La Malinche." In *Literatura Chicana: Texto y Contexto*, edited by Antonia Castañeda, Tomás Ybarra-Frausto, and Joseph Sommers, 304-06. New York: Prentice-Hall, 1972.

Girard, René. *Violence and the Sacred*. Translated by Patrick Gregory. Baltimore: Johns Hopkins University Press, 1977.

Gonzales, Sylvia. "Chicana Evolution." In *The Third Woman: Minority Women Writers of the United States*, edited by Dexter Fisher, 418-22. Boston: Houghton Mifflin, 1980.

Hawkesworth, Mary E. "Knowers, Knowing, Known: Feminist Theory and Claims of Truth."

Signs 14, no. 3 (Spring 1989): 533-557.

Jacques Lafaye. *Quetzalcóatl y Guadalupe: La Formación de la conciencia en México (1531-1813)*. Translated by Ida Vitale and Fulgencio López Vidarte. México: Fondo de Cultura Económica, 1983.

Kristeva, Julia. "Women's Time." Translated by Alice Jardine and Harry Blake. *Signs* 7, no. 1 (1981): 13-35.

Kristeva, Julia. "The Ethics of Linguistics," *Desire in Language: A Semiotic Approach to Literature and Art*. Translated by Thomas Gora, Alice Jardine, and Leon S. Roudiez. Edited by Leon S. Roudiez, 23 – 25. New York: Columbia University Press, 1980.

Limón, José E. "La Llorona, The Third Legend of Greater México: Cultural Symbols, Women, and the Political Unconscious." *Renato Rosaldo Lecture Series Monograph*, 59-93, no. 2. Tucson: Mexican American Studies and Research Center, University of Arizona, 1986.

Lopez, Yolanda M. "Guadalupe Walking" *Fem* 8, no. 34 (1984): front cover.

Maranda, Pierre. "The Dialectic of Metaphor: An Anthropological Essay on Hermeneutics." *The Reader in the Text: Essays on Audience and Interpretation*. Edited by Susan R. Suleiman and Inge Crosman. 184-85. Princeton, NJ: Princeton University Press, 1980.

Mohanty, Chandra T. "Under Western Eyes: Feminist Scholarship and Colonial Discourses." *boundary* 2 12, no. 3 (1984): 333-58.

Mohanty, S. P. "Us and Them: On the Philosophical Bases of Political Criticism." *Yale Journal of Criticism* 2, no. 2 (1989):1-31.

Moraga, Cherríe. *Loving in the War Years: Lo que nunca pasó por sus labios*. Boston: South End Press, 1983.

Ong, Walter J. *The Presence of the Word: Some Prolegomena for Cultural and Religious History*. New Haven: Yale University Press, 1967.

Ong, Walter J. *Orality and Literacy: The Technologizing of the Word*. New York: Methuen, 1982.

Ortner, Sherry B. "Is Female to Male as Nature is to Culture?" In *Woman, Culture, and Society*, edited by Michelle Zimbalist Rosaldo and Louise Lamphere, 67-88. Stanford: Stanford University Press, 1974.

Pacheco, José Emilio. *Islas a la deriva*. México: Siglo XXI, 1976.

Paz, Octavio. *The Labyrinth of Solitude: Life and Thought in Mexico*, translated by Lysander Kemp. New York: Grove Press, 1961. Originally published in 1950.

Paz, Octavio. "The Sons of La Malinche." In *Introduction to Chicano Studies: A Reader*, edited by Livie Isauro Durán and H. Russell Bernard, 17-27. New York: Macmillan, 1973.

Phillips, Rachel. "Marina/Malinche: Masks and Shadows." In *Women in Hispanic Literature: Icons and Fallen Idols*, 97-114. Edited by Beth Miller. Berkeley: University of California Press, 1983.

Reyes, Alfonso. *Visión de Anáhuac (1519)*. México: El Colegio de México, 1953. Originally published in 1915.

Rich, Adrienne. *On Lies, Secrets and Silence: Selected Prose, 1966-1978*. New York: Norton, 1979.

Rich, Adrienne. *Of Woman Born: Motherhood as Experience and Institution*. New York: W.W. Norton, 1976.

Rich, Adrienne. "Compulsory Heterosexuality and Lesbian Existence." In *Women, Sex and Sexuality*, edited by Catharine R. Stimpson and Ethel Spector Person, 62-91. Chicago: University of Chicago Press, 1980.

Rodríguez, Gustavo A.. *Doña Marina*. México: Imprenta de la Secretaría de Relaciones Exteriores, 1935.

Said, Edward W. *The World, The Text, and the Critic*. Cambridge: Harvard University Press, 1983.

Sánchez, Marta. *Contemporary Chicana Poetry: Critical Approaches to an Emerging Literature*. Berkeley: University of California Press, 1985.

Sosa Riddell, Adaljiza. "Chicanas and El Movimiento." *Aztlán* 5, nos. 1-2 (1974): 155-65.

Tafolla, Carmen. In "La Malinche." *Five Poets of Aztlán*, edited by Santiago Daydi-Tolson, 193-95. Binghamton, NY: Bilingual Press, 1985.

Todorov, Tzvetan. *The Conquest of America: The Conquest of the Other*. Translated by Richard Howard. New York: Harper and Row, 1985.

Villanueva, Alma. "La Chingada." In *Five Poets of Aztlán*, 140. Edited by Santiago Daydi-Tolson. Binghamton, NY: Bilingual Review Press, 1985.

Wolf, Eric R. "The Virgen de Guadalupe: A Mexican National Symbol." *Journal of American Folklore* 71, no. 279 (1958): 34-39.

CHICANA LITERATURE

A SEXUAL AND RACIAL CHALLENGE FROM THE
PROLETARIAT TO THE PATRIARCHY[1]

↦ ↤

Translated by Ariadna Molinari Tato and Alí Siles

THIS TEXT IS BASED on two claims that, in my opinion, bring together its diverse thematic facets:

1) Literature is the theoretical discourse of a historical process.

2) A critical perspective can only arise clearly when we cannot find a tradition that collects our attitudes and when we realize that we are facing a foreign tradition that we have never belonged to or that we no longer accept unquestionably.

The main Chicano literary attitudes displayed both by men and women gather around the search for self-determination, self-definition, along with a process of self-invention in the interstices between cultures. These attitudes materialize into a critical perspective that is aware of the historical traces it provides and whose vision produces a theoretical discourse on the historical process regarding individuals and families both in their most intimate moments as well as in cognitive stances. The bibliography of the last three decades (1960s-1990s) would include well over a hundred authors. Their published books are mostly written in English and include the occasional Spanish phrase, but their affective impact usually requires interpretations that go beyond their literal meaning. The selection of phrases in Spanish is very specific and reflects a Mexican system of cultural signification. Thus, in linguistic terms, it brings into play at least two cultures: North American and Mexican. However, the occasional use of Spanish

---

1. *Editors' Note*: This essay was first published as "La literatura de la chicana: Un reto sexual y racial del proletariado," *Mujer y literatura mexicana y chicana: Culturas en contacto* 2, ed. Aralia López González, Amalia Malagamba, and Elena Urrutia. (https://doi.org/10.2307/j.ctvhno9nt.31). It appears here in English for the first time translated from the Spanish by Ariadna Molinari Tato and Alí Siles. The translation is copyrighted by Universidad Nacional Autónoma de México (UNAM)/Centro de Investigaciones y Estudios de Género (CIEG), 2023, and it is published with permission from UNAM/CIEG.

is not the only form of cultural juxtaposition used to forge the self-definition and the self-invention mentioned above; there is also the appropriation of the English language as one's own communication tool. From my point of view, this process is analogous to the historical process of appropriating the Spanish language as a tool for communication in México and Latin America. For instance, Chicana author Ana Castillo avoids literary workshops facilitated by North Americans because she fears losing her own voice, given the pressure to integrate to English language usage in those contexts. Nonetheless, she writes in English (and sometimes in Spanish) but tries to elude its dominant influence. She has a working-class background and insists on that positioning as a significant starting point. Many other authors also refuse to attend those workshops and prefer organizing their own, led by Chicanos. For them, it is a matter of protecting and cultivating their own voices and themes—i.e., self-definition and self-invention. On the other hand, writers such as Sandra Cisneros, Gary Soto, Barbara Brinson Curiel, and Alberto Ríos have participated in writers' workshops in North American universities and have freely agreed to appropriate the poetic and narrative techniques therein to serve their own purposes. For example, Sandra Cisneros, also from a working-class background, tells us of the literary muteness she experienced in front of her peers during a workshop in Iowa, a predominantly white American setting. She found it impossible to describe the atmosphere of her barrio in the same way her peers did their home neighborhoods: i.e., with exquisitely trimmed lawns, big gardens, and beautiful houses. It was not until her second year of studies that she was able to break that literary silence and decided to write about the ghetto, the barrio, the garbage, the cockroaches, and the rats, which meant exposing her experiences, her privacy. This reminds me of an anecdote Rosario Castellanos used to tell: When she arrived at Distrito Federal, the Mexican capital, she thought she could write about very sophisticated and intellectual people; in other words, she thought she could create a world of fantasy, but the pettiness of the countryside she came from constantly pushed through to come out in her work. In Cisneros' case, what pushed to come out from her was the world of the barrio. Within this linguistic framework there are many labels used to refer to different kinds of Chicano literature: resistance literature, social protest literature, performance literature, proletariat literature, mainstream literature (compliant with the dominant Anglo-American tradition), feminist literature, and gay literature. The sum of these labels and their corresponding texts certainly provide a stimulating and enriching panorama. During the last decade, Chicana literary production has greatly increased.

This current generation of women writers grew in the shade of the Chicano sociopolitical movement and of the Anglo-American feminist movement. The former is characterized by predominantly men's voices and cultural perspectives, whereas the latter showcases the feminist voices of white middle-class women. Notwithstanding, in the 80s, Chicana writers were driven by the political and literary challenge posed by the publication of *This Bridge Called my Back*,[2] a volume edited by Chicana authors Cherríe Moraga and Gloria Anzaldúa that denounces North American feminist racism and sexism in general, as those attitudes marginalized women of color who were also in need of emancipation. The book put together a series of testimonies that portrayed the experiences of socially marginalized women, including Chicana, Cuban, Puerto Rican, Asian, Black, and Indigenous women. It also helped insist on the impossibility of analyzing the social and historical situation of women of color, as well as their critical, theoretical, and literary production, without taking into consideration the three social orders and analytical categories that have always determined their experiences: gender/sex, race/culture, and socioeconomical status. As a matter of fact, that volume inaugurated the study of Chicanas and other women of color in North American universities.

When studying the literary production of Chicana writers, we realize that there is an obsession with their genealogy and the circumstances of their immediate family. This theme also seems to obsess men writers, but their perspective is different from women's. For instance, the men writers' position towards the father can be summarized in the following paradigmatic figures:

1) *Yo soy Joaquín (I am Joaquín)*, by Corky Gonzales[3]

2) *Pocho*, by José Villarreal[4]

3) *Y no se lo tragó la tierra*... (... And the Earth Did Not Swallow Him), by Tomás Rivera[5]

---

2. Cherríe Moraga and Gloria Anzaldúa, eds., *This Bridge Called my Back: Writings by Radical Women of Color* (Watertown, MA: Persephone Press. 1981).

3. Rodolfo "Corky" Gonzales, *Yo soy Joaquín (I am Joaquín)*, translated by Juanita Domínguez. 1967.

4. José Villarreal, *Pocho* (Garden City, NY: Doubleday, 1959).

5. Tomás Rivera, *Y no se lo tragó la tierra*... (... *And the Earth Did Not Swallow Him*), trans. Herminio Rios (Berkeley: Quinto Sol Publications, 1971).

4) *Bless me, Ultima,* by Rudolfo Anaya[6]

These works show 1) the affirmation of Mexican genealogy in the face of the hostile Anglo-American patriarch; 2) the rejection of the Mexican patriarch and the individual search for new models; 3) the Bildungsroman, that is the evolution of the youngster/man; and 4) the pachuco as a speculative myth that provides reflections about racism, the change of linguistic codes, challenging attitudes, and, as Rosario Castellanos would say, a desire for "another way of being." That is what Octavio Paz posed in the first chapter of *The Labyrinth of Solitude*: the pachuco emerges in between two cultures but disavows both.[7] The pachuco is a sociohistorical figure that has inspired many Chicanos, but he does not write for himself; he merely works as a mirror with many faces.

In contrast, Chicana writers have been rejecting both the Mexican and the Anglo-American patriarchy and their father figures for the last decade: 1) they remain silent about the father, but let his oppressive and repressive force cast a shadow that can be read between the lines—as in Moraga's play *Giving Up the Ghost*—[8] or 2) they express their attitude clearly, just like Ana Castillo, and say things like: "I stopped loving my father a long time ago. What remained was the patterns of slavery." This claim is made through an epigraph, attributed to Anaïs Nin, that opens Castillo's epistolary narrative, *The Mixquiahuala Letters*.[9] There, she reveals that the patterns of slavery are the Catholic Church and its rigid ideology regarding masculinity and femininity, as well as sexual patterns, namely the ideological heterosexism that crushes both men and women. This ideology causes women to suffer a very specific economic and social abandonment, and both men and women to have an overdetermined life, without the chance to free themselves from sociocultural and historical restraints. (It should be noted that authors such as Rivera, Villareal, Islas, among others, also condemn Catholicism and the Catholic Church.) In other words, for Castillo, the chance to invent "another way of being" cannot exist in a world where the definitions of masculinity and femininity are expressed as a natural, social, or religious dogma that is out of our control, nor when they are presented as binary oppositions— where the meaning of one concept depends inextricably on the meaning of the other. To discuss this subject, I will begin by quoting a statement from Juan

---

6. Rudolfo Anaya, *Bless Me, Ultima* (Berkeley: TQS Publications, 1972).
7. Octavio Paz, *Labyrinth of Solitude* (New York: Grove Press, 1961) 9-28.
8. Cherríe Moraga, *Giving Up The Ghost* (Los Angeles: West End Press, 1986).
9. Ana Castillo, *The Mixquiahuala Letters* (Binghamton, NY: Bilingual Press/Editorial Bilingüe, 1986) np.

José Arreola's *Homage to Otto Weininger,* a social philosopher of womanhood who represented a huge pain in the neck for Rosario Castellanos: "Like a good romantic, I wasted my life pursuing a bitch."[10] It could be interpreted that all good romantics wasted their lives pursuing the muse, which has now become a bitch due to the degradation caused by the exploitation of romanticism, but I dare remind you that it is probably the woman worker—she who barely raises her voice—the one who has a front row seat to the romantic show and is most familiar with degradation.

Nevertheless, the woman writer, according to the romantic contract, was expected to stay silent and be nothing but an inspiration—whether as muse or "bitch"—but now she has decided to approach this bankrupt romantic contract from an entirely different perspective. For instance, we could review and appropriate Arreola's statement and rephrase it as follows: "Like any good romantic woman, I have lost over a decade following not one, but many dogs." And that is how Castillo defines love: "What is love? In the classic sense, it is an instrument to cause a woman to be submitted to a man." In other words, Castillo demystifies romantic love following a path different from Arreola's. Although irony abounds in the works of Chicana writers like Castillo and Cisneros (especially in Cisneros' collection of poems *My Wicked Wicked Ways*), they experience irony differently.[11] After following many dogs—if we extend Arreola's metaphor—they realize that dogs only want a wife, which they interpret to be a housemaid (it would be necessary to specify how this dynamic works in countries where there are still housemaids) and not the object of love they *a priori* used to think she was. Once the muse/bitch becomes a poet and learns how to write, she can only conclude she has fallen into a very deep trap. However, for this woman poet, the objects of love are not abstract beings, such as a "friend" or a "beloved," but someone with a first name, such as Álvaro, Sergio, Alexis, Francisco, Guillermo, Ricardo, or Rodrigo. When they are given such concrete names, the romantic experience does not only allude to the ideology inscribed in the romantic contract, but also to an experience that becomes profoundly social. I emphasize this difference because other poets, like Chicana writer Lucha Corpi or Mexican author Rosario Castellanos, do not give concrete names to their love objects and only refer to them using metaphors, such as "love," "friend," or

---

10. Juan José Arreola, "Homage to Otto Weininger," *Confabulario and Other Inventions,* trans. George D. Schade (Austin: University of Texas Press, 1964), 37-38.

11. Sandra Cisneros, *The House on Mango Street* (Houston, TX: Arte Público Press, 1984) and *My Wicked Wicked Ways* (Bloomington: Third Woman Press, 1987).

just "X." It should be noted that the very change in the name of the loved one suggests a change in attitude; when using the beloved's first name and revealing his feet of clay, he becomes one of many mortals, a mere domestic dog. The demystification of the heterosexual romantic contract goes hand in hand with a rejection of religion, which clearly suggests that the new attitude towards women's sexuality requires a different vision of both the father/parent and the father/priest. In other words, it is possible to get three figures "with one stone": the spiritual father, the familial father, and the lover. All this requires having a room of one's own or even a house of one's own, something Sandra Cisneros dreams of in *The House on Mango Street*. Thus, the appropriation of women's sexuality, its practice, and its definition rely upon the financial independence of all women. But how to achieve that?

Another figure that has been reclaimed and reviewed is that of the mother. At first, both women and men Chicano writers thought of themselves as an intellectual revolutionary miracle. Given our families' socioeconomic circumstances, it is truly miraculous that so many of them were able to take hold of the written word, against all odds, and reclaim their genealogy. From that point of view, this generation is very special, since its vision unfolds towards the peasantry/working class and the social and intellectual middle class. Thus, their own bodies function as a prism that illuminates several social and ideological orders. Taking this socioeconomical framework into account, women writers have displayed an ambivalent and contradictory attitude towards the mother figure. On the one hand, she is seen as a working woman who has sacrificed herself working in the fields and factories to support her family; on the other, when she is seen as the figure responsible for relaying traditional cultural patterns, she is thought to betray her daughter's interests or to abandon her so that she can find her own way in an extremely hostile environment for women of color. Among the most passionate claims about the mother figure, we find those by Alma Villanueva and Cherríe Moraga. They seek solidarity with the mother, but contingent upon her changing. Alma Villanueva suggests that, in case it is necessary, the daughter will have to become her own mother, given the abandonment she has suffered.

Ultimately, the daughter will forge—in her own way for herself—the mother figure In that vein, Chicana poets and essayists have recovered the figure of the *soldadera* from the Mexican Revolution and reconstructed an authentically revolutionary feminine image whose desires were betrayed by the racism and sexism of two patriarchies.

Another motherly figure that has been reclaimed and reconstructed to give a voice to the visions of contemporary women writers is the mute and mistreated image of the Malinche. There are two Mexican authors whose perspectives on the Malinche have influenced Chicano literature significantly: Octavio Paz and Carlos Fuentes. In fact, fragments of their writings about the Malinche were included in anthologies of Chicano studies in the 70s.[12] Consequently, Chicana writers have examined the masculine idea of the Malinche and reconstructed her profile in many ways:

1) She has been defended as a slave whose historical circumstances had never been taken into consideration or taken seriously.

2) She has been identified as a myth of the patriarchal imagination used to control women's voices.

3) She has been represented as the redeeming goddess women have been waiting for, a goddess in their own image and likeness.

4) Finally, she has been thought of as a figure that can truly explain the sociohistorical experience of indigenous and *mestiza* women in this continent, i.e., a figure in the margins of the legitimate and *criolla* society, an unprotected outlaw, a "non-woman."

In other essays I explain further these visions of the Malinche and the current imagery of the biological and cultural mother of our time. What I wish to highlight here is that motherly figures in contemporary literature are extremely complex and have functioned as multi-faceted mirrors that currently help decipher the daughter's subjectivity. Thus, if it is true that women (and men) have been the practical actualization of metaphysics, it is inevitable to ask what metaphysics and ideology are, and how they are actualized through our experiences. In other words, consciously capturing this cultural operation is a necessary step towards social transformation.

At this point I will circle back to two of the figures discussed by Octavio Paz in *The Labyrinth of Solitude* whom he describes as being exiled and excluded from cultures that consider themselves to be more authentic and legitimate,

---

12. Octavio Paz, "The Sons of La Malinche," in *Introduction to Chicano Studies: A Reader*, ed. Livie Isauro Durán and H. Russell Bernard (New York: Macmillan, 1973), 17-27. See also Carlos Fuentes, "The Legacy of La Malinche," in *Literatura Chicana: Texto y Contexto*, ed. Antonia Castañeda, Tomás Ybarra-Frausto, and Joseph Sommers (New York: Prentice-Hall, 1972), 304-06.

and that have been reclaimed by writers and narrators of Chicano culture: the pachuco, reclaimed by men; and the Malinche, reclaimed by women.[13] The parallels between both figures are numerous:

> 1) They have access to several linguistic codes that shed light on their existential and historical situation.
>
> 2) They have been denied decent treatment and have been banished from the circles of decent people.
>
> 3) For them, rebellion is a form of survival in conflictive cultural environments where the excluded can barely find refuge.
>
> 4) They represent symbols of a current orphanhood and lawlessness that has been the purview of the aristocracy and the bourgeoisie.

To my understanding, the genealogy of both figures is still unknown, so it is not surprising that the same group that reclaims the slur "Chicano" to revaluate it also reclaims these sociohistorical figures with similar intentions.

To conclude, I offer a quotation from Gloria Anzaldúa's latest book, *Borderlands/La Frontera: The New Mestiza,* specifically from the chapter called "*La conciencia de la mestiza*/Towards a New Consciousness."[14] Inspired by José Vasconcelos, Anzaldúa claims that:

> The new *mestiza* copes by developing a tolerance for contradictions, a tolerance for ambiguity. She learns to be an Indian in Mexican culture, to be Mexican from an Anglo point of view [and she learns to be pocha from a Mexican point of view]. She learns to juggle cultures. She has a plural personality, she operates in a pluralistic mode—nothing is thrust out, the good the bad and the ugly, nothing rejected, nothing abandoned. Not only does she sustain contradictions, she turns the ambivalence into something else.... In attempting to work out a synthesis, the self has added a third element which is greater than the sum of its severed parts.[15]

---

13. Paz, *Labyrinth,* 9-28, 65-88.

14. Gloria Anzaldúa, "*La Conciencia de la Mestiza*: Towards a New Consciousness," in *Borderlands/La Frontera (*San Francisco: Aunt Lute Books), 1987), 99-120.

15. Anzaldúa, "*La Conciencia de la Mestiza*: Towards a New Consciousness," 101.

BIBLIOGRAPHY

Anaya, Rudolfo A. *Bless Me Ultima*. Berkeley: Quinto Sol Publications, 1972.

Anzaldúa, Gloria. "*La Conciencia de la Mestiza*: Towards a New Consciousness." In *Borderlands/La Frontera*, 99-120. San Francisco: Spinsters/Aunt Lute, 1987.

Arreola, Juan José. "Homage to Otto Weininger." In *Confabulario and Other Inventions*. Translated by Goerge D. Schade and illustrated by Kelly Fearing, 37-38. Austin: University of Texas Press, 1964.

Fuentes, Carlos. "The Legacy of La Malinche." In *Literatura Chicana: Texto y Contexto*. Edited by Antonia Castañeda, Tomás Ybarra-Frausto, and Joseph Sommers, 304-06. New York: Prentice-Hall, 1972.

Castillo, Ana. The *Mixquiahuala Letters*. Binghamton, NY: Bilingual Press/Editorial Bilingüe, 1986.

Cisneros, Sandra. *The House on Mango Street*. Houston: Arte Público Press, 1984.

Cisneros, Sandra. *My Wicked Wicked Ways*. Bloomington: Third Woman Press, 1987.

Gonzales, Rodolfo. *Yo soy Joaquín (I am Joaquín)*. Translated by Juanita Dominguez. 1967.

Moraga, Cherríe. *Giving Up the Ghost*. Los Angeles: West End Press, 1986.

Moraga, Cherríe and Gloria Anzaldúa, editors. *This Bridge Called my Back: Writings by Radical Women of Color*. Watertown, MA: Persephone Press, 1981.

Paz, Octavio. *The Labyrinth of Solitude: Life and Thought in Mexico*. Translated by Lysander Kemp. New York: Grove Press, 1961. Originally published in 1950.

Paz, Octavio. "The Sons of La Malinche." In *Introduction to Chicano Studies: A Reader*. Edited by Livie Isauro Durán and H. Russell Bernard, 17-27. New York: Macmillan, 1973.

Rivera, Tomás. *Y no se lo tragó la tierra... (...And the Earth Did Not Swallow Him)*. Translated by Herminio Rios. Berkeley: Quinto Sol Publications, 1971.

Villarreal, José. *Pocho*. Garden City, NY: Doubleday, 1959.

CHICANA FEMINISM

IN THE TRACKS OF "THE" NATIVE WOMAN[1,2]

→ ←

AS SPAIN PREPARES TO celebrate the quincentenary of "the discovery" in 1992 contemporary Chicanas have been deliberating on the force of significations of that event. It took almost 400 years for the territory that today we call México to acquire a cohesive national identity and sovereignty. Centuries passed before the majority of the inhabitants were able to call themselves Mexican citizens. As a result, on the Mexican side of the hyphen in the designation Mexican-American, Chicanas rethink their involvement in México's turbulent colonial and postcolonial history, while also reconsidering, on the American side, their involvement in the capitalist neocolonization of the population of Mexican descent in the United States.[3]

In the 1960s armed with a post-Mexican-American critical consciousness, some people of Mexican descent in the United States recuperated, appropriated and recodified the term Chicano to form a new political class.[4] Initially, the new appellation left the entrenched (middle-class) intellectuals mute because it emerged from the oral usage in working-class communities. In effect, the new name measured the distance between the excluded and the few who had found a place for themselves in Anglo-America. The new Chicano political class began to work on the hyphen eager to redefine the economic, racial, cultural and

---

1. *Editors' Note:* This essay was first published in *Cultural Studies* 4, no. 3 (1990): 248–256. Subsequently, it was published in *Living Chicana Theory*, ed. Carla Trujillo (Berkeley, CA: Third Woman Press, 1998), 371-82; *Between Woman and Nation: Nationalisms, Transnational Feminisms, and the State*, ed. Caren Kaplan, Norma Alarcón, and Minoo Moaellem (Durham, NC: Duke University Press, 1999), 63-71; *Chicano Cultural Studies Reader*, ed. Angie Chabram-Dernersesian (New York: Routledge, 2006), 183-190; *Cultural Representation in Native America*, ed. Andrew Jolivétte (Lanham, MD: AltaMira Press, 2006) 119-130; and *Understanding Others: Cultural and Cross-Cultural Studies and the Teaching of Literature*, ed. Joseph Trimmer and Tilly Warnock (Urbana: National Council of Teachers of English, 1992), 96-106. We include the version published in *Cultural Studies*, 1990.

2. I would like to thank Gloria Anzaldúa, Rosa Linda Fregoso, Francine Masiello, and Margarita Melville for their reading and comments on this essay. Responsibility for the final version is, of course, mine.

3. Mario Barrerra, Carlos Muñoz, and Charlie Ornelas, "The Barrio as Internal Colony," in *People and Politics in Urban Society*, ed. Harlan Hahn (Los Angeles: Sage, 1972), 465-98.

4. See Rodolfo Acuña, *Occupied America: The Chicano's Struggle Toward Liberation* (San Francisco: Canfield Press, 1972) and Carlos Muñoz, *Youth, Identity, Power: The Chicano Movement* (London: Verso, 1989).

political position of the people. The appropriation and recodification of the term Chicano from oral culture was a stroke of insight precisely because it unsettled all of the identities conferred by previous historical accounts. The apparently well-documented terrains of the dyad México/United States were repositioned and reconfigured through the inclusion of the excluded in the very interiority of culture, knowledge, and the political economy. Thus, the demand for a Chicano/a history became a call for the recovery and rearticulation of the record to include the stories of race/class relations of the silenced against whom the very notions of being Mexican or not-Mexican, being American or not-American, and being a citizen or not a citizen had been constructed. In brief, the call for the story of Chicanas/os has not turned out to be a "definitive" culture as some dreamed. Rather the term itself, in body and mind, has become a critical site of political, ideological and discursive struggle through which the notion of "definitiveness" and hegemonic tendencies are placed in question.

Though the formation of the new political Chicano class was dominated by men, Chicana feminists have intervened from the beginning. The early Chicana intervention is available in the serials and journals that mushroomed in tandem with the alternative press in the United States in the 1960s and 1970s. Unfortunately, much of that early work by Chicanas often goes unrecognized which is indicative of the process of erasure and exclusion of raced ethnic women within a patriarchal cultural and political economy. In the 1980s, however, there has been a re-emergence of Chicana writers and scholars who have not only repositioned the Chicano political class through a feminist register but who have joined forces with an emergent women-of-color political class that has national and international implications.[5]

In the United States the 1980s were, according to the Ronald Reagan administration, the decade of the Hispanic—a neoconservative move assisted by the US Census Bureau[6] and the mass media, to homogenize all people of Latin American descent and occlude their heterogeneous histories of resistance to domination, in other words, the counter-histories to invasions and conquests. At the same time, in the 1980s, a more visible Chicana feminist intervention has given new

---

5. Andrée Nicola McLaughlin, "Black Women, Identity, and the Quest for Humanhood and Wholeness: Wild Women in the Whirlwind," in *Wild Women in the Whirlwind*, ed. Joanne M. Braxton and Andree N. McLaughlin (New Brunswick, NJ: Rutgers University Press, 1990), 147-80.

6. Martha Giménez, "The political construction of the Hispanic," in *Estudios Chicanos and the Politics of Community*, ed. Mary Romero and Cordelia Candelaria (Boulder: National Association for Chicano Studies, 1989), 66-85.

life to a stalled Chicano movement.⁷ In fact, in the United States, this appears to be the case among most raced ethnic minorities. By including feminist and gender analysis into the emergent political class, Chicanas are reconfiguring the meaning of cultural and political resistance and redefining the hyphen in the name Mexican-American.⁸

To date most writers and scholars of Mexican descent refuse to give up the term Chicana. Despite the social reaccommodation of many as Hispanics or Mexican-Americans, it is the consideration of the excluded evoked by the name Chicana that provides the position for multiple cultural critiques—between and within, inside and outside, centers and margins. Working-class and peasant women, perhaps the "last colony," as a recent book announces,⁹ are most keenly aware of this. As a result, when many a writer of such racialized cultural history explores her identity, a reflectory and refractory position is depicted. In the words of Gloria Anzaldúa:

> She has this fear
> that she has no names
> that she has many names
> that she doesn't know her names
> She has this fear
> that she's an image that comes and goes clearing and darkening
> the fear that she's the dreamwork inside someone else's skull . . .
> She has this fear that if she digs into herself
> she won't find anyone that when she gets 'there'
> she won't find her notches on the trees . . . She has this fear that she
> won't find the way back.¹⁰

The quest for a true self and identity which was the initial desire of many writers involved in the Chicano movement of the late 1960s and early 1970s has given way to the realization that there is no fixed identity. "I" or "She" as

---

7. Guillermo Rojas, "Social Amnesia and Epistemology in Chicano Studies," in *Estudios Chicanos and The Politics of Community*, eds. Mary Romero and Cordelia Candelaria (Boulder: National Association for Chicano Studies, 1989), 54-65.

8. Cherríe Moraga and Gloria Anzaldúa, eds. *This Bridge Called My Back: Writings by Radical Women of Color* (New York: Kitchen Table Press, 1983); Norma Alarcón, "Traddutora, Traditora: A Paradigmatic Figure of Chicana Feminism," *Cultural Critique*, no. 13 (1989): 57-87; Norma Alarcón, "The Theoretical Subject(s) in *This Bridge Called My Back* and Anglo-American Feminism," in *Making Face, Making Soul/Haciendo Caras*, ed. Gloria Anzaldúa (San Francisco: Aunt Lute Books, 1990).

9. Maria Mies *et al.*, *Women: The Last Colony* (London: Zed, 1989).

10. Gloria Anzaldúa, *Borderlands/La frontera: The New Mestiza* (San Francisco: Spinsters/Aunt Lute, 1987), 43.

observed by Anzaldúa, is composed of multiple layers without necessarily yielding an uncontested "origin." In the words of Trinh T. Minh-ha, "things may be said to be what they are, not exclusively in relation to what was and what will be (they should not solely be seen as clusters chained together by the temporal sequence of cause and effect), but also in relation to each other's immediate presences and to themselves as non/presences."[11] Thus, the name Chicana, in the present, is the name of resistance that enables cultural and political points of departure and thinking through the multiple migrations and dislocations of women of "Mexican" descent. The name Chicana is not a name that women (or men) are born to or with, as is often the case with "Mexican," but rather it is consciously and critically assumed and serves as point of redeparture dismantling historical conjunctures of crisis, confusion, political and ideological conflict and contradictions of the simultaneous effects of having "no names," having "many names," not "know(ing) her names," and being someone else's "dreamwork." However, digging into the historically despised dark *(prieto)* body in strictly psychological terms, may get her to the bare bones and marrow, but she may not "find the way back" to writing her embodied histories. The idea of plural historicized bodies is proposed with respect to the multiple racial constructions of the body since "the discovery." To name a few, indigenous (evoking the extant as well as extinct tribes), criolla, morisca, lobra, cambja, barchina, coyota, samba, mulatta, china, chola. The contemporary assumption of *mestizaje* (hybridism) in the Mexican nation-making process was intended to racially colligate a heterogeneous population that was not European. On the American side of the hyphen, *mestizas* are non-white, thus further reducing the cultural and historical experience of Chicanas. However, the *mestiza* concept is always already bursting its boundaries. While some have "forgotten" the *mestiza* genealogy, others claim an indigenous, black or Asian one as well. In short, the body, certainly for the past 500 years in the Américas, has been always already racialized. As tribal "ethnicities" are broken down by conquest and colonizations, bodies are often multiply racialized and dislocated as if they had no other contents. The effort to recontextualize the processes recovers, speaks for, or gives voice to, women on the bottom of a historically hierarchical economic and political structure.[12]

It is not coincidental that as Chicana writers reconstruct the multiple names of the *mestiza* and Indian, social scientists and historians find them in the

---

11. Trinh T. Minh-ha, *Woman/Native/Other* (Bloomington: Indiana University Press, 1989), 94.

12. Gayatri C. Spivak, "Can the Subaltern Speak?" in *Marxism and the Interpretation of Culture,* ed. Cary Nelson and Lawrence Grossberg (Urbana and Chicago: University of Illinois Press, 1988), 271-313.

segmented labor force or in the grip of armed struggles. In fact, most of these women have been (and continue to be) the surplus sources of cheap labor in the field, the canneries, the maquiladora border industries, and domestic service. The effort to pluralize the racialized body by redefining part of their experience through the reappropriation of "the" native woman on Chicana feminist terms, marked one of the first assaults on male-centered cultural nationalism on the one hand,[13] and patriarchal political economy on the other.[14]

The native woman has many names also—Coatlicue, Cihuacóatl, Ixtacihuátl, etc. In fact, one has only to consult the dictionary of *Mitologia Nahuátl,* for example, to discover many more that have not been invoked. For many writers the point is not so much to recover a lost "utopia" nor the "true" essence of our being, although, of course, there are those who long for the "lost origins," as well as those who feel a profound spiritual kinship with the "lost"—a spirituality whose resistant political implications must not be underestimated, but refocused for feminist change.[15] The most relevant point in the present is to understand how a pivotal indigenous portion of the *mestiza* past may represent a collective female experience as well as "the mark of the Beast" within us—the maligned and abused indigenous woman.[16] By invoking the "dark Beast" within and without, which many have forced us to deny, the cultural and psychic dismemberment that is linked to imperialist racist and sexist practices are brought into focus. These practices are not a thing of the past either. One has only to recall the contemporary massacres of the Indian population in Guatemala, for example, or the continuous "democratic" interventionist tactics in Central and South America, which often result in the violent repression of the population.

It is not surprising, then, that many Chicana writers explore their racial and sexual experience in poetry, narrative, essay, testimony and autobiography through the evocation of indigenous figures. This is a strategy that Gloria Anzaldúa uses and calls "La herencia de Coatlicue/The Coatlicue state." The "state"

---

13. Alarcón, "Traddutora, Traditora," 7-87.

14. Margarita Melville, ed., *Twice a Minority: Mexican American Women* (St. Louis: C. V. Mosby, 1980); Magdalena Mora and Adelaida R. del Castillo, eds. *Mexican Women in the United States: Struggles Past and Present* (Los Angeles: Chicano Studies Research Center, University of California,1980); Teresa Córdova, et al. eds., *Chicana Voices: Intersections of Class, Race, and Gender* (Austin: Center for Mexican American Studies, 1986); Vicki L. Ruiz, and Susan Tiano, eds., *Women on the US-Mexican Border: Responses to Change* (Winchester, MA: Allen & Unwin, 1987); Patricia Zavella, *Women's Work and Chicano Families: Cannery Workers of the Santa Clara Valley* (Ithaca: Cornell University Press, 1987).

15. Paula Gunn Allen, "Who is your mother? Red Roots of White Feminism," in *The Graywolf Annual Five: Multicultural Literacy,* ed. Rick Simonson and Scott Walker (Saint Paul: Graywolf Press, 1988), 13-27.

16. Anzaldúa, *Borderlands,* 43.

is, paradoxically, an ongoing process, a continuous effort of consciousness to make "sense"of it all. Every step is a *"travesía,* a crossing" because "Every time she makes 'sense' of something, she has to 'cross over,' kicking a hole out of the old boundaries of the self and slipping under or over, dragging the old skin along, stumbling over it."[17] The contemporary subject-in-process is not just what Hegel would have us call the *Aufhebung*—that is, the effort to unify consciousness "is provided by the simultaneous negation and retention of past forms of consciousness within a radical recomprehension of the totality,"[18] as Anzaldúa's passage also suggests. The complex effort to unify, however tenuously, Chicanas' consciousness which is too readily viewed as representing "postmodern fragmented identities" entails not only Hegel's *Aufhebung* with respect to Chicanas' immediate personal subjectivity as raced and sexed bodies, but also an understanding of all past negations as communitarian subjects in a, doubled relation to cultural recollection and re-membrance, and to our contemporary presence and non/presence in the sociopolitical and cultural milieu. All of which together enables both individual and group identity as oppressed racialized women. In order to achieve unification, the Chicana position previously "empty" of meanings emerges as one who has to "make sense" of it all from the bottom through the recodification of the native woman. As such the so-called postmodern decentered subject, a decentralization which implies diverse, multiply-constructed subjects and historical conjunctures, in so far as she desires liberation, must move towards provisional solidarities especially through social movements. In this fashion one may recognize the endless production of differences to destabilize group or collective identities on the one hand, and the need for group solidarities to overcome oppressions through an understanding of the mechanisms at work, on the other.[19]

The strategic invocation and recodification of "the" native woman in the present has the effect of conjoining the historical repression of the "non-civilized" dark woman—which continues to operate through "regulative psychobiographies" of good and evil women such as that of Guadalupe, Malinche, Llorona and many

---

17. Anzaldúa, *Borderlands*, 48, 49.

18. Scott Warren, *The Emergence of Dialectical Theory: Philosophy and Political Inquiry* (Chicago: University of Chicago Press, 1984), 37.

19. Andrée Nicola McLaughlin, "Black Women, Identity, and the Quest for Humanhood and Wholeness: Wild Women the Whirlwind," in *Wild Women in the Whirlwind: Afra-American Culture and the Contemporary Literary Renaissance,* ed. Joanne M. Braxton and Andrée Nicola McLaughlin (New Brunswick, NJ: Rutgers University Press, 1990), 147-80; L.A Kauffman, "The Anti-Politics of Identity," *Socialist Review*, no. 1 (1990): 67-80.

others—with the present moment of speech that counters such repressions.[20] It is worthwhile to remember that the historical founding moment of the construction of *mestiza(o)* subjectivity entails the rejection and denial of the dark Indian Mother as Indian which have compelled women to often collude in silence against themselves, and to actually deny the Indian position even as that position is visually stylized and represented in the making of the fatherland. Within these blatant contradictions the overvaluation of Europeanness is constantly at work. Thus, México constructs its own ideological version of the notorious Anglo-American "melting pot" under the sign of *mestizo(a)*. The unmasking, however, becomes possible for Chicanas as they are put through the crisis of the Anglo-American experience where ("melting pot") whiteness not *mestizaje* has been constructed as the Absolute Idea of Goodness and Value. In the Américas, then, the native woman as ultimate sign of the potential reproduction of *barbarie* (savagery) has served as the sign of consensus for most others, men and women. Women, under penalty of the double-bind charge of "betrayal" of the fatherland (in the future tense) and the mother tongues (in the past tense), are often compelled to acquiesce with the "civilizing" new order in male terms. Thus, for example, the "rights" of women in Nicaragua disappear *vis-à-vis* the "democratizing" forces of the US, the Church's "civilizing-of-women" project, and traditional sexisms notwithstanding Sandinista intentions.[21] In this scenario, to speak at all, then, "the" native woman has to legitimize her position by becoming a "mother" in hegemonic patriarchal terms which is near to impossible to do unless she is "married" or racially "related" to the right men.[22] As a result the contemporary challenge to the multiple negations and rejections of the native racialized woman in the Américas is like few others.

For Chicanas the consideration of the ideological constructions of the "non-civilized" dark woman brings into view a most sobering reference point: the overwhelming majority of the workers in maquiladoras, for example, are *mestizas* who have been forcefully subjected not only to the described processes but to many others that await disentanglement. Many of those workers are "single," unprotected within a cultural order that has required the masculine protection

---

20. Gayatri C. Spivak "The Political Economy of Women as Seen by a Literary Critic," in *Coming to Terms: Feminism, Theory, Politics,* ed. Elizabeth Weed (London: Routledge, 1989) 227.

21. Maxine Molyneux, "Mobilization Without Emancipation: Women's Interests, the State, and Revolution in Nicaragua," *Feminist Studies* 11 no.2 (1985): 227-54.

22. Aída Hurtado, "Relating to Privilege: Seduction and Rejection in the Subordination of White Women and Women of Color," *Signs: Journal of Women in Culture and Society* 14 no.4 (1989): 833-55.

of women to ensure their "decency," indeed to ensure that they are "civilized" in sexual and racial terms. In fact as Spivak and others have suggested "the new army of 'permanent casual' labor working below the minimum wage—[are] these women [who today] represent the international neo-colonial subject paradigmatically."[23] These women (and some men) who were subjected to the Hispanic New World "feudal mode of power," which in México gave way to the construction of *mestizo* nationalism; and who were subjected to an Anglo-American "feudal mode of power" in the isolation of migrant worker camps and exchange labor, which in the US gave rise to Chicano cultural nationalism of the 1960s; in the 1990s find themselves in effect separated in many instances from men who heretofore had joined forces in resistance. Though work in the fields continues to be done with kinship groupings, the "communal mode of power" under the sign of the cultural nationalist family may be bankrupt, especially for female wage-workers. Although, of course, the attempt to bring men and women together under conservative notions of the "family" continues as well. In this instance "family" may be a misnaming in lieu of a search for a more apt name for communitarian solidarity.

Whether it be as domestic servants, canners or in the service industry in the United States, or as electronic assemblers along the US/Mexican border, these "new" women-subjects find themselves bombarded and subjected to multiple cross-cultural and contradictory ideologies. A maze of discourses through which the "I" as a racial and gendered self is hard put to emerge and runs the risk of being thought of as "irrational" or "deluded," in their attempt to articulate their oppression and exploitation. In the face of Anglo-European literacy and capitalist industrialization which interpellates them as individuals, for example, and the "communal mode of power" (as mode of de-feudalization),[24] which interpellates them as "Mothers" (the bedrock of the "ideal family" at the center of the nation making process, despite discontinuous modes of its construction), the figure and referent of Chicanas today is positioned as conflictively as Lyotard's *différend*. She is the descendant of native women who are continuously transformed into *mestizas,* Mexicans, emigrés to Anglo-America, "Chicanas," Latinas, Hispanics—there are as many names as there are namers.

Lyotard defines a *différend* as "a case of conflict, between (at least) two parties, that cannot be equitably resolved for lack of a rule of judgment applicable to both

---

23. Spivak, "The Political Economy," 223.
24. Spivak, "The Political Economy," 224.

arguments. One side's legitimacy does not imply the other's lack of legitimacy."[25] In appropriating the concept as a metonym for both the figure and referent of the Chicana, for example, it is important to note that though it enables us to locate and articulate sites of ideological and discursive conflict, it cannot inform the actual Chicana *différend* engaged in a living struggle as to how she can seize her "I" or even her feminist "We" to change her circumstances without bringing into play the axes in which she finds herself in the present—culturally, politically, and economically.

The call for elaborated theories based on the "flesh and blood" experiences of women of color in *This Bridge Called My Back*[26] may mean that the Chicana feminist project must interweave the following critiques and critical operations: (1) multiple cross-cultural analyses of the ideological constructions of raced "Chicana" subjects in relation to the differently positioned cultural constructions of all men and some Anglo-European women; (2) negotiate strategic political transitions from cultural constructions and contestations to "social science" studies and referentially grounded "Chicanas" in the political economy who live out their experiences in heterogenous social and geographic positions. Though not all women of Mexican/Hispanic descent would call themselves Chicanas, I would argue that it is an important point of departure for critiques and critical operations (on the hyphen/bridge) that keep the excluded within any theory-making project. That is, in the Mexican-descent continuum of meanings, Chicana is still the name that brings into focus the interrelatedness of class/race/gender into play and forges the link to actual subaltern native women in the US/México dyad, (3) in negotiating points one and two, how can we work with literary, testimonial and pertinent ethnographic materials to enable "Chicanas" to grasp their "I" and "We" in order to make effective political interventions. This implies that we must select, in dialogue with women, from the range of cultural productions, those materials that actually enable the emergence of I/We subjectivities.[27]

Given the extensive ideological sedimentation of the (Silent) Good Woman and the (Speech-producing) Bad Woman that enabled the formations of the

---

25. Jean-François Lyotard, *The Differend: Phrases in Dispute*, trans. Georges Van den Abbeele (Minneapolis: University of Minnesota Press, 1988), xi.

26. Cherríe Moraga and Gloria Anzaldúa, eds. *This Bridge Called My Back: Writings by Radical Women of Color* (New York: Kitchen Table: Women of Color Press, 1983) (Originally published 1981.)

27. Olivia Castellano, "Canto, locura y poesía: The Teacher as Agent-Provocateur," *The Women's Review of Books* 8, no.5 (1990): 18-20.

cultural nationalist "communal modes of power", Chicana feminists have an enormous mandate to make "sense" of it all as Anzaldúa desires. It requires no less than the deconstruction of paternalistic "communal modes of power," which is politically perilous since often it appears to be the "only" model of empowerment that the oppressed have, although it has ceased to function for many women as development and post-industrial social research indicates. Also, it requires the thematization and construction of new models of political agency for women of color who are always already positioned cross-culturally and within contradictory discourses. As we consider the diffusion of mass media archetypes and stereotypes of all women which continuously interpellates them into the patriarchal order according to their class, race (ethnicity), and gender, the "mandate" is (cross-culturally) daunting. Yet, "agent provocateurs" know that mass media and popular cultural production are always open to contestations and recodifications which can become sites of resistance.

Thus, the feminist Chicana, activist, writer, scholar and intellectual has to on the one hand locate the point of theoretical and political consensus with other feminists (and "feminist" men), and on the other continue with projects that position her in paradoxical binds. For example, breaking out of ideological boundaries that subject her in culturally specific ways, and not crossing over to cultural and political areas that subject her as "individual/autonomous/neutralized" laborer. Moreover, to reconstruct differently the raced and gendered "I's" and "We's" also calls for a rearticulation of the "You's" and "They's." Traversing the processes may well enable us to locate points of differences and identities in the present to forge the needed solidarities against repression and oppression. Or, as Lorde and Spivak would have it, locate the "identity-in-difference" of cultural and political struggle.[28]

---

28. Audre Lorde, *Sister/Outsider* (Trumansburg, NY: Crossing Press, 1989); Spivak, "Can the Subaltern Speak?" 1988.

BIBLIOGRAPHY

Acuña, Rodolfo. *Occupied America: The Chicano's Struggle Toward Liberation.* San Francisco: Canfield Press, 1972.

Alarcón, Norma. "Traddutora, Traditora: A Paradigmatic Figure of Chicana Feminism." *Cultural Critique,* no. 13 (1989): 57-87.

Alarcón, Norma. "The Theoretical Subject(s) of *This Bridge Called my Back* and Anglo-American Feminism." In *Making Face, Making Soul/Hacienda Caras: Creative and Critical Perspectives of Feminists of Color,* edited by Gloria Anzaldúa, 356-69. San Francisco: Aunt Lute Books. 1990.

Allen, Paula Gunn. "Who is your mother? Red Roots of White Feminism." In *The Graywolf Annual Five: Multicultural Literacy,* edited by Rick Simonson and Scott Walker, 13-27. Saint Paul: Graywolf Press, 1988.

Anzaldúa, Gloria. *Borderlands: La Frontera. The New Mestiza.* San Francisco: Spinsters/Aunt Lute, 1987.

Anzaldúa, Gloria, ed. *Making Face, Making Soul/Haciendo Caras.* San Francisco: Aunt Lute Books, 1990.

Barrera, Mario, Carlos Muñoz, and Charlie Ornelas. "The Barrio as Internal Colony." In *People and Politics in Urban Society,* edited by Harlan Hahn, 465-98. Los Angeles: Sage, 1972.

Castellano, Olivia "Canto, Locura y Poesia: The Teacher as Agent-Provocateur." *The Women's Review of Books,* 8 no.5 (1990): 18-20.

Córdova, Teresa, Norma Cantú, Gilberto Cardenas, Juan García, and Christine M. Sierra, editors. *Chicana Voices: Intersections of Class, Race, and Gender.* Austin: Center for Mexican American Studies, 1986.

Giménez, Martha. "The Political Construction of the Hispanic." In *Estudios Chicanos and the Politics of Community,* edited by Mary Romero, and Cordelia Candelaria. 66-85. Boulder: National Association for Chicano Studies, 1989.

Hurtado, Aída. "Relating to Privilege: Seduction and Rejection in the Subordination of White Women and Women of Color." *Signs: Journal of Women in Culture and Society,* no. 4 (1989): 833-55.

Kauffman, L.A. "The Anti-Politics of Identity." *Socialist Review,* no. 1 (1990):67-80.

Lorde, Audre. *Sister/Outsider.* Trumansburg, NY: Crossing Press, 1989.

Lyotard, Jean-François. *The Differend: Phrases in Dispute.* Translated by Georges Van den Abbeele. Minneapolis: University of Minnesota Press, 1988.

McLaughlin, Andrée Nicola. "Black Women, Identity, and the Quest for Humanhood and Wholeness: Wild Women in the Whirlwind." In *Wild Women in the Whirlwind: Afra-American Culture and the Contemporary Literary Renaissance,* edited by Joanne M. Braxton and Andrée N. McLaughlin, 147-80. New Brunswick, NJ: Rutgers University Press, 1990.

Melville, Margarita, editor. *Twice a Minority: Mexican American Women.* St Louis: C. V. Mosby, 1980.

Mies, Maria, Veronika Bennholdt-Thomsen, Claudia von Werlhof, editors. *Women: The Last Colony.* London: Zed. 1989.

Molyneux, Maxine. "Mobilization without Emancipation: Women's Interests, The State, and Revolution in Nicaragua." *Feminist Studies,* no. 2 (1985): 227-54.

Mora, Magdalena, and Adelaida R del Castillo, eds. *Mexican Women in the United States: Struggles Past and Present.* Los Angeles: Chicano Studies Research Center, University of California. 1980.

Moraga, Cherríe and Anzaldúa, Gloria eds. *This Bridge Called My Back: Writings by Radical Women of Color.* New York: Kitchen Table: Women of Color Press. 1983 (Originally published 1981.)

Muñoz, Carlos. *Youth, Identity, Power: The Chicano Movement.* London: Verso, 1989.

Rojas, Guillermo. "Social Amnesia and Epistemology in Chicano Studies." In *Estudios Chicanos and The Politics of Community,* edited by Mary Romero and Cordelia Candelaria, 54-65. Boulder: National Association for Chicano Studies, 1989.

Ruiz, Vicki L. and Susan Tiano, eds. *Women on the US-Mexican Border: Responses to Change.* Winchester, MA: Allen & Unwin, 1987.

Spivak, Gayatri C. "Can the Subaltern Speak?" In *Marxism and the Interpretation of Culture,* edited by Cary Nelson and Lawrence Grossberg, 271-313. Urbana and Chicago: University of Illinois Press, 1988.

Spivak, Gayatri C. "The Political Economy of Women as Seen by a Literary Critic." In *Coming to Terms: Feminism, Theory, Politics,* edited by Elizabeth Weed, 218-29. London: Routledge, 1989.

Trinh, T. Minh-ha. *Woman, Native, Other.* Bloomington: Indiana University Press, 1989.

Warren, Scott. *The Emergence of Dialectical Theory: Philosophy and Political Inquiry.* Chicago: University of Chicago Press, 1984.

Zavella, Patricia. *Women's Wark and Chicano Families: Cannery Workers of the Santa Clara Valley.* Ithaca: Cornell University Press, 1987.

ON FEMININE CULTURE ACCORDING TO ROSARIO CASTELLANOS[1]

→ ←

Translated by Mónica Mansour

IN ROSARIO CASTELLANOS' INTELLECTUAL and vital formation, there are two fundamental topographical axes: Chiapas and México City. Her literary work and her philosophical and political positions were developed under their influence. Even though Castellanos was born in México City on May 25, 1925, her first fifteen years were spent in Comitán, Chiapas. Since the mid-nineteenth century, the Castellanos family owned large haciendas in Chiapas and lived in the Rosario Hacienda, on the Jataté River, near Comitán, as well as in the same town until 1940. After that year and the displacements due to Cárdenas' Agrarian Reform, and the need to give education to the daughter, whose inheritance had diminished, the family moved definitively to México City. Nevertheless, during the 1950s, after her parents' death, Castellanos returned to live in Chiapas in different periods.

Based on key events of the provincial experience, Rosario Castellanos creates a personal, political, and intellectual autobiographical fable for herself. This can be found in her lectures, like the one given at Indiana University in 1966, interviews, autobiographical essays, and in her first novel; *Balún Canán*.[2] The autobiographical impulse is inserted in fragments in her texts. However, here we will underscore some elements that may answer the fundamental question in Castellanos' work: What is feminine culture?

---

1. *Editors' Note:* This essay was first published as Chapter 3 in Alarcón's book *Ninfomanía: El discurso feminista en la obra poética de Rosario Castellanos* (Madrid: Editorial Pliegos, 1992), and it appears here in English for the first time translated from the Spanish by Mónica Mansour. The translation is copyrighted by Universidad Nacional Autónoma de México (UNAM)/Centro de Investigaciones y Estudios de Género (CIEG), 2023, and it is published here with permission from UNAM/CIEG.

2. In order to reconstruct parts of the life of R. Castellanos I have used the following: Rosario Castellanos, *Mujer que sabe latín...* (México: SepSetentas, 1973); "Rosario Castellanos" in *Hispanic Arts* I, no. 2 (Autumn, 1967): 67-70; Rhoda Dybvig, *Rosario Castellanos: Biografía y novelística* (México: Ed. de Andrea, 1965); "Rosario Castellanos," in *Los narradores ante el público* (México: Joaquín Mortiz, 1966), 89-98; Rosario Castellanos, *El uso de la palabra,* ed. José Emilio Pacheco and Danubio Torres Fierro (México: Ediciones de Excélsior, 1974).

The novel *Balún Canán*, a hybrid *bildungsroman*[3] mainly narrated by a seven-year-old girl, represents three significant relationship axes: between the girl and her nanny, her brother, and her parents. Castellanos says that when she began writing *Balún Canán*, although she was not very sure of what would happen in the story, she had already decided that one of the main events would be her brother's death.[4] Her lectures and essays constantly point out that his death traumatized her parents and consequently herself. Her brother's death threw her into chaos, uncertainty, and confusion; it also incited a totalizing crisis in the family and revealed the family values concerning sexuality. A way of life taken for granted was simultaneously destroyed and demystified.

In *Balún Canán*, the brother is called Mario. (Before this novel there is a similar short story named "First Revelation."[5] It recounts the death of a younger brother seen from the point of view of the first-person narrator, a little girl. It is the first rough version of a key aspect of the novel.) The relationship between brother and sister is the subtext of the novel. The young narrator, who has no name and is always called the girl, points out that it is true that she and her nanny are inseparable, and barely acknowledged by the family. On the contrary, Mario receives all the parents' attention. The girl is above all a separate and marginalized spectator of the family. Concerning her creative work, Castellanos underlines the dichotomy between a girl's and a boy's experience. This dichotomy begins with the name which identifies the person. If Mario's name and that of other characters are mentioned over and over, the girl is only identified by her gender and the nanny by her role as nurturer (which harmonizes with the expectations of her sex) or by her race. Here the fact stands out that if the girl and the nanny are socially distanced from the others, they resemble each other through marginalization. Neither one possesses individuality or personhood in the eyes of others. Therefore, it is not surprising that, in another context, Castellanos says that, for her, writing and definition (self-naming in itself) are initially motivated by the desire to see oneself represented, objectivized, to recognize and understand oneself: "But what is my name? Who do I look like? Who am I different from? Pen in hand I begin a search which has had its truces as much as it has had its findings, but which is still not finished."[6] In order not to be one thing among many others, similarities and differences must be

---

3. Dybvig, *Rosario Castellanos* 15-16.
4. Elena Poniatowska, "Rosario Castellanos," *México en la cultura*, no. 26 (1958): 7, 10.
5. Rosario Castellanos, "Dos Poemas," in *Poesía no eres tú*, (México: Fondo de Cultura Económica, 1972), 56.
6. Castellanos, *Mujer que sabe latín . . .* , 196.

clarified and identified. Thus, Castellanos chooses writing by means of memory (autobiographical) as the instrumental vehicle for her description of herself.

For Castellanos, memory is a cognitive instrument useful for safeguarding experience and rescuing it from oblivion. Her philosophical conviction regarding this is reinforced through Henri Bergson's *Matter and Memory*, which she read preparing for her master's thesis in philosophy. The Bergsonian text also suggests two titles for her poetry, *The Rescue of the World* and *Memorable Matter*. She quotes the following fragment of Bergson's book:

> The main and primary characteristic of the spirit is memory. Memory represents the abolition of the most immediate temporal barrier. Preserving the past and maintaining it alive, constantly available, and acting according to our will, is to stretch our sense of time beyond the present, it is to infuse coherence in our evolution, and our development. But it is also ... the first ransom we pay for the most elementary form of death: oblivion.[7]

Taking possession of memory, however, is not only a mission of rescuing oneself and the world, nor only the pleasure of giving coherence to the chaotic multiplicity of past events, through literature, for example. Memory is at the service of the subject's will, who strives to understand by means of remembering what happened, understanding which, on the other hand, can lead us to reconciliation with reality. Evidently, memory mediated by will helped Castellanos to understand what had happened, but reconciliation with the cultural context is never achieved. Thus, a great temporal and spatial tension is established between understanding and the dilemma. Self-reflection together with reflection on the cultural context as they simultaneously reflect and criticize each other make Castellanos' work a compendium of paradox and irony, within the frame of the sociohistorical situation that produces them.

The girl narrator in *Balún Canán* is overwhelmed with pain and blames herself for her brother's passing. Even though it is not directly stated that the girl wished for her brother's death, while he is agonizing in his delirium he says that the key to the secret chapel that the siblings had stolen must be returned so that he can be cured. The girl does not do it, maybe fearing punishment or maybe wishing for Mario to disappear, either due to rivalry or childish jealousy.

---

7. Rosario Castellanos, "Sobre cultura femenina," in *América: Revista Antológica*, (1950): 73. [This is not a direct quote of Bergson's book but is taken by Castellanos from a translation by Martín Navarro, "*Materia y Memoria. Ensayo sobre la relación del cuerpo con el espíritu*, (Madrid: Imprenta de Victoriano Suárez,1900)].

She feels paralyzed and does nothing. She listens and watches him die. In the confusion and commotion at home due to his death, the girl is subjective to her elders, who do not speak to her. The girl observes all the Indians walking down the street, looking for her nanny who disappeared. When she does not find her, she feels betrayed. Furious, the girl says that all the Indians look the same. When she goes back home she comments: "When I got home I looked for a pencil. And with my unskilled and clumsy writing, I wrote Mario's name, Mario on the bricks in the garden, Mario on the walls of the corridor, Mario on the pages of my notebooks."[8] During a revealing lecture, around ten years after *Balún Canán* was published, Castellanos confesses that:

> In order to exorcise the ghosts around me, all I had within reach was words. But once they were pronounced, their power evaporated, it was diluted in the air, it was lost. I had to fix them in a stronger substance, in a more resistant matter. The whitewash on the walls, where I wrote the name of the dead boy, would peel off.[9]

Castellanos discovers that, for her, the permanence of words is greater when documented than when spoken; the past risks being lost, including its reality when relayed by the spoken word. For Castellanos, in art, and writing, the naming and representation of objects is equivalent to owning the object itself. When giving them a linguistic existence, she exercises control over things. Thus, without a doubt, she can say: "I only consider as lived what has been written."[10] Castellanos adopts this phenomenological perspective especially referring to herself in order to objectify herself in writing as a female being, and in order to break that circle, placing herself as a contingent subject. At the end of her life, she questions her own perspective focusing more directly on the socio-political scene regarding women.

Balún Canán ends with the death of the brother and the girl's attempt to reverse this fact by writing and invoking Mario's name; for Castellanos, her brother's death begins a series of experiences that mark and structure her adulthood. That is, her brother dies, but her memory of him does not. According to Castellanos, the brother's death cast her away "forever from the line of sight of parents blinded by pain and nostalgia."[11] The parents' reaction to the death of

---

8. Rosario Castellanos, *Balún Canán* (México: Fondo de Cultura Económica, 1973), 291.
9. Castellanos, "Los narradores ante el público," 89-90.
10. Castellanos, "Los narradores ante el público," 89.
11. Castellanos, "Los narradores ante el público," 89.

their only son had such an impact on Rosario that decades later she uses that experience to differentiate the Israeli and the Mexican attitude towards death. She writes that for Israelis:

> The important thing is life, not death. Contrary to what we do: we have turned suffering into something elegant, which gives the person who is grieving a certain aura of superiority.... I am able to appreciate the importance of this because I grew up in an environment where sadness prevailed: my brother died when he was seven and my parents, who died fifteen years later, were never able to recover from that loss and never left their mourning clothes. After some time, I rebelled [...] against all of that....[12]

Being bound by her parents to an "elegant suffering" is unforgettable. It appears in her poems, her prose, sometimes with rage, sometimes with distancing. Thus, words become weapons and instruments for self-defense and self-appropriation. Castellanos is passionate about words because at an early age, she discovers that through words she can become real, she can prove she exists, and that others also exist. Not only do they lead to what is real, but they are symbolic instruments that allow her to distinguish herself from what surrounds her. This differentiation and consequently a separation, according to her, is like being cured of a disease: "I am apart, forever separated from what I once harbored within me as you harbor... a disease."[13] The written word as a form of liberation from diseases is a discovery in adulthood; for the girl, the spoken word in itself, with its sounds and cadences, is a source of magic. Pronounced words may help to fall asleep, and invoke dreams that deny painful truths and facts such as the brother's death and the parents' neglect. The girl does not have to be

> ... she whom death has discarded in order to choose someone else, someone better, my brother. I am not she whom her parents have abandoned in order to weep, thoroughly, their grief. I am not that unfortunate figure who wanders down deserted corridors and who does not go to school nor outings or anywhere. No. I am almost a person. I have the right to exist....[14]

Even dead, the brother is the parents' and also death's favorite.

---

12. Esperanza Brito de Martí, "Rosario Castellanos," ¡Siempre! (14 nov. 1973): 42.
13. Castellanos, Mujer que sabe latín..., 195.
14. Castellanos, Mujer que sabe latín..., 193.

We cannot emphasize enough Castellanos' discovery through personal experience that fighting against silence with words, spoken or written, allows her to emerge as a concrete, significant, and individualized entity. The effects of silence, marginalization, and the inability to name and to speak, particularly as the place given to Indians and women, become one of the outstanding topics of her work. In her passionate impulse towards words, Castellanos finds a companion in Jean-Paul Sartre. He points out in his autobiography *The Words* that:

> [. . .] as a result of discovering the world through language, for a long time I took language for the world. To exist was to have an official title somewhere on the infinite Tables of the Word; to write was to engrave new beings upon them or —and this was my most persistent illusion— to catch living things in the trap of phrases: if I combined words ingeniously, the object would get tangled up in the signs, I would have a hold on it.[15]

Passion for words together with the conviction that objects can be possessed and dominated through them, leads to writing in itself for the young Sartre, a situation analogous to that of Castellanos when she tells us that once she began writing with professional intentions, she experienced many difficulties in controlling writing so it would say and mean something specific. Language and writing follow their own path, which though amusing is incomprehensible to others.

This coincidence in attitude between Sartre and Castellanos is a result of an isolated childhood, with only the company of books, books that of course differ in both cases. If during her youth, Castellanos understood language as a vehicle for personal salvation from a critical situation, in adulthood, as we shall see, her literary vocation arises as a response to an urgent situation in which she was in extreme danger.[16]

The power of language, as well as critical situations in which human beings may be immersed, have become common topics in the twentieth century. Ludwig Wittgenstein in his *Tractatus Logico-Philosophicus*, believed that the crisis was due to the loss of precision in self-expression, which threatened man's perception of reality. In *Philosophical Investigations*, Wittgenstein abandons the possibility of clearly representing the relationship between word and object. He insists that "we must always take into account the context, the workings of the language in

---

15. Jean-Paul Sartre, *The Words*, trans. Bernard Frechtman (New York: Vintage Books, 1981), 182.
16. Castellanos, *Mujer que sabe latín . . .* , 191.

which words are enunciated," emphasizing that the process of teaching how to name experiences and sensations begins during childhood through adults. The dilemma between the wish to determine meanings and the fact that meanings depend on the sociocultural and historical context has been debated not only by Castellanos but by many during all the twentieth century.[17]

Octavio Paz emphasizes the liberating power of the word. In 1949 the title for his first collection of poems is *Libertad bajo palabra* (*Liberty through Words*) and he considers the word a source of change, a manner of "liberty that invents itself and invents me every day."[18] Evidently this literary attitude had an influence on Castellanos. However, Paz's concern for words frequently becomes formal aestheticism, evading their socio-cultural function; specifically, the words that can re-invent their hermetic existence *a priori*. Paz prefers the intertextual play of words, in which they refer to one another. He prefers subscribing to poetic aestheticism that, according to Barthes, "destroys the spontaneous functionality of language [...] retains only the superficial form of relationships."[19] Paz defines this self-described modernist poetic branch as an avant-garde experience that implies "the denial of the outside world."[20] Thus, the liberating search, that in Paz's case is called by Jason Wilson "the poetics of self-knowledge,"[21] results in ethics and aesthetics considerably different from those of Castellanos, although she is also interested in self-knowledge. For Castellanos, the outside world is important because that externality is socially and culturally structured and is intimately linked to the search for self-knowledge.

For Castellanos, existence is set in a contingent historical time. From this place, life frequently is perceived as a nebulous and fragmented process that requires and needs order and naming, considering the socio-historical context in which events take place. Virginia Woolf, for example, reveals how words helped her put existence in order:

> [...] a blow in my life is immediately followed by the wish to explain it. I feel that I have had a blow; but it is not, as I thought as a child, simply a blow from an enemy hidden behind the cotton wool of daily life; it is or will become a revelation of some order; it is a token of some real thing behind appearances; and I make it real by putting it

---

17. John Passmore, *A Hundred Years of Philosophy* (New York: Penguin Books, 1978), 432.
18. Octavio Paz, *Libertad bajo palabra* (México: Fondo de Cultura Económica, 1968), 10.
19. Roland Barthes, *Writing Degree Zero* (Boston: Beacon Press, 1970), 46, 47.
20. Octavio Paz, *Corriente alterna*. (México: Siglo XXI Editores, 1970), 7.
21. Jason Wilson, *Octavio Paz: A Study of His Poetics* (New York: Cambridge University Press, 1979), 66.

into words. It is only by putting it into words that I make it whole; this wholeness means that it has lost its power to hurt me; it gives me, perhaps because by doing so I take away the pain, a great delight to put the severed parts together."²²

Through the drive to explain "the blows in life," believing that experience is not only contingent but that it also belongs in a sense to an order not evident in appearances, Woolf produces meanings for herself. The inter-relationship between immediate personal experience and words suggests the order in which they belong, and for Barthes both are a way of conceiving literature and a "confrontation of the writer with the society of his time;" which "on the other hand, considering this social purpose, takes the writer back, by means of a tragic reversal, to the sources, that is, to the instruments of creation."²³ In other words, the literary text is unfolded simultaneously into two perspectives: one that grasps a sociocultural truth and one which reinserts the prevailing system, by means of the word, trapped in networks of meanings; that is, it mystifies and demystifies at the same time. At that moment critique must intervene.

Despite Barthes' observations, the idea of making real the nebulous or the appearances, or explaining them, is an intentional attitude toward language that Simone Weil also shares with Castellanos. According to Weil, it is an effort to "face the world."²⁴ For Castellanos, language is a means whose power lies in the possibility of helping her understand, examine, define, and rebuild her experience. She says: " . . . when I was a teenager my best friend was almost mute [. . .] I was possessed by a kind of frenzy that forced me [. . .] to define my moods, and interpret my dreams and remembrances. I had not the slightest idea of who I was or who I was going to be, and I urgently needed to organize and formulate myself by means of words and not action."²⁵ However, as we shall see, the critical positions adopted by Castellanos related to her cultural heritage will also lead her to concur with Barthes' perspective.

The biographical drama, which in Woolf's terms is a "shock and blow" (trauma) to being, is accentuated in Castellanos after her brother's death. After the closing of private schools in Chiapas, by order of the Cárdenas government, Castellanos' parents, who suffered financial setbacks due to the Cárdenas agrarian

---

22. Virginia Woolf, *Moments of Being* (New York: A Harvest/HBJ Book, 1976), 72.
23. Barthes, *Writing Degree Zero*, 15, 16.
24. Simone Weil, *Lectures on Philosophy* (London: Cambridge University Press, 1978), 68.
25. Rosario Castellanos, *Los convidados de agosto* (México: Ediciones Era, 1977), 11.

reform, refused to send Rosario to a public school, which deprived her of social contact even more. To make matters worse, unlike Sor Juana, she did not have a good library. Her father had a collection of books on engineering and the complete works of Shakespeare in English, which he had acquired when studying in Philadelphia. Thus, aside from the textbooks used for homeschooling, newspapers were her only intellectual stimulus as well as an expurgated copy of the *Arabian Nights*, Amado Nervo's poetry, and a book by Gregorio Martínez Sierra that she received on her 13th birthday. According to Castellanos, these books were considered good reads for decent young people.

In a story ironically titled "Mexican History,"[26] Castellanos creates a protagonist who is her double. It is the true story of Cecilia, a provincial teenager. Cecilia was "abnormal," and her abnormality was that she spoke. She said everything that came to her mind and refused to be silent. She was constantly disciplined by her parents, she had to be punished, they made fun of her. Cecilia's story ends happily because her parents are forced to move from the province to México City, where Cecilia hopes to get a higher education. Moving was the only alternative, because if not they would have had to lock their daughter up in an insane asylum, since the neighbors considered her crazy. Cecilia's story, told sarcastically by Castellanos, shows not only her desire to make silence disappear and to name reality with words; it is also an echo of what happened in the 1940s, when Castellanos was a teenager, and she went through "a first psychoanalytic treatment that was equivalent to a diploma of adaptation to my circumstances."[27]

In Cecilia's story, the fact that she speaks, names, and defines is what makes her parents' life difficult in their provincial town. In other words, Castellanos uses vital experiences with manifold interpretations. In her comments on her own life, she says that the cause for moving to México City was the loss of family-owned lands. Also, now her education was not only a financial need, but it replaced that of the son. Castellanos has said that before her brother's death, her parents were not concerned about her education because they saw her as destined to marry, preferably one of the landowners of Chiapas, which would keep the land within the group of Ladino landowners.

Castellanos considers Cárdenas' agrarian reform very important because it forced many landowners of large estates to return the land to the Indians. About this historical event, she says:

---

26. Rosario Castellanos, "Historia mexicana," in *El uso de la palabra*, in *Excélsior*, trans. José Emilio Pacheco and Danubio Torres Fierro. México: Ediciones de Excélsior (1974): 48-51.

27. Rosario Castellanos, *Hispanic Arts* 1, no 2 (1967): 69.

> This national phenomenon had very deep repercussions on me. On the one hand, the certainty of my racial, social, and economic superiority, which, had I continued living in Chiapas, faithful to its traditions, I would have enjoyed with no distress as one of the inherited gifts, and on the other hand it forced me to find something to hold on to, values to be conquered and possessed in order to feel worthy of living.[28]

For Castellanos, Cárdenas was: "The man of [her] destiny." The historical forces of Cárdenas' reforms outside the provinces were very important in forming her social consciousness, opposite to the inherited ones: a kind of "divine right" to privilege, and on a personal level helped her escape the ritual and repetitive character of provincial women's life. However, if Castellanos did escape that life, this did not happen to many of her "neighbors in the province." As a consequence, these women become subjects of her narrative together with those who evade their situation by plunging into a phantasmagoric world.

Nevertheless, as Castellanos points out in another context, the Aristotelian "zoon politikon" moves her much later in life.[29] She believes that from adolescence until she was almost thirty there was a slow pace from "the most hermetic of subjectivities to the disturbing discovery of the other's existence, and lastly the rupture of the ideal model of couples, in order to integrate into the social, which is the sphere in which poets define, understand, and express themselves."[30]

What Castellanos calls "the most hermetic of subjectivities" is probably better explained by what she says about Cecilia in "Mexican History:" "Cecilia did not see the others... she saw herself reflected in them and that image annoyed and saddened her."[31] The U.S. poet Adrienne Rich has commented that women are "hungry for images,"[32] images that they themselves have created or that reflect alternatives to understanding their lives through them. It seems that the young Castellanos suffered from a "hunger for images" and a lack of alternatives to fulfill herself. In the 1940s, when she was trying to discover the perimeter of her existence as well as the images that had defined her, she was still not aware that in order to update what would later be her concept of literature, namely that "which

---

28. Castellanos *Hispanic Arts,* 67.
29. Castellanos, *Mujer que sabe latín...*, 203.
30. Castellanos, *Mujer que sabe latín...*, 203.
31. Castellanos, "Historia mexicana," 49.
32. Observations made during a lecture in Indiana University, Spring, 1979.

would provide knowledge on masculine and feminine humanity,"[33] she would have to insert and rediscover herself within the literary and social text. Her early writing, which was never published, was poetic meditations about the "depths" of the vanity of vanities and of life, and a concept of love as a vague mystic fervor. Therefore, her "amazement" when she discovered Delmira Agustini's poetry, and love as erotic passion in the work of Pablo Neruda. Within the context of the rigid moral world in the provinces, love was not allowed to be considered a feeling that included eroticism. In the 1970s, after having acquired some intellectual distance, Castellanos points out that "within an alienated society, one of the most alienated creatures is a woman who has no access to authenticity, not even through creativity."[34] The search for authenticity is limited or suppressed by the social, economic, and moral obstacles, in a way in which creativity itself is condemned to repeating "depths" that lead either to the denial of the individual self or to producing a closed (hermetic) self. In the 1940s, however, Castellanos does not appear to have a clear understanding of women's alienation, because of the cultural context in which she was raised. At the same time, that context is produced within a colonial framework. The most important aspect perceived at the time is that self-expression and self-understanding are imperative goals, and these can be achieved by means of the written word. During her youth, she probably did not even suspect that one day she would say:

> Perhaps create a work (. . .)
> Work? To change the face of nature?
> To add some books to the bibliographical lists?
> Vary the course of history?
>
> But this–again—is matter for men
> and for time measured in the way of men
>
> and according to the criteria
> with which they accept or refuse.[35]

The young writer who hoped to "change the face of nature" had not yet decisively understood that her alienation was not only the result of the family environment or of life in the provinces, but that it was based on a much vaster patriarchy and that it possessed the very criteria with which "nature, history, and

---

33. Naomi Lindstrom, "Rosario Castellanos: Representing Woman's Voice," *Letras femeninas* 5, no. 2 (1979): 230.
34. Castellanos, *El uso de la palabra*, 231.
35. Castellanos, "El retorno," in *Poesía no eres tú*, 340.

literature" have been defined. Moreover, books as such cannot change the order of things: they have to be accompanied by some form of collective social action. The Mexican poet José Emilio Pacheco has said that the readers of Castellanos did not truly understand her literary intentions: "When rereading her books, we will see that no one in this country, at the moment, had such a clear awareness of what the double condition of being a woman and a Mexican means, nor made this awareness the topic of their writing, the central line of their work. Naturally, we did not know how to read her."[36] The fact that her readers could not read the exploratory efforts of Castellanos in the representation of women and their interrelations is based on the prevailing ideology of criteria "with which they accept or refuse." That is why Castellanos tries to clarify her project through her essays. Pacheco agrees with Castellanos in that being a woman and a Mexican is a "double condition," echoing Castellanos' idea that women suffer not just a double alienation, but of the coloniality that persists in the Third World: social and cultural/racial and economic. The idea that women are doubly alienated, marginalized, or oppressed, and even triply by the continuing colonizing of the underclasses, is accepted by women of ethnic minorities in the United States, be they African American, Puerto Ricans, Chicanas, Asian Americans, and Indigenous populations. This shows that even in the context of a nation like México, where we would suppose that women only feel the impact of the local patriarchal oppression, she also shows the impact of international sociocultural relations and their power to affect women. Castellanos perceives México as a Third World country and culture, produced by a colonial past and a capitalist neo-colonialism, and open to a future that cannot evade its connections or dependence on the international Anglo-European patriarchy in all levels of life. To short-circuit the analysis of women's condition, examining the culture in which she was raised, is closing the mind to the inherent interdependence as well as the linked axes that connect women in a global context. Castellanos understood this phenomenon very well, excellently dramatized in the farce *The Eternal Feminine*, published posthumously, and in several essays. *The Eternal Feminine* links a series of acts that represent female characters of different social stereotypes, histories, and myths. Castellanos concludes the play, by urging Mexican women to invent their own feminist consciousness since imported forms cannot be easily accepted or assimilated. Castellanos' more militant and

---

36. Castellanos, *El uso de la palabra*, 8.

clear feminist positions can be found in her essays collected in *The Use of the Word (El uso de la palabra)*.

This "militant" aspect of Rosario Castellanos' feminist thought develops during the last ten or fifteen years of her life, approximately between 1960 and 1974. Along with Virginia Woolf and Simone de Beauvoir, she anticipates much of the contemporary feminist thinking in Europe and the United States, mainly through deconstructive strategies. But, as Castellanos says, the "zoon politikon" reaches her late, and by the end of the 1940s, when she is deciding on an academic field of study, she chooses philosophy, partly because it focused, as she says, on "the major questions."[37] Her parents had encouraged her to study something pragmatic, such as chemistry or law. Although she had attended some literary classes, the way in which literature was taught at the time disappointed her, because "the listing of dates and names, the catalogue of styles, and the analysis of literary devices did not help me in the least to understand anything."[38] The wish to "confront the world" was not made easier even by reading contemporary poets, except for Alfonsina Storni whose use of irony she admires, and Mistral, whose use of images she admires. Concerning the answers to the "major questions" or to understanding them, most of the Latin American women poets that Castellanos knew of at the time reflected a "closed (hermetic) subjectivity." It must be said that Castellanos was starting to define herself as a writer, contrary to her forerunners. In searching for predecessors who would be useful for distinguishing themselves from orthodoxies, she feels a great affinity with Storni and Sor Juana Inés de la Cruz, as well as with Gabriela Mistral, although her admiration for the latter excludes accepting Mistral's values developed in her poetry.[39]

After studying philosophy, Castellanos receives her master's degree with a dissertation called *On Feminine Culture (Sobre cultura femenina*, 1950). The dissertation reveals that one of Castellanos' "major questions" was the position of women in culture, their work within it, and their relationship with it, especially the advanced and erudite culture regarding philosophy, art, and writing. The answers referring to herself as a cultural being or to support her professional purposes were not found in philosophy. On the contrary, what she discovers

---

37. Castellanos, *Mujer que sabe latín...*, 205.
38. Castellanos, *Mujer que sabe latín...*, 204-205.
39. For the development of this perspective, see chapter IV of my book, *Ninfomanía: El discurso feminista en la obra poética de Rosario Castellanos* (Madrid: Pliegos de Bibliofilia, 1992).

investigating the selected texts is that, as cultural beings or agents, women do not exist. All done with the twists and turns of irony.

Castellanos' dissertation is situated between the extremes of reconciliation and rebellion. It is serious and comical, it is an affirmation of feminine culture by means of negative arguments, and it is an ironic denial of the need to express oneself culturally because women satisfy their need for immortality through motherhood. She concludes with a feminist position concerning the discourse of difference, but she denies feminism within the text, especially as a discourse of equality. It is a series of contradictions comically developed. By punctuating her text with sarcasm, contradiction, paradox, and irony, Castellanos brings into question her conclusion that she is reconciled with the examined philosophies.

The last chapter invites women to reinsert themselves by means of examining their unique experiences and moving away from the masculine representation they have inherited and internalized. Castellanos claims that the metaphysical (onto[theo]logical) representations of femininity are true because they have undoubtedly reflected preceding women and exert ideological control over contemporary women. She denies her solidarity with "feminist women and men" because she considers their claims and optimism false. Castellanos argues that feminists before 1950 do not make the effort of confronting the totalizing masculine supremacy, which is evident for her, since:

> It is he who invents the devices to dominate nature, and to make human transit on earth more comfortable, easier, and pleasant. It is he who carries out the commercial enterprises, conquests, explorations, and wars. It is he who gives speeches, organizes politics, and passes laws. It is he who writes the books and reads them, who sculpts statues and admires them. It is he who discovers truths and believes them and expresses them. It is he who has communication with God, officiates at his altars, interprets the divine will, and executes it. It is he who designs women's clothes and who approves the designs of clothes. It is he....[40]

Castellanos sees patriarchy, sometimes sarcastically, sometimes seriously, as having control and possession of the world, from the most frivolous fashion to the divine. The insertion of some exceptional women in masculine culture cannot change the world, nor women's situation, nor her own. From this

---

40. Castellanos, *Sobre cultura femenina*, 79.

perspective, urging women to reinsert themselves is much more radical than it seems, because it is the challenge to conscientiously discover and reconstruct themselves and their world.

On Feminine Culture reveals a young woman fighting the intellectual, social, economic, political, and historical environment of her time, in short fighting against patriarchy and its byproducts. However, when she presented this dissertation to the academic jury it provoked laughter. It seems that Castellanos, in the oral defense of her text, stated that "women writers are writers because they have no children."[41] Many of her comments defending her thesis show that Castellanos did not take that academic ritual very seriously, and it is very probable that laughter saved a situation that could have turned into a difficult political moment, albeit academic. Nevertheless, Castellanos, seriously and according to evidence, derived from this work that motherhood and writing were not easily compatible. When writing her thesis she obtained moral and intellectual support from Virginia Woolf's *Three Guineas*, written on the eve of World War II. There, Woolf analyzes and mocks the fact that patriarchy is the owner of military forces and higher education. Castellanos also reveals similarities and differences with Simone de Beauvoir's *The Second Sex*.[42] It is difficult to know whether Castellanos read this book before writing her dissertation. Victor Baptiste reports that Castellanos has been called the Simone of México, and that Octavio Paz sent her a copy of *The Second Sex* from Paris in 1950.[43] Although Simone de Beauvoir's influence on the whole work of Castellanos is evident, I doubt the book arrived in time for the preparation of *On Feminine Culture*. In any case, Castellanos mentions Woolf in her bibliography and not de Beauvoir. The important and interesting point in the work of these two women who question philosophy as women is that, in spite of the noticeable difference in the philosophy books they deal with, they coincide in key aspects.

According to Simone de Beauvoir, masculine thought has conceived man as transcendence, and woman as immanence. In the terms used by Castellanos, man is an actor and a maker, and woman a purely natural being. In de Beauvoir's argument, women's participation in culture is not rare, but it is limited between the extremes of acceptance or rebellion; that is, submission or revolt. Castellanos ironically accepts the philosophical assertion that women do not have the

---

41. Poniatowska, "Rosario Castellanos," 7.
42. Simone de Beauvoir. *The Second Sex,* trans. and ed. H.M. Parshley (New York: Vintage Books, 1974).
43. Victor Baptiste. "La obra Poética de Rosario Castellanos." PhD Diss., (Urbana: University of Illinois, 1967), 6.

need nor the tendency towards participation in culture. Thus, she declares that the little evidence of such participation must be somehow justified.[44] In other words, if philosophers say so, it must be true, or how could a student reject this position? Castellanos' rhetorical strategy is to reverse the predicament of feminine participation in culture. Instead of arguing, as has been done among feminists, that in fact there is a provable feminine cultural production in the work of some women, even though they are few, Castellanos decides to justify the exceptions by means of the philosophical discourse that *a priori* she regards as true.

If "once upon a time" men and women had access to eternity, men through art and women through motherhood, this is no longer the case. According to Castellanos, motherhood has been degraded and no longer enjoys social value. Since many women are aware of that, for some time they have chosen to do things differently from the "biology is destiny" mandate. In this aspect, Castellanos seems to agree with de Beauvoir in the assertion that the sex that "gives birth" has been devalued. De Beauvoir points out that "Life is not the supreme value for man; on the contrary, life must serve more important purposes than life itself... It is not in giving life but in risking life that man is raised above the animal; that is why superiority has been accorded in humanity not to the sex that brings forth but to that which kills."[45] Castellanos does not acknowledge the superiority of men; however, she states that, from a cultural perspective, the sex that "brings forth" seems not to have any value. On thinking of the philosophical equation woman=nature, Castellanos believes that the reproductive function no longer confers any sense of permanence, and consequently, any value for the existent individual. She argues that the maximum value of the Western world is granted to institutions and art, which have been produced mostly by men.

Castellanos focuses on a fundamental question: women's participation in culture. Given her lack of documentation and preparation, the philosophers she consults to deal with the matter —Schopenhauer, Weininger, Simmel, Moebius—her rage together with the intuition that something was wrong, the discontinuity in her dissertation was inevitable. In fact, the ironization of the opposing philosophical terms that mediate their meanings becomes a deconstruction that does not manage to be theorized in her thesis. As a result, *On Feminine Culture* can be better defined as a document by means of which Castellanos maintains a prolonged dialogue with the authorities in her search

---

44. Castellanos, *Sobre cultura femenina*, 32.
45. Beauvoir, *The Second Sex*, 72.

for self-knowledge. She succeeds in demystifying them through the support of extreme strategic positions, be it on the side of culture or of nature, with the aim of invalidating all of them: them and herself. In contrast with the fact that women need to make use of cultural production to obtain permanence, Castellanos protects her faith in writing and in feminine cultural production.

In the first chapter of her dissertation, Castellanos summarizes the ideas of the mentioned philosophers only to conclude that for them feminine culture does not exist. In the second chapter she says that culture "is a world different from the one in which I vegetate."[46] Castellanos is aware that philosophy excludes women because when philosophers refer to them, it is to marginalize them as participants in the epistemological and ontological project of rational culture. She emphasizes that the "authorities" agree that women are not rational beings. It is odd that Castellanos, when reviewing the different father philosophers she consulted, never mentions José Ortega y Gasset. Ortega, for example, has said explicitly: "The more man one is, the more he feels full of rationality. All he does and actualizes, he does and actualizes for a reason, especially for a practical reason." And it is not possible to assume that Ortega is referring to humanity when he says "man" because he continues his thought: "Woman's love, the divine offering of the ultra-interiority of her being that the impassioned woman realizes, is perhaps the only thing that is not actualized through reason. The nucleus of the feminine mind, no matter how intelligent, is occupied by an irrational force. If man is the rational being, woman is the irrational being."[47] Castellanos probably did not know of these texts of Ortega, or maybe she did not wish to question any Hispanic philosopher, because she would have had to defend her points of view before Ortega's admirers or her colleagues. At another time, Castellanos wrote an essay in which she places Ortega among "the bourgeois intellectuals who, in spite of having discovered that history moves unceasingly, they continue to confuse their peculiar form of culture and civilization with the only possible culture and the only possible civilization..."[48] As a Spanish philosopher, in effect, his point of view is a colonizing one.

In short, the examined philosophers believe that the active creation of culture is masculine, an activity for which woman is not "naturally" endowed. Instead of disagreeing with the authorities, Castellanos chooses to agree with them and

---

46. Castellanos, *Sobre cultura femenina*, 34.
47. José Ortega y Gasset, "Landscape with a Deer in the Background," in *On Love: Aspects of a Single Theme* (New York: Meridian, 1957), 151-168.
48. Rosario Castellanos, *Juicios sumarios* (Xalapa, Veracruz: Universidad Veracruzana, 1966), 417-418.

is ironic in her choice. Refusing direct tactics, she assumes the inferior position assigned to her sex in the way of Sor Juana Inés de la Cruz in *The Answer (La Respuesta)* and Virginia Woolf in *Three Guineas*. When adopting this position, which is also an interpretive method, Castellanos argues that given the fact that she is a woman, she is constitutionally incompetent to use the methods elaborated by men; for example, logic, since the authorities mentioned in the first chapter said so. She writes:

> ... not only does my feminine mind feel completely off-center when I try to make it work according to certain invented norms, practiced by men and dedicated to masculine minds, but my feminine mind is far beneath those norms and it is too weak and scarce to rise and reach their level... But is there a specific way of thinking for us women?... The most venerable authors assert that it is a direct, dark, inexplicable, and usually accurate intuition. Well, then, I shall let myself be guided by my intuition.[49]

Implicitly, Castellanos also assumes some of Woolf's questions and answers; for example, "what is this 'civilization' in which we find ourselves? What are these ceremonies and why should we take part in them? What are these professions and why should we make money out of them? Where in short is it leading us, the procession of the sons of educated men?"[50] In the example of the very comical chapter on methodology, Castellanos seems to have followed Woolf's advice against "intellectual prostitution" and "you must refuse to sell your brain for the sake of money. [. . .] But directly the mulberry tree begins to make you circle, break off. Pelt the tree with laughter."[51] In effect, philosophy is mocked. Culture is a world very different from the one she vegetates in. Castellanos covers up her nonconformity with ironic mocking and once in a while finds an opportunity to openly say: "an attitude is banned for me: that of feeling offended by the defects that those gentlemen whom I have read and quoted, accumulate on the sex I belong to."[52]

The exposition of her work intends to conform to the orthodox expectations of those documents: statement of the problem, method, research, and conclusions. However, when stating in the conclusions that women do not feel the

---

49. Castellanos, *Sobre cultura femenina*, 33.
50. Virginia Woolf, *Three Guineas* (New York: Harcourt Brace Jovanovich, 1966), 63.
51. Woolf, *Three Guineas,* 80.
52. Castellanos, *Sobre cultura femenina*, 31.

need to participate in cultural activities, because "[a] woman satisfies her need to become eternal through motherhood,"⁵³ the statement does not specify that in the chapter where this topic is analyzed, she made fun of masculine fears regarding women when she says: "Every woman is, before marriage, a potential Circe. And after marriage, a full Circe. And every unmarried man is a candidate to be Circe's victim. And once married, a candidate is metamorphosed into . . . victim."⁵⁴ The "authorities" deny the existence of feminine culture and declare that the fate of woman is motherhood. Castellanos then tries to prove that women do not feel the need to participate in culture because they have access to eternity through motherhood. Her exaggerated interpretation of women's wish to be mothers transforms men into studs:

> A woman chases a man and fools him with the lure of beauty, of happiness, of pleasure, but deep down she is working for the possible offspring, and in a man, she looks not for the human being but for the male, not the person but the father. She tries to separate her partner from any interest that gravitates outside the sexual and family orbit because she wants to make him the most adequate instrument for her purposes.⁵⁵

Castellanos reduces to absurdity the philosophers' positions concerning women and that of women concerning men. She mocks masculine anxiety of paternal legitimacy: "He does not have, cannot have the absolute and harrowing evidence that the child is his."⁵⁶

As a method, ironic rhetoric in *On Feminine Culture* is useful to Castellanos to achieve distancing and not take direct responsibility for comments and criticism, as well as to support the notion that woman represents irrationality itself. On one hand, Castellanos does not want to back the idea that there has been no feminine cultural production; on the other, she also does not want to defend all women considering only a few, as "feminist men" do.⁵⁷ Nevertheless, once she places herself outside the culture "created almost exclusively by men"⁵⁸ and she accepts the notion that there is no feminine culture because it has not

---

53. Castellanos, *Sobre cultura femenina*, 101.
54. Castellanos, *Sobre cultura femenina*, 80.
55. Castellanos, *Sobre cultura femenina*, 84.
56. Castellanos, *Sobre cultura fernenina*, 83.
57. Castellanos, *Sobre cultura femenina*, 89.
58. Castellanos, *Sobre cultura femenina*, 89.

been necessary for women since motherhood is enough to make them eternal, Castellanos gets trapped in her own rhetoric. In other words, she uses conceptual dichotomies to exploit to absurdity sexual differences; but this puts her in a negativist impasse. Irony is not a suitable device to initiate positive action for and by women. The trap obviously emerges in the last chapter, where it is clear that she wants to support a positive feminist manifesto with cultural objectives, and she had already "proved," with a rationalistic mask, that women do not need to produce culture. Thus, in Castellanos' dissertation, the frustrating contradiction of two positions is revealed: the wish to participate culturally as a feminine subject, and the fact that philosophy, as we know it, opens no space for feminine subjectivity, except negatively. This is due to the fact that philosophy has produced meanings based on opposing concepts, such as culture-nature, man-woman, and reason-emotion in which women (the feminine) are placed *a priori* in the negative position. From this deconstructive practice, Castellanos learns how to pivot onto(theo)logical philosophic systems.

It is very possible that Castellanos could have avoided these rhetorical traps if she had proposed writing a feminist manifesto from the beginning. But to declare oneself a feminist in 1950 (and even today) would have been difficult, since feminists have been ridiculed during all of the 20th century, and even Simone de Beauvoir in *The Second Sex* and Virginia Woolf in *Three Guineas* deny it. Nevertheless, we must remember that Castellanos suspected that the matter of women was (and is) much more complex than what was postulated in the mid-20th century. Castellanos, then, proposes a paradoxical strategy by denying feminism in the context of philosophy on the one hand, and of herself and her women readers on the other, asserting it without using the term.

Once Castellanos has established that literature has been one of the few cultural openings for women, she considers this is due to its mimetic basis, and she adds:

> If it is imperative for women to write, we should hope, at least, that they do it by delving deeper and deeper into their own being... What we would hope is that she reverses the direction of that movement (since she does not reverse the direction of the movement that separates her from her femininity confining her to an imitation of the male), turning it towards her own being, but with such an impetus that she will exceed the immediate and despicable periphery of appearances and plunge so deeply that she will reach her true, and until now

unviolated root, putting aside the conventional images presented by the male to form her own image, her image based on her personal untransferable experience, image that may coincide with the other one but that may also differ. And once that depth is reached (which tradition does not acknowledge or falsifies, and which the usual concepts do not reveal), she should make it emerge to the conscious surface and liberate it through expression.[59]

Castellanos believed it was possible to write as a woman, without moving away from femininity, because if she moved away she would fall into the opposite term, masculinity, in the imitation of the male. In other words, even though Castellanos questions the traditional values of the binary relation, she does not move out of the system but places herself in the historical ontological margin as a contingent feminine subject. This is how she values the "untransferable experience." It is obvious that Castellanos was an avant-garde feminist theorist, coinciding in her position with many contemporary writers, for example, the North American poet Adrienne Rich who in the 1970s began theorizing feminism. Compare the quoted fragment of Castellanos with the following by Rich:

> Feminism begins but cannot end with the discovery by an individual of her self-consciousness as a woman. It is not, finally, even the recognition of her reasons for anger, or the decision to change her life... Feminism means finally that we renounce our obedience to the fathers and recognize that the world they have described is not the whole world. Masculine ideologies are the creation of masculine subjectivity; they are neither objective, nor value-free, nor inclusively "human." Feminism implies that we recognize for us, the distortion, of male-created ideologies, and that we proceed to think, and act, out of that recognition.[60]

Castellanos' feminist trajectory is often inhibited and complicated, not only because of "the quantity and quality of internal resistances that have to be overcome in order to express oneself, recognizing an objective fact,"[61] but also because of her other main concern: the socio-economic oppression of one cultural group by another and the attempt to understand their colonizing

---

59. Castellanos, *Sobre cultura femenina*, 97.
60. Adrienne Rich, *On Lies, Secrets and Silence* (New York: W.W. Norton, 1979), 207.
61. Castellanos, "La liberación de la mujer aquí," in *El uso de la palabra*, 58.

methods. The model for the latter arises from her experience in Chiapas and is brilliantly expressed in *Oficio de Tinieblas* [*The Book of Lamentations*]. In *On Feminine Culture*, Castellanos discovers that women constitute a rhetorical fantasy first constructed by philosophers; this brings about her wish to put aside "the conventional images of femininity that males provide for her to form her own image."[62] This is a calling for self-awareness, self-construction, and self-definition that can differ from the inherited thinking.

More than one commentator has been confused by the title of the thesis: *On Feminine Culture*. Margit Frenk Alatorre in her review in 1950 takes Castellanos literally and says that "the author has surrendered to a fatalist pessimism and, due to her own position as an intellectual woman in the midst of a masculine, and sometimes hostile, world, has seen all doors as closed and has considered life as something definitely and inflexibly fixed by the fundamental trends of human nature."[63] Apparently, Frenk Alatorre wished for a more "reasonable," more measured, more "serious" discussion, and feels disappointed by the "method" chosen by Castellanos. She is successful in making us question the conceptual dichotomies, that is, a binary logic, and in her final declaration, Castellanos refuses to place herself as a "disembodied spirit," term used by Adrienne Rich referring to intellectual women who, in order to escape the trap of the body, "have insisted they are first of all human beings" and consequently have "minimized their physicality and their connections with other women."[64]

As Sor Juana and Virginia Woolf did, Rosario Castellanos controls and disguises her intellectual rage by means of the self-conscious presupposition of her inferiority based on her sex. For example, she says that "From his point of view, I (and with me all women) am inferior [...] From my point of view, traditionally shaped by his, I also am."[65] The consciousness of assigned inferiority given by his sex comes not only from the masculine hostile intellectual environment which Frenk Alatorre mentions but also has its roots in rejection. According to Poniatowska, they said to her: "Why did your brother die and not you? You should have died so that our son could have inherited the estate."[66] The emphasis on the importance of the son over the daughter cannot be clearer. It

---

62. Castellanos, *Mujer que sabe latín...*, 202.
63. Margit Frenk Alatorre, "Sobre cultura femenina," *México en la cultura*, no. 97 (1950): 7.
64. Adrienne Rich, *Of Woman Born* (New York: Bantam Books, 1977) 21-22.
65. Castellanos, *Sobre cultura femenina*, 31-33,
66. Elena Poniatowska, "Rosario Castellanos," *La Cultura* en *México*, no. 1106 (1974): 8.

is very probable that Castellanos lived with this lament until her parents died in 1948 and with its echo for the rest of her life.

Poniatowska adds that what Castellanos most wanted "was to implant herself in people with love."[67] This leads to the appearance of a crucial dilemma for Castellanos and her subsequent work: how to reconcile the rejection produced because of her sex with the need to love and be loved? Before solving this dilemma—if it can be solved—Castellanos again, as in the writing of her dissertation, assumes a challenging position which is like mental salvation. She declares in *Two Poems* (1950):

> I shall be silent someday, but I will have said before
> that the man who walks down the street is my brother,
> that I am where
> the woman with vegetable attributes is.

Simultaneously, she refuses to relinquish her sisterhood with all women, those with "vegetable attributes" according to philosophers, and she also refuses to relinquish the notion of universal siblinghood. She continues in the same poem:

> Beyond my skin and further inside
> my bones, have I loved.
> Beyond my mouth and its words,
> beyond the knot of my tormented sex.
> I shall not die of disease
> nor old age, anguish, or fatigue.
> I shall die of love, I shall surrender
> to the deepest bosom.
> I will no longer be ashamed of these empty hands
> nor of this hermetic cell called Rosario.[68]

At the same time, she refuses to be defeated by rejection and loneliness, she chooses love as a path to universal and personal salvation. However, at this moment of her career, that is 1950, Castellanos has not yet built a definition of love. It is a promising concept and feeling, but how should it be experienced, how should it be lived, given, and received? As some Chicanas of our time have wondered, can we build a decolonial love?

---

67. Poniatowska, "Rosario Castellanos," 8.
68. Castellanos, "Dos Poemas," in *Poesía no eres tú*, 51.

Simone de Beauvoir has said that "love has been assigned to the woman as her supreme vocation"[69] and that woman, often without questioning herself, has given herself to her "task," and the consequences are that "she has nothing to hold on to in order to understand the world, she does not transcend her (domestic) subjectivity, her freedom remains frustrated... She has only one way of authentically using her freedom, and that is by projecting it through positive action in society."[70]

Notwithstanding de Beauvoir's observations, the critical dilemma for Castellanos is that when dedicating herself to literature, and even perceiving it as a social act, she is distanced from the "positive action in society" itself. In other words, for a long time, her feminism is in fact textual, dedicated to naming and protesting against the unfolding of the feminine difference in the onto(theo)logy that is her cultural heritage. Castellanos preferred to rescue the sense of the feminine body and spirit, that is, how women are perceived or how they perceive themselves, and what is the ideology from which she writes. This wish is what motivates much of her work, including *On Feminine Culture, Balún Canán,* and her collection of poems, *Poesía no eres tú [Poetry is not you]*. To the question of 'Why write?' she responds in a late poem:

> I write because one day, as a teenager,
> I leaned towards a mirror and no one was there.[71]

---

69. Beauvoir, *The Second Sex,* 743.
70. Beauvoir, *The Second Sex,* 752-753.
71. Castellanos, "Entrevista de Prensa," in *Poesía no eres tú,* 303.

BIBLIOGRAPHY

Alatorre, Margit Frenk. "Sobre cultura femenina." *México en la cultura,* no. 97 (December 10, 1950).

Baptiste, Victor. "La obra poética de Rosario Castellanos." PhD Dissertation. University of Illinois, 1967.

Barthes, Roland. *Writing Degree Zero.* Boston: Beacon Press, 1970.

Beauvoir, Simone de. *The Second Sex.* Translated and edited by H.M. Parshley. New York: Vintage Books, 1974

Bergson, Henri. *Materia y Memoria. Ensayo sobre la relación del cuerpo con el espíritu.* Translated by Navarro. Madrid: Imprenta de Victoriano Suárez, 1900.

Brito de Martí, Esperanza. "Rosario Castellanos." ¡*Siempre!* (14 nov. 1973).

Castellanos, Rosario. *Mujer que sabe latín . . . .* México City: SepSetentas, 1973.

Castellanos, Rosario. "Dos Poemas." In *Poesía no eres tú.* México: Fondo de Cultura Económica, 1972.

Castellanos, Rosario. *El uso de la palabra,* In *Excélsior.* Translated by José Emilio Pacheco and Danubio Torres Fierro. México: Ediciones de Excélsior, 1974.

Castellanos, Rosario. *Juicios sumarios.* Xalapa, Veracruz: Universidad Veracruzana, 1966.

Castellanos, Rosario. "Entrevista de Prensa." In *Poesía no eres tú.* México: Fondo de Cultura Económica, 1972), 303.

Castellanos, Rosario. *Balún Canán.* México: Fondo de Cultura Económica, 1973.

Castellanos, Rosario. *Sobre cultura femenina.* México: *América Revista Antológica.* Ediciones de América, 1950.

Castellanos, Rosario. *Los convidados de agosto.* México: Ediciones Era, 1977.

Dybvig, Rhoda. *Rosario Castellanos: Biografía y novelística.* México: Ed. de Andrea, 1965.

Lindstrom, Naomi. "Rosario Castellanos: Representing Woman's Voice." *Letras femeninas* 5, no. 2 (1979): 29-30.

Ortega y Gasset, José. "Landscape with a Deer in the Background." In *On Love: Aspects of a Single Theme.* New York: Meridian, 1957.

Passmore, John. *A Hundred Years of Philosophy.* New York: Penguin Books, 1978.

Paz, Octavio. *Libertad bajo palabra.* México: Fondo de Cultura Económica, 1968.

Paz, Octavio. *Corriente alterna.* México: Siglo XXI Editores, 1970.

Poniatowska, Elena. "Rosario Castellanos." *México en la cultura,* no. 26 (1958): 7, 10.

Poniatowska, Elena. "Rosario Castellanos." *La Cultura* en *México,* no. 1106 (1974).

Rich, Adrienne. *Of Woman Born.* New York: Bantam Books, 1977.

Rich, Adrienne. *On Lies, Secrets and Silence.* New York: W.W. Norton, 1979.

"Rosario Castellanos." In *Los narradores ante el público.* 89-98. México: Joaquín Mortiz, 1966.

"Rosario Castellanos." In *Hispanic Arts* 1, No. 2 (Autumn, 1967): 67-70.

Sartre, Jean-Paul. *The Words.* Translated by Bernard Frechtman. New York: Vintage Books, 1981.

Weil, Simone. *Lectures on Philosophy.* London: Cambridge University Press, 1978.

Wilson, Jason. *Octavio Paz: A Study of His Poetics.* New York: Cambridge University Press, 1979.

Woolf, Virginia. *Moments of Being.* New York: A Harvest/HBJ Book, 1976.

Woolf, Virginia. *Three Guineas.* New York: Harcourt Brace Jovanovich, 1966.

PART II

THEORETICAL SUBJECTS

THE THEORETICAL SUBJECT(S) OF *THIS BRIDGE CALLED MY BACK* AND ANGLO-AMERICAN FEMINISM[1]

→ ←

This Bridge Called My Back: Writings by Radical Women of Color, edited by Chicana writers Cherríe Moraga and Gloria Anzaldúa,[2] was intended as a collection of essays, poems, tales, and testimonials that would give voice to the contradictory experiences of "women of color." To make explicit this end, the editors wrote:

> We are the colored in a white feminist movement.
> We are the feminists among the people of our culture.
> We are often the lesbians among the straight.[3]

By giving voice to such experiences, each according to her style, the editors and contributors believed they were developing a theory of subjectivity and culture that would demonstrate the considerable difference between them and Anglo-American women, as well as between Anglo-European men and men of their culture.

As a speaking subject of an emergent discursive formation, the writer in *Bridge* was aware of the displacement of her subjectivity across a multiplicity of discourses: feminist/lesbian, nationalist, racial, and socioeconomic. The peculiarity of her displacement implied a multiplicity of positions from which she was driven to grasp or understand herself and her relations with the real, in the Althusserian sense of the word.[4] The writer in *Bridge*, in part, was aware that these positions were often incompatible or contradictory, and problematic, since many readers would not have access to the maze of discourses competing

---

1. *Editors' Note:* This essay was previously published in *Criticism in the Borderlands: Studies in Chicano Literature, Culture, and Ideology*, ed. Hector Calderón and José David Saldívar (Durham, NC: Duke University Press, 1991), 28-42. Also in *Making Face, Making Soul: Creative and Critical Perspectives by Feminists of Color* (San Francisco: Aunt Lute Foundation, 1990) 356-369; *The Postmodern Turn: New Perspectives on Social Theory* (Cambridge UP, 1994), 140-152; *The Second Wave: A Reader in Feminist Theory* (Routledge, 1997), 288-299; and *The New Social Theory Reader: Contemporary Debates 2001*), 309-320. We include the version from *Criticism in the Borderlands.*.

2. Hereinafter cited as *Bridge*, the book has had four editions. I use the second edition, published by Cherríe Moraga and Gloria Anzaldúa, eds, *This Bridge Called my Back: Writings by Radical Women of Color*, (New York: Kitchen Table, Women of Color Press, 1983). The first edition was published by Persephone Press, 1981.

3. Moraga and Anzaldúa, *Bridge*, 23.

4. Louis Althusser, *Lenin and Philosophy and Other Essays*, trans. Ben Brewster (New York: Monthly Review Press, 1971).

for her body and her voice. This self-conscious effort to reflect on her "flesh and blood experiences to concretize a vision that [could] begin to heal [their] 'wounded knee'"[5] led many a *Bridge* speaker to take up a position in conflict with multiple inter- and intracultural discursive interpretations in an effort to come to grips with "the many-headed demon of oppression."[6]

Since its publication in 1981, *Bridge* has had a diverse impact on feminist writings in the United States. Teresa de Lauretis, for example, claims that *Bridge* has contributed to a "shift in feminist consciousness,"[7] although her explanation fails to clarify what the shift consists of and for whom. There is little doubt, however, that *Bridge* along with eighties writings by many women of color in the United States has problematized many a version of Anglo-American feminism and has helped open the way for alternate feminist discourses and theories.

Presently, however, the impact among most Anglo-American theorists appears to be more cosmetic than not because, as Jane Flax has recently noted, "The modal 'person' in feminist theory still appears to be a self-sufficient individual adult."[8] This particular "modal person" corresponds to the female subject most admired in Western literature which Gayatri Chakravorty Spivak has characterized as the one who "articulates herself in shifting relationship to . . . the constitution and 'interpellation' of the subject not only as individual but as 'individualist.'"[9] Consequently, the "native female" or "woman of color" can be excluded from the discourse of feminist theory. The 'native female,' the object of colonialism and racism, is excluded because, in Flax's terms, white feminists have not "explored how our understanding of gender relations, self, and theory is partially constituted in and through experiences of living in a culture in which asymmetric race relations are a central organizing principle of society."[10]

It is clear that the most popular subject of Anglo-American feminist theorizing is an autonomous, self-making, self-determining subject who first proceeds according to the *logic of identification* with regard to the subject of consciousness, a notion usually viewed as the purview of man, but now claimed for women.[11] And

---

5. Moraga and Anzaldúa, *Bridge*, 23.

6. Moraga and Anzaldúa, *Bridge*, 195.

7. Teresa de Lauretis, "Feminist Studies/Critical Studies: Issues, Terms, and Contexts," *Feminist Studies/ Critical Studies*, ed. Teresa de Lauretis (Bloomington: Indiana University Press, 1987), 10.

8. Jane Flax, "Postmodernism and Gender Relations in Feminist Theory." *Signs* 12, no. 4 (1987): 640.

9. Gayatri Chakravorty Spivak, "Three Women's Texts and a Critique of Imperialism," *Critical Inquiry* 12, no. 1 (1985): 243-44.

10. Flax, "Postmodernism and Gender Relations in Feminist Theory," 640.

11. See Julia Kristeva, "Women's Time," trans. Alice Jardine and William Blake, *Signs* 7, no. 1 (1981): 19.

believing that in this respect she is the same as man, she now claims the right to pursue her own identity, to name herself, to pursue self-knowledge, and in the words of Adrienne Rich to effect "a change in the concept of sexual identity."[12]

Though feminism has problematized gender relations as "the single most important advance in feminist theory,"[13] it has not problematized the subject of knowledge and her complicity with the notion of consciousness as "synthetic unificatory power, the centre and active point of organization of representations determining their concatenation."[14] The subject (and object) of knowledge is now a woman, but the inherited view of consciousness has not been questioned at all. As a result, some Anglo-American feminist subjects of consciousness have tended to become a parody of the masculine subject of consciousness, thus revealing their ethnocentric liberal underpinnings.

In 1982 Jean Bethke Elshtain noted the "masculine cast" of radical feminist language, specifically citing the terms "raw power, brute force, martial discipline, law and order with a feminist face—and voice."[15] Also, in critiquing liberal feminism and its language, she wrote that "no vision of the political community that might serve as the groundwork of a life in common is possible within a political life dominated by a self-interested, predatory individualism."[16] Althusser has argued that this tradition "has privileged the category of the 'subject' as Origin, Essence, and Cause, responsible in its internality for all determinations of the external object. In other words, this tradition has promoted Man, in his ideas and experience, as the source of knowledge, morals and history."[17] By identifying in this way with this tradition, standpoint epistemologists have substituted, ironically, woman for man.

This logic of identification as a first step in constructing the theoretical subject of feminism is often veiled from standpoint epistemologists because greater attention is given to naming female identity and describing women's

---

12. Adrienne Rich, *On Lies, Secrets and Silence: Selected Prose, 1966–1978* (New York: W. W Norton & Company, 1979), 35.

13. Flax, "Postmodernism and Gender Relations in Feminist Theory,"627.

14. Michael Pêcheux, *Language, Semantics and Ideology*, trans. Harbans Nagpal (London: Macmillan, 1982), 122.

15. Jean Bethke Elshtain, "Feminist Discourse and Its Discontents: Language, Power, and Meaning," *Signs* 7, no. 3, (1982): 611.

16. Elshtain, "Feminist Discourse and Its Discontents," 617.

17. Louis Althusser, quoted in Diane Macdonell, *Theories of Discourse* (Oxford: Basil Blackwell, 1986), 76

ways of knowing as being considerably different than men's.[18] By emphasizing "sexual difference," a second step takes place, often called oppositional thinking (counteridentifying). However, this gendered standpoint epistemology leads to feminism's bizarre relationship with other liberation movements, working inherently against the interests of non-white women and no one else.

Sandra Harding, for example, argues that oppositional thinking (counteridentification) with white men should be retained even though "There are suggestions in the literature of Native Americans, Africans, and Asians that what feminists call feminine versus masculine personalities, ontologies, ethics, epistemologies, and world views may be what these other liberation movements call non-Western versus Western personalities and world views.... I set aside the crucial and fatal complication for this way of thinking—the fact that one-half of these people are women and that most women are not Western."[19] She further suggests that feminists respond by relinquishing the totalizing "master theory" character of our theory making: "This response to the issue (will manage) to retain the categories of feminist theory... and simply set them alongside the categories of the theory making of other subjugated groups... Of course, it leaves bifurcated (and perhaps even more finely divided) the identities of all except ruling-class white Western women."[20] The apperception of this situation is precisely what led to the choice of title for the book *All the Women Are White, All the Blacks Are Men, But Some of Us Are Brave*, edited by Gloria T. Hull, Patricia Bell Scott, and Barbara Smith.[21]

Notwithstanding the power of *Bridge* to affect the personal lives of its readers, *Bridge's* challenge to the Anglo-American subject of feminism has yet to affect a newer discourse. Women of color often recognize themselves in the pages of *Bridge* and write to say "The women writers seemed to be speaking to me, and they actually understood what I was going through. Many of you put into words feelings I have had that I had no way of expressing.... The writings justified some of my thoughts telling me I had a right to feel as I did."[22] However, Anglo feminist readers of *Bridge* tend to appropriate it, cite it as an instance of

---

18. For an intriguing demonstration of these operations, see Seyla Benhabib, "The Generalized and the Concrete Other: The Kohlberg-Gilligan Controversy and Feminist Theory," in *Feminism as Critique*, eds. Seyla Benhabib and Drucilla Cornell (Minneapolis: University of Minnesota Press, 1987), 77-95.

19. Sandra Harding, *The Science Question in Feminism* (Ithaca, NY: Cornell University Press, 1986), 659.

20. Harding, *The Science Question in Feminism*, 660.

21. Gloria T. Hull, Patricia Bell Scott, and Barbara Smith, eds, *All the Women Are White, All the Blacks Are Men, But Some of Us Are Brave* (New York: Feminist Press, 1982).

22. Moraga, "Foreword" in Moraga and Anzaldúa, eds, *This Bridge Called My Back*, 14.

difference between women, and proceed to negate that difference by subsuming women of color into the unitary category of woman/women. The latter is often viewed as the "common denominator"²³ between us, though it is forgotten that it is our "common denominator" in an oppositional (counteridentifying) discourse with some white men that leaves us unable to explore relationships among women.

Bridge's writers did not see the so-called "common denominator" as the solution for the construction of the theoretical feminist subject. In the call for submissions, the editors clearly stated: "We want to express to all women—especially to white middle-class women—the experiences which divide us as feminists; we want to examine the incidents of intolerance, prejudice, and denial of differences within the feminist movement. We intend to explore the causes, and sources of, and solutions to these divisions. We want to create a definition that expands what 'feminist' means to us."²⁴ Thus, the female subject of *Bridge* is highly complex. She is and has been constructed in a crisis-of-meaning situation which includes racial and cultural divisions and conflicts. The psychic and material violence that gives shape to that subjectivity cannot be underestimated nor passed over lightly. The fact that not all of this violence comes from men in general but also from women renders the notion of "common denominator" problematic.

It is clear, however, that even as *Bridge* becomes a resource for the Anglo-American feminist theory classroom and syllabus, there's a tendency to deny differences if these differences pose a threat to the "common denominator" category. That is, solidarity would be purchased with silence, putting aside the conflictive history of groups' interrelations and interdependence. In the words of Paula Treichler, "How do we address the issues and concerns raised by women of color, who may themselves be even more excluded from theoretical feminist discourse than from the women's studies curriculum? . . . Can we explore our 'common differences' without overemphasizing the division that currently seems to characterize the feminism of the United States and the world?"²⁵ This exploration appears impossible without a reconfiguration of the subject of feminist theory, and her relational position to a multiplicity of others, not just white men.

Some recent critics of the "exclusionary practices in Women's Studies" have noted that gender standpoint epistemology leads to a "tacking on" of "Material about minority women" without any note of its "significance for feminist

---

23. de Lauretis, "Feminist Studies/Critical Studies," 14.
24. Moraga and Anzaldúa, Introduction to the first edition, *Bridge,* xxiii.
25. Paula Treichler, "Teaching Feminist Theory," in *Theory in the Classroom*, ed. Cary Nelsen, ed. (Urbana: University of Illinois Press, 1986), 79.

knowledge."²⁶ The common approaches noted were the tendency to (1) treat race and class as secondary features in social organization (as well as representation) with primacy given to universal female subordination; (2) acknowledge that inequalities of race, class, and gender generate different experiences and then set aside race and class inequalities on the grounds that information was lacking to allow incorporation into an analysis; (3) focus on descriptive aspects of the ways of life, values, customs, and problems of women in subordinate race and class categories with little attempt to explain their source or their broader meaning.²⁷ In fact, it may be impossible for gender standpoint epistemology to ever do more than a "pretheoretical presentation of concrete problems."²⁸

Since the subject of feminist theory and its single theme—gender—go largely unquestioned, its point of view tends to suppress and repress voices that question its authority, and as Jane Flax remarks, "The suppression of these voices seems to be a necessary condition for the (apparent) authority, coherence, and universality of our own."²⁹ This may account for the inability to include the voices of women of color in feminist discourse, even though they are not necessarily underrepresented in reading lists.

For standpoint epistemologists, the desire to construct a feminist theory based solely on gender, on the one hand, and the knowledge or implicit recognition that such an account might distort the representation of many women and/or correspond to that of some men, on the other, gives rise to anxiety and ambivalence for the future of that feminism, especially in Anglo-America. At the core of that attitude is the often unstated recognition that if the pervasiveness of women's oppression is virtually universal on some level, it is also highly diverse from group to group and that women themselves may become complicitous with that oppression. "Complicity arises," says Macdonell, "where through lack of a positive starting point either a practice is driven to make use of prevailing values or a critique becomes the basis for a new theory."³⁰

The inclusion of other analytical categories such as race and class becomes impossible for a subject whose consciousness refuses to acknowledge that "one becomes a woman" in ways that are much more complex than simple opposition

---

26. Maxine Baca Zinn, Lynn Weber Cannon, Elizabeth Higginbotham, and Bonnie Thornton, "The Costs of Exclusionary Practices in Women's Studies," *Signs*, vol. 11, no. 2 (1986): 296.

27. Baca Zinn et al., "The Costs of Exclusionary Practices in Women's Studies," 296.

28. Baca Zinn et al., "The Costs of Exclusionary Practices in Women's Studies," 297.

29. Flax, "Postmodernism and Gender Relations in Feminist Theory," 633.

30. Diane Macdonell, *Theories of Discourse* (Oxford: Blackwell, 1986.), 62.

to men. In cultures in which asymmetric race and class relations are a central organizing principle of society, one may also "become a woman" in opposition to other women. In other words, the whole category of woman may also need to be problematized, a point that I shall take up below.

Simone de Beauvoir and her key work *The Second Sex* have been most influential in the development of feminist standpoint epistemology.[31] She may even be responsible for the creation of Anglo-American feminist theory's "episteme:" a highly self-conscious ruling-class white Western female subject locked in a struggle to the death with "Man." De Beauvoir shook the world of women, most especially with the ramifications of her phrase, "One is not born, but rather becomes, a woman."[32] For over 400 pages of text after that statement, de Beauvoir demonstrates how a female is constituted as a "woman" by society as her freedom is curtailed from childhood. The curtailment of freedom incapacitates her from affirming "herself as a subject."[33] Very few women, indeed, can escape the cycle of indoctrination except perhaps the writer/intellectual because "She knows that she is a conscious being, a subject."[34] This particular kind of woman can perhaps make of her gender a project and transform her sexual identity.

But what of those women who are not so privileged, who neither have the political freedom nor the education? Do they now occupy the place of the Other (the "Brave") while some women become subjects? Or do we have to make a subject of the whole world?

Regardless of our point of view on this matter, the way to becoming a female subject has been effected through consciousness-raising. In 1982, in a major theoretical essay, "Feminism, Marxism, Method, and the State: An Agenda for Theory," Catherine A. MacKinnon cited *Bridge* as a book that explored the relationship between sex and race and argued that "consciousness-raising" was *the* feminist method.[35] The reference to *Bridge* is brief. It served as an example, along with other texts, of the challenge that race and nationalism have posed for Marxism. According to her, Marxism has been unable to account for the appearance of these emancipatory discourses nor has it been able to assimilate them. Nevertheless, MacKinnon's major point was to demonstrate the epistemological challenge that

---

31. Simone de Beauvoir, *The Second Sex,* trans. H. M. Parshley (New York: Vintage Books, 1974).
32. De Beauvoir, *The Second Sex,* 301.
33. De Beauvoir, *The Second Sex,* 316.
34. De Beauvoir, *The Second Sex,* 761.
35. MacKinnon, Catherine A., "Feminism, Marxism, Method, and the State: An Agenda for Theory," *Feminist Theory* 7, no. 3 (1982): 336-381.

feminism and its primary method, "consciousness-raising," posed for Marxism. Within Marxism class as a method of analysis had failed to reckon with the historical force of sexism. Through "consciousness-raising," (from women's point of view) women are led to know the world differently. Women's experience of politics, of life as sex objects, gives rise to its own method of appropriating that reality: the feminist method.[36] It challenges the objectivity of the "empirical gaze" and "rejects the distinction between knowing subject and known object."[37] By having women be the subject of knowledge, the so-called "objectivity" of men is brought into question. Often this leads to privileging women's way of knowing in opposition to men's way of knowing, thus sustaining the very binary opposition that feminism would like to change or transform. Admittedly, this is only one of the many paradoxical procedures in feminist thinking as Nancy Cott confirms, "It acknowledges diversity among women while positing that women recognize their unity. It requires gender consciousness for its basis, yet calls for the elimination of prescribed gender roles."[38]

However, I suspect that these contradictions or paradoxes have more profound implications than is readily apparent. Part of the problem may be that as feminist practice and theory recuperate their sexual differential through "consciousness-raising," women reinscribe such a differential as feminist epistemology or theory. With gender as the central concept in feminist thinking, epistemology is flattened out in such a way that we lose sight of the complex and multiple ways in which the subject and object of possible experience are constituted. The flattening effect is multiplied when one considers that gender is often solely related to white men. There's no inquiry into the knowing subject beyond the fact of being a "woman." But what is a "woman" or a "man" for that matter? If we refuse to define either term according to some "essence," then we are left with having to specify their conventional significance in time and space, which is liable to change as knowledge increases or interests change.

The fact that Anglo-American feminism has appropriated the generic term for itself, leaves many a woman in this country having to call herself otherwise, that is, "women of color," which is equally "meaningless" without further specification. It also gives rise to the tautology, Chicana women.

Needless to say, the requirement of gender consciousness only in relationship to man leaves us in the dark about a good many things, including interracial and

---

36. MacKinnon, "Feminism, Marxism, Method, and the State," 536.
37. MacKinnon, "Feminism, Marxism, Method, and the State," 536.
38. Nancy F. Cott, *The Grounding of Modern Feminism* (New Haven, CT: Yale University Press, 1987), 49.

intercultural relations. It may well be that the only purpose this type of differential has is as a political strategy. It does not help us envision a world beyond binary restrictions, nor does it help us reconfigure feminist theory to include the "native female." It does, however, help us grasp the paradox that within this cultural context one cannot be a feminist without becoming a gendered subject of knowledge which makes it very difficult to transcend gender at all and to imagine relations between women.[39]

In *Feminist Politics and Human Nature*, Alison M. Jaggar, speaking as a socialist feminist, refers repeatedly to *Bridge* and other works by women of color unrepresented in feminist theory.[40] Jaggar claims that socialist feminism is inspired by Marxist and radical feminist politics though the latter has failed to be scientific about its insights. *Bridge* is cited various times to counter the racist and classist position of radical feminists.[41] Jaggar charges that "Radical feminism has encouraged women to name their own experience but it has not recognized explicitly that this experience must be analyzed, explained and theoretically transcended."[42] In a sense Jaggar's charge amounts to the notion that radical feminists were flattening out their knowledge by an inadequate methodology, that is, gender consciousness-raising.

Many of Jaggar's observations are a restatement of *Bridge*'s challenge to Anglo-American feminists of all political persuasions, be it liberal, radical, Marxist, or socialist, the types sketched out by Jaggar. For example, Jaggar's "A representation of reality from the standpoint of women must draw on the variety of all women's experience"[43] may be compared to Barbara Smith's view in *Bridge* that "Feminism is the political theory and practice to free *all* women: women of color, working-class women, poor women, physically challenged women, lesbians, old women, as well as white economically privileged heterosexual women."[44] Jaggar continues, "Since historically diverse groups of women, such as working-class women, women of color, and others have been excluded from intellectual work, they somehow must be enabled to participate as subjects as

---

39. For a detailed discussion of this theme, see Judith Butler, "Variations on Sex and Gender: Beauvoir, Wittig, and Foucault," *Praxis* 5, no. 4 (1986): 128-142.
40. Alison M. Jaggar, *Feminist Politics and Human Nature* (New Jersey: Rowman & Allanheld/Harvester Press, 1983).
41. Jaggar, *Feminist Politics and Human Nature*, 249-50, 295-96.
42. Jaggar, *Feminist Politics and Human Nature*, 381.
43. Jaggar, *Feminist Politics and Human Nature*, 386.
44. Smith, *Bridge*, 61.

well as objects of feminist theorizing."[45] Similarly, writers in *Bridge* appear to think that "consciousness-raising" and the naming of one's experience would deliver some theory and yield a notion of "what feminist means to us."[46] However, except for Smith's statement, there is no overarching view that would guide us as to "what feminist means to us." Though there is a tacit political identity—gender/class/race—encapsulated in the phrase "women of color" that connects the pieces, they tend to split apart into "vertical relations" between "culture of resistance" and the "culture resisted or from which excluded." Thus, the binary restrictions become as prevalent between race/ethnicity of oppressed versus oppressor as that between the sexes.

The problems inherent to Anglo-American feminism and race relations are so locked into the "Self-Other" theme that it is no surprise that *Bridge*'s coeditor Moraga would remark, "In the last three years I have learned that Third World feminism does not provide the kind of easy political framework that women of color are running to in droves. The *idea* of Third World feminism has proved to be much easier between the covers of a book than between real live women."[47] She refers to the United States, of course, because feminism is alive and well throughout the Third World largely within the purview of women's rights or as a class struggle.[48]

The appropriation of *Bridge*'s observations in Jaggar's work differs slightly from the others in its view of linguistic usage implying to a limited extent that language is also reflective of material existence. The crucial question is how indeed can women of color be subjects as well as objects of feminist theorizing? Jaggar cites María Lugones' doubts,

> We cannot talk to you in our language because you do not understand it.... The power of white Anglo women vis-a-vis Hispanas and African-American women is in inverse proportion to their working knowledge of each other.... Because of their ignorance, white Anglo women who try to do theory with women of color inevitably disrupt the dialogue. Before they can contribute to collective dialogue, they need to "know the text," to have become familiar with an alternative way of viewing the world.... You need to learn to become unintrusive,

---

45. Jaggar, *Feminist Politics and Human Nature,* 386.
46. Moraga and Anzaldúa, *Bridge,* xxiii.
47. Moraga, Foreword to the 2nd edition, *Bridge,* n.p.
48. See Miranda Davies, *Third World: Second Sex* (London: Zed Books, 1987).

unimportant, and patient to the point of tears, while at the same time open to learning any possible lessons. You will have to come to terms with the sense of alienation, of not belonging, of having your world thoroughly disrupted, having it criticized and scrutinized from the point of view of those who have been harmed by it, having important concepts central to it dismissed, being viewed with mistrust."[49]

Lugones' advice to Anglo women to listen was post-*Bridge*. But we should recall that one of *Bridge*'s breaks with prevailing conventions was, of course, linguistic. If prevailing conventions of speaking/writing had been observed many a contributor would have been censored or silenced. So would have many a major document or writing by minorities. *Bridge* leads us to understand that the silence and silencing of people begin with the dominating enforcement of linguistic conventions, the resistance to relational dialogues, as well as the disenablement of peoples by outlawing their forms of speech.

As already noted, Anglo-American feminist theory has assumed a speaking subject who is an autonomous, self-conscious individual woman; yet, it has also taken for granted the linguistic status which founds subjectivity. In this way, it appropriates woman/women for itself and turns its work into a theoretical project within which the rest of us are compelled to fit. By forgetting or refusing to take into account that we are culturally constituted in and through language in complex ways and not just engendered in a homogeneous situation, the Anglo-American subject of consciousness cannot come to terms with her [his] own class-biased ethnocentrism. She is blinded to her own construction not just as woman but as an Anglo-American one. Such a subject creates a theoretical subject that could not possibly include all women just because we are women.

Against this feminist backdrop many "women of color" have struggled to give voice to their subjectivity, as evidenced in the publication of the writings collected in *Bridge*. However, the freedom of women of color to posit themselves as multiple-voiced subjects is constantly in peril of repression precisely at that point where our constituted contradictions put them at odds with women different from themselves.

The pursuit of a "politics of unity" solely based on gender forecloses the "pursuit of solidarity" through different political formations and the exploration of alternative theories of the subject of consciousness. There is a tendency in

---

49. María C. Lugones and Elizabeth V. Spelman, "Have we got a theory for you! Feminist Theory, Cultural Imperialism and the Demand for 'The Woman's Voice,'" *Women's Studies International Forum*, 6, no. 6 (1983): 386.

more sophisticated and elaborate gender standpoint epistemologists to affirm "an identity made up of heterogeneous and heteronomous representations of gender, race, and class, and often indeed across languages and cultures"[50] with one breath and with the next to refuse to explore how that identity may be theorized or analyzed, by reconfirming a unified subjectivity or "shared consciousness" through gender. The difference is handed over with one hand and taken away with the other. If it were true, as Teresa de Lauretis has observed, that "Self and identity . . . are always grasped and understood within particular discursive configurations,"[51] it does not necessarily follow that one can easily and self-consciously decide "to reclaim (an identity) from a history of multiple assimilations"[52] and still retain a "shared consciousness." Such a practice goes counter to the homogenizing tendency of the subject of consciousness in the United States. To be oppressed means to be disenabled not only from grasping an "identity," but also from reclaiming it.

To grasp or reclaim an identity in this culture means always already to have become a subject of consciousness. The theory of the subject of consciousness as a unitary and synthesizing agent of knowledge is always already a posture of domination. One only has to think of Gloria Anzaldúa's essay in *Bridge*, "Speaking in Tongues: A Letter to Third World Women Writers."[53] Though de Lauretis concedes that a racial "shared consciousness," may have prior claims than gender, she still insists on unity through gender, "the female subject is always constructed and defined in gender, starting from gender."[54] One is interested in having more than an account of gender; there are other relations to be accounted for. De Lauretis still insists, in most of her work, that "the differences among women may be better understood as differences within women."[55] This position returns us all to our solitary, though different, consciousness, without noting that some differences are (have been) a result of relations of domination of women by women, that differences may be purposefully constituted for the purpose of domination or exclusion, especially in oppositional thinking.

Some of the writers in *Bridge* thought at some point in the seventies that feminism could have been the ideal answer to their hope for liberation. Chrystos,

---

50. de Lauretis, "Feminist Studies/Critical Studies," 9.
51. de Lauretis, "Feminist Studies/Critical Studies," 8.
52. de Lauretis, "Feminist Studies/Critical Studies," 9.
53. Gloria Anzaldúa, "Speaking in Tongues: A Letter to Third World Women Writers" in *This Bridge Called My Back,* eds. Cherríe Moraga and Gloria Anzaldúa (New York: Kitchen Table Press, 1983), 165-74.
54. de Lauretis, "Feminist Studies/Critical Studies," 19.
55. de Lauretis, "Feminist Studies/Critical Studies," 14.

for example, states her disillusionment as follows, "I no longer believe that feminism is a tool which can eliminate racism or even promote better understanding between different races & kinds of women."[56] The disillusionment is eloquently reformulated in the theme poem by Donna Kate Rushin, "The Bridge Poem."[57] The dream of helping the people who surround her to reach an interconnectedness that would change society is given up in favor of self-translation into a "true self." In my view, the speaker's refusal to play "bridge," an enablement to others as well as self, is the acceptance of defeat at the hands of political groups whose self-definition follows the view of self as unitary capable of being defined by a single "theme." The speaker's perception that the "self" is multiple ("I'm sick of mediating with your worst self / On behalf of your better selves"[58]) and its reduction harmful gives emphasis to the relationality between one's selves and those of others as an ongoing process of struggle, effort, and tension. Indeed, in this poem, the better "Bridging self" of the speaker is defeated by the overriding notion of the unitary subject of knowledge and consciousness so prevalent in Anglo-American culture.

Difference, whether it be sexual, racial, or social, has to be conceptualized within a political and an ideological domain.[59] In *Bridge*, for example, Mirtha Quintanales points out that "in this country, in this world, racism is used *both* to create false differences among us *and* to mask very significant ones—cultural, economic, political."[60]

Consciousness as a site of multiple voicings is the theoretical subject, par excellence, of *Bridge*. These voicings or thematic threads are not viewed as necessarily originating with the subject, but as discourses that transverse consciousness and which the subject must struggle with constantly. Rosario Morales, for example, says "I want to be whole. I want to claim myself to be Puerto Rican, and U.S. American, working class & middle class, housewife and intellectual, feminist, Marxist and anti-imperialist."[61] Gloria Anzaldúa observes, "What am I? *A third world lesbian feminist with Marxist and mystic leanings*. They would

---

56. Moraga and Anzaldúa, *Bridge*, 169.

57. Donna Kate Rushin, "The Bridge Poem," *This Bridge Called My Back*, eds. Cherríe Moraga and Gloria Anzaldúa, (New York: Kitchen Table Press, 1983), xxi-xxii.

58. Rushin, "The Bridge Poem," xxii.

59. Monique Wittig, cited in Elizabeth Meese, *Crossing the Double-Cross: The Practice of Feminist Criticism* (Chapel Hill: University of North Carolina Press, 1986), 74.

60. Moraga and Anzaldúa, Introduction to the first edition, *Bridge*, 153.

61. Rosario Morales, "We're All in the Same Boat" in *This Bridge Called My Back*, eds. Cherríe Moraga and Gloria Anzaldúa, 11.

chop me up into little fragments and tag each piece with a label."[62] The need to assign multiple registers of existence is an effect of the belief that knowledge of one's subjectivity cannot be arrived at through a single "theme." Indeed the multiple-voiced subjectivity is lived in resistance to competing notions for one's allegiance or self-identification. It is a process of disidentification[63] with prevalent formulations of the most forceful theoretical subject of feminism.

The choice of one or many themes is both a theoretical and a political decision. Like gender epistemologists and other emancipatory movements, the theoretical subject of *Bridge* gives credit to the subject of consciousness as the site of knowledge but problematizes it by representing it as a weave. In Anzaldúa's terms the woman of color has a "plural personality." Speaking of the new *mestiza* in *Borderlands/La Frontera*, she says, "She learns to juggle cultures. The juncture where the *mestiza* stands, is where phenomena tend to collide."[64] As an object of multiple indoctrinations that heretofore have collided upon her, their new recognition as products of the oppositional thinking of others can help her come to terms with the politics of varied discourses and their antagonistic relations.

The most remarkable tendency in the work reviewed in this essay is the implicit or explicit acknowledgment that, on the one hand, women of color are excluded from feminist theorizing on the subject of consciousness and, on the other, that though excluded from theory, their books are read in the classroom and/or duly (foot)noted. Given these current institutional and political practices in the United States, it is almost impossible to go beyond an oppositional theory of the subject. However, it is not the theory that will help us grasp the subjectivity of women of color. Socially and historically, women of color have been now central, now outside antagonistic relations among races, classes, and genders. It is this struggle of multiple antagonisms, almost always in relation to culturally different groups, and not just genders, that gives configuration to the theoretical subject of *Bridge*. It must be noted, however, that each woman of color cited here, even in her positing of a "plurality of self," is already privileged enough to reach the moment of cognition of a situation for herself. This should suggest that to privilege the subject, even if multiple-voiced, is not enough.

---

62. Moraga and Anzaldúa, Introduction to the first edition, *Bridge*, 102.
63. Pêcheux, *Language, Semantics and Ideology*, 158–59
64. Anzaldúa, *Borderlands* 79.

BIBLIOGRAPHY

Althusser, Louis. *Lenin and Philosophy and Other Essays*, translated by Ben Brewster. New York: Monthly Review Press, 1971.

Anzaldúa, Gloria. *Borderlands/La Frontera: The New Mestiza*. San Francisco: Spinsters/Aunt Lute, 1987.

Beauvoir, Simone de. *The Second Sex*. Translated by H. M. Parshley. New York: Vintage Books, 1974.

Benhabib, Seyla. "The Generalized and the Concrete Other: The Kohlberg-Gilligan Controversy and Feminist Theory." *Feminism as Critique*, 77-95. Edited by Seyla Benhabib and Drucilla Cornell. Minneapolis: University of Minnesota Press, 1987.

Butler, Judith, "Variations on Sex and Gender: Beauvoir, Wittig, and Foucault" *Praxis* 5, no. 4 (1986): 128-142.

Cott, Nancy F. *The Grounding of Modern Feminism*. New Haven, CT: Yale University Press, 1987.

Davies, Miranda. *Third World: Second Sex*. London: Zed Books, 1987.

De Lauretis, Teresa. "Feminist Studies/Critical Studies: Issues, Terms, and Contexts." *Feminist Studies/Critical Studies*, 1-9. Edited by Teresa de Lauretis. Bloomington, IN: Indiana University Press, 1987.

Elshtain, Jean Bethke. "Feminist Discourse and Its Discontents: Language, Power, and Meaning." *Signs* 7, no. 3 (1982): 603-621.

Flax, Jane. "Postmodernism and Gender Relations in Feminist Theory." *Signs* 12, no. 4 7): 621–643.

Harding, Sandra. *The Science Question in Feminism*. Ithaca, NY: Cornell University Press, 1986.

Hull, Gloria T. Patricia Bell Scott, and Barbara Smith, editors. *All the Women are White, All the Blacks Are Men, But Some of Us Are Brave*. New York: Feminist Press, 1982.

Jaggar, Alison M. *Feminist Politics and Human Nature*. New Jersey: Rowman & Allanheld/Harvester Press, 1983.

Kristeva, Julia. "Women's Time." translated by Alice Jardine and William Blake. *Signs* 7, no. 1, (1981): pp. 13–35.

Lugones, María C. and Elizabeth V. Spelman. "Have we got a theory for you! Feminist Theory, Cultural Imperialism and the Demand for 'the Woman's Voice.'" *Women's Studies International Forum* 6, no. 6 (1983): 573-581.

Macdonell, Diane. *Theories of Discourse*. Oxford: Basic Blackwell, 1986.

MacKinnon, Catherine A. "Feminism, Marxism, Method, and the State: An Agenda for Theory." *Feminist Theory* 7, no. 3 (1982): 515-544.

Meese, Elizabeth. *Choosing the Double-Cross: The Practice of Feminist Criticism*. Chapel Hill

NC: University of North Carolina Press. 1986.

Moraga, Cherríe and Gloria Anzaldúa, editors. *This Bridge Called My Back*. 2nd edition. New York: Kitchen Table Press, 1983.

Pêcheux, Michael. *Language, Semantics and Ideology*, translated by Harbans Nagpal. London: Macmillan, 1982.

Rich, Adrienne. *On Lies, Secrets and Silence: Selected Prose, 1966–1978*. New York: W. W. Norton & Company, 1979.

Spivak, Gayatri Chakravorty. "Three Women's Texts and a Critique of Imperialism." *Critical Inquiry* 12, no. 1 (1985): 235-61.

Paula Treichler, "Teaching Feminist Theory." In *Theory in the Classroom*, edited by Cary Nelsen. Urbana: University of Illinois Press, 1986.

Zinn, Maxine Baca, Lynn Weber Cannon, Elizabeth Higginbotham, and Bonnie Thornton. "The Costs of Exclusionary Practices in Women's Studies." *Signs* 11, no. 2 (1986): 290–303.

NYMPHOMANIA

THE DISCOURSE OF DIFFERENCE[1]

→ ←

Translated by Ariadna Molinari Tato

IN THE POETRY COLLECTION *En la Tierra de en Medio* [In the Land in Between], the feminist starting point for articulating the feminine in Rosario Castellanos' work—a phrase that is evocative of Nepantla (an in-between land), where Sor Juana Inés de la Cruz was born—there is a ten-line poem (intended to evoke and displace the "Tenth Muse") titled "Nymphomania." Apart from the lines themselves, a series of contextual relationships are at stake: the land in between (Nepantla/México); Sor Juana, who, in her own words, pulled herself out of the feminine standard by becoming a nun; and Rosario Castellanos herself, who is not herself, but the Woman, an entity who might only correspond to the realm of Nymphomania. According to the *Diccionario ideológico de la lengua española* [Ideological Dictionary of Spanish], "nymphomania" is a uterine fury: a state of fervor, anger, madness.[2] The same dictionary describes *uterine fury* as "a genital agitation that makes women develop an insatiable desire to surrender to copulation."[3] Copulation, in turn, means "tethering, bonding one thing with another, copulating in order to generate."[4] In grammar, however, the copula is the link between the predicate and the subject, what is asserted about the subject in a clause. In the surface of the poem itself, "the insatiable (sexual) desire to surrender to copulation" is sub-textualized, and it is revealed that what is wanted "again and again, yet once more" is to taste "the infinite." The title of the poem, "Nymphomania," is the only "evidence" we have that somehow the infinite is linked to the insatiable sexuality through the desire to taste it. The key lies in "copula." Copula is a two-fold term for predicating:

---

1. *Editors' Note:* This essay was originally published as Chapter 1 in Norma Alarcón's book, *Ninfomanía: El discurso feminista en la obra poética de Rosario Castellanos* (Madrid: Editorial Pliegos, 1992), 9-17. It appears here in English for the first time translated from the Spanish by Mónica Mansour. The translation is copyrighted by Universidad Nacional Autónoma de México (UNAM)/Centro de Investigaciones y Estudios de Género, (CIEG), and it is published here with permission from UNAM/CIEG.

2. Julio Casares Sánchez, *Diccionario ideológico de la lengua Española* (Barcelona: Editorial Gustavo Gili, 1942).

3. Casares, "uterine fury."

4. Casares, "copulation."

(1) for generating in terms of biological reproduction, and (2) for generating meanings, for asserting qualities of the subject in clauses. Without it, without the copula, there are no clauses, no generation. Copula, then, is the Woman, capitalized, as an already ontologized being whose affirmed value is the "uterine fury," nymphomania. But the Woman, as copula, is not strictly speaking the object either, because it is the term that predicates the meanings of the subjects, that binds the subject with what is objectified, and if she occupied the position of the subject the only thing that could be asserted about her is herself, as copula, as uterine fury, as nymphomania. It could very well be suggested that Castellanos implicitly reverses Lacan's propositions about the Phallus, which represents the plenitude of symbolism, while the Woman does not exist as a subject because she suffers the lack of the Phallus, and thus inscribes herself negatively, as an absence, in the table of ontological symbolisms.[5] Through her critical intervention, however, Castellanos conversely suggests that this is not an actual lack, but that she is the copula: the logic that generates meanings and the "biologic" that generates reproductions. As a copula, she functions as a generator that helps to affirm or deny the qualities of the masculine subject that already includes the specular feminine in the table of ontological symbolism. Thus, the need to taste the infinite, to inquire about the Self on behalf of the Woman, can only be called nymphomania. Logically, Rosario Castellanos is right about the absurdity represented by the onto(theo)logical patriarchal systems.[6] The poem can be found below:

> *Nymphomania*
>
> I had you in my grasp:
> All of humanity in a nutshell.
> What a hard and wrinkled rind!
> And within, the simulacrum
> of the two cerebral hemispheres
> which, obviously, do not aspire to act upon
> but to be devoured, lauded
> by that neutral flavor, so unsatisfactory,
> which demands of the infinite

---

5. Jacques Lacan, *Écrits*, trans. Alan Sheridan (London: Thavistock, 1972).

6. The work of Jacques Derrida exposes the construction of these systems, particularly the ontological and the phenomenological. See, for instance, *Of Grammatology*, trans. G. C. Spivak (Baltimore: John Hopkins University Press, 1976); and *Writing and Difference*, trans. A. Bass (Chicago: Chicago University Press, 1978).

to be tasted again and again, yet once more.⁷

Within (ontological) humanity there is a simulacrum, a copy of the copy of the human that represents the conceptual oppositions through the two "cerebral hemispheres," whose functions and meanings oppose each other *a priori*: reason-emotion, intelligence-sensibility, etcetera. Thus situated, nymphomania, which according to the dictionary is a feminine quality, in fact, belongs to both man and woman. What is proposed is a transvaluation of what has already been valued *a priori* as masculine and feminine, respectively.

When Rosario Castellanos, as an interrogating subject, began her research "on feminine culture," she stumbled upon the fact that, from a perspective situated in the onto(theo)logical philosophical system, neither the Woman nor her substantial cultural production existed, as they were negative points. Within this same system, women were assigned the term opposite to culture; that is, nature. Along with this ontological system, there is a theological system as well. And, regarding the theological system, Saint Augustine's exposition is both important and useful. In *The City of God*, he organizes the Old and the New Testament around "two cities:" the heavenly city and the earthly one.⁸ According to Celia Amorós, they "respectively correspond to two opposing genealogical series: the inhabitants of the heavenly city are the children of promise—the promise of true inheritance—and grace; the inhabitants of the Earthly city belong to the order of nature—which hereby opposes grace—, and are creatures of the perishable and the ephemeral."⁹ The two systems, in fact, offer three propositions that refer to the essential Woman, which correspond to the three propositions Jacques Derrida makes about Nietzsche's work.¹⁰ Although Rosario Castellanos never read Derrida, she did read Nietzsche, which I think suggests that in her deconstruction of the onto(theo)logical system, Castellanos captured the three propositions that can be extracted from the philosopher's work. Would it be outrageous to suggest that Castellanos learned to deconstruct from Nietzsche, as many contemporary French theorists have certainly done too? I argue, then, that the propositions Derrida lists for Nietzsche match those that Castellanos presents in her poetic work:

---

7. Rosario Castellanos, *Meditation on the Threshold: A Bilingual Anthology of Poetry by Rosario Castellanos*, trans. Julian Palley (Tempe, AZ: Bilingual Press/Editorial Bilingüe, 1988), 139.

8. Saint Augustine, Bishop of Hippo, *City of God*. 354.

9. Celia Amorós, *Hacia una crítica de la razón patriarcal* (Madrid: Anthropos, 1985), 88-89.

10. Jacque Derrida, *Spurs: Nietzsche's Styles*, trans. Barbara Harlow (Chicago: University of Chicago Press, 1979).

1. The Woman as a figure of lies, of untruths (earthly city)

2. The Woman as a figure of truth itself (heavenly city)

3. The Woman as a simulator, an actress, a Dionysian being, a maenad; basically, a being with multiple masks.

The strategy is not precisely to revert the system and propose an antithesis, but to interrogate it as "Nymphomania" does. What is sexual about it? Everything and nothing. Eve allows Rosario Castellanos to create a strategic opening for situating herself both inside and outside the theological system as a figure of fall/guilt/body/flesh/lies/death. This figure allows Castellanos to extract the metaphors/concepts already linked to the figure itself within the textual heritage. If she identified herself with Mary, who in Castellanos' work (and in Nietzsche's) is the figure of truth, and the one who proves the divine existence, she would put herself on the side of truth and would, in fact, have nothing to say; she would only have to reproduce it by living it. By placing herself next to Eve and her accompanying series of links, Rosario Castellanos opens a radically contingent space, the I who is now, in the interval between past and future, where my difference is exposed. She owns the word itself through the lie, the mirror/Eve that inversely reflects the Logos, Eve the metaphor herself, the (cerebral) simulacrum. She owns the simulacrum in order to investigate it as feminine and as negativity because it is mediated by Eve. This is the only way one can understand Rosario Castellanos' efforts to feminize the possession of the word and of poetry.[11] Thus, thou art not poetry, Woman, as Gustavo Adolfo Bécquer would say, nor am I; poetry is the artifice of writing, which means Rosario Castellanos tried to denaturalize art, since it has been seen consistently as a mimesis of nature, and as a mimesis of nature it is mediated by what has been qualified *a priori* as feminine.[12]

This can be rephrased following Simone de Beauvoir and Luce Irigaray. (The former influenced Castellanos, but the latter did not.) According to Simone de Beauvoir in *The Second Sex*, for the male subject, the Woman has represented the Other; that is, she is the Other within the ontological system where the man identifies with the Being/subject. That is why she argues that "one is not born, but

---

11. See Chapters III and IV, Norma Alarcón, *Ninfomanía: El discurso feminista en la obra poética de Rosario Castellanos* (Madrid: Editorial Pliegos,1992), 19-55.

12. *Editors' note:* Alarcón is referencing Gustavo Adolfo Bécquer, whose often-quoted verse holds that woman is poetry. Castellanos' poem, "Poetry is not you" is a response to Bécquer's claim.

rather becomes, a woman."[13] Becoming a woman diverges into two roads: either the woman becomes a woman by following the ideological patterns received from the onto(theo)logical system (which can vary throughout history, even if history is under its influence,) or the woman chooses herself as subject, which is what de Beauvoir suggests, and from then onwards she turns herself and the world into a project in and of itself. In a way, Rosario Castellanos travels both roads. On the one hand, she chooses to be a subject, a practitioner of writing who defines herself as project-praxis, but only after trying to appropriate poetry for herself; on the other hand, she uses this practice to investigate her cultural heritage, that is to say, the patterns she received and should imitate. Consequently, her poetics deals with many paradigmatic figures. Castellanos' poetic work is simultaneously an imitation, a repetition, and even a parody of feminine representations and their masks, as well as a displacement. Her (speaking) poetic self continuously unfolds between what was (or should have ethically been) and what is not the contingent radical difference. Thus, her poetry becomes a long essay/draft that points towards a future that is still non-existent, the exact dilemma where the (feminist) discourse of difference lies today. Does the Woman represent an identity point of reference using the received and elaborated meanings, or is she a background that is reread through the process of being a woman/women in the contingent social circumstances? Moreover, to what an extent are the received meanings reinscribed due to their massive influence in the social arena? That is, one can only think simultaneously inside and outside the valued and prevailing systems. The position of contemporary feminism is, above all, to critique what prevails so as to displace it, transform it, and change it. In the end, that was also Rosario Castellanos' purpose throughout her work.

Luce Irigaray, unlike de Beauvoir, does not appropriate the notion of Woman as a subject, but alongside de Beauvoir she claims that the theory of the subject is masculine; however, she emphasizes that this theory has always been appropriated by the masculine subject, which is why it is impossible for women to place themselves within that same concept.[14] That is, within this onto(theo)logical system, it is impossible to speak as a "woman/subject," except when taking the masculine place. By situating as a female being and owning it, one can perceive how the Woman is already negatively situated within the system, how she is already both: the other and the not-other. Irigaray wonders why not double the

---

13. Simone de Beauvoir, *The Second Sex* (New York: Vintage Books, 1974).
14. Luce Irigaray, *Speculum of the Other Woman*, trans. Gillian C. Gill (Ithaca: Cornell University Press, 1985).

misunderstanding to the limits of exhaustion. The misunderstanding, the mistake is already situated in the Order of Meanings; inside this mirror of order, she may find a voice strong enough to shape the imaginary orb of the masculine subject.[15] This means that, within the onto(theo)logical system, the Woman cannot keep up to date by and for herself, as de Beauvoir states, and this is unresolvable since it is mediated by the notion of Being. She remains the "simultaneous co-existence of opposites," of binary terms already in opposition, "she is equally *neither one nor the other*. Or is she rather between the one and the other—that elusive gap between two discrete bodies?"[16] This is the site where the difference I call the place of the contingent radical subject is executed, which Rosario Castellanos figures as Eve, for instance, or as a marginalized being, in order to discuss what has been received and inherited. As a contingent radical subject herself, the Woman is unnecessary for the system, but as a non-subject, negatively subjected by the system, she is essential; herein lies the danger of adjusting to the inherited paradigms and thus essentializing the female identity mediated by them. Rosario Castellanos intended to get around that same essentialization. And, although she tried to control the word and the meaning through self-awareness, she had in mind that they had a previous textual existence that controlled her.[17] That is what causes the effect of conflicting texts within her work.

Regarding de Beauvoir's suggestion that women should choose themselves as subjects for and by themselves, Castellanos chooses herself for and by herself as a writer who explores difference as a site where she is neither one nor the other, where she is between one and the other. It should be noted that she did not choose herself as a philosopher, although she studied philosophy. Thus, when Castellanos introduces the theme of otherness, the Other is always elsewhere; she points out to her "male friend" that she is not the Other, but that the Other is a third party, something external that lies between them.

In *Hacia una crítica de la razón patriarcal*, Celia Amorós has observed that nowadays feminist discourses follow two currents: the discourse of equality and the discourse of difference. The former takes us to the contemporary social realm, where the battles for integration and against the legal, economic, and political subordination of women are fought. The latter introduces us to the realm of patriarchal "reason," the symbolic core that needs to be translated and decodified. In this philosophical-ontological realm, the Woman as difference

---

15. Irigaray, *Speculum of the Other Woman*, 143-44.
16. Irigaray, *Speculum of the Other Woman*, 165.
17. Alarcón, *Ninfomanía*, 29-55.

has been marginalized from subjectivity itself.[18] Amorós' proposed method for decodification is a skeptical, critical, and even suspicious attitude. The critical attitude is the criticism of the difference. By choosing the figure of Eve, for instance, Castellanos "writes the body," but contextualizes it historically. This means that the inherited textualization on which difference operates, through Salomé, for instance, situates her within the binary opposition of man-woman, which executes meanings both within and outside the system.[19]

Critics have pejoratively qualified Castellanos' early works as "feminine," and her more mature work has been positively classified as "feminist," since its protest is more effective thanks to irony.[20] The deconstruction of the masculine symbolic order is understood as something that occurs in her later works, where irony is more evidently emphasized.[21] When the inscribed and reinscribed repetition of the "traditional poetic rhetoric" is read in her early works, that is, the multiplicity of images and metaphors taken from the mystical-romantic heritage,[22] it is qualified as a repetition of the "feminine:" narcissistic, self-absorbed, sentimental, subjective, etc. It is a repetition, but a self-aware and necessary repetition that questions the heritage, that demystifies it through Eve. The irony is the conscious discovery of the inherited mirror and the dismemberment of the mirror where she is and is not. As a poet, Castellanos often describes it as super rhetorical; as an essayist, though, she once described it as a draft in which she poured her knowledge about the feminine. In the face of a strictly aesthetic evaluation, Castellanos falters; outside the aesthetic, she amasses value. If her work is explored as a summary of her knowledge of "the feminine," our critical intervention should consider that, in order to make that draft, Castellanos was forced to reinscribe the poetic tradition both from inside and from outside. Her voice does not only dominate the knowledge "on feminine culture," but also the poetic technique that she has to practice for making her work "aesthetically" admissible. Thus, irony is a distancing technique where there is always a female intermediary (the Other Woman, the one from the inherited symbolic and social texts) between the "I" and the body. Onto(theo)logy is the mirror of the man that the Other Woman inhabits, as well as the mirror that she (the contingent

---

18. Amorós, *Hacia una crítica de la razón patriarcal*, 72-73.
19. Alarcón, *Ninfomanía*, 101-128.
20. Rosario Castellanos, *Meditation on the Threshold: A Bilingual Anthology of Poetry by Rosario Castellanos*, trans. Julian Palley (Tempe, AZ: Bilingual Press/Editorial Bilingüal, 1988.)
21. Alarcón, *Ninfomanía*, 101-154.
22. Alarcón, *Ninfomanía*, 57-100.

subject) observes. That Woman (as a symbol and concept) is not us (the social beings) but could potentially be at any time. Standing between the female speaker and the system, the mirror/Woman looks at him, the builder, and at her, the one who observes the multiple superimposed masks that she is expected to reflect. Therefore, from this perspective, she must break the mirror and disperse a multiplicity of representations where all and none are true. She breaks the mirror and doubles and reinscribes the figures until she reaches exhaustion again, and again, yet once more. In that sense, writing is also Nymphomania: surrendering to the copula(tion). Rosario Castellanos' poetic reinscriptions open "the true battlefield," as Amorós describes in a different context, where "the reorganization of a cultural order whose unconscious interiorization does not represent women as oppressed and depressed psychology."[23] The problem of "constituting our own discourse as women are radically assuming the symbol's contradiction and possibilities to overcome them."[24] Rosario Castellanos understood all of this before contemporary feminism. The criticism that she practices intervenes in her poems by focusing on the construction of the feminine, its cultural representation, and the strategies that the female speaker chooses to distance herself from that construct. She offers us fables, parodies, and paradigmatic figures for us to unravel and find out as much as possible about those paradoxes that constitute the feminine. It is a strategy that she also used in her prose and that still needs to be critically explored.

---

23. Amorós, *Hacia una crítica de la razón patriarcal*, 71.
24. Amorós, *Hacia una crítica de la razón patriarcal*, 70.

BIBLIOGRAPHY

Alarcón, Norma. *Ninfomanía: El discurso feminista en la obra poética de Rosario Castellanos.* Madrid: Editorial Pliegos, 1992.

Amorós, Celia. *Hacia una crítica de la razón patriarcal.* Madrid: Anthropos, 1985.

Augustine, Saint, Bishop Of Hippo, 354. *City of God.*

Beauvoir, Simone de. *The Second Sex.* New York: Vintage Books, 1974.

Casares Sánchez, Julio. *Diccionario ideológico de la lengua Española.* Barcelona: Editorial Gustavo Gili, 1942.

Castellanos, Rosario. *Meditation on the Threshold: A Bilingual Anthology of Poetry by Rosario Castellanos.* Translated by Julian Palley. Tempe, AZ: Bilingual Press/Editorial Bilingüe, 1988.

Derrida, Jacques. *Of Grammatology.* Translated by Gayatri Chakravorty Spivak. Baltimore: John Hopkins University Press, 1976

Derrida, Jacques. *Writing and Difference.* Translated by Alan Bass. Chicago: Chicago University Press, 1978.

Derrida, Jacques. *Spurs: Nietzsche's Styles/Eperons: Les Styles de Nietzsche.* Translated by Barbara Harlow. Chicago: University of Chicago Press, 1979.

Irigaray, Luce, *Speculum of the Other Woman.* Translated by Gillian C. Gill. Ithaca: Cornell University Press, 1985.

Lacan, Jacques, *Écrits.* Translated by Alan Sheridan, London: Thavistock, 1977.

COGNITIVE DESIRES

AN ALLEGORY OF/FOR CHICANA CRITICS[1]

→ ←

AS I WRITE THIS I cannot help but realize that it is 1992, the year of the quincentenary, marking the "encounter," as the Anglo-Spanish promoters call it, between Europeans and the indigenous in the Americas for whom it is more of an agonistic than celebrative occasion. Thus for those of us who continue to exist on the downside of the "encounter," remembrance is more the commemoration of a deadly collision that continues to kill and produce anger and grief in the context of multinational capitalist "development" and exploitation that carries over into institutions, even academic ones, in ways that we have yet to clarify. In my view, then, the academic allegory for Chicana critics refers to that woman of Mexican descent who claims the name Chicana, lives in the United States, may even be a descendant of natives or long-time residents, and, most importantly, refuses to forget that she is also the descendant of peoples, some of whose names have disappeared, who have been engaged in continuous conflict with state and institutional power structures that wish to repress the memory of the unsavory consequences of conquest, colonization, dislocation, discrimination, and their historical transformation. Though the allegory is one pertaining to an academic power structure, I would like to make the connection that the consequences of imperialisms and their multiple transformations are not only pertinent to the political economy but cognitive as well, for it is within academic institutions that knowledge production may be "recycled" into narratives that support the national(istic) status quo. Cognitive desire, then, is not just a "hunger of memory" that is subsumed by categories produced elsewhere, but a "hunger of memory" desirous of its own productive intervention in the retrieval and making of cognitive symbols and concepts that may help us apprehend our experience of the political economy in conjunction with jurisprudence, history, ethnography, and literary mediation. It is, after all, the conditions of the political economy,

---

1. *Editors' Note:* This essay was published previously in *Listening to Silences: New Essays in Feminist Criticism*, ed. Elaine Hedges and Shelley Fisher Fishkin (New York and Oxford: Oxford University Press, 1994), 260-273. It was also published in a slightly different version in *Chicana (W)rites: On Word and Film*, ed. Maria Herrera-Sobek and Helena Maria Viramontes (Berkeley: Third Woman Press, 1995), 185-200;. The version published here is from *Listening to Silences*.

especially in the twentieth century, that have made migrants of many of us. Not just migrant workers in the agribusiness fields, but in many other enterprises of industrial development locally and globally, as well as the migration of peoples from third-world areas to the Euro/American terrain.

To tell the tale, then, I will start out with an academic anecdote from the United States-Mexican border, a border on the verge of another radical transformation as the groundwork is already being laid out so that the North American Free Trade Agreement may kick into place.[2] A ground was prepared by the establishment of maquiladora shops starting in the early 1960s when the Chicano Movement (1965–1975) was just beginning, and Chicanas were struggling for self-defined positions within it and experiencing exclusion there as well as in the contemporary Women's Movement, whose own momentum was simultaneous with all of these events. Is it an ironic coincidence that simultaneous with the cry of liberation by Euro-American women and minority populations in the United States, the multinationals began the construction of shops whose workers are primarily women, not only on the United States–Mexican border but all over the globe? Certainly for the women working in the maquiladoras under polluted, life-threatening conditions, their quietist and exploited group history dovetails into global shifts in the political economy of the metropolis which places them in a contradictory double-bind between necessity and economic "opportunity," which, given the unsafe working conditions, put them at risk. For me, there is a tenuous connection between women working in the actual border shops, who put their lives at risk, and Chicana critics who work in an interstitial zone that is constantly on the move, given its structural displacements within the academy. That is, the latter displacements parallel those of the former and remain nonequivalent. Thus, though each lives within different economies of signifying circuits, "we" nevertheless share experiences of dislocation that contribute to cultural productions. Since the emergence of Chicana critics can be traced no further back than about 1965, applying the name retroactively is much like calling Sor Juana Inés de la Cruz a modern woman. Thus, the scenario on the border that opens up the allegory is a necessary step in the travails of the Chicana critic since it implicates both Mexicans and Anglo-Americans in the production of

---

2. See Vicki L. Ruiz and Susan Tiano, eds. *Women on the U.S.–Mexico Border: Responses to Change* (Boston: Allen & Unwin, 1987); M. Patricia Fernández Kelly and Anna M. Garcia, "Invisible Amidst the Glitter: Hispanic Women in Southern California Electronics Industry," in *The Worth of Women's Work; A Qualitative Synthesis,* ed. Anne Statham, Eleanor M. Miller, and Hans O. Mauksch (New York: State University of New York Press, 1988), 265-89.

meaning for her. Such a critic, who could only take shape through this fabulous construction, is a paradigmatic woman of multiple incarnations. The construction aims to situate the Chicana critic in the locus of *la différend*, the site of a conflict, collision, or contest opposed to judicial litigation, or (constitutional) law, indeed opposed to anything that presupposes for its interpretation an inherent monological rationality. My contention is that heretofore the Chicana critic has not taken account of her insider/ outsider/insider status with respect to multiple discourse structures, some of which cannot easily be translated into each other.[3] To pursue the nexus or intersectionality of the multiple discourse structures that surround the Chicana critic is in a sense to come to terms with the modes through which her disappearance is constantly promoted through the speech of others no matter how unintentional, and against which she struggles through counter—and disidentificatory discourses. In the process, one may come to terms on theoretical grounds with how the speech of the border shop worker may be drowned out, so that one may then ask the purposefully naive question, "Can the subaltern speak?"[4] The struggle is for histories actual and imaginary that give substance and provide an account of her position within the culture and the political economy.

SCENARIO ON THE BORDER: (DIS)IDENTIFYING THE PLAYERS

AT A RECENT CONFERENCE in the Mexican border city of Tijuana, two women—as it happened, one Anglo-American and the other European—presented, sequentially, Spanish-language written papers on the same work: *Querido Diego, Te Abraza Quiela* by the Mexican-Polish writer Elena Poniatowska.[5] Poniatowska grew up speaking French and Spanish—French, the preferred language of the Polish aristocracy, and Spanish as a result of her Mexican upbringing and education. The audience included Poniatowska herself, a handful of Chicanas—some of whom fully understood Spanish, others not—a few Anglo-American scholars who pursue Spanish-language literary studies, and local community women, who fully understood Spanish but not the interpretive apparatus. The rest of the audience were Mexican women who were literary scholars and intellectuals from the Colegio de México, a co-sponsor of the conference with the Colegio

---

3. Jean-François Lyotard, *The Differend: Phrases in Dispute*, trans. George Van de Abbeele (Minneapolis: University of Minnesota Press, 1988), 9-10.

4. Allusion to Gayatri C. Spivak, "Can the Subaltern Speak?" in *Marxism and the Interpretation of Culture*, eds. Cary Nelson and Lawrence Grossberg (Basingstoke: Macmillan, 1988), 271–313.

5. Elena Poniatowska, *Querido Diego, te abraza Quiela* (México: Era, 1978).

de la Frontera Norte. As you may anticipate, given the diverse social identities and their discursive formations, the potential for cross-purposed dialogue and misrecognition was rife. I cannot pursue the ramifications for each player, but I will attempt them for Chicanas, most of whom were actually critics or writers. Theoretically, the various players could, if they so desired, place themselves in the nodal point of *la différend*. However, I would guarantee a different outcome for each. It is my intention to be as impartial as possible, especially insofar as the Chicana critic does not have a "word to her name" except the proprietary claim to the term of recent recodification—Chicana.[6] On the other hand, to enter the inquiry through the term Chicana already bespeaks bias. As such she is, like most women of color in the United States, a recent arrival on the stage of the Western critical (mostly male) tradition. This is not to say that she does not claim female ancestors; however, they cannot be said to exist at the interstice and intersection of the multiple discourses that give shape to the Modern and Postmodern, which cannot be assumed to be sequential either, but to be implicitly or explicitly interferential.

On the San Diego–Tijuana border, the two speakers presented completely different interpretations of Quiela, the writer of the letters addressed to Diego (Rivera) that represent the fictive textualization of a historically real Russian-born artist's ill-fated romantic attachment to Diego Rivera. The Anglo-American critic interpreted the letters as an instance of the social production of female oppression based on the account given in the text of Quiela's experiences, which would ultimately silence her but for Poniatowska's intervention. The European critic interpreted the letters as an instance of the symbolic construction of femininity, a near-perfect sample of a quietist *écriture feminine*.[7] The first interpretation was motivated by a sociopolitical desire to demonstrate that Quiela's inequality, overdetermined gender identity, and experience are so negative that no sane woman should want to assume such a position, a calculated move to put the romantic in crisis and lead listeners to disidentification with Quiela. The second interpretation was motivated by an aestheticist textual desire to demonstrate Quiela's elegantly constructed pathos, a phallocratic production of femininity and its correlative embodiment. The first interpreter insisted on a heterosexist social referentiality

---

6. See Norma Alarcón, "Chicana Feminism: In the Tracks of 'the' Native Woman," *Cultural Studies*, vol.4 no.3 (1990): 248-56.

7. Toril Moi, *Sexual/Textual Politics: Feminist Literary Theory* (London: Metheuen, 1985). By citing Moi, I do not mean to endorse her typology vis-à-vis the Anglo-Americans and the French, let alone her characterization of lesbians and U.S. women of color; rather, I refer the reader to a readily available bibliography.

that called for political positions beyond the text, while the second insisted on a self-referential (inter)textuality, which nonetheless appealed to the audience to share in the work's aesthetic pathos. The first was firmly embedded in the liberal self-other experiential paradigms of some Anglo-American bourgeois feminist theories which, though still historically interesting, are not complex enough to explain our diverse socio-symbolic formations, positionalities, or heterogenous histories; the second was embedded in French feminist appropriations of crosshatched Derridean-Lacanian deconstructive practices which, though also important theoretical contributions, remain an autonomous system, difficult to transpose and map onto sociosymbolic formations outside the bourgeois Eurocentric intellectual tradition. However, the possibility of resonance with the non-European is not necessarily precluded. The "new" feminist "identity politics" of women of color forged through a "politics of cultural difference" that have emerged and developed since World War II require multiple theoretical and paradigmatic conjunctions that only now are beginning to be addressed. However, I will elaborate on this below as I return to the allegory of "the" Chicana critic who configures in part such conjunctions.

The interpreters, who were clearly fully invested in their respective positions, were unable to negotiate a passage between themselves, though they both had a clear claim to the literary discipline. When both finished, the silence in the room was stunning. Since neither the audience nor the presenters were forthcoming with questions or responses; Poniatowska herself was asked to comment on the interpretations of her work. Were those her intentions? Did either or both critics hit upon the meaning of the work? Poniatowska, who is the contemporary champion of the silenced in México, in fact, giving voice to a forgotten Russian artist, and who feels that if the sociopolitically oppressed are silenced someone must intervene for them, refused to comment on the grounds that the work in question is too close to her. The work was a vehicle for the exploration and displacement of one of her intimate personas. Since Chicanas had been explicitly invited to the conference with the aim of building bridges with *Mexicanas*, and one kept waiting for dialogue to take place, I for one wondered how it ever could under the circumstances. Further, if for argument's sake, anyone was looking for some sort of Mexican social identity and experience in the work or a Mexican interpretation of it, and she had asked, she would have been taken for a fool. The only things Mexican there were the border, constructed and reconstructed as it rubs against/with the United States; a large portion of the silenced audience who carried Mexican passports in case they wanted to cross to the United States; Chicanas who carried proper identification not so much to enter México as to return to the United States; and Diego Rivera, the recipient of Quiela's letters. That is, texts and cultural productions may cross borders, but some people risk arrest without *señas de identidad* (signs of identity), to quote the title of a Spanish novel published in Franco's Spain. People may be more closely tied—whether they want to or not—to nationally conferred identities than some texts. The fact that one needs "signs of identity" should tip us off to the requirements of subordination to the nation-state that (non)citizens must comply with and the fact that the inside/outside/inside occupied by Chicanas is not just symbolic but socio-political as well, regardless of the documentation status, since the Immigration and Naturalization Service may not wait for it. Racism (or the particular historical constructions of Mexicanness) makes her subject to a constant demand for the production (proof) of "ethnic" identity and citizenship in both México and the United States. Placing her in continuous movement from inside/outside/inside, as I have stated.

Since the interpreters had given us divergent interpretations of the socio-symbolic formation of femininity based not only on work widely recognized as Mexican, but based on letters addressed to a Mexican, to ask what any of it had to do with a Mexican identity and experience was to risk being seen as an ignorant déclassé given to excessive referential quibbling and maybe even essentializing, which ironically drew one nearer to the Anglo-American than the European with whom most of the Mexicanas sympathized, apparently because the former was too "aggressive" (read too "anti-men"). And yet there is that documentation required by law burning a hole in one's pocket and the knowledge that the aim of the conference was to clarify the proximity or overlap between Mexicanas and Chicanas through literature, our "medium," though apparently, the organizers took the meaning of "magical" mediations as the primary meaning of medium. It became increasingly clear that there was no productive strategy for effecting the avowed goals of the Mexicanas, and frankly, it reminded one of the National Women's Studies Association, where the organizers often feel that if you have a "caucus" you are participating. For me, however, this particular event marked the collapse of the enterprise. Indeed the major accomplishment was one that most Chicanas already knew of, and that was the marked class differences between us Mexicanas and Chicanas. Also, it would appear that it was such class differences that might draw Chicanas closer to the Anglo-Americans who did not deny historical socioreferentiality, thus opening up the possibility of addressing class positions, while the taboo of referentiality in the other interpretive system made it impossible even to speak of Quiela and Poniatowska as entities formed through cultural emblems drawn from a different aesthetic.

Such recognized differences make a difference in the constellation and concatenation of texts and critical tools. As in the case of African-American women, as Hortense Spillers notes, Chicanas "maintain no allegiances to a strategic formation of texts," which further draws them to a "logological" (textually Eurologocentric) feminist discourse. In fact, the Euro-American "process of aligning with prior acts of the text (is) the subtle component of power that bars... women of color as a proper subject of inquiry from the various topics of contemporary feminist discourse."[8] That is, the Euro-American canon formations demand privileged priority over the inquiries of women of color, a fact which may lead to contradiction, contestation, deconstruction, resistance, disidentification, or the production of alternative discursive practices. My claim, however, goes further to include the critical speaker who is positioned by that "subtle component of power" as a nonspeaker (a silent subaltern) because the privileged linguistic practices cannot hear, translate, or transcode (with a residue of nonequivalence) what is said.

In any case, the disjunction between purported aims and expectations and the actual events contributed to the increasing gap between Mexicanas and Chicanas, which resulted in our marginalization and silence. We became spectators to a textual performative that claimed to incorporate us. Could it be that such interstices are potential sites for the actual productive and bridging dialogues? In this particular scenario, the only speech possible was to remark on the discursive weave, which did not afford an opportunity for a positive Chicana intervention. Thus Chicanas were placed in a negative position whereby if they had wanted to speak, it would have been to note their exclusion from an event that supposedly included them in the conference's goals, most certainly its title: *Mujer y Literatura Mexicana y Chicana: Culturas en Contacto*.[9] In the end, Poniatowska herself intervened by stating that when it came to feminist activism, the Mexicanas were *mosquitas muertas* (loosely translated, wallflowers),

---

8. Horense Spillers, "Interstices: A Small Drama of Words," in *Pleasure and Danger: Exploring Female Sexuality*, ed. Carole S. Vance (London: Pandora, 1989), 80, 89.

9. The most recent anthology printed as a result of these conferences is *Mujer y literatura Mexicana y chicana: Culturas en contacto*, 2, ed. Aralia López-González, Amelia Malagamba, and Elena Urrutia (México: El Colegio de México/Colegio de la Frontera Norte, 1990).

which angered her countrywomen no end. To this day, she told me recently, that some of those who were there do not speak to her.

The exchange between Chicanas and Mexicanas does not appear at this time to be as extensive as one might expect. Bourgeois Mexicanas in general tend to find distasteful an identification with their "prole" kin, who are not *gente decente*, the "customary" epithet through which raced-class positions are segregated in Hispanic societies. Few upper-class Latin American women would admit to being colleagues to someone who could have been the household maid but for the grace of a minoritized education in the United States. And now the woman who could have been their maid talks back, often with a class-inflected speech, and has gone the way of many maids in Latin America, to the maquiladoras scattered all over the continent, and not just on the United States-Mexican border.

Speaking in Tongues: Cruising the Academy

Most Chicana critics are likely to come in contact with Anglo-American critics who have learned to pretend to some extent that this is a classless society where economic conditions, previously, at least since World War II, have enabled a pretense that now begins to crumble. Within the Anglo-American context, then, Chicana critics are often subtly but forcefully compelled to choose between the Anglo-American and the European interpreters characterized above. Moreover, it becomes increasingly apparent that there is an implicit "two-class theory" in the practitioners of the approaches, not so much because each is inherently of a different class, so much as the fact that the Europeans recognize class divisions and the Anglo-Americans "bracket" them. It is often the institutionalized prerogative of both the Anglo-American and the European to decide where we belong, which may foreclose almost all possibilities for self-propelled inquiry on the part of Chicanas.

In effect, these maneuvers recall the old "add and stir" method that a previous generation of Euro-American feminists protested and have successfully contested, thus radically changing the "cognitive map" of feminism and Women's Studies. Since each practitioner of the critical discourses in question is more interested in strengthening her position than bridging the disparate discourses, there are no adequate sources to aid the observer/reader in negotiating, not necessarily resolving, their paradoxes and contradictions. Moreover, more often than not, our students are taught those positions in isolation from each other. If the Chicanas call for a change of critical discourse so that our text may be included in a more dialogized fashion than is possible within the containing "add and stir" method, we may be told to go to Ethnic Studies.

If there is an Ethnic/Chicano Studies Program and Chicanas take refuge there, we may be compelled to historicize (following a male-head-of-household genealogical story) and sociologize (quantitative empiricism) our text into the "raced masculine model" at the expense of whatever feminist insight we may have had, as there too there is an "add and stir" containment. If there is no Ethnic/Chicano Studies Program, a Chicana may get bounced around between the Spanish and English departments, where she may not be better off than before, since at this time it is a toss-up as to who can silence most. The tendency of many departments is to neocolonize rather than enable critical thinking on her part, which would mean providing the pedagogical conditions for her speaking intervention and for exercising her interpretive agency. A Chicana critic may be inside studying and teaching, but outside the legitimate curricular mission of the department. If, as a feminist, she decides to insist on taking refuge in a Women's Studies Program, she may once again be faced with the cited interpreters of the text who are indeed sympathetic to her pathos and her unbelievable oppression. Yes, they'd be happy to take her text but not her, except as a seasonal worker. On the other hand, she may be glad to learn that her text is already in the curriculum—feminist sociology, anthropology, or regional history—all of which claim their own inherent rationality. Her feminist critical voice may be muted, but she is now (through the text) part of a guided international tour.

Indeed, taking the long view since the emergence of Chicana critics in the 1960s, after a decade or more of carrying "our text" around looking for a home for both of them, a Chicana critic may realize that she has become typed in one or both of two ways: (1) she is a minority woman narcissistically obsessed with herself through her text; (2) she is a wonderful resource. To employ some Marxist and Freudian vocabulary for a moment, in the first instance she is being so particularistic as to have no use-value; in the second instance she returns as a sample of the repressed and oppressed, and her use-value is theoretically reinstated. Thus, in the first instance, she is erased from the scene even as her text accrues exchange value because pluralism and diversity are more simply satisfied with texts than with actual people. Since her text acquired exchange value through the 1970s, in the 1980s another generation of Chicana critics emerged, even as the previous ones have disappeared. In the 1990s the successors of those from the

1970s and 1980s, plus a new crop of writers, are now often seasonally employed, joining the ranks of migrant/segmented, albeit intellectual, labor.

Aside from the fact that the successors have acquired a great deal more book knowledge, we may well wonder how our lot has changed from that of our parents or grandparents, who actually were migrant field or segmented manufacturing laborers. Successors should not completely despair, though, for at this juncture we have also acquired many kin in the Third World, where intellectuals travel around various schools and universities in order to make a living. This is not so much a misery-loves-company interpretation as perhaps a reminder that within the United States, we are viewed in a similar fashion to Third World intellectuals, inside/outside/inside, and it is worthwhile to investigate the ground of such views. Yet I do not speak of just any Third World intellectuals, as my discussion of *Mexicanas* should have demonstrated, but a genealogy of writers and thinkers who have been or are engaged in contestatory inquiries rather than sheer mimicry, though the latter should be identified as well. The Chicana critic is now, and perhaps has always been, positioned as a Third World intellectual, as are *Mexicanas*, and it was being inside the United States that has led her to (mis)recognize the position. That is, if upper-class *Mexicanas* favor "quietist" European interpretive theories over Anglo-American ones, which may align them away from Chicanas, through her status in the United States academy, the Chicana critic is repositioned as Third World intellectual, thus realigning her from another angle with the *Mexicanas*. In other words, boundary crossing has been largely a mental exercise because our *señas de identidad* are inappropriately embodied; that is, the very rage at our embodied history as Chicanas can find no adequate "inherently rational" (monological), in Spillers' terms "logological," discourse with which to sweep up the letters of her name. Moreover, the social contradictions at work cannot be easily overcome through symbolic representation at conferences.

If a Chicana critic has had time to meditate about her lot, she now realizes that the only thing she might have had was her version of the (socio) text, and not the text itself. It is plain to see, if she is still on the fringes of the academy, that the text she thought was hers may be claimed by everyone. Thus, without having read Saussure, Derrida, Foucault, Lacan, or even Marx, she has discovered that the text/signifier is a commodity, and almost from the beginning she was a "signifying problem" rather than a participant of the "political economy of the signifier." If she still harbors an attachment to her text for some bizarre reason, she now keeps it a secret, lest she once again shows her déclassé status by identifying too closely with it. You, so the accusation went last time she mentioned her attachment, are essentializing, as the version of the text you've hung onto demonstrates. Essentializing is back, however, as the new journal *Differences* proclaims, so she can essentialize again, but she had better watch her mouth, for it is only permissible as a rhetorical strategy. In fact, of course, many of us are déclassé, but it's best not to show it, except theoretically.

My no-win narrative of/for Chicana critics and our text is what Bateson, in *Steps to an Ecology of Mind*, called the double-bind.[10] Since the term has been popularized, it is hard to remember that it is the kind of bind that actually produces psychosis. Most people, as Bateson notes, will do anything to escape the double-bind, or they risk psychosis, at which point psychoanalysis is of no use whatsoever. His solution for escaping the double-bind is to proceed to a higher epistemological or metanarrative ground; however, I think that one must discern and unravel the double-binds that cross our path since our path is culturally, politically, and economically located such that we live out the double-binding *différend* effect, and such junctures help us identify contradictory practices that require transformation. Moreover, there is no "talk cure" for psychosis. By the time a person is indeed psychotic, a protective wall has been erected that no one can talk themselves through—neither the one "inside" nor the one "outside." However, in the United States it is very difficult to tell what's inside and what's outside because we all share the same political boundary rights, or so we are told. Here again, we are in good company. Because of colonialism and the multinationals' international division of labor, a lot of the Third World cannot tell what's inside and what's outside either, as selected discourses, processes, and procedures cross borders with capitalist bureaucratic structures. As the Chicana poet Lorna Dee Cervantes has remarked in conversation, criticism is not enough to assist us out of a critical situation, yet it is often necessary for its clarification.

Survivalists have had at least three options. The first is the Richard Rodríguez option, whereby one can affirm that "the child who learns to read about his nonliterate ancestors necessarily separates himself from their way of life."[11] Many people experience this as an incontrovertible force that calls for abandonment, as obviously he did. Today, paradoxically, he finds himself writing about the successor ancestors and makes his living writing about *los pobres*. They are,

---

10. Gregory Bateson, *Steps to An Ecology of Mind* (San Francisco: Chandler Publishing, 1972), 10.

11. Richard Rodríguez, *The Hunger of Memory: The Education of Richard Rodríguez* (New York: Bantam, 1988), 169.

however, now at a safe distance as some reductive version of the nonliterate other. Thus, he preserves his psychic well-being by denying his metonymic relationship to others while simultaneously affirming it through his brand of journalistic transliterations, and by offering us an oversimplified but coherent story. The second is the orthodox Marxist option, where we could join the generic class struggle and change the subject, or forget the subject as well as forget the raced cultural history of the group. This version of the déclassé has invited us to view the "marginalized" as some monolith without any clue with regard to the social formation or the conditions of our existence nor recognition of our protestations along the way. The third is the resource option already mentioned, except that in the late 1980s and probably in the decade ahead, some may obtain, as a result of the success of our differential text and pluralism, a nonmigratory position, albeit segmented. (The "segmentation" could be turned into a less fractured account if the academy, in general, were supportive of (feminist) cultural studies; however, the disciplined departmental investment continues to dominate.)

If past generations of Chicana critics still desire to stage a comeback, we may discover that our "essentializing" obsolescence has returned under a new market-commodified value that has opened up what Trinh T. Minh-ha calls "planned authenticity." She explains, "as a product of hegemony and a remarkable counterpart of universal standardization, it constitutes an efficacious means of silencing the cry of racial oppression." That is to say, the minoritized are granted voice as long as they speak as "authenticators" of cultural experiences without pursuing the dialectical reconfiguration of knowledge production vis-à-vis the "other" (dominant). Anglo-Europeans now tell us, "We no longer wish to erase your difference. We demand, on the contrary, that you remember and assert it. At least, to a certain extent."[12] What extent? Here again, the Chicana critic is on dangerous ground. How much difference is enough? Let's say she decides to risk, and in the parlance of today take the "window of opportunity" that has opened up to her. Since conferences today are often clearly staged events, perhaps even "minoritizing" spectacles, commodified shows, our older Chicana critic may coincide in the same panel with her younger "sister;" the younger critic, unlike herself, has been schooled in representation, thematization of othering, and textual difference focusing on the constructed nature of identity, while the older critic may continue to "essentialize" social difference. In a sense, we are back in

---

12. Trinh T. Minh-ha, *Woman, Native, Other: Writing Postcoloniality and Feminism* (Bloomington, IN: Indiana University Press, 1988), 13.

Tijuana, though our critics are no longer Anglo-American or European. They are us, and we find ourselves unable to speak with each other even in theory.

Moving On: Subjects-in-Process

IN THEORY, THE PERILS of this fabulous Chicana critic are endless because, as Cornel West would say, a minoritized intellectual who tries to work with and on the same terms as the dominant/dominating is always on the defensive or, I would add, such an intellectual may already be bidding to occupy a dominant/dominating pose.[13] In fact, our relationship to the hegemonic political economy, institutions, and the symbolic order has always been asymmetrical, though we are purportedly assured juridical symmetry, i.e., equality. However, as Rosaura Sánchez points out, the terms of the boundaries can be reduced or extended to include us or exclude us by processes and manipulations beyond our control. At this juncture we all discover, as Sánchez suggests, that we do not possess much of our identity, difference, or experience because some of these are fixed elsewhere; that is, they are not as self-determined as one may pretend, but fixed by political and economic agendas and stereotyping public policies as well as by texts.[14] Resistance through self-determined identity formations, in effect, is a powerful force often doused by official (legalistic) maneuvers, commodifying discourses, and the mass media, which keep themselves busy producing, erasing, modifying, and transcoding identities. Precisely because there is a continuous drive for hegemonic containment toward a stasis that assures its control, resistance movements cannot afford to let up the pressure. If some of this sounds familiar to theory buffs, I want to emphasize that most of us learn this "in the flesh," as social movements continually testify. It is for this reason, for example, that the Chicana poet Lorna Dee Cervantes can say that (proto)deconstruction is the social *modus operandi*, not just the textual theory, of the politically marginalized/excluded, which, I would add, generates the "politics of difference" as initially sketched out by Audre Lorde.[15]

The desire for critical agency on the part of Chicana critics and writers presupposes subjects-in-process who construct provisional (self-determining)

---

13. Cornel West, "The Dilemma of the Black Intellectual," *Cultural Critique*, no. 1 (1985) :109–24.
14. Rosaura Sánchez, "Ethnicity, Ideology and Academia," *Cultural Studies* 4, no. 3 (1990): 294-302.
15. Audre Lorde, "The Master's Tools Will Never Dismantle the Master's House," in *This Bridge Called My Back: Writings by Radical Women of Color*, ed. Cherríe Moraga and Gloria Anzaldúa (Watertown, MA: Persephone Press, 1981), 98-106.

"identities"[16] that subsume a network of discursive and signifying practices and experiences imbricated in both the historical and imaginary shifting national borders of México and the United States. A subject-insertion into such a geographical economy and politics presupposes not only specific historical sociosymbolic texts but a situated contemporaneous horizon of meanings and intentions that swerve away from those produced and enunciated by Euro-Americans and Europeans, especially when the latter produce hegemonic structures and discourses of containment. Identity formations through differentially theorized experience, in this instance through the term Chicana, a historically raced/gendered/class position forged through the interstices of two nation-states—signal and proposes a subject-in-process. Such a subject-in-process is desirous of self-determination, yet is "traversed through and through the world and by others.... It is the active and lucid agency that constantly reorganizes its contents, through the help of these same contents, that produces by means of a material and in relation to needs and ideas, all of which are themselves mixtures of what it has already found there before it and what it has produced itself."[17] Through the speaking critical subject-in-process, cultural production reintroduces what was there before in new and dynamic combinatory transculturations. A bi- or multi-ethnicized, raced, and gendered subject-in-process may be called upon to take up diverse subject positions that cannot be "unified" without double-binds and contradictions. Indeed, what binds the subject positions together is precisely the difference from the perceived hegemony. The contradictions between subject positions move the subject to recognize, reorganize, reconstruct, and exploit differences through political resistance and cultural productions, and to see herself "in-process."[18] It is not a matter of doing away with "the discourse of the other" (whomever or whatever the other, hegemonic or not, is) "because the other is in each case

---

16. Commenting on the shift that the notion of identity has undergone in women's discourses, Trinh T. Minh-ha claims in *Woman, Native, Other* that the shift does not lead to "a theory of female identity" but rather "to identify as points of re-departure of the critical processes by which I have come to understand how the personal—the ethnic me, the female me—is political." Trinh T. Minh-ha, *Woman, Native, Other: Writing Postcoloniality and Feminism* (Bloomington: University of Indiana Press, 1989), 4.

17. Cornelius Castoriadis, *The Imaginary Institution of Society*, trans. Kathleen Blamey (Cambridge: The MIT Press, 1987), 106.

18. The notion subject-in-process (on-trial-/in-question) was first introduced by Julia Kristeva to refer to the double identitarian status of the speaking subject vis-à-vis the law on the one hand and, on the other, the transformative and unsettling movements she undergoes in writing, in culture, as agent vis-à-vis her place in the symbolic order. See, for example, *Desire in Language: A Semiotic Approach to Literature and Art*, ed. Leon S. Roudiez, trans. Thomas Gora, Alice Jardine, and Leon S. Roudiez (New York: Columbia University Press, 1980), 17-19.

present in the activity that eliminates [it]."[19] The traces of a process of elimination (however unintended) may construct the subject as much as the efforts to incorporate. A critical subject-in-process who reorganizes "contents" upon the demands of the contingent historico-political moment may discover that it is in the inaugural transitional moment from being traversed to reconfiguration that the political intention, as well as the combinatorial transculturating, takes place. Through such "moments," one can discover diverse cultural narrative formations, translations, and transcodifications that generate texts that are "hybrid" or "syncretic," and far from wanting to remain at rest in that taxonomy, make a bid for new discourse formations, bringing into view new subjects-in-process. In Gloria Anzaldúa's terms, these are the "borderlands" through which the border "theory circuits" of geopolitics and critical allegories find resonance but the zones of figurations and conceptualizations remain nonequivalent.[20] That is, the very contingent currents through which the geopolitical subject-in-process is dislocated, forced into (im)migration, will retain an irreducible difference that refuses to neatly correspond to the critico-discursive dislocated subject-in process.

It is my hope that through the writing of this essay, I have presented to the reader an exemplum, a practice, and a theory of the speaking subject-in-process, who in this instance stands in as a Chicana critic positioned in the interstice between nation-states.

---

19. Castoriadis, *The Imaginary Institution of Society*, 107.
20. Gloria Anzaldúa, *Borderlands/La Frontera: The New Mestiza* (San Francisco: Aunt Lute Books 1987), 20.

BIBLIOGRAPHY

Alarcón, Norma. "Chicana Feminism: In the Tracks of 'the' Native Woman." *Cultural Studies* 4, no. 3 (1990): 248-56.

Anzaldúa, Gloria. *Borderlands/La Frontera: The New Mestiza*. San Francisco: Spinsters/Aunt Lute, 1987.

Bateson, Gregory. *Steps to an Ecology of Mind*. San Francisco: Chandler Publishing, 1972.

Castoriadis, Cornelius. *The Imaginary Institution of Society*. Translated by Kathleen Blamey. Cambridge: The MIT Press, 1987.

Differences. no.1 (1989).

Fernández Kelly, M. Patricia and Anna M. García, "Invisible Amidst the Glitter: Hispanic Women in Southern California Electronics Industry." In *The Worth of Women's Work: A Qualitative Synthesis*, edited by A. Strathram, Eleanor M. Miller, and Hans O. Mauksh, 265-89. New York: State University of New York Press, 1988.

Kristeva, Julia. *Desire in Language: A Semiotic Approach to Literature and Art*. Edited by Leon S. Roudiez. Translated by Thomas Gora, Alice Jardine, and Leon Roudiez. New York: Columbia University Press, 1980.

López-González, Aralia, Amelia Malagamba and Elena Urrutia, editors. *Mujer y literatura Mexicana y Chicana: Culturas en contacto*, 2. México: El Colegio de México/Colegio de la Frontera Norte, 1990.

Lorde, Audre. "The Master's Tools Will Never Dismantle the Master's House." In *This Bridge Called My Back: Writings by Radical Women of Color*, edited by Cherríe Moraga and Gloria Anzaldúa, 98-106. Watertown, MA: Persephone Press, 1981.

Lyotard, Jean-François. *The Differend: Phrases in Dispute*. Translated by George Van de Abbeele. Minneapolis: University of Minnesota Press, 1988.

Moi, Toril. *Sexual/Textual Politics: Feminist Literary Theory*. London: Metheuen, 1985.

Poniatowska, Elena. *Querido Diego, te abraza Quiela*. México: Biblioteca Era, 1978.

Rodríguez, Richard. *The Hunger of Memory: The Education of Richard Rodríguez*. New York: Bantam, 1988.

Ruiz, Vicki L. and Susan Tiano, editors. *Women on the U.S.–Mexico Border: Responses to Change*. Boston: Allen & Unwin, 1987.

Sánchez, Rosaura. "Ethnicity, Ideology and Academia." *Cultural Studies* 4, no. 3 (1990): 294-302.

Spillers, Hortense. "Interstices: A Small Drama of Words." *Pleasure and Danger: Exploring Female Sexuality*, 73-100. Edited by Carole S. Vance. New York: Routledge, 1984.

Spivak, Gayatri Chakravorty. "Can the Subaltern Speak?." In *Marxism and the Interpretation of Culture*, edited by Cary Nelson and Lawrence Grossberg, 71–31. Basingstoke:

Macmillan, 1988.

Trinh, T. Minh-ha. *Woman, Native, Other: Writing, Postcoloniality, and Feminism.* Bloomington: Indiana University Press, 1988.

West, Cornel. "The Dilemma of the Black Intellectual." *Cultural Critique*, no. 1 (1985): 109–24.

TROPOLOGY OF HUNGER

THE "MISEDUCATION" OF RICHARD RODRÍGUEZ[1]

→ ←

THE HISTORICAL CONDITION OF our times is to have "ethnicity," albeit reconfigured and remapped in the aftermath of the civil rights movement in the United States. The Marxist mandate to acquire a class consciousness has been too limited to account for all the elements in the formation of raced ethnic groups in the context of the Américas. It increasingly appears as well that in the Euro-American terrain the formation of a proletarian class consciousness has become more of a step on the way to the formation of an unstable bourgeois liberal subject, given the hegemony of the ideology, than to becoming the "subject of history." Consequently, the contemporary entwinement of modernism (in the guise of aesthetics, positivism, enlightenment capitalist liberalism, and their conditioned Marxist contestations) and postmodernism (marking the refractedness and sinister side of the enlightenment project of progressive rationality, the multiplicity of life-world group formations, and the crisis of the male-biased liberal, political subject) gives rise to complex questions with respect to the cartography of culture and politics pertinent to the so-called ethnic canon, especially in its currently subordinated position to the nation and its canon.[2] Thus, the primary questions before us are, What is an American? What is América? What are the Américas?

It is not enough to assume ethnic identity in the context of the nation. One must pursue the conditions of its production and constitution and the structural and rhetorical forms engaged in the process. The extent to which ethnicity (raced or not) and gender can or cannot be refused is also of paramount importance given the constitutive contradictions to which the speaking/writing subject is

---

1. *Editors' Note:* This essay was originally published in *The Ethnic Canon: Histories, Institutions, and Interventions,* ed. David Palumbo-Liu (Minneapolis: University of Minnesota Press, 1995), 140-152.

2. David Harvey, *The Condition of Postmodernity* (Cambridge, MA.: Blackwell, 1989). Fredric Jameson, *Postmodernism or, The Cultural Logic of Late Capitalism,* (Durham, NC: Duke University Press, 1991). Ernesto Laclau and Lilian Zac, "Minding the Gap: The Subject of Politics," in *The Making of Political Identities*, ed. Ernesto Laclau and Lilian Zac (New York: Verso, 1994), 11-39.

subjected with respect to questions of identity-in-difference.³ For the "aesthete" like Richard Rodríguez, contradictions emerging from sociopolitical inequalities and spheres of institutional power may be turned into biting, (un)witty, and playful ironies as he insists in the too absolutist separations of the public and the private in classical liberal terms. The boundaries and traffic between the aesthetic and the political are a debatable nexus of analysis and discourse through the structures produced.⁴

Perhaps no other U.S. writer of Mexican descent has simultaneously embraced and undermined the political subject of bourgeois classical liberalism as has Richard Rodríguez. Indeed, Rodríguez's salient critical apparatus entails the deployment of the extremely dichotomized political categories of the private and the public, such that the private pertains to culture and experience, and the public to the (unquestioned) institutional or public political sphere of the nation-state. It is clear that his anti-affirmative action and anti-bilingual education positions assume a bourgeois classical liberal understanding of the public sphere. In the words of Nancy Fraser, such understanding of the public sphere assumes "that it is possible for interlocutors in a public sphere to bracket status differentials and to deliberate 'as if' they were social equals...and that a single, comprehensive public sphere is always preferable to a nexus of multiple publics."⁵ The call for "as if" they were social equals requires the construction of a "public persona" with a greater or lesser degree of dissonance with the "private" one. Under these conditions, the demand for group representation as people of Mexican descent (that is, as an ethnicized group) in the public sphere makes no sense, must be subsumed under the private and thereby rendered irrelevant—along with non-English languages—to the public sphere. English becomes, then, the common denominating language of the public sphere and

---

3. Trinh T. Minh-ha, *Woman, Native, Other: Writing Postcoloniality and Feminism* (Bloomington: Indiana University Press, 1989); Gloria Anzaldúa, *Borderlands/La Frontera: The New Mestiza* (San Francisco: Spinsters/Aunt Lute, 1987); and Gayatri Chakravorty Spivak, "Can the Subaltern Speak?" in *Marxism and the Interpretation of Culture,* eds. Cary Nelson and Lawrence Grossberg (Urbana: University of Illinois Press, 1988).

4. It is interesting to note that Richard Rorty's *Contingency, Irony, and Solidarity* relegates irony to privatized aesthetic spheres, blocking off questions of its sociopolitical implications. For further comment on Rorty, see also Honi Fern Haber's *Beyond Postmodern Politics: Lyotard, Rorty, Foucault* (NewYork: Routledge, 1994). I would question, however, the feasibility of leaping to beyond. In his work *Chicano Narrative: The Dialectics of Difference*, Ramon Saldívar also pursues the too absolute a separation between the private and the public in Rodríguez's work and attendant problems.

5. Nancy Fraser, "Rethinking the Public Sphere: A Contribution to the Critique of Actually Existing Democracy," in *Between Borders: Pedagogy and the Politics of Cultural Studies,* ed. Henry A. Giroux and Peter McClaren (New York: Routledge, 1994), 80.

all differences may be erased. The mandate, under these conditions, is for the formation of bourgeois classical liberal political subjects devoid of difference, devoid of (produced or constructed) "ethnic" trappings, indeed of gender and sexuality. In the liberal political context of Euro-America, then, it is no accident that the most sustained critique and challenge of the domains of the private and the public continue to emerge from feminist theorists, since it is what counts as private and/or public that becomes a salient issue in contemporary politics and demands for radical democracy.[6]

In a sense, Rodríguez's deployment of these political categories in his work is part of a noncritically acquired education that in effect leads him to the (unsustainable) refusal of ethnicity, except as a private phenomenon that is then opposed to his construction of a public persona. Notwithstanding the historical naiveté of his political positions—which make him a popular public speaker in neoconservative spheres—it is the structural and rhetorical traffic between experienced culture and politics, which he cannot neatly sever into the private and the public, that undermines the political public persona to which, in his view, we should all aspire.

Rereading *Hunger of Memory* and other of his works from the hierarchical structure and discourse generated through the pivotal scene in the section "Complexion" enables us to track the double-binds, which are often played for ironic effects, and the political economy's constitutive contradictions, which become inescapable for people of Mexican descent in the United States on the one hand, and for the (im)migrant's location on the other. A simultaneous reading of the constitutive contradictions of (im)migrants from the point of view of a Mexican location requires a reading of the displacement of campesinos/Indians from the economy and their exclusion from forming a public persona under Mexican conditions. In effect, the Chiapas neo-Zapatista movement is a recent dramatic example, in México, of the political economy's productive processes and the displaced people's claims to citizenship in the Mexican nation-making history.[7]

The section titled "Complexion" in Rodríguez's *Hunger of Memory* may be said to be structured by the mediating category of (im)migration. This analytical maneuver enables the displacement of a reading of the work as "merely" that of an emblematic passage into a self-making, self-determining Anglo-American political

---

6. Carole Pateman, *The Disorder of Women: Democracy, Feminism and Political Theory* (Stanford: Stanford University Press, 1989); Fraser, "Rethinking the Public Sphere"; and Zillah R. Eisenstein, *The Color of Gender: Reimagining Democracy* (Berkeley: University of California Press, 1994).

7. Roger Burbach, "Roots of the Postmodern Rebellion in Chiapas," *New Left Review* 205 (1994): 113-24.

liberal subject and brings into relief the salient constitutive contradictions that (im)migrants of Mexican descent undergo as they cross and recross the geopolitical border México–United States.[8] Moreover, it offers the possibility of reading Rodríguez's "ironic" mapping since his clear intentions are often enunciated by marking his privileged difference from (im)migrants, whom he wittily calls *los pobres*. (The only other Spanish term used is *los gringos*.) He points to his entry into the public sphere as a citizen-subject who "could act as a public person—able to defend my interests, to unionize, to petition, to speak up—to challenge and demand."[9] On the other hand, Rodríguez situates the (im)migrant as silent: "Their silence is more telling, they lack a public identity. They remain profoundly alien. Persons apart. People lacking a union obviously, people without grounds."[10] As (im)migrants subject to the waged-work realm of private capital and cultural spaces, Rodríguez underlines their lack of a "public identity" through which to defend their "rights" as workers. If they have a "public persona" at all it is as *collectivized* (im)migrants, displacing the possibility of *individualized* "rights" claims, thus highlighting the liberal justice system's vexed question of the rights of individuals versus the rights of (raced, gendered, and ethnicized) groups, as groups, a tension that is deeply implicated in the formation of the nation. As if proximity to (im)migrants bespoke a contagious disease, Rodríguez claims his "rights" as citizen-subject, reconfirming liberal ideology, and declares, "I would not shorten the distance I felt from *los pobres* with a few weeks of physical labor. I will not become like them. They were different from me."[11]

By marking the economic difference in Spanish-language terms, the (im)migrants are not just any (im)migrants but Mexican ones (or Latino ones), making as much the point that citizenship is as dependent on economic well-being as on speaking English. As a result, through the substitution of *los pobres* for (im)migrants, Rodríguez undermines the liberal "as if" proposition of social equality; that is, economic inequality becomes a sociopolitical one as well. By reversing the substitution of the ideological romanticization of the U.S. formation, (im)migration narrative is put on trial as it is revealed that (im)migrants are impoverished people with virtually no rights. In this scenario, *los pobres* as (im)migrants are constituted as the other of the bourgeois classical liberal political subject. Thus the political economy's constitution of this grouping (i.e.,

---

8. Roger Rouse, "Mexican Migration and the Social Space of Postmodernism," *Diaspora* 1, no. 1 (1991): 8-23.
9. Richard Rodríguez, *Hunger of Memory: The Education of Richard Rodríguez* (Boston: Godine, 1982): 138.
10. Rodríguez, *Hunger of Memory*, 138.
11. Rodríguez, *Hunger of Memory*, 135-36.

immigrants) is rejected for the pleasures of the hyperindividualized citizen-subject. On the one hand, it is precisely the tension between groupings (via the processes of the political economy) and individuals that historically overdetermined minoritized subjects put in evidence; on the other hand, Rodríguez's "refusal" to recognize this tension leads him to forget his (im)migrant status via the father, which, interestingly enough for us as readers, produces the unintended "irony" that undermines his claimed grounds. Moreover, the very "Complexion" that produces the relationality to the (im)migrants (discussed shortly) and undermines his separationist politics may well have the effect of turning him into an alien in Governor Pete Wilson's California. The separatist's politics are double and simultaneous (1) from (im)migrants, (2) between the private and the public, such that (im)migrants become part of the private sphere and silenced.[12]

Yet Rodríguez's marking of his difference works not only in the direction of the (im)migrant worker but also in the direction of the "authentic" (i.e., Anglo-American) nonalien, without much grasp of the production of an alie(n)ation insofar as the (im)migrant has no "grounds" for a "public persona." The autobiographical impulse moves toward dis-alie(n)ation through the desire not to be ethnicized as "Chicano" or "Mexican American" but rather one who is an "American," as Rodríguez claims in his essay "An American Writer." Terms such as Mexican American often function in his work as "merely" sociological categories unrelated to the practice of aesthetic writing—which again is a hyperindividualized project in Rodríguez and bound to compete as an aesthetic object in the aesthetic sphere of debate.

Euro-American liberal "rhetoric, in its Americanizing power to interpellate selfhood along consensual lines of upward mobility, social regeneration, and affirmative self-making," has often been the critical reading par excellence of autobiography.[13] Given the fact that such is the salient self-identity narrative in *Hunger of Memory*, the work implicitly falls in line with the "Americanist discourse, which no matter how critical it gets of existing society, only is granted professional legitimacy and social currency if it can evoke an affirmative relation to 'America' as the process of national self-affirmation and international

---

12. The political twists and turns of the private and the public are being played out in California through its Proposition 187, which was passed in the 1994 elections. The Proposition would have schools report undocumented (im)migrant children to the Immigration and Naturalization Service, which goes against children's protected educational rights under the Family Educational and Privacy Act. See the *San Francisco Chronicle*, August 13,1994: A1, A15.

13. Rob Wilson, "Producing American Selves: The Form of American Biography," *Boundary 2* (summer 1991): 118.

self-assertion."[14] This form of critical reading becomes the corresponding partner to notions of the public and the private in liberal political discourse, which calls for the homogeneous making of the citizen-subject. Rodríguez follows the ideology of what Wilson refers to as "the master-narrative of Americanization,"[15] through the mediating categories of the public and the private, thus promoting the (hyper)individuation of liberal political philosophy, which has often found its ideal discursive genre in autobiography on the one hand, and capitalist formation on the other.[16]

Nevertheless, as mentioned earlier, Rodríguez is aware of his undeniable, metonymically articulated relation to the (im)migrant via racialization and language. Through this evident relation, "White America" would want him to "claim unbroken ties with [the] past."[17] What he would relegate to the past is constantly present in the figure of the dark complected (im)migrant. A "clean" break with the past becomes impossible in a nation whose very formation has been constituted through racializations. Thus, he is actually trapped in-between the "past" that is not past and the "future" that is not present. Desire, which is ever the future, is "misrecognized" by Rodríguez in the salient ideology of "Americanization." It has been the "misrecognition" of choice for many (prima facie male) (im)migrants. Rodríguez, however, does not consciously seize the historical entrapment, which is the one that often pertains to minoritized intellectuals in the United States.

Wit, with its concomitant use of inversions, irony, sarcasm, parody, and contradiction, is even more salient in Rodríguez's more recent work. Having learned the difference in socioeconomic class from the British, who until recently believed themselves a pale island, he has also learned the racist difference in Anglo-America, but he is too polite to say so. México, whose "melting-pot" ideology has called for miscegenation, becomes, in his wit producing grammar, an assimilationist country, while the United States, with its myth of assimilationism, becomes the country of criminalized miscegenation. He does not have to use an imaginary past—which in any case he cannot remember—as a shield because he carries it on his face—"Look at this Indian face!"[18] Indeed, he is not supposed to

---

14. Wilson, "Producing American Selves," 124.

15. Wilson, "Producing American Selves," 109.

16. Michael Sprinker, "Fictions of the Self: The End of Autobiography," in *Autobiography: Essays Theoretical and Critical*, ed. James Olney (Princeton: Princeton University Press), 1980.

17. Rodríguez, *Hunger of Memory*, 5.

18. Richard Rodríguez, "An American Writer," in *The Invention of Ethnicity*, ed. Werner Sollors (New York: Oxford University Press, 1989), 10.

remember, since just about the time of the Anglo-America of Manifest Destiny Mexicans began to make much of their *mestizaje*, or what Rodríguez calls their assimilationist policy. Thus, if the Anglo-American nation-state formation is murderously manifested, the Mexican one is forcefully miscegenated and vice versa. One can very well ask what might be Rodríguez's aim through this baroque wit, characterized in literature by complexity of form and bizarre, ingenious, and often ambiguous imagery; characterized as well by grotesqueness, extravagance, or flamboyance.

The cover of the November 1991 issue of *Harper's* promotes Richard Rodríguez's essay "Mexico's Children" (subsequently collected in *Days of Obligation: An Argument with My Mexican Father*), as "The end of cultural and racial purity: Mixed Blood—a celebration of our *mestizo* world."[19] Between covers, Rodríguez proclaims: "I have come at last to Mexico, the country of my parents' birth. I do not expect to find anything that pertains to me."[20] (A Mexican national anonymous reader said he did not read much that pertained to him; in fact, the essay seemed to him a form of "Chicano" writing!) Rodríguez, however, concludes his tourism by remarking that "the Indian stands in the same relation to modernity as she [*sic*] did to Spain: Willing to marry, to breed, to disappear in order to ensure her inclusion in time; refusing to absent herself from the future.... I take it as an Indian achievement that I am alive, that I am Catholic, that I speak English, that I am an American."[21] Indian, Catholic, English, American are four trope-producing terms that Rodríguez employs for the concatenation of his cultural and political persona. To round out the visit to México, he states: "Mexico City: Europe's lie.... Each looks like mine.... where, then, is the famous conquistador? We have eaten him... we have eaten him with our eyes. I run to the mirror to see if this is true. It is true."[22] (Rodríguez plays here with a Mexican idiom applied to those that look too directly at another: "Comérselo con los ojos.") These observations bind two transformative effects—masculine into feminine and conquistador into Indian, respectively—turning through the consuming eyes.

In this later work, where he works tropes through the Indian face Rodríguez contradicts an earlier position. In "Late Victorians," for example, he had

---

19. Richard Rodríguez, "Late Victorians: San Francisco, AIDS, and the Homosexual Stereotype." *Harper's* (October 1990): 57-65.
20. Rodríguez, "Late Victorians," 51.
21. Rodríguez, "Late Victorians," 56.
22. Rodríguez, "Late Victorians," 56.

elected—"barren skeptic" that he is—to be a "reader of St. Augustine, curator of the earthly paradise, inheritor of the empty mirror." As curator, he administers by and large a rhetorical museum, and the mirror is empty. He has chosen the role of spectator, "shift[ing] my tailbone upon the cold, hard pew."[23] This "American Writer" does not fail to remind us that he too is a professional (ironic) Aztec: "God it must be cool to be related to Aztecs."[24] In the course of everyday transactions the body is textualized by others. He observes to his Anglo-American audience, "I am one of you,"[25] as he exclaims, "Look at this Indian face!"[26] He is told by both San Francisco and Berkeley liberals, as well as his grandmother, to maintain his culture, "whatever that means."[27] Americans end up sounding like one another, he observes, and "We do not, however, easily recognize our common identity."[28] But he claims to retain "aspects of culture, the deepest faiths, and moods of my ancestors, an inheritance deeper sometimes than I dare reveal to you, formal you."[29] The theme of secretive, in this instance, privatization continues, and the clue to the put-down of his Anglo-American audience is in that "formal you." If Americans do not differentiate linguistically between an informal "private" you and a formal "public" you, he begs the privilege to invoke the Hispanic usage, albeit embroiled in the baroque effects of colonization. He distances himself from "you" through linguistic practices that are alien to the "egalitarian" linguistic mask of Anglo-America.

Rodríguez's baroqueness is not book-learned from Indo-Hispanic América but from his orally rooted and disenfranchised father who learned the proper grammatical address, and from the British from whom he learned about manners, socioeconomic class, and the forms appropriate to it—especially those that deploy the wit/conceit of the upper classes or the aristocracy. The implication is that the colonized servants learn "conceit" from the aristocrats or upper classes and subsequently hold up a mirror, albeit rhetorical. In a sense, this accounts for Rodríguez's fondness for the pastoral, the form of impersonation "felt to imply a beautiful relation between rich and poor," where the elite get to be shepherds for a day and conduct a "courtship between contrasted social classes."[30] According

---

23. Rodríguez, "Late Victorians," 66.
24. Rodríguez, "An American Writer," 10.
25. Rodríguez, "An American Writer," 11.
26. Rodríguez, "An American Writer," 10.
27. Rodríguez, "An American Writer," 10.
28. Rodríguez, "An American Writer," 4.
29. Rodríguez, "An American Writer," 11.
30. Kenneth Burke, *A Grammar of Motives* (Berkeley: University of California Press, 1969), 123

to Burke, William Empson's *Some Versions of Pastoral*, which Rodríguez read, was a "response to a vogue for 'proletarian' literature," and thereby "profoundly concerned with the rhetoric of courtship between contrasted social classes."[31] Thus, it should be no surprise that Rodríguez would use the conceits of the form as the devices to propel his rejection of self-proclaimed Chicano "proles" on the one hand, and the "egalitarian" mask of Anglo-America on the other, through the very fulcrum of middle-class America, the "universal" class and its bourgeois liberal subject.

In many ways, Rodríguez places in question those who are fond of claiming citizenship by saying "I am an American" and think they know what they mean. To this Rodríguez replies implicitly, "so am I"—though most of his book learning has been English/British through education (recently he has added Octavio Paz and Carlos Fuentes to the list), his socioeconomic and political life is (Anglo) American, and his affective life is represented through working-class Mexican Spanish (which he cannot write). If the aristocrats can play at being shepherds, Rodríguez can play at being an aristocrat. He acts the aristocrat and simultaneously courts him. But he can also play at being an American and fly east from California, "against the grain of America, into the dark."[32] Rodríguez's rhetorical impersonations involve what Butler has called a complex "double inversion that says appearance is an illusion."[33] In Rodríguez's vocabulary, the outside appearance is Indian/feminine but the "essence" inside the body is aristocratic/masculine. At the same time, it symbolizes the opposite: the appearance outside is aristocratic/masculine but the "essence" inside is Indian/feminine, operating via the tropes produced as a result of "eating through the eyes." Enacted impersonations place the truth of identity in question while simultaneously producing other possibilities as in the case of "neoethnicity" gambits. For example, a book by Danny Santiago (*Famous All over Town*), an Anglo whose name was James, won a Casa de las Américas Prize as a Chicano book.[34] More recently, the Cherokee tale *The Education of Little Tree* was discovered not to have been written by a Cherokee but by Asa (Ace) Carter, a white supremacist who wrote speeches for former Alabama governor George C. Wallace and worked for the Ku Klux Klan.

---

31. Burke, *A Grammar of Motives*, 123.

32. Rodríguez, "An American Writer," 3.

33. Judith Butler, "Gender Trouble, Feminist Theory and Psychoanalytic Discourse," in *Feminism/Postmodernism*, ed. Linda Nicholson (New York: Routledge, 1990), 337.

34. Danny Santiago, *Famous All Over Town* (New York: Plume/Penguin, 1984).

The complicity between the demand for authenticity and its subsequent commodification, and the ease with which we can pass as "authentic" by learning the "right" things, come with the territory of having "ethnicity" in the Américas today. In a sense it is an additional aspect of its production in advanced capitalist nations. Richard Rodríguez says with Trinh T. Minh-ha "Like you/not you," the "in-between zones are the shifting grounds on which the (doubly) exiled walk."[35] And to mark this duplicity, Rodríguez translates the style of the drag queen through the rhetorical museum of the Indian. Much, one might say—as Derrida's Nietzsche in *Spurs*—translates the style of the man through the rhetorical museum of the feminine. In the Trinh T. Minh-ha citations, the exile is double because the Insider is Outsider, the Outsider is Insider, "Outside in Inside Out." Further in the never-ending play of the rhetorical, Rodríguez reveals his "ethnicity" because he is an American, and he reveals his Americanness because he is an "ethnic." "I suspect," he says, "ethnicity is only a public metaphor, like sexuality or age, for a knowledge that bewilders us."[36] But in the United States, for example, those that continue to be "ethnic" (or in México, "Indians") are those who are unable to miscegenate, that is, they could not actually pass for or impersonate an "Anglo-American." Manifest Destiny is the move of Anglo-America toward the South and then the West, and from both we read América against the grain: "Undercutting the Inside/Outside opposition, her intervention is necessarily that of both a deceptive insider and a deceptive outsider."[37] In the rhetorical museum of (wo)man, the impersonator is virtually always feminine.[38] Yet this baroque wit, which we insist on calling "postmodern," is an inversion of the pastoral for Rodríguez, for we have the "shepherd" playing at the "aristocrat," or, shall we say the Caliban playing at Prospero: "I have taken Caliban's advice. I have stolen their books. I will have some run of this isle."[39] Rodríguez's performance of raced ethnicities finds resonance in the Supreme Court's nation-defining statement in the Bakke decision, which claims that "all groups in the United States are a minority, each of which so far as 'racial and ethnic distinctions' go is rooted in our Nation's constitutional and demographic history."[40] According to this vision, the United States is a "nation of minorities,"

---

35. Trinh, *Woman, Native, Other*, 70
36. Rodríguez, "An American Writer," 9.
37. Trinh, *Woman, Native, Other*, 70.
38. Trinh, *Woman, Native, Other*, 74.
39. Rodríguez, *Hunger of Memory*, 3.
40. *Regents of University of California v. Bakke*, 1221.

each of which had to struggle "to overcome prejudices not of a monolithic majority, but of a 'majority' composed of various minority groups of whom it was said—perhaps unfairly in many cases—that a shared characteristic was a willingness to disadvantage other groups.""[41] Since the civil rights movement puts in crisis the myth of the "melting pot" of nation-making Anglo-America, ethnic raconteurs and "disadvantaging majorities" from all academic disciplines including jurisprudence are all now embroiled in "identity" formation discourses.

Is a bourgeois pastoral subject all a "true" American can have? Rodríguez's fascination with the pastoral is due to the paradigmatic and ideological function that he saw in the form. However, since the form itself is ironically mannered, he is drawn deeper into its wit, very self-conscious of the fact that not all is as is, perhaps a variation on the *ser/parecer* theme of the Spanish baroque itself. Tomás Rivera observed of *Hunger of Memory* that Rodríguez's use of the verb *to be* is one of locatedness, of place, rather than of predication.[42] Rivera gets at this by noting that in Spanish there are two verbs to signify *to be, ser* and *estar* (contrast this with *ser/parecer*—that is, *ser* pivots two contrastive verbs). Rivera theorizes that the first reflects interiority and the second exteriority, and that the core of "our" life is the family, the interiority, the intimate—completely the reverse of what Rivera assumes that Rodríguez claims. Rivera sees Rodríguez as claiming that the core of his life is the "public" one because he silences his immediate family, refusing to educate himself on Hispanic culture, his genealogical family as well. I think Rivera is preliminarily on the right track on his observations of the use of to be—as *being* and as *situatedness*. It is the play between those possibilities, including *ser/parecer*, that Rodríguez puts into play through his usage of tropes in the English language. However, Rivera glides too easily from individual interiority to the family to the private and presumes that they correspond in too symmetrical a fashion to *ser*, leaving *estar* to designate the "public": No assessment has been made of Rivera's linguistic claims on *Hunger of Memory*; at this point this becomes an instance of the traffic between Spanish and English.

For Rodríguez the use of the Spanish language is something to savor. The contrast of Spanish and English is a contrast between gliding and stumbling, mellifluous sliding and screeching. He sentimentalizes the working-class users of Spanish (shepherds?) from the point of view of English usage (aristocrats?). Spanish, for Rodríguez, represents his parents, who betrayed him by insisting

---

41. *Regents of University of California v. Bakke*, 1221.

42. Tomás Rivera, "Richard Rodríguez's *Hunger of Memory* as Humanistic Antithesis," *MELUS* 11, no. 4 (1984): 5-13.

that he do as the nuns say and learn English. He does so with a vengeance (as we have come to learn) in order to hurt his parents— and, in a childish way, both to keep the intimacy of what his parents offered and to distance himself from them. Through this emotionally charged relationship, he privatizes Spanish, relegating it to the domestic sphere, and severs it (unsuccessfully) from English, which is relegated to the public sphere. His rage at the break—the discontinuity between home and school, past and present that every Spanish-speaking child experiences in the United States—is displaced toward Chicanos who demand bilingual education. Moreover, he refuses to claim, as Rivera would want him to, a heritage that is not his, playing on the finer point of possession/dispossession—the political displacement and dispossession of his father from México. To claim a heritage is to use it as a shield, yet simultaneously he relegates his (im)migrant father to silence.

Insofar as judicial affirmative action narratives have hitched constitutional consistency and coherence to the privileged rights of the individual who is above "political and social judgments" pertinent to groups, Rodríguez is in complete agreement with the system. According to the Supreme Court, "Nothing in the constitution supports the notion that individuals may be asked to suffer otherwise impermissible burdens in order to enhance the societal standings of their ethnic groups."[43] It will not be suffered that the individual's worth will be tarnished by "stereotypes of groups"; moreover, "innocent individuals should not be forced to bear the burdens of redressing grievances not of their making."[44] The pursuit of self-possessed individuality in Richard Rodríguez takes place according to the Constitution of the United States as coded in the Fourteenth Amendment. Yet he also demonstrates, unwittingly, the limits of the refusal to play the Anglo-American ethnic game. Anglo-America's politics continue to be predicated on acquiring visibility through ethnicity, not race, a factor that makes the justices shutter as it may imply a "two-class theory." It was the incorporation of race into the Constitution that henceforth made denial impossible, yet that is eroded through the ethnic dance. In my view, the hidden episteme in Rodríguez's pastoral is the rage at our embodied history, for while his wit may pass muster, his face does not. As a result, the face becomes a weapon along with wit. How else can he tell us that his body is as textualized as his speech? Yet he knows what he is about as he asserts, "There are those in America who would anoint me to

---

43. *Regents of University of California v. Bakke*, 1223.
44. *Regents of University of California v. Bakke*, 1223

play out for them some drama of ancestral reconciliation.... But I reject the role."[45] Who are the ancestors? Who are those?

Richard Rodríguez's "bad faith," if I may use such an antiquated existential phrase, and even on occasion his egregious politics, lie in the silencing of the disenfranchised—(im)migrant labor. He does so politically by continuing to allow his bioexemplum to serve as the preferred citation of right-wing liberals. In some sense, Rodríguez demonstrates that neoconservative liberal cynicism knows no bounds, as it rhetorically feeds its own trope machine by the selective filtering of the discourses of emancipation. In *Hunger of Memory*, as George Yúdice has observed, "arguments against affirmative action and bilingual education, because these policies construct a certain minority identity, are a significant indictment of liberal morality (or hypocrisy to be more exact)."[46] Rodríguez's unsustainable refusal of a minoritized identity blunts the edge of his anger, as he prefers to advance his "public" and "scholarship boy" persona, which has become a carbon copy of the literate dominant even as he admits that such an obedient and imitative persona voids him of critical thinking. He has discovered, however, that totalizing self-construction is elusive.

Caught within the limitations of a self-avowed spectatorship, the demands of participatory democracy, the textualization of the body, and the will to conserve some notion of the "American" way, Rodríguez has been as much silenced by some criticism as he has silenced the Mexican (im)migrant. Displacement and dislocation are at the core of the invention of the Américas. However, it is not the dispossessed (im)migrant laborer or Indian as presence but her absence from the public sphere, as citizen-subject, that continues to drive the nation-making processes. Rodríguez's major unintended question may well be, "Can the Subaltern Speak?"[47] To which his answer is no because she lacks a public persona. Yet he would deprive her of the possibility of a public persona by insisting on an identitarian figuration of the public sphere, while simultaneously performing the tropology of differences as an aesthetic project closed off from the sociopolitical sphere. Thus, in Rodríguez's writing trajectory, difference is aesthetic and private, identity is political and public and must be subordinated to prevailing hegemonic views of the public sphere. One might well say, from this point of view, that not even the Supreme Court justices agree completely!

---

45. Rodríguez, *Hunger of Memory*, 4.
46. George Yúdice, "Marginality and the Ethics of Survival," in *Universal Abandon? The Politics of Postmodernism*, ed. Andrew Ross (Minneapolis: University of Minnesota Press, 1988), 222.
47. Spivak, "Can the Subaltern Speak?"

BIBLIOGRAPHY

Anzaldúa, Gloria. *Borderlands/La Frontera: The New Mestiza.* San Francisco: Spinsters/Aunt Lute, 1987.

Burbach, Roger. "Roots of the Postmodern Rebellion in Chiapas." *New Left Review* 205 (1994): 113-24.

Burke, Kenneth. *A Grammar of Motives.* Berkeley: University of California Press, 1969.

Butler, Judith. "Gender Trouble, Feminist Theory and Psychoanalytic Discourse." In *Feminism/Postmodernism.* Edited by Linda Nicholson, 324-340. New York: Routledge,1990.

Eisenstein, Zillah R. *The Color of Gender: Reimagining Democracy.* Berkeley: University of California Press, 1994.

Fraser, Nancy. "Rethinking the Public Sphere: A Contribution to the Critique of Actually Existing Democracy." In *Between Borders: Pedagogy and the Politics of Cultural Studies.* Edited by Henry A. Giroux and Peter McClaren, 74-98. New York: Routledge, 1994.

Jameson, Fredric. *Postmodernism, or, The Cultural Logic of Late Capitalism.* Durham, N.C.: Duke University Press, 1991.

Haber, Honi Fern. *Beyond Postmodern Politics: Lyotard, Rorty, Foucault.* New York: Routledge, 1994.

Harvey, David. *The Condition of Postmodernity.* Cambridge, MA.: Blackwell, 1989.

Laclau, Ernesto, and Lilian Zac. "Minding the Gap: The Subject of Politics." In *The Making of Political Identities.* Edited by Ernesto Laclau, 11-39. New York: Verso, 1994.

Pateman, Carole. *The Disorder of Women: Democracy, Feminism and Political Theory.* Stanford: Stanford University Press, 1989.

Regents of University of California v. Bakke, 438 U.S. 265, 98 S.Ct.2733, 57 L.ed.2d 750 (1978)

Rivera, Tomás. "Richard Rodríguez's *Hunger of Memory* as Humanistic Antithesis." *MELUS* II no. 4 (1984): 5-13.

Rodríguez, Richard. "An American Writer." In *The Invention of Ethnicity.* Edited by Werner Sollors, 3-13. New York: Oxford University Press, 1989.

Rodríguez, Richard. *Days of Obligation: An Argument with My Mexican Father.* New York: Viking, 1992.

Rodríguez, Richard. *Hunger of Memory: The Education of Richard Rodríguez.* Boston: Godine, 1982.

Rodríguez, Richard. "Late Victorians: San Francisco, AIDS, and the Homosexual Stereotype." *Harper's* (October 1990): 57-65.

Rodríguez, Richard. "Mixed Blood, Columbus's Legacy: A World Made Mestizo." *Harper's* (November 1991): 47-56.

Rorty, Richard. *Contingency, Irony, and Solidarity.* Cambridge: Cambridge University Press, 1989.

Rouse, Roger. "Mexican Migration and the Social Space of Postmodernism." *Diaspora* 1, no. 1 (1991): 8-23.

Spivak, Gayatri Chakravorty. "Can the Subaltern Speak?" In *Marxism and the Interpretation of Culture,* edited by Cary Nelson and Lawrence Grossberg. Urbana: University of Illinois Press, 1988.

Sprinker, Michael. "Fictions of the Self: The End of Autobiography." In *Autobiography: Essays Theoretical and Critical,* 321-342, edited by James Olney. Princeton, N.J.: Princeton University Press, 1980.

Trinh, T. Minh-ha. *Woman/Native/Other.* Bloomington: Indiana University Press, 1989.

Wilson, Rob. "Producing American Selves: The Form of American Biography." *Boundary* 2 (1991): 104-29.

Yúdice, George. "Marginality and the Ethics of Survival." In *Universal Abandon? The Politics of Postmodernism,* edited by Andrew Ross, 214-136. Minneapolis: University of Minnesota Press, 1988.

ANZALDÚA'S *FRONTERA*

INSCRIBING GYNETICS[1]

→ ←

The Inscription of the Subject

IN OUR TIME THE very categorical and/or conceptual frameworks through which we explicitly or implicitly perceive our sociopolitical realities and our own subjective (private) contextual insertion are very much in question. There is a desire to construct our own (women of color) epistemologies and ontologies and to obtain the interpretive agency with which to make claims to our own critical theory. Theoretically infused writing practices, such as those found in anthologies like *This Bridge Called My Back: Writings by Radical Women of Color*;[2] *All the Women Are White, All the Blacks Are Men, But Some of Us Are Brave*,[3] and *Making Face/Making Soul: Haciendo Caras, Creative and Critical Perspectives by Feminists of Color*,[4] are salient testaments to that desire for inscription in a different register—the register of women of color.

The self that writes combines a polyvalent consciousness of "the writer as historical subject (who writes? and in what context?), but also writing itself as located at the intersection of subject and history—a literary and sociological practice that involves the possible knowledge (linguistic and ideological) of

---

1. *Editors' Note:* This essay was originally published in *Anuario de Letras Modernas, no. 6, Facultad de Filosofía y Letras* (México: Universidad Nacional Autónoma de México, 1994), 143-159. Subsequently, it was republished in *Diaspora and Geographies of Identity* (Durham, NC: Duke University Press, 1996), 41-54; *Chicana Feminisms: A Critical Reader*, ed. Patricia Zavella, Gabriela F. Arredondo, Aída Hurtado, Norma Klahn, and Olga Nájera-Ramírez (Durham, NC: Duke University Press, 2003), 354-376; and *Decolonial Voices: Chicana and Chicano Cultural Studies in the 21st Century*, ed. Arturo J. Aldama and Naomi H. Quiñonez (Bloomington: Indiana University Press, 2002), 113-128. The version published here is from *Chicana Feminisms: A Critical Reader*, 2003.

2. Cherríe Moraga and Gloria Anzaldúa, eds., *This Bridge Called My Back: Writings by Radical Women of Color* (Watertown, MA: Persephone Press, 1981).

3. Gloria Hull, Patricia Bell Scott, and Barbara Smith, eds., *All the Women Are White, All the Blacks Are Men, But Some of Us Are Brave: Black Women's Studies* (New York: Feminist Press, 1982).

4. Gloria Anzaldúa, ed., *Making Face, Making Soul: Creative and Critical Perspectives by Feminists of Color* (San Fransico: Aunt Lute Books, 1990).

itself as such."⁵ Self-inscriptions, as focal points of cultural consciousness and social change, weave into language the complex relations of a subject caught in the contradictory dilemmas of race, gender, ethnicity, sexualities, and class, a transition between orality and literacy, and the "practice of literature as the very place where social alienation is thwarted differently according to each specific context."⁶

Self-inscription as focal point of cultural consciousness and social change is as vexed a practice for the more "organic/specific" intellectual as it is for the "academic/specific" intellectual trained in institutions whose business is often to continue to reproduce his hegemonic hold on cognitive charting and its (political) distribution in the academy itself. As a result, it should be no surprise that critics of color, in a context different from that of *Bridge* and thus differently articulated, nevertheless critique through their exclusion, their absence or displacement in the theoretical production and positions taken by Euroamerican feminists and African Americanists. "The black woman as critic and more broadly as the locus where gender-, class-, and race-based oppression intersect, is often invoked when Anglo-American feminists and male Afro-Americanists begin to rematerialize their discourse."⁷ Thus, cultural/national dislocations also produce cognitive ones as the models that assume dominance increasingly reify their discourse through the use of nonrevised theories, thus resembling more and more so-called androcentric criticisms. In other words, Smith says, "When historical specificity is denied or remains implicit, all the women are presumed white, all the blacks male. The move to include black women as historical presences and as speaking subjects in critical discourse may well then be used as a defense against charges of racial hegemony on the part of white women and sexist hegemony on the part of black males."⁸ Thus the "black woman" appears as a "historicizing presence," which is to say that, as the critical gaze becomes more distanced from itself as speaker, it looks to "black women" as the objective difference that historicizes the text in the present, signaling the degree to which such theorists have ambiguously and ambivalently assumed the position of Same/I

---

5. Trinh T. Minh-Ha, "Not You/Like You: Post-Colonial Women and the Interlocking Questions of Identity and Difference," in *Making Face/Making Soul: Haciendo Caras. Creative and Critical Perspectives by Women of Color*, ed. Gloria Anzaldúa (San Francisco: Aunt Lute Books, 1990), 6.

6. Trinh, "Not You/Like You," 245.

7. Valerie Smith, "Black Feminist Theory and the Representation of the 'Other,'" in *Changing Our Own Words: Essays on Criticism, Theory and Writing by Black Women*, ed. Cheryl A. Wall (New Brunswick, NJ: Rutgers University Press, 1989), 44.

8. Smith, "Black Feminist Theory and the Representation of the 'Other,'" 44-45.

as mediated by current critical theories. In this circuitous manner, the critical eye/I claims Same/Not Same, an inescapability that itself needs elaboration through the narratives that incorporate the historical production of differences for the purpose of exclusion, repression, and oppression. The inscription of the subject takes place in a polyvalent historical and ideological context that demands larger frames of intelligibility than that of a self/other duality.

Insofar as the critical discourses of Euroamerican feminists transform white patriarchal thought via the critical infusion of gender and sexuality, and racialized men challenge a white supremacist patriarchy via the critical infusion of race, women of color who are minimally intersected by these are excluded from what become accepted critical discourses in institutions. Though it is no small critical achievement to transform conceptual frames of intelligibility through the inclusion of a culturally produced category of difference, the fact remains that women of color, by our mere existence and self-inscription, continue to question those critical hermeneutics that silences the very possibility of another critical practice that does not foreclose inclusion or at least reveals an awareness of the exclusions that make the construction of our work possible. The work of women of color emerges through the critical and material gap produced by multiple exclusions in the silences of the text that further may implicitly suggest inclusion such that we *appear* to be working together in opposition to the "Name of the Father and the Place of the Law." Are we?

Smith goes on to affirm that as black feminist theorists emerge they challenge "the conceptualizations of literary study and concern themselves increasingly with the effect of race, class, and gender on the practice of literary criticism."[9] My intention here is not so much to produce a "literary criticism" for Chicanas, nor do I want to be limited by the reach of what are perceived as "literary texts." I want to be able to hybridize the textual field so that what is at stake is not so much our inclusion or exclusion in literary/textual genealogies and the modes of their production, which have a limited though important critical reach, but to come to terms with the formation and displacement of subjects as writers/critics/chroniclers of the nation and the possibility that we have continued to recodify a family romance, an oedipal drama in which the woman of color in the Americas has no "designated" place. That is, she is elsewhere. She is simultaneously presence/absence in the configurations of the nation-state and its narrative representation. Moreover, the moment she emerges as a "speaking

---

9. Smith, "Black Feminist Theory and the Representation of the 'Other,'" 46-47.

subject-in-process" the heretofore triadic manner in which the modern world has largely taken shape becomes endlessly heterogeneous and ruptures the "oedipal family romance" that is historically marked white in the United States. The underlying structure of social and cultural forms in the organization of Western societies has been superimposed through administrative systems of domination—political, cultural, and theoretical—and subsequent counter-nation-making narratives have adapted such forms in the Americas that are now disrupted by the voice of writers/critics of color such as Chicanas so that we must "make familia from scratch."

In an earlier essay, "Chicana Feminism: In the Tracks of 'the' Native Woman,"[10] I appropriated as metonym and metaphor for the referent/figure of the Chicana the notion of the "differend" from Lyotard, which he defines as "a case of conflict between (at least) two parties that cannot be equitably resolved for lack of rule of judgment applicable to both arguments. One side's legitimacy does not imply the other's lack of legitimacy."[11] In part, her conflictive and conflicted position emerges as Smith affirms when the oppositional discourses of "white" women and "black" men vie for her "difference" as historical materialization and/or a shifting deconstructive maneuver of patriarchy, "The Name of the Father and the Place of the Law." Yet one must keep in mind that Lyotard's disquisition on the term doesn't negotiate well the transitions between textual and political/juridical representation. As Fraser and Nicholson have noted, "There is no place in Lyotard's universe for critique of pervasive axes of stratification, for critique of broad-based relations of dominance and subordination along lines like gender, race and class."[12] Relations of dominance and subordination arise out of the political economy and the ways the nation has generated its own self-representation in order to harness its population toward its own self-projection on behalf of the elite. As such, the formation of political economies, in tandem with the making of nations, provides the locations from which historical material specificity arises and generates its own discourses. These discourses philosophically may or may not coincide with theories of textual representation, which may be held hostage through a discipline. The shift from theories of symbolic self-representation to

---

10. Norma Alarcón, "Chicana Feminism: In the Tracks of 'the' Native Woman," *Cultural Studies* 4, no. 3 (1990), 248-256.

11. Jean-François Lyotard, *The Differend: Phrases in Dispute* (Minneapolis: University of Minnesota Press, 1988), 12.

12. Nancy Fraser and Linda J. Nicholson, "Social Criticism without Philosophy: An Encounter between Feminism and Postmodernism," in *Feminism/Postmodernism*, eds. Nancy Fraser and Linda J. Nicholson (New York: Routledge, 1990), 23.

juridical and phenomenological ones is not seamless; indeed, the interstice, discontinuity, or gap is precisely a site of textual production—the historical and ideological moment in which the subject inscribes herself contextually. In other words, the located historical writing subject emerges into conflictive discourses generated by theories of representation, whether juridical or textual/symbolic. Each is rule-governed by different presuppositions, and a Chicana may have better fortunes at representing herself or being represented textually than legally as a Chicana. That is, the juridical text is generated by the ruling elite, who have access to the state apparatus through which the political economy is shaped and jurisprudence is engendered, whereas representation in the cultural text may include representations generated by herself. However, insofar as the latter are, as it were, "marginalia," they not only exist in the interstices, they are produced from the interstices. She, akin to Anzaldúa's "Shadow Beast," sends us in as "stand-ins," reinforcing and ensuring the interstitiality of a *differend*, as the very nonsite from which critique is possible. Her migratory status, which deprives her of the "protection" of "home," whether a stable town or a nation-state, generates an "acoherent" though cogent discourse that it is our task to revise and inscribe.

It is, I believe, in the spirit of the above remarks, which are as much produced by my reading of Anzaldúa as hers are produced by her "hunger of memory," and by a coming into "being," which Anzaldúa understands to be both the truth and a fiction, a truth as the Shadow Beast who is continually complicit with and resistant to the stand-in, conscious will, and who "threatens the sovereignty" of conscious rulership, that the Shadow Beast ultimately undermines a monological self-representation, because it kicks out the constraints and "'bolts' at the least hint of limitations."[13]

Inscribing Gynetics

GLORIA ANZALDÚA IS A self-proclaimed Chicana from Hargill, Texas, a rural town in what is known as El Valle, the Valley. It is an agricultural area notorious for the mistreatment of people of Mexican descent, African Americans, and displaced indigenous peoples. Indeed, many of the narratives that emerge from that area tell of the conflictive and violent relations in the forging of an anglicized Texas out of the Texas-Coahuila territory of New Spain as well as of the eventual production of the geopolitical border between México and the United

---

13. Gloria Anzaldúa, *Borderlands/La Frontera* (San Francisco: Spinsters/Aunt Lute, 1987), 12.

States. These borderlands are spaces where, as a result of expansionary wars, colonization, juridico-immigratory policing, and coyote exploitation of emigrés and group-vigilantes, formations of violence are continuously in the making. These have been taking place as misogynist and racialized confrontations at least since the Spanish began to settle México's (New Spain) "northern" frontier of what is now the incompletely Angloamericanized Southwest. Subsequently, and especially after the end of the Mexican-American War in 1848, these formations of violence have been often dichotomized into Mexican/American, which has the effect of muting the presence of indigenous peoples yet setting "the context for the formation of 'races.'"[14]

Consequently, the modes of autohistoricization in and of the borderlands often emphasize or begin with accounts of violent racialized collisions. It is not surprising, then, that Anzaldúa should refer to the current U.S./Mexican borderline as an "open wound" from Brownsville to San Diego, from Tijuana to Matamoros, where the former are considerably richer than the latter and the geopolitical line itself artificially divides into a two-class/culture system; that is, the configuration of the political economy has the "Third" World rub against the "First." Though the linguistic and cultural systems on the border are highly fluid in their dispersal, the geopolitical lines tend to become univocal, that is, "Mexican" and "Anglo."

Of Hargill, Texas, and Hidalgo County and environs, Anzaldúa says, "This land has survived possession and ill-use by five powers: Spain, México, the Republic of Texas, the United States, the Confederacy, and the U.S. again. It has survived Anglo-Mexican blood feuds, lynchings, burnings, rapes, pillage."[15] Hidalgo is the "most poverty-stricken county in the nation as well as the largest home base (along with Imperial Valley in California) for migrant farmworkers." She continues "It was here that I was born and raised. I am amazed that both it and I have survived."[16]

Through this geographic space, then, people displaced by a territorialized political economy whose juridical centers of power are elsewhere, in this case México, D.F., and Washington, D.C., attempt to reduce the level of material dispossession through the production of both counter- and dis-identificatory discourses. That is, the land is repossessed in imaginary terms, both in the

---

14. David Montejano, *Anglos and Mexicans in the Making of Texas, 1836-1986* (Austin: University of Texas Press, 1987), 309.

15. Anzaldúa, *Borderlands/La Frontera*, 90.

16. Anzaldúa, *Borderlands/La Frontera*, 98.

Lacanian and Althusserian sense. I return below to a more elaborate discussion of this proposition, which I also characterize as dialogically paradigmatic and syntagmatic, respectively, yielding a highly creative heteroglossia.

However, before turning to Anzaldúa's attempt to repossess the borderlands in polyvalent modes, let's quickly review one area of counter-identificatory or oppositional discursive productions that are based on a self/other dualistic frames of intelligibility. Thus, for example, Américo Paredes and now his follower José E. Limón claim El Valle as the site where the corrido originated. That is, in the Américas in the Valley of a landmass now named Texas a completely "new" genre emerged, the corrido. As such, Limón strategically moves the emergence toward disengagement from claims of the corrido's origins in the Spanish romance—Spain's own border ballads. The Paredes-Limón move could be contextualized as a racialized-class-culture-based one, where "people" of Mexican descent mediate their opposition to Anglos via the corrido. The trans*form*ation and trans*figuration* in raced-class crossing remains unexplored.[17] That is, the metamorphoses of the Spanish ballad form are induced by the emergence of an oppositional hero in the U.S.–México border whose race-class position is substantially different from Spanish ballad heroes, who are often members of the aristocracy. Limón's strategy is in contradiction to that of María Herrera-Sobek's in her book *The Mexican Corrido: A Feminist Analysis*,[18] where she aligns the corrido with the peninsular origins theory, in which border ballads also emerged in the making of Spain. Herrera-Sobek's lack of desire to disengage the formal origins from Spain in its Spanish-language form and relocalize them in Texas could be a function of an implicit feminist position. The representation of women, be it in the romance or the corrido, reenacts a spectacularly Manichaean or romantic scenario in patriarchal tableaux. Why claim a "new" genre when what we have is a "new" dispossessed figure with claims to becoming a hero for "his" people in a different formation—people of Mexican descent, Chicanos/as.

The point of my analysis, however, is to call attention to the need to "repossess" the land, especially in cultural nationalist narratives, through scenarios of origins that emerge in the self-same territory—be it at the literary, legendary, historical, ideological, critical, or theoretical level—producing in material and imaginary terms "authentic" and "inauthentic," "legal" and "illegal" subjects.

---

17. José E. Limón, *Mexican Ballads, Chicano Poems: History and Influence in Mexican-American Social Poetry* (Berkeley: University of California Press, 1992), 7-42.

18. María Herrera-Sobek, *The Mexican Corrido: A Feminist Analysis* (Bloomington: Indiana University Press, 1990).

That is, the drive to territorialize/authenticate/legalize and deterritorialize/deauthenticate/delegalize is ever present, thus constantly producing "(il)legal"/(non)citizen-subjects both in political and symbolic representations in a geographic area where looks and dress have become increasingly telling of one's (un)documented status.[19] It should be no surprise, then, that the corrido in the borderlands makes a paradigmatic oppositional hero of the persecuted in the figuration of the unjustly outlaw(ed), the unjustly (un)documented—in Anzaldúa's terms, Queers.

Thus, also, in Anzaldúa's terms, the convergence of claims to proper ownership of the land "has created a shock culture, a border culture, a third country, a closed country."[20] Here, the "detribalized" and dispossessed population is not only composed of "females, . . . homosexuals of all races, the darkskinned, the outcast, the persecuted, the marginalized, the foreign"[21] but is also possessed of the "faculty," a "sensing," in short, a different consciousness, which is represented by the formulation of the consciousness of the "new *mestiza*," a reconceptualized feminist consciousness that draws on cultural and biological miscegenation.

If, however, Gregorio Cortéz becomes a paradigmatic oppositional corrido figure of Texas-Mexican ethnonationalism, given new energy after the publication of Paredes' *With a Pistol in His Hand*,[22] Anzaldúa crosscuts masculine-coded "Tex-Mex" nationalism through a configuration of a borderland "third country" as a polyvocal rather than univocal Imaginary and Symbolic. She says, "If going home is denied me then I will have to stand and claim my space, making a new culture—*una cultura mestiza*—with my own lumber, my own bricks and mortar and my own feminist architecture."[23] To the extent that she wavers in her desire for reterritorialization à la Gregorio Cortéz's oppositional paradigm, the "third country" becomes a "closed country," bounded; to the extent that she wants to undercut the "Man of Reason," the unified sovereign subject of philosophy, she constructs a "crossroads of the self," a *mestiza consciousness*. Anzaldúa's conceptualization of the *mestiza* as a produced vector of multiple culture transfers and transitions resonates simultaneously with Jameson's version of the Lacanian pre-individualistic "structural crossroads," that is, "in frequent

---

19. Debbie Nathan, *Women and Other Aliens: Essays from the U.S.-Mexican Border* (El Paso: Cinco Puntos Press, 1991).
20. Anzaldúa, *Borderlands/La Frontera*, 11.
21. Anzaldúa, *Borderlands/La Frontera*, 38.
22. Américo Paredes, *With a Pistol in His Hand: A Border Ballad and Its Hero* (Austin: University of Texas Press, 1971).
23. Anzaldúa, *Borderlands/La Frontera*, 22.

shifts of the subject from one fixed position to another, in a kind of optional multiplicity of insertions of the subject into a relatively fixed Symbolic Order."[24] It has resonance with Cornelius Castoriadis' version as well:

> The subject in question is . . . not the abstract moment of philosophical subjectivity; it is the actual subject traversed through and through by the world and by others . . . . It is the active and lucid agency that constantly reorganizes its contents, through the help of these same contents, that produces by means of a material and in relation to needs and ideas, all of which are themselves mixtures of what it has already found there before it and what it has produced itself."[25]

Notwithstanding the different locations of each theorist, Anzaldúa, Jameson, and Castoriadis, the resonance is inescapable. (As is the resonance with Trinh Minh-Ha, cited at the beginning of this essay.)

That transversal simultaneity is one where the speaking subject-in-process is both traversed "by the word and by others" and takes hold so as to exercise that "lucid agency that constantly reorganizes . . . contents" and works in what the subject has produced herself. Now, the relatively fixed Symbolic Order that Anzaldúa's text crosscuts is differently reorganized as she shifts the targets of engagement. It is now cutting across Eurohegemonic representations of Woman, now Freudian/Lacanian psychoanalysis "I know things older than Freud,"[26] through Jungian psychoanthropology and the rationality of the sovereign subject as she in nonlinear and non-developmental ways shifts the "names" of her resistant subject positions: Snake Woman, La Chingada, Tlazolteotl, Coatlicue, Cihuacoatl, Tonantzin, Guadalupe, La Llorona. The polyvalent name insertions in *Borderlands* are a rewriting of the feminine, a feminist reinscription of gynetics. Of such revisionary tactics, Drucilla Cornell says, in another context, "in affirmation, as a positioning, as a performance, rather than of Woman as a description of reality."[27] Because the category of Woman in the case of Chicanas/Latinas and other women of color has not been fully mapped nor rewritten across culture-classes, the multiple-writing, multiple-naming gesture must be

---

24. Fredric Jameson, *Postmodernism, or, the Cultural Logic of Late Capitalism* (Durham, NC: Duke University Press, 1991), 354.

25. Cornelius Castoriadis, *The Imaginary Institution of Society*, trans. Kathleen Blamey (Cambridge, MA: MIT Press, 1987), 106.

26. Anzaldúa, *Borderlands/La Frontera*, 26.

27. Drucilla Cornell, *Beyond Accommodation: Ethical Feminism, Deconstruction and the Law* (New York: Routledge, 1991), 7.

carried out given the absence of any shared textualization. Thus, a text such as Anzaldúa's is the racialized "ethnic" performance of an implicitly tangential Derridean deconstructive gesture that "must, by means of a double gesture, a double science, a double writing, practice an *overturning* of the classical opposition *and* a general *displacement* of the system."²⁸ That is, through the textual production of, and the speaking position of, a "*mestiza* consciousness" and the recuperation and recodification of the multiple names of "Woman," Anzaldúa deconstructs patriarchal ethnonational oppositional consciousness on the one hand, and its doublet, "the Man of Reason"—an oppositional consciousness, which, as stated earlier, is given shape through the dualism of self (raced-male subject) and other (white-male subject).

Insofar as Anzaldúa implicitly recognizes the power of the nation-state to produce "political subjects" who are now legal, now illegal, deprived of citizenship, she opts for "ethnonationalism" and reterritorialization in the guise of a "closed/third country." Although she rejects a masculinist ethnonationalism that would exclude the Queer, she does not totally discard a "neonationalism" (i.e., the "closed/third country") for the reappropriated borderlands, Aztlán. However, it is now open to all of the excluded, not just Chicanos, but all Queers. That is, the formation of a newer imaginary community in Aztlán would displace the ideology of the "holy family"/ "family romance" still prevalent in El Valle and elsewhere in the Southwest, which makes it possible for many to turn away from confronting other social formations of violence.

The imaginary utopic community reconfirms from a different angle Liisa Malkki's claim that our confrontation with displacement and the desire for "home" brings into the field of vision "the sedentarist metaphysic embedded in the national order of things."²⁹ The counterdiscursive construction of an alternate utopic imagined community reproduces the "sedentarist metaphysic" in (re) territorialization. Malkki continues, "Sedentarist assumptions about attachment to place lead us to define displacement not as a fact about sociopolitical content, but rather as an inner, pathological condition of the displaced."³⁰ Anzaldúa has clear recognition of this in the very concept of a *mestiza* consciousness as well as in her privileging of the notion of migratoriness, the multiplicity of our

---

28. Jacques Derrida, *Margins of Philosophy,* trans. Alan Bass (Chicago: University of Chicago Press, 1982), 329.

29. Liisa Malkki, "National Geographic: The Rooting of Peoples and the Territorialization of National Identity among Scholars and Refugees," in "Beyond 'Culture': Space, Identity, and the Politics of Difference," ed. James Ferguson and Akil Gupta, special issue, *Cultural Anthropology* 7, no. 1 (1992): 31.

30. Malkki, "National Geographic," 32-33.

names, and the reclamation of the borderlands in feminist terms that risk the "pathological condition" by representing the nonlinearity and the break with a developmental view of self-inscription: "We can no longer blame you nor disown the white parts, the male parts, the pathological parts, the queer parts, the vulnerable parts. Here we are weaponless with open arms, with only our magic. Let's try it our way, the *mestiza* way, the Chicana way, the woman way."[31] Indeed, the hunger for wholeness—*el sentirse completa*—guides the chronicles, and that hunger is the same desire that brings into view both the migratoriness of the population and the reappropriation of "home." In the Américas today, the processes of sociopolitical empire and nation-making displacements over a 500-year history are such that the notion of "home" is as mobile as the populations, a "home" without juridically nationalized geopolitical territory.

THE SHADOW BEAST MOVES US ON

THE TROPE OF THE Shadow Beast in the work of Gloria Anzaldúa functions simultaneously as a trope of a recodified Lacanian unconscious, "as the discourse of the Other," and as an Althusserian Imaginary through which the real is grasped and represented.[32] The Shadow Beast functions as the "native" woman of the Américas, as a sign of savagery—the feminine as a sign of chaos. The speaking subject as a stand-in for the "native" woman is already spoken for through the multiple discourses of the Other as both an unconscious and an ideology. Thus, the question becomes: What happens if the subject speaks both simultaneously and, implicitly grasping her deconstruction of such discursive structures, proposes the New Consciousness? "This almost finished product seems an assemblage, a montage, a beaded work with several leitmotifs and with a central core, now appearing, now disappearing in a crazy dance.... It is this learning to live with *La Coatlicue* that transforms living in the borderlands from a nightmare into a numinous experience. It is always a path/state to something else."[33]

The Lacanian linguistic unconscious sets in motion a triangulated paradigmatic tale of mother/daughter/lesbian lover. The Althusserian Imaginary, on the other hand, sets in motion syntagmatic conjunctions of experience, language, myth, folklore, history, Jungian psychoanthropology, and political

---

31. Anzaldúa, *Borderlands/La Frontera*, 88.

32. Jacques Lacan, *Ecrits*, trans. Alan Sheridan (New York: Norton, 1977); Louis Althusser, *Lenin and Philosophy and Other Essays*, trans. Ben Brewster (New York: Monthly Review Press, 1971).

33. Anzaldúa, *Borderlands/La Frontera*, 66, 73.

economy. Some of these are authorized by "academic"-type footnotes that go so far as to appeal to the reader for the authorizing sources that will "legitimate" the statement. Some of these conjunctions in effect link together multiple ideologies of racist misogyny as it pertains to Indians/*mestizas*. Simultaneously, the Shadow Beast is metonymically articulated with Snake Woman, Coatlicue, Guadalupe, La Chingada, and others and concatenated into a symbolic metaphor through which more figures are generated to produce the axial paradigm—the totalizing repression of the lesboerotic in the fabulation of the nation-state. The chronicle effect, however, is primarily produced through the syntagmatic movement of a collective text one may call "panmexican," yet relocated to the borderlands, thus making the whole of it a Chicano narrative. The indigenous terms and figurations have filtered through the Spanish-language cultural text; the code-switching reveals the fissures and hybridity of the various incomplete imperialist/neocolonial projects. The terms and figurations preserved through the oral traditions and/or folk talk/street talk coexist uneasily with "straight talk," that is, standard Spanish and standard English, all of which coexist uneasily with scholarly citations. The very "Symbolic Order" that "unifies" in Anzaldúa's text the production, organization, and inscription of *mestiza* consciousness is granted the task of deconstruction of other symbolic structures.

In short, then, Coatlicue (or almost any of her metonymically related sisters) represents the non(pre)-oedipal (in this case non[pre]-Columbian) mother, who displaces and/or coexists in perennial interrogation of the "Phallic Mother," the one complicitous in the Freudian "family romance." Coatlicue is revised and released as non(pre)-oedipal and non-Phallic Mother:

> And someone in me takes matters into our own hands, and eventually, takes dominion over serpents—over my own body, my sexual activity, my soul, my mind, my weaknesses and strength. Mine. Ours. Not the heterosexual white man's or the colored man's or the state's or the culture's or the religion's or the parents'—just ours, mine.... And suddenly I feel everything rushing to a center, a nucleus. All the lost pieces of myself coming flying from the deserts and the mountains and the valleys, magnetized toward that center. Completa.[34]

Anzaldúa resituates Coatlicue through the process of the dreamwork, conjures her from nonconscious memory, through the serpentine folklore of her youth.

---

34. Anzaldúa, *Borderlands/La Frontera*, 51.

The desire to center, to originate, to fuse with the feminine/maternal/lover in the safety of an Imaginary "third country," the borderlands disidentified from the actual site where the nation-state draws the juridical line, where formations of violence play themselves throughout miles on either side of the line: "She leaves the familiar and safe homeground to venture into the unknown and possibly dangerous terrain. This is her home/this thin edge of/ barbwire."[35] The sojourner is as undocumented as some maquila workers in southern California. In this fashion, the syntagmatic narratives, as an effect in profound structural complicity with ideologies of the nonrational Shadow Beast, contribute to the discursive structuration of the speaking subject, who links them to figures (like Coatlicue) of paradigmatic symbolism recodified for ethical and political intent in our time, engaged in the search, in Anzaldúa's vocabulary, for the "third space." Anzaldúa destabilizes our reading practices, as autobiographical anecdotes, anthropology, ideology, legend, history, and "Freud" are woven together and fused for the recuperation, which will not go unrecognized this time around. In a sense, reconstitution of completeness for the subject is a reweaving of the subject through "inter-disciplinary" thinking, or, its inverse, "disciplinary" thinking has produced a fragmentation of the most excluded subject in the Symbolic Order. The (im)possibility that Anzaldúa presents is the desire for wholeness, or is it a totalization for Queers?

When Anzaldúa says she knows "things older than Freud," notwithstanding the whispering effect of such a brief phrase, she is, I think, announcing her plan to re(dis)cover what his system and, in Lacanian terms, the patronymic legal system displace. This is so especially with reference to the oedipal/family-romance drama. The Freudian/Lacanian systems are contiguous to rationality, the "Man of Reason," the subject-conscious-of-itself-as-subject, insofar as such a subject is its point of their departure.[36] Thus, the system that displaces the Maternal Law substitutes it with the concept of the "unconscious," where the so-called primal repression is stored so that consciousness and rationality may be privileged, especially as the constituted point of departure for the discovery of the "unconscious." Further, it constitutes itself as the science-making project displacing what will thereafter be known as mythological systems, that is, the "unconscious-as-the-discourse-of-the-Other"'s multiple systems of signification to which the maternal/feminine is also imperfectly vanished.

---

35. Anzaldúa, *Borderlands/La Frontera*, 13.
36. Lacan, *Ecrits*.

In a sense, Anzaldúa's eccentricity—affected through non-Western folk/myth tropes and practices as recent as yesterday in historical terms, through the testimonies textually conserved after the conquest and more recently excavated in 1968 by workmen repairing México City's metro—constructs a tale that is feminist in intent. It is feminist insofar as through the tropic displacement of another system she re(dis)covers the mother and gives birth to herself as inscriber/speaker of/for *mestiza* consciousness. In Julia Kristeva's words, "Such an excursion to the limits of primal regression can be phantasmatically experienced as a 'woman-mother.'"[37] However, it is not as a "woman-mother" that Anzaldúa's narrator actualizes the lesboerotic "visitation" of Coatlicue, but as daughter and "queer." In contrast, Kristeva gives us a sanitized "homosexual facet of motherhood," as woman becomes a mother to recollect her own union with her mother. Though in her early work, Kristeva posited the semiotic "as the disruptive power of the feminine that could not be known and thus fully captured by the masculine symbolic," she has "turned away from any attempt to write the repressed maternal or the maternal body as a counterforce to the Law of the Father."[38] We are left instead with a theorization of the "maternal function" in the established hierarchy of the masculine symbolic.[39] Anzaldúa's narrator, however, represents the fusion without the mediation of the maternal facet itself. In Kristeva's text the "sanitization" takes place on the plane of preserving rather than disrupting the Freudian/Lacanian oedipal/family-romance systems, not to mention the triadic Christian configuration.[40]

Anzaldúa's rewriting of the feminine through the polyvalent Shadow Beast is an attempt to reinscribe, on the one hand, what has been lost through colonization. She says, "Let's root ourselves in the mythological soil and soul of this continent."[41] On the other hand, she wants to reinscribe it as the contemporaneous codification of a "primary metaphorization," as Irigaray has posited—the repressed feminine in the Symbolic Order of the Name of the Father and the Place of the Law as expressed in the Lacanian rearticulation of Freud and the Western metaphysic.[42] According to Irigaray, the psychic organi-

---

37. Julia Kristeva, *Desire in Language: A Semiotic Approach to Literature and Art*, trans. Thomas Gora, Alice Jardine, Leon S. Roudiez, ed. Leon S. Roudiez (New York: Columbia University Press, 1980), 239.
38. Cornell, *Beyond Accommodation*, 7.
39. Cornell, *Beyond Accommodation*, 7.
40. Kristeva, *Desire in Language*, 239.
41. Anzaldúa, *Borderlands/La Frontera*, 68.
42. Judith Butler, "Gender Trouble, Feminist Theory, and Psychoanalytic Discourse," in *Feminism/Postmodernism*, ed. Linda J. Nicholson (New York: Routledge, 1990), 324-340.

zation for women under patriarchy is fragmented and scattered, so that this is also experienced as dismemberment of the body.[43] "The nonsymbolization" of her desire for origin, of her relationship to her mother, and of her libido acts as a constant to polymorphic regressions (due) to "too few figurations, images of representations by which to represent herself."[44] I am not citing Irigaray so that her work can be used as a medium for diagnostic exercises of Anzaldúa's work as "polymorphic regressions." On another plane of interpretation, this could be understood as a representation symptomatic of the histories of dismemberment and scattering, which have their own polyvalence in the present for Chicanas. Anzaldúa's work is simultaneously a complicity with, a resistance to, and a disruption of Western psychoanalysis through systems of signification drastically different from those of Irigaray herself. Yet the simultaneity of conjunctures is constitutive of Anzaldúa's text. Indeed, what Irigaray schematizes as description is the multiple ways the "oedipal/family-romance," whatever language form it takes, makes woman sick even as it tries to inscribe her resistance as illness already. The struggle for representation is not an inversion per se. Rather, the struggle to heal through rewriting and retextualization yields a borrowing of signifiers from diverse, potentially monological discourses, as Anzaldúa does to push toward the production of another signifying system that not only heals through re-membering the paradigmatic narratives that recover iconographic figures, memory, and history but also rewrites and codifies the heterogeneity of the present. The desire is not so much a counterdiscourse as that for a disidentificatory one that swerves away and begins the laborious construction of a new lexicon and grammars. Anzaldúa weaves self-inscriptions of mother/daughter/lover that, if unsymbolized as "primary metaphorization" of desire, will hinder "women from having an identity in the symbolic order that is distinct from the maternal function and thus prevent them [us] from constituting any real threat to the order of Western metaphysics"[45] or, if you will, the national/ethnonational "family romance." Anzaldúa is engaged in the recuperation and rewriting of that feminine/ist "origin" not only in the interfacing sites of various symbolizations but on the geopolitical border itself—El Valle.[46]

---

43. Luce Irigaray, *Speculum of the Other Woman*, trans. Gillian C. Gill (Ithaca: Cornell University Press, 1985).
44. Irigaray, *Speculum of the Other Woman*, 71.
45. Irigaray, *Speculum of the Other Woman*, 71.
46. Sonia Saldívar-Hull, "Feminism on the Border: From Gender Politics to Geopolitics," in *Criticism in the Borderlands: Studies in Chicano Literature, Culture, and Ideology*, ed. Héctor Calderón and José D. Saldívar (Durham, NC: Duke University Press, 1991), 203-220.

Anzaldúa's Shadow Beast, intratextually recodified as Snake Woman, La Llorona, and other figurations, sends her stand-in forth as an Outlaw, a Queer, a "mita y mita," a fluid sexuality deployed through a fluid cultural space, the borderlands, which stand within sight of the patronymic law and where many, except those who possess it, are Outlaws, endlessly represented as alterities by D.C. and D.F. *Borderlands/La Frontera* is an "instinctive urge to communicate, to speak, to write about life on the borders, life in the shadows," the preoccupations with the inner life of the subject and with the struggle of that subject amid adversity and violation with the "unique positionings consciousness takes at these confluent streams" of inner/outer. An outer that is presented by the Texas-U.S., Southwest/Mexican border "and the psychological borderlands, the sexual and spiritual borderlands."[47] A self that becomes a crossroads, a collision course, a clearinghouse, an endless alterity who, once she emerges into language and self-inscription, so belated, appears as a tireless peregrine collecting all the parts that will never make her whole. Such a hunger forces her to recollect in excess, to remember in excess, to labor to excess, and produce a text layered with inversions and disproportions, which are effects of experienced dislocations, vis-à-vis the text of the Name of the Father and the Place of the Law. Chicanas want to textualize those effects.

The contemporaneous question, then, is how this can continue to be rewritten in multiple ways from a new ethical and political position, and what it might imply for the feminine in our historical context, especially for women of Mexican descent and others for whom work means migrations to the electronic, high-tech assembly work on both sides of the U.S.–Mexican border.

---

47. Anzaldúa, *Borderlands/La Frontera*, Preface.

BIBLIOGRAPHY

Alarcón, Norma. "Chicana Feminism: In the Tracks of 'the' Native Woman." *Cultural Studies* 4, no. 3 (1990): 248–256.

Althusser, Louis. *Lenin and Philosophy and Other Essays.* Translated by Ben Brewster. New York: Monthly Review Press, 1971.

Anzaldúa, Gloria. *Borderlands/La Frontera: The New Mestiza.* San Francisco: Spinsters/Aunt Lute, 1987.

Anzaldúa, Gloria. *Making Face/Making Soul: Haciendo Caras. Creative and Critical Perspectives of Feminists of Color.* San Francisco: Aunt Lute Books, 1990.

Butler, Judith. "Gender Trouble, Feminist Theory, and Psychoanalytic Discourse." In *Feminism/Postmodernism.* Edited by Linda J. Nicholson, 324-340. New York: Routledge, 1990.

Castoriadis, Cornelius. *The Imaginary Institution of Society.* Translated by Kathleen Blamey. Cambridge, MA: MIT Press, 1987.

Cornell, Drucilla. *Beyond Accommodation: Ethical Feminism, Deconstruction and the Law.* New York: Routledge, 1991.

Derrida, Jacques. *Margins of Philosophy.* Translated by Alan Bass. Chicago: University of Chicago Press, 1982.

Fraser, Nancy, and Linda J. Nicholson. "Social Criticism without Philosophy: An Encounter between Feminism and Postmodernism." In *Feminism/Postmodernism,* edited by Nancy Fraser and Linda J. Nicholson, 19-38. New York: Routledge, 1990.

Herrera-Sobek, María. *The Mexican Corrido: A Feminist Analysis.* Bloomington, IN: Indiana] University Press, 1990.

Hull, Gloria, Patricia Bell Scott, and Barbara Smith, editors. *All The Women Are White, All the Blacks Are Men, but Some of Us Are Brave: Black Women's Studies.* New York: Feminist Press, 1982.

Irigaray, Luce. *Speculum of the Other Woman.* Translated by Gillian C. Gill. Ithaca: Cornell University Press, 1985.

Jameson, Fredric. *Postmodernism, or, the Cultural Logic of Late Capitalism.* Durham, NC: Duke University Press, 1991.

Kristeva, Julia. *Desire in Language: A Semiotic Approach to Literature and Art.* Edited by Leon S. Roudiez, translated by Thomas Gora, Alice Jardine, and Leon S. Roudiez. New York: Columbia University Press, 1980.

Lacan, Jacques. *Ecrits.* Translated by Alan Sheridan. New York: Norton, 1977.

Limón, José E. *Mexican Ballads, Chicano Poems: History and Influence in Mexican-American Social Poetry.* Berkeley: University of California Press, 1992.

Lyotard, Jean-François. *The Differend: Phrases in Dispute.* Minneapolis: University of Minnesota Press, 1988.

Malkki, Liisa. "National Geographic: The Rooting of Peoples and the Territorialization of National Identity among Scholars and Refugees." In "Beyond 'Culture': Space, Identity, and the Politics of Difference," edited by. James Ferguson and Akil Gupta, special issue, *Cultural Anthropology* 7, no. 1 (1992): 24–44.

Montejano, David. *Anglos and Mexicans in the Making of Texas, 1836-1986.* Austin: University of Texas Press, 1987.

Moraga, Cherríe, and Gloria Anzaldúa, editors. *This Bridge Called My Back: Writings by Radical Women of Color.* Watertown, MA: Persephone Press, 1981.

Nathan, Debbie. *Women and Other Aliens: Essays from the U.S.–Mexican Border.* El Paso, TX: Cinco Puntos Press, 1991.

Paredes, Américo. *With a Pistol in His Hand: A Border Ballad and Its Hero.* Austin: University of Texas Press, 1971. Originally published in 1958.

Saldívar-Hull, Sonia. "Feminism on the Border: From Gender Politics to Geopolitics." In *Criticism in the Borderlands: Studies in Chicano Literature, Culture, and Ideology.* Edited by Héctor Calderón and José D. Saldívar, 203-220. Durham, NC: Duke University Press, 1991.

Smith, Valerie. "Black Feminist Theory and the Representation of the 'Other.'" In *Changing Our Own Words: Essays on Criticism, Theory and Writing by Black Women.* Edited by Cheryl A. Wall, 38-57. New Brunswick, NJ: Rutgers University Press, 1989.

Trinh, T. Minh-Ha. *Woman, Native, Other: Writing Postcoloniality and Feminism.* Bloomington: Indiana University Press, 1989.

Trinh, T. Minh-Ha. "Not You/Like You: Post-Colonial Women and the Interlocking Questions of Identity and Difference." In *Making Face/Making Soul: Haciendo Caras. Creative and Critical Perspectives by Women of Color,* edited by Gloria Anzaldúa, 371-375. San Francisco: Aunt Lute Books, 1990.

CONJUGATING SUBJECTS IN THE
AGE OF MULTICULTURALISM[1]

→ ←

THIS ESSAY IS NECESSARILY layered as I attempt to write and connect circuits of signification arising in specific historical locations, while also attempting to bring into view their relationality through processes of appropriation, translation, and recodification. Terms such as subject(ivity), *différance*/difference, identity, experience, history, resistance, *negritude*, and *mestizaje* are implicated in such processes. These, however, will be threaded through the term *essential(ism)* to bring into relief the politics of "identity" on the one hand, and the cultural politics of "difference" on the other, as well as the consideration of the complex possibilities of "identity-in-difference" as a privileged nexus of analysis. Moreover, following, implicitly or explicitly, the diverse uses or charge of the vexed term *essentialism* may aid the reader to weave the layered text. (May my "instructions" be simpler to follow than those for assembling a bicycle.)

In the preface to her book *Between Past and Future: Eight Exercises in Political Thought*,[2] Hannah Arendt meditates on the "lost treasure" of the generation that came of age during and after World War II. That "lost treasure," I suggest to you, is the loss of a *grand récit*, or a coherent metanarrative, or exhausted versions of some metaphysics. (As an aside, conquest, displacement, migration, and colonization have had similar effects for non-Europeans. Thus, it may be argued that that global war had the effect of putting in question both in the "center" and the "periphery" the value of modernity, reason, and enlightenment; that is, highlighting their dark sides. Moreover, the unique historical role of the United States in this potential binarization gives its entry into the debates of modernity and postmodernity peculiar twists.)

---

1. *Editors' Note:* A version of this essay was originally published as "Conjugating Subjects: The Heteroglossia of Essence and Resistance," in A*n Other Tongue: Nation and Ethnicity in the Linguistic Borderlands*, ed. Alfred Arteaga (Durham, NC: Duke University Press, 1994), 125-138. A revised version, "Conjugating Subjects in the Age of Multiculturalism," was later published in *Mapping Multiculturalism*, ed. Avery F. Gordon and Christopher Newfield (Minneapolis and London: University of Minnesota Press, 1996), 127-148. The version published here is from *Mapping Multiculturalism,* 1996.

2. Hannah Arendt, *Between Past and Future: Eight Exercises in Political Thought* (New York: Penguin Books, 1978).

Arendt points out that the loss is beset by a "namelessness." It is an unwilled situation. It was without testament. It had no story. She resolves the metaphors by suggesting that the "lost treasure" be named "tradition—which selects and names, which hands down and preserves, which indicates where the treasures are and what their worth is." However, because there no longer seems to be a "willed continuity in time and hence, humanly speaking neither past nor future," she asserts that we face a situation totally unforeseen by any tradition, because no "testament had willed it for the future."[3]

Through that moment of virtually total social and political breakdown, Arendt suggests, there set in a recognition of the existential experience of the rupture between "thought and reality." That is, "thought and reality [had] parted company."[4] Arendt locates the moment of recognition in the aftermath of World War II, "when it began to dawn upon modern man that he had come to live in a world in which his mind and his tradition of thought were not even capable of asking adequate, meaningful questions, let alone of giving answers to its own perplexities."[5] In a sense, that West European experience, which promotes the growth of existentialism with its inversion of the "essence-existence" binary[6] and which is followed by poststructuralism, attempts to interrogate and contest through these theoretical trends the assertion that "Modern[ist] philosophy began with a loss of the world... [indeed] the autonomous bourgeois subject... began with the withdrawal from the world."[7]

The most recent challenges to that subject have emerged with a larger degree of convergences than we have recognized. Although Arendt was writing in the 1950s, that same decade promotes the proliferation of the "new" social movements on a global scale and their concomitant "politics of identity-indifference." Thus, for example, even as Arendt is rewriting the epistemological politics of Western philosophy, Simone de Beauvoir is rewriting the ontological and epistemological sexual politics in *The Second Sex*.[8] Moreover, in the United States, even as Jacques Derrida was addressing the French Philosophical Society in January 1968 with his groundbreaking theorization of *différance,* people of Mexican descent, under the recodified name Chicano, signaling *différance,* were mobilizing in Los

---

3. Arendt, *Between Past and Future*, 6.
4. Arendt, *Between Past and Future*, 6.
5. Arendt, *Between Past and Future*, 9.
6. Jean-Paul Sartre, *Search for a Method,* trans. Hazel Barnes (New York: Alfred A. Knopf, 1963).
7. Seyla Benhabib, *Situating the Self: Gender, Community and Postmodernism in Contemporary Ethics* (New York: Routledge, 1992), 205-207.
8. Simone de Beauvoir, *The Second Sex*, trans. H. M. Parshley (New York: Vintage Books, 1974).

Angeles for the school walkouts of March 1968.[9] In brief, with broad strokes I am attempting to convey the convergence of discourses of identity-in-difference as linked to the "essence-experience" binary that it has taken so long to recognize as the patriarchal "West" engages in resistances of its own.

The potential of the discourse of identity-in-difference and its nuances was derailed by the oversimplified hegemonization of a universalized concept of woman aided and abetted by the media, for example.[10] The hegemonization of feminism as woman brought on an attack by a patriarchal media commodification of feminism on the assumption that feminism entailed a strictly recodified appropriation of the autonomous, self-determining, bourgeois, unified subject presumed to be male-owned, as if that kind of subject was essential to maleness. That is, if women claimed that facet of the subject as well, what was man to do? In other words, feminism was read by the Reaganomic media as a mimetic inversion of an essential aspect of maleness, thus producing anxiety. These processes of identification and counteridentification between unified man and unified woman barely permitted the articulations (in both senses of the word—enunciation and linkage) of a politics of identity-in-difference by "women of color" to be heard in the United States. Historically, racialized women were not heard until postmodernism in the 1980s invaded the hegemonic 1970s liberal agenda of feminism. Poststructuralist theory made it possible to mis(manage) a variety of other feminist discourses (i.e., socialist, radical, Marxist, "of color" etc.).[11]

By working through the "identity-in-difference" paradox, many racialized women theorists have implicitly worked in the interstice/interface of (existentialist) "identity politics" and "postmodernism" without a clear-cut postmodern agenda. Neither Audre Lorde's nor Chela Sandoval's notion of difference/differential consciously subsumes a Derridean theorization—though resonance cannot be denied and must be explored—so much as represents a process of "determinate negation," a naysaying of the variety of the "not yet," that's not it. The drive behind the "not yet/that's not it" position in Sandoval's work is termed "differential consciousness," in Lorde's work, "difference;" and in Derrida's work, *différance*. Yet each invokes dissimilarly located circuits of signification codified by the context of the site of emergence, which nevertheless does not obviate their agreement on the "not yet," which points toward a future. The difficulties of articulating these sites across languages, cultures, races, genders, and social

---

9. Carlos Muñoz, *Youth, Identity, Power: The Chicano Movement* (London: Verso, 1989).
10. Susan Faludi, *Backlash: The Undeclared War Against American Women* (New York: Crown Publishers, 1991).
11. Alison M. Jaggar, *Feminist Politics and Human Nature* (Totowa, N.J.: Rowan and Allanheld, 1983).

positions are painfully hard but yield a space for debate beyond "ethnocentrisms" without denying them.

Arendt herself, in an effort to theorize the critical interstitial intervention of the existential and historical subject who has lost the testamental "treasure," turns to Kafka to provide her with the poetics for a theorization of the gap. It is there, in the interstice, that Arendt thinks the simultaneity of time-and-space, thought-and-event will henceforth take place. Kafka's valuable parable is as follows:

> [S]he has two antagonists: the first presses her from behind, from the origin. The second blocks the road ahead. She gives battle to both. To be sure, the first supports her in her fight with the second, for it wants to push her forward, and in the same way the second supports her in her fight with the first, since it drives her back. But it is only theoretically so. For it is not only the two antagonists who are there, but she herself as well, and who really knows her intentions? Her dream, though, is that some time in an unguarded moment—and this would require a night darker than any night has ever been yet—she will jump out of the fighting line and be promoted, on account of her experience in fighting, to the position of umpire over her antagonists in their fight with each other.[12]

Arendt translates Kafka's forces into past and future. The fact that there is a fight at all is due to the presence of the [wo]man. Her insertion, her inscription, breaks up the motion of the forces, their linearity. This causes the forces to deflect, however lightly, from their original direction. The gap where she stands is an interstice or interval.[13] It is a time-space from which she can simultaneously survey what is most her own and that "which has come into being" through her "self-inserting appearance." Arendt falters, as does every theorist including Derrida, as to what precisely drives one to that differential self-insertion through which "a double gesture, a double science, a double writing, practice an *overturning* of the classical opposition *and* a general displacement of the system."[14] (Psychoanalysis and its theory of the unconscious provide for some a venue for understanding such impulses *within* the subject; for others it is the experience of "otherization" *between* subjects.) However, anyone outside of contexts that

---

12. Arendt, *Between Past and Future*, 7.
13. Jacques Derrida, *Margins of Philosophy*, trans. Alan Bass (Chicago: University of Chicago Press, 1982).
14. Derrida, *Margins of Philosophy*, 329.

entail "classical oppositions" proper to the West's systematizing reasoning processes is likely to practice more than "double" gestures and writings. Thus Gloria Anzaldúa, through the textual production, self-insertion, and speaking position of a *"mestiza* consciousness" disrupts the possibility of such tidiness.[15] A different tactic with similar effects is that of Luce Irigaray, who disrupts the tidiness of deconstruction's use of the feminine by introducing the contingent woman outside of metaphysical circuits of representation and meaning.[16] The one who engages the essentialization of Woman and renegotiates symbolization.

Both Anzaldúa and Irigaray have been suspected of essentializing: the first on the basis of race, that is, *mestizaje,* and the second on the basis of the female body. The charges against Anzaldúa are made at conferences, or muttered in classrooms and academic hallways, while those against Irigaray are subject to extensive debates with a healthy bibliography.[17] (In the United States, the debate on race and [anti]essentialism has been largely left to African-American theorists and Diana Fuss,[18] while the debate with respect to Chicanas and Latin Americans and other groups is largely obscured as the discourses of race continue to binarize into black and white.)

Taking up the question of essentialism and race from another angle, Jean-Luc Nancy resists the possibility of turning *mestizaje* into "a substance, an object, an identity ... that could be grasped and 'processed.'" He deplores the notion that one could be a *mestiza* or a *mestizo.* "Everything" he continues, "everyone—male, female—who alters me, subjects me to *mestizaje.* This has nothing to do with mixed blood or mixed cultures. Even the process of 'mixing' in general, long celebrated by a certain theoretical literary and artistic tradition—even this kind of 'mixing' must remain suspect: it should not be turned into a new substance, a new identity."[19]

---

15. Gloria Anzaldúa, *Borderlands/La Frontera: The New Mestiza* (San Francisco: Spinsters/Aunt Lute, 1987).

16. Luce Irigaray, *Speculum of the Other Woman,* trans. Gillian C. Gill (Ithaca, N.Y: Cornell University Press, 1985). For commentary on deconstruction's use of the feminine, see Rose Braidotti, *Patterns of Dissonance: A Study of Women in Contemporary Philosophy,* trans. Elizabeth Guild (New York: Routledge, 1991); Gayatri C. Spivak, "Displacement and the Discourse of Women," in *Displacement: Derrida and After,* ed. Mark Krupnik (Bloomington: Indiana University Press, 1983), 169-196.

17. See Judith Butler, *Gender Trouble: Feminism and Subversion of Identity* (New York: Routledge, 1990); *Revaluing French Feminism: Critical Essays on Difference, Agency & Culture,* eds. Nancy Fraser and Sandra Lee Bartky (Bloomington: Indiana University Press, 1992); Toril Moi, *Sexual/Textual Politics* (London: Methuen, 1985); Jean-Luc Nancy, "Cut Throat Sun," in *An Other Tongue,* ed. Alfred Artega (Durham, NC: Duke University Press, 1994), 113-123.

18. Diana Fuss, *Essentially Speaking: Feminism, Nature and Difference* (New York: Routledge, 1989).

19. Nancy, "Cut Throat Sun," 123.

Even as he wants to valorize the notion of *mestizaje,* indeed claim the term *mestizo* for himself, he cautions against "biologisms" or even cultural mixing, and cautions against ultimate *meaning* by having us place ourselves "on the border, on the very border of *meaning.*"[20] To be pinned down by meaning and intentionality, to mean, is to essentialize. The pursuit of identity as a quest for meaning closes off possibility. This quest for meaning can also appear, in postmodernist terms, as the drive to privilege our constructedness through the deconstruction of our essential(izing) quest for identity meaning. Jena-Luc Nancy speaks of the constructed subject who is traversed by the world and by others in such ways that he is never pure. The subject is unbounded and open to the other through *mestizaje,* "[s/he who] alters me, subjects me to *mestizaje.*"[21] Significance cannot come to rest, cannot stop; intersubjectivity as well as interaction with the world is always at play. However, we are indeed in the face of a paradox/contradiction. For Nancy does not want us to mistake his meaning of the term. In wanting to set it free and make it open to the future in specific ways, we are cautioned that this does not mean "mixed blood" or "mixed cultures," one of the modes in which Anzaldúa, for example, employs the term. With that prohibition he closes up the time and space of *mestizaje;* it is now under control, yet of course open to the future "toward infinity." Thus, is Nancy subjected to the politics of his own location, "a twentieth-century Frenchman, . . . of Spanish and Viking, of Celt and Roman." What I mean to say is that the politics of his own location, his own time and space, leads him to appropriate and recodify the notion such that now it refers to the specificity of his own history, the "melting pot" that is France. Although he too is a *mestizo,* it is a kind open to the drift of the future, "on the border, on the very border of *meaning.*" Indeed, one may view Anzaldúa's work as doubly located on the "border of meaning." That is, the U.S.–Mexican geopolitical border as juridical sociopolitical division, which simultaneously opens up the past and the future as unfolding "borders of meaning" wherein Kafka's (wo)man struggles. Insofar as there is meaning, it emanates from the prohibition itself. The historical discussion of "mixed blood" in the Américas, including its juridical normalizations, further problematizes Nancy's prohibition since it might silence the legal history of the racialization of the pre-and post-Columbian subject, of (post)slavery African Americans, and of migratory/diasporic travails of others such as Chicanos.

---

20. Nancy, "Cut Throat Sun," 123.
21. Nancy, "Cut Throat Sun," 123.

Another example of a different kind of prohibition, yet with similar silencing effects, appears in Frantz Fanon's rejection of Jean-Paul Sartre's translation of negritude into class on the grounds that the former is too particularistic/concrete and the latter abstract and universal, whereas Fanon suggests that the former is a "psychobiological syncretism" a methodical construction based on experience.²² Fanon notes that in Sartre's system *negritude*

> "appears as the minor term of a dialectical progression: The theoretical and practical assertion of the supremacy of the white man is its thesis; the position of negritude as an antithetical value is the moment of negativity." . . . Proof was presented that my effort was only a term in the dialectic . . . I defined myself as an absolute beginning. So I took up my negritude, and with tears in my eyes I put its machinery together again. What had been broken to pieces was rebuilt, reconstructed by the intuitive lianas of my hands.²³

The very inflected force of the selected theoretical frameworks from a universalizing center expels the narratives and the textualization of difference and resistance.

It may be true that the expulsion itself produces a resistance; that is, resistance becomes the site of the emergence of meaning itself and its concomitant practices should there be no other resistance to deflect the projected course of meaning. But in Sartre, as Fanon reads him, the coexistence of prohibitions and resistances forecloses conditions of possibility for the renegotiation of relations and structures. The very emergences of syncretic new subjects, recodified on their own terms and rehistoricized anew, are dismissed without taking up the task of piercing beneath, uncovering the structure, relations, and possibilities that present themselves as the conditions of the possibility of the new subject appearing as it does. The maneuver to avoid the probing is done through a reobjectification of the "new subject" a reification or a denial of the historical meaning posited by the differential signifier. As a result the difference is not fully engaged as a resistance to the monologizing demands of the West. The desire to translate as totalizing metaphorical substitution without acknowledging the "identity-in-difference" so that one's own system of signification is not disrupted through a historical concept whose site of emergence is implicated in our own

---

22. Frantz Fanon, "The Fact of Blackness," in *Anatomy of Racism,* ed. David Theo Goldberg (Minneapolis: University of Minnesota Press, 1990), 120.
23. Fanon, "The Fact of Blackness," 120, 124.

history, may be viewed as a desire to dominate, constrain, and contain. Sartre's desire reflects the "center's" own resistance to renegotiating meaning and structure.

Sartre allows the possibility that racial difference may be ontologized in the process of exploring *mestizaje* or *negritude* as "psychobiological syncretism" leads to a prohibition rather than a careful evaluation of how the drive to decolonize, to free up the subject from subjection, has embattled her inscription as represented by Kafka's allegorical parable. If to "ontologize difference" in the pursuit of identity and meaning as modes of resistance to domination entails essentializing by relying on the concept of an authentic core that remains hidden to one's consciousness and that requires the elimination of all that is considered foreign or not true to the self, then neither Anzaldúa nor Fanon are essentialists at all. Both are quite clear that the pursuit of identity through "psychobiological syncretism" is one engaged through the racial difference imputed to them as a stigma that is now revalorized through reconstruction in historical terms. In fact both acknowledge the impossibility of regaining a pure origin.

Where does the terror of the "ontologization of difference" come from if not from the possibility that the result will continue to be inequality in the face of a liberal legal subject that has been naturalized on masculine terms?[24] This particular fear is more pronounced in feminist theory than in antiessentialist theories of race because, as I stated earlier, the latter is dominated by men who do not bother to remark gender. The possibilities that the combination of gender with race may transform our mode of speaking about the constructedness of the subject from both the outside *and* the inside are virtually unexplored by men.

Derrida's considerations on the "two interpretations of interpretation" as "irreconcilable" yet "live[d] simultaneously and reconcile[d] . . . in an obscure economy"[25] have not been explored precisely as simultaneous and irreconcilable in conjunction with the "obscure economies" that emerge, such as Kafka's parable for example.[26] The two interpretations noted by Derrida are (1) "The one that seeks to decipher . . . truth or an origin which escapes play and the order of the sign, and which lives the necessity of interpretation as an exile; and (2) the one that no longer turned toward the origin, affirms play and tries to pass beyond

---

24. Michèle Barret and Anne Phillips, *Destablizing Theory: Contemporary Feminist Debates* (Stanford: Stanford University Press, 1992).

25. Jacques Derrida, *Writing and Difference,* trans. Alan Bass (Chicago: University of Chicago Press, 1978), 292-93.

26. Derrida, *Writing and Difference,* 293.

man and humanism."[27] Further, it is not a question of choosing one or the other since both are irreducible and to choose is to trivialize. Thus, Derrida continues, "we must conceive of the common ground, and the *différance* of this irreducible difference."[28] The fact that the resistant texts of minoritized populations in the United States are often read as interpretation number one and charged with essentializing (as is the case in Fuss's treatment of African-American women critics and the debate on Irigaray, for example) is a misreading in light of the theorists' own resistance to conjugating interpretations of interpretation and conjugating significance for the present. It is often the case as well that no one claims an "immutable origin;" however, the anxiety of pursuing the "*différance* of this irreducible difference" continues to surface as a charge of essentialism on the one hand, and a fear of losing ground on the equality battlefront, given patriarchal resistance to equality via a naturalized liberal subject whose criteria we all must be, on the other. That is, while identity now labors under a charge of essentialism, difference is now checked by the charge of inequality. The double-bind of *différance* emerges in the struggle between the age-old metaphysics of *being* and the liberally inspired politics of *becoming*—dare I say the past and the future?

Fuss struggles with this double-bind, justifying "the stronger lesbian endorsement of identity and identity politics" on the basis that it may indicate that "lesbians inhabit a more precarious and less secure subject position than gay men."[29] Interestingly, she argues for the progressiveness (i.e., antiessentialism) of lesbian scholarship by arguing via Heidegger for the metaphysical unity of identity as a fictional coherence that "theories of 'multiple identities' fail to challenge effectively."[30] The unity of identity even as fictional coherence can be maintained and thereby make "identity politics" theoretically acceptable if one does away with the claim of "multiple identities;" that is, *différance* must be relocated to the "space *within* identity" and withdrawn from the "spaces *between* identities."[31] A theory of the fictional unity of identity via the Freudian-Lacanian unconscious is selected by Fuss, in my view, in order to salvage, through complementariness, the autonomous, self-determining, liberal bourgeois subject that is important to the kind of struggle made necessary by currently hegemonic views of juridical

---

27. Derrida, *Writing and Difference*, 292.
28. Derrida, *Writing and Difference*, 293.
29. Fuss, *Essentially Speaking*, 98.
30. Fuss, *Essentially Speaking* 103.
31. Fuss, *Essentially Speaking*, 103.

equality.³² In the process, however, she discards "the spaces *between* identities" which are paramount to cross-cultural exploration and analysis of "women of color." Thus, one of the major questions that arises in these theoretical debates is, what is behind the antiessentialist position? Certainly it is one that too readily assumes that the other is, of course, being essentialist. What are the stakes in such oppositional arguments wherein one is either implicated in Derrida's interpretation number one or interpretation number two, but not, shall we say, engaged in a struggle such as that of Kafka's (wo)man?

In Anzaldúa's terms, "*mestiza* consciousness" reveals a "tolerance for contradictions," paradox, and ambiguity because the term *mestiza* projects a confluence of conflicting subject positions that keep "breaking down the unitary aspect of each new paradigm."³³ M.Y. Mudimbe designates an "intermediate space between the so-called ... tradition and the projected modernity of colonialism." It is apparently an urbanized space in which "vestiges of the past, especially the survival of structures that are still living realities (tribal ties, for example), often continue to hide the new structures (ties based on class or on groups defined by their position in the capitalist system);" at any rate, this intermediary space "could be viewed as the major signifier of underdevelopment. It reveals the strong tension between a modernity that often is an illusion of development, and a tradition that sometimes reflects a poor image of a mythical past."³⁴ These in-between/interstitial zones of instability present us with paradigms of "obscure economies." In these zones theoretical frameworks are both affirmed and resisted, especially when experiential and historical meanings are erased and differences go unengaged, their irreducibility unnamed despite the risk of misnaming.

In resonance with Anzaldúa, Chela Sandoval claims that:

> U.S. Third World feminism represents a central locus of possibility, an insurgent movement which shatters the construction of any one of the collective ideologies as the single most correct site where truth can be represented.... What U.S. Third World feminism demands is a new subjectivity, a political revision that denies any one ideology as the final answer, while instead positing a *tactical subjectivity* with

---

32. Kimberlé Crenshaw, "Demarginalizing the Intersection of Race and Sex: A Black Feminist Critique of Antidiscrimination Doctrine, Feminist Theory and Antiracist Politics," *University of Chicago Legal Forum* 1, Article 8 (1989): 139-167.

33. Anzaldúa, *Borderlands/La Frontera*, 79-80.

34. V. Y. Mudimbe, *The Invention of Africa: Gnosis, Philosophy, and the Order of Knowledge* (Bloomington: Indiana University Press, 1988), 5.

the capacity to recenter depending upon the kinds of oppression to be confronted. This is what the shift from hegemonic oppositional theory and practice to a U.S. third world theory and method of oppositional consciousness requires.[35]

Sandoval calls attention to the many "women of color" who have pointed the way toward the development of a "new subject of history" and as such a "new political subject." Aída Hurtado has claimed that "women of color" develop political skills "like urban guerrillas trained through everyday battle with the state apparatus."[36] For Moraga, feminist "guerrilla warfare" is a way of life. "Our strategy is how we cope" on an everyday basis, "how we measure and weigh what is to be said and when, what is to be done and how, and to whom . . . daily deciding/risking who it is we can call an ally, call a friend."[37]

Citing Audre Lorde's remarks at a 1979 conference commemorating the thirtieth anniversary of the publication of *The Second Sex*, Sandoval points to the fact that "ideological differences" must be seen as "a fund of necessary polarities between which our creativities spark like a dialectic. Only within that interdependency" of historical and ideologically positioned differences "can the power to seek new ways of being in the world generate . . . the courage and sustenance to act where there are no charters."[38] In a sense, if, as Moraga also claimed, feminists of color are "women without a line,"[39] coalescing with Sandoval, then the "new subject of history" is the one who struggles "to insure our survival,"[40] who is always "challenging women to go further,"[41] who in my view engages a politics of the "not yet," in the interstice between past and future. As Sandoval herself states, the "politics of the not yet" waged by U.S. Third World feminists is that of "differential consciousness" that posits no "ultimate answers, no terminal utopia . . . no predictable final outcomes. . . . Entrance into this new order requires an emotional commitment within which one experiences

---

35. Chela Sandoval, "U.S. Third World Feminism: The Theory and Method of Oppositional Consciousness in the Post-Modern World," in "Theorizing Nationality, Sexuality, and Race," ed. Ann Kibbey, special issue, *Genders* 10 (spring 1991): 14.

36. Aída Hurtado, cited in Sandoval, "U.S. Third World Feminism," 14-15.

37. Cherríe Moraga, Preface to *This Bridge Called My Back: Writings by Radical Women of Color*, eds. Cherríe Moraga and Gloria Anzaldúa (Watertown, MA.: Persephone Press, 1981), xix.

38. Sandoval, "U.S. Third World Feminism," 15.

39. Moraga, Preface to *This Bridge Called My Back*, xix.

40. Barbara Smith and Beverly Smith, "Across the Kitchen Table: A Sister-to-Sister Dialogue," in *This Bridge Called My Back*, ed. Cherríe Moraga and Gloria Anzaldúa (Watertown MA: Persephone Press, 1981), 127.

41. Smith and Smith, *This Bridge Called My Back*, 127.

the violent shattering of the unitary sense of self, as the skill which allows a mobile identity to form.... Citizenship in this political realm is comprised of strategy and risk."[42]

Who is this "new subject of history" whose "identity-in-difference" politics was so dramatically documented in *This Bridge Called My Back* and given form in the context of second-wave, that is, contemporary, feminism, whose existential writings foreshadowed, *avant la lettre*, the poststructuralist subject, yet emerged as a paradoxical, contradictory subject whose own pursuit of "identity politics" was fissured by every other sentence through an affirmation of difference that questioned every category of import to the formation of a new society? Categories such as nation, class, race, gender, sexuality, and ethnicity were intermittently questioned and disrupted. In brief, her very constitution as a "speaking subject" called attention to contradiction and difference as her constitutive ground through discursive political and intersubjective practices. When Sandoval publishes her essay ten years later, she calls it "differential consciousness." She gives it a name that at its core signals a situated (located in the interval/gap/interstice/time-space) subject whose practice "cannot be thought *together*."[43] It cannot be thought simultaneously because the reinscription is thought out from the site of displacement, which is subject to misnaming, misrecognition, misalliance, as well as hitting the mark. It cannot be thought together because it aims to situate that which has no place and through naming may fall short of the mark. The name may never be quite "it" because names are "relatively unitary ... structures" whose oppositional status one may not intend, yet may take over. When Sandoval claims that the differential consciousness that calls for entering the "between and amongst" demands a mode of consciousness once relegated to the province of intuition and psychic phenomena, but which now must be recognized as a specific practice, she is in effect moving us toward and/or finding the relationality between the inside, as affirmed by Fuss (per the discussion earlier) and the outside as the cross-cultural, intersubjective site; that is, she poses the challenge of resistance to oppositional hegemonies through a *différance* that works inside and outside on multiple planes—a factor that works itself out through a "speaking subject" conscious that she can be "constituted by discourse and yet not be completely determined by it."[44] Benhabib asks, "What psychic, intellectual or other sources of creativity and resistance must we attribute

---

42. Sandoval, "U.S. Third World Feminism," 23.
43. Derrida, *Margins of Philosophy*, 19.
44. Benhabib, *Situating the Self*, 218.

to subjects for such [agential variation to discursive subject determination] to be possible?"[45] Hannah Arendt called it "spirit" others call it "aesthetics" yet others have called it a "project" a "sparking dialectic." Anzaldúa calls it the "Shadow Beast." All grope for the impulse. As stated earlier, some have settled for the "unconscious"—a metaphor for the drives and impulses toward structural and symbolic change in the name of feminism.

The critical desire to undercut subject determination through structures and discourses, in my view, presupposes a subject-in-process who constructs *provisional* identities, or Sandoval's *tactical subjectivity*, which subsume a network of signifying practices and structural experiences imbricated in the historical *and* imaginary shifting national borders of México and the United States for Chicanas, for example. (Other "borders" that mediate [im]migration might be invoked.) A subject-insertion into such a geographical economy and politics may presuppose not only specific historical sociosymbolic texts but a situated contemporaneous horizon of meanings and intentions that swerve away from those produced and enunciated by Euro-Americans and Europeans, especially when the latter produce structures and discourses of containment that resist change. Identity formations through differentially theorized experience and history—in this instance, through the term Chicana, thus signaling a historically raced/gendered/classed position forged through the interstices of two nation-states—propose a subject-in-process, desirous of self-determination yet "traversed through and through by the world and by others.... It is the active and lucid agency that constantly reorganizes its contents, through the help of these same contents, that produces by means of a material and in relation to needs and ideas, all of which are themselves mixtures of what it has already found there before it and what it has produced itself."[46] Through the speaking critical subject-in-process, cultural production reintroduces what was there before in new and dynamic combinatory transculturations. A bi- or multiethnicized, raced, and gendered subject-in-process may be called upon to take up diverse subject positions that cannot be unified without double-binds and contradictions. Indeed, what binds the subject positions together may be precisely the difference from the perceived hegemony and the identity with a specific autohistory. The paradoxes and contradictions between subject positions move the subject to recognize, reorganize, reconstruct, and exploit difference through political resistance and

---

45. Benhabib, *Situating the Self*, 218.
46. Cornelius Castoriadis, *The Imaginary Institution of Society*, trans. Kathleen Blarney (Cambridge, M.A.: MIT Press, 1987), 102-103.

cultural productions in order to reflect the subject-in-process. It is not a matter of doing away with the discourse of the other "because the other is in each case present in the activity that eliminates [it]."[47] The traces of a process of elimination may construct the subject as much as the efforts to incorporate.

A critical subject-in-process who reorganizes "contents" upon the demands of the contingent moment and context may discover that it is in the inaugural transitional moment from being traversed to reconfiguration that the political intention as well as the combinatory transculturating takes place. Through such time-spaces one can discover diverse cultural narrative formations, translations, appropriations, and recodifications, which generate texts that are "hybrid" or "syncretic" and, far from wanting to remain at rest in that taxonomy, make a bid for new discourse formations bringing into view new subjects-in-process. In Gloria Anzaldúa's terms, these are the "borderlands" through which the "theory circuits" of geopolitics and critical allegories find resonance but the zones of figurations and conceptualizations remain non-equivalent; that is, the very contingent currents through which the geopolitical subject-in-process is dislocated and forced into (im)migration will retain an irreducible difference that refuses to correspond neatly to the subject's account of herself and the theory we produce to account for her appearance.

As transnational geopolitics with a concomitant production of "new" subjects of history come into contact with theoretical and critical allegories of the liberal political subject, the "new citizen subject;" in Chela Sandoval's terms (see earlier discussion), and the "cultural politics of difference, or identity-in-difference," are subsumed under "multiculturalism." However, as I will argue, "multiculturalism" and the "cultural politics of difference" are neither equivalent nor homologous. The term "multiculturalism" appears to be a quick metaphoric fix signaling inclusion that both comprehends the commodifications of difference and refuses to hear the implications for the production of knowledge and the material grounds that give rise to revised social and political histories as well as the "cultural politics of difference;" that is, "multiculturalism" serves a functional end in the political economy of culture that fails to grasp the substantive claims generated through what Cornel West has named "the new cultural politics of difference." Yet, "multiculturalism" has, in our time, become the discourse of choice for a multiplicity of national and transnational agendas to name the traffic in goods and peoples, the referential subjects of this complex discursive

---

47. Castoriadis, *The Imaginary Institution of Society*, 106.

economy. Like most ideological formations, "multiculturalism" harnesses and distorts the production of the interpellated.[48]

Etienne Balibar suggests that the current multiculturalism has become a lightning rod that produces a neoracism. It is, after all, the "unmeltables" who are the metaphoric subjects, daily in the media, of multiculturalism's discourse. The currently renewed, "genetic"-based attack on African Americans' "measured" IQ levels suggests that, at the end of the twentieth century, the so-called nineteenth-century racist biologism converges with the end-of-the-twentieth-century culturalism to bespeak the racialized panic of our "liberal" society and the age-old questions of administering heterogeneity. As the media "educates" the public, both IQs and multiculturalism are raced, permitting "liberal" discourse to assume a mediating position in the face of right-wing attacks on "unmeltables." How, one might ask, is that position articulated, and is it possible to make productive critical interventions in the contemporary discourse of multiculturalism as mediated by politically liberal critiques, or is it the kind of octopus that ensnares one in its multiple tentacles? Jürgen Habermas, I think, does a creditable job of outlining the potential multicultural tentacles—feminism, ethnic minorities, nationalism, Eurocentrism as Western cultural hegemony, philosophical discourses, the question of rights and political correctness—especially as these are embroiled in producing discourses that also narrate the "cultural politics of difference."[49] However, the point of my analysis at this juncture is to do a preliminary mapping of how liberal academic thinkers mediate the "cultural politics of difference" and have it end up recodified as "multiculturalism." In brief, the question might well be, What is the ground

---

48. I use the term "transnational" as a mediating analytical category that enables a nexus for critical intervention across and between nation-states and opens up a ground for the critique of the representations, practices, and discourses that emerge in the conjunctural constitutiveness of historical subjects. This approach would beg the question of how one can generate a postnationalist critical discourse. For further discussions of transnational critique see Frederick Buell, *National Culture and the Global System* (Baltimore: Johns Hopkins University Press, 1994). For further discussion of "The New Cultural Politics of Difference," see Cornel West, *Keeping Faith: Philosophy and Race in America* (New York: Routledge, 1993), 3-32.

49. Etienne Balibar, "Is There a Neo-racism?" *Race, Nation, Class: Ambiguous Identities* (London: Verso, 1991), 17-28; Charles Murray, *The Bell Curve: Intelligence and Class Structure in American Life* (New York: Free Press, 1994).

for the formation of a critical and political culture that is not equivalent to a recodification as "multiculturalism?"⁵⁰

Even an eminent intellectual such as Arthur Schlesinger Jr., for example, is reduced to incoherent, murky thinking when faced with multiculturalism and its implications for the location from which he reads it. He fears a dismantling of "his" institutions. Insofar as he reads Afrocentrism as the total negation of what he thinks he stands for, clear thinking collapses and his text, *The Disuniting of America,* becomes the occasion for hysteria and paranoia.⁵¹ The hysteria enters in when he deploys unremarked contradictory arguments in a surreal stream-of-consciousness fashion, and the paranoia when he sees the nation-state crumbling before him as a result of the "cultural politics of difference" or of "multiculturalism," as school boards have recoded it.⁵² The recoding in itself is a disservice to a complex cultural and political questioning that at a minimum goes back to the constitution of the nation-state, leading up to and unfolding from the Constitution itself. In this context, "multiculturalism" becomes a wimpy kind of name that returns one to the notion of cultural contribution to the making of the nation, which permits a kind of blindness in which "American" culture becomes fused with the "political contract" and the rest is pasted on such that most nonwhites will remain not-American, but "raced ethnics" in perpetuity. There is, however, the possibility of seeing "American" culture as the consistent failure to make good on its ideal horizon of meanings and on the institutional interpretation of the political contract. "We the people" can be analyzed along its historical trajectory as in effect meaning some and not others, hence the desire for a strong revisionist historical and social map that is tied to a reconstructionist project. On the other hand, when "the cultural politics of difference" are practiced as a strictly oppositional formation of a minoritized "we the people" held up to a capitalized "We the People," another kind of boundary is constructed, which in effect converges as well with some liberal understandings of multiculturalism

---

50. Charles Taylor, Kwame Anthony Appiah, Jürgen Habermas, Steven C. Rockefeller, Michael Walzer, and Susan Wolf *Multiculturalism: Examining the Politics of Recognition,* ed. Amy Gutman (Princeton: Princeton University Press, 1994), 116-122. David Palumbo-Liu is cognizant of the fact that once a discourse such as multiculturalism makes a bid for hegemonic mediation of identity-in-difference, perhaps the best that minoritized intellectuals can do is to turn our critical mapping lens through it as well. Consequently, he calls for a critical multiculturalism. As he notes, ideologically, multiculturalism becomes a recodification of pluralism for the era of trans-nationalisms and globalisms. See the introduction to his edited anthology, *The Ethnic Canon: Histories, Institutions, and Interventions* (Minneapolis: University of Minnesota Press, 1995), 1-27.

51. Arthur Schlesinger Jr., *The Disuniting of America* (New York: W.W. Norton, 1998).

52. See Michael Bérubé, "Disuniting America Again," *Public Access: Literary Theory and American Cultural Politics* (London: Verso, 1994), 225-242.

as celebratory heterogeneous representations. These responses, in my view, are symptomatic of deep dialogic complicity in the formation of all "American" subjects, though some are constantly on trial as to their "Americanness." To see one's self-representation textualized is not to come to terms with its dialogic construction and contestation. Grasping the dialogic constructions, however, creates passages that undermine, for example, Stuart Hall's observation that "far from collapsing the complex questions of cultural identity and issues of social and political rights, what we need is *greater distance between them [sic]*. We need to be able to insist that rights of citizenship and the incommensurability of cultural difference are respected and the *one is not made a condition of the other [sic]*."[53] How can we simultaneously deal with the contemporary desire to renegotiate the "political contract" maintaining distant equilibrium between equal citizenship rights and cultural difference, when faced with a history where "rights of citizenship" have been conditioned by identitarian sameness with the contingently historical bourgeois liberal subject and not in conjunction with difference—that is, race, gender, sexuality, and social position—but its expulsion? At this juncture the traffic between cultural and political practices is heightened and highly dependent on whether one is or is not viewed as a social equal and on asking what is producing social and political inequality. Moreover, if indeed the construction of differences has been historically produced in a dialogical manner between discrete sets of social relations, one must question, as I have earlier, the boundaries that such an analytic and interpretative nexus produces and that make it impossible to grasp articulations across the "cultural politics of difference or identity-in-difference." The fact that the latter often appears virtually impossible, indeed, does tend to make it homologous to "multiculturalism."[54]

Consequently, and in fairness to Stuart Hall, I would argue that although there may be a distinction to be made with respect to the "incommensurability of cultural difference" and "rights of citizenship," the struggle of the "cultural politics of difference" is precisely about the "distance between them" and how the distance is functioned. What is involved in the "distance between them" that we take, or what is at stake in making or not making one "a condition of the other"? Such "distance" should be functioned in more as an analytical

---

53. Stuart Hall, *New Times: The Changing Face of Politics in the 1990s,* ed. Martin Jacques (London: Verso, 1991), 35.

54. Carl Gutiérrez-Jones makes a solid argument for the interfacing juncture of aesthetics and legal culture in *Rethinking the Borderlands: Between Chicano Culture and Legal Discourse* (Berkeley: University of California Press, 1995).

pause for critique and productive resolutions than as unquestioned separation of spheres of interest. It would be more productive, then, to ask with Cornel West, what the political consequences are of (strategic) cultural identity-in-difference formations as an effect of previous overdetermination of culturally raced identities. As distinct from liberalized "multiculturalist" discourses, the "cultural politics of difference" "acknowledge[s] the uphill struggle of fundamentally transforming highly objectified, rationalized and commodified societies and cultures in the name of individuality and democracy."[55] In effect the raced-ethnic overdeterminations have taken place *a priori* in the Américas, certainly in the United States, "in the name of individuality and democracy," as tied to economic opportunity and desire.

Multiculturalism is only the latest discourse on the "table" to rehearse once again the discursive positional traps that emerge from deep-seated structural inequalities, which, moreover, have been sedimented over hundreds of years. Because "multiculturalism" in the United States is often perceived through the ongoing ethnic genocide and fighting in Eastern Europe, it gives rise in the United States to paranoia, on the one hand, which only seems to have the effect of triggering more racism, on the other, especially in light of a much-publicized economic decline and restructuration.[56] Thus, "multiculturalism" a name never advanced in the first place by U.S. activists and intellectuals of the "cultural politics of difference;" has moved from revising the K-12 curriculum to focusing on the academy, and is served up as rethinking the foundational epistemology, but not practice, of liberalism. As demonstrated in the recently reissued meditation on "the politics of recognition" by Charles Taylor in a collection sold as *Multiculturalism and the Politics of Recognition,* liberalism is not the same for the Canadian thinker as it is for Jürgen Habermas, a German one. (The question, What are the historical and political conditions that make the difference possible? is beyond the scope of this essay; certainly, however, the geographic position of each exerts pressure on his thinking. In short, the Américas are not Europe.) While, on the one hand, Taylor appears as a benign patriarch for whom boundaries may be blurred, questioned, or reasserted periodically, and who even invokes, though he doesn't account for, a dialogic subject/group formation, Habermas, on the other, wants to draw boundaries everywhere and exercise a strong control over their porosity and permeability. "Constitutional

---

55. West, *Keeping Faith: Philosophy and Race in America*, 30.

56. See Michael A. Bernstein and David E. Adler , eds., *Understanding American Economic Decline*, (Cambridge: Cambridge University Press, 1994).

patriotism" and "procedural consensus" are the twin pillars for the hard-and-fast universalism Habermas proposes.[57]

Charles Taylor provides philosophical merit to the discourse of multiculturalism with his meditative and critical essay "The Politics of Recognition," which has been translated into Italian, French, and German. In a sense this signals the modes through which some European and Euro-American thinkers understand what I've been calling with Cornel West "the cultural politics of difference." To codify the latter as "multiculturalism" is tantamount to an effort to displace "the cultural politics of difference" embraced by many intellectuals in the United States and to rethink them through an invocation of liberal epistemological foundations. At the core of this rethinking is the question of individual rights and citizenship as a unit.

Taylor's invocation of liberal epistemological foundations has the virtue of sincerely trying to explore the contradictions that "the cultural politics of difference" (or, as he entitles them, "the politics of recognition") has uncovered in the liberal political agenda. Taylor perceives two modes of politics: (1) the politics of difference "as an individual and also as a culture;" and (2) the claim to cultural equal worth.[58] He admits that the liberal principle of blindness to difference has not been successful in its application and that perhaps "the very idea of such a liberalism may be a kind of pragmatic contradiction, a particularism [of liberal thought] masquerading as the universal."[59] Moreover, he cannot imagine a "common project" that is compatible with differentiation, but he would like to. As a result, he wonders if there is not a middle ground wherein there is a "willingness to be open to comparative cultural study of the kind that must displace our horizons in the resulting fusions."[60] Borrowing from H. G. Gadamer, he hits upon the possibility of a coming "fusion of horizons" that "operates through our developing new vocabularies of comparison, by means of which we can articulate these contrasts."[61] The gesture to dialogism and conversation is not given up by Taylor even though "equal worth" cannot be demanded as a right. Such "equal worth" can only be accomplished or established through conjunctural conversations, otherwise they polarize into demands of cultural

---

57. Charles Taylor, Kwame Anthony Appiah, Jürgen Habermas, Steven C. Rockefeller, Michael Walzer, and Susan Wolf, *Multiculturalism: Examining the Politics of Recognition*, ed. Amy Gutman (Princeton: Princeton University Press, 1994), 135.

58. Taylor et al., *Multiculturalism*, 42-43.

59. Taylor et al., *Multiculturalism*, 44.

60. Taylor et al., *Multiculturalism*, 68.

61. Taylor et al., *Multiculturalism*, 67.

"equal worth" and "self-immurement within ethnocentric standards."[62] Stated from this angle, there is a strong desire on Taylor's part to understand the "cultural politics of difference" and the flaws it uncovers in the liberal political and aesthetic project. He questions procedural liberalism and finds it inhospitable because it continues to pretend a blindness to differences and "pretends to offer a neutral ground in which people of all cultures can meet or coexist."[63]

In appropriating G. H. Gadamer's notion of "fusion of horizons," Taylor is actually proposing, though not specifying, different "reading" practices. Gadamer's project is to outline the reading practices appropriate to the "hermeneutic experience" wherein the "conversation" takes place between the critical reader and the literary object. It is a practice that, in his view, may account for but surpasses historicism, such that the aesthetic is the teleological site for the "fusion of horizons between reader and text."[64] Taylor swerves from this ethnocentric project to insist on conversation between diverse ethnocultural critical readers and claimed texts. From this point of view, "equal [cultural] worth" is deferred through the conversation and the criterion of worth is as yet undetermined. Gadamer's ethnocentric project is undergirded by an insulated diachronism that insists, as Habermas notes in another context, on "the ontological priority of linguistic tradition before all possible critique."[65] Taylor's repositioning of "fusion of horizons" as the outcome to be achieved through conjunctural conversations between critical readers of different cultural formations disrupts and displaces Gadamer's map of the "hermeneutic experience." In fact, it opens it up to the possibility of a nonethnocentric critical discourse.

Given the desire for dialogism, Taylor's good intentions are too slippery for his interlocutors. His implicit understanding that there's more here than a "politics of recognition," which is only a first step for the conversation to take place, leads to a concomitant reciprocity of I's and We's that become polylogical given their formations in the context of nation making, which, no matter how veiled, is understood in the context of Canada, as I then understand it in the context of the United States; that is, a history hovers throughout the discussion. His interlocutors, however, panic over the emphasis given to collective groups'

---

62. Taylor et al., *Multiculturalism*, 68, 72.
63. Taylor et al., *Multiculturalism*, 62.
64. H.G. Gadamer, "The Hermeneutical Experience." *Philosophy Looks at the Arts: Contemporary Readings in Aesthetics*, ed. Joseph Margolis (Philadelphia: Temple University Press, 1987), 501.
65. Cited in Christopher Norris, *Contest of Faculties: Philosophy and Theory after Deconstruction* (London: Methuen, 1985), 26.

goals, which perhaps undermines the attachment to individual rights and individual freedom and the construction of citizenship on these grounds rather than collective goals. (See, for example, the comments by Steven Rockefeller and Michael Walzer in the volume.) The possibility of conversations that may give rise to uncontrolled "fused horizons" is a source of panic to them. And perhaps no one in the volume speaks to it more forcefully than Jürgen Habermas, while Rockefeller and Walzer retreat to notions of "universal identity as human beings" completely divorced of the nation-form that confers identities, whether they be a "matter of citizenship, gender, race, or ethnic origin."[66] The more sophisticated Habermas understands that the question of the nation-form cannot be obliterated. The nation-form cannot eschew its relationality to its subjects. Given this, then, one has to return to that which is fundamental for the nation, its legal system and its conferring of basic rights, which are individual and in contradiction to collective rights. The latter may be protected as cultural lifeworlds, but subject to the political culture of the nation-form, "the ethical integration of groups and subcultures with their collective identities must be uncoupled from the abstract political integration that includes all citizens equally."[67] What is that "abstract political integration"? Isn't that often made substantive and hence not abstract through the narrative of the nation-form, which continually strategizes to include or exclude citizenship and aestheticized "hermeneutic experience?" What does it mean to have "constitutional principles" interpreted or thoroughly distanced "from the perspective of the nation's historical experience" when the narrative of that very national experience is in question, as is the case in Canada, the United States, and the Américas?

Taylor sees the "common political culture" as something to be achieved, while Habermas takes it to be in place, resting on the constitutional rights and principles "from the fixed point of reference of any constitutional patriotism that situates the system of rights within the historical context of a legal community."[68] We get closer to Habermas's desire here, since it would appear that it is not so much the "nation's historical experience" in general and the formation of its subjects, as it is the "historical context of a legal community" that should prevail. I take this to suggest that it is the "historical legal community" that will have priority over any other notion or version of history. This is confirmed by the assertion that "in complex societies the citizenry as a whole can no longer

---

66. Taylor et al., *Multiculturalism*, 88.
67. Taylor et al., *Multiculturalism*, 133-134.
68. Taylor et al., *Multiculturalism*, 134.

be held together by a substantive consensus on values but only a consensus on the procedures for the legitimate enactment of laws and the legitimate exercise of power."[69] A strong proceduralism is the glue that will hold society together, not conversations over time that seek "fusion of horizons" as utopic possibility. In the age of poststructuralist thought, the question of universality will now reside in the rationality of the legal community.

In a sense, Habermas faults Taylor for too much philosophical thinking and not enough legalistic politics. At stake in the latter is the strong preservation of individual rights and freedom as the hallmark of citizenship. The swipes at poststructuralist thought that are taken by most in the book are conditioned by its deconstruction of the transcendental and sovereign subject on which "enlightened" modernity has depended for the maintenance of its self-contradictory empowered legitimacy and which subsequently makes it necessary to speak of two levels of integration, those that aspire to "our" political culture and those that remain in a "subpolitical level" that is, "ethnics" or, as Habermas refers to these, "lifeworlds" as a reconfiguration of pluralism now coded as multiculturalism. Consequently, the latter are misrecognized as culturally bounded in discrete forms and may claim the right to participate in the "political culture" by discarding "difference." What difference is at this level of discourse, I presume, is adjudicated by the modern liberal subject of the contingently prevailing political culture-in-law. What is citizenship continues to be on trial and, I suppose, will be juridically administered by the self-legitimated "political culture." While Taylor emphasizes the cultural discussion and postpones the political outcome, Habermas emphasizes the political legal culture and contains rather than postpones the cultural outcome. The former is portrayed as too philosophical and involved in questions of intersubjectivity; the latter ultimately and implicitly discards the intersubjective dimension except in a discussion of feminism, a version that appears to be already and conveniently homogenized by Habermas into his liberalism—a curious exception, to say the least, yet a minimalist gesture to the epistemological problems that feminism has raised so successfully.[70] That gesture remains too isolated from the *a priori*s of legal history and its production of the "political culture" already in place. On the other hand, the "cultural politics of difference" is already embroiled in claims

---

69. Taylor et al., *Multiculturalism*, 135.
70. Taylor et al., *Multiculturalism*, 115-117.

of the historical experience of the nation-making form, which is also a political culture whose adjudications have indeed been intersubjective throughout.[71]

The clarity of thought in Habermas should not be underestimated, especially its apparent administrative resolutions in "the historical context of a legal community." It interpellates a historically constructed Anglo-America and those who have been able to seek protection and entitlement through that proceduralism. Insofar as the theorists and practitioners of the "cultural politics of difference," each in turn and formed around their historical constitutedness, have engaged in a dialogism with the proceduralist "center" we have not been able to produce a notion of the coalitional subject. White paranoia and panic have reached extreme proportions in California, as reflected in the negative adjudication of Rodney King's rights[72] and those of (im)migrants via the passage of Proposition 187 and of the upcoming (irony not intended) California *Civil Rights* Initiative.

---

71. Priscilla Wald, "Terms of Assimilation: Legislating Subjectivity in the Emerging Nation," in *Cultures of United States Imperialism*, ed. Amy Kaplan and Donald E. Pease (Durham, NC: Duke University Press, 1993), 59-84.

72. Robert Gooding-Williams, ed., *Reading Rodney King, Reading Urban Uprising* (New York: Routledge, 1993).

BIBLIOGRAPHY

Anzaldúa, Gloria. *Borderlands/La Frontera: The New Mestiza*. San Francisco: Spinsters/Aunt Lute, 1987.

Arendt, Hannah. *Between Past and Future: Eight Exercises in Political Thought*. New York: Penguin Books, 1978.

Balibar, Etienne. "Is There a Neo-racism?" In *Race, Nation, Class: Ambiguous Identities*. London: Verso, 1991.

Beauvoir, Simone de. *The Second Sex*. Translated by H. M. Parshley. New York: Vintage Books, 1974.

Benhabib, Seyla. *Situating the Self: Gender, Community and Postmodernism in Contemporary Ethics*. New York: Routledge, 1992.

Bernstein, Michael A. and David E. Adler, editors. *Understanding American Economic Decline*. Cambridge: Cambridge University Press, 1994.

Bérubé, Michael. "Disuniting America Again." In *Public Access: Literary Theory and American Cultural Politics*, 225-242. London: Verso, 1994.

Braidotti, Rose, *Patterns of Dissonance: A Study of Women in Contemporary Philosophy*. Translated by Elizabeth Guild. New York: Routledge, 1991.

Buell, Frederick. *National Culture and the Global System*. Baltimore: Johns Hopkins University Press, 1994.

Butler, Judith. *Gender Trouble: Feminism and Subversion of Identity*. New York: Routledge, 1990.

Castoriadis, Cornelius. *The Imaginary Institution of Society*. Translated by Kathleen Blarney. Cambridge: MIT Press, 1987.

Crenshaw, Kimberlé. "Demarginalizing the Intersection of Race and Sex: A Black Feminist Critique of Antidiscrimination Doctrine, Feminist Theory and Antiracist Politics." In *The University of Chicago Legal Forum* 1989, iss. 1, article 8, 139-167. 1989.

Derrida, Jacques. *Margins of Philosophy*. Translated by Alan Bass. Chicago: University of Chicago Press, 1982.

Derrida, Jacques. *Writing and Difference*. Translated by Alan Bass. Chicago: University of Chicago Press, 1978.

Faludi, Susan. *Backlash: The Undeclared War against American Women*. New York: Crown Publishers, 1991.

Fanon, Frantz. "The Fact of Blackness." In *Anatomy of Racism*, edited by David Theo Goldberg and translated by Charles Lam Markmann, 108-126. Minneapolis: University of Minnesota Press, 1990.

Fraser, Nancy and Sandra Lee Bartky. *Revaluing French Feminism: Critical Essays on Difference, Agency & Culture*. Bloomington: Indiana University Press, 1992.

Fuss, Diana. *Essentially Speaking: Feminism, Nature and Difference.* New York: Routledge, 1989.

Gadamer, H.G. "The Hermeneutical Experience." In *Philosophy Looks at the Arts: Contemporary Readings in Aesthetics,* edited by Joseph Margolis, 499-517. Philadelphia: Temple University Press, 1987.

Gooding-Williams, Robert, editor. *Reading Rodney King, Reading Urban Uprising.* New York: Routledge, 1993.

Gutiérrez-Jones, Carl. *Rethinking the Borderlands: Between Chicano Culture and Legal Discourse.* Berkeley: University of California Press, 1995.

Hall, Stuart and Martin Jacques, editors. *New Times: The Changing Face of Politics in the 1990s.* London: Verso, 1990.

Hurtado, Aída. "Relating to Privilege: Seduction and Rejection in the Subordination of White Women and Women of Color." In *Signs* 14, no. 4(1989), 833-855.

Irigaray, Luce. *Speculum of the Other Woman.* Translated by Gillian C. Gill. Ithaca, NY: Cornell University Press, 1985.

Jaggar, Alison M. *Feminist Politics and Human Nature.* Totowa, NJ: Rowan and Allanheld, 1983.

Moi, Toril. *Sexual/Textual Politics.* London: Methuen, 1985.

Moraga, Cherríe, and Gloria Anzaldúa, editors. *This Bridge Called My Back: Writings by Radical Women of Color.* Watertown, MA: Persephone Press, 1981.

Mudimbe, V.Y. *The Invention of Africa: Gnosis, Philosophy, and the Order of Knowledge.* Bloomington, IN: Indiana University Press, 1988.

Muñoz, Carlos. *Youth, Identity, Power: The Chicano Movement.* London: Verso, 1989.

Murray, Charles and Richard Hernstein. *The Bell Curve: Intelligence and Class Structure in American Life.* New York: Free Press, 1994.

Nancy, Jean-Luc. "Cut Throat Sun." In *An Other Tongue,* edited by Alfred Artega, 113-123. Durham, NC: Duke University Press, 1994.

Norris, Christopher. *Contest of Faculties: Philosophy and Theory after Deconstruction.* London: Methuen, 1985.

Palumbo-Liu, David, editor. *The Ethnic Canon: Histories, Institutions, and Interventions.* Minnesota: University of Minnesota Press, 1995.

Rorty, Richard. *Contingency, Irony, and Solidarity.* Cambridge: Cambridge University Press, 1989.

Sartre, Jean-Paul. *Search for a Method.* Translated by Hazel Barnes. New York: Alfred A. Knopf, 1963.

Sandoval, Chela. "U.S. Third World Feminism: The Theory and Method of Oppositional Consciousness in the Postmodern World." In "Theorizing Nationality, Sexuality, and Race," ed. Ann Kibbey, special issue, *Genders* 10 (spring 1991): 1-24.

Schlesinger, Arthur M., Jr. *The Disuniting of America: Reflections on a Multicultural Society.* British Columbia: Whittle Books, 1991.

Smith, Barbara and Beverly Smith "Across the Kitchen Table: A Sister-to-Sister Dialogue," in *This Bridge Called My Back*, edited by Cherríe Moraga and Gloria Anzaldúa, 113-127. Watertown, MA: Persephone Press, 1981.

Spivak, Gayatri Chakravorty. "Displacement and the Discourse of Women." In *Displacement: Derrida and After*, edited by Mark Krupnik, 169-196. Bloomington, I.N.: Indiana University Press, 1983.

Taylor, Charles, Kwame Anthony Appiah, Jürgen Habermas, Steven C. Rockefeller, Michael Walzer, and Susan Wolf. *Multiculturalism: Examining the Politics of Recognition.* Edited by Amy Gutman. Princeton: Princeton University Press, 1994.

Wald, Priscilla. "Terms of Assimilation: Legislating Subjectivity in the Emerging Nation." In *Cultures of United States Imperialism*, edited by Amy Kaplan and Donald E. Pease, 59-84. Durham, NC: Duke University Press, 1993.

West, Cornel. "The New Cultural Politics of Difference." *October*, 53 (1990): 93-109.

West, Cornel. *Keeping Faith: Philosophy and Race in America.* New York: Routledge, 1993.

ANZALDÚAN TEXTUALITIES

A HERMENEUTIC OF THE SELF AND THE COYOLXAUHQUI IMPERATIVE[1]

→ ←

If I had the words for all of the images in my head, life would be much easier.

—stated to me in a critical literacy workshop for middle school girls

INTRODUCTION

THE FOLLOWING CRITICAL ESSAY is a preliminary and provisional attempt to bring into relief what I think are the structures and theory of praxis in the work of Gloria Anzaldúa as it is currently given to us in the corpus of her published work.[2] Ironically, Anzaldúa does not appear to have mentioned the concept-metaphor[3]

---

1. Editor's Note: This essay was published in *El Mundo Zurdo 3: Selected Works from the 2012 Meeting of the Society for the Study of Gloria Anzaldúa*, ed. Larissa M. Mercado-López, Sonia Saldívar Hull, and Antonia Castañeda (San Francisco: Aunt Lute Books, 2013), 189-208.

2. I want to thank and acknowledge the work of AnaLouise Keating who has been bringing to our attention through edited collections some of the scattered publications by Gloria Anzaldúa and Norma Cantú's foundational work in the formation of the Society for the Study of Gloria Anzaldúa. I also want to thank and acknowledge Steve Martinot's published work on the formation and structures of White Identity in the U.S. Moreover, I could not have finished this piece without the assistance of Christina Gutiérrez.

3. Scattered in her critical work Gayatri Spivak uses the hyphenated notion of "Concept-Metaphor." I have decided to deploy it in this essay because I think that Anzaldúa is constructing her own "concept-metaphor" epistemology which she appropriates from pre-Columbian mythography and terms. Through that appropriation she recodes them for her philosophical vision. I interpret "concept-metaphor" through the hyphen as Spivak's effort to bring into relief the relationality and/or correlativity between terms that are customarily used separately in the Anglo-European critical corpus. Both terms signal a substitution for differently located "referents" that may be erased depending on the specified genre of the text from philosophy to science. Anzaldúa herself states, "... I have to have a central metaphor like La Llorona or La Prieta. Within that central metaphor are these concepts, like working within the interface between different realities—nepantla space." See "Quincentennial: From Victimhood to Active Resistance." Interview with AnaLouise Keating, in *Gloria Anzaldúa: Interviews/Entrevistas*, ed. AnaLouise Keating (New York: Routledge, 2000), 176. Thus, in order to provide critical consistency to my structuration of this particular line of thought in Anzaldúa's work, I will be adhering to this "concept-metaphor" theoretical perspective as much as is possible. I was able to find at least one reference to the idea of decolonization when Anzaldúa points out to the ways "we attempt to decolonize ourselves" as we work through the violence internalized from the societies we live in" (Gloria Anzaldúa, *Making Face, Making Soul / Haciendo Caras: Creative and Critical Perspectives of Feminists of Color* (San Francisco: Aunt Lute Books, 1990), xvii.

of decolonization for her life-long project to heal the inner wounds and the sociopolitical and economic wounds of colonization. In fact, however, I think that her project's *telos* was a quest for personal and political decolonization, a project that begins with processes entailed in a self-reconstruction of a damaged self due to trauma suffered. Chela Sandoval writes, "We had each tasted the shards of 'difference' until they had carved up our insides; now we were asking ourselves what shapes our healing would take."[4] With few exceptions, such as the concept-metaphors of psyche, spirit, being, self, other, and consciousness, Anzaldúa deeply distrusts and often rejects epistemologies offered by white hegemonic Western forms of Reason. These forms, in fact, cannot help the speaking subject[5] of color make sense of her experience. In the process, Anzaldúa develops her own concept-metaphors by (largely) drawing on her readings of Jung and Jungian-style notions of the psyche-spirit, symbols, and shadow; the pre-Colombian legacy of cosmological and mythographic figures and terms; and her personal experience that is often narrated in a testimonial and anecdotal style in her early work from *Bridge* to *Borderlands*. In my view, these texts provide a narrative praxis entwined with theory of praxis that become the initial ground for the later development of her thought. Further, these texts, combined with interviews of that period are, in my estimation, continuously and diversely rethought and reinscribed in later work as she relentlessly pursues meanings for experiences both personal and political. For Anzaldúa, one's experiences must not be let go without inquiry as to their meanings.

At a minimum through this conjunctive assemblage that structures praxis and theory of praxis, Anzaldúa tries to transform the chaos of experiences into order—an order which, in effect, is constantly in peril of becoming once again an agonistic chaos as she depicts, for example, in La Facultad and The Coatlicue State.[6] As attentive readers of Anzaldúa's work in print know, her work is a cornucopia of possibilities for lines of inquiry, as such what I do in this essay represents what I believe to be one important "line." Thus, Anzaldúa's philosophical self-grounding in the inner and outer experiences of the self remains to be explored further. In brief, Anzaldúa draws from a variety of systems of knowledge, to achieve her own "system," to achieve what she projected for

---

4. Anzaldúa, *Making Face, Making Soul*, xxvii.

5. For elaboration of the notion of the "speaking subject" see Julia Kristeva's "The System and the Speaking Subject," in *The Kristeva Reader*, ed. Toril Moi (New York: Columbia University Press, 1986), 24-33.

6. Gloria Anzaldúa, *Borderlands/La Frontera: The New Mestiza* (San Francisco: Spinsters/Aunt Lute, 1987), 38-39 and 41-51.

herself in El Mundo Zurdo section of "La Prieta"[7] and in *Borderlands*, where she states that she wants

> the freedom to carve and chisel my own face, to staunch the bleeding with ashes, to fashion my own gods out of my entrails. And if going home is denied me then I will have to stand and claim my own space, making a new culture—*una cultura mestiza*—with my own lumber, my own bricks and mortar and my own feminist architecture.[8]

Indeed, she did.

Theory-In-The-Flesh

THE INVOCATION FOR "THEORY-IN-THE-FLESH" put forth by Cherríe Moraga was one that referred to the contributors of the section "Entering the Lives of Others: Theory in the Flesh" in *This Bridge Called My Back*.[9] It also prompted readers to explore their personal and political structures of experience. For many it was an understanding that it was these very personal and political structures of experience, memory, and history that conditioned an outsidedness rooted in the violence of slavery and colonization within the Anglo-American nation-state, though not limited to it. Hence, for example, Audre Lorde's title for her collection of essays *Sister Outsider* has been virtually as foundational to a queer and feminist women-of-color consciousness as *Bridge* has been.[10]

The interpellation to do "theory-in-the-flesh" was responded to by many who understood and knew that their work was being carried out on the outer margins of the socioeconomic, political, and academic weave. Laboring from the outer margins of a highly stratified society these women-of-color understood that if their work was heard at all it was in sound bytes that dehistoricized and dematerialized their work thereby silencing it—with a few exceptions. However, many queer feminist women-of-color in general heard what they had to say between and amongst each other, as Chela Sandoval analyzes in her work, *Methodology of the Oppressed* and reiterates in her more recent essay "After Bridge:

---

7. Gloria Anzaldúa, "La Prieta," in *This Bridge Called My Back: Writings by Radical Women of Color*, ed. Cherríe Moraga and Gloria Anzaldúa (New York: Kitchen Table/Women of Color Press, 1983), 198-209.
8. Anzaldúa, *Borderlands/La Frontera*, 22.
9. Moraga, *Bridge*, 21-23.
10. Audre Lorde, *Sister/Outsider: Essays and Speeches* (Crossing Press, 1984).

Technologies of Crossing" in *This Bridge We Call Home*, Anzaldúa's last edited book with AnaLouise Keating.[11]

At the 2010 meeting of the Society for the Study of Gloria Anzaldúa, for example, Laura E. Pérez commented that *Borderlands* "was an invitation into the deeper recesses of the margins," which at the time she could not bear.[12] However, a few years later she had embraced the book and was claiming that Anzaldúa "presents us with a new philosophical framework outside of Western binary thought."[13] It is a claim that I think first returns us to that invitation to delve "into the deeper recesses of the margins" which in Anzaldúa's work are structured by a confrontation with her internalized otherness, the source of her trauma and wound.[14]

Confronting Internalized Otherness

FOR ANZALDÚA "THEORY-IN-THE-FLESH" EMERGES from her confrontation with her trauma and wound that has also generated what she names a Shadow Beast, that is, the negativity within the self that threatens her quest for self-integration, healing, and wholeness every step of the way. Eventually, as I will discuss, that quest is mediated by the concept-metaphors of Coatlicue, Nepantla and Coyolxauhqui and the practice of making and unmaking and remaking as a lived necessity. In an early interview with Christine Weiland, Anzaldúa gives us a glimpse of a theoretical view of the praxis towards self-transformation and self-reintegration that she subsequently details in The Coatlicue State in

---

11. Chela Sandoval, "After Bridge: Technologies of Crossing" in *this bridge we call home: radical visions for transformation*, ed. AnaLouise Keating (New York: Routledge, 2002), 21-26.

12. Laura Pérez, "The Performance of Spirituality and Visionary Politics in the Work of Gloria Anzaldúa," in *El Mundo Zurdo 2: Selected Works from the 2020 Meeting of the Society for the Study of Gloria Anzaldúa*, ed. Sonia Saldívar Hull, Norma Alarcón, and Rita Urquijo Ruiz (San Francisco: Aunt Lute Books, 2012),13.

13. Pérez, "The Performance of Spirituality and Visionary Politics," 14.

14. From the beginning of her published work Anzaldúa launches a testimonial and anecdotal inquiry of the Self in the flesh, for example in *Bridge* "La Prieta" where she first speaks of her vision of El Mundo Zurdo (208-209) for transcending her agonistic life formation experiences, and "Speaking in Tongues: A Letter to 3rd World Women Writers." Also in *Borderlands,* the turmoil of the internalized unwanted otherness is given greater personal depth as torment of the self, for example, the chapter called *"La Herencia de Coatlicue*: The Coatlicue State" as well as interviews of that period which depict, reinscribe, and rescript her agony. A recent book by the noted neurobiologist Antonio Damasio, *Self Comes to Mind: Constructing the Conscious Brain* (New York: Pantheon, 2012), maps the ways in which indeed one can insist on the idea of "theory-in-the-flesh" from the bottom of the organism's knowledges. Also the work of noted neuropsychologist Candace B. Pert lends itself to the idea of "theory-in-the-flesh" in her book *Molecules of Emotion: Why You Feel the Way You Feel* (New York: Simon & Shuster, 1999).

Borderlands.¹⁵ It entails a confrontation with the negative and violent otherness of self in its interiority—"You make the inner changes first, and then you make the other changes... Sometimes you can do both at the same time: work to create outer change, through political movement, at the same time that you're trying to do meditation and developing yourself."¹⁶ For Anzaldúa, confronting the internalized otherness opens the possibility of self-transformation, as it can become a transition from wallowing in a state of victimhood by diminishing the internalized self-contempt. However, that confrontation may have to be repeated as internalized otherness, is not easily swept away completely, if ever.

Western philosophy can be said to begin and end with the question of the Other.¹⁷ Anzaldúa's psychic, spiritual, political and intellectual journey, however, starts with inquiries into her own otherness within that compels her to pierce the "mystery of the self" and to explore "the center of the self."¹⁸ In effect, there is a double alienation at work—the one that alienates her from a desired integral interiority of self and the alienation and exile from society and the world. In the healing work for the interiority of self, Anzaldúa recognizes her double alienation. She says,

> I feel a great isolation and separateness and *differentness* from everyone, even though I have many allies. Yet as soon as I have these thoughts—that I'm in this alone, that I have to stand on the ground of my own being, that I have to create my own separate space—the exact opposite thoughts come to me: that we are all in this together, juntas, that the ground of our being is a common ground, la Tierra.¹⁹

To assuage that loneliness she has to both create and imagine a community for herself.

---

15. Gloria Anzaldúa, Interview, "Within the Crossroads: Lesbian/Feminist/Spiritual Development" with Christine Weiland, in *Gloria Anzaldúa: Interviews/Entrevistas*, ed. AnaLouise Keating (New York: Routledge, 2000) 72-127.

16. Anzaldúa, "Within the Crossroads," 101.

17. Though Western philosophy may "begin" and continue to our day with the question of the Other, its focus has been Anglo-European. In fact, though the concept and practice of othering has been deployed against the racialized enslaved and colonized people of color, locally and globally, the effects of that theory and practice have not been reckoned with, unpacked, nor engaged by whites in general—men or women. A self-decolonizing praxis and theory of practice is now being formulated by some people of color, especially queer feminists of color.

18. Moraga and Anzaldúa, *Bridge*, 169.

19. Gloria Anzaldúa, "Bridge, Drawbridge, Sandbar, or Island," in *The Gloria Anzaldúa Reader*, ed. AnaLouise Keating (Durham, NC: Duke University Press, 2009), 141.

What are the sources of that doubled alienation and that sense of living in exile which are the product of the traumatic wound? They are multiple—as a colonized-raced-daughter, as a colonized-raced-student, as a colonized-raced-woman, as queer and poor, in short, as a social being in the world where her very interiority and exteriority of self is other. Also, she is the other of multiple communities and least the other in a "community of women of color writers."[20] Though this may provide solace, it does not eradicate the otherness experienced within—inside herself. That internalized multiple sense of otherness is agonistic and a result of damage, injury, and woundedness arising from her own structures of experience many of which are narrativized in her writings. However, she believes that through writing she will achieve the expulsion of that other within her (the Shadow Beast) by putting into praxis and theory of praxis the overarching Coyolxauhqui "method," which she subsequently transforms into "the Coyolxauhqui imperative"—the vision of reaching out, of being all in this together. Thus to Spivak's question "Can the Subaltern Speak?"[21] Anzaldúa juxtaposes "Can the Subaltern Write?" She gives an affirmative answer to both questions, and urges women to speak and write in "Speaking in Tongues: A Letter to 3rd World Women Writers."[22]

She wills herself to write "Because the world I create in the writing compensates for what the real world doesn't give me."[23] In fact the real world produces in her the experience of inner-otherness-in-the-flesh which threatens to overwhelm and devour her, as depicted in The Coatlicue State. In brief, I think that her project is to decolonize herself and reach out to others to do the same through both speaking and writing—to exorcize otherness by transcoding it into language. She insists, "And as we internalized this exile we came to see the alien within us and too often as a result, we split away from ourselves and each other."[24] "Speaking and writing are the tools for piercing that mystery.... it is the quest for the self, for the center of the self, which we women-of-color have to think as 'other....'"[25] It is a process of self-disalienation. In order to get rid

---

20. Anzaldúa, Bridge, 171.
21. Gayatri C. Spivak, "Can the subaltern speak?" in Marxism and the Interpretation of Culture, ed. Cary Nelson and Lawrence Grossbery (Urbana: University of Illinois Press, 1988), 271-313.
22. Gloria Anzaldúa, "Speaking in Tongues: Letter to 3rd World Women Writers," in This Bridge Called my Back: Writings by Radical Women of Color ed Cherríe Moraga and Gloria Anzaldúa (New York: Kitchen Table/Women of Color Press, 1983), 165-173.
23. Anzaldúa, "Speaking in Tongues," 169.
24. Anzaldúa, "Speaking in Tongues," 169.
25. Anzaldúa, "Speaking in Tongues," 169.

of that otherness, we must confront it and revolt. Her project for excavating and disclosing this otherness diverges quite a bit from that of Simone de Beauvoir in *The Second Sex* by focusing on her inner structures of experience first which are not those of a white bourgeois privileged woman. In fact, de Beauvoir's theorization of being Other is one of white women in relation to a European white heteropatriarchy.

Though Anzaldúa succeeds in writing and speaking "about life on the borders, life in the shadows,"[26] she puts in question towards the end of her life her success in having dissolved the body/mind/spirit split which was one of her goals, and states, "Though your body is still *la otra* and though pensamientos dualisticos still keep you from embracing and writing corporally *con esa otra*, you dream of the possibility of wholeness."[27] The structured inner and outer experience of otherness must be confronted and dissolved through acts of decolonization over and over again through the positional locations she elaborates for this confrontational act—largely The Coatlicue State, Nepantla and the Coyolxauhqui method and imperative. Nepantla is an "in-between" space through which a "third critical space" is seized and pivoted to encompass diverse situations and worlds. It is an interstitial space, a space in-between multiple social worlds. Caught between multiple sociopolitical and cultural worlds, the interfaces of lifeworlds are a consistent current and undercurrent in Anzaldúa's development and hermeneutic of the self. Though initially Nepantla is a "liminal state between worlds, between realities, between systems of knowledge, between symbology"[28] thus elaborating the praxis of self-healing by creating an "in-between" space that facilitates self-transformation,[29] the concept-metaphor of Nepantla is also reframed for her vision of public acts by Nepantleras, a correlative concept-metaphor coined by Anzaldúa.

---

26. Anzaldúa, *Borderlands*, Preface.

27. Anzaldúa, "... now let us shift, 563.

28. Gloria Anzaldúa, "Toward a Mestiza Rhetoric: Gloria Anzaldúa on Composition, Postcoloniality, and the Spiritual," Interview with Andrea Lunsford, in *Gloria Anzaldúa: Interviews/Entrevistas*, ed. AnaLouise Keating (New York: Routledge, 2000), 268.

29. Anzaldúa, *Entrevistas*, 5.

Between Chaos and Order/Between Imaginal Consciousness and Reasoning Consciousness

IT IS NOT INACCURATE to say that Anzaldúa waged a life-long battle to dissolve the Western Cartesian split of body-mind-spirit.[30] She did so by first focusing on her own embodied life formation and situation. Very distrustful of the western academy's alienating forms of reason, she says "Something has to emerge out of the chaos and raw material of your life."[31] This is a major reason for her call to "de-academize" theory and construct theories of our own, a decolonial project to say the least.[32]

Though she starts her devotion to writing the colonized body calling it "autohistoria," it is also clear that she was evolving an "automythography," which, entwined in process, would eventually yield a visionary philosophy of the personal and the political. In *Borderlands*, she declares, "I write the myths in me, the myths I am, the myths I want to become."[33] Fifteen years later in "now let us shift...the path of conocimiento . . . inner work, public acts," she tells us, "As a modern-day Coyolxauhqui, you search for an account that encapsulates your life, and finding no ready-made story, you trust her light in the darkness to help you bring forth (from the remnants of the old personal/collective autohistoria), a new personal myth."[34] Through the 80s and 90s Anzaldúa continued pivoting Coyolxauhqui's meanings for her and the centrality of this concept-metaphor in her work. From the position of an in-between Nepantla consciousness, Coyolxauhqui is a theory and praxis and theory of praxis encompassed by *compostura* and *decompostura*, which is subject to revision as an ultimate *compostura* proves elusive. That is, it may have to be performed over and over again.

Though many of her early writings tend to emphasize testimonio and autohistoria by the time she publishes *Borderlands* the entwinement with an automythography begins in earnest. They are, in effect, interwoven and assembled currents that feed each other—autohistoria and automythography. One could also say that an automythography envisioned earlier by Anzaldúa reaches an elaborated vision that culminates in the three essays I will be discussing. However,

---

30. For a fascinating account of this process as "selfcraft" see Chapter 6 of Edwina Barvosa's *Wealth of Selves: Multiple Identities, Mestiza Consciousness and the Subject of Politics* (Texas A & M University Press, 2008).
31. Anzaldúa, "Putting Coyolxauhqui Together: A Creative Process," in *How We Work*, ed. Marla Morris, Mary Aswell Doll, and William F. Pinar (New York: Peter Lang, 1999) 259.
32. Anzaldúa, *Making Face, Making Soul*, xxvi.
33. Anzaldúa, *Borderlands*, 93.
34. Anzaldúa, "now let us shift," 559-560.

a sample of an earlier vision is thematized in the section of "La Prieta" called "El Mundo Zurdo (The Left-Handed World)" where she states:

> I believe that by changing ourselves we change the world, that travelling El Mundo Zurdo path is the path of a two-way movement—a going deep into the self and an expanding out into the world, a simultaneous recreation of the self and a reconstruction of society. And yet I am confused as to how to accomplish this.... I build my own universe, El Mundo Zurdo.[35]

By the time she publishes the last essay completed in her lifetime ("Let us be the healing of the wound: The Coyolxauqui imperative—la sombra y el sueño"), the confusion has been dispelled and she has built her own universe, which she continually offers to her listeners and readers. That universe entwines autohistoria and automythography and she resolves the confusion for herself in a visionary philosophy drawn from praxis and theory of praxis. One could also say it is drawn from experience and theory of experience, which she depicts and analyzes as a speaking subject in a process of reconstructing the self and its constructed heterogeneity.

In her essay "Putting Coyolxauhqui Together: A Creative Process," Anzaldúa appears to have for the first time pulled the "bones" together which she articulates into a skeletal architecture, thereby providing the epistemologic/automythographic structure for her creative process which she had already rehearsed in "Tlilli, Tlapalli: The Path of the Red and Black Ink."[36] Through that structure she depicts and details her embodied internal struggle to pull the "bones" together. It is an agonizing effort to produce any piece of the embodied writing she desires in the finished product given the interruptive force of the chaotic emotions undergone in the process of weaving writing itself. In her eyes these products of writing are always flawed in the face of the ideal perfection she seeks and which blocks her repeatedly in the effort to write. As readers we can empathize with the arduous processes undertaken and in fact come to understand why so much written material remained either in her computer or files, which is now relegated to the Anzaldúa Archives[37] which I am sure many will consult in years to come.

---

35. Anzaldúa, "La Prieta" in *Bridge*, 232-233.

36. Anzaldúa, *Borderlands*, 65-75.

37. Editor's Note: Alarcón is referring to the Gloria Evangelina Anzaldúa Papers at the Nettie Lee Benson Latin American Collection, The University of Texas at Austin Library.

In this essay, she gathers the "bones" for structuring the skeletal articulation, which are represented by the concept-metaphors of La Llorona, la naguala, el cenote, Nepantla, the shadow [elsewhere noted as Shadow Beast], and Coyolxauhqui, who has the healing powers of a shaman. These guide her in the fleshing out of the text as well as herself. Though she does not mention Coatlicue by name, she addresses brooding depressions for which Coatlicue is the salient figure and at times a metonym of La Llorona. With the exception of the Shadow Beast, all of these concept-metaphors, figures and symbols have been appropriated from the pre-Colombian indigenous mythographic narrative tradition and legacy. However, Anzaldúa recodifies these for herself with the exception of La Llorona who retains her salient post-conquest meanings, especially grief. She is still a woman who wails for the loss of her children and is condemned to a perpetual grief in her search for them. Anzaldúa says, "My symbol for la herida de colonialism and the trauma of Conquest is La Llorona."[38]

For Anzaldúa the call to write comes from La Llorona, "the dark mother... the ghost woman who wails the loss of her children." She is closely linked to la naguala, the virtual twin "musa bruja... that incites [her] to write... [and] will carry [her] through from beginning to end."[39] The response to the call is motivated by the need to make sense and give meaning to the chaos and raw materials of her life which have been constituted by the founding wound and trauma of her personal experience as initially narrated in "La Prieta" and scattered throughout subsequent interviews and writings. It is important to note that in the creative process depicted in this essay, Coyolxauhqui in pieces is closely linked to La Llorona and la naguala. It is the call to put Coyolxauhqui together again and restore her to wholeness from the dismemberment and fragmentation she underwent at the hands of her brother, the God of War. From this point of view, Coyolxauhqui's disarticulated body is put in tension with the desire to reassemble her own body in pieces into a wholeness which will be represented by the final written product, from *decompostura* to *compostura*, and back again as required by situation. Through this internal tension, Anzaldúa maps her strenuous inner struggle to write her "entrails." That mapping entails a diving into El Cenote, the concept-metaphor or symbol for the inner recesses of the self, including the unconscious when possible and in a fully conscious way. The praxis of confronting the violent inner recesses of the self as depicted in

---

38. Anzaldúa, *Entremundos*, 55.
39. Anzaldúa, "Putting Coyolxauhqui Together," 242.

The Coatlicue State have evolved into a theory of praxis for embodied writing which is now represented by El Cenote as the cavern for the imaginal–El Cenote, which in other texts Anzaldúa also refers to as the dark cave, marks the site of "the cavernous theater of dreams,"[40] a state of awake-dreaming. El Cenote yields "visual, aural, or olfactory memory of some trivial incident [that] triggers a stream of images. Subliminal events in your body or sensations provoked by its organs appear and vanish like fleeting fish, leaving behind a flash of el cuerpo's *(sic)* knowledge."[41]

To begin the work of deciphering and organizing the "bones" and to capture the awake-dreaming stream of inner focused Nepantla consciousness, she invokes la naguala who enables talking "about the work of embodying consciousness"[42] and to capture that stream in her "net of words."[43] That is she attends "to the imaginal with the goal of translating it on paper"[44] and catches it in her "net of words." La naguala, *musa bruja*, is, however, also linked to Nepantla, which in a relay play together begin to decipher and organize the contents of El Cenote, "a mental network of subterranean rivers of information that converge and well up to the surface."[45] In naguala space her perception is "hyperempathic" and she becomes "shifting and fluid, the boundaries of self-identity blur. . . ." This state alternates between "hyperempathy and excessive detachment, a seamless change from one to the other."[46]

Nepantla is invoked to create "a wider space in [her] mind." The Nepantla liminal position assists her in fielding the confusion and disorder, "[i]t enables switching from one perception channel to another."[47] Nepantla's wider scope allows her "to make connections, allowing the various scenarios to merge and come into focus." Nepantla is shaman-like. Its work "is a mysterious dreaming or perception which registers the workings of all states of consciousness . . . moves from rational to visionary states, from logics and poetics, from focused to unfocused perception, from inner to outer world. Nepantla is the twilight landscape beween self and the world, between imagery of the imagination and

---

40. Anzaldúa, "Putting Coyolxauhqui Together," 245.
41. Anzaldúa, "Putting Coyolxauhqui Together," 245.
42. Anzaldúa, "Putting Coyolxauhqui Together," 249.
43. Anzaldúa, "Putting Coyolxauhqui Together," 247.
44. Anzaldúa, "Putting Coyolxauhqui Together," 244.
45. Anzaldúa, "Putting Coyolxauhqui Together," 244.
46. Anzaldúa, "Putting Coyolxauhqui Together," 250.
47. Anzaldúa, "Putting Coyolxauhqui Together," 252.

the harsh light of reality.[48] Nepantla in this creative process operates "in the liminal spaces,"[49] navigating the interstice between an overly ordered side and "bacchanalian chaos, always attempting to join the two in a seamless web."[50]

> Nepantla averiguan *(sic)* el conflicto. It provides associations and connective tissue ... and interweaves multiple, superimposed strands of thought.... The imaginal consciousness, the dreaming naguala, seizes the booty that El Cenote renders up and turns into sentient worlds, while Nepantla interlaces those worlds into a coherent whole.[51]

However, the achievement of "a coherent whole" the one that will be the reassembling of Coyolxauhqui is not without obstacles. The naguala can shapeshift into a virulent *musa bruja* who has the capacity to "rise up from the depths," and drag her "into the deep waters of the cave."[52] In that cave she becomes possessed by the Shadow Beast which she "can't deny, can't hide from the shadow side of writing."[53] She is in effect thrown into chaos which throws her into depression, or the Coatlicue state. She feels that she must confront the dark cave and the Shadow Beast and admit that it is part of her. She posits that it is her own "irrationality" that catapults her into the Coalicue state and fears that she may not "emerge with the message from the source," suspecting that her "irrationality" arises from a desconocimiento (ignorance or denial) of herself which she has to confront. In brief she will have "to accept the imperfections"[54] in the work, "accept its partial incoherences.... like a person's life all art is a work in progress."[55] Thus she hopes that "[t]his Coyolxauhqui will emerge from the cave's cauldron...."[56]; that is, from El Cenote which is both the source for creativity and the source that may envelop her in a chaos that she must process.

Throughout this creative process Anzaldúa's high intensity self-questioning continually begs the question of whether she has succeeded in putting Coyolxauhqui together again from the depths of El Cenote, the dark cave. The cave, the cauldron is always at play. Has Coyolxauhqui been reassembled without

---

48. Anzaldúa, "Putting Coyolxauhqui Together," 252.
49. Anzaldúa, "Putting Coyolxauhqui Together," 252.
50. Anzaldúa, "Putting Coyolxauhqui Together," 252.
51. Anzaldúa, "Putting Coyolxauhqui Together," 252-53.
52. Anzaldúa, "Putting Coyolxauhqui Together," 255.
53. Anzaldúa, "Putting Coyolxauhqui Together," 255.
54. Anzaldúa, "Putting Coyolxauhqui Together," 259.
55. Anzaldúa, "Putting Coyolxauhqui Together," 259.
56. Anzaldúa, "Putting Coyolxauhqui Together," 259.

succumbing to white western modes of rationality which would disembody the work? Resisting the epistemological methodologies of white Western rationality, she wants to give coherence and order to the chaos on her own terms, constructing her own universe, her own concept-metaphors (epistemologies). She wants to capture the language of the awake-dreaming of the inner imaginal world into a "net of words" that does not mimic white western rationality. In this fashion she moves from a first semiological plane of disorder to a second semiological order that is all her own construction.[57]

Conocimiento

In "now let us shift... the path of conocimiento... inner work, public acts," Anzaldúa reiterates and restages some of the key concept-metaphors mapped out in the depiction of the creative process as well as *Borderlands*. These are aligned with the "path of conocimiento.... Conocimiento questions conventional knowledge's current categories, ossifications, and contents."[58] "Conocimineto comes from opening all your senses, consciously inhabiting your body and decoding its symptoms."[59] For Anzaldúa, conocimiento is an "overarching theory of consciousness, of how the mind works."[60] It is a concept-metaphor that she recodifies from the Spanish language's customary usages. It reflects

> an awareness, the awareness of facultad [as depicted in La Facultad in *Borderlands*] that sees through all human acts whether of the individual mind and spirit or the collective, social body. The work of conocimiento—consciousness work—connects the inner life of the mind and the spirit to the outer worlds of action. In the struggle for social change I call this particular aspect of conocimiento spiritual activism.[61]

---

57. For further elaboration on this issue against the grain of Western "rationalist epistemology," see Amala Levine's "Champion of the Spirit: Anzaldúa's critique of Rationalist Epistemology," in *EntreMundos/Among Worlds*, ed. AnaLouise Keating (New York: Palgrave Macmillan, 2005), 171-184
58. Anzaldúa. "now let us shift," 541.
59. Anzaldúa. "now let us shift," 542.
60. Anzaldúa. *Interviews*, 177.
61. Anzaldua, *Interviews*, 178. This is a restaged conceptualization inspired by Roland Barthes' euro-centered theorization in "Myth Today" collected in his book *Mythologies* as well as Jacques Derrida's theorization and critique of Levi-Strauss's theorization of myth in "Structure, Sign, and Play in the Discourse of the Human Sciences," collected in *Writing and Difference*. In brief, by reading Anzaldúa through her cultural location I transfer euro-centered critical theory to the U.S. That is, it crosses the Atlantic.

Traumatic events such as an earthquake or an encounter have the power to throw her into chaos "shattering the mythology that grounds [her],"[62] which had already been depicted and rehearsed in "La Facultad" in *Borderlands*. That is, the contingent narrative of the self that grants a precarious sense of wholeness is always liable to interruption and disruption. In fact, though unmentioned, La Facultad's irruption is the first stage-space of conocimiento.[63] This type of chaotic disruption catapults her into Nepantla. The shattering emerges from the outer world and in Nepantla, the second stage-space of conocimiento, she is situated in the liminal space "where the outer boundaries of the mind's inner life meet the outer world of reality, in a zone of possibility."[64] In restaging the concept-metaphors used for mapping the creative process, here Coatlicue represents "depths of despair, self-loathing and helplessness" and is the third stage-space of *conocimiento*.[65] Earlier I referred to this as self-contempt, which encompasses the emotions listed here.[66] Through some form of action (the fourth stage-space of *conocimiento*), she can work herself out of depression, and her "desire for order" (fifth stage-space of *conocimiento*) leads to restructuring the pieces together "to create a new narrative articulating [her] personal reality."[67] If you will, this will be administered by the Nepantla state of consciousness. Each *arrebatamiento*—that is shock, *susto*, and trauma—reopens the wound. It constitutes a "loss of the familiar" which motivates the effort to reintegrate herself or put Coyolxauhqui together, which in this instance is herself. It instantiates the sixth stage-space of *conocimiento*. However, the resulting reintegration and reinscription in the Coyolxauhqui stage-space may fail as it is tested out in the world and may not "live up to your ideals.... Disappointed with self and others, angry and then terrified at the depth of your anger, you swallow your emotions, hold them in, blocked from your own power, you are unable to activate the inner resources that could mobilize you."[68] The Shadow Beast and

---

62. Anzaldúa, "now let us shift," 544.
63. AnaLouise Keating has been expanding and critiquing in her work Anzaldúa's notion of "spiritual activism." I refer the reader especially to her edited collections of Anzaldúa's work. For additional reflections on conocimiento and Coyolxauhqui consciousness, see Irene Lara's "Daughter of Coatlicue: An Interview with Gloria Anzaldúa" in *EntreMundos*. Also many of the essays collected in *this bridge we call home* critically rethink aspects and influence of Anzaldúa's work and *Bridge*, as well as essays collected in *El Mundo Zurdo* and *El Mundo Zurdo 2*.
64. Anzaldúa, "now let us shift," 544.
65. Anzaldúa, "now let us shift," 545.
66. Anzaldúa, "now let us shift," 545.
67. Anzaldúa, "now let us shift," 545.
68. Anzaldúa, "now let us shift," 545.

the Coatlicue State recur, bringing forth an embattlement with the unwanted aspects of the self, which can be paralyzing. These unwanted aspects of the self have, in effect, been constituted by that internalized otherness that may require repeated confrontation.

The seventh stage-space, after failure, can bring forth a new development in her self-narrativization/automythography. It is a critical turning point of transformation:

> you shift realities, develop an ethical, compassionate strategy with which to negotiate conflict and difference within self and between others, and find common ground by forming holistic alliances. You include these practices in your daily life, act on your vision—enacting spiritual activism."[69]

In fact, in the previous passage Anzaldúa is more fully narrativizing the transformation that is possible after each "fall" into the Coatlicue State.[70] Throughout, she struggles with the shadow/Shadow Beast, that is, "the unwanted aspects of the self."[71] Simultaneously, throughout, she maintains the liminal space of Nepantla, which does the liminal work that pivots the inner-outer consciousness. Thus each *arrebatamiento* is a "chance to reconstruct yourself."[72] She is bound to rewrite and re-interpret "the story you imagined yourself living in...."[73]

In this essay, the concept-metaphor of Nepantla receives a broader and larger characterization and definition than ever before in the Anzaldúan corpus. It is home and it represents both transition and "site of transformation."[74] If earlier in "Putting Coyolxauhqui Together..." she had stated "Nepantla averigua el conflicto," within, now it is the liminal space "where different perspectives come into conflict... [it] is the zone between changes where you struggle to find equilibrium between the outer expression of change and your inner relationship to it."[75] She realizes, however, that though "your head and heart decry the mind/body dichotomy, the conflict in your mind makes your body a battlefield where beliefs fight each other.[76]" I think that the different perspectives that come into

---

69. Anzaldúa, "now let us shift," 545.
70. Anzaldúa, "now let us shift," 545.
71. Anzaldúa, "now let us shift," 545.
72. Anzaldúa, "now let us shift," 547.
73. Anzaldúa, "now let us shift," 547.
74. Anzaldúa, "now let us shift," 548.
75. Anzaldúa, "now let us shift," 548-49.
76. Anzaldúa, "now let us shift," 549.

conflict and make themselves evident to Nepantla consciousness are a restaging of Anzaldúa's theory of Mestiza Consciousness; however, the specific *mestizaje* of that theory in *Borderlands* is now hybridized beyond the specificity of Mexican history of *mestizaje* itself. That is, she is expanding the earlier theory to encompass other possibilities.

As she restages the Coatlicue State and the Shadow Beast[77] "being lost in chaos occurs when you are between 'stories' before you shift from one set of perceptions and beliefs to another, from one mood to another,"[78] she insists, however, that "the body is the basis for the conscious sense of self, the representation of self in the mind,"[79] though not without question, always tripping into self-doubt and negativity. Nevertheless, she goes forth continuously "re-interpreting [her] past... reshap[ing] her present."[80] "You are sure of one thing: the consciousness that's created our social ills (dualistic and misogynist) cannot solve them—we need a more expansive conocimiento [that is, as stated earlier, a more expansive consciousness.]. The new stories must partially come from outside the system of ruling powers."[81] She is quite clear that

> Coyolxauhqui personifies the wish to repair and heal as well as re-write the stories of loss and recovery, exile and homecoming... stories that lead out of passivity and into agency, out of devalued into valued lives. Coyolxauhqui represents the search for new [concept-] metaphors to tell you what you need to know, how to connect and use the information gained, and, with intelligence, imagination, and grace, solve your problems and create intercultural communities.[82]

The politico-spiritual activism of knowledge outside of religious metaphysics, sharing and exchange that the concept-metaphor of Nepantla represents becomes the neologism of Nepantleras. They can function as mediators that "averiguan el conflicto," inner and outer, and call "on the connectionist faculty to show the deep common ground and interwoven affinities among all things and people."[83] Nepantla is the pivoting liminal space where Nepantleras can operate to effect that politico-spiritual activism. Are these politico-spiritual activists

---

77. Anzaldúa, "now let us shift," 550-51.
78. Anzaldúa, "now let us shift," 553.
79. Anzaldúa, "now let us shift," 555.
80. Anzaldúa, "now let us shift," 556.
81. Anzaldúa, "now let us shift," 562.
82. Anzaldúa, "now let us shift," 563.
83. Anzaldúa, "now let us shift," 567-68.

to be the leaders of a "new tribalism" that Anzaldúa invokes? The ones who "begin building spiritual/political communities"?[84] She says, "By compartiendo historias, ideas, las Nepantleras forge bonds across race, gender and other lines, thus creating a new tribalism."[85] I interpret the possibility of creating a "new tribalism" as the construction of an alternate spatio-temporality that remains to be elaborated further as Anzaldúa is no longer just speaking of a *cultura mestiza* that only refers to people of Mexican descent as in *Borderlands,* but is now a formulation that shows "the deep common ground and interwoven kinship among all things and people" as cited above. It would be a "new tribalism" of the excluded and the outcasts from the hegemonic Anglo-European world and heteronormative patriarchy.

The Coyolxauhqui Imperative

In "Let us be the healing of the wound: The Coyolxauhqui Imperative—la sombra y el sueño," Anzaldúa begins by saying, "the day the towers fell [reference to 9/11/01], me sentí como Coyolxauhqui, la luna. I fell in pieces into that pitch-black brooding place."[86] La Llorona howls with grief and loss and Anzaldúa feels the imperative to "speak" *esta herida abierta.* Most of the concept-metaphors and symbols discussed in "Putting Coyolxauhqui Together: Creative Process" are restaged and reiterated here as they also were in "now let us shift . . . " The key concept-metaphors elaborated upon to depict the creative process in the exploration of the structure of inner experience are again deployed here, to reiterate the path of transformation we must take not just in healing our personal inner wounds, but also our political wounds which are caused by the leaders of exploitation, injury and imperialism. That is, I think, that imperialism's inner Shadow Beast produces an exteriority of sheer destructiveness that affects us all—the outcasts, the excluded, the dispossessed, and the *atravesados,* all of which are addressed in *Bridge* and *Borderlands,* and reiterated throughout her work.

In depicting the shadow (alternately in other texts Shadow Beast), which is a negativistic form of embodied consciousness, Anzaldúa states,

> As I see it, this country's real battle is with its shadow—its racism, propensity for violence, rapacity for consuming, neglect of its responsibility to global communities and the environment, and unjust

---

84. Anzaldúa, "now let us shift," 576.
85. Anzaldúa, "now let us shift," 574.
86. Anzaldúa, *The Gloria Anzaldúa Reader,* 303.

treatment of dissenters and the disenfranchised, especially people of color... In order to understand our complicity and responsibility we must look at the shadow.[87]

There's ambiguity in the latter statement as one is not quite clear if that "shadow" is our own that depicts our complicity, or the "shadow" of perpetrators of destruction. Both, I would say.

Throughout the piece she interweaves a detailing of the predatory logic of Imperialism's actions both locally and globally with the concept-metaphors and symbolic figures she had elaborated for processes of creativity, healing and transformation. Now, however, as in "now let us shift..." she invokes these to help us "to put a psycho-spiritual-political frame on our lives' journeys...."[88] Just as she had confronted her Shadow Beast at every turn (a self-wounding negative consciousness) which is closely linked to the wound of trauma, shock or *susto*, she calls upon us to now also perceive it as a "collective shadow—made up of the destructive aspects, psychic wounds, and splits in our own culture."[89]

Though we can perceive the destructive effects of Imperialism's shadow (Beast) upon all of us, what could possibly be the wound to be healed that spurs the emergence of the Shadow Beast within predatory imperialists? It is difficult to imagine healing the wound of the predator, even if we can speculate about it as we would that of a serial killer. Following Anzaldúa's thought, its very predatoriness is conditioned by the wound (trauma) that generates imperialism's Shadow (Beast). It's like calling upon us to discover and heal the wound of our rapists, whose act of rape is a product of their own Shadow, which is not analogous to that of his victims and in fact is producing it for his victims. Would there be a relationality that needs to be discerned so that we are not complicit due to ignorance or *desconocimineto*? But in fact, that is what Anzaldúa appears to be calling upon us to do through the path of *conocimiento*, as mediated by Nepantla and Coyolxauhqui positions and generating the Nepantleras who will carry out through *conocimiento* the assemblage of a psycho-spiritual-political frame. Though this interpretation may disturb some of us, it is possible. However, I think, it is possible as well to imagine a correlative interpretation based on alternate thinking posed in this essay as well. That is, we must avoid taking

---

87. Anzaldúa, *The Gloria Anzaldúa Reader*, 304.
88. Anzaldúa, *The Gloria Anzaldúa Reader*, 314.
89. Anzaldúa, *The Gloria Anzaldúa Reader*, 311.

a vengeful position which spells more destruction, for we must not exchange "one wound for another."[90]

Conocimiento which emerges from our confrontation with our personal wounds and Shadow Beasts will not necessarily be an option chosen by Imperialism and its supporters. As such it must be our *conocimientos*. Anzaldúa transfers the path of *conocimiento*, drawn from the structures of her inner experiences, into the public realm. We have allowed Bush to "kill off the dream (*el sueño*) of what our culture could be—a model of democracy."[91] Through *desconocimiento* (ignorance and/or denial) we have been complicitous, and it is now time to take responsibility as we continually work as well on the *conocimientos* that emerge for us in the public sphere.

To that end, Nepantla and Coyolxauhqui are involved for the transition from lethal crisis to transformation:

> The Coyolxauhqui imperative is to heal and achieve integration... Coyolxauhqui is my symbol for the necessary process of dismemberment and fragmentation, of seeing that self or the situations you're embroiled in differently. It is also my symbol for reconstruction and reframing, one that allows for putting the pieces together in a new way. The Coyolxauhqui imperative is an ongoing process of making and unmaking.[92]

Let us remember that the "unmaking" is a result of repeated traumatic assaults and of *desconocimiento*, an aspect of the Shadow (Beast) that has not been confronted. Without confrontation there's no *conocimiento*. Since it is doubtful that Imperialism will be confronting its Shadow (Beast) and miraculously reach *conocimiento* of the destructive force embedded in its logical forms of thought and doing, we must begin "to think not in terms of 'my' country, or 'your' nation but 'our planet.'"[93] And with our *conocimientos* in hand of both inner and outer structures of experience, "let us be the healing of the wound."[94] Let us bring a different future into being. Just as we confront our personal wound/ Shadow Beast to yield *conocimiento* for ourselves, transferring the "method" to the public realm demands that we become aware of Imperialism's path and logic

---

90. Anzaldúa, *The Gloria Anzaldúa Reader*, 307.
91. Anzaldúa, *The Gloria Anzaldúa Reader*, 307.
92. Anzaldúa, *The Gloria Anzaldúa Reader*, 312.
93. Anzaldúa, *The Gloria Anzaldúa Reader*, 312.
94. Anzaldúa, *The Gloria Anzaldúa Reader*, 314.

of destruction and combine a psycho-spiritual-political activism that can lead us to confront our social sickness, much of it a result of predatory actions and forms of thinking. It is up to us to do it.

Through *conocimientos*—that is, the knowledge we produce—and psycho-spiritual-political activism (non-religious), we can confront the Shadow Beast, the negative and nihilistic consciousness of Imperialism's predators, which can be seen, I think, as serial killers and mutilators. Build a "new tribalism" dedicated to discovering our interconnectedness across race, gender, class, sexuality and ethnicities to bring forth the "new stories from outside ruling powers." Let us remember that Anzaldúa uses the terms story and stories in ways that also invoke non-fictional stories, and invoke the idea of putting information together, for which Nepantla and Coyolxauhqui go hand in hand. Thus, whether they be factual or fictive, the stories can disclose the logic and structures of predatoriness and the wound that motivates and defines it, as simultaneously we give structure to the "new tribalism" (politics) based on our human interconnectedness which may assist in disclosing the logic of predatoriness—that is Empire's own criminal mind. Does this heal the predator's wound too? If it does not, we can at a minimum persuade many to confront their inner and outer *desconocimientos* in order to create a different future and an alternate world for ourselves, which may include the dream of a people's democracy that changes the current character of the Imperialist Corporate State. Can we do that Nepantler@s through the Nepantla and Coyolxauhqui imperative and method? Can we starve the destructive political spirit of the predator with our own political thought and action?

Conclusion

THE TWENTY-FIRST CENTURY APPEARS to be inaugurated by a "decolonial turn." Taking the lead in the Americas, for example, there has been The Zapatista Movement (EZLN) launched in 1994. The anti-colonial movements of the Twentieth Century from India to Cuba and U.S. Civil Rights Movements, which include subsequent post-colonial critical thought which in effect are still engaging forms of resistance to the Corporate State's local and global neocolonialism but have not done enough to reach "l@s de abajo." The relentless machine of the Corporate State's neocolonialist operations continues to fiercely recolonize "l@s de abajo" as well as others who have not thought of themselves as colonized such as white people in the U.S. L@s de abajo, if you will, in recent decades have been pursuing another line of inquiry in an effort to free themselves from colonial structures of experience and knowledge. L@s de abajo have been formulating praxes and theory of praxes in order to generate alternative spaces for new forms of political thought and action and Gloria Anzaldúa is one of them.

There is being work done to this end, for example, in Bolivia and other parts of South America. In the United States, the effort in decolonizing knowledge has been spearheaded by Anzaldúa and Moraga's *This Bridge Called My Back* and scholars such as Emma Pérez, Chela Sandoval, Arturo Aldama, and Naomi Quiñones in their published work to name a few. The work of New Zealander Linda Tuhiwai Smith, and other indigenous-based scholars have also been taking a lead in the decolonizing of praxis and knowledge. Recently Paola Bacchetta has transnationalized the decolonial thought of Anzaldúa in her essay "Transnational Borderlands: Gloria Anzaldúa's Epistemologies of Resistance and Lesbians 'of color' in Paris,"[95] and with her colleague Jules Falquet in Paris has translated into French the decolonial work of Chicanas and Latinas in *Les Cahiers du CEDREF.*

In brief, I cannot do justice to the proliferating bibliography of the "decolonial turn" at this time. However, it could be that our earlier focus on anti-colonial movements and resistance has not been well understood as also including decolonizing form of thought and action, and the implications in the context of the stratification of academically produced knowledge and of capitalist structures of power. I believe so.

---

95. Paola Bacchetta, "Transnational Borderlands: Gloria Anzaldúa's Epistemologies of Resistance and Lesbians 'of Color' in Paris," in *El Mundo Zurdo: Selected Works from the Society for the Study of Gloria Anzaldúa 2007 to 2009,* ed. Norma Cantú, Christina L. Gutiérrez, Norma Alarcón and Rita E. Urquijo-Ruiz (San Francisco: Aunt Lute, 2010), 109-128.

BIBLIOGRAPHY

Anzaldúa, Gloria. *Borderlands/La Frontera: The New Mestiza*. San Francisco: Spinsters/Aunt Lute, 1987.

Anzaldúa, Gloria. "Bridge, Drawbridge, Sandbar, or Island." *The Gloria Anzaldúa Reader*. 140-56. Edited by AnaLouise Keating. Durham, NC: Duke University Press, 2009.

Anzaldúa, Gloria. Interview. "Daughter of Coatlicue: An Interview with Gloria Anzaldúa." By Irene Lara. *Entre Mundos/Among Worlds: New Perspectives on Gloria Anzaldúa*. 41-55. Edited by AnaLouise Keating. New York: Palgrave Macmillan, 2008.

Anzaldúa, Gloria. Interview. "Quincentennial: From Victimhood to Active Resistance." By AnaLouise Keating. *Gloria Anzaldúa: Interviews/Entrevistas*, edited by AnaLouise Keating, 177-78. New York: Routledge, 2000.

Anzaldúa, Gloria. Interview. "Toward a Mestiza Rhetoric: Gloria Anzaldúa on Composition, Postcoloniality, and the Spiritual." By Andrea Lunsford. *Gloria Anzaldúa: Interviews/Entrevistas*, edited by AnaLouise Keating, 251-80. New York: Routledge, 2000.

Anzaldúa, Gloria. Interview. "Within the Crossroads: Lesbian/Feminist/Spiritual Development." By Christine Weiland. *Gloria Anzaldúa: Interviews/Entrevistas*, edited by AnaLouise Keating, 72-127. New York: Routledge, 2000.

Anzaldúa, Gloria. "La Prieta." *This Bridge Called My Back: Writings by Radical Women of Color*, edited by Cherríe Moraga and Gloria Anzaldúa, 198-209. New York: Kitchen Table: Women of Color Press, 1983.

Anzaldúa, Gloria. *Making Face, Making Soul/Haciendo Caras: Creative and Critical Perspectives by Women of Color*. San Francisco: Aunt Lute Books, 1990.

Anzaldúa, Gloria. "now let us shift... the path of conocimiento... inner work, public acts." In *This Bridge We Call Home: Radical Visions for Transformation*, edited by Gloria Anzaldúa, and AnaLouise Keating, 540-78. New York: Routledge, 2002.

Anzaldúa, Gloria. "Putting Coyolxauhqui Together: A Creative Process." In *How We Work*, edited by Marla Morris, Mary Aswell Doll, and William F. Pinar, 241-62. New York: Peter Lang, 1999.

Anzaldúa, Gloria. "Speaking in Tongues." In *This Bridge Called My Back: Writings by Radical Women of Color*, edited by Cherríe Moraga and Gloria Anzaldúa, 165-74. New York: Kitchen Table: Women of Color Press, 1983.

Bacchetta, Paola. "Transnational Borderlands: Gloria Anzaldúa's Epistemologies of Resistance and Lesbians 'of Color' in Paris." In *El Mundo Zurdo: Selected Works from the Society for the Study of Gloria Anzaldúa 2007 to 2009*, edited by Norma Cantú, Christina L. Gutiérrez, Norma Alarcón and Rita E. Urquijo-Ruiz, 109-128. San Francisco: Aunt Lute, 2010.

Barthes, Roland. "Myth Today." In *Mythologies*. Translated by Annette Lavers. Farrar, Straus and Giroux, 1972.

Barvosa, Edwina. *Wealth of Selves: Multiple Identities, Mestiza Consciousness and the Subject of Politics*. Texas A & M University Press, 2008.

Damasio, Antonio *Self Comes to Mind: Constructing the Conscious Brain*. New York: Pantheon, 2012.

Derrida, Jacques. "Structure, Sign, and Play in the Discourse of the Human Sciences." In *Writing and Difference*. 2nd edition, New York: Routledge, 2001.

Keating, AnaLouise, ed. *The Gloria Anzaldúa Reader*. Durham, NC: Duke University Press, 2009.

Keating, AnaLouise, "Risking the Personal: An Introduction." *Gloria Anzaldúa:Interviews/ Entrevistas*. 1-15. Edited by AnaLouise Keating. New York: Routledge, 2000.

Kristeva, Julia. *The Julia Kristeva Reader*. Edited by Toril Moi. New York: Columbia University Press, 1986.

Levine, Amala Levine. "Champion of the Spirit: Anzaldúa's critique of Rationalist Epistemology." In *EntreMundos/Among Worlds*. 171-184. Edited by AnaLouise Keating. New York: Palgrave Macmillan, 2005.

Lorde, Audre. *Sister Outsider: Essays and Speeches*. Freedom, CA: The Crossing Press, 1984.

Moraga, Cherríe and Gloria Anzaldúa. Editors. *This Bridge Called My Back: Writings by Radical Women of Color*. New York: Kitchen Table: Women of Color Press, 1983.

Pérez, Laura E. "The Performance of Spirituality and Visionary Politics in the Work of Gloria Anzaldúa." *El Mundo Zurdo 2: Selected Works From the 2010 Meetings of the Society for the Study of Gloria Anzaldúa*, edited by Sonia Saldívar-Hull, Norma Alarcón, and Rita Urquijo Ruiz, 13-27. San Francisco: Aunt Lute Books, 2012.

Pert, Candace B. *Molecules of Emotion: Why You Feel the Way You Feel*. New York: Simon & Schuster, 1999.

Saldívar-Hull, Sonia, Norma Alarcón, and Rita Urquijo-Ruiz. Editors. *El Mundo Zurdo 2: Selected Works from the 2010 Meeting of the Society for the Study of Gloria Anzaldúa*. San Francisco: Aunt Lute Books, 2012.

Spivak, Gayatri C. "Can the Subaltern Speak?" In *Marxism and the Interpretation of Culture*, edited by Cary Nelson and Lawrence Grossbery, 271-313. Urbana and Chicago: University of Illinois Press, 1988.

PART III

IMBRICATIONS/CONJUGATIONS/MEDIATIONS

...BUT YOU DON'T LOOK MEXICAN[1]

→ ←

MAKING THE WORLD SAFE for democracy and freedom in our times has come to mean, in practice, making the world available for the exploitative transactions of transnational corporate capital which in fact is now postnational. With the assistance of the State, corporate capital has been disarticulated from the nation through deregulations, privatizations, and the quest for serf and/or disposable labor. The State too, then, as an agent of disarticulations, is in effect disarticulated from the Nation.

Democracy and freedom which were touted as the political ideals of the Modern nation-state have been rendered "post modern" by the flourish of the "legal" presidential pen in the USA given that under globalization these ideals have been reterritorialized and redefined for the benefit of transnational corporate capital and against the people of the national territories, some of whom may have become "enemies" of the State in the State's own eyes, for it covets an absolute autonomy. The State and its institutions are on a course to crush dissent. As such, some, like Mexican migrants, are now subjected to the mandates of corporate capital and criminalized by the State if they do not submit, moreover, for example, intellectuals who question "official" histories risk losing their academic careers. Already in a previous decolonizing era, Frantz Fanon had stated in *The Wretched of the Earth* that "what the factory owners and finance magnates of the mother country expect from their government is not that it should decimate the colonial peoples, but that it should safeguard with the help of economic conventions their own 'legitimate interests.'"[2] That is, the modernist ideals of democracy and freedom have not been intended for those who are earmarked for colonization whether it is under the Modern State or the transnational Postmodern State. Safeguarding the interests of exploitative

---

1. *Editors' Note:* This essay was originally published in *Cien años de lealtad: en honor a Luis Leal/One Hundred Years of Loyalty: In Honor of Luis Leal*, ed. Luis Leal, Sara Poot Herrera, Francisco Lomelí, and María Herrera-Sobek (Goleta, CA, Monterrey, NL, and México City: University of California, Santa Barbara, Universidad Nacional Autónoma de México, Instituto Tecnológico y de Estudios Superiores de Monterrey, Universidad del Claustro de Sor Juana, 2007). 259-272.

2. Frantz Fanon, *The Wretched of the Earth*, trans. Richard Philcox (New York: Grove, 1961), 65.

corporate capital whether under modern or postmodern conditions has been the mandate of the colonizing Anglo-American and European states.

In the USA there has been a restructuration of private and public life as well as a dismantling of previous relations between its people and political economy under modernist conditions. In our times, in USA, there's a periodic interpellation of "the" national consciousness in the name of securing their "way of life," democracy and freedom against the forces of *terrorismo* while simultaneously ignoring and/or repressing the populace whose national consciousness diverges from the State's new self-imposed mandate, making the world safe for capital's mobility and exploitation of resources and people. The State is now in the protectionist service of corporate capital and not necessarily the people and simultaneously claiming that it makes the world safe for democracy and freedom. In fact, it is a disarticulation of State and nation that México is now also embracing and in effect constructing color lines that have become more evident, and putting in question its claims to non-racist modes of thinking and practice. One must ask if today the nation is a phantom, an imaginary entity that serves the State more than its population.

However, as Fanon also suggests, the making of the Modern nation-ştate itself was set in motion through a racist consciousness which had been generated in colonialists before "discovery" and accelerated through the colonial period in the Américas as people of color and/or non-westerners were subjected to the exploitative colonial order. In the Américas when the organization of national formations and independence from former colonial territories is undertaken, it is carried out by those whose hegemonic drive had already drawn color lines between themselves and other inhabitants of the territories notwithstanding the rhetoric of "liberators." That is to say that the racist hierarchy of the previous colonial era remained in place subjecting the indigenous and imported African population to the colonial order and the nation-state in formation. From this point of view, then, in the Américas, we are in the grip of a struggle to recolonize through the force of a "Neoliberalism" that entails the partnership of corporate capital and the State and which is being strongly contested as apartheid continues to rule for those who have always already been targeted for colonization and subjection by the Anglo-European West with the assistance of client states like México. In fact, the practices of Western capitalist exploitation and the State across historical eras of colonialism, Modernity's recolonization, and now postmodernity's neocolonization have produced a de facto segregated population that are in effect "*sujetos sobrantes*/subjects-in-excess" to those who claim the Nation and the State as theirs. For if there is a nation, it is now one that is managed by the State for transnational corporate capital's "legitimate interests" and whose agents now eschew any responsibility for, or accountability to, the people who inhabit the national territory and whose subjection is requisite. From this point of view, "democracy and freedom" have been "rhetorical commodities" for USA's white population, though they are also disappearing for them under the new conditions produced by the Postmodern State whose primary work is now so visibly in the service of continuous destabilization of other nations, wars, militarization and transnational corporate capital.

In her book, *Methodology of the Oppressed*,[3] Chela Sandoval posits that US women of color and Chicanas who emerged in the 70s and 80s are "new subjects of history" seeking social justice through activism. It has been an activism that has been transcoded from the "barrios and streets" to the written literary and critical text. For these new subjects of history, a transformation of consciousness occurred through diverse forms of activist protest which verbalized and put into language our situatedness in the world which is grasped as we seek to delineate our relationality to others, and in the USA, specifically white others. These new subjects of history bring to awareness and practice multiple forms of consciousness which give substance to a subjectivity that is non-singular in identity formations. There is no singular positionality of the subject of consciousness, but a multiplicity made possible through a hybrid cultural and political experience that Gloria Anzaldúa actually named a new *mestiza* consciousness of history and experience itself in the case of Chicanas. As such these new subjects of history put in the question all dualisms of "self and other," for indeed each term colligates vectors of history and experience that complicate the oversimplified conceptualization of the dualism "self and other." The self as well as the other is rendered more complex than modernist thought would have had us believe. The rejection of the singularity of self and consequently consciousness, introduces forms of self-decolonization as well as that of a decolonized critical consciousness. However, it does not necessarily bring forth decolonization from the structures of power that are "proper" to the institutions of the nation-state, modernist or postmodernist.

---

3. Chela Sandoval, *Methodology of the Oppressed* (Minneapolis: University of Minnesota Press, 2000).

As new subjects of history we find ourselves in a double-bind situation wherein we can observe and experience both the forms that self-decolonization have taken AND simultaneously are treated as *sujetos sobrantes*/subjects-in-excess to the Nation and to the State. Among people of color descent in the USA there are several groups that have been relegated to a place of excess and exclusion in the historical trajectory of modernity and postmodernity—migrants, indigenous populations, people and women of color, and Chicanas. For the structures of power, we are *sujetos sobrantes*/subjects-in excess whose genealogies and present conditions of existence mark the forms and locations of exclusionary rhetoric, representation, and practice. As the rhetoric, representation and practices of anti-immigrant forces from the streets to the Congress, for example, pose, through cultural and political contestation the question of who is and who is not an American, not only does racism continue to flourish, but, in effect, the new subjects of history are positioned as *sujetos sobrantes*/subjects-in-excess who have no "legitimate" claim on the Nation or the State. In effect, the question of ownership of the officialized national territory emerges once again as the white nativist project.

As subjects-in-excess what we have in common is our political and historical situatedness outside the making of the racially regulated n"ation state." Throughout the 20th century the demand upon us has been to "assimilate" into the forms of culture and political economy that the state offers as it simultaneously revises what is Mexican and what is American within the marked geopolitical territories. As *sujetos sobrantes* we are objects of contempt, marginalization and hatred even as we are subjects of a self-decolonization that deconstructs globalization without recourse for structural change except continuous protest. As self-decolonizing subjects of history who have a deep awareness of the ways in which we have been *sujetos sobrantes*, we have developed multiple forms of political and cultural consciousness that continuously keep in mind the questions of how have we been constructed under the force of colonization and what will be the transformative positions through which we will remake and reinvent ourselves. An alternative way of stating this would be, how has colonization made us subjects-in-excess and how will our own self decolonization transform the world and the current structures of neocolonizing power. As we continue to give form and substance to a "postcolonial" consciousness and imaginary, even in the face of postmodern global colonialism, in resistance we constantly seek the tools that will also transform the structures of both older and newer colonialisms which hold us in contempt. The Chicana critic and theorist Gloria Anzaldúa has called this the "new *mestiza* consciousness," and Chela Sandoval has named it a dynamic "differential consciousness" of resistance and transformation as learned through the work of USA's Third World Women, and especially women of color of which Chicanas have been part.

At the core of these new forms of consciousness is the conviction that we have been positioned and constructed through the white supremacist lens that has been instrumental to the making of the modern nation-state for which raced and gendered inequity has been the order of business. It is, in fact, our embodiment that generates geopolitical and symbolic borders that render us *sujetos sobrantes* as the "Third World grates against the first and bleeds" as Gloria Anzaldúa has noted.[4] Yet, as we know, that friction does not only lie at the official geopolitical border but is perceived by white supremacists wherever we find ourselves in the cartography of structures of relentless marginalization according to our color as embodied and as such becomes culturally and politically marked. White supremacist demands for assimilation require that we erase all traces of "foreignness" while simultaneously having the color of our skin perpetuate the perception of "foreignness." In white supremacist USA, for example, the migrant crisis of our times has made evident that white is the color of the State and the Nation regardless of citizenship. The people who experience rejection and insult most violently are those who are visibly not white and betray roots which are not Anglo-European. In the Anglo-European imaginary to be Mexican is *a priori* a lack of "*pureza de sangre*." The taxonomies of *mestizaje* of the colonial era obtain an obscure economy of significations as our colorizations are depicted as that of peanuts, café au lait, the hue of a chicharrón or a cajeta, as well as negroide. All of these colorizations betray our impurity at first sight and signal not only danger but our non-white historical genealogy in the eyes of white supremacists. (In her novel *Caramelo*, Sandra Cisneros suggests some of these colorizations.)[5]

In "La Prieta" Gloria Anzaldúa, born in the Rio Grande valley of Texas, tells us that though her family was sixth generation "American" they were still marked as Mexican.[6] In effect the takeover of the territory from Indians and Mexicans initiated a form of racist nativism that situated all but whites as foreigners, intruders and *atravesados* as Anzaldúa might say. Where we are born is

---

4. Gloria Anzaldúa, *Borderlands/La Frontera* (San Francisco: Spinsters/Aunt Lute, 1987),

5. Sandra Cisneros, *Caramelo* (New York: Knopf, 2002).

6. Gloria Anzaldúa, "La Prieta," in *This Bridge Called my Back: Writings by Radical Women of Color*, ed. Cherríe Moraga and Gloria Anzaldúa (New York: Kitchen Table, Women of Color Press, 1983, 198-209).

not immediately indicative of our nationality because at first sight s/he who is "American" is white and vice versa. To be of Mexican descent as mediated by our skin is equivalent to not being American and so it is to our times throughout the USA. Though racism blocks the paths to "assimilation," it has become a general ideological discourse today through the work of the Harvard political theorist Samuel Huntington who decries that we of Mexican descent do not become assimilated Americans thereby putting the Nation in danger of disappearing. Thus, we receive a slap on both sides of our faces—blockage via racism, and the charge of not assimilating which is blocked by racism.

However, the traces of that Anglo and European desire for "*pureza de sangre*" can also be found in the midst of our families who have consumed that desire as well and demonstrate it through an internalized racism that is inflected in the family itself. In "La Prieta" Anzaldúa tells us that her mother cautioned her against playing in the sun. Rosario Castellanos[7] was also cautioned in Comitán, Chiapas, because if she got any darker, like Gloria, she would be mistaken for an Indian, and as Gloria also remarks "you don't want people to say you are a dirty Mexican." Being taken for an Indian transforms one into a dirty Mexican, and ultimately being taken for a Mexican puts one in danger of being taken for an Indian. It is the color of our skin that puts in motion the dirtiness of being Indian or Mexican. In effect, for white supremacists there is something like looking Mexican, and it is dark and dirty.

It was much later in life, and after much rejection, that Anzaldúa acquired the awareness that she and her family continued to be Mexican regardless of birth place and time spent in the USA. Neither time nor space erase the lack of "pureza de sangre." Our very skin signals our impurity. She remarks, "It has taken me over 30 years to unlearn the belief instilled in me that white is better than brown—something some people of color never will unlearn." Indeed, this becomes among the first steps in self-decolonization, for it is colonization and neocolonization that teaches us that whiteness is better than brownness or blackness. In fact, José Vasconcelos, the early 20th century theorist of *mestizaje*, claimed that a proportionate mode of miscegenation would assuage the aesthetic problem of being non-white, non-peninsular, non-European. Beauty is linked to desire for "*pureza de sangre*," and degrees of darkness to tainted blood.

---

7. Rosario Castellanos, *Balún Canán* (México, Fondo de Cultura Económica, 1957) and *Oficio de tinieblas* (México: Joaquín Mortiz, 1962).

At the center of modern subjectivity are whiteness and the forms of thought and practice that secure a pinnacle of superiority and worthiness. As such without an acknowledgement on our part of our non-white roots, be they indigenous or African, no matter how minute or remote, no matter how much we think that the embodied racialized root has been overcome or surpassed, we will not be confronting our formation in racist thought and practice. That in that obscure economy of the taxonomies of *mestizaje*, indigenous and African men and women are part of our genealogy and in fact have been "*la teta de la nación.*" Rosario Castellanos recognizes this in her characterization of "La Nana" in her novels *Balún Canán* and *Oficio de tinieblas* where she allegorizes the racist hierarchizations in the making of Chiapas itself which may well serve as paradigms for other locations in the Mexican terrain.[8]

Anzaldúa comments, "We say *nosotros los mexicanos* (by *mexicanos* we do not mean citizens of México, we do not mean national identity, but a racial one.) We distinguish between *mexicanos del otro lado* and *mexicanos de este lado*. Deep in our hearts we believe that being Mexican has nothing to do with which country one lives in."[9] To that we may add that it has nothing to do with which country one is born in either. For Anzaldúa, "Being Mexican is a state of soul—not one of mind, not one of citizenship."[10]

Here she is in implicit agreement with Bonfil Batalla's theory of "*El México profundo*"[11] which has also been deeply racialized through the desire for "*pureza de sangre*" which continues to operate through those economies of miscegenation produced by the official record of *mestizaje* and indigeneity which are part of our genealogy, experience and historical consciousness. Through the ideologies and mythographies of who is and who is not a modern subject, the indigenous continue to be seen as not "civilized," as are Mexicans in general. We are suspect as to our "civilized" status for above all the modern subject has been constituted as white and male, preferably Anglo and/or European. That subject carries with it an implicit philosophy of the individual which is not only distinct from any notion of community, but actually against it. "It is easier to repeat the racial-racist patterns and attitudes, especially those of fear and prejudice, that we have inherited than to resist them ... thus we pay homage not to the power

---

8. Castellanos, *Balún Canán* and *Oficio de tinieblas*.
9. Anzaldúa, *Borderlands/La Frontera*, 62
10. Anzaldúa, *Borderlands/La Frontera*, 62
11. Guillermo Bonfil Batalla, *México Profundo: Reclaiming a Civilization*, trans. Philip A. Dennis (Austin: University of Texas Press, 1996).

inside us, but to the power outside us, masculine power, external power, patriarchal power. I see Third World people... not as oppressors but as accomplices to oppression by unwittingly passing on to our children and our friends the oppressor's ideologies... we are not screaming loud enough in protest," says Anzaldúa.[12] In fact, the work of Anzaldúa constitutes a loud protest to being held hostage as a *sujeto sobrante*/subject-in-excess in both USA and México through the emergent political subjectivity called Chicana whom she characterizes as "the new *mestiza*" subject of a new political and cultural consciousness who has seized the effects of the ruling modern white masculine subject. Those effects have evolved through disciplinary practices that have also brought forth intolerable fragmentations. That is to say, the self of such a subject is not singular. It is a plurality that takes form through the fragmentations of a racist-sexist colonialism and which are held in tension by the cultural and political subject that has been called Chicana. When I say that I am a Chicana, for example, I do not speak of a singular identity. I speak of a self-decolonized critical political subject who is simultaneously aware of being both inside modernity and postmodernity as well as a subject-in-excess to both. Such an excess subject deconstructs modernity and postmodernity and reconstructs the modes of her excess status within those white patriarchal schemas, practices, and symbols.

"Chicanos did not know we were a people until 1965... With that recognition we became a distinct people. Something momentous happened to the Chicano soul—we became aware of our reality and acquired a name and a language... that reflected that reality. Now that we had a name, some of the fragmented pieces began to fall together," says Anzaldúa.[13] Many people of Mexican descent have rejected that name without recognizing that it has given form to a critical perspective of a self-decolonized subject that addressed both USA and México and that implicitly has spoken of our radical heterogeneity as people of Mexican descent. That rejection of the name, in my view, makes visible the internalized racism that Anzaldúa addresses in her work and forecloses in effect our transnational and diasporic status in modernity and postmodernity

In 1955 when my parents migrated to the USA by crossing the official geopolitical border that marks the separation of the territory, and which is ritualized through the presentation of documents, I instantly became a person of Mexican descent. Since I was only eleven years old and had barely begun to

---

12. Anzaldúa, "La Prieta," 207.
13. Gloria Anzaldúa, *Borderlands La Frontera*, 63

learn the history of the making of México, I did not know what being a person of Mexican descent meant outside of my family. I had already, however, learned that I was a güera and that a greater value was attributed to that embodiment in social terms, that is, in relation to others which included extended family and neighbors. I had already been indoctrinated to the greater social value of whiteness. This was disrupted by our migration to Chicago.

In Chicago and the Midwest I became a person of Mexican descent, I became an ethnicity that was perceived as negatively different from that of whites, Anglos and others of European descent. Notwithstanding my *"güera"* status, it was an ethnicity that was/is not white, an ethnicity that has been deeply racialized. I was born to a people who are perceived as a non-white race. In Anglo America, even new immigrants from Europe after WWII saw me as such when they got past the phenotype to the accent, the name, the Spanish language we spoke at home. In a sense I became a Mexican in and through the eyes of others during my adolescence, which is to say that if a child is taught to distinguish herself by coloring in the family, she learns what Mexican is in and through the eyes of Anglos. Thus, ironically, though I was born in México with a thoroughly Mexican genealogy, I became a Mexican in the USA. Becoming a Mexican in the USA is to learn all of the ways in which we are rejected and maligned because México itself is *a priori* a racialized country in Anglo America as are most Latin American countries. I was not aware of what African Americans call PASSING, which is passing as if one was white due to phenotype. My first sense that I was "passing" without knowing the dynamics as understood by African Americans, was the remark, "but you don't look Mexican." Later it would become something like "but you don't speak like a Mexican." The question of whether I looked Mexican or did not look Mexican had not occurred to me. However, I slowly learned that my father looked Mexican and was the object of police profiling and scrutiny, and that my mother did not look Mexican and was scrutinized suspiciously when she spoke Spanish. Spanish is a racialized language in the USA.

What does a Mexican look like in the Anglo-American imaginary? She is anywhere from slightly dark to chocolate dark and those of us who are *güeras* and declare we are of Mexican descent immediately become an object of suspicion for we are descendants of a people who is not white. I have come to think of this phenomenon as the "unofficial" one-drop rule form of thinking, an echo of the "official" one-drop [of blood] rule which legally defined who would continue to be of African descent in the USA terrain, and thereby not have access to the same citizen rights and privileges as whites. Change of the law has not necessarily changed perception. There's also the official "blood quantum" rule which defines who is an Indian in the USA. Cultural racism is structured into the political and juridical domains to determine non-whiteness. What is the "one-drop/blood quantum" that produces "looking or not looking Mexican"? Our indigenous and African genealogies. If one does not look Mexican at first sight, inquiry into our name and speech makes the "rule" become operant and one is an object of suspicion—underlying this perception is the foundational belief in *"pureza de sangre."* Notwithstanding the scientific repudiation of such beliefs, the sociocultural determinations of our inferiority continue to be governed by the notion of *"pureza de sangre."* The desire for "pureza de sangre" has gone underground, we don't hear it as we used to, we are however, disciplined and policed by other means—re you or are you not white? As long as this is the "hidden" structuring agenda of thought and practice among white supremacists, the call for assimilation is a red herring for it has already been blocked. On the other hand, who would want to assimilate to a political and juridical culture whose power is dedicated to continuous racism, continuous destabilization of non-white nations, wars of aggression, the protection of the new order of corporate capitalism, rampant militarization, and oblivious to the mutilation of the planet itself?

BIBLIOGRAPHY

Anzaldúa, Gloria. "La Prieta." In *This Bridge Called my Back: Writings by Radical Women of Color,* edited by Cherríe Moraga and Gloria Anzaldúa. New York: Kitchen Table, Women of Color Press, 1983.

Anzaldúa, Gloria. *Borderlands La Frontera/The New Mestiza.* San Francisco: Spinsters/Aunt Lute, 1987.

Bonfil Batalla, Guillermo. *Mexico Profundo: Reclaiming a Civilization,* translated by Philip A. Dennis. Austin: University of Texas Press, 1996.

Castellanos, Rosario. *Balún Canán.* México: Fondo de Cultura Económica, 1957.

Castellanos, Rosario. *Oficio de tinieblas.* México: Joaquín Mortiz, 1962.

Cisneros, Sandra. *Caramelo.* New York: Alfred A. Knopf, 2002.

Fanon, Frantz. *The Wretched of the Earth.* Translated by Constance Farrington. New York: Grove Press, 1963.

Sandoval, Chela. *Methodology of the Oppressed.* Minneapolis: University of Minnesota Press, 2000.

IMBRICATIONS[1]

→ ←

IN *This Bridge Called My Back: Writings by Radical Women of Color*, Cherríe Moraga has an essay entitled "La Güera."[2] That work carries an epigraph by Emma Goldman that reads: "It requires something more than personal experience to gain a philosophy or point of view from any specific event. It is the quality of our response and our capacity to enter into the lives of others that helps us to make their lives and experiences our own."[3] Contra Emma Goldman, I would amend the statement as follows—when allowed to enter the lives of others our capacity to understand that privilege calls for reciprocity on the one hand, and on the other requires that we understand that we CANNOT "make their lives and experiences our own." I personally think that we must respect the distance marked by the impossibility of making someone else's lives and experiences our own, for in my view a dispossession takes place of that which is exclusively theirs, as are our own lives and experiences. There is an irreducible difference between each one of us, that continuously disturbs our social pretense that we are the same. As Trinh Min Ha says, "like you not you."[4]

The encounter with, and the entrance into the lives and experiences of others may draw us to each other, however, each is unique and that uniqueness manifests itself through that irreducible difference each one of us possesses. What are those irreducible differences that plague us and maybe even be a repressed plague? As I enter Anzaldúa's textualized life and experience in her most intimate self-disclosures in the work, I calibrate the distance between us and recognize that her experience and life are not my own, while simultaneously learning from her. This, however, does not prevent us from joining her in her vision of EL MUNDO ZURDO. On the one hand our similarities and differences are acknowledged, and on the other we come together in her vision. In fact, she

---

1. *Editors' Note:* This previously unpublished paper was delivered at El Retorno, at the University of Texas, Río Grande Valley in Edinburg, Texas in May 2009.

2. Cherríe Moraga, "La Güera," in *This Bridge Called My Back: Writings by Radical Women of Color*, ed. Cherríe Moraga and Gloria Anzaldúa (New York: Kitchen Table, Women of Color Press, 1983), 27-34.

3. Moraga, "La Güera,"27.

4. Trinh T. Min-Ha, "Not You/Like You: Post-Colonial Women and the Interlocking Questions of Identity and Difference," in *Inscriptions: Feminism and the Critique of Colonial Discourse*, ed. Deborah Gordon (Santa Cruz, CA: University of California, Santa Cruz Center for Cultural Studies, 1988), 71-77.

points to that which can bring us together, that is, our affinities open the door to saying "AS if our own" lives and experiences. However, "as if" is not the actual lives and experiences of others and can never be our own. We live within a paradoxical tension between wanting to be same and not same simultaneously, which is hypocritical and risks delusional thinking.

In the late 1970s when Anzaldúa was in her 30s, I believe a profound life transition was taking place within her as she embarks on the struggle to write "La Prieta" which is published in *Bridge*. She tells us that it took her two years to write it. She is terrified by her own feelings and thoughts which she wants to render onto the blank page. Going through the process and pain of writing this essay-testimonio, is also the process of becoming her own woman, not somebody else's. She can then declare in that same piece: "The mixture of bloods and affinities, rather than confusing me, has forced me to achieve a kind of equilibrium. Both cultures deny me a place in *their* universe."[5] That is the Anglo-American culture and the Mexican/Xicanx culture. "Between them and among others, I build my own universe, El Mundo Zurdo. I belong to myself and not to any one people."[6] In fact, I think, this is her response to the potential fragmentation she would have to live through. Many want her allegiance—La Raza, The Chicano Movement, the feminists, the lesbians, the Marxists, the gay movement, the revolutionary socialists, the New Age, the mystics, the magic/occult groups, the artists, the *tercermundisatas*.[7]

In the poem "Arriba mi gente," in *Borderlands*,[8] she appears to contradict herself, as *"mi gente"* may signal only Raza to some, given its Spanish language rendition of EL MUNDO ZURDO, but I suggest that it would be no more than a misleading translation/interpretation, for the "tent" of EL MUNDO ZURDO is capacious. She calls to a *"pueblo de almas afines / encenderemos los campos / con una llamarada morada– / la lumbre de El Mundo Zurdo . . . /* In a spirit as one / all people arising." And, in an echo of Enriqueta Vásquez's cry *"despierten*

---

5. Gloria Anzaldúa, "La Prieta," in *This Bridge Called my Back: Writings by Radical Women of Color*, ed. Cherríe Moraga and Gloria Anzaldúa (New York: Kitchen Table Press, 1983), 209.

6. Anzaldúa, "La Prieta," 209.

7. Anzaldúa, "La Prieta," 205.

8. Gloria Anzaldúa, *Borderlands/La Frontera: The New Mestiza* (San Francisco: Spinsters/Aunt Lute, 1987), 214-215.

hermanos," Anzaldúa says, "*Mi gente, despierta.*"⁹ It is I think the vigilant search for Affinities that works against what would otherwise be a fragmentation of the self, and she dares to say, even though she fears misunderstanding, that she loves whites. She says, "I have been terrified of writing this essay because I will have to own up to the fact that I do not exclude whites from the list of people I love..."¹⁰

I suggest to you that by centering herself through these affinities, she begins to engage the "enormous contradiction in being a bridge."¹¹ That is, the apparent contradictions exposed by the cross-pollination that diverse people bring to the "crossroads." The site where the *atravesados* gather. But it is the (un)conscious act of "bridging" which eventually also leads to the title for the collection—*This Bridge Called My Back*—which alerts us to her life-long pursuit, and further enables the recentering of the induced fragmentations of her self in the sociopolitical sphere. As I type this on May 10th, which is coincidentally Mother's Day in both Anglo-American and Mexican/Chican@ cultures, I imagine that like Anzaldúa many mothers perform this task of being a bridge and a crossroads; however, I dare say that many women/mothers may not consciously grasp this as Anzaldúa did. To do so is, in my view, a feminist revolutionary act that extracts us from the clutches of patriarchal binary logic. Bridging became her home, this bridge is our home. In geopolitical terms the facticity of the borderlands is the home in which we perform that bridging as we also discover many symbolic borderlands as well.

However, before reaching this juncture in "La Prieta," probably among her first published prose texts, Anzaldúa has to defy her terror and fear of "tak[ing] a trip back into the [formative roots] of the self, [and] travel to [the] deep core of [those] roots, to discover and reclaim [her] colored soul..."¹² and her stigmatized sexuality and poverty. Plumbing to the depths of her self-formation requires, as she notes, "opening the door to memory" which is dangerous because "it brings back images that haunt, old ghosts, and the old wounds."¹³ However, the danger must be risked, for the haunting of ourselves may corrode our being through an

---

9. *Editors' Note:* "Despierten Hermanos" was the title of the column Enriqueta Vásquez published. For more information see: "Despierten Hermanos," in *Enriqueta Vasquez and the Chicano Movement: Writings from El Grito del Norte,* ed. Lorena Oropeza and Dionne Espinoza (Houston: Arte Público Press, 2007) and Gloria Anzaldúa, "Arriba mi gente," *Borderlands,* 214-215.

10. Anzaldúa, "La Prieta," 206.

11. Anzaldúa, "La Prieta," 206.

12. Anzaldúa, "La Prieta," 195.

13. Anzaldúa, "La Prieta," 198.

accumulated self-hatred[14] as a result of our color, sexuality, and poverty. And, she says, "It is only now [in the 1970s] that the hatred of myself, which I spent my adolescence of my life cultivating, is turning to love."[15] She implies that love is blocked and cannot be felt or known when hatred and self-hatred, perhaps a core emotion in victimization and rejection, rules us. What are the roots of our experienced self-hatred? It may not be skin color, sexuality, and poverty, as it is for her, it may be something else such as being seen as worthless, however, one must acknowledge hatred and/or self-hatred, and ask what are those roots? One cannot expunge what one denies, and denial must be confronted. What are the images that haunt, old ghosts, and old wounds that corrode our present, and in effect block us from an access to bridging our affinities with others in a regenerative "postmodern love," or a "decolonial love" as Chela Sandoval proposes in her book *Methodology of the Oppressed*?[16]

In "La Prieta" Anzaldúa is challenging herself and her readers to ask hard questions that may need answering for the purpose of self-transformations. In the poem "Letting Go," which is subsequently printed in its entirety in *Borderlands*,[17] Anazldúa writes: "Nobody's going to save you / No one's going to cut you down, / cut the thorns thick around you."[18] How can anyone outside of ourselves save us when our memories and wounds are beyond their reach, understanding, and knowledge? One must have the will to change, without that desire, no amount of assistance can help. "La Prieta" is a sample of how Anzaldúa consciously begins the act of saving and loving herself and her innermost being. She refuses pity and self-pity.

Nevertheless, in that same poem, she declares, "It's not enough / opening once./ Again you must plunge your fingers/into your navel . . . / There is no one who/will feed the yearning. Face it, you will have to do it yourself."[19] It is a repetitive act, it is hard to expunge cancerous emotions that have been foundational to our own innermost existence. "Letting Go" is a repetitive act that releases the poison and "like a fish to the air / you come to the open / only between breathings. / But already gills / grow on your breasts."[20] Metaphorically speaking we have the capacity to be "amphibians," which is to say "go under

---

14. Anzaldúa, "La Prieta," 202.
15. Anzaldúa, "La Prieta," 202.
16. Chela Sandoval, *Methodology of the Oppressed* (Minneapolis: University of Minnesota Press, 2000).
17. Anzaldúa, *Borderlands*, 186-188.
18. Anzaldúa, *Borderlands*, 187.
19. Anzaldúa, *Borderlands*, 187.
20. Anzaldúa, *Borderlands*, 188.

water" (the threatening dark side of life) and "rise above water," (the break into the light") perhaps in exploring the depth of these metaphors here and in other works gave Anzaldúa the title for her posthumously published book: *Light in the Dark / Luz en lo Obscuro*.[21]

As we let go, over and over, so that the undertow of some emotional states subsides and the light shines through, guilt and shame are companions in the process. She knows it and defies those emotions that block us from our fulfillment. If your family gave you a Xtian education, they also used "guilt and shame" as the whipping sticks to make us conform to that which we cannot defy until later in life, if ever, as Anzaldúa suggests in "La Prieta."[22] The victimization does make us wonder what it is that we have done to deserve such treatment, and it may take time to understand that we didn't do anything to deserve such hostility directed at us. One's contingent and constructed life-formation, especially in our youth, is inescapable and must be confronted over and over again until the poison is extracted or dematerialized keeping in mind the self-transformation we desire. However, it is a never-ending process that becomes less burdensome in time.

In "La Prieta" the three sources that constitute self-hatred are her skin color, sexuality and poverty. From birth Anzaldúa is stigmatized by her family, and her mother. Her mother had first hand in her formative stigmatization. It may not be the mother's intention, however, continually calling attention to Anzaldúa's medically abnormal bleeding, mimicking menstruation, was not subjected to exploration of treatments for an infant and thereafter. "In her eyes and in the eyes of others I saw myself reflected as 'strange,' 'abnormal,' 'queer' I saw no other reflection. Helpless to change that image, I retreated into books and solitude and kept away from others"[23]—a characteristic I share with Anzaldúa and may well be the "origin" of shyness. Mothers and daughters place each other in double-binds and often do not recognize them as such, which is imperative if one wants to dissolve the binds. The binds that tie shouldn't be so negative and nasty. These ties should not become a double-bind operating within the relationship.

Though she retreated into books and self-isolation, "unknowingly," she says, "I took the transformation of my own being . . . into my hands."[24] An intuition perhaps, that it was up to her, and only her, to save herself from the abjection

---

21. Gloria Anzaldúa, *Light in the Dark/Luz en lo obscuro: Rewriting Identity, Spirituality, Reality*, ed. AnaLouise Keating (Durham, NC: Duke University Press, 2015).

22. Anzaldúa, "La Prieta," 199–200.

23. Anzaldúa, "La Prieta," 199.

24. Anzaldúa, "La Prieta," 202.

that rejection produces. However, as she notes, it took her over 30 years to unlearn "the belief instilled in me that white is better than brown . . . something that brown people never will unlearn."[25] She has convinced me that writing "La Prieta" was one of Anzaldúa's steps to unlearning such ideology. That is to write it down and thereby shed the silent perniciousness. Did it take just as long to unlearn self-hatred over her reproductive organs, which was seen as "la seña," as if a sign of the devil because she began to bleed at birth. (She does not mention the amount of blood in infancy and so on.) It was an apparent aberration from normative development in her reproductive physiological system. Later, there's her refusal of heteronormative sexuality which she discards with searing words. Not only does she say that the "traditional role of la mujer was a saddle" she did not want to wear,[26] but six pages later declares that her "life-blood [was being] sucked out of [her] by [her] role as woman nurturer—the last form of cannibalism."[27] Certainly, there is a harsh contradiction between this position and the one she actually undertook later in life as a pedagogue of nurturing and bridging among students and peers. She lowers the temperature of her rage of roles assigned by virtue of being a woman, who is stereotyped. However, we learn later that she wanted to do it on her own terms, and not be obliged to meet expectations or assumptions about woman/women.

Self-hatred is produced in us through the eyes of others who hold up mirrors, hostile expressions and venomous images—name calling, irritation, and anger at our own existence. The so-called "Mirror Stage" which in Lacanian psychoanalytic theory is presented as an ideal paradigm for the nurturing development of the baby-child, is foundationally violated. As such the baby-child will eventually be faced with the need to acquire a loving wholeness with her own eyes, with her own hands, with her own will for her self-transformation. This is not easily attained. For she will have to go through the embodied turmoil, pain, and terror of not only not acknowledging her self-hatred but undoing it. In my view self-hatred is produced in moments of irrationality in engaging with the other. It is the irrationality that demands that we come to terms with the ways in which hatred was instilled in us—a kind of madness in our human relations that has to be undone.

This undoing leads Anzaldúa to believe, I think, that "The pull between what is and what should be," is to know that "by changing ourselves, we change the

---

25. Anzaldúa, "La Prieta," 202.
26. Anzaldúa, "La Prieta," 202.
27. Anzaldúa, "La Prieta," 208

world, that traveling El Mundo Zurdo path is the path of a two-way movement—a going deep into the self and expanding out into the world, a simultaneous recreation of the self and a reconstruction of society. And yet I am confused as to how to accomplish this."[28] There is an irrationality, she believes, in the violence we perpetrate upon each other, so she adds, "I'm trying to create a religion not out there somewhere, but in my gut. I am trying to make peace between what has happened to me, what the world is, and what it should be."[29] That is a tall order she envisages for herself. I venture the opinion that the mission for herself resides in her gut, anticipating the construction that will emerge from her gut. What is the gut? It is popular to speak of the gut in Anglo-American culture as a site of insight, i.e., I feel it in my gut. In Chinese Traditional Medicine what this may translate into is Chi or Qi—the system that strives toward mental, physical and emotional harmony. Chi is the essence of who you are. It is not overreaching to suggest these possibilities for Anzaldúan thought given her search for self-transformative methods, a lifelong quest.

She rejects Anglo-American feminists (white women) insofar as "they attempt to speak for us,"[30] Indeed, her self-transformation is grounded and founded, I think, in learning to speak for herself as a woman of color, as a Chicana, as a thinker. In an interview with Karin Ikas, Anzaldúa states, "I wasn't as political and feminist in the beginning. I was always rebellious and political when it came to the cultural stuff, but not to the degree I was later when I wrote *Borderlands*."[31] It may be that dealing with the "cultural stuff" in "La Prieta" enabled her to speak for herself, and acquire the self-transformation that puts rebellion and the anger that fuels it, in becoming the political subject that undertakes more than the "cultural stuff." I would argue with Anzaldúa and say that she was being a feminist with all that "cultural stuff"; however, that cultural-political voice acquired extensions in *Borderlands* as she came to terms with her political and historical legacies that had links with the more personal ones. In brief, Anzaldúa planted many of the thematic seeds in "La Prieta" that would continue to evolve in the rest of her life's work.

In her book, *MeXicana Encounters: The Making of Social Identities in the Borderlands*, Rosalinda Fregoso states that she explores "the vital role of culture in

---

28. Anzaldúa, "La Prieta," 208.
29. Anzaldúa, "La Prieta," 204.
30. Anzaldúa, "La Prieta," 206.
31. Karin Ikas, "Interview with Gloria Anzaldúa," in *Borderlands/La Frontera: The New Mestiza*, 2nd ed. (San Francisco: Aunt Lute Books, 1999), 228-229.

the formation of social identities in the Borderlands."[32] In the term "MeXicana," Fregoso wants to mark "the interface between MeXicana and Chicana" drawing attention to the historical material and discursive effects of "contact zones" (term introduced by Mary L. Pratt) and exchanges among and between various communities on the México–U.S. border, living in the shadows of colonizations in almost 175 years of conflict, interactions, and tensions. That is, since the Treaty of Guadalupe Hidalgo in 1848, "MeXicana," Fregoso states, "references processes of transculturaltion, hybridity and cultural exchanges—social and economic interdependency and power relations structuring the lives of inhabitants on the borderlands."[33] The term MeXicana reflects the complicated imbrication of "Chicanas" and "Mexicanas" in the formation of subjects in the nation. "We have a shared history of being othered."[34]

On the other hand, in her new book *Postnationalism in Chicana/o Literature and Culture*, Ellie Hernández, who like Fregoso was born and bred to adulthood in the Texas Borderlands, states that she uses the term Chicana/o with reference to USA's "born residents of Mexican descent and displaced immigrants."[35] In this text I find myself marked, if you will, as a "displaced immigrant," for I was not born in USA but in a borderlands town *del otro lado*, in México. In one book I find myself "imbricated" and in the other I find that I am a "displaced immigrant," albeit of Mexican descent like Chicanas. Clearly, going by the title of this paper, I prefer "imbrication," though I have modified the term in two ways. First, I want to call attention to the "X" of Xicana which has no difference in sound than Chicana, though with an X it is used by women of Mexican descent who are emphasizing their indigenous roots in modes that differ from Chicanas. These subtle distinctions are facilitated by the philological and etymological pronunciation of the X which on the one hand is pronounced as in Chicana, and on the other keeps the spelling in Nahuátl, thereby recognizing the indigeneity that in fact is also proper to Chicana. The other is the @ (ampersand sign) which runs together the feminine marker, "a," and the masculine marker "o." The Spanish language is a gendered language and called a romance language. I call to our attention that the masculine marker is open even as it is given form

---

32. Rosalinda Fregoso, *MeXicana Encounters: The Making of Social Identities in the Borderlands* (Berkeley: University of California Press, 2003), xiii.
33. Fregoso, *MeXicana Encounters*, xiv.
34. Fregoso, *MeXicana Encounters*, xiv.
35. Ellie Hernández, *Postnationalism in Chicana/o Literature and Culture* (Austin: University of Texas Press, 2009), 2.

by the fluid movement of the "a" which in effect circles itself opening to the outside, suggesting in my view, that the circularity of the hermeneutic mode of interpretation is open ended, neither feminine nor masculine, yet both at the same time. It calls attention to both the a/o and it is so queer. I focus and play with the glyph in its queerness.

I sensed the imbrications during the Chicano Movement (approx. 1965-1975) and distanced from the O with the Chicana feminist movement, women of color feminism, and white women's feminism of the late 1960s and 1970s, though like Anzaldúa I also distanced myself from the white feminist movement when I realized that even though we were speaking for ourselves, it was irrelevant to white women. They could not hear us. They have apparently been unable to come to terms with their sociohistorical and political white privilege of their position as settler colonialists. On the other hand, some believe that *Bridge*, for example, reflects victims, and not survivors claiming sociohistorical and political self-representation that marks a difference and requires engagement and not dismissal in the name of universal sisterhood which appears as a missionary colonial rescue position or permanent deferral. They often cannot hear the voice of those that have been othered, stuck in their own othered position by white men. It is in the "contact zone" or border contact of sociohistorical and political othering that new terms of engagement have yet to be generated for the future. Indeed, that form of othering of ourselves has also led us to other whites in multiple ways. Will we get stuck there? If so, it would go against the grain of Anzaldúa's thought and desire.

The process of disidentification with the hegemonic nation-state, be it México or USA, has gathered its own cultural, historical, and political justifications. Anzaldúa takes a third path and occupies a third space in order to reconstruct herself and bring forth El Mundo Zurdo.

BIBLIOGRAPHY

Anzaldúa, Gloria. *Borderlands: La Frontera/The New Mestiza*. San Francisco: Aunt Lute Books, 1987.

Anzaldúa, Gloria. *Light in the Dark/Luz en lo obscuro: Rewriting Identity, Spirituality, Reality*. Edited by AnaLouise Keating. Durham, NC: Duke University Press, 2015.

Anzaldúa, Gloria. "Arriba mi gente." In *Borderlands: La Frontera/The New Mestiza*. 214-215. San Francisco: Aunt Lute Books, 1987.

Anzaldúa, Gloria. "La Prieta." In *This Bridge Called My Back: Writings by Radical Women of Color*. 189-200. Edited by Cherríe Moraga and Gloria Anzaldúa. New York: Kitchen Table, Women of Color Press, 1983. (Originally published in 1981)

Fregoso, Rosa Linda. *MeXicana Encounters: The Making of Social Identities in the Borderlands*. Berkeley: University of California Press. 2003.

Hernández, Ellie. *Postnationalism In Chicana/O Literature and Culture*. Austin: University of Texas Press, 2009.

Ikas, Karin, "Interview with Gloria Anzaldúa." In *Borderlands: La Frontera/The New Mestiza*, 2nd ed. 227-246. San Francisco: Aunt Lute Books, 1999.

Lacan, Jacques. *Ecrits*. Translated by Alan Sheridan. London: Tavistock, 1977.

Min-Ha, Trinh T. "Not You/Like You: Post-Colonial Women and the Interlocking Questions of Identity and Difference." In *Inscriptions: Feminism and the Critique of Colonial Discourse*, ed. Deborah Gordon. Santa Cruz, CA: University of California, Santa Cruz Center for Cultural Studies, 1988.

Moraga, Cherríe. "La Güera." In *This Bridge Called My Back: Writings by Radical Women of Color*. Edited by Cherríe Moraga and Gloria Anzaldúa, 27-34. New York: Kitchen Table, Women of Color Press, 1983. (Originally published in 1981)

Sandoval, Chela. *The Methodology of the Oppressed*. Minnesota: University of Minnesota Press, 2000.

Vásquez, Enriqueta. "Despierten Hermanos." In *Enriqueta Vasquez and the Chicano Movement: Writings from El Grito del Norte*. Edited by Lorena Oropeza and Dionne Espinoza. Houston: Arte Público, 2006.

ANZALDÚA'S INSURRECTION OF SUBJUGATED KNOWLEDGES

AN INTERVIEW WITH NORMA ALARCÓN[1]

→ ←

The challenge for us is to further inquire into the conditions of possibility for the transformations of knowledge production that we can bring off...I believe that we continue to be part of the insurrection of subjugated knowledges and that our mere existence is transgressive.

–Alarcón "Conjugations"

Yolanda Venegas: Can you tell us about when you first read *Borderlands* and started teaching it?[2]

Norma Alarcón: In order for you to understand how I would teach Anzaldúa now, I have to tell you about how I first encountered *Borderlands*, about my initial response to her prose and I think I'm going to shock you a little bit.

Borderlands came out in 1987 and that fall was my first semester of teaching at Berkeley. And Gloria Anzaldúa just sent me a copy of her book, which was a very pleasant surprise and I felt flattered that she would reach out because I felt that she was someone that was known at least in certain parts of the country, and you know, I just came out of the Midwest and arrived in the Bay Area. And I looked at the book and then I said well, I'll figure out what to do with it later because I already have my syllabus for that year. I was too nervous to introduce new things.

---

1. *Editors' Note*: This is an edited transcript of an audio-recorded interview for *Anzaldúan Pedagogies: Teaching and Learning Con el Corazón Con Razón en la Mano*, an anthology in progress edited by Yolanda Venegas and Irene Lara. Vanegas, Lara, and Macarena Hernández were present at the initial interview, which was conducted in New Orleans, Louisiana, on December 20, 2017. Follow-up interviews and edits were conducted via Zoom, email, and mail between Alarcón, Venegas, and Lara in 2022.

2. First published in 1987, Gloria Anzaldúa's *Borderlands/La Frontera: The New Mestiza* (Aunt Lute Books) is now in its 5th edition.

And then she called me and she wanted to have coffee with me, and I said, oh shit, she wants to know what I think of the book. That's what writers do–I mean what's the first thing Sandra [Cisneros] asks me about anything? "What do you think of it?" So she wants to have coffee and I say oh shit she wants to know what I think of the book. And I better hurry up and look at it and make the date. You can't get out of this one, it's too cowardly. I could've postponed it for a year, but I felt cowardly to do that.

I said, "Well, let's make a date of whenever you think you're going to be up here" and she was already. She was still living in Oakland, I think. She was not in Santa Cruz yet. So I looked at the book and I said, "Oh my god what is this?" I had just gotten my PhD, I had only been teaching two years and I had been teaching straight literature, along with all the rules and regulations of "good" critical thinking and "good" prose. And I look at her book and I said, "what the fuck?" And I am a publisher and on one hand I wish she had asked me to publish it and on the other hand, I asked myself "Would you have published it the way it is?" And my answer was no.

I had been wrestling with the question of what to publish.[3] I had a lot of submissions and was wrestling with the questions of: What do I publish? What don't I want to publish? Well, I wanted to publish things that were really exemplifying a new voice, a new entry into a political sphere because even if it's literature, once you take speech and you take action you are acting in some way politically you know. I was wrestling with all these questions and I thought well, you've caught yourself in a contradiction here because on the one hand you wish she had asked you if you would want to publish it and on the other you are asking would you do this and I am saying no.

See that's why I'm shocking you.

Because my editorial and publisher's voice said I cannot publish this. The poetry was different. I separated the book into the poetry section and the prose section. I could not see myself publishing the prose section the way it was. Ah...You know my editor's head immediately went to correct it. I could not assign this book and have undergraduates think that I thought it was a sample of good prose writing. That was the difficulty on my end. I think part of this problem emerges because there was no category in which to put

---

3. Norma Alarcón was the founder and managing editor of Third Woman Press.

the book. A category that would then give you a frame of what the author intends. Sometimes you feel like she's rambling, other times she feels like she dropped this point and she doesn't pick it up for three pages and I have to run over there to pick it up. But I also know that she is strong headed with respect to being edited and it may have been hard for anyone to say to her I need more substantive order as you proceed so that things are not jumping around. That's the experience I had, initially.

So when I met her for coffee, I said okay, if you take the lead, you can sort of, not allow her to make too embarrassing questions for you. So I took the lead by telling her that I liked her poetry better. I was looking at the book, as carefully as I could to see what positive things I could say. And they all came out of the poetry, not the prose. Initially, the prose to me was incoherent, incomprehensible, and I wanted to correct it.

Norma: There was a rhythm in her movement of speech, the code-switching, that gave it a certain kind of Tex-Mex flavor in some parts of it. The code-switching was an aspect that readers were not necessarily used to. They are used to it in Texas, in fact, it is a salient feature of the Valley in south Texas to have these linguistic code-switches. But that also can take you by surprise if you are not used to it and one of the difficulties for me was that I had learned to separate my languages. I was a Spanish speaker that learned English and I was immersed in an English language school so I learned to separate by languages rather than blend them unless it was a very informal situation like with my family and my parents who didn't know much English at the time. Formally and outside my doorstep I was accustomed to separating languages and this is the way I encountered *Borderlands*, and with Gloria having coffee.

Irene Lara: But why did you feel uncomfortable talking to Gloria about that, about your take on that?

Norma: Because–I didn't want to alienate her as a potential friend. I wanted to know her and I did not think that I should come upon her as an academic, straight-shirt kind of thing or even as an editor, I just wanted us to get to know each other before we got into other subjects. I had just arrived in California and I wanted to have friends, which in the end, from that moment on we were. In her own way Gloria could read me, kindly.

Irene: But wasn't she trying to reclaim that working-class Spanish, wasn't that part of her point too?

Norma: I don't think she was reclaiming it; I think it's genuine.

Irene: You think that's her voice?

Norma: Yes, I think that's her voice. She may have repressed some of it for the demands of the Anglo world. "Speak English!" *Borderlands* should be treated as her authentic voice. It wasn't until after *Borderlands* that her voice began to change somewhat not only in terms of her lectures but also in terms of further writing and interviews that her voice began to change. That is what happens with us as we interact with other people, our way of thinking and expressing ourselves changes. I do think that it is her voice and we need to respect that, this is *what* she was telling us and this is *how* she was telling us.

One could say that she was reclaiming what her teachers wanted to wash away with soap as it was practiced in the U.S. classrooms of the 1950s before she went off to university. Teachers did wash their mouths and put them in separate rooms and so on and so forth. However, it was what kids learned at home, it's genuine, it took her years to erase those modes of talking and writing. And again these things happen because she is out in the world exchanging, learning, and she is an avid learner and reader. You have to keep that in mind as you progress through her work and her life that she is constantly learning and shifting her perception of things because she is eager to know and to learn. She championed the voices of women no matter what and that is to her credit. I heard her say so and do so. Also, she would not want shame to silence her and she would not want shame to silence any women whatsoever. Of course, shame is a big theme of hers especially in the beginning as part of the stigma of her life and she didn't want shame to be a silencer for her or other women. This was already part of her way of encouraging others and so in that sense she was not only a learner but a teacher. Constantly. She was always under construction until the end of her life. Self-construction.

Irene: Okay.

Norma: I think that's her voice and the reason I say that is not only because of the year she was born, like me, but also her parents, and she was a reader, as she says in her essays in *Bridge*.⁴ She was a reader of popular literature, but in English, not a reader of popular literature in Spanish.

When I was a child in México, for the first eleven years of my life, I was a reader of popular literature in Spanish. So even then fotonovelas have appropriate correct Spanish. Even the fotonovelas did not give you bad tenses or palabras mochas.

Norma: In Coahuila, in my town, you wouldn't have Spanglish. But in the Valley where Gloria grew up, you do.

I was very uncomfortable to be an academic with her; to have the academic response. And I didn't want to have an academic response, that's for sure. But I did want to correct her. Also, I myself was brought up against superstition and against certain folklore that is superstition. And that, again, is the difference between the city and the country. Even though I was from a small town, it already was citifying itself if you will.

Irene: Modernizing.

Norma: My hometown where my parents grew up, they grew up on the edge of modernizing. My father's family were into *curanderas*. My mother's family were into medical doctors. Since my mother had the last word on some things, I was brought up with medicine and healers, gente del pueblo, del rancho.

Even though I was from a small town I had citified myself, became an urban dweller especially in Chicago style English both in the school and in the street and this made a difference between us. And this is important to note among all of us and something that she also says that we have to note and respect our differences in order to form alliances, to reach out for our commonalities in order to move forward while simultaneously respecting our differences.

Yolanda: Right.

---

4. *Bridge* is a tender abbreviation for *This Bridge Called My Back: Writings by Radical Women of Color*. First published in 1981, the third expanded and revised edition of *This Bridge Called My Back* was published by Third Woman Press in 2002. Most recently published by SUNY Press in 2021, *Bridge* is now in its fifth edition. Gloria E. Anzaldúa, "La Prieta," in *This Bridge Called My Back: Writings by Radical Women of Color*, ed. Cherríe L. Moraga and Gloria E. Anzaldúa (Third Woman Press, 2002), 220–33; and Gloria E. Anzaldúa, "Speaking in Tongues: Letter to Third World Woman Writers," in *This Bridge Called My Back: Writings by Radical Women of Color*, ed. Cherríe L. Moraga and Gloria E. Anzaldúa (Third Woman Press, 2002), 183–93.

Norma: My mother even went so far as to call healers superstitious. And the thing is that in a way, Gloria's first half, the prose half of *Borderlands,* made me very uncomfortable because that was what I learned not to do in perfecting my Spanish language and becoming educated by getting a Ph.D. in Spanish.

Irene: And here she was with a book that broke all the rules, published.

Norma: And here she was bringing the *pueblo* back into my face. My experiences with *gringas* from childhood was what today I would call informal ethnographic critical gaze. The playground: *Where did you get your clothes? Where did you come from?* The cafeteria: *Is that what you eat? Who makes your lunch?* Imagine that. All I wanted was to be friends with them and all they wanted to do was interrogate me. I was an object of scrutiny. It took me three years to make a non-Mexican friend only to discover that her family was too racist to have her befriend a Mexican. I lost a friend. She was open to me but her family was not.

When *Borderlands* was published, the readers of Mexican descent, especially in Texas, responded as if they were encountering a long-lost *hermana* with respect to Anzaldúa. The response was that they had found a long-lost friend. Sonia Saldívar-Hull says that in the Introduction to the second edition of *Borderlands.*[5] The tolerance of some professors and graduate students for responses that were little less than self-indulgent *testimonios* shocked me. Again this is me. If initially in 1987 I had been trained in a particular way as an academic, and had to rethink myself, I didn't mind. I welcomed doing that. On the other hand, here comes the critic to one of the first conferences on Anzaldúa and everybody's response is that they found a long-lost friend and I thought they were going to present papers. So here is the academic in me coming out. I think they are going to present papers and they are all kind of embracing their lost *hermana*. I thought, what is this? Where am I? Then again, it's on me and it brings out the critic in me, which is my training. I was responding from the point of view of training. You go to conferences, people present papers. So, I go to a conference in Texas, in San Antonio, downtown UTSA and I expect orderly papers. I expect papers that elucidate the text for me. Because that is what I went there for, to have the text elucidated for

---

5. Sonia Saldívar-Hull, "Introduction to the Second Edition," in *Borderlands/La Frontera: The New Mestiza*, 2nd edition (Aunt Lute Books, 1999), 1-15.

me from their point of view. Here I am willing to listen and they are not elucidating the text—They are elucidating themselves.

That only speaks about me. That for me, reading Anzaldúa and paying close attention to how she was being received, moving around this world was to experience certain jolts. But it also speaks to me that I welcomed the jolts. I think that we should be open to that. This is part of dialogue, this is part of conversation, this is part of exchange with people. I had to step back and watch the reception because I thought, "I want to be part of this yet my expectations are not what is happening here." I had to come to terms with the fact that there was a deep-seated need to be allowed to have such a personal response. I was used to a personal response in the classroom, you might remember Yolanda and Irene, that students were allowed to have a personal response and object to this or that, yet here this was a celebration of themselves because they had a text that spoke directly to them in a very personal text. That was my point of view. The critic in me was asking: What is the reception that's going on here? What is going on in this culture of Mexican descent that Gloria is such a heroine? So, I said "ok, let's see what happens after this. I have to watch the reception here." As you will mention to your students, Gloria has global receptivity.

Yolanda: Norma what was the conference?

Norma: It was one of the first ones on Gloria Anzaldúa, in San Antonio. It was the 2009–that was the large one. I think it was 2009.[6]

Norma: In terms of teaching the essays and *Borderlands*, it means that the teacher, the one that teaches has to be prepared for a variety of responses, from love to rejection. Accept them and handle them, because they are meaningful wherever they may come from and the serious pedagogue should take these as serious statements from their students. Because then it is a way in which you can then return to their interests. As long as they are passionate about what and how they want to learn, and you can see that this is what they want to do—love and rejection, you have to go with it and be prepared to handle it while all the while respecting the voice of the writer.

---

6. *Editors' Note:* The Society for the Study of Gloria Anzaldúa first met at a conference titled *Prietas y Güeras* at the University of Texas at San Antonio in 2007. Subsequently, starting in 2009, the conferences have been titled El Mundo Zurdo and held every 18 months.

As I began teaching *Borderlands*, the critic in me was asking what is the reader's reception? What is the reception from a reader that is alien to the text and what is the reception from a reader that considers Anzaldúa a long-lost friend? The reception of the text becomes part of the story of the text itself. If you are going to teach Anzaldúa, you have to be curious about what the students' reception means and use that to guide your students through their own frames of intelligibility.

Norma: I'm a critic, I consider myself a critic of Gloria Anzaldúa, and not a fan. And what I mean by a fan is that it helps no one to be merely a fan. That is what a naïve reading is for. The first reading of the text is a naïve reading where you allow yourself to have whatever response you have, the students are allowed to have whatever response they have, but then they have to step back and think, not only about their response, but also about how they can come back to the book itself. Do you know what I mean?

Irene: You're not going to automatically put her on a pedestal and romanticize.

Norma: Absolutely...

Irene: Because you respect her.

Norma: Here's what I have done that I think is extremely respectful and what I advise young scholars to think about as they begin to teach Anzaldúa. The reason I did the "Textualities" essay the way I did was by way of trying to point out the development of her thinking, of how she was constructing and reconstructing herself in her lifelong journey in the pursuit of knowledge, in the pursuit of knowing herself.[7] That is part of her mission, for herself, to know herself. She had struggled on her own terms to be educated, to educate herself. First of all she trusted herself and how she generated her education for herself. She was resistant to authority. She was resistant to tradition. One of the reasons I adore her is her resistances to the exterior world that surrounded her. Her resistances are part of what we learn from her that she resists, and we may be resisting with her and we have to think about how those resistances

---

7. When Norma references "Textualities," she is referring to Norma Alarcón, "Anzaldúan Textualities: A Hermeneutic of the Self and the Coyolxauhqui Imperative," in *El Mundo Zurdo 3: Selected Works from the 2012 Meeting of the Society for the Study of Gloria Anzaldúa*, ed. Larissa M. Mercado-López, Sonia Saldívar-Hull, and Antonia Castañeda (Aunt Lute Books, 2013), 189–208.

are taking place. She wanted to squeeze out of academic institutions what she could without being erased.

Simultaneously she undertakes a continuous rebellion against the academy even as she wants to be there. Not easy to do. And that is one of the major contradictions that she navigates, that is, wanting to change the academy and wanting to be in it too. That is what you do, you learn to work with that contradiction. First because you have some respect for the academy, the academic institution, but at the same time, you want more from it.

The whole school experience in the Valley,[8] the experience at the University of Texas, Austin, the experience in the fields of Indianapolis where she was sent to teach bilingual education to the migrants. Throughout all these experiences she was an intellectual activist. Whatever some of our responses may be in terms of her text she was an intellectual activist from the very beginning. And her struggle would be harder because she was an intellectual activist. People don't like it when you talk back, people don't like *osiconas*. She has that aspect of *osicona* in her *Borderlands* chapter "How to Tame a Wild Tongue."[9]

And she did struggle to become educated with all the things against her that were there. You know, the whole school experience in the Valley, the experience in Austin. But she wanted to achieve an education and she struggled for that Ph.D. very hard. Very, very, hard and I could even say that she made her life harder in the struggle because the level of her resistance did not allow her to listen too much to her professors at all. I don't blame her for that. You don't want to listen to your professors, don't, I don't care. But just remember if you're paying a price, and if you're paying a price, what is it? I resisted professors. We all have resisted professors. But I tried to imagine, you know, for me, Gloria Anzaldúa *develops* from the time she writes those essays in *Bridge* to the time of *Borderlands*, until the end. From my point of view tracking the development of her thought is critical to the *how* of teaching Anzaldúa.

Irene: Absolutely.

Norma: Every step of the way is a development or self-reconstruction as she calls them. But the leap in development for Gloria happens with *Haciendo*

---

8. Gloria grew up in the Rio Grande Valley in South Texas, along the Texas-México borderlands.
9. Gloria Anzaldúa, "How to Tame a Wild Tongue" in *Borderlands/La Frontera: The New Mestiza* (San Francisco: Spinsters/Aunt Lute, 1987), 53–64.

Caras.¹⁰ This is the time when she had already moved to Santa Cruz and was studying in Santa Cruz. And you can read in her introduction that she was picking up a lot of information, a lot of critical information, a lot of concepts and metaphors that she was putting to her own use, but they were part of the Santa Cruz curriculum and the History of Consciousness Program that she wanted to be in, and could not, so she was sent to Literature.

Knowing Santa Cruz, the way I came to know it, I can see why they didn't want her in History of Consciousness and insisted that she go to Literature. Part of the reason would be, I think, that History of Consciousness, well on the one hand, Gloria herself was a consciousness that one could make history of and some have.

Irene: They wanted to study her and not talk with her.

Norma: In other words, she was interesting because here was a fascinating consciousness that could be studied, but she was "not equipped" to study the history of consciousness as they taught it. But I think, when she went into that, I think her style began to change. She started to be a writer and a thinker that had tremendously improved upon herself. Developed. And this is the way I have studied Gloria Anzaldúa. This is the way I would teach Anzaldúa if I was to teach her now. This is the way I have come to study Gloria Anzaldúa because I want to ask the hard questions of what the struggle actually is when you have a desire to be an intellectual and an activist intellectual at that.

I wanted to be an intellectual and I actually wanted to be an intellectual somewhat different from what the academy produced. In general, the academies I was in teach you along the lines of disciplines. We are all familiar with that disciplining as Foucault called it. I had to follow a disciplinary methodology. Discipline oriented instruction follows the lines of employment the Ph.D. candidate can aim for. In my case, I was trained to eventually teach in a Spanish department with a Latin American curriculum and I was fortunate to end up in Chicano and Ethnic Studies because I could experiment with curriculum which would not be the case in my time within a discipline. In a sense when I met Gloria in 1987 at that faithful Cody's Café in Berkeley, I was a person that had been trained in a discipline meeting someone that had

---

10. Gloria Anzaldúa, ed., *Making Face, Making Soul/Haciendo Caras: Creative and Critical Perspectives by Feminists of Color* (San Francisco: Aunt Lute Books, 1990).

rebelled against any discipline because she was fed up with trying to be put into one discipline. And I feel free today after retirement because I don't have to be an intellectual keeping an ear out for the academy. And I like that. But I don't know if in the long run, Gloria was kind of pushed into saying that she was an artist and a literary person, instead of something else because I think she had the makings of a high-powered intellectual myself. And that she was always thinking and developing her own thought, but her own thought was also very preoccupied with whatever her own internal trauma was and making sense of her trauma.

I don't know if you have noticed as you read her work from beginning to end, so to speak, that she is constantly trying to make sense of her trauma. Constantly. One way or another she's always trying to make sense of her trauma and inventing metaphors or appropriating terminology that she redefines and this and that and the other, but always trying to make sense of her trauma and helping others to make sense of their trauma. And I'm not sure that people *read that* about Gloria; that Gloria is interested in helping you think through your trauma. So the answers she has for you are answers that she has gotten from studying her trauma.

Yolanda: I want to stay with what you are saying about how Gloria is always writing about her trauma.

Norma: Correct.

Yolanda: Because I think, part of what is really important in her work, in the writing process she models for us, is that she sees that process of returning to your trauma to make meaning as the source of her emancipation. It's liberatory. It's a reintegration of the self as in putting Coyolxauhqui together again.[11] That's powerful for her you know?

Norma: Yes. In "Anzaldúan Textualities" I address the fact that she points to the necessity of engaging in an inner healing of the self to transform the disorder of our interiority before or simultaneously as the disorder of our

---

11. See, for example, Gloria Anzaldúa, "Putting Coyolxauhqui Together: A Creative Process," in *How We Work, Counterpoints* 90, ed. Marla Morris, Mary Aswell Doll, and William F. Pinar (Peter Lang, 1999), 241–61; and Gloria Anzaldúa, "Let us be the healing of the wound: The Coyolxauhqui imperative—La sombra y el sueño," in *Light in the Dark, Luz en Lo Oscuro: Rewriting Identity, Spirituality, Reality*, ed. AnaLouise Keating (Durham, NC: Duke, 2015), 9–22.

exteriorities.[12] To experience in the raw experience, transcodified into some grammatically rational interpretation of the situatedness of our experiences and finally assign sociohistorical meaning or if you will, the imagination's meaning for it. Yes, the inner work of healing our multiple traumas is part of the Coyolxauhqui imperative. The fragmentation of our interiority has to be assembled in order to transition into assembling the fragmentation of our exterior world which has in fact broken the coherence of our own interiority. In other words, the disorder of our world as we have experienced it in itself produces trauma but at the same time both have to be addressed, interiorly and exteriorly, and she never gives up on that notion as a kind of dialectic through which to effect self transformation. Remember that one of her quests is to become whole and integral and I assume in our world as it's going right now there are lots of people out there that want to figure out just what could make our world whole again.

The greatest tool for the facilitation of healing in the undergraduate classroom is a serious approach to journal keeping and writing. Speaking and writing are key. It is very difficult to figure out how to have students keep a journal of the classroom, of the text, of what they experience and perceive in class and outside of class as they encounter the text. It is difficult for the professor to have students keep a journal because they expect you to read everything they write and of course this is labor intensive, yet you can pick and choose what to read and it is worthwhile to teach students the importance of writing in their own self-construction.

Yolanda: I want to ask you a question, going back to where you started with your first reaction to *Borderlands,* when did you first start using Anzaldúa in your teaching if it wasn't that first year in Berkeley, when did you, do you remember? And was it something from *Bridge* that you first put in your course reader or was it something from *Borderlands*?

Irene: Or *Haciendo Caras*?

Yolanda: When did you first start to integrate Gloria into your classes and what pieces were they?

---

12. Alarcón, "Anzaldúan Textualities."

Norma: I waited a few years after I started teaching to introduce her, but the first time I did it I decided to do it by reading her and Cherríe Moraga side by side, *Loving in the War Years*[13] and *Borderlands* side by side.

Yolanda: Which pieces do you remember?

Norma: I put together Cherríe Moraga and Gloria Anzaldúa in a seminar I did at Cornell for graduate students.

I never taught the whole book to undergraduates. It would have taken up half the semester to teach it, I thought. Maybe I made things too complicated, but it would have taken too long to teach *Borderlands* and I didn't want them to just read it and whatever because the challenge with the prose part of *Borderlands,* in terms of teaching it to undergraduates, is that you have to help them to enrich the book. Most undergrad students I've had have a hard time understanding poetry. That is a task of its own I think. If you want to include some of the poetry I suggest that you select some of the poems that enhance or shed more light on the prose as well as elucidate the prose more. You can do a back and forth with the poetry and prose so that they shed light on each other. If you are mostly going to read the prose part of *Borderlands* with undergrads or even grads, first I would situate the book historically and allow students to talk back to the text or to the instructor.

Students are free to respond in any way they wish but they have to get a hold of their responses and put them together in various ways, noting what ideological formation they are coming from and noting how they are situating themselves. I ideologically came to terms with what they were expressing and tried to then put some of it back together so that they go away with something that is more coherent than the varied expressions of 30 people in a classroom.

When I had graduate students read Gloria and Cherríe side by side at the same time, they could try and help, we could make sense of it together and they would be more willing to participate and also it would be a small number of them. They [Cornell grad students] did not like Gloria, they did not think she was a good writer, which is what I expected. Cherríe is the English speaker. It's important to say, Cherríe is an Anglophone speaker and Gloria is not. And she's not an Hispanophone speaker either. She is a mixed-language, borderland, del rancho [speaker].

---

13. Cherríe Moraga, *Loving in the War Years: lo que nunca pasó por sus labios* (South End Press, 1983).

So I taught her in the graduate classroom. They did not like Gloria. One big criticism was to bring aliens into the narrative.

Irene: The supernatural.

Norma: Another was the idea of choosing to be a lesbian, that became a big debate. And they all loved Cherríe. They all loved Cherríe.

Irene: Do you think part of it was that Cherríe provided an intelligibility that they could tap into?

Norma: That's a good word for it.

Irene: I learned it from you.

Norma: Yes, she did, she did. Something they could talk to very easily. They were all English Majors.

Gloria validated certain things for me because I also thought about the notion of multiple selves. So that for me, personally, Gloria was a person who talked about multiple selves without shame, without apprehension. She did attempt to justify it one way or another because she is obviously very conscious that she lives in a culture that may pathologize it. She did validate for me the notion of multiple selves, and in my work, I try to put it in a frame of intelligibility that would make it critical and theoretical.

Yolanda: Thinking back to that *mestiza* consciousness undergraduate class you taught at Berkeley, what were you after in teaching Anzaldúa, what was your objective?

Norma: We only read the *mestiza* consciousness chapter, right?

Yolanda: When teaching Anzaldúa what were your teaching objectives or did you have an overall umbrella objective and did that shift depending on the class or who your students were?

Norma: When I taught Anzaldúa at all in undergraduate classrooms, it would be chapters.

Two of my favorite chapters were "Tlilli Tlapalli" and "*La conciencia de la mestiza*"[14] because they're easy and neat to work with undergraduate students without going off the deep end of frustration, irritation, or negative thinking. In "Tlilli Tlapalli" she talks about making an assemblage because there she was theorizing about what she thinks she has done.

She calls what she has done an assemblage. That to me made sense and clued me into the fact that Gloria was re-thinking what she had done, in the previous chapters, and realized that they were an assemblage. That she was assembling some things together. She had an awareness that these things if they were coherent, they were so, from a poetic point of view and not a prose point of view. If you read her text carefully, she teaches us how to read her, how to critique her, and I would say even how to teach her work. Follow me on that?

Anzaldúa knew that for Anglophones, Women of Color and Third World Women writers might as well be speaking in tongues. So many are expressing their experience in an Anglophone social and cultural world. Don't let that deter you from speaking and writing, she says. Don't be ashamed of that in an Anglophone dominant culture with the pathologizing that comes with that. Let me add that the imperialist American Psychological Association has multiplied the number of volumes which are distributed globally. This is dangerous for both men and women I think. That is, that their own diagnostic manual has become a kind of psychological *Bible* for the rest of the world.

Poetry coheres in different ways than prose does. Prose demands a lot more rationality than Gloria gives us in *Borderlands*.

Except after *Haciendo Caras*. When you compare it to her early work you can see her prose, her intelligibility growing by leaps and bounds. To follow her train of thought you have to be willing and open to her non-coherent rambling at times. As a reader you have to see the patterns. In the classroom you have to teach students to see the patterns in that sinuous style that she has that may not seem as clear to the naïve reader. I often have a compulsion to unscramble her thinking. And in fact, I do, in order to discern the thematics that obsess her, especially in *Borderlands*, the book in which she launches, I

---

14. Gloria Anzaldúa, "Tlilli, Tlapalli: the Path of the Red and Black Ink" and "*La conciencia de la mestiza*: Towards a New Consciousness" in *Borderlands/La Frontera: The New Mestiza* (San Francisco: Spinsters/Aunt Lute, 1987), 65-75, 77-91.

think, her own foundational self-reconstructions, that she continues to pursue in subsequent texts.

Irene: And what do you mean by rationality?

Norma: Intelligible.

Yolanda: That you can follow her train of thought?

Norma: Yes. As I have been noting *Borderlands* resists academically generated writing genres. In the second edition of *Borderlands* (1999) she calls it creative nonfiction. Earlier she had called it *autohistoria* and automythography. Anzaldúa uses the notion of *autohistoria*, a form of *testimonio*, and automythography to explain to us and to herself as well what she is doing in her text. The autohistoria which can be seen as a variety of life stories and anecdotes are entwined with automythography. Both terms allude to a double movement in the text. One referencing experience and the other the extant pre-Columbian mythologies which she appropriates and recodifies for her own self-construction, for her own understanding of experience itself. Sonia Saldívar-Hull calls it *testimonio* or *testimonio* pedagogy. *Borderlands* defies categories from the academy or book marketing and Duke publishing house markets it as Chicana and Women's Studies. Putting marketing aside, the other terms are useful because she uses them to explain to the reader and to herself what she is doing.

Irene: Norma, can you talk about other parts of *Borderlands* that were important in teaching Anzaldúa?

Norma: The *facultad* chapter is a tremendous, a fascinating piece.[15] I think she's doing really in-depth work on trauma there, but she never brings out that this *facultad* may be like post-traumatic stress disorder that she is trying to address.

When you suffer from PTSD, largely an existentially produced malady, and stream of consciousness flows by quickly, like a river, images and words may seem to snowball on you, silently, without necessarily making any sense, unless verbalized or scripted for oneself or through another. It may be frightening; however it may be possible to distance yourself from your flow

---

15. "*La facultad*" is the last section of the third *Borderlands* chapter, "Entering Into the Serpent." Gloria Anzaldúa, "Entering Into the Serpent" in *Borderlands/La Frontera: The New Mestiza* (San Francisco: Spinsters/Aunt Lute, 1987), 25-39.

of consciousness and become an observer of that phenomenon. When I was detoxing from my psychotropics, I called what was happening in my brain "tsunami swarms" because of the intensity of energy in your brain being released by taking away the drugs. In releasing that energy, the imagery just flowed and I called them swarms because they would come in pushes, balloon size, like a swarm of bees and thoughts and so on. I myself started being able to connect *la facultad* vis-à-vis trauma, that people who suffer with PTSD have these kinds of experiences.

In that section on la facultad she is trying to legitimize these forms of thought that are part of our experience, I think. I had students that expressed a strong affinity to that section on la facultad. They expressed a strong rapport with it so I asked myself what am I missing that this is the way they feel? I think that this section validates for some, their personal experience and they walk away from the text feeling that they possess, or they have la facultad, that is the name they can call it. A concept emerges from which to organize the psychic effects of violence such as physical and emotional abuse. Anzaldúa speaks of the psyche, that part of our mind that does not communicate well, it produces a sensing of our ambience, feelings and emotions, that are not verbalized in an intelligible way even to ourselves and our interiority. The idea of a sixth sense can be seen by acknowledging that our skin is one of our senses. She calls the use of *la facultad* a survival tactic especially for the oppressed, females, homosexuals of all races, the prosecuted, the marginalized, the foreign. Why Anzaldúa prefers to call it *la facultad* rather than our psychic energy may be part of her resistance to being defined by the terms of the colonizing west without necessarily denying that the term psyche exists. It also enables an organization of these phenomena with a term that is not obliged to embrace the concept of psyche. This gives us a different axis, a different way of organizing what is actually happening that better serves us and shift us away from the pathologizing frameworks of western psychology.

Irene: These ways of knowing.

Norma: I would say these ways of possible knowing. In "La facultad"[16] and other sections the modes she verbalizes are actually the interior experiences that are often non-verbal or non-linguistic which she notes are part of our brain function that does not speak yet the sensing experiences interior to

---

16. Anzaldúa, "Entering Into the Serpent," 38-39.

ourselves or exterior have to be verbalized or scripted in order to acquire an elaboration into knowing. That is of knowing by writing out what has happened rather than just accepting that tumultuous thinking as knowing itself. It has to be verbalized. It has to be scripted. In a way I am making the claim here that some of our experiences of consciousness are not necessarily clear but they have a value that needs to be extracted and we extract it in the verbalization to others, in a repartee, or we extract it by writing it up at which point you are transforming that into knowledge. You are scripting an interior experience that needs clarification in the face of the others and even in the face of yourself as your cogence demands it. If it demands it at all. Actually, one could say that by writing her own experiences in this section and others as well Anzaldúa is giving words to a suffering to which others respond, hence the affinity and rapport with her, not only in this section, but in other sections as well. In terms of teaching it in the classroom, this is why it becomes important to see how your students respond in rapport or not, in affinity or not. And then you can go from there. I believe that she is learning to know herself. I was fascinated from the point of view of my students who felt empowered with the idea of possessing la facultad. We need to come to terms with these layers of experience, especially many of us who have been deeply violated as Franz Fanon knew in his work.

Irene: Right, yeah.

Norma: Because we have been-

Irene: You had to develop that to survive.

Norma: Well the thing is you don't develop *la facultad* in the sense that philosophy or education would say you develop it, *la facultad* sort of comes to you from being abused. It comes from a hard life. It comes from abuse and violence. It is a manifestation of our post-traumatic stress disorders.

Yolanda: Norma, in your "Anzaldúan Textualities" essay, why do you use "concept-metaphor"? What does this enable that "concept" or "metaphor" does not?

Norma: I adopted Spivak's hyphenated notions of concept and metaphor.[17] Although of course we will continue to use each notion separately depending

---

17. In "Anzaldúan Textualities," Norma elaborates on her application of Gayatri Spivak's "Concept-Metaphor" to engage with Gloria's work. See Norma's endnote #2. Alarcón, "Anzaldúan Textualities," 204-206.

on context, I find its hyphenization useful for cultural studies that crosses disciplinary borders. It is important I think for the scholarly student to both understand the notion of concept and metaphor. The notion of concept and metaphor slide into each other in so far as both signal that these notions are substituting for a reality that is an objective correlative or referencing an objective correlative, which may have a more robust reality claim than the metaphor or the concept involved. If you tell a social scientist that the concept that is part of his or her epistemological thread is actually a metaphor as well, he or she will deny it. For example, race, class, and gender. Largely because metaphor has been the province of literary critical thinking. Moreover, social scientists are more protective of their disciplinary border. A lot is at stake for them. Specifically funding in grants from the government, foundations, and right-wing think tanks. Those of us in literary and cultural studies are not only disciplinary border crossers, we are also aware that the literary imagination cannot be contained or should not be contained, and we need to defend forms of expansive consciousness, which, for example, Anzaldúa pursued.

Yolanda: We can see *la facultad* is important in teaching Anzaldúa, can you tell us about some of the other really important ideas, Anzaldúan concepts in your teaching?

Norma: *Mestiza* consciousness was to me I think, one of those that empowered the notion of multiple selves and hybridity. It's more than a border, it's a consciousness that expands, and more than that, it overflows. And that's a very important thought in her work I think, *mestiza* consciousness, because it makes us pay attention to how being from multiple cultural backgrounds and learning from other cultures transforms our consciousness and you can either go ahead and leave it all mixed up if you want. *Aya tú*, good luck with that, or you can learn to pull out the threads and then weave them. And not all the threads will weave with each other, but you can pull out the threads and weave them into your own *tapiz*, as Ana Castillo calls it and then write in an intelligible, rational way in terms of grammatical logic, that's what I mean by that, rather than a form of fancy reasoning.[18]

It's hard to escape the logistics of grammar. If we do so we are also escaping parts of our culture and making our own at risk of unintelligibility. On the

---

18. *Tapiz* here is in reference to Ana Castillo's "Un Tapiz: The Poetics of Concientización," in *Massacre of the Dreamers: Essays in Xicanisma* (University of New Mexico Press, 1994), 163–179.

other hand if women are to rupture what Anzaldúa calls the cultural tyranny of patriarchy we must engage in an invention of ourselves that breaks the cultural barriers that imprison our thought. For example, our drive for revising and expanding philosophical conceptualizations from The Enlightenment to the present. We must continue to undo and unlearn the stronghold and stranglehold that patriarchy has on our world and on us. It's rather sad that our antipatriarchal drive is often felt to be emasculating by some men.

I'm just telling you my trajectory with Gloria because I didn't teach her methodically in every classroom I had. I taught pieces in the undergraduate classroom depending on the syllabus goals, not goals with Gloria, but how Gloria fulfilled the goals of the syllabus, and I would choose some chapters like "Mestiza Consciousness."[19] I did not choose the chapter with La facultad because I felt that I had to do a great big lecture about how I understood it and undergraduates might get confused.

Yolanda: Did you teach the concept of Shadow-Beast? If so, can you tell us why you taught it and how?

Norma: Anzaldúa appears to use the concept-metaphor Shadow-Beast, which is in fact drawn from Jungian thought, in *Borderlands* for the first time. I would have to do a review of earlier work to see if she mentioned it earlier. In *Borderlands,* Anzaldúa defines the Shadow-Beast as the "rebel in" her, the "part of" her "that refuses to take orders from [her] conscious will, [the Shadow-Beast] threatens the sovereignty of my rulership" she says on page 38.[20] In this contextualization, I interpret this as an active energy that refuses limitations and turns against what she calls her conscious will. It is both a negative and a positive energy in so far as its negativity threatens to destroy her and its positivity leads her to resist limitations. I wonder if it's rage?

Anzaldúa tends to select useful concept-metaphors in elaborating what I see as her existential thinking throughout and each needs elaboration by tracking its usages contextually throughout time since their meaning shifts depending on context. The Shadow-Beast does not shift as radically as Coyolxauhqui

---

19. Norma is referring to the frequently anthologized "*La conciencia de la mestiza*/Towards a New Consciousness," the seventh and last chapter in *Borderlands*. Anzaldúa, *"La consciencia de la mestiza,"* 77-91.

20. In the 1987 first edition of *Borderlands*, Gloria says this on page 16 (the second page of the second chapter). Gloria Anzaldúa, *"Movimientos de rebeldía y las culturas que traicionan,"* in *Borderlands/La Frontera: The New Mestiza* (Aunt Lute Books, 1987), 16.

does. At times she only says shadow and not shadow beast. You can pull them apart or you can see how they work together. I bring them together because they are interrelated.

Since the concept-metaphor has strong psychological valence in her work, it must be addressed and taught, I think. One strategy for teaching is to first track it across her text to see how it is deployed for example, in elaborating the place it may have in *la facultad* even though it doesn't explicitly appear in that section on *la facultad*. Another is to elaborate its linkage with the psychoanalytic concept of the psyche. To me it appears that Anzaldúa fluctuated between Jung and Freud. Although she does say she "know[s] things older than Freud."[21]

Yolanda: When you taught graduate students, you taught the whole book?

Norma: Yes, the prose book yes.

Yolanda: No, that's a good point, how did your students respond to your attempts to teach *Borderlands* in grad school? In Ethnic Studies?

Norma: Some of my Native-American students hated the whole Aztlán chapter, the first chapter,[22] and they had all kinds of quarrels with it, and they all had different points of view about it, and I never wanted to teach that chapter of Gloria's because I felt that was a waste of time. It was a waste of time if the students were not willing to look at that chapter as this is Gloria's version of the world, but wanted to read it as Gloria's version is all wrong. The question of how the American continent was populated is not why we read Anzaldúa.

Yolanda: Right, but were they reading it for accuracy from a Chicana perspective?

Norma: I don't read Gloria for accuracy from any perspective. I read Anzaldúa from the point of view of her intentions and motivations for writing as she did. For telling the stories that she needed to tell in her critique of culture broadly speaking, that desires border crossing of many kinds. I read for her recodification of sources in her lifelong struggle to transform herself, ourselves, in order to transform the cultures that oppress us generally or resist colonization, which is continuous with imperialist cultures.

---

21. Anzaldúa, *Borderlands*, 26.
22. Gloria Anzaldúa, "The Homeland, Aztlán/*El otro México*," in *Borderlands/La Frontera: The New Mestiza* (Aunt Lute Books, 1987), 1–14.

Yolanda: It's the imagination.

Norma: Yeah, and also most writers know that on the one hand, but on the other, they all suffer the delusion that they are original. In other words, they know it's not so, they know they're not original. But they all have the delusion that they are. So when you start to quiz them on where they got this and where they got that and what book did you read for this and what book did you read for that, which you could do with Gloria with all her footnotes, you can see which mythographers she read, which anthropologists she read, and all that sort of thing.

In Gloria's case, I would say follow her delusion. Make sense of her delusion, and I do it with other writers too. First make sense of their delusion, their sense of what is theirs, original, creative, and then do your critical work.

Irene: I'm really curious about "Speaking in Tongues," did you ever teach "Speaking in Tongues"? From *This Bridge*? Her "Letter to Third World Women Writers"?[23]

Can you speak to those experiences and how you taught that piece, what your objectives were when teaching that piece? How the students responded?

Norma: I did teach that piece and I do like "Speaking in Tongues" because I think "Speaking in Tongues" addresses a very interesting linguistic phenomenon, and well and this is why in teaching the work of Gloria, I pick out pieces, but they are pieces that are going to serve some other objective than the study of Gloria Anzaldúa, you follow me? Because if it was just a seminar on Gloria Anzaldúa then you would run it completely different and I would work a great deal with the concept of assemblage, where *mestiza* consciousness begins to be introduced and how it is developed, for example and other concepts that she brings out and are there throughout.

All the concept-metaphors I mention in my "Textualities" essay are crucial. Since many deploy the term *conocimiento*, I think it would be important to deepen it more in its significance especially since Anzaldúa gives it quite a bit of neurological weight. It needs deepening and that deepening can come from her own text.

---

23. Anzaldúa, "Speaking in Tongues," 183–93.

Her recodification of precolombian mythographies as well as her notion of *mestizaje* that is not equivalent to that of Mexican nationalism are also crucial. Many will try to conflate the way Gloria used *mestizaje* to the Mexican nationalist approach and she is not using it that way. She is giving it a different cultural value. Not in the sense of a Chicano nationalist. She is using it to elucidate consciousness.

The fact that she wants to break out of ideological notions of identity that harness our imagination is also crucial to discuss. In *Borderlands* she says I belong to myself and not to any one people. These are variations of the theme throughout her work. She says I am going deep into the self and expanding out into the world. A simultaneous recreation of the self and a reconstruction of society. I would say that these are variations of her pursuit for self-invention for her. She cannot find her sociocultural existentiality in the context of her experiences so she says, "If both cultures deny me a place in their universe, between them and among others I build my own universe."[24] This very pursuit to build her own universe is also what motivates her not to be constrained by notions of identity. If I am going to have an identity, I am going to build my own, she says. This could be in some ways liberating to your students in case they have resistances to being labeled it can become important for them to think and write about what they want to build for themselves.

But when I selected the pieces of Gloria work, it was for a purpose, a point I wanted to make for the rest of the syllabus. "Speaking in Tongues" is one of them because, and I think I taught it from the point of view that you're not monolingual, and when you're not a monolingual person, the way that you may handle your language makes you not make sense to others. The United States is not a culture that encourages or prizes multilingualities. Quite a bit of the Anglophone population is constantly saying "speak English please." Not

---

24. We could not find where Gloria directly says this, however, this is Gloria's sentiment throughout her opus. For example, "And if going home is denied me then I will have to stand and claim my own space, making a new culture–*una cultura mestiza*–with my own lumber, my own bricks and mortar and my own feminist architecture" (Anzaldúa, *Borderlands*, 22). Also, in a 1983 interview Gloria critiques nationalism and declares herself to be "a citizen of the universe" (Christine Weiland, "Within the Crossroads: Lesbian/Feminist/Spiritual Development. An Interview with Christine Weiland," in *Interviews/Entrevistas: Gloria E. Anzaldúa*, ed. AnaLouise Keating (Routledge, 2000), 118), inviting us, in AnaLouise Keating's words, "to move beyond the binary-oppositional frameworks we generally use in identity formation and social change" (AnaLouise Keating, "'I'm a Citizen of the Universe:' Gloria Anzaldúa's Activism as Catalyst for Social Change," *Feminist Studies* 34, no. 1/2, The Chicana Studies Issue, (Spring–Summer 2008): 61, https://www.jstor.org/stable/20459180).

even please, it is a demand. It is part and parcel of the cultural penchant to enforce assimilation of the multitudes of immigrants that have been deployed in this territory for more than a couple of centuries. The Anglophone demand is part and parcel of the demand for assimilation, which has been sought since settler colonialism founded the Anglo nation. I doubt that Latinos in general will be assimilating thoroughly since we have been seeking bilinguality and biculturality. Also we are from this continent and the distance between us and our ancestors across the border South of the U.S. is not as huge as that of those that crossed the Atlantic or the Pacific.

If you mix up your theories, like if you start mixing Hegel and Marx and Nietzsche all in the same essay and don't separate them as entities that can be drawn together this way, but just mix them up, it's like speaking in tongues. A variety of things are thrown together and that many people experience this in their lives because they're multilingual and have had to struggle to be both what they are and monolingual. Again, unraveling the threads, and in "Speaking in Tongues" the question is language, how do you unravel the language? How to write it?

For me, in "Speaking in Tongues," she's already imagining as she concludes her essay, and I mention this in one of my essays, she's already imagining her corpus, the major aspects of her thought are all thrown together into one paragraph towards the end of that essay.[25] And if you reread it with all of her work in mind, in your background and you're looking at it and you're in-between, you can see it. You can see the back and forth. So that for me [shows] she had already imagined her corpus in little pieces. That she unravels as time goes on. Some more than others. Marx becomes nothing. Well, she can live it, she can live poverty. But as a thinker, he's not much of anything in her work. However her work is Marxian, can you hear it?

Norma: So I don't know if that satisfies you.

Irene: No, that does!

---

25. Norma traces Anzaldúa's development in her essay "Anzaldúan Textualities: A Hermeneutic of Self and the Coyolxauhqui Imperative."

Norma: I read all of her interviews.[26] I think that one thing I would recommend young professors is to read all of her interviews and then select out the ones that will serve your objectives in the course, or your objectives, if the course is about Anzaldúa, or your objectives about reading the prose half of *Borderlands*. You know what I mean?

To me it was very fascinating and I didn't read all of her interviews until I got to Texas because then I had time. Importantly, not all of them are gathered, because I found one that wasn't, and it's a good one to have, if you want to teach about how Gloria began to think more professionally about her creative craft, there's a great essay that I mention in my work that I published.

Yolanda: Just to finish up, in the years that I knew you, Anzaldúa was always there as a part of your teaching in different contexts you know?

Norma: She gave me insights. But the way that she spoke about "Speaking in Tongues" gives you a different insight, and Anzaldúa was always in my mind because she gave me some ideas, she legitimated some thought that I had had, that now I found that she had. And there were things that were problematic for me that I had to iron out for myself. Like the whole thing with la facultad. Though she makes it seem like a mysterious gift, I don't think it's mysterious myself. I think it is part of our wounds of traumatization, our modes of life struggle that are part of colonization wherever we come from as Latinx in the U.S. as well as the colonization imposed upon us by white supremacists— the "Speak-English onlys." Such are the effects of imperialism and settler colonialism. This is part of the conquest, invasion and expropriation that we have suffered in this continent. La facultad is trying to break us out of that violence.

Yolanda: Maybe she was trying to re-write the fact that Mexicanos have been pathologized, that's a part of our narrative history, right? To try to explain whenever academics wrote about us, it was in that register, so it was perhaps writing against that, so instead of pathologizing, I'm just guessing of course, she was looking for a term that would undo some of that, that would turn that upside down, por eso es La Facultad.

---

26. In her "Anzaldúan Textualities" essay, for example, Norma cites: Keating, *Interviews/Entrevistas* and Irene Lara, "Daughter of Coatlicue: An Interview with Gloria Anzaldúa," in *EntreMundos/AmongWorlds: New Perspectives on Gloria E. Anzaldúa*, ed. AnaLouise Keating, 41–55.

Norma: I agree with you, I agree that she was looking for a term that would not only justify certain propensities, but that would also recuperate them in a positive pedagogical manner.

Irene: To decolonize the victimizer discourse, or victim discourse. That we're not victims.

Norma: We refuse to continue to be victims. But what she doesn't do in that section "La facultad"–that is why it becomes an incomplete thought for me–what she doesn't do is to develop what she says about how it's a part of our ontological self. I wanted more development of that.

Irene: So it's something that we all have, it's human.

Norma: A part of our ontological self. By the fact of being women everyone around you is willing to compromise your freedom and your future so there has to be resistance to being compromised in that way. I was nine years old when I noticed that my freedom and my life were being compromised. I am sure that Gloria noticed too, this is why her rebellion. So the question to your students is: "How old were you when you noticed that your life was being compromised by other people telling you who you were?" This is important in teaching *Borderlands*, that this is part of the question in that book. So that students can grasp that this is an underground question going through the book *Borderlands*: "Who am I? Historically, in situatedness, in learning?" The difficulty with that is that you as a teacher have to keep that together because Gloria doesn't help you. She jumps around what you might call a formal historical approach, a more informal historical approach, a sociopolitical environment, but all of these become modes that are undergirded and underpinned by the questions: "Where do I fit in this world?" and "Who am I?" And in writing this book I am discovering it as much as you. There is a way of reaching out to the reader in that way but the reader has to not forget that the major question of inquiry is "Who am I in this world?" where everybody knows what to tell me about who I am? School, work, the field, the workplace, everywhere I go. And you, as the teacher critic, have to keep it together. You take a bridge position between the text and the student responses.

Yolanda: I think she is also teaching us how writing becomes a tool for critical intellectual inquiry. Her text is in fact documenting her effort to answer that question for herself. Her text answers the question of how do we use writing in our own critical self-construction.

Norma: Castellanos said something decades ago when I was doing all that research on her.[27] She said something that puzzled me, "no doy por vivido sino lo redactado."[28] This is what she said in an interview in one of those sessions they had at the Bellas Artes. My interpretation of that is that writing enables the capture of something that is very fleeting and that is everyday experience as you move about your life. It becomes fleeting and the only way to capture that is to seize those things into writing.

Yolanda: Norma as a way to end this interview, I want to turn to your "Conjugations" essay.

In that essay you write: "In a sense, even today, I hope for a frame of intelligibility that can give form to a sociopolitical collectivity that together could transform our current state of affairs. Dreamers have a hard time dying, as dreamers anyway."[29] So my ending question to you is what do you have to say to dreamers today who want to teach an Anzaldúan "insurrection of subjugated knowledges"?[30]

Norma: One of the major thoughts that comes to mind is something that I left at the end of my "Textualities" essay, and that is the suggestion by Gloria in her own work that she sees that there is something of the Shadow Beast in certain sectors of the Anglo-American population.[31] She sees Anglo-American culture as being itself beset by their own Shadow Beast that needs to be addressed. By them perhaps. By us perhaps. I would like to develop that from the point of view of her empathetic response to the very suggestion that there is a Shadow Beast to be reckoned with among Anglo-Americans. I say empathetic because she is not just denouncing it in and of itself and making an enemy of white supremacists. Her response is more empathetic

---

27. Norma wrote her dissertation on Mexican writer Rosario Castellanos. See Norma Alarcón, *Ninfomanía: El discurso feminista en la obra poética de Rosario Castellanos* (Madrid: Editorial Pliegos, 1992).

28. Rosario Castellanos, "Rosario Castellanos," *Los narradores ante el público* (INBA/Joaquín Mortiz, 1966), 89.

29. Norma Alarcón, "Conjugations: The Insurrection of Subjugated Knowledges and Exclusionary Practices," *Chicana/Latina Studies* 13, no. 2 (Spring 2014): 204, https://www.jstor.org/stable/43941440.

30. Alarcón, "Conjugations," 224. See Norma's "Conjugations" essay where she re-situates Michel Foucault's claims about "the insurrection of subjugated knowledges" in his book, *Power/Knowledge: Selected Interviews and Other Writings, 1972-1977* (New York: Vintage, 1980).

31. Alarcón, "Anzaldúan Textualities," 200-203.

from the point of view of saying that there is a shadow beast within that sector of Anglo-American culture and society and to the degree that she wants to discuss what that shadow beast might be she is being empathetic, rather than just saying I denounce you. And I conclude my "Textualities" essay without judgment necessarily but also expressing the difficulty that it suggested to me personally of doing that. It's like embracing your serial killer I said in the essay. And this is why I want to bring out that aspect of her work, and that is a deep empathy for humanity that rises to the level of compassion. This is part of her work I think. An empathetic address. I am not sure that it is an insurrection of subjugated knowledges, but it is expanding an aspect of her work that is not necessarily mentioned.

Irene: That is really wonderful to engage in these ideas and wrap up the interview in that way because that is her thread with spiritual activism. It's in *Borderlands* when she talks about learning to "see through serpent and eagle eyes"[32] and not wanting to be in this *encontronazo*, in this *bronca*, that is not ultimately transformative. In terms of teaching an Anzaldúan "insurrection of subjugated knowledges," I think those are subjugated knowledges too. Those wisdom traditions of trying to survive by cooperating, by figuring a way through that is not just about inverting the hierarchy where we are now the masters. Her empathy is a form of subjugated knowledge I would say. Her boldness in what people would see as her naïve spirituality, and she resisted that and tried to pave her own universe. And that is a dream. That is part of the dreaming that is happening. We are trying to create "otro modo de ser humana y libre."[33]

Norma: Yes. Spirituality has been slowly suppressed in late Modernity in the industrialized nations. Also, it is often tied to standard religions which is not helpful. I believe that spirituality arises from the spirit-in-the-flesh flowing through our bodies in the molecules of emotion that are in constant motion within us.

Gloria had great faith in the secular idea (I think) of spiritual activism. She generated her own narrative to account for her spirit in all its guises in order to share her spirit with us. I believe that she desired a plenitude of identity,

---

32. Anzaldúa, *Borderlands*, 78.

33. Rosario Castellanos, "Meditación en el Umbral," in *Meditación en el umbral: Antología poética* (México: Fondo de Cultura Económica, 1985), 73.

after all she did say *que quería sentirse completa*. The torture of the fragmented spirit is a suicidal one. She did a monumental self-cleansing, moving through the debris of experiences violent to the spirit. A violence that kills the spirit. Don't stereotype violence which is not all about blows, knives and guns.

Perhaps that's what the existentialists meant when they clamored for authenticity of the self. The feeling of plenitude in our chiaroscuro identity. How else can one transcend the flesh and yet return to it in ecstasy and for ecstasy? One can't imagine clearly "*otro modo de ser*" until we find the praxis that leads us to the feeling of plenitude of identity, not just one's own, but also in relation to those around us.

BIBLIOGRAPHY

Alarcón, Norma. "Conjugations: The Insurrection of Subjugated Knowledges and Exclusionary Practices." *Chicana/Latina Studies* 13, no. 2 (Spring 2014): 202–224.

Alarcón, Norma. "Anzaldúan Textualities: A Hermeneutic of the Self and the Coyolxauhqui Imperative." In *El Mundo Zurdo 3: Selected Works from the 2012 Meeting of the Society for the Study of Gloria Anzaldúa*. Edited by Larissa M. Mercado-López, Sonia Saldívar-Hull, and Antonia Castañeda. San Francisco: Aunt Lute Books, 2013.

Alarcón, Norma. *Ninfomanía: El discurso feminista en la obra poética de Rosario Castellanos*. Madrid: Editorial Pliegos, 1992.

Anzaldúa, Gloria E. "Speaking in Tongues: Letter to Third World Woman Writers." In *This Bridge Called My Back: Writings by Radical Women of Color*. Third edition. Edited by Cherríe L. Moraga and Gloria E. Anzaldúa. Berkeley: Third Woman, 2002.

Anzaldúa, Gloria E. "La Prieta." In *This Bridge Called My Back: Writings by Radical Women of Color*. Third edition. Edited by Cherríe L. Moraga and Gloria E. Anzaldúa. Berkeley: Third Woman Press, 2002.

Anzaldúa, Gloria. *Borderlands/La Frontera: The New Mestiza*. San Francisco: Spinsters/Aunt Lute, 1987.

Anzaldúa, Gloria. "Putting Coyolxauhqui Together: A Creative Process." In *How We Work, Counterpoints* 90. Edited by Marla Morris, Mary Aswell Doll, and William F. Pinar. New York: Peter Lang, 1999.

Anzaldúa, Gloria. "Let us be the healing of the wound: The Coyolxauhqui imperative—La sombra y el sueño." In *Light in the Dark/Luz en lo Oscuro: Rewriting Identity, Spirituality, Reality*, edited by AnaLouise Keating. Durham, NC: Duke University Press, 2015.

Anzaldúa, Gloria, editor. *Making Face, Making Soul/Haciendo Caras: Creative and Critical Perspectives by Feminists of Color*. San Francisco: Aunt Lute Books, 1990.

Castellanos, Rosario. "Meditación en el Umbral." In *Meditación en el umbral: Antología poética*. México City: Fondo de Cultura Económica, 1985.

Castellanos, Rosario. "Rosario Castellanos." In *Los narradores ante el público*. México: INBA/Joaquín Mortiz, 1966.

Castillo, Ana. "Un Tapiz: The Poetics of Concientización." In *Massacre of the Dreamers: Essays in Xicanisma*. Albuquerque: University of New Mexico Press, 1994.

Foucault, Michel. *Power/Knowledge: Selected Interviews and Other Writings, 1972-1977*. New York: Vintage, 1980.

Keating, AnaLouise. "'I'm a Citizen of the Universe:' Gloria Anzaldúa's Activism as Catalyst for Social Change." *Feminist Studies* 34, no. 1/2, The Chicana Studies Issue, (Spring–Summer 2008): 53–69.

Keating AnaLouise, editor. *EntreMundos/AmongWorlds: New Perspectives on Gloria E. Anzaldúa*. New York: Palgrave/Macmillan, 2005.

Keating AnaLouise, editor. *Gloria E. Anzaldúa: Interviews/Entrevistas.* New York: Routledge, 2000.

Keating AnaLouise, editor. *Light in the Dark, Luz en lo Oscuro: Rewriting Identity, Spirituality, Reality.* Durham, NC: Duke University Press, 2015.

Lara, Irene. "A Daughter of Coatlicue: An Interview with Gloria Anzaldúa." *EntreMundos/ AmongWorlds: New Perspectives on Gloria E. Anzaldúa.* Edited by AnaLouise Keating. New York: Palgrave/Macmillan, 2005.

Moraga, Cherríe. *Loving in the War Years: lo que nunca pasó por sus labios.* Boston: South End Press, 1983.

Moraga, Cherríe L. and Gloria E. Anzaldúa, editors. 1981. *This Bridge Called My Back: Writings by Radical Women of Color.* Expanded and Revised 3rd edition, Berkeley: Third Woman Press, 2002.

Saldívar-Hull, Sonia. Introduction.In *Borderlands/La Frontera: The New Mestiza* by Gloria Anzaldúa, 1987, 2nd edition, San Francicso: Aunt Lute Books, 1999.

Weiland, Christine. "Within the Crossroads: Lesbian/Feminist/Spiritual Development. An Interview with Christine Weiland." *Gloria E. Anzaldúa: Interviews/Entrevistas.* Edited by AnaLouise Keating. New York: Routledge, 2000.

NEPANTLA—PRODUCTIONS OF PATHOLOGIES AND HEALING[1]

UNDER CONSTRUCTION

→ ←

Norma Alarcón, Marisa Belausteguigoitia, and Romana Radlwimmer

THE FOLLOWING PAGES REPRESENT an account of the Mesa Redonda "Nepantla—Productions of Pathologies and Healing" with Norma Alarcón, Marisa Belausteguigoitia, and Romana Radlwimmer at the International Conference El Mundo Zurdo 2016. The moderator of the Mesa Redonda was Sara A. Ramírez, and present in the audience and active discussants were, amongst others, María Lugones, Laura Pérez, Sonia Saldívar-Hull, Elvia Niebla, Irene Lara, and Josie Méndez-Negrete. In our conversation, we ponder the production of cultural, physical, physiological, psychological, emotional, and spiritual pathologies as experienced on all levels, for instance in educational, medical, or political structuring. We approach the pathological states by questioning and affirming the ongoing presence of Eurocentric patriarchy and its contemporary strategies of seduction and the absence of cultural memory of resistance. We reflect on Alarcón's philosophical elaborations on *desire* inside Academia and ask in which ways Anzaldúa's *nepantla* can lead us into a state of healing. The healing we envision through the round table is a shared thinking and feeling process along conceptual categories and in a creative space of expression.

Marisa Belausteguigoitia: Yesterday, Romana and I thought about how exciting it was to have Norma with us. We were thinking of a format for the round table and thought: How can you contain Norma. *(Laughter in the audience)*

---

1. *Editors' Note:* This edited transcript of a round table panel was first published in *El Mundo Zurdo 6: Selected works from the 2016 Meeting of the Society for the Study of Gloria Anzaldúa*, ed. Sara A. Ramírez, Larissa M. Mercado-López, and Sonia Saldívar-Hull (San Francisco, Aunt Lute Books, 2018), 73-88. This account was transcribed by Marisa Belaustreguigoitia and Romana Radlwimmer and edited by Sara A. Ramírez. Speakers, other than those listed as authors, gave their permission to have their words included and verified the content of their comments.

Romana Radlwimmer: How to contain Norma in a format. *(Laughter in the audience)*

Marisa: ... in a way that we could enjoy her and develop a conversation, so we could listen to her and hear each other. We came up with this idea: instead of having a PowerPoint, we are going to have points of power. Ten points of power.

Romana: Well ... it got out of hand ... *(Laughter in the audience)*

Norma Alarcón: Can we have seven? I prefer seven. *(Laughter in the audience)*

Marisa: We are going to try to generate a conversation—with Sara and with you, the public, included—around different issues: texts, definitions, ideas, fashions, and especially with a selection of Anzaldúa's drawings from the Benson Library. Nepantla, la mano zurda, el cuerpo, theory in the flesh—all these concepts were drawn by Anzaldúa. We know that these drawings came in images in Spanish. We also want to honor the sort of Spanish she spoke, the Spanish of the Southwest, the Spanish of Texas. We will show you some images and we can react to them.

So our first point of power shows the upper part of the arm. It shows flesh. It is the arm of one of my students *(shows PowerPoint image with a tattoo)*. The image represents academia placed upside down, or queer. It is queer, leaning, inclined, *atravesada. La academia que se atraviesa, la academia de los atravesados.* It is Gelen's arm, one of my former graduate students. Students are, in México and the US, *atravesando* their sexuality, along conceptual categories: the erotic on the political and the political on the erotic. They are investing in new encounters of desire, but also want to make things appear, beyond academic borders: in the political realm, in the aesthetic realm, in the pedagogical, and in the body, the corporeal one. Do you think that students may find in academia, in texts like *Borderlands*, a sort of suspended classroom? A state of interruption of the culturally dominating narratives? A device to think "outside" or at the borders of academia? When do you think that the classroom, as Nepantla, provides an interruption? An interruption of being "Western," being "women," being "students." Suspend to act upon, to be able to interrupt. The classroom we are working on is a sort of Nepantla: *estado suspendido*, in Anzaldúa's words—wider space in their minds. Do students analyzing Anzaldúa in the classroom interact—in Norma's words— with "the construction of political structures?" The theory of the practice; the theorizing from the flesh. Now we want reactions on the tattoo of a student, a tattoo turning academia on its head. P*uesta de cabeza, o si no: atravesada. Los atravesados en* Borderlands *son los queer, los migrantes.* Norma, what do you have to say about academia *puesta de cabeza*? Is that possible?

Norma: *(Laughs, then reflective)* Well, it has to be done all over again, because it already got started. *Eso de ponerla de cabeza,* it already got started, when people of color and women started walking, when women-of-color started walking into the academy. So that already got started. If young people today don't know that it is because they don't know enough recent history. They don't know the history of the last fifty years. If young people do not know the history of the last fifty or sixty years, then not only are they apparently ignorant, but also we have the kind of election we are having right now—*I* think. So, if a student is saying "I am going to put it on its head," I have to say: "It already got started. Catch up." How do you catch up? In doing it again, because it's never over. I think it has to be done over and over again for a long time because patriarchy is very solid, and very strong. *Ponerla de cabeza* is a movement, and it is a movement that already started. And if twenty-year-olds feel that they have to do it—yes they do, but they have to take it up where it already started. And if they don't know about it, they are in trouble, with their lives, let alone the Academy: with their lives, their bodies. That doesn't make me feel that the political world is going to turn around or change. We can't do it, those of us who are older. I can't do it. We tried and we have had our chance. We keep doing it. But if the fifteen–to twenty-year-olds aren't catching up, then we can't turn it upside down again.

Marisa: It will be eventually turned around.

Norma: I feel that the strength of patriarchy is incommensurable and very devastating to think about. So I don't want to think about it. *(Laughs)*

Marisa: You feel it. You feel it actually in your body. That's part of the pathologies we want to talk about, *¿no?*

(Comment from the audience)

Norma: That's Laura Pérez.

Laura Pérez: When speaking about patriarchy, it seems that there is a new seduction, right? A modernization of patriarchy's techniques, new seductions directed towards women, young women. I have these attacks of perplexity and disbelief when I see the difficulty of penetrating patriarchal thought that views itself as progressive. I think about Bernice Johnson Reagon's "coalition is not home," and it helps me to get back up.[2] What are your thoughts about how patriarchy is seducing?

Norma: Well, you are already putting your finger on it by calling attention to cultural consumption and marketing. This is the way it stays in place. This is outside the academy, but it is within a capitalist structure. It is cultural consumption, rather than just the capitalist structure. They are ahead in the game, incredibly, because they are coming from how to constantly sell something. And they are not going to sell it to me. I mean, they are not going to sell me potato chips or any junk food anymore. But it's part of the cultural consumption. It is clothing or food and all of that. It stays in place due to that capitalist structure of consumption and marketing.

(Comment from the audience) Isn't it a sign of optimism that we have never had a woman president and now we might have one?

Norma: Not for me, but I'd rather not talk about that, because I don't want to go into American politics.

Romana: We have been circling two intriguing fields. The one is desire, the other one is the cultural memory of resistance. These two fields are also linked. Where we are missing the memory of resistance, we have a desire for it. This is relevant to my approach to academia. It is closely linked to my academic history. When I first enrolled in a European university at the start of the new millennium, a lot changed. The so-called "Bologna process" has altered European university structures and is functioning all over Europe nowadays. The way I tend to construct it today is that in my time as a university student, the system was much more open to the study process than it is now. You lived with the sensation that you were able to take the time you needed. You could venture into research at an early stage, into arts, into the interstices between the academy and community, into community. You could follow

---

2. Bernice Johnson Reagon, "Coalition Politics: Turning the Century" in *Home Girls: A Black Feminist Anthology*, ed. Barbara Smith (New Brunswick, NJ: Rutgers University Press, 2000) 343-355.

their connections and create your own artistic and intellectual interstices. There was a certain freedom of time and space. My parents's generation went to universities in the 1960s, and the 1970s, *y pues metieron caña,*[3] they fought for it. *Mi generación lo disfrutaba. Yo lo disfrutaba.* Until today, academia has ideally been a place of creation and knowledge exchange, an infinite space. This is what I was looking for, and what I meant to find, partly. I found thought; I found friendship, and so many interesting things. I found—and here we are again with a notion so central to your work, Norma—desire. Desire, as a cultural concept. My desire of finding this infinity. *¿Pero qué tipo de libertad nos puede dar* the academy? *¿Qué tipo de libertad nos está negando?* Nowadays, in my teaching in Europe, I see the effects of Bologna which established all over a "universal," entre comillas, European system of Bachelor and Master degrees, where students have to be very quick, technically quick. It seems that they have to produce and produce, that they lack the time to navigate between university and community, lack the time to go abroad without counting credits and knowing exactly when to return to the foreseen, lack the time to experience arts, and go to the theaters. They prefer to watch their movies at home, and I ask them: What about the experience of going to a critical movie theater, and having discussions there?—Or what you told me, María *(asking María Lugones)*, that you were invited to Germany—which I took very personally—and your audience did not discuss anything with you. They invite María Lugones to Germany and there is no discussion! What does this tell me about my generation, or about this younger in-between-generation that you were talking about, Norma? What does this all tell me about the cultural economies produced around consuming? So, the Academy is a very ambiguous space for me. Yes, patriarchy is in place, and I agree with the difficulty of recognizing it. It is so well disfrazado . . . I don't want to use the term "*disfrazado.*" It looks so pretty and colorful, but it's really patriarchy, right?

Marisa: Norma and Romana, you are pointing to the absence of history: the dehistorizing, dematerializing, and colonizing of history.

---

3. Radlwimmer explains: "The Bologna process is the restructuring of European higher education launched especially in the first decade of the new millennium. Advantages are, for instance, an easier transfer in studies and creditability of study results between the universities of different European countries. Study and internship programs abroad (such as ERASMUS) have become more easily accessible. Critiques of the reform of European higher education aim at the economization of education and the administrative predominance over critically open thinking structures."

Norma: I am not speaking of history as if I were a historian. I sort of always get in trouble with historians. I say, you are out of my field of discourse. If you are an academic historian, don't even try, okay? *(Laughs and laughter in the audience)*

Marisa: Norma, isn't your elaboration of *desire* a way to interrupt this marketing, and cultural consumption and composition? You are one of the few scholars who elaborate on an Epistemology of Desire. I don't know if I can make this equation: isn't the theory of practice related? The things you *do* with Lacan, Kristeva, and Derrida, you use them to establish some kind of mobile subject-in-process and then you say "good-bye." You stay with what you exactly need because you know them very well. In the logic of desire, there is also a current of Anzaldúa present. You sit Anzaldúa next to Derrida, Kristeva and Lacan. At the same time, your work is not appropriating that grammar, what you do is not European, *es muy . . . (searching for the right expression)*

Norma: *Chueco. (Laughter in the audience)*

Marisa: *Chueco*, yes. Well, Lacan is *muy europeo*.

Norma: Oh yes.

Marisa: And you— *¡Lo pones de cabeza!*

Norma: You want an example of the patriarchy in psychoanalysis: Lacan!

Romana: Abuelito Lacan.

Marisa: But you had to go through him to talk about desire, *y luego desecharlo*. I love the way you use patriarchy. You use and dispose of it. *Los usas y los despachas*. We want to pick on your epistemologies and ontologies to unpack *lo que dice Laura, que es la constante reinvención del patriarcado, del capitalismo, la estructura de la academia.*

Norma: Well, I was in conversation with Romana a couple of days ago, when I was going through this transformation *(points to her orange-purple hair. Laughter in the audience, comments from the audience: Looks lovely! . . . Yeah!).*

Romana: As you might notice, we went through this transformation together (points to her pink hair). *(More laughter in the audience)*

Norma: I don't know which hour of the day it was, but I do remember something that she provoked in me, what was true of me, and I said to her: When I was a girl, I wanted to be a reader and a writer. When I was in college, I wanted to be an intellectual, and the only way to be an intellectual in college was through the disciplinary method, of getting degrees. I couldn't say, at this point, that my professors were academic intellectuals. Not intellectuals. Some of the philosophers I pick on are intellectuals, and never had been academics. I pick them not because of that. It was kind of a being drawn to them. In retrospect, I discovered they were not academics. They never had an academic job. I discovered at an older age that the philosophers I was drawn to did not teach in the academy, or did not teach at all. Other than Derrida there was… *(audience starts giving names and Norma affirms them, comes up herself with new names)* Irigaray, Simone de Beauvoir, Hannah Arendt, Cixous, yes, Sartre. Deleuze and Guattari, who were not teaching in any academy. They were invited—that's another story. But it's not being a professor in the academy. I didn't realize that that was my problem *(laughs, and laughter in the audience)*. Academic departments were disciplined. They were disciplinary academics, men and women. From that point of view, women are embedded in the patriarchal structure. They can call it "gender" or whatever they want to call it, but they are in the patriarchal structure. Here is one way of seeing "gender" as part of the patriarchal structure. When I was in Berkeley in the late 80s, the women grabbed at "gender" really quickly, because it made them acceptable in the academy. The guys were not going to fight them by using the term "gender." That was OK with the guys—the male professors. Other than that, gender was not relevant. Keep gender out *(laughs)*. That was at least at the time I was there. Back to the story: my problem was that I did not understand that, quote-unquote, I liked the intellectual life. The life of thought. What Hanna Arendt called in one of her titles: *The Life of the Mind*. I think that is what Gloria, in her own register, liked. And she had no choice but to like it, from my point of view. My point of view on Gloria would be—in me, this might be a point except that she went ahead and did something with it—that she was all her life under the affliction of post-traumatic stress disorder. Post-traumatic stress disorder is a terrific emotional chaos for the person who suffers from that. Might get schizophrenic, but might play with it *(laughs)*. I am saying that to Josie, who is pretty well-versed in it. Her research, not herself. *(Laughter in the audience)*

Romana: In the next point of power we quote one of your works which reflects on desire and on the mind, which reflects on, as you call it, cognitive desire: "Chicana critics . . . work in an interstitial zone which is constantly on the move given its structural displacement within the Academy."[4] Would you like to comment on that, Norma?

Norma: I think we have been, since we started here, talking about cognitive desire, maybe even we started our conversation a few days ago. It´s constantly on the move because of its constant displacements, so you also have to keep moving. Barbara Smith said in *Bridge* about dealing with white women, having to always say "Not yet!" and throwing the stone even further. So we have become a politics of "not yet." You haven't got it—*yet.*

Romana: Okay, I am quoting Norma Alarcón here: "Clarify what the shift consists of and for whom."[5] What kind of interstitial zone, what kind of Nepantla are we talking about? What shifts are we talking about, and between which actors?

Norma: The interstitial zone—personally I think—has to be specified by each one of us, by each one of you. Of myself, I can try to specify my interstitial zone. That interstitial zone that we are working on, given the displacements, is the one that we are already on track on. In other words, our self-education, as well as our formal education, our own historical moment in time.

Marisa: Could you specify your own interstitial zone?

Norma: My own interstitial zone?—I had to get out of Berkeley *(laughs and laughter in the audience)* to get my next interstitial zone.

Romana: And what do pathologies have to do with the interstitial zone?

Norma: It has to do with embracing the pathologies whatever they are, even if you still don't know what they are. Embrace pathologies. Give up medication. If your son, for instance, doesn't want medication, I feel and understand deeply why. With medication, he doesn't feel himself. With medications, at some point, you don't know who you are. One cannot understand and hence embrace pathologies without getting rid of medication.

---

4. Norma Alarcón, "Cognitive Desires: An Allegory of/for Chicana Critics," *Chicana (W)rites on Word and Film,* ed. María Herrera-Sobek and Helena María Viramontes, Berkeley: Third Woman Press, 1995), 186.

5. Norma Alarcón,"The Theoretical Subject(s) of *This Bridge Called My Back* and Anglo-American Feminism."[1990], in *Feminist Theory Reader: Local and Global Perspective,* ed. Carole R. McCann and Seung-Kyung Kim (New York: Routledges, 2003). 404

Romana: Norma, Marisa, do you—and everybody else in this room—think pathologies are multilayered, coming in many forms? Medical issues, medications sold as healing; academic questions; institutions. Are these the pathologies? And in which sense are we talking about healing?

Marisa: In other words, what makes us sick?

Romana: The next point of power shows the Anzaldúan drawing of a hand. *La mano zurda* connects with the production of pathologies and healing. Would you like to talk about that, Marisa?

Marisa: Pathologies are the underlying theme of this conversation. Gloria Anzaldúa´s *trabajos*, all of them, relate to healing. Norma is a critic, an intellectual who gives us deep reading, and reading Anzaldúa through Norma is another world. On the point of power, you see the left hand, *la mano zurda*. Let's not forget what makes us sick, and not forget the position of academia turned upside down. This is what Anzaldúa wrote about the left hand: "To activate the conocimiento and communication we need the hand. The hand is an agent of action. It is not enough to speak and talk and write and communicate. It is not enough to see and recognize and know. We need to act upon what we know, to do something about it. The left hand has always been sinister and strange, associated with the female gender and creativity. But in union with the right, the left hand can do great things."[6] If you look at the point of power, at Anzaldúa´s drawing, what do you see in the hand?

(Audience answers) La lengua.

Marisa: *La lengua* is hanging, like *fotografías de la gente cansada*. The right to rest is present here. The shape of the tip of the tongue is accentuated, *también es muy común decir: lo tengo en la punta de la lengua*. At the tip of the tongue. The urgency to spill/spell things out. *Los ojos representan* an understanding. *Pero la lengua es el órgano privilegiado*, it is a symbol for breaking silence. And it is a split tongue.

Norma: I would like to remind us that the privileged sense in European philosophy is linked to the eyes. The visual is the privileged sense of European life.

(Comment from the audience) Is that the third eye?

---

6. Anzaldúa, Gloria, "The New Mestiza Nation," in *The Gloria Anzaldúa Reader*, ed. AnaLouise Keating (Durham, NC: Duke University Press, 2009), 212.

Norma: No, not the third eye.

Romana: It is the eye coming from above, seeing everything, but not being seen. What comes to mind here is one of the institutional pathologies. It has to do with the first point of power with academia turned upside down, and Norma and I have had conversations about this. I am referring to the constant construction of distance and superiority. That connects with the eyes you mentioned, Norma: the produced necessity to be up there, to be in control, to go against something, somebody, to watch from a distanced point of view. So in my perspective, a certain kind of distance is pathological.

Marisa: The left hand is important, what is coming from the left?

Romana: Yes, that's right, and that is the healing: the left hand as an option for healing. Healing comes through: it means critical intimacy. As Anzaldúa says, not to be detached. Against pathologies, the left hand engages in a process of healing the prevailing visions of distance.

Marisa: *La mano zurda inclina,* inclines academia. One of the healing operations could be theorizing from the flesh, activating knowledge, and constructing the political structures of experience. In Nepantla classrooms we are very interested in inclining Academic, and activating it. Classrooms are supplied with all these texts and all these ways of distancing. But there is also an expected distancing from the academic and from disciplinary thought, in a way of tending to understand things—not yet spelled out—that is at the tip of our tongues. That tip in so many tongues shows—as Norma already pointed brilliantly out—that it already got started. *Eso de poner la academia y el mundo de cabeza* started when people of color and women-of-color walked into the academy. It already got started. Norma, you were teaching for so many years.

Norma: My whole life.

Marisa: The classroom has been a space for you, an interval. Did you feel the magic of your classroom? But *magic* sounds like a soft word: the *power* of your classroom. As students, we were seduced by your power. You did an incredible job in constructing and deconstructing minds, bodies and desires. Anzaldúa talks about public arts, inner works, *compartir*... *La mano zurda* is also the hand that can go into classrooms. Norma, what was your experience?

Norma: Well, one thing I have to say, especially to younger people, is that I came into a field that was under construction and invention. Two fields really: "Ethnic Studies" and "Women Studies" in general. They were under construction. Even though my formal course work was in the Spanish Department at Indiana University. That was my formal "education." But I was working and playing with two fields that were under construction. That gave me a freedom that others do not have, or cannot have, or have not had. Our fight was to have—a territory under construction *(laughs)*. That was our fight. But even that territory for some of you younger people is already being under construction, and disciplined, if you will. And you pay for it if you want to get out of those tracks. So, I was fortunate in that sense. Especially as someone who wanted to be an intellectual, an academic philosopher, a literary critic, whatever it was. I had a mentor who was very supportive of whatever it was because I was helping him with that construction. I was his graduate student and he was a professor, but I was helping him with the construction. He had things of his own. He didn't care what I did as long as I was building, so to speak, using this metaphor. I think deconstructing and constructing will continue to be a constant struggle, but it may feel less of a struggle if you historicize that period of time. Take civil rights in the US context. If you historicize that period into the 21st century, you can also visualize how your struggle has changed. It is not the same as it was in the 70s—for me—or late 60s. It would not be the same anymore. Even the language of the struggle would have changed. Keep in mind that it will continue to be a struggle, because the academy continues to be, and will continue to be, a patriarchal structure. Because it is the easiest thing it can be. It's its tradition.

Romana: And a colonial structure.

Norma: Yes. And it goes hand in hand with capitalism.

Romana: It all goes together: the patriarchal structure, the colonial structure, the heterosexist structure.

Norma: The political economy, with the academy thrown in to validate it. The academy validates the political economy. Maybe not the Philosophy Department in itself, but parts of the academy, too, in the way the Philosophy Department does help to maintain the tradition and to only push it just a little bit: guys that manifest on the one hand novelty and on the other the traditional patriarchal philosophy.

Romana: From the level of assistant professors, we tend to think that things are getting easier when ascending the hierarchy of the academy, but that's not necessarily the case. Binaries and hierarchies are not easy. Those who live a culture of resistance and maintain its memory will be regarded as a non-existing place in the traditional academy. Right now, I am in a beautiful situation to be in a place where I feel encouraged to construct, so in a certain sense what you just said, Norma, echoed in me. Academic careers are at times imagined as linear processes, you go and go and all of a sudden you "have" all the power. But this is really very relative. And also, do we want to be in and construct these imagined places where "all power" is? I don't think so, at least I would rather not.

Marisa: Sonia wants to say something.

Sonia Saldívar-Hull: When we do, we construct something outside of that condition you described. We have been trying to build a Women's Studies Department here at the University of Texas, San Antonio. It is a very liberating project in some ways. But I am contracted as an English professor. When the women's studies working group included questions of race and class next to the masculine and feminine, we were constructing something new. By now we exist as a new women-of-color decolonial women's studies program, a victory indeed, but we have no money. We pay the costs with our invisible labor. It's heteropatriarchal capitalism. There is a price to pay: overwork, depression, PTSD and so on.

Marisa: That's pointing to the next point of power, where we talk with Anzaldúa about the psychopathies of our creative life. Which aspects of your life do you exclude or marginalize? Which power struggles do you engage in? What are you paying for? From here, we do question pathologies. We engage in other questions, but all of a sudden pathologies pop up again. It is like an iceberg. What makes us sick? But I also wanted to hear the audience—Laura, Sonia—about what Norma said and about life in the classroom in the many years of experience you have.

Romana: So many voices present... *las y los estudiantes aquí,* what do you think?

Marisa: Irene, Sara, Elvia, and María, we heard already what you said this morning in your keynote.

Laura Pérez: Irene and I were walking over with a young student who is now a healer in Berkeley. And we were talking about healing and how we need it, and how Berkeley needs it, and how Ethnic Studies needs it. The note that we ended on was on what happens in the classrooms. The student was complimenting the space she has had, the space Irene is creating. I don't know about others, but I do know that a lot of my energy in creativity has gone into rethinking the space of the classroom. I had to give myself a lot of permission. It's been an act of practice. It's been the creation and inhabitation of, in Norma's words, an interstitial space. To be able to think and enact a gap where we can acknowledge and provide the language for what *we* think is real, of what we think is interesting. All of us, including the faculty, experience this continual denial; the violence of continual appropriation and public degradation of the work. I find it really difficult to imagine a rich space, where all we do is lecture. I personally have always found this really difficult to take, I get very ADHD. I also think there is something about the politics of how we teach and how it is that we treat the other: whether we are treating them as a receptacle, or whether we treat ourselves as the ones who want to perform as the ones in power. For me, it has been very healing to teach another point of view.

Josie Méndez-Negrete: I am having a conversation with myself. It begins with notions of pathologies of whatever type. The reason for that is, as a sociologist I always see it as a binary that locks you into a structural argument whereby the pathologies become individual practices, possessions, and emotions. In reality, we need to look at the structure or the systemic quality. That is, how to be able to understand how in the academy we can make a difference and direct people to take ownership of the knowledge they engage with. The presupposition for me always is that students bring knowledge into my classroom and that it increases the knowledge base for all of us—especially for me, because I may be able to unpack things that they have not yet seen, because they have not done what Norma did, to step outside and to see how the structure is limiting. The way I see it is that this has been a good place for us because Norma is here.

Marisa: Norma, a question that is at the tip of my tongue: What kind of power struggles did you engage with, were you *arrasada por ellas*?

Norma: Well... *(Laughter in the audience)* Let's see. My colleagues thought I was Eurocentric, that I was using European texts. Not all my texts were European. Okay, here is the contradiction, really: just because we want to undo patriarchy doesn't mean we want to throw all of it out.

Marisa: What do we want to keep?

Norma: For myself, I thought I had to learn a sense of order that I could then throw out. Aristotle is all about methodology and method. So how do you throw it out? You can't throw out what you don't know. What is dysfunctional about patriarchy that I would throw out? We can't get away from knowing something about patriarchy, because we are imprinted from the time we are born. Mom and Dad do it all. No matter how hard they try, there is also the television and other media, doing it. The question is, how do you enable someone to throw it out? How can a person enable herself to throw it out?

Sonia: I think you, Norma, and others have enabled some of us to throw it out. I don't need to go to Aristotle to engagee a methodology. Sara teaches our Methodology courses. Where do you go?

Sara Ramírez: I go to Anzaldúa. The research class is a space where I "decolonize" the classroom space. We are no longer using Eurocentric conceptualizations of methodology, epistemology, and ontology, which tell us who is human and what knowledge can be valued. So, I do ask students, for instance, at the very beginning of the class: Can plants tell you their properties? And they laugh: of course, plants don't talk! Then eventually we get into ontology and epistemology, which allow them to understand the different values we assign to what we believe to be living and non-living. And at the very end of class they understand. "Oh, plants can speak to us. Alright, we have to consider non-Eurocentric epistemologies." I go to Anzaldúa, to Shawn Wilson, another indigenous scholar, Linda T. Smith, and scholars who have been influenced by others, like Aristotle. There is a history behind our methodology. In my dissertation, I consult European philosophers. I bring them together. But I sometimes question why I have to do that.

Norma: When I learn about Buddhism, I feel a deep existentialism of inner being. But I also like to read existentialism as the Europeans do it. When a speaker conjugates Buddhist philosophy and existentialist philosophy, I am ecstatic. I am happy. I like conjugations. It could be a generational thing. I grew up adoring some philosophers, and I am not going to give them up for Gloria.

Laura: Not even did Gloria herself.

Norma: She didn't. I went into Kierkegaard in her archives, and I said, "Ha, so you have been reading Kierkegaard!"

Josie: She read Sartre. She read a lot, to understand them and refute them, and to provide an alternative.

Norma: She is reading Kierkegaard, and she is trying to understand herself. But anyway, that's what I mean by— No, I don't know what I mean about whatever. I am just telling you what gives me pleasure.

Sonia: Pleasure?

Marisa: What gives you pleasure, Sonia?

Sonia: Rejecting the patriarchs. See, I am feeling ecstatic right now *(Laughs, and laughter in the audience)*.

Norma: I do reject patriarchy's structures. But I still like the male body. Sorry. *(Laughs and laughter in the audience)* The young one. *(Laughs, more laughter in the audience)*

Laura: I think that's very classic, like in the classical world. *(Laughter in the audience)*

Norma: *(laughs)* Very Greek! *(Laughter in the audience)*

María Lugones: The old women in the codices were all into bodies, the young ones.

(Comments and laughter from the audience)

Norma: Oh, I haven't seen that! . . . Which codices?

María: In these long poems that the Europeans translated. . .

Norma: In the Aztec codices?

María: Yes. I also wanted to say that I like it if students show a sense of history, a sense that is not necessarily activated and that has to do with society. Right now, we have the Black Lives Matter movement. There is a sense of solidarity. In history, we decided to have women of color. As we are doing that, we are connecting directly to the classroom. The classroom is not just in there, in the edifices, it is also out there, it is where we are thinking, in the rebellion against the discourse, pushing against the disciplines. I was feeling small.

Norma: Why small?

María: The academy has always made me feel small.

Marisa: We relate to that.

Laura: I just want to say something really quickly. I want to acknowledge and emphasize one of the things you said, Norma. It is also about you, too, María. I think historically, and in the flesh, it is incredibly important to be women thinkers. Women thinkers, everywhere I have looked, have always existed, in different cultures, in different times. And it is incredibly difficult to be that. Norma made a distinction between what it means to be an academic. Would an academic's work be called "intellectual"? I really appreciate the distinction you have made. I think what it means to be an intellectual is something very creative, something very individual, without being individualist. It has to do with what is our destiny, with what is our path.

María: As I engage with people in the disciplinary construction, *es como una cosa que se te mete. Son bichos...*

Norma: What I learned in the struggle, being in Berkeley, was the rhetoric of a person in the disciplines. So I did. I *did* do that. But I did not *do* it in my work. But I had to because you are listening to your overwhelmingly powerful colleagues. I am not talking about Ethnic Studies anymore either, although that was another vocabulary, oh my god. Anyway! *(Laughs)* So it was in the interstices of the powerful academy and Ethnic Studies, which had its own power. Those interstices: that would be my disciplinary location of a certain period of my life. That interstice. Both Ethnic Studies and the academy make you feel small, inconsequential, and so on and so forth. But one of my methodological problems has been anger and rage.

Marisa: One of mine also.

Norma: I think if you possess those things, perhaps you want to let them go onto your colleagues, so to speak, or you want to channel them into your work. And I can tell you that my work has been channeled by rage and anger. I recommend them if you know how to control them.

Sara: Audre Audre Lorde discusses rage and anger in her essay, "The Uses of Anger: Women Responding to Racism" in *Sister Outsider*.[7]

Marisa: Right... Now, Norma, how do you translate that anger and rage?

Norma: The strategy is to control it. It is like having a rope. *Una reata*, in Spanish. It can go out of control. And that's okay when you are being creative at the desk. Like Gloria talked about it, with the hand, the creativity of the intellectual life. But you know, Laura Pérez comes to my door and I have to tell her: "Hey, Manita. Let's have *un calmante*, first, before we talk." *(Laughs and laughter from the audience)* Because I am in a rage right now.—And then you acknowledge that you are in a rage. But you are not afraid of it, and it's all yours. See, I am not trying to be a docent in rage. I am saying: I already had it. I am asking you: do you already have it? And what are you gonna do with it? And this is what I would say to you, María. And this is a way not to feel small.

María: No. Small also in the sense of how you were thinking about it.

Norma: Oh! Well, this is all rage theory. *(Laughs, and laughter in the audience)*

María: In my case I think going with people to build spaces even if they don't last very long. My rage goes, in them. And it makes me happier.

Norma: Happier?

María: Yes, happier.

Norma: Well, it's intellectual pleasure. It is also a fulfilment of desire. Not sex, directly.

Sonia: But supposed to be.

Marisa: Desire under construction...

---

7. Audre Lorde, "The Uses of Anger: Women Responding to Racism," in *Sister Outsider: Essays and Speeches* (Berkeley: Crossing Press, 2007).

Romana: In Norma's words, to conjugate pleasure, anger, and power, inside and outside the classroom.

Sara: Well, on *that* note... *(Laughter in the audience)* We actually ran out of time. Thank you so much for this great discussion.

BIBLIOGRAPHY

Alarcón, Norma. "Cognitive Desires: An Allegory of/for Chicana Critics." In *Chicana (W)rites on Word and Film,* edited by María Herrera-Sobek and Helena María Viramontes, 185-200. Bereley: Third Woman Press, 1995.

Alarcón, Norma. "The Theoretical Subject(s) of This Bridge Called My Back and Anglo-American Feminism." [1990] In *Feminist Theory Reader: Local and Global Perspective,* edited by Carole R. McCann and Seung-Kyung Kim, 404-414. New York: Routlege.2003.

Anzaldúa, Gloria. "The New Mestiza Nation." In The Gloria Anzaldúa Reader, edited by AnaLouise Keating, 203-216. Durham, NC: Duke UP, 2009.

Lorde, Audre. "The Uses of Anger: Women Responding to Racism" In *Sister Outsider: Essays and Speeches.* Berkeley: Crossing Press, 2007.

Reagon, Bernice Johnson. "Coalition Politics: Turning the Century." In *Home Girls: A Black Feminist Anthology,* edited by Barbara Smith, 343-355. New Brunswick, NJ: Rutgers University Press, 2000..

CONJUGATIONS

THE INSURRECTION OF SUBJUGATED KNOWLEDGES AND
EXCLUSIONARY PRACTICES[1]

→ ←

Alienated from her mother culture, alien in the dominant culture, the woman of color does not feel safe within the inner life of her Self. Petrified *she can't respond her face caught between los intersticios, the spaces between the different worlds she inhabits.*

Gloria E. Anzaldúa, *This Bridge We Call Home: Radical Visions for Transformation*

We cut our teeth in anger.

Audre Lorde, "The Uses of Anger: Women Responding to Racism"

THE TEXT THAT FOLLOWS is an abbreviated memoir of my collision course with the University of California, Berkeley (UCB), the Department of Ethnic Studies (ES), and other departments. I have been, to say the least, an idealist Chican@ feminist who happened to be the only one in the whole institution for the first decade of my tenure there. Being the only one may not be healthy, especially for a beginner in the academy, because it invisibly begins to isolate one when sympathetic and understanding mentors to lend support do not exist in the institution.

Indeed, I question whether feminism can be defined without saying that it harbors an idealist political philosophy that calls for a thorough transformation of our society, that seeks to deconstruct and reconstruct the world so that it is habitable for girls, women, and our queer futurity—to cite part of the title of José Muñoz's book. I have found that my feminist idealism will not yield to pragmatism because it feels like giving up on the future we want to have and in which we want to live. Thus, to Freud's confusion on what do women want, I would say we want to dismantle a racist and misogynist heteronormative patriarchy

---

1. *Editors' Note:* This essay was first published in *Chicana/Latina Studies*, no. 2 (2014): 201-224.

that sucks the life out of women and some men from birth. The demands of my Chican@ feminist idealism are in a constant struggle with pragmatism.

For this brief memoir I selected some recollections of what I deemed to be key situations and incidents of cumulative frustrations, tensions, and contradictions which reveal the violence of the daily grind that queer and feminist women of color may endure in the context of a hegemonic white heteronormative patriarchal research institution. I was a participant-observer of my own work-life and I gather here some aspects of the structural logic and players of the atmosphere into which I was thrown. In providing an assessment of situations and incidents experienced, I make commentaries and may supply interpretations that spatio-temporal distance allows. What I did not fully recognize at the time was that I was actually working against the grain of the institution; in fact, in the end, I did recognize it, however it was too late to do me any good. The major question for me, then, becomes what is the good to understand and know, *a priori*, one is a personification of working against the grain. How does understanding and knowing help anyone of us to protect ourselves from the cumulative violent effects of the daily grind so as to prevent our own exhaustion and collapse?

The Domestication of the Insurrection of Subjugated Knowledges

I CAME OF AGE in the tumultuous 1960s and early 1970s. I was deeply influenced by the multitudinous activities and rhetorics of those times. These included queer and feminist women of color in the United States as well as non-hegemonic feminists of color all over the world. Moreover, there was a spectacular array of ethno-race movements, anti-colonialist movements in the third world, hegemonic white feminisms, and hegemonic white-male left antiwar movements. The latter two mostly came from the Anglo-American middle-classes. In brief, a historical and sociopolitical consciousness awakened. At the time I perceived this potential sociopolitical collectivity as sectors and fragments of the Anglo-American nation-state, some of which were in solidarity with planetary anticolonial movements, and all of which would in time interconnect and form alliances and maybe even create some coherence because they were all written on pages of dissent from, and revolt against, the ruling classes. Or thus it was the way I read so at the time! I was in error, of course, to read them in this manner, for I had not entered into my reading the calculus that each sector had a different frame of intelligibility—which to our day has not been overcome, or so it seems to me. In a sense, even today, I hope for a frame of intelligibility that can give form to a sociopolitical collectivity that together could transform our current state of affairs. Dreamers have a hard time dying, as dreamers anyway.

Clearly, this was an idealistic perception, perhaps enabled by my immigrant status and relative isolation in Bloomington, Indiana, where these radicals sometimes stopped by to visit on their way from west to east or vice versa. Our own activist and rhetorical hub was small in comparison and went largely unnoticed, though not without some local accomplishments. I have come to think that this relative isolation nurtured an idealistic euphoria that carried me into the halls of academe, and, in time and almost overnight, I was demographically transferred from being a woman with unskilled working-class roots of Mexican descent to a woman of Mexican descent in the pigeon hole identification of middle-class, as my income increased from that of an answering-service telephone operator (remember Lily Tomlin). I was the first in my family, and even among acquaintances, to go to college.

The dust in my *huaraches* would not be so easily wiped out, however, just because of a raise in wages. One remains a commodity on a different level—exchange value level. One may leave the cadres of surplus/use labor for the cadres of unrepresentable exchange value labor in the white academy that ends up as a footnote that serves the needs of the preferably white and/or assimilated expert. In fact, I had first found out about us of Mexican descent in the library catalogue at Indiana University in the late 1960s. We existed in print in the bib and I ask myself, Are we headed in a similar direction today, albeit, digitalized? After all, it is the more high-class commoditized and assimilated experts that get to speak their expertise in the academy or to the viewing public on corporate media.

When I arrived at the University of California, Berkeley, in the fall of 1987, to undertake my new job in the Department of Ethnic/Chican@ Studies, I was terribly excited by the prospect of working at a university, which had undergone a student insurrection that had managed to establish a department in the flagship campus of the University of California system. I believed that we were part, along with many third world others, of what Foucault had referred to as "The insurrection of subjugated knowledges."[2] In fact, in my job talk on Chican@ literature for the department, I had foregrounded that statement and further suggested that that statement referred to all of us across all disciplines in the department who were affecting a transformation in the production of knowledge that would reach all disciplines in the humanities and social sciences. After all, these disciplines were being challenged in the Chican@ print culture of 1960s-1980s. Hardly! What was actually afoot in these divisions was a process of liberal subsumption a la capitalist methodologies of domestication, as well as a dematerialized appropriation, when suitable to dominant paradigms of the local sense of legitimized theory and scientificity. Though we did change as a people in general, what stayed the same was the elite ruling structure of the academy and its (neo)liberal adept and subtle practices of exclusion, albeit, with tokens of domesticated inclusion! The university may well have imagined that insofar as they had responded to the students' insurrection over the exclusionary practices of access to the academy, as a progressive institution, they had done their duty and had complied with a long-neglected moral obligation. That is, the days of the white man's burden were over.

As if that was not enough, I was hired to teach Chican@ literature in a department fully dominated by patriarchal social scientists and historians for whom literature was a secondary or even tertiary (after education) player in what I mistakenly had taken for an insurrection. That is to say, that literature did not carry much value. The insurrection was dead, a death enforced by the white academy's maneuvering of rules, protocols, and policy. And, as my medical doctor said to me ten years after a critical comment I made about the university, "Be careful what you say, you know those men in suits." He did not mention those women in fashionable suits. By this time, however, this same doctor had concocted, with the approval of his consulting psychiatrist, a cocktail

---

2. Michel Foucault speaks of "the insurrection of subjugated knowledges" in his book *Power/Knowledge: Selected Interviews and Other Writings 1972-1977*, ed. Colin Gordon (New York: Vintage, 1980), 81. He speaks of suppressed knowledge, "those blocks of historical knowledge which were present but disguised within the body of functionalist and systematising (sic) theory. . .a whole set of knowledges that have been disqualified as inadequate... naïve knowledges, located low down on the hierarchy, beneath the required level of cognition or scientificity" (82). That is, "discontinuous, disqualified, illegitimate knowledges against the claims of a unitary body of theory" (83). His position, however, is stated in the context of Eurocentric hegemonic production of knowledge, which he is critiquing and, in effect, denouncing. I have re-situated his claim in my own context of Anglo-Eurocentric hegemonic production of knowledge and denouncing its marginalization of our work both as queer and feminist women of color, as well as that of people of color in general.

of psychotropics so that I could keep working with all of those suits! But, I am getting ahead of the story.

Cumulative Double-Binds and Piquetitos

AT FIRST, I WAS a bit anxious because I had been a second-choice hire in the Chicano Studies program of the Department of Ethnic Studies, which housed us, Native Americans, and Asian Americans. I quickly put this concern behind me since I was quite happy to get out of the Midwest. I could now avoid an unsavory career path in an intolerable Spanish department that was rife with *burguesismo*, offered a strictly monolingual curriculum, and was dominated by Anglos. My Chican@ Studies expertise had been developed through a praxis of formulating literary courses in the newly founded program of Chicano-Riqueño Studies by my wonderful graduate school mentor Luis Dávila, a Chicano from the San Antonio, Texas—Westside! During the 1960s and 1970s many of us were acquiring our expertise in Chican@ Studies through praxis and praxis theory with explicit or implicit historical materialist perspective. Indeed, it had been through an insurrectional print culture that a renaissance literary field had been emerging, as well as for other disciplinary venues, and it was up to us to affirm our academic legitimacy. However, from the point of view of many an institution—including University of California, Berkeley—legitimacy was constantly questioned by the hegemonic disciplines, some of whose pedigrees went back to the beginning of the twentieth century. Also by the late 1970s the right-wing think-tank industry had begun to bloom. Moreover, I thought that I had found a home for Third Woman Press (1979-2004) other than my own house. In fact, I had not.

The most important aspect of my new job on the margins of long-standing literary disciplines—English and Spanish—were my classes in Chican@ literature and comparative women of color literatures. This provided me with a center that straddled the other two major literary fields. Not only did it provide a center but also creative spaces for the study and analysis of new insurrectional voices. I was told by an English Department professor of the beloved left that I could not teach my classes in his department the way I did in Ethnic Studies. It took a while to discover that my insurrectionary frame of intelligibility would not be welcome. However, my course offerings opened the door for affiliation with Women's Studies, which changed its name to Gender and Women's Studies, when, as it were, the theoretical concept of "gender" arrived, displacing "women and experience" and muting feminist expression, routing the notion of "the personal is political" which had been a mainstay of earlier feminist thought. That is, postfeminism had arrived!

On the other hand, the atmosphere of the Ethnic Studies Department was one of constant tensions that were difficult to understand for a newcomer who was unaware of, at a minimum, the previous ten years of the faculty's forms of accommodation to each other and the university. Also, the linkage to African American Studies was tenuous. African American Studies had been successful in getting a department of their own and separated from the others in the mid-1970s. And, all of the programs in Ethnic Studies wanted a department of their own—a form of self-determination. My question then, and even now, was why was there no sense of collectivity? Were we not all in the same bargain basement of the grand elite Department Store? It is quite apparent now that I needed a mentor, not to explain our location in the basement, but to explain the tensions among the basement players. However, no such mentor was forthcoming in the department, and I mostly had to live out those tensions in silence. There was very little point in speaking since people would look at me and continue as if I had said nothing. As I learned much later, the mission of the founding players in the Ethnic Studies Department was to not only have a department of one's own but also a college of one's own. Ironically, these patriarchal players were as idealistic as I was; however, we were out of sync.

The department's code of honor was one of team-player consensus. That meant that despite the vibrant tensions, the faculty and staff had to hold together in consensus with whatever strategy of resistance was developed against the administration. However, the issue-strategies were developed outside of discussion and debate. In a sense, one was expected to be compliant, and to me it soon became clear that we were in a raced-class war of positions and indeed, within the department, race and class dominated the curriculum as concepts of choice. That is to say, a heteronormative patriarchy of color emerged against a white supremacist heteronormative patriarchy that is also fond of team players, too. In a sense, the classroom was the only space for self-expression for me where my own voice could be mediated by and through the discussion of texts by queer and feminist women of color. In that pedagogical setting it was possible to address race, class, gender, and sexuality as interconnected and fused multiple modes of experience which could be articulated freely. A factor which put the exclusivity of race and class in question and exposed it as a structured heteronormative patriarchal stranglehold in the university as a whole.

Many of the tensions among the programs and faculty were a result of competition for adequate funding, not just for the department as a whole but between the programs themselves. This form of competition is not necessarily unusual in the elite Department Store, for they too had to compete for funding and there was resentment about losing some of the wealth to Ethnic Studies and African American Studies. The Department Store felt entitled on the grounds of their long-standing legitimacy as disciplines which waged their own competitive lobbying and varied depending on their own status in relation to the most legitimated core of all—mirror, mirror on the wall, who is the fairest one of all? I dare say that in the pecking order of legitimacy both Anglo Americanists and Latin Americanists were second-class citizens, though in relation to us they did not see themselves that way. We, on the other hand, were travelling third class or worse. The resentment may have been attenuated among some through the liberal ideology of progress which, in my view, comprised the academic supportive left. We were the poor relations, or as we say in Spanish, *los arrimados y arrimadas*, which actually prompted the student hunger strike of 1999 in which I took part—students camping out on the lawns of California Hall at the University of California, Berkeley (UCB) administration building. Little did I know that I would be typed a troublemaker among administrators with which Ethnic Studies concurred at some point. All along, however, all of us had been profiled by the administration, a symbolic demographic captivity, sui generis.

However, and perhaps even more alarming to me, there were tensions among the cadre of faculty of color as to which program had the more legitimate roots of oppression and capitalist exploitation—another form of competition—in the course of genocide, slavery, and dehumanization during colonization and the creation of the Anglo-American nation-state. As far as I can tell these tensions remain in the political theater of our times, mediated by ideologies of pluralism and somewhat supplanted by a dematerialized multiculturalism, diversity, and postracialism. To add to these tensions, there was competition as to which program was more academically worthy. This valuation in particular was made known to me by a member of the faculty who told me not long after hire that the Chicano Studies program was the weakest academic program in the department, and perhaps I could help change that. Who needs mentors like this one? I got no explanation for the remark in passing. Why me? I had scarcely published anything and the short essay published in *This Bridge Called My Back* had been called "shrill" and "too" militant—read "feminist"—by my former employer.

A few years later I was told by a sympathetic left white woman that I and a graduate student of the time had been sowing confusion among the faculty about our sexuality, making them think we were lesbians. What faculty was getting confused, where did the confusion come from? How? And why did it matter so much? Was it that intellectual activist feminism was read as de facto lesbianism? The latter had been a tactic of many a patriarchal sociopolitical movement in order to intimidate the women around it. It is a tactic that has survived to our times and makes heteronormative-oriented women fear feminism. Even recently I heard it from an old guard leftist white man in San Antonio when I responded to a question about Third Woman Press. He asked, "Are you one of those angry lesbians?" "Are you homophobic?" I asked, which silenced him momentarily. In the department, moreover, a male colleague wondered out loud to me how he was going to use my piece in the game. At the time, the contextual implication was that of a piece on a chess board, which in itself is insulting. I learned in time that he was a master of sexual innuendo as he liberally dispensed with double entendres and ambiguity, or as we might say otherwise, Mexican-style—*indirectas*. Weapons of the weak? Many a lesbian or hetero feminist student was brought to tears by this tactic of humiliation which, of course, I got to hear about. A full professor teaching a course in pedagogy devoted class time to a critique of women's bodies when they made presentations. This finally spilled out into formal complaints to the chair. I advocated for his removal from class and tried to generate a women's caucus in Ethnic Studies, but my fellow women faculty were reluctant and voted no with their feet. Similarly, another student was told by another male faculty after stating ideas for a dissertation, "And who is going to read you? Another angry Chicana?"

Repeated trivialization and intimidation were continuous tactics of oppression for both the students and the faculty who lent support. Within the department, there were queer and feminist women of color who were screamed at and shut down for questioning male professors on the exclusive race and class conceptualization of history and society in their courses. What about gender and sexuality? They are irrelevant. I found that most of the orthodox Marxists in California agreed. Given that consensus, as such, these professors felt emboldened to strike us down verbally. One of the most stunning declarations of the irrelevancy of women to the methodological frame of intelligibility regarding socioeconomic issues occurred during my second year at UCB. I attended a lecture on urban gangs. When the Latino professor finished his presentation on the social formation and economy of gangs, I asked how the young women involved with gangs figured into his model. The professor replied without preamble that they did not because they were parasites in the gang economy. In effect, my question was as irrelevant as the young women. I felt shut down by his disrespect. I sensed contempt in his nonchalant demeanor. No one in the room spoke out further. In Southern California, there was a joker, who can also be contemptuous, who was given to refer publicly to the cluster of Chicana professors in Northern California campuses as "*las brujas del norte.*" Obviously, I was one of them. Can't you take a joke? It occurs to me that the founding of Mujeres Activas en Letras y Cambio Social (MALCS) in the mid-1980s may have prompted such disrespectful and injurious name-calling.

The ideologies of raced heteronormativity in these patriarchally-structured and organized universities, for me, allows these baiting attitudes meant to trivialize, put us down, intimidate and/or provoke us into a combative response or put us on the defensive with a call not to get emotional—at which point you want to punch them. Women may be seen always already as too emotional—no, the young women are not parasites, no we are not witches, yes, feminism is relevant to the sociopolitical and economic struggle. We may not have the critical tools or knowledge other than anger at our command to expose the misogynist frame of intelligibility and referents. Often, we may not be familiar with their framing. It is outside our field and often difficult to deconstruct. These Latinos/Chicanos were not alone with the attitude toward the courageous women who dared to be feminist or make reference to feminism. Several years later I encountered this attitude from prominent Latin Americanists. One thought that the Ejército Zapatista de Liberación Nacional (EZLN) women's feminist laws, which comprised a demand for freedom to make choices about their lives, were irrelevant; another was reported by a solid source to have been telling audiences in Latin America that feminism was irrelevant. Thusly colonized, oppressed, and exploited indigenous women and intellectual feminist women from the bourgeoisie were being told that they were irrelevant and to conform to the extant patriarchal paradigm.

Then, there is the native informant syndrome where the colonizer gets to play anthropologist and it comes from all directions. I call it a native informant approach to conversation because we may be treated as if it was our responsibility to educate the questioner about ourselves and our culture. I am not speaking here of students in the classroom but of faculty who want to get some information on the run. There is no reciprocity and no dialogue. After the American Cultures Center was formed, some of us in Ethnic Studies were invited to form a panel and make presentations on our ethnic research and identity—a classic case of interpellation to assume our proper positions. When I got to the door I saw that the majority were white men and women. Were these the ones who had been for or against the Center? A bit of both? Through the center we were now officially included—in a manner of speaking—in the undergraduate curriculum of American, dematerialized multicultural/pluralist style. In the face of those people in suits I felt like I was part of a dog and pony show; little did I know that there would be many more times for me—tokenization. I changed my mind about my presentation and on the spur of the moment decided to do a philosophical meditation on the concept of identity. I was a nervous wreck and I could not even remember what I said. My intention was to bore them with utterances with which they might already be familiar. From then on, unless it was a specifically Chican@ conference, though I accepted invitations to be part of dog and pony shows, I made sure that my presentation took a feminist women of color critico-theoretical perspective—some Chican@ colleagues were known to say that my work was "blather/babble." The critico-theoretical perspective was very disappointing to a white woman faculty at another elite institution, who wanted the facts and not the theory. I referred her to a vast bibliography on the subject. What is this? I can read your theory and you cannot read mine?

From my very first graduate seminar in Ethnic Studies (ES) I became controversial. I put two volumes of readings arranged in constellations that included the critical research of both men and women of color, as well as pertinent theoretical critiques by U.S. critics and Eurocentric ones. One of my goals was to generate dialogue and debate points of connections or disconnections in the readings. I was eager to go through the course myself, since this was my first seminar and I was experimenting. I wanted to see if it was possible to constellate different "frames of intelligibility" such that there might be interconnections to discover and simultaneously localize and explain the frames. From my point of view the seminar went well since at a minimum lively debate and dialogue took place, as well as some visceral protests about having to read this or that. On the other hand, some students volunteered points of view on why this or that might be important. My two volumes of readings must have circulated among the faculty because one fine morning I discovered an op-column in my mailbox. An orthodox Marxist was waxing eloquent about the perils of poststructuralism—rebranded as postmodernism for Anglo-American localized reproduction and consumption—some of which I had included in the readers. A warning that I be cognizant of the perils? Was I out of bounds? Regardless, I continued my seminars in this style throughout the years. I guess I never presented enough textual or verbal evidence that I was a historical materialist. Since the anti-Eurocentric perspective was general in the department, perhaps using some Eurocentric, albeit selected, poststructuralist work was held against me. It turned out to be that it would always be so. I almost had a mutiny in a seminar. Fortunately, it was quelled by discussion and debate.

What I call the anti-essentialist movement that actually displaced the earlier feminist debate on the dichotomous nature-culture binary hit the academic airwaves by the end of the 1980s and continued with a strong theoretical force of gender constructionism. Despite its good intentions, motivations, and insights, this movement emerged from a cadre of younger white privileged women whose major focus was to challenge the university's heteronormative patriarchal apparatus of symbolic power. However, it subtextually acquired a white-raced-class postfeminist position that excluded and shut down the voices of queer and feminist women of color, as well as some men of color who could not address their historical experiences of colonizing oppression and exploitation without being charged with essentializing. Even readings included in my seminar packets were now taboo on the basis of essentialism as the anti-essentialist movement reached an academic firestorm and constructed its own exclusionary firewall. Indeed, oppression and exploitation were a construction, but such a construction was not addressed as the result of a racist and misogynist capitalist colonization of the insurrectionary speaking subject—one of which were queer and feminist women of color. Ironically, the very challenge to the legacy of dead white men (as a feminist on campus called them) did not take into account that the heirs of the legacy were in the strongly structured power of the university itself and it was not merely symbolic. It was during this period that Barbara Christian published her essay, "The Race for Theory."[3] When I brought it to the reading circle of Latin Americanists that had invited me to join them, the question was "So what's the point?" One's exchange value reaches a limit and it may well constitute what Chela Sandoval calls the apartheid of theoretical domains in her

---

3. Barbara Christian, "The Race for Theory," *Cultural Critique*, no. 6 (1987): 51–63.

book, *Methodology of the Oppressed*.⁴ When does one know that one's exchange value has reached its limit? That is my question to all of us queer and feminist women of color.

I was living through intensely irritating and anger-producing double-binds and paradoxes. The academic success of privileged white women enabled the political economy of the heirs of dead white men to keep on with its institutionalized racism and diverting our attention with postfeminist tokenizations. In a sense, then, in general, Ethnic Studies became even more inappropriate as the explicit or implicit historical materialism was tarred with the reductionist label of identity politics, which became essentialism. Of course, the Anglo-Eurocentric disciplines did not look into the mirror of their own identity politics. I was caught in another double-bind, this time in ES, due to my feminist interventionary focus and my interest in a poststructuralism that would further enable that focus. However, what was not understood about my interest was the inquiry into the possible critical tools it provided for the analysis of the continuing force of white supremacist and colonial legacies of European modernities and Enlightenment reason, which in my view continued to dominate the (neo)capitalist structures of the university and its hegemonic hold on the production of knowledge—locally and globally. In old-fashioned terminology, the enormous (post)modernist capacity of the university and the nation-state to co-opt ideas of worth, dematerialize and depoliticize them, and stir in the marketing structure appears insurmountable at times to me.

The Psychotropic Denouement

AFTER TEN YEARS OF intense psychic battering—by which I mean the abuse of feelings, emotions, and self-perception—in the daily grind of life in the high-class Department Store, sensing myself on the verge of a psychotic breakdown, I agreed to medicate myself with a cocktail of psychotropics and sleeping pills so that I could continue to function on the job. My practice of rational(ized) suppression of feelings and emotions had not worked well enough. In effect, the patriarchal structure and organization of the university, whether of white hegemony or Ethnic Studies, had slipped in under the radar of self-suppression. Clearly, I had deceived myself that such a strategy would help me survive the climate generated by the suited ones and the general atmosphere in which I was

---

4. Chela Sandoval, *Methodology of the Oppressed* (Minneapolis: University of Minnesota, 2000).

working. I had been, if you will, the only out feminist Chicana in the university achieving the rank of full professor in humanities and social sciences. In fact, I had acquired such a rank because the previous, still moderately liberal, administration perceived me as having exchange value of some minimal sort in its tokenization practices. The promotion in rank was a result of negotiation with an outside work offer. Many a student of color had his/her share of psychic battering in this institution.

The first few years under psychotropic influence provided relief from disabling psychic symptoms, though I had also been diagnosed with diabetes. Like magic I lapsed into emotional indifference within a few months. The daily grind of double-binds and *piquetitos* were muted as if I had dosed myself with flea spray against vermin. However, I slowly discovered that the only job I could complete was to prepare, show up, and teach my classes—always with a tinge of fear and anxiety that my work was not good enough, though the latter was not a new feeling. On the other hand, the drugs protected me from any deep sensing of disrespect and negations in the university-at-large, while helping me maintain a positive attitude with students in the classroom and with those who sought intellectual and moral support for their projects. The majority were queer and feminist women of color who brought their experiences of insult and negation to my office door or over coffee in a shop nearby.

Nevertheless, as the years passed, the simulated lobotomy produced by psychotropics began to show itself when a wave of anger would appear and then quickly dissipate. My brief periodic waves of anger began to make me more aware of what I began to think of as the blackout of my spirit-being. Apparently, anger was the only emotion to make it through, however brief. My organism was getting choked by numbness, as if there was no one within. This sense of being-less-ness within was most emphatically felt when several white women of the beloved left remarked to me about some keynote speakers at the Practicing Transgression Conference I had organized with students: "Are 'they' still saying that?" One of the speakers they insulted with this line of questioning was Gloria E. Anzaldúa. The conference was intended to celebrate the 3rd edition of *This Bridge Called My Back*, published by Third Woman Press,[5] which may well have been received by these venerable white women of the beloved left, as "oh, they are still saying that." It was already known to me that at least one member of the

---

5. Cherríe Moraga and Gloria Anzaldúa, eds., *This Bridge Called My Back: Writings by Radical Women of Color* (Berkeley: Third Woman Press, 2002).

Gender and Women's Studies Department was going around saying that *Bridge* was a collection of "victim speakers." Thus, the department that had become a champion of "agency" was hard put to recognize agency in the work of queer and feminist women of color. My own participation in that department had failed to convince anyone that it was time they hired a Chicana, African American, and/or Native American woman. I even tried for a Latin Americanist. I had also failed to convince the Spanish Department to hire someone on U.S. Latin@ Studies, by the way. In their neoliberal democracy of borders, I was their token! Such was my demoralizing conclusion.

Fortunately, I had earned sabbatical leave the spring semester of 2002, wherein I collapsed with exhaustion and clinical depression. The anti-depressants, which are now sometimes called mood stabilizers, were failing. I knew then that I had to do something about this state of affairs. My first instinct was to get a job elsewhere, which I did not get, and that was good because there was no elsewhere in the academic market, though I apparently still had a bit of exchange value going for me in the interview market. By the fall of 2003, I decided to take the plunge into detoxification, cold turkey style. What were the risks? I did not know, but I was celebrating my sixtieth birthday with detoxification on my own and by the seat of my pants! My situation had become unbearable. In my view, the death of my spirit was at stake.

One of the first effects of detoxification was the loosening of my imaginary and my tongue. One of the first casualties of my loosened tongue was a white male of the beloved left who claimed to be a supporter of people of color. I said to him, "I bring out the Nazi in you, don't I?" And, if you will, I began to speak in tongues, and brought out the Nazis within multiple others. Further, for my Spring 2004 Gender and Women's Studies course on feminist theory I constructed a course that took the students back to the future by reading some texts from an earlier phase of feminist works. While it seemed to please some students, others complained loudly that this was not feminist theory! Too many feminists and not enough gender trouble—as if feminists did not have gender trouble! I did not finish the class. Needless to say, the department became angry with me. So did Ethnic Studies since I did not finish the class there either. (I did do final grading for both courses.) Both departments began to find out about my loose tongue!

Early during that same semester, I was being pressed by the dean to submit my case for review. I told him that I could not do it because even looking at the files for submitting my case made me literally sick. Another effect of detoxification, I could not bring myself to look at my own work. He must have heard my refusal well enough because he offered me the funds to hire a graduate student to help me do the job. I submitted my case, which was quickly expedited since I got my letter of assessment and worth within two months. Unprecedented! I think the administration was ready for me. I was on the dean's list of troublemakers of color—and Chicano/Ethnic Studies concurred. I think that for the latter I had become a loose can(n)on! Maybe that is what a Chicana feminist is to the patriarchy nearest to her. By this time, Ethnic Studies had refused to take me back full time, with one exception. A few years before, I had transferred part of my appointment to Gender and Women's Studies and Spanish, seeking relief from a hostile environment, thinking that moving around campus would help. Not so: within a couple of years the daily grind of racist tensions laden with class privilege had gotten to me. I wanted to return to Chican@/Ethnic Studies if only to have just one office and one place to work from, regardless of the problems. But as I said, I was turned down, and what faced me was working in three hostile departments, not to mention the university-at-large.

Thus, it was that in mid-April of 2004, I received my letter of the evaluation of my case. I had been detoxing for five months already; as a result, another effect was to loosen the rage that was aroused by the letter. The pay increase was a pittance; Third Woman Press was worth nothing and merited no mention. It never had. My request for equity went nowhere. Obviously, there is no equity for a troublemaker or a loose can(n)on. And as one colleague had put it, "the university wants good citizens." I guess I had a lot of gender trouble of my own making, which makes me laugh ironically these days, or as we say, *calavera* laughter. *¡Así es!*

My self-righteous rage rose within, and I marched to my Women's Studies class to let the students know there would be no class that day because I was going on strike. I had witnessed the efforts of other professors of color that followed the rules and protocols of rebuttal, and I was too exhausted and enraged to go that route, especially since Ethnic Studies had refused my request for return full time. Did the students understand my explanations for my wildcat strike? I will never know. What I do know is that I walked out of the classroom with my enraged spirit on automatic pilot all the way home, *el coraje en vuelo*. Once I was home I immediately went to my computer to write my letter of rebuttal. I wrote the administrators—with copies to Ethnic Studies and others—calling them "deaf, dead, dicks" and waxing eloquent in justifying my strike, further stating that I would not return until they addressed my grievances. Their idea of addressing my grievances was to ask me to submit to a psychological evaluation. Knowing to some extent the American Psychiatric Associations preferred modes of treatment and pill-pushing, there was no way that I was going to submit to a gringo-trained psychologist, especially hired by the university to serve internal needs. A friend pointed out to me that my terms of refusal were already ground enough for the suited university to declare me irrational. After all, there are rules and protocols for undertaking a strike—even in labor unions! When all is said and done, I had only one advocate within the ivory tower. She was a queer and feminist woman of color. That is poetic justice!

If in Ethnic Studies and Chicano Studies I seemed to be performing a latter-day Malinche, among many a white progressive I had become a tokenized part of their dog and pony shows. That is, whatever exchange value I had possessed circulated as cheap tokenization. Yet another double-bind, caught between the resistance-to-theory court among many colleagues of color and tokenization in the white progressive circles of the university. Most egregious tokenizations came from anticolonialist Latin Americanists and blatant *piquetitos* from the white women, beloveds of the left who wondered if "they"—queer and feminists of color—were still saying "that." In brief, I was inspired to detoxify by our own title to the 2002 conference: Practicing Transgression: Radical Women of Color for the 21st Century, which is indeed an insurrection of subjugated knowledges.

Conclusion

IF "[A]LL EXPERIENCE IS [transformed into] meaning of experience," (rephrasing Jacques Derrida)[6] as Gloria E. Anzaldúa did, I think that I have suggested some meanings in the course of writing this memoir. There is, as well, a profound disillusionment for a feminist idealist who got a front row seat on the degradation of the very notion of university, which, regardless of its continuous false claim to being a public university, has been mimicking the structural corporate model—and today hardly any university is spared from that model; maybe they never were. My medical doctor who had himself been subsumed into the corporate model of practice already knew and had warned me to be careful, perhaps as careful of speech and practice as he was. It seemed preposterous

---

6. Jacques Derrida, *Positions,* trans. Alan Bass (Chicago: University of Chicago Press, 1982), 30.

that the university could not tolerate criticism and critique of its own practice and theory. Yet, Fall 2012, students and faculty were brutally assaulted by the university's police force for their critical Occupy Berkeley sit-in. In comparison, the ethnic students' hunger strike of Spring 1999 was relatively peaceful. The violent police methods against protesting students escalated as the years passed. The so-called public university has become more privatized and a more free market participant than ever, highly regulated by police discipline in order to maintain its rules of order, global neocapitalist structure and organization, and the dead white men's legacy in high-tech suits.

The political economy of the university, in my view, is already threaded with violence in collegial voicing. It was there already when I arrived in 1987, but I did not know how to read it *in situ*—liberal ambiguities, American exceptionalism, UCB's mantra of excellence, and progressive bosom friends who claimed to be supportive—where equality is nil, especially for queer and feminist women of color. If one does not assimilate into its codes of governance, in the production of knowledge itself, there are punishments tailored for all of us, meted out in the devaluation of the faculty's work, like arranging a promotion to full professor with a $1 raise since merit of research cannot be denied, or denying tenure if a faculty's research goes against the grain of corporate interests and/or ideological interests. These are just two cases I was witness to.

Departments like Ethnic Studies, as well as other dissenting studies, are contained and used as symbolic markers of neoliberal patriarchal benevolence. Can you imagine if the study of right-wing movements turned its lens on the university itself or if Ethnic Studies turned its critical lenses on the university's corporate structure and organization.

One thing is still certain: we queer and feminist women of color are wedged in or caught in the crossfire of multiple patriarchies inside and outside the university. The challenge for us is to further inquire into the conditions of possibility for the transformations of knowledge production that we can bring off—small, medium, and large. But who/what are our horizontal alliances? I believe that we continue to be part of the insurrection of subjugated knowledges and that our mere existence is transgressive. I may be alienated from the university, but not from myself, kindred-spirit intellectuals nor the library. Is it silly to be such an idealist? A good old Anglo-Americanized pragmatic individual would probably say, "Of course." I, and others, might say, "Never!" Because one's idealism can be the template for evaluation of the transformation of the production of knowledge and practices that are actually taking place in both the local and global university. It is another way of saying, "Not yet." For me, there is no transformation in the way I imagined it; however, the globalized high-tech, in their current transformation, is producing the intellectuals of the future that are handmaidens to the global and patriarchal corporatization of the planet.

My parents would not have understood anything I have said. They did not even understand the metaphor-concept Chican@. As my mother once told me, "*Ay, hablas muy bonito pero ¿quién te entiende?*" Her response to a paper I had given in Spanish. On the other hand, if she and my father could have understood what I have written above, they might have asked, "*¿Quién te manda?*" mimicking the good old pragmatist—though I hope not. Life without rational(ized) suppression and the un-repression that detoxification produced is good. I think of my unconscious as a vacuum cleaner bag that was emptied out. As some might say in my birthplace, *la regaste*. Indeed, no regrets!

BIBLIOGRAPHY

Anzaldúa, Gloria. *Borderlands/La Frontera: The New Mestiza*. San Francisco, Aunt Lute, 1987.

Christian, Barbara. "The Race for Theory." *Cultural Critique*, no. 6 (1987): 51–63.

Derrida, Jacques. *Positions*. Translated and annotated by Alan Bass. Chicago: University of Chicago Press, 1982.

Foucault, Michel. *Power/Knowledge: Selected Interviews and Other Writings, 1972-1977*. Edited by Colin Gordon. New York: Vintage, 1980.

Moraga, Cherríe and Gloria Anzaldúa, editors. *This Bridge Called My Back: Writings by Radical Women of Color*. Berkeley: Third Woman Press, 2002.

Sandoval, Chela. *Methodology of the Oppressed*. Minneapolis: University of Minnesota, 2000.

Epilogue

CRITICAL THINKING AS A PEDAGOGICAL MOVIDA

DOUBLE-BINDS, ACCENTS, AND CONTRADICTIONS FOR
STUDENT SPEAKING-SUBJECTS

Marisa Belausteguigoitia Rius

> True voyage is return
>
> Ursula K. Le Guin, *The Dispossessed*

AN EPILOGUE CAN BE understood as a journey of return, a way of reading and making sense backwards. Octavia Butler's epilogues, to give an example, represent her way to paradoxically introduce—at the end of the story—her fears, anecdotes, passions, accents, and hidden meanings; there, in the afterword, she unveils invisible triggers and unexpected streams, without spoiling the narrative's plot.[1]

Following this logic, this epilogue discloses some of the *accents* which make Norma Alarcón a critical pedagogue and an extraordinary, rebellious thinker. I would like to share my ideas of Alarcón's pedagogical imperative to help readers understand the ways in which she wrestles with theory, relates to students as critical thinkers and free subjects, and encourages learning other ways of understanding not only Chicana theory and discourse but also the ways in which academic thinking can be critical, creative, generating interventions on urgent social matters, especially today when teaching from a critical stance has become dangerous.

What does it mean to end this book with an episode on pedagogy? What kind of emphasis can be drawn from Norma's relation to the classroom, to knowledge production, to students, and to critical thinking as a way of teaching that recognizes students as *speaking subjects* and *subjects-in-process*? *Speaking* and *in-process-subjects* imply teaching as a pedagogical maneuver, which involves transitions from self to other, from universal thinking to situated knowledges, from color-blind arguments to intersectional debates. These "maniobras" are

---

1. An example of this is the afterword to *Bloodchild*. There, she clarifies that the story is not about slavery, as some readers have interpreted, but rather serves multiple purposes: as a love story; as a coming-of-age story; as a pregnant man story or as an attempt to confront and mitigate her personal fear of botflies: parasites that lay eggs under the skin. Octavia Butler, *Bloodchild* (New York: Seven Stories Press, 1996).

relevant to reading, writing, and assessing critical interventions to generate "another future than the one forged by oppressors."[2]

Employing this critical pedagogy means to make visible the most important function of the university. It means to teach and to occupy the classroom as a creative maneuver, with a critical turn. It means to pay attention to racial, sexual, class and gender differences. Pedagogy as a critical intervention represents today an incommensurable challenge to creating the paths—or even inventing them—to produce what has to be seen.

To finish this book with a pedagogical turn means first and foremost focusing on the classroom and Norma Alarcón's critical pedagogies in a historical moment when teaching race, class, and gender differences is persecuted and punished in the USA and other parts of the world. The right-wing extremists in the USA want to make critical thinking invisible if not totally disappeared for the sake of white supremacist ideologies.

Pedagogy under such a lens works more as mechanism of administration of critical knowledge, as an activation of a currently passive academia, and revelation of passion and forms of creativity rooted in an approach to the university as an institution that fosters social justice and social change. Pedagogical practice, in this Freireian way, represents a political, ethical, and aesthetic tool, which works more on the desire to learn and understand than on the mastery of a specific topic.[3]

This epilogue makes visible Norma's pedagogical intervention, especially on Anzaldúa's paradoxical notion of consciousness as the *desire* to be at both sides at the same time "estar en las dos orillas a la vez."[4] Anzaldúa understood ambivalence, errantry, and mobility as fundamental parts of the New Mestiza and her strategic, paradoxical, and ambivalent form of consciousness. Alarcón's critical pedagogies—not exactly defined in what she writes but on what and how she teaches—do integrate both the unrest, the concern, the paradoxes of ambivalence, marked by Anzaldúa as constitutive of a New Mestiza and Chicana Identity, but also an urgency of accentuation.

On the last Zoom meeting we held to address editorial concerns on *Forced*, we discussed grammatical conventions, especially the issue of diacritical marks

---

2. Norma Alarcón, "What Kind of Lover Have You Made Me, Mother: Towards a Theory of Chicanas' Feminism and Cultural Identity through Poetry." *Women of Color: Perspectives on Feminism and Identity* 1, no. 1 (1985): 105.

3. Alarcón, "What Kind of Lover," 102

4. Gloria Anzaldúa, *Borderlands/La Frontera: The New Mestiza* (San Francisco: Spinsters/Aunt Lute, 1987), 139.

(accents) on Spanish-language names (Alarcón, Anzaldúa, Pérez) and those of other languages. Norma was adamant to follow the rule of accentuation in Spanish and place them on all which carry them, even the ones of renegades, those whose last names have lost their accents. Norma explained the act of preserving the accent on a name, as being political and also technical; political because Mexicans in the US and Chicanxs, carry marks on their tongues, bodies and names that make them visible and, today, deportable. To exhibit those marks is to construct a statement on whose accents matter and whose bodies can become in/valuable. It means make visible—as a form of pedagogy—what needs to be seen; the technical issue is related to how easy it is today to add an accent; keyboards did not facilitate them in the past.

Alarcón and Anzaldúa do carry bold, visible and strong accents; being both inscribed in pedagogy and their critical way of creating and disseminating knowledge, one inflection I do think is worthy to underscore.

When I was a doctoral student at the University of California at Berkeley from 1994 to 2000, Alarcón was my advisor; quickly she became my friend. México and its history, as well as her knowledge of politics, literature, Mexican cuisine, language, and culture, were some of the many bridges that cemented our friendship and my learning of her multiple layers of knowledge and uncommon ways of transmitting such knowledge. Alarcón analyzed the Zapatista rebellion (1994) and made sense of their novel and extravagant political strategies: the Women's Revolutionary Laws, the construction of politics based on irony and humor, their extensive and irregular use of time in negotiations with the government, the necessity of translation, and the innovative use of ski masks and postscripts. How could a starving, hurting, repressed, and excluded Indigenous community construct such an amazing repertoire of unusual, eccentric, and efficient strategies of representation, communication, survival, and political struggle?

Some of the answers to this question may be found in this book, in the capacities, paradoxes, and dilemmas of mediation, translation, and interpretation revealed in her critical revision of consciousness as processing multiple voicings. One example of Alarcón's skills on mediation, multiple voicing, and interpretation was the comparison and analysis of Gloria Anzaldúa and subcomandante Marcos that she helped me construct for my Ph.D dissertation, which entailed a critical reading and appropriation of Gloria Anzaldúa in our Mexican context.

Critical Thinking as a Pedagogical Maneuver

AS A GRADUATE, I was very interested in working with Norma Alarcón because of her unique theoretical capacity derived from the expertise acquired in the fields of critical theory, literature, psychoanalysis, deconstruction, philosophy, French feminist discourses, and cultural, queer, and gender studies, along with her work to enhance the function of the university also as building self-determination, consciousness, body, and word. "Timelines have to be redrawn, epistemologies revised, and ontologies rewritten,"[5] assesses Alarcón in her opening text. At that time, Chicana discourse and writing was pretty much unknown to me and to Latin American academia.

I applied to the Ethnic Studies Program because I sought to work with her, drawn by her way of constructing knowledge and conjugating different frames of intelligibility with writers such as Rosario Castellanos and Juana Alegría, other Mexican and Latin American intellectuals, and Chicana writers and theorists like Ana Castillo. Further, I was attracted to her work, and her critical readings of the figure of Malinche.[6] It was not common that Ethnic Studies professors were knowledgeable of Chicana writing and discourse, Latin-American Literature and at the same time on Lacanian psychoanalysis, French Feminist thinkers and postmodern, queer literature. I needed those theoretical frames to situate my doctoral dissertation around subcomandante Marcos and Gloria Anzaldúa as mediators of struggles for equality and democracy. It was the 90's and those were the battles.

Clearly Norma taught me how to contest—within this complex canon—foundational figures like Octavio Paz, José Emilio Pacheco or Carlos Fuentes, through radical readings coming from female writers like Rosario Castellanos or Sor Juana Inés de La Cruz. Through her teaching she unveiled the many ways in which the experience of female intellectuals and writers has been misrepresented and trivialized to students.

Along with other students, my attention was immediately captured by Alarcón, a dynamic Chicana feminist whose graduate seminar on Women of Color and Ethnic Studies was life-altering. We recognized in Professor Alarcón the power to convey, draw, and relate theory, experience, and histories in novel

---

5. See page xxii in her Preface to this book.
6. Norma Alarcón, "The Theoretical Subject(s) of *This Bridge Called My Back* and Anglo-American Feminism,," in *Criticism in the Borderlands: Studies in Chicano Literature, Culture, and Ideology*, ed. Héctor Calderón and José Saldóvar, 28-42. Durham, NC: Duke University Press, 1991

formulations. She gave us an anticipated version of ourselves interrupting, enjoying, and intervening critically and powerfully in the many worlds that constitute us. Norma Alarcón was a force in the classroom, in the department, on campus, as an editor, and as a mentor, and without a doubt one of the most important and transcendental influences in our lives, and in the academic and activist community, both on and off campus.

Many conversations with Norma, our cohort, and other academics inside and outside the classroom focused on the exceptional use of politics and critical pedagogies of Chicanas that were unmaking forms of representation of themselves as being uncivilized, dirty, and indecent. This pedagogical strategy—almost a visual dispositive—invited Anglo, Mexican, and global citizens to unveil and re-read the political and narrative forms of representation of dark women, and so of the nation, in critical ways. This unveiling pedagogy was rooted in her unique appropriation of critical theory, driven by the incorporation of French feminist thinkers, particularly Julia Kristeva and Luce Irigaray, alongside with different Chicana poets, writers and intellectuals.

Building on deconstruction and a poststructural critique, she ignited her classes, her writing, and her academic performance.[7] Her pedagogy—a master performance in the unveiling of narratives, scripts, and un/doing of representations that shape modernity and its promises—analyzed the challenges Women of Color in general and Chicanas in particular posed to euro-centered epistemologies. Her poststructural and decolonial analyses during the 1990's performed an eloquent and efficient demolition of the structure—as a pedagogical act—that built the promises of equality, freedom, and citizenship, which had been, and continue to be inaccessible for Women of Color in the United States.

Through her approaches to theory, history, and politics, as movements that link academia and theory-in-the-flesh to representation, Norma taught us the power of theory and how to pervert and redeploy hegemonic relations for our own critical thinking, collective projects, and modes of reinvention and reversal. During my six years at UC Berkeley, my cohort and I witnessed her power to disrupt the Ethnic Studies curriculum through the analytics of gender and sexuality; to teach amazing syllabi drawn from the relations of gender and nation-state, psychoanalytical and Derridean philosophy; to surprise us with

---

7. Those theoretical fields were not popular inside the Ethnic Studies canon. Norma Alarcón was strongly criticized by her fellow faculty members for the incorporation of such a critical field in the realm of Ethnic Studies, a more activist and sociological field. For more on those tensions see "Conjugations. The Insurrection of Subjugated Knowledges and Exclusionary Practices" in this volume.

her use of theory around Chicana discourse and writing; to disrupt academic and Anglo time by spending a whole day with us commenting on our writing; and to mesmerize us when taking part in strikes, hunger strikes, and other forms of resistance in order to support the expansion of Ethnic Studies inside the university.[8]

One of the most remarkable decolonial practices of recovery and reappropriation, of voice as critical pedagogy, was quotidian and related to her use of time inside Anglo-American academia. Her pedagogical labor was exercised against the grain. An example of this was the interruption of the regularly scheduled and programmed office or advising hours; Professor Alarcón's office hours also occurred off campus, with a beginning but no end. The students she was advising could spend the whole day talking, reading, understanding and eating in her home. The kind of critique she was trying to convey to us took time to grasp; a mixture of critical theory from her own standpoint, poststructuralist thinking blended into Chicana interstices. Chicana critical thinking was developed by the persistent underlining of double-binding, paradoxical, ironic, and contradictory maneuvers recognized as critical moves and/or elucidating entrapments. She created complex intervals of understanding, encouraging deep dialogue, incandescent critical views and extremely productive and unexpected theoretical conjugations instead of what restricted time in the formalized script of regular office hours would allow.

Throughout Alarcón's academic work one could witness eccentric and extraordinary ways of redirecting critical maneuvers, pedagogical interventions, theoretical interruptions, to develop routes that could reverse mechanisms of dispossession, be they pedagogical, intellectual, or related to the emergence of students voices

These enlightening theoretical and critical interventions would frequently be conjugated with tensions among academic authorities. One of these disagreements was raised at the hunger strike in 1999, which she actively joined. The strike was held as a protest against budget cuts and in favor of Ethnic Studies visibility. At

---

8. In 1995, Norma Alarcón and Irene Tinker conducted a project called "International Gender Systems in Comparative Perspective: A Research and Training Program for the U.C Berkeley Campus" to promote the incorporation of gender issues into area studies and general undergraduate education, and to enhance comparative and international research on the Berkeley campus by reciprocally linking the programmatic activities of International and Area Studies with the Women's Studies Department and the Beatrice Bain Research Group. They proposed a three-tiered program of activities designed to integrate gender and women studies at the levels of teaching, curricular development, and training. She also restructured the graduate curriculum of the Department of Ethnic Studies.

that time, she was teaching around the *movidas* (maneuvers) to acquire a richer and more varied voice, which could respond and be heard inside unequal power relations. I remember she was then the Chair of Women and Gender Studies; I visited her during the Hunger Strike and witnessed her frustration with university authorities and her complete involvement with students.

As difficult as it is to build an academic community with a shared vision and language, Norma Alarcón gathered students, professors, activists, and artists around her innovative way of developing theoretical and pedagogical maneuvers against fierce academic apartheid. She enlarged frameworks to view the difficulties and divisions that fragment intellectual work in the university. Norma intervened in the construction of a much-needed way of thinking about consciousness in opposition, through a paradoxical theoretical upheaval: an interlude in-between semiotics, modernity, and poststructuralism that focuses on the development of new strategies for social change, social organization, and social justice. In many ways, that coalitional consciousness, across racialized, sexualized, and gendered theoretical domains, such as white male poststructuralism, hegemonic feminism, third world feminism, postcolonial discourse, and queer theory, have a possibility of resonating and constructing interventions where "the master's tools cannot dismantle the master's house," but can unlock a door or open a window to look inside and understand its architecture.

What Norma Alarcón taught us vis-à-vis those master thinkers was to be confident to enter, stray inside, but mostly to be careful enough to design–from the beginning—more than one exit. Regarding male intellectuals and theorists, "they will leave you all confused, they, without a doubt, will abandon you," stated Alarcón in one of our conversations. She managed to make use of their tools inside her own project and territory and leave them before they turned their backs on her. She "rides with" them but makes sure she is not the last to leave. This exact move, abandoning before she is abandoned, is the one she perfects while on rides with Derrida, Nietzsche, and Lacan. This in order to construct definitions of women which will ground her early study on Rosario Castellanos and the full range of paradoxical, ironic, and contradictory systems of critical construction she manages to build as early as the mid-1980s.

Teaching on master houses' design was extremely efficient for giving her students voice to explore and decipher "high" theory that could keep students confused and silent. I must emphasize that these theoretical *movidas* were performed inside the Ethnic Studies program with students who held strong stances against theory or were very critical of whatever could be understood as such. This tension represented a challenge to Alarcón's teaching, which she faced with extraordinary patience. Teaching with a pedagogy centered on the unveiling of contradictions played on rhetorical figures such as irony—as a way to create a distance and at the same time produce a sort of ambiguous thinking—which she learned to master from her reading of Rosario Castellanos.

Alarcón performed the very act of thinking out loud, with the full potentiality of paradoxes—which helped us to think through an economy of irony as the incorporation of contradictions—to create a dimension in which every single student, be they graduate or undergraduate, could not only think but develop conversations despite tensions and contradictions.

An example of the seeming contradictions—taught to undergraduates—of European vis-à-vis decolonial thinkers, was her reading of Audre Lorde and Virginia Woolf, on their work on anger. Audre Lorde considers anger as the matrix for a creative force, while Virginia Woolf represents it as a force which distracts the vision that helps us reach the incandescence for creative and critical thinking.[9] Notwithstanding the racial and class politics which surround them, students were able to read, make sense around differences, and also enjoy and learn about different writing styles. This pairing of European or hegemonic thinkers with those emanating from the Ethnic Studies canon, emphasized Norma Alarcon's capacity of listening to protests against Eurocentric theory, while fostering visible contradiction and underlining theoretical *misfits* as possible centers for creativity and enunciation of the multiple voices that conform different positioning.

In a similar way, addressing Sor Juana Inés de la Cruz (1987) and Rancière (1991) on silence, Anzaldúa (1987) and Octavio Paz (1994) on *mestizaje*, Audre Lorde and Virginia Woolf on anger, produced constant acts of convergence and conversation of opposite thinkers and theorists, especially efficient with the students who resisted Theory. This capacity to listen, surprise, amaze and convince, created an extraordinary pedagogical performance. She herself acknowledges this act of conjugation of opposites with her students, by dedicating this book to them: "To all of my students who enjoyed the critical challenge and in turn challenged me."

---

9. Virginia Woolf, *A Room of One's Own* (New York: Harcourt Brace, 1989) and Audre Lorde, "The uses of anger," in *Sister Outsider: Essays and Speeches* (Suecia: Lennart Sane Agency AB, 1984), 124-33.

Norma was not interested in nurturing students and engaging in care practices women have been forced to enact, but in bridging all borders in her teaching. In one of our conversations around pedagogy she stated what I confirmed from the beginning, the confidence and absolute support in her students: "Grad students should have all the freedom in the world to do the project they want even if it is not in my 'specialty.'"

She understands students in the classroom and in her life also as *subjects-in-process,* capable of constructing futures of *self-determination.*[10] The theoretical move that would transit from *(sujetos sobrantes) subjects-in-excess* to *subjects-in-process*; concepts refashioned from Kristeva[11] "to recognize, reorganize, reconstruct and exploit difference through political resistance and cultural production and to see themselves 'in-process.'"[12] Alarcón is interested in assessing and constructing a *historical subject*—a *subject-in-process*—out of Chicana poetry and writing as a form of intervention, and interruption of both theoretical discourse and some of the restricted horizons of Chicanas' discourse and narrative, in order to "redirect and transform her future"[13] She did not call this activity a pedagogy, as bell hooks most certainly did. Rather than focusing on the act of speaking from the open wounds, as bell hooks and other decolonial thinkers did, Norma invites students to speak from an imagined horizon, where they can be full agents of the word over the open wound, or even more preferable, a closed one, a scar which makes pain recognizable, but not the ruler of action and word.

I want to close this epilogue with a final accent on the different ways Alarcón's critical pedagogies contributed to and enriched Mexican academic practices, especially those held at the Gender Studies Program at the Universidad Nacional Autónoma de México (UNAM), a public university in México City

The Word over the Wound: Pedagogical turns in Mexican Academia

I have worked for more than 40 years in Education and the Women and Gender Studies Program at UNAM. On my return to México in 2001, after six years as a PhD student at Berkeley, one of my goals was to expand the reach, partly through translation, of Anzaldúa and other Chicana authors for Latin American audiences. I have undertaken this work within the framework of critical

---

10. Norma Alarcón, "Cognitive Desires: An Allegory of/for Chicana Critics," in *Listening to Silences: New Essays in Feminist Criticism*, ed. Elaine Hedges and Shelley Fisher Fishkin (Oxford University Press, 1995), 270.
11. Julia Kristeva, *The Subject in Process* (New York: Routledge, 1998), 133-173.
12. Alarcón, "What Kind of Lover," 88.
13. Alarcón, "What Kind of Lover," 88.

pedagogies, which work against assimilation and towards an understanding of such worlds, such words, such writers in a Mexican context.

My formation with Norma helped make many different interventions on Mexican academia possible. In many ways these academic activities were inspired by my experience at Berkeley, especially the one derived from her editorial and pedagogical practices. Soon after my return, I was appointed chair of Women Studies at UNAM (2004-2013) and was also designated Chair for another period (2021-2025). In both phases at the Gender Studies Program we performed diverse pedagogical maneuvers developed with a strong input on Chicanx writing and discourse, centered on the students, the classroom, the construction of graduate seminars and undergraduate courses, dissertation topics, postdoctoral students, international research project, and a special program of publication and translation. At the Gender Studies program we were able to translate into Spanish Gloria Anzaldúa's *Borderlands/La Frontera: The New Mestiza* (an extraordinary linguistic intervention done by Norma Cantú and Claire Joysmith), Chela Sandoval's *Methodologies of the Oppressed,* and several essays by Norma Alarcón, some of which appear part of this volume, and other Chicana writers and thinkers.

A significant number of our students at UNAM (80% approximately) are first generation; they come from working class families and are mixed with a small percentage of the most selected privileged students of Mexican youth, due to the academic status of our university. Similar to the subjects Anzaldúa understands as *atravesados*,[14] these students are considered more of an obstacle to the *excellence of learning*; they may be even perceived as potentially "dangerous" as migrants are considered "transgressors" in the United States.

Public universities like UNAM offer students real possibilities to transform the closed walls of the university classroom into an opening space that can speak not only excellence in knowledge, but also on historically grounded reasons for their disadvantage and disenfranchisement. Almost one third of our students have family members in the US and—as much as our prison numbers are not as high as the US ones—they have had violent contact with police or experienced strong forms of justice inequality. *Los atravesados* do have a place in our classrooms.

Particularly relevant was the work on prisons we have developed from 2007 until today. A group of academics, professors, students, activists, artists and lawyers at UNAM work with women in prison who mostly did not finish middle

---

14. Anzaldúa defines *Los atravesados* as "the squint-eyed, the perverse, the queer, the troublesome, the mongrel, the mulato, the half-breed, the half dead; in short, those who cross over, pass over, or go through the confines of the 'normal' " See *Borderlands/La Frontera: The New Mestiza* p.25.

school and "... have been silenced before uttering a word, or having spoken, have not been heard."[15] The skills I developed around the *Mestiza Consciousness* and the construction of these women as *subjects-in-process* or *speaking – subjects*, learned with Norma, helped me understand the politics, the pedagogies, the theory and language intervention to develop *New Mestizas* out of women in prison.

With Norma I learned the paradox of words. On the one hand we need them to explain and make visible the unfair and unequal ways in which many of our students live; and on the other, we cannot let words trap us in the realities they describe, we need to set them free, invent new ones, to mobilize whatever project or idea student develop.

This allows theory to become both the incessant striving for words that fit reality to transform it and the excessive and errant expansion of new projects that cannot be articulated or figured out in advance

As much as Norma does not understand herself as a pedagogical critical thinker, she helped me figure out the classroom as one of the most radical spaces for changing the future and fostering crucial transformation in our students. These spaces—our classrooms—and with them our deep, intellectual, affective and joyful relation to our students, are being severely challenged. If Norma were to be active inside these classrooms today, I am sure she would be incandescent and precise, ironic and clear. I figure we would be holding long, strong, inspiring conversations at her home, sharpening our vocabulary, inventing forms of consciousness intervention and developing all our accents, the ones in our last names, and the ones on our tongues and bodies.

---

15. Gloria Anzaldúa, Introduction to *Making Face/ Making Soul. Haciendo Caras: Creative and Critical Perspectives by Women of Color*, ed. Gloria Anzaldúa. San Francisco: Aunt Lute, 1990, xvii.

BIBLIOGRAPHY

Alarcón, Norma. "What Kind of a Lover Have You Made Me, Mother: Towards a Theory of Chicanas' Feminism and Cultural Identity through Poetry." *Women of Color: Perspectives on Feminism and Identity* 1, no. 1 (1985): 85-110.

Alarcón, Norma. "Cognitive Desires: An Allegory of/for Chicana Critics." In *Listening to Silences: New Essays in Feminist Criticism*, edited by Elaine Hedges and Shelley Fisher Fishkin, 199–211. New York: Oxford University Press, 1994.

Alarcón, Norma. "The Theoretical Subject(s) of *This Bridge Called My Back* and Anglo-American Feminism." In *Criticism in the Borderlands: Studies in Chicano Literature, Culture, and Ideology*, edited by Hector Calderón y José David Saldívar, 28–42. Durham, NC: Duke University Press, 1991.

Anzaldúa, Gloria. *Borderlands/La Frontera: The New Mestiza*. San Francisco: Spinsters/Aunt Lute, 1987.

Anzaldúa, Gloria, editor. *Making Face, Making Soul/Haciendo Caras: Creative Perspectives on Women of Color.* San Francisco: Aunt Lute Books, 1990

Butler, Octavia. *Bloodchild*. New York: Seven Stories Press, 1996.

De la Cruz, Sor Juana Inés. *Respuesta a Sor Filotea de la Cruz*. México, D.F.: Fontamara, 2014.

Kristeva, Julia. "The Subject in Process." In *The Tel Quel Reader*, edited by Patrick French and Roland-François Lack, 133-173. New York: Routledge, 1998.

Le Guin, Ursula K. *The Dispossessed*. New York: Harper Perennial. Modern Classics, 2014.

Lorde, Audre. "The Uses of Anger." In *Sister Outsider: Essays and Speeches*, 124-133. Suecia: Lennart Sane Agency AB, 1984.

Paz, Octavio. *El Laberinto de la Soledad*. México: Fondo de Cultura Econnómica, 1994

Rancière, Jacques. *The Ignorant Schoolmaster: Five Lessons in Intellectual Emancipation.* Stanford: Stanford University Press, 1991.

Sandoval, Chela. *Methodology of the Oppressed*. Minneapolis: University of Minnesota Press, 2000.

Sayers Peden, Margaret. *A Woman of Genius: The Intellectual Autobiography of Sor Juana Inés de la Cruz*. Salisbury, CT: Lime Rock Press, 1987.

Woolf, Virginia. *A Room of One's Own*. New York: Harcourt Brace, 1989,

Norma Alarcón in Saltillo, Coahuila, México, 1971. Photo by Manuel Alarcón Ortiz.

DR. NORMA ALARCÓN is Professor Emerita in the Departments of Ethnic Studies, Spanish and Portuguese, and Gender and Women's Studies at the University of California, Berkeley. She was the founder and publisher of Third Woman Press, which began as a journal and gave voice to many Latina writers. She is the author of *Ninfomanía:el discurso feminista en la obra poética de Rosario Castellanos* (1992) and co-editor, among others, of *Between Woman and Nation: Nationalisms, Transnational Feminisms, and the State* (1999). Her writings have had an impact across disciplines in the humanities and social sciences and range from Chicana feminism and Chicana literature to topics such as gender, race, feminist politics, the U.S.–México border, women of color feminisms, and contemporary social justice issues. Her work has been published both in the U.S. and in México. In her critical essays that have been reprinted in anthologies and journals, Alarcón challenged dominant epistemologies and theories for interpreting the experiences of Chicanas and women of color and carved out a space for deeper conversation about resistance and difference. Alarcón earned her Ph.D. from Indiana University. She has received the National Association for Chicana and Chicano Studies Scholar Award, the Mujeres Activas en Letras y Cambio Social Tortuga Award, and was recognized for her contributions to Chicana and Chicano Literature by the Modern Language Association.

DR. NORMA E. CANTÚ was born in Nuevo Laredo, Tamaulipas and raised in Laredo, Texas; she is a daughter of the US–México borderlands. Cantú taught at what is now Texas A&M International University for twenty years; she then taught and retired as Professor Emerita, from the Department of English, University of Texas at San Antonio. She currently serves as the Norine R. and T. Frank Murchison Professor of the Humanities at Trinity University in San Antonio, Texas, where she teaches Latinx and Chicanx Studies, folklore, and creative writing. She earned her Ph.D. from the University of Nebraska, Lincoln. She served as a senior arts specialist with the National Endowment for the Arts Folk and Traditional Arts Program. Author of the award-winning novels *Canícula: Snapshots of a Girlhood en la Frontera* and *Cabañuelas*, she also published the poetry collection, *Meditación Fronteriza: Poems of Love, Life, and Labor* and has edited or co-edited over a dozen anthologies. Her most recently published anthologies are *Chicana Portraits: Critical Biographies of Twelve Chicana Writers* and the co-edited *¡Somos Tejanas! Tejana Identity and Tejanidad*, as well as her single-authored book *Fiestas in Laredo: Matachines, Quinceañeras, and George Washington's Birthday*. She lives in San Antonio, Texas.

DR. MARISA BELAUSTEGUIGOITA, Professor at the School of Pedagogy in the Humanities at the Universidad Nacional Autónoma de México, she is chair of the Gender Studies Center at UNAM (CIEG/UNAM). Her work focuses on the relationship between critical pedagogies, artistic and juridical practices focused on women's access to justice. Her most recent work in English includes: "Strikes, Stoppages, Occupations: Mexican Feminist Writing of the Walls" in *Critical Times* (2022) and *Critical Terms in Latin American Thought. Historical and Institutional Trajectories in Latin American Culture* coedited with San Miguel y Ben Sifuentes-Jáuregui (2016, Spanish version 2018). Professor Belausteguigoitia has been one of the most active scholars involved in translating, teaching and researching the work of Chicanas and Chicana discourse and theory in México. She has coordinated the Spanish language translation and publication of *Methodology of the Oppressed* by Chela Sandoval (2013) and Gloria Anzaldúa's *Borderlands: La Frontera. The New Mestiza* (2015), both at CIEG/UNAM press. She has received several awards: Omecíhuatl by the Women Institute in México City INMUJERES DF, 2010); Margherita von Brentano's award Freie Universität Berlin (2013). Her documentary "Nos Pintamos Solas," on Imprisoned Women in México City, co-directed with

Mariana X. Rivera was awarded best director and best film by the Film Festival FICFUSA 2015 in Colombia. She was also the *2019 Andrés Bello Distinguished Chair for the Study of Latin American Cultures,* at KJCC, NYU.

DR. DIONNE ESPINOZA is Professor in the Department of Women's, Gender, and Sexuality Studies at Cal State LA. Her research and teaching interests center the voices, archives, and critical theories of Chicana feminist writers and activists from the sixties to the present. In addition to articles in the fields of Chicana history and literature, she has co-edited two award winning books: *Chicana Movidas: New Narratives of Women's Activism and Feminism in the Movement Era* (with María Cotera and Maylei Blackwell, University of Texas Press, 2018) and *Enriqueta Vasquez and the Chicano Movement: Writings from El Grito del Norte* (with Lorena Oropeza, Arte Publico Press, 2006). She is currently revising her book manuscript *Bronze Womanhood: Chicana Activism and the Chicano Movement Narrative.*

OUR MISSION   Founded in 1982, Aunt Lute Books is an intersectional, feminist press dedicated to publishing literature by those who have been traditionally underrepresented in or excluded by the literary canon. Core to Aunt Lute's mission is the belief that the written word is critical to understanding and relating to each other as human beings. Through the centering of voices, perspectives, and stories that have not been traditionally welcomed by mainstream publishing, we strengthen ties across cultures and experiences, promoting a broader range of expression, and, we hope, working toward a more inclusive and just future.

LAND ACKNOWLEDGMENT   We, Aunt Lute Books, acknowledge that we do our work of uplifting marginalized voices and striving toward justice via the written word on the unceded ancestral homeland of the Ramaytush Ohlone who are the original inhabitants of the San Francisco Peninsula. As the indigenous stewards of this land and in accordance with their traditions, the Ramaytush Ohlone have never ceded, lost, nor forgotten their responsibilities as the caretakers of this place, as well as for all peoples who reside in their traditional territory. As Guests, we recognize that we benefit from living and working on their traditional homeland. We wish to pay our respects by acknowledging the Ancestors, Elders and Relatives of the Ramaytush Community and by affirming their sovereign rights as First Peoples.

You may buy books from our website.

www.auntlute.com

aunt lute books

P.O. Box 410687
San Francisco, CA 94141
books@auntlute.com

All material printed herein is copyrighted.
Reproduction is not permitted without express written permission.
This book would not have been possible without the kind contributions of the Aunt Lute Founding Friends:

Anonymous Donor	Diana Harris
Anonymous Donor	Phoebe Robins Hunter
Rusty Barceló	Diane Mosbacher, M.D., Ph.D.
Marian Bremer	Sara Paretsky
Marta Drury	William Preston, Jr.
Diane Goldstein	Elise Rymer Turner

www.ingramcontent.com/pod-product-compliance
Lightning Source LLC
Chambersburg PA
CBHW070603230426
43670CB00010B/1389